D1262041

Foreword

With respect to military aircraft and aerial weapons development in the United States, the period from the end of World War Two through to the Korean Conflict is little discussed as a whole. The general sense of many students of aviation history is that this was a period of lackluster progress yielding marginal systems with few truly capable or enduring products emerging. I hope to demonstrate in the coming pages that this notion is misleading.

This volume focuses on the influence of America's World War Two aviation development and experience, subsequent aviation technological advances, and world events in shaping American choices in military aircraft and associated weapons' development during the few years following the war. It shows how air warfare weapons from the last conflict were carried forward and altered, how new systems evolved from these, and how the choices fared in the next war—Korea. The period was one of remarkable progress in a short period via a great many aircraft and weapons programs and associated technological progress—as much or more than during World War Two for the same number of years. These systems were of immense importance influencing and growing the engineering, production, and operational capabilities to exploit for the next generation of weapons that soon followed. Other than World War Two itself, few if any other periods are quite comparable.

Space does not permit detailed descriptions of the aircraft and weapons, their development, production, and service history. Instead, emphasis is on the innovative features or new technology and how these contributed to advancing American military aviation, influencing the evolution of follow-on models or types. Included are prototype, experimental, and research aircraft that are equally important in understanding the history of American aircraft development.

With the goal of highlighting the progress of aircraft technological development, no effort is made to trace every military solicitation and responding proposal, nor every project and program. Space would not permit this in any event. Likewise, no effort is made to compare with work undertaken outside the United States apart from that which served as motivation for American efforts. Being a discussion of hardware development, specific personalities are largely left unstated. The Korean War chapter also highlights progress and equipment adaptation, so it is not a history of the air war. Likewise, specific dates beyond month and year are neglected because this suitably shows chronological progression. Tabulated characteristics are provided for those aircraft that entered production or represented significant technological advances influencing others that followed. These show progress in greater detail by permitting comparison with earlier machines. A glossary is provided to explain technical terms that may be unfamiliar to the reader.

Although nautical air miles per hour (knots) began to be used as the principal measure of aircraft airspeed during this period, miles per hour (and the conversion to kilometers per hour) will be held in the text to permit ready comparison with subjects from my World War Two books (see the bibliography). The phrase "Korean Conflict" was used at the time, in addition to "Police Action," to downplay the West's heating confrontation with the Communist powerhouses, the Soviet Union and China. While it has since been more routinely called a war, the term "Conflict" will be retained to avoid confusion with references to World War Two.

The author welcomes all feedback and additional research material, especially photographs. He may be contacted at williamnorton@earthlink.net.

Bill Norton
Tehachapi, California, 2021

Acknowledgments

For their kind assistance, the author wishes to thank the following individuals and organizations, in alphabetical order: the Air Force Test Center History Office, the American Aviation Historical Society, Dennis Jenkins, Gerry Balzer, the Grumman History Center, the Jay Miller Collection, the Museum of Flight, the National Archives, the National Museum of Naval Aviation, the National Museum of the United States Air Force, the Naval Aviation Archives, the San Diego Air and Space Museum, and Tony Landis.

Contents

Foreword 3

Acknowledgments 5

Glossary 9

Acronyms and Abbreviations 16

1   Altered Landscape 21

2   Flight Research 55

3   Mission Imperatives 99

4   Fighters Evolve 133

5   Second Generation Fighters 169

6   Deviant Fighters 201

7   Bombers Transform 220

8   Transport and Assault 273

9   Helicopters Ascend 314

10   Sea Missions 353

11   Special Types 385

12   Aerial Weapons 425

13   The Test: Korea 447

14   Precipitous 466

Endnotes 482

Bibliography 493

Index 504

Glossary

Aeroelasticity: The combination of aircraft flexure (elasticity) and airloads acting on the structure, some unsteady, producing a variety of static and oscillatory responses that may be unstable.

Afterburning (AB): Also known as augmentation, reheat, and secondary combustion, this is the injection of fuel into the hot exhaust of the turbine, forward of the nozzle, to produce additional jet engine thrust.

Air-cooled engine: A piston aero engine employing the passing air to cool the cylinders and other components. This requires a properly formed cowling and baffling encircling the engine, and usually cowl flaps to regulate the flow of air while reducing cooling drag.

Aircraft category, class, type, and model: For the purpose of this text, category refers to the nature of the aircraft such as lighter than air, airplane, rotorcraft, and the like. Class refers to the purpose of the aircraft, such as airplanes with the role of fighter, transport, liaison light-plane, and the like. Type refers to specific "make" from a manufacturer, such as Douglas AD Skyraider. Model is, then, a specific production series such as AD-1, AD-2, etc.

Airfoil: A wing cross-sectional shape determining flight lift characteristics.

Airload: The distributed air pressure forces acting on an aircraft structure during flight.

Angle of attack: Angle between the wing's mean chord line and the incident airflow.

Anhedral: The aero surface is angled down, the tip lower than the root.

Anti-ice: The systems aboard an aircraft that work to prevent atmospheric ice from accumulating on the exterior in flight that can compromise safety. These were commonly heated elements like windscreens and aero surface leading edges (usually from heated air passed locally within the structure), and alcohol or glycol fluid emitted to be spread across a surface by the passing airflow or, for the propeller, radial acceleration.

Arrestment: Means of capturing and decelerating an airplane landing on an aircraft carrier deck. This usually consists of a series of parallel cables stretched across the deck, one of which is engaged by a tailhook hanging below the aft fuselage of a landing aircraft. The cable is laid out and gradually restrained by an energy absorption system below deck.

Aspect ratio: The arithmetic square of the wingspan divided by the area of the wing. A high aspect ratio wing is comparatively long and narrow.

Assisted take-off: In the context of land-based aviation, this consists of small rocket motors attached to the aircraft to provide additional thrust to get an aircraft off in a shorter distance or a heavy aircraft off in a standard distance. These were referred to as rocket-assisted take-off (RATO) and Jet-Assisted Take-Off (JATO, also used to refer to the Aerojet bottled rocket products).

Augmentation: A means of providing additional thrust from a turbojet engine, usually for a brief period, by such means a water injection and afterburning.

Axial-flow jet engine: A turbine engine through which air flows along the longitudinal axis without being radially redirected as through a centrifugal compressor.

Backside of the power curve: This is the region of the aircraft's velocity versus drag curve—airspeed versus thrust or power required—in which thrust (throttle or propeller pitch) controls flight path angle while pitch attitude (longitudinal control input) controls airspeed. An increase in thrust alone will decrease flight path angle, but not necessarily result in an airspeed increase.

Bombsight: An optical device for estimating the impact point of bombs dropped from an aircraft at a considerable altitude.

Boundary layer: The thin layer of air adjacent to a surface in an airstream in which the flow goes from zero velocity at the surface to freestream velocity. A thick or turbulent layer would possess greater skin friction drag than a thin or laminar boundary layer.

Boundary layer control: This involves forcing the boundary layer to a smooth laminar profile by either sucking off the air at the surface or blowing air out to energize the layer and keep it attached for more of the surface length rather than separate into a turbulent layer.

Buzz: A form of flutter in which a control surface rotates at high frequency at a small angle due to airflow instability.

Camber: The curvature of an airfoil contributing to lift.

Catapult: A means of launching an airplane off an aircraft carrier deck, usually by a bridle between the aircraft and a shuttle in a slot along the deck. The shuttle is propelled by a hydraulic or gas piston below deck to accelerate the aircraft to take-off velocity.

Ceiling: Combat ceiling is the altitude at which the climb rate decays to 500 fpm. Service ceiling equates to 100 fpm and absolute ceiling to 0 fpm.

Center of gravity: The point at which the aircraft would balance if suspended from that point, or the center of gravitational attraction acting on the mass of the vehicle. A center of gravity too far forward or too far aft could render the airplane uncontrollable.

Centrifugal-flow jet engine: A turbine engine in which air flows through a centrifugal compressor, redirecting the air radially outward to pass through combustors on the outer perimeter of the powerplant.

Chaff: Metallic strips of length matched to expected opposition radar wavelengths, carried by a bomber or support aircraft to confound detection by an enemy air defense system.

Chord length: The width of a wing or the line between the leading and trailing edges, usually referred to as a mean chord for a tapered wing.

Circular error probable: Defines average accuracy with half the launched missiles or bombs impacting within that radius.

Compound helicopter: A helicopter with an additional propulsion device facilitating greater forward airspeed than otherwise achievable with the rotor(s) alone. The added device is usually a tractor or pusher propeller and added wings.

Compressibility effects: Refers to the effects on aircraft performance, stability, and control resulting from air compressing into shock waves on the aircraft surfaces as it approaches the speed of sound. These include such hazards as Mach tuck and locked-in steep dives.

Constant-speed propeller: Mechanically changing the blade pitch to automatically maintain steady rotational speed (rpm), giving more efficient thrust generation for airspeed, throttle setting, and aircraft attitude.

Contra-rotating propeller: Also known as a dual-rotation propeller or "contraprop," this employs two propellers, front to back, turning in opposite directions on coaxial power shafts.

Control authority: Aircraft response resulting from control surface deflection, as a function of flight condition. The limits of the response define the authority (such as ability to trim the aircraft) and so may suggest loss of control if operating beyond such limits of authority.

Counter-rotating propeller: Propellers on opposite sides of the aircraft (as in a twin-engine installation) that rotate in opposite directions to eliminate torque effects.

Critical Mach number: The flight velocity at which compressibility shocks first begin to appear on the aircraft (see also transonic flight).

De-ice: The systems aboard an aircraft that work to shed atmospheric ice from exterior surfaces in flight. These were usually pneumatically inflated leading-edge rudder boots or thermal heating.

Dihedral: The aero surface is angled up, the tip higher than the root.

Dive brakes: Flaps or other deployed surfaces intended to limit the dive speed of the aircraft, thereby reducing the recover g or preventing exceedance of the critical Mach number.

Dive flaps: Flaps beneath the wing restoring some lift lost via compressibility to allow recovery from a dive for which pullout is rendered ineffectual by compressibility effects.

Drag: The resistance of the air to the passage of an aircraft. It is made up of induced drag from the creation of lift and profile drag that includes skin-friction drag, the overall frontal area offered to the incident air, cooling drag from air passing through a cowling and engine baffling, and other elements.

Drag parachute: Also known as deceleration or braking chute, it is at the rear of the airplane and deployed on landing to assist in slowing the aircraft, supplementing wheel brakes.

Drogue parachute: A relatively small parachute deployed to provide the force to extract a larger chute.

Drooped ailerons: Ailerons that can be biased to a downward-deflected neutral angle about which normal differential up-down displacement is still performed for aircraft roll control. The droop enhances overall lift (as well as drag) and is usually performed for a low-speed landing approach.

Dual-rotation propeller: (see contra-rotating propeller)

Feathering: Turning constant-speed (variable pitch) propeller blades edge-wise to the line of flight to stop rotation and reduce drag when an engine has ceased operating during flight.

Flaps: An articulated portion of a wing trailing edge that enhances lift at the expense of drag and is usually employed on a landing approach to allow a reduced landing speed. The split flap is a lower portion of the trailing edge that rotates down. The Fowler flap slides aft and down, increasing wing area and usually creating a slot between the wing main plane and flap surfaces through which air accelerates.

Flutter: An unstable oscillation of a portion of the aircraft or control surface that can grow to catastrophic amplitude. The instability is induced by unsteady airloads interacting with the elastic deformation of the structure or control surface rotation at like frequencies (resonance).

Fully articulated rotor: Possessing flapping and lead/lag hinges.

Ground resonance: An on-gear instability at certain rotor speeds that could make the rotorcraft oscillate dangerously and risk an overturn or other structural damage.

Gunsight: A mechanism for aligning aircraft projectile weapons with a target. This is usually in front of the pilot or gunner, allowing a visual sighting through an optical device that may also compensate for firing errors.

Hardpoint: A strengthened structural portion within the bottom surface of a wing or fuselage with fittings for carriage of weapon or fuel tank mounts.

Inlet pressure recovery: This is seeking as near to freestream pressure as possible within the turbine engine inlet ducting given the range of operating conditions and losses via friction and other effects.

Inline engine: A reciprocating engine in which the pistons are arranged in one or more longitudinal lines parallel to the central power shaft. An upright or inverted V-arrangement was typical of engines for high-performance combat aircraft.

Intercooler: One or more heat exchangers cooling supercharged air, passing to the carburetor, to void engine knock or to further increase the air density. The intercooler drops the air temperature before the addition of fuel while an aftercooler decreases the heat of the charged fuel-air mixture before reaching the engine.

Irreversible flight controls: These are fully powered, as opposed to boosted, with the pilot only controlling hydraulic servo valves to move surfaces. There is no natural aerodynamic feedback to the cockpit controls. An artificial feel must be provided to the pilot for expected response to inputs.

Laminar flow: Boundary layer of air adjacent to a surface in an airstream with an even pressure distribution, as opposed to turbulent, and possessing less skin-friction drag. A laminar flow wing is one with an airfoil designed to maintain laminar flow for more of the chord length, before becoming turbulent towards the trailing edge, than typical airfoils.

Liquid-cooled engine: A piston engine employing recirculated liquid to cool the cylinders and other components. The liquid is itself cooled via one or more radiators open to the passing air.

Load factor: Also known as normal load factor, this is a measure of maneuvering acceleration in the vertical axis of an aircraft defined as units of gravitational pull on the surface of the Earth (1 g). This is a primary criterion for structural design to ensure the airframe can withstand maneuvering airloads and inertia, plus a factor of safety.

Mach number: The speed of sound at the aircraft's operating altitude.

Mach tuck: A compressibility effect in which shocks on the wing cause the center of pressure to move aft and the horizontal tail to lose effectiveness. Both allow the aircraft's nose to drop and speed to increase, which exacerbates the instability.

Military and maximum power: Military power is full throttle without augmentation while maximum would be with added augmentation such as afterburner.

Plane guard: This is standing by in the event an aircraft went into the sea while launching from or recovering to a carrier. This role had been performed by nearby ships until assumed by helicopters. A helicopter from the carrier can respond more quickly and potentially save aircrew lives. The helicopter could be on the deck, possibly with engines running, or in the air during intensive flight operations.

Power loading: The ratio of aircraft gross weight to engine take-off power.

Pressurization: A system that pumps compressed air into the sealed aircraft's interior volume to maintain pressure at a safe "cabin altitude" for occupants as the aircraft climbs into the rarefied air at high altitude.

Prop wash: The flow of air off a propeller passing back over the aircraft directly aft (assuming a tractor propeller). The prop wash can create asymmetrical rates on the aircraft, but also ensures control effectiveness at low aircraft velocities for those surfaces within the wash.

Propeller reversing: The ability to reverse the pitch on a constant-speed propeller to reverse the thrust for slowing on landing or backing the aircraft on the surface.

Propeller synchronization: The process of ensuring similar rpm for each propeller on a multi-engine aircraft to prevent an annoying rhythmic noise.

Pulsejet engine: Similar to a ramjet, the air for combustion enters through one-way shutters or valves at the intake that are then slammed shut under the pressure of combustion. When the resulting pressure wave exits the engine nozzle to produce thrust, the shutters are blown open again. The cycle continues in an intermittent fashion. Like the ramjet, the engine requires some forward airspeed to start.

Radar or radio altimeter: A device measuring height above the ground or sea by reflected electromagnetic waves and permitting safer night flying at low altitude.

Radial engine: A reciprocating engine in which the pistons are arranged radially about the central power shaft. One or two rows of these radially grouped cylinders are typical.

Radio control: The remote control of an aircraft or missile in flight via radio signals causing specific responses permitting desired behavior or actions.

Ramjet: An engine using an inlet accelerated to high speeds to compress the air for combustion and so eliminating rotating compressor and turbine components, though it lacks low-speed thrust. The areas of the inlet diffuser, combustion section, and exit area must be carefully matched to ensure efficient operation, especially if supersonic flight is intended.

Retreating blade stall: The blades on the side of the rotor disk advancing into the incoming "relative wind" effect during forward flight experiences greater lift than on the retreating side that experiences the relative wind as a tail wind. The dissymmetry of lift across the disk is dealt with by flapping or cyclical coarsening of blade pitch on the retreating side to ensure uniform lift across the disc and avoid an uncontrollable roll. This coarsening of pitch has the limitation of any airfoil where the angle of attack reaches the point of flow separation extent, reducing lift to unacceptable levels.

Roll reversal: Moving an aileron trailing edge down increases the nose down twist of the wing structure, reducing the roll rate generated. This could decrease effectiveness to zero or even reverse the roll sense.

Shocks: The compression front of air as it flows around a body near sonic speeds. These shocks increase drag and can have a profound effect on the stability and control of the aircraft.

Slats: A segment of a wing-leading edge that slides forward to increase the wing camber (inflexion) and add lift. This usually creates a slot between the surface and the wing main plane through which air is accelerated to energize the flow downstream and delay stall.

Slot: A narrow spanwise opening between the lower and upper surface of a wing, allowing the high-pressure air below to accelerate up and over the top of the wing to energize the airflow and delay stall. Also, a gap created when moving a control surface or flaps, the flow through the slot enhancing the effect of the surface deflection.

Specific fuel consumption: Ratio of fuel burned to the unit of thrust produced.

Specifications: An agreement between a contractor and the military as to the characteristics of an aircraft or other product yet to be designed and built.

Spin: An out-of-control condition produced by the stall of one wing coupled with a high yaw angle. The result is a descending flight path with the aircraft rotating about a vertical axis. Classical recovery is by arresting the yaw and then pushing the nose over to break the stall, then pulling out the resulting dive.

Stall: The turbulence and separation of air on a wing or other surface due to a high angle of attack and adverse pressure gradients within the boundary layer that causes an enormous loss of lift.

Static margin: Distance between the center of pressure and the aircraft center of gravity that determines static stability of the aircraft.

Supercharger: A spinning compressor impeller, usually driven off the engine accessory gear case, through which the fuel-air mixture from the carburetor is ported and compressed to higher density before passing into the intake manifold. This "boosts" power output and especially helps maintain intake pressure nearer sea level, even at the lower air density at altitude, for sustained high performance.

Swept wing: A wing in which the mean chord line is less than 90 degrees to the aircraft centerline. An aft sweep is most common, meaning the mean chord line—

typically measured at the quarter chord line—is farther forward at the root than at the tip.

Telemetry: The transmission by radio of sampled data from an aircraft to a ground station for safe observation of results during a flight event.

Torque: The aircraft lateral displacement tendency created by a propeller, especially at high power on take-off and low speed on landing. This is a combination of mechanical effects from turning the heavy prop as well as the asymmetrical airflow effects on the aircraft elements aft of the propeller.

Transonic flight: Airspeeds at which, at the lower velocity, the critical Mach number at which shocks have begun to form on portions of the airframe and, at an upper end, the flow over the exterior surface is likely entirely immersed within shocks. Flight in this regime is accompanied by a great increase in aircraft drag and changes in stability.

Turbojet: A turbine (jet) engine for which the motive output is an accelerated mass of air for thrust.

Turboprop: A turbine (jet) engine for which the principal motive output is shaft torque to a propeller.

Turbosupercharger: A turbine spun by engine exhaust gases that, in turn, spins a compressor to "charge" air taken in via a ram air duct. This air is then passed to the carburetor or supercharger.

Twin-spool engine: A turbine engine possessing a low-pressure/low-speed compressor and turbine on one shaft and a high-pressure/high-speed pair on a nested shaft such that these could run at different rpms. This allows more compressor stages for greater power with less risk of compressor stall and surges when off the ideal design condition.

Variable exit area nozzle: The adjustable nozzle of a turbojet engine that optimizes the area for the ideal exit pressure and so improves thrust production. It allows some compensation for the slow change in the rotation speed of engines owing to inertia (lag time in rpm to throttle) or to prevent compressor stalls. This became especially critical in go-around decisions or bolter calls for which rapid response could be critical.

Water injection: The introduction of a metered flow of water (usually a water–alcohol mixture) into the turbine engine compressor to increase mass flow while also aiding engine cooling.

Wind tunnel: A fabricated tunnel in which fans cause air motion through a test section in which a model of an aircraft or part thereof is mounted for collection of such data as forces, moments, and pressure distribution. In a full-scale wind tunnel, the test section is large enough to mount the entire aircraft and operate it remotely.

Wing loading: Aircraft gross weight divided by wing area. High wing loading via high aircraft weight or a small wing (reducing structural weight and aircraft drag) implies lower maneuverability than at lower wing loading. Also, without devices like Fowler flaps, landing speed—and by association landing distance—can be uncomfortably high at high wing loading.

Wingtip vortex: As air flows from the high-pressure zone beneath the wing to the low-pressure zone above, with aircraft forward velocity, the flow becomes a vortex trailing behind the wingtip. Many aircraft configurations and flight condition parameters determine the size and strength of the vortex.

Acronyms and Abbreviations

AAA:	anti-aircraft artillery
AAB:	army air base
AAF:	army air field
AAM:	air-to-air missile
AB:	afterburner, afterburning
ADC:	Air Defense Command
AEC:	Atomic Energy Commission
AEW:	airborne early warning
AMC:	Air Materiel Command
AoA:	angle of attack
APU:	auxiliary power unit
AR:	aerial refueling
ARDC:	Air Research and Development Command
ARH:	active radar homing
ARS:	Air Rescue Service
ASR:	air-sea rescue
ASW:	anti-submarine warfare
ATAR:	Anti-Tank Aircraft Rocket
ATO:	assisted take-off
ATSC:	Air Technical Services Command
att.:	attitude
aux.:	auxiliary
BLC:	boundary layer control
BuAer:	Bureau of Aeronautics
C:	Centigrade
CAA:	Civil Aeronautics Authority
cal:	caliber
CAS:	close air support
casevac:	casualty evacuation
CEP:	circular error probable

CG:	center of gravity
CIC:	Combat Information Center
cm:	centimeter, centimeters
COD:	Carrier Onboard Delivery
CP:	center of pressure
D. C.:	District of Columbia
DAC:	Douglas Aircraft Company
DoD:	Department of Defense
ECCM:	electronic counter-countermeasures
ECM:	electronic countermeasures
ELINT:	electronic intelligence
EW:	electronic warfare
ext.:	external
F:	Fahrenheit
FCS:	fire control system
FDSC:	Flush Deck Super Carrier
FFAR:	Folding-Fin Aircraft Rockets
FICON:	Fighter Conveyor
FOD:	foreign object damage
fpm:	feet per minute
fps:	feet per second
FRI:	Flight Refueling Incorporated
FRL:	Flight Refueling Limited
g:	acceleration due to gravity
gal:	U.S. gallons
GE:	General Electric
GW:	gross weight
hp:	horsepower
HVAR:	High Velocity Aircraft Rockets
int.:	internal
JATO:	Jet-Assisted Take-Off
JCS:	joint chiefs of staff
kg:	kilograms
km:	kilometer, kilometers
kN:	kilo-Newtons
kPa:	kilo-Pascals
kph:	kilometers per hour
kton:	kilotons
kW:	kilowatt, kilowatts
l:	liter, liters
lab:	laboratory
LABS:	Low Altitude Bombing Systems
lb:	pound, pounds
lbf:	pounds force

LORAN:	Long Range Navigation
LOS:	line of sight
LOX:	liquid oxygen
LSD:	Landing Ship, Dock
LST:	Landing Ship, Tank
m:	meter, meters
MAD:	magnetic anomaly detection
MATS:	Military Air Transport Service
max.:	maximum
MBC	Mobile Base Concept
McAir:	McDonnell Aircraft
MG:	machine gun, machine guns
mm:	millimeter, millimeters
mod, mods:	modification, modifications
mph:	statute miles per hour
mpm:	meters per minute
mps:	meters per second
MTBF	mean time between failures
N:	Newton, Newtons
NAA:	North American Aviation
NACA:	National Advisory Committee for Aeronautics
NADC:	Naval Air Development Center
NAF:	Naval Aircraft Factory
NAMU:	Naval Aircraft Modification Unit
NAS:	Naval Air Station, National Academy of Sciences
NATC:	Naval Air Test Center
NATO:	North Atlantic Treaty Organization
nav	navigation, navigator
NEPA:	Nuclear Energy for the Propulsion of Aircraft
NOTS:	Naval Ordnance Test Station
NRL:	Naval Research Laboratory
OLS:	optical landing system
ONR:	Office of Naval Research
ops:	operations
P&W:	Pratt & Whitney
Pax River:	NAS Patuxent River
PDRK:	People's Democratic Republic of Korea
PR:	photoreconnaissance
prop:	propeller
psi:	pounds per square inch
R&D:	research and development
RAF:	Royal Air Force
Razon:	Range and Azimuth only
RCM:	radio countermeasures

recce:	reconnaissance
recip:	reciprocating engine
RFP:	request for proposals
rpm:	revolutions per minute
S&C	stability and control
SAC:	Strategic Air Command
SAR:	search and rescue
SARH:	semi-active radar homing
SECDEF:	secretary of Defense
SECNAV:	secretary of the Navy
SFC:	specific fuel consumption
SHORAN:	Short Range Navigation
sonar:	sound, navigation and ranging
spec, specs:	specification or specifications
SSF:	Seaplane Strike Force
STOL:	short take-off and landing
TAC:	Tactical Air Command
TNT:	trinitrotoluene
tric, trics:	tricycle
U.K.:	United Kingdom
U.N.:	United Nations
U.S.A. or U.S.:	United States of America
USAAF or AAF:	United States Army Air Forces
USAF:	United States Air Force
USCG:	United States Coast Guard
USMC:	United States Marine Corps
USN:	United States Navy
USS:	United States Ship
USSR:	Union of Soviet Socialist Republics
VDT:	variable discharge turbine
VHF:	very high frequency
VIP:	very important person
VSTOL:	vertical/short take-off and landing
VTOL:	vertical take-off or landing
WADC:	Wright Air Development Center
WALC:	water-denatured ethyl alcohol
Wright-Patt:	Wright-Patterson AFB

1

Altered Landscape

The world-spanning, cataclysmic conflict of 1939–1945 had wrought profound changes in air warfare and the underlying technologies. The airplane and associated weapons were shown to have great potential for influencing the course of a war. However, these weapons depended on rapidly evolving technology. Many new weapons were being developed by the end of the conflict that would make aircraft safer, easier to operate, and more effective. The United States of America was well placed to exploit these technologies in the aftermath. It had survived the war without adverse impact to its industries and with no rebuilding to perform. The supply of raw materials was assured in a world where American influence was vast. The U.S. had to maintain a presence in many locales across the globe to avoid chaos as nations recovered.

There had been profound changes to air elements of the U.S. armed forces compared to 1939. A large standing military was to be maintained, avoiding the errors of the interwar years. However, there was so little concern with threats to the country that demobilization and defense cuts were deep. Forces were still equipped to comparatively enormous levels. The number of aircraft, bases, aircraft carriers, personnel with extensive experience, and support from the citizenry were still considerable. Given the destruction wrought during the war and the outcome, the U.S. was left in an enviable position with tremendous military power and monetary influence to bring to bear if this became necessary. There was also a national commitment to continue the technological growth of the force that the Germans had shown was behind in a few fields. The country was full of pride and awareness of its new place as the dominant military and economic power in the world, willing to maintain these resources. The government, however, was reluctant to fund the services to levels many felt appropriate, even in peacetime.

The U.S. came to rely on the new A-bomb as a cornerstone of its defense posture. The potential for preventing or ending a war with a single weapon, or the threat of such bombing, was very compelling. It also appeared to be a potentially less costly approach to defense. Enormous resources were devoted to these weapons and their delivery systems, although at the expense of more traditional arms.

The United States ended World War Two as the dominant military power in all respects. Its airpower had achieved remarkable feats of arms and would remain the largest force of airplanes ever fielded. This is suggested by a mass flyover of naval F4U and F6F airplanes during the surrender ceremony aboard the USS *Missouri* anchored in Tokyo Bay, September 2, 1945. (*U.S. Department of Defense*)

Although planning for the postwar U.S. military structure was mature at the time hostilities ended, political forces intervened. The United States Army Air Forces had initially planned to retain seventy-eight groups, but this proved impractical given demobilization and the budget squeeze. In eight months, the USAAF dropped 78 percent from 2.2 million personnel to 485,000, and airbases 77 percent from 783 to 177. A vast number of aviation units were deactivated or merged. The aircraft inventory went to 35,000 machines by October 1945, with 11,000 stored, then 23,200 with 15,000 stored—a 34 percent overall decrease with 66 percent drop in active machines. Many aircraft remained in former warzones to fulfill occupation duties, but most were eventually rotated home or salvaged in place. A large number of World War Two-era aircraft remained in service, though mostly in reserve and Air National Guard units, and more stored. Valuable knowledge and skills were inevitably lost. However, the Reserve and Air National Guard were composed mostly of combat veterans and so the embers to rekindle capabilities were retained.

The naval air arm struggled in a similar fashion. The navy's carrier fleet was greatly downsized at the end of hostilities, ultimately to fifteen active ships and more "mothballed." Consequently, air groups were deactivated or placed in reserve status. Essex-class vessels (ninety-seven aircraft accommodated) had a mix of long and short decks, with production halted at the end of the war. There were also three of the larger Midway-class flattops (133 aircraft) begun near the end of the war, all commissioned between 1945 and 1947. Seaplane tenders were reduced from thirteen large and fifty-four small vessels to four large and ten small.

Weapon system development programs also suffered in the immediate postwar period. Many were truncated or terminated, leaving only those seen as most worthy in the forecast circumstances of the new era. Within two years of the war, the defense budget had shrunk 84 percent, and ongoing development or research projects were reduced by half or more. Half the defense spending was to service debt from the war. The surviving programs proceeded at a more deliberate pace than during the conflict, with the armed services working to ensure delivery of weapons their warfighters needed and that met specifications ("specs") for the available budget.

World Theater

The postwar international milieu was unsettled. It demanded American attention to contain violence as societies and countries worked to settle into some new normalcy in the wake of the calamitous violence and border adjustments. Some of these struggles yielded "tectonic" shifts with profound future implications, to include China "falling" to communists, border divisions in Southeast Asia, and nationalist struggles in the Middle East. Where airpower was a factor, American equipment and sometime personnel were dominant. The deployed U.S. military units helped contain the violence and prepare for contingencies. America's greatest focus was the growing confrontation with communism and the Union of Soviet Socialist Republics, especially in the seam zone between Eastern and Western Europe as the Soviet Bloc solidified behind the "Iron Curtain."

The former ally began to appear as the principal threat to western democracy and influence almost immediately following the war. Their occupation of Eastern Europe and parts of Asia as part of the war's immediate aftermath became permanent thereafter, and they established Soviet-style communist governments controlled from Moscow. The free flow of people across these frontiers became tightly controlled. The enormous standing Red Army could, it was feared, overwhelm Western Europe, even with American military presence. With the aid of resources seized in occupied Germany, the USSR continued to press on with the development of new weapons matching western capabilities. In this way, they made steady progress that undermined America's lead. The U.S. attempted to keep track of this progress via airborne reconnaissance to include the growing field of electronic intelligence (ELINT).

The North Atlantic Treaty Organization (NATO) was formed in 1949 as a defense pact against the threat, and Germany was urged to rearm while other nations increased their military forces. This was accelerated with the advent of the Korean Conflict. The U.S. was the principal contributor of military might, with sizable forces stationed in Europe, and sold weapons to most of the other members—especially warplanes.

Reconnaissance moved to jet aircraft in an effort to stay ahead of opposition jet interceptors. The RB-45C outnumbered the pure bomber versions of the C-model Tornado, this image emphasizing the revised nose and aerial refueling receptacle on the spine. This reflected the diminishing value of this jet as a combat aircraft in the rapidly evolving jet bomber field, but great need for high-altitude, high-speed recce aircraft. The aircraft contributed importantly during the Korean Conflict and performed penetration missions over hostile nations in the Far East until strengthening air defenses precluded this. (*San Diego Air & Space Museum*)

The war ended with the Americans possessing the only atomic bombs and the only true strategic bomber in the B-29. With the demonstration in the capitulation of Japan, this appeared a profound "game-changer" in warfare and to make strategic bombardment the preeminent military element. However, other nations were determined to create the same capabilities for their defense. The Soviets reverse-engineered the B-29 and manufactured it as the Tupolev Tu-4, displaying it in 1947. However, significant manufacturing of the Tu-4 took years to ramp up. In August 1949, the Soviets detonated their first nuclear device. The U.S.A. was put on notice that it was no longer invulnerable. Given the Soviet propensity for expanding communism by fomenting discord throughout the world and the American promotion of competing democratic ideals, a dangerous new international contest emerged.

The revelation of Soviet nuclear capability caused a shift in military funding. The intelligence community was warning that the USSR would soon have hundreds of A-bombs and intercontinental bombers.[1] It would be vital that these aircraft be destroyed quickly and efficiently, preferably on the first intercept. The air force began deploying interceptors to bases far removed from the continental U.S., particularly Alaska and Greenland, to confront the bombers. However, those fighters did not possess the performance for the jet bombers eventually expected. The Berlin Blockade, fall of China, hardening of the Eastern Europe occupation, and support for insurgencies worldwide all appeared to show a steady march of communism. All played into widespread anxiety and a consequent surge of rearmament. The outbreak of the Korean Conflict in June 1950 was seen as another move to assert communist rule by force, with the North Koreans supported by the USSR and China. This brought America and many allies together in a shooting war, though constrained. Numerous weapon development programs received funding, intended to not only wage the conventional war in the Far East, but also prepare to meet further aggression elsewhere. Indeed, the majority of the funding went to strategic systems, with nuclear bomb manufacturing accelerated to include developing the markedly more powerful hydrogen bomb. American war plans were then to deliver A-bombs on the Soviet homeland while conventional forces were mustered and deployed to Europe. Many more weapons and delivery systems were required. The Cold War and arms race were birthed, with weapons technology the determiner of military prowess via the ability to wreak devastation in a bid to deter aggression.

Reorganization

In this postwar environment, some U.S. organizational contraction was inevitable. However, more profound changes came with the National Defense Act of 1947. The War Department was reorganized as the National Military Establishment with a secretary of defense (SECDEF). It also formally established the joint chiefs of staff (JCS) upon which sat the military chief of each service, with a service represented as the chairman on a rotating basis. The act created the United States Air Force (USAF) in September 1947 as a separate service besides the army and U.S. Navy (USN), and identified the Marine Corps (USMC) as independent under the Department of the Navy, with their air wings equipped by the department. The National Military Establishment became the Department of Defense (DoD) in August 1949 with the three individual service secretaries then falling under SECDEF authority.

All of these changes were under the edict of "unification" for a reasoned distribution of roles and missions, plus the associated weapon systems. Decreasing redundancy sought efficient application of scare defense funds. For example, within the DoD was a Research and Development Board and a Munitions Board to coordinate those resources across the services for maximum efficiency. However, the goal was only partially met due to inter-service competition and bickering. Each feared they would be under-represented in budget decisions. With airpower seen as such a decisive element, the USAF was graced with a sizable slice of the "pie."

The budget squeeze, evolving technologies, and the creation of the USAF all created disputes over roles and responsibilities. The USAF and navy argued over nuclear weapon delivery and strategic objectives, plus basic air combat operations (ops) ashore. The navy perceived that the USAF wanted to push naval air out of business or, at best, take it over. The army insisted it retain anti-aircraft defenses, to include defense of US territory, while the air force insisted on possessing the air role in continental air defenses.

A meeting of the service chiefs in Key West, Florida, during March 1948, defined the divisions. While the USAF retained the primary role in strategic air warfare, the navy had a collateral function, interpreted to include attacking inland targets and employing atomic weapons. While the Key West Agreement, and results of a subsequent meeting in Newport, Rhode Island, in August 1948, found middle ground in each area of dispute, underlying suspicion and pushing the limits of the agreement continued.

There was also movement in industry. Tens of thousands of employees were let go, and excess manufacturing floor space was left vacant or turned to other endeavors. Goodyear decided not to compete in the aircraft market and to concentrate on its automobile market. Likewise, the aircraft and aero-engine divisions of Ford Motor Company and General Motors (Eastern Aircraft) were closed and the plants turned back to producing cars. The Stinson division of Consolidated-Vultee was sold off to Piper in 1948. More significantly, Curtiss-Wright was unable to win meaningful contracts, especially production, and ultimately sold its aircraft assets to North American Aviation (NAA) of Inglewood, California, in 1951. Military project profits began to return in 1950 and 1951 as development efforts moved to production, spurred by the Korean Conflict.

The War Department/DoD, concerned about so many aircraft plants concentrated on the west coast and northeastern seaboard, among other factors, sought to disperse them via "encouragement" of the manufacturers to relocate. Yet, industry consolidation and defense infrastructure realignment were closely monitored to ensure this did not undermine essential capabilities. Among the adjustments was Chance Vought Aircraft's move from Stratford, Connecticut, into the former NAA factory in Dallas, Texas, during 1948 and 1949. This was no mean feat as it meant breaking down and packing 13,500 tons of equipment and moving it 1,700 miles (2,736 km), then erecting all the equipment back into an operable industrial plant. Also coming along were 13,000 key personnel and their families. The plant offered more space and better weather. At USN urging, Bell Aircraft broke out its helicopter division and moved it from Buffalo, New York, to a new facility in Fort Worth, Texas, in 1951. Vultee moved from Downey to San Diego to concentrate the California resources of Consolidated-Vultee—commonly referred to as Convair. In 1952, Northrop was able to establish a presence in the high desert above Los Angeles, near Edwards AFB, at Palmdale. Aircraft assembled in Hawthorne were flown to Palmdale for final equipment installation and acceptance flights outside the dense Los Angeles basin. Some aircraft manufacturers were favored by the individual services. These were not firm divisions, but the unofficial alignment also tended to edge out firms that might have had good solutions to offer.

As rapidly as the American aircraft industry expanded to meet the demands of total war, it shrank after. Manufacturing capacity was much reduced, but it rose again as the Korean Conflict freed money for a higher volume of acquisitions. This image shows a small portion of the Republic Aviation plant in Farmingdale, New York, on Long Island, where F-84F fighters are being assembled for the U.S. Air Force. (*National Museum of the United States Air Force*)

Aircraft development and production programs required the labor of thousands of engineers at the airframer and engine manufacturer plants as well as subcontractors. At times, these became a scare commodity and risked pacing an aircraft program. This image shows engineers at work at the Lockheed Aircraft "Skunk Works" in Burbank, California. (*Air Force Test Center*)

Until mathematical and then computer tools replaced it, the ship building practice of lofting was continued in aircraft construction. These Lockheed, Burbank, employees are transferring blueprint lines to full-scale on metal sheets, especially curves, using a variety of techniques to include projectors and flexible strips held by weighted hooks. When cut out, these templates aided in constructing the jigs for the production line. (*National Archives*)

Army Struggles

The end of the war had left Army Ground Forces with an organic air arm composed of liaison airplanes. With the formation of the USAF, all air elements were stripped away except this corps of light airplanes. The army's aircraft were to be acquired through the air force or navy, or by direct commercial purchase. The USAF conducted primary flight and mechanics training for the army. By late 1945, there was agreement that the army could also train on helicopters, but there was no follow-up until 1947. Under the Key West Agreement, the limitations were more clearly defined as helicopters of no more than 4,000 lb (1,814 kg) and fixed-wing 2,500 lb (1,134 kg). These supported unarmed liaison and light battlefield transport duties. All other missions were to be executed by the USAF.

Postwar funding only allowed aircraft to be procured at a low rate, and so machines from the war predominated for many years. Specialized liaison airplanes developed during the war, with tremendous utility, were either passed by or bought in only small numbers. The service was preparing in summer 1950 to seek battlefield transport helicopters, and the Korea experience emphasized this need. The USAF resisted relaxing the weight restrictions until finally arbitrated in October 1951. There would be no weight restrictions and aircraft were limited to battlefield missions only. The army had also been dissatisfied with USAF training of its aviators, contributing to the ill-preparedness of the corps. The 1951 agreement included allowing the army to take over this activity.

As when the USAAF had been formed, the emergence of the USAF was accompanied by concerns from the "ground pounders" that the airmen would neglect their obligations to the army as it pursued strategic bombers and jet fighters. Only the next war would demonstrate any validity of their concerns.

The army aviation fleet degraded from want of funds and replacement aircraft. By the start of the Korean Conflict, the army possessed 525 liaison and 143 passenger airplanes, plus fifty-seven utility helicopters. Many of the fixed-wing airplanes were World War Two liaison or trainer types and commercial machines with no warzone role. The years of combat permitted hundreds more aircraft to be acquired. From 481 aircraft taken up in the fiscal year 1949–1950, 3,637 were ordered in 1952 and 702 the following year. By the end of 1952, the service operated 1,534 liaison and 320 passenger airplanes plus 647 utility helicopters and seventy-two cargo choppers. Helicopter procurement funding for the army increased from $2 million to $42.4 million in 1951. The emergency and the growing capability of helicopters, with the USMC acquiring troop transports, led to the army seeking similar machines. After

The army retained a corps of liaison light-planes after the creation of the U.S. Air Force, but they were poorly funded and equipped. The Ryan L-17 Navion was a commercial purchase intended only for stateside or rear area liaison work. Yet the emergency required "all hands on deck" and so the aircraft was operated on improvised fields in Korea supporting combat operations as seen here in the company of an L-19. (*National Museum of the United States Air Force*)

more arguments with the USAF, it was agreed in November 1952 that the army could operate heavier helicopters for small unit assault. This agreement also re-imposed a weight limitation on light airplanes at 5,000 lb (2,268 kg), though subject to review.

Air Force Strides

In March 1946, the USAAF had reorganized into three operational commands. These, created from the Continental Air Force, were Air Defense Command (ADC), Tactical Air Command (TAC), and Strategic Air Command (SAC). There were still numbered air forces and regional commands, such as Caribbean Air Command and Alaskan Air Command. It added Continental Air Command in December 1948 to administer the reserve and air guard forces. Air force and navy transport elements were merged into Military Air Transport Service (MATS), which included the Air Weather Service. For what had become an air force with a global mission, weather prognostication and planning products had taken on great importance, requiring expanded and more reliable resources. In the weapon system development arena, aircraft engineering and acquisition functions were separated, with Air Technical Services Command becoming Air Materiel Command (AMC) and grounded at what had become Wright-Patterson AFB, joining two nearly contiguous bases. Although opposed by the air staff, research and development (R&D) took equal footing with the establishment of Research and Development Command in January 1950, soon renamed Air Research and Development Command (ARDC). Most of the laboratories, engineering shops, and flight test activities fell under the Wright Air Development Center (WADC) within ARDC. The service also established a deputy chief of staff of development to further strengthen R&D.

The USAF had initially envisioned a force of seventy groups to include twenty-five groups of heavy bombers, seventeen of day fighters, and three of all-weather interceptors. The all-weather interceptors were soon raised to six. However, budget shortfalls constrained the force to forty-eight groups including seven of day fighters and five all-weather, with tactical aviation particularly reduced. The year 1949 was particularly tight, and the following year looked equally grim. Even the forty-eight-group force that eventually solidified included units that were skeleton teams or reflected on paper only.

An Air Policy Commission was formed in 1948 to assess the best means of answering the nation's air warfare requirements. The resulting 1949 report endorsed rapidly expanding the air force, the principal holder of the relevant missions. Yet, building the desired force composition remained a never-ending push against funding inertia.

At the end of 1945, the USAAF had been formulating characteristics of the next generation of aircraft, taking advantage of new technologies, and these continued to evolve in the face of emerging or envisioned threats. Exploiting all the advances made during the war was expected to enhance USAF mission effectiveness and remain the dominant airpower team in the world.

The air force felt that the strategic bomber had proven a decisive weapon during the war, despite the mixed conclusions of the bomber survey that followed. The introduction of nuclear weapons only enforced the conclusion that strategic bombers remained the preeminent element in modern warfare, and so nurturing such a force was the number one priority. Anything that did not contribute to this mission was bound to play second fiddle when it came to funding during an era of shrinking defense budgets. Bringing jet fighters and bombers, with all associated systems and air weapons, to a mature and operationally effective level was essential.

Particularly the intercontinental B-36 was brought along through budget battles and development challenges. Defending the bombers with escort fighters was the next necessity, as emphasized by the lessons of the past war. One goal was to grow bomber speed to make escort unnecessary, limiting attacks to a tail intercept where a tail gun alone could deal with the threat. In the meantime, their lack meant that the bombers would be expected to fly individual paths to separate targets, thus swamping enemy defenses. Bomber formations appeared anachronistic in the age of atomic bombs, especially when the bombers were bought in the low hundreds instead of the thousands during the war.

The long-range bomber escort became a protracted and vexing problem, consuming many resources. The perceived growing threat of Soviet bombers carrying A-bombs motivated the USAF to invigorate its high-speed and all-weather interceptor programs, plus any reliable communications links, to equip ADC. "All-weather" became important for this mission, seeking to avoid a situation such as the Battle of

The new U.S. Air Force worked to create the best stable of aircraft to include jet trainers. Lockheed created a prototype trainer offshoot of the P-80 Shooting Star fighter under their own funding and this attracted USAF interest, then the first of many production contracts as the T-33A in January 1948. The U.S. Navy also acquired the machines as the TV-2. The T-bird became a legend and served around the world for decades in many roles apart from the training of many thousands of pilots. (*National Archives*)

the Bulge during the last war when air support was grounded by weather, sparing the Germans from that concern in pressing their offensive. Requirements were aimed at intercept and strike in inclement weather but came to include night ops as well given the commonality in aircraft equipment. Radar and anti-ice protection were all features of such aircraft.

The advent of atomic weapons small enough to be carried by fighter-bombers brought notions of tactical employment. Such could rapidly affect the conduct of a war. In particular, the diversion of forces to Korea, leaving reduced resources available to defend Europe from Soviet adventures, were seen as one motivation. Consequently, TAC took on the nuclear strike mission in November 1950, and aircraft began to be modified or built new for the mission.

Navy Evolution

The U.S. Navy had won significant victories during the war and facilitated others. The carrier air wings had emerged as the most powerful element of naval power. The end of the conflict found the USN without peer adversary, with none on the foreseeable horizon. The tensions with the USSR were primarily focused in Europe. The Red Navy was no menace and so little influence on force composition decisions. Furthermore, the role strategic bombing played in the victory, and with very capable army air forces aircraft based throughout the world, appeared to diminish the traditional role of sea power and naval air. These conclusions were the motivation behind the deep cuts in carriers and naval aircraft.

The USAAF/USAF role as the sole delivery force for atomic weapons, and the new air force perceived as the darling of the services, created deep resentment within the navy. Although it was permitted to employ nuclear weapons as part of its sea control mission, it did not initially possess the means to do this. The USAF defended its new roles and missions jealously and resisted navy efforts to grow its power-projection means with an A-bomb delivery capability. The two services vociferously argued the value and vulnerabilities of their respective assets. The competition was evident when the new service emphasized its presence by stenciling "United States Air Forces" on all its aircraft. The USN responded in kind with "United States Navy" or just a large "NAVY." When the air force set out to take and hold every official aviation record, the navy followed suit.

The navy sought ways to deploy aircraft capable of carrying the exceptionally large and heavy A-bombs of the era, necessarily from aircraft carriers after the Key West Agreement. The Midway and Essex ships were unsuitable for the heavy aircraft associated with the mission. Consequently, the Flush Deck Super Carrier (FDSC, no structure protruding above the deck) was conceived, and the USS *United States* (CVA-58)—the first of five in the class—was ordered in August 1948. This was to be a 65,000-ton vessel, compared with 45,000 tons for the Midway and the 27,000-ton Essex. It was also costly, and the budget did not seem to support both the new carrier and continued acquisition of the USAF's B-36. The national debate about the choice became embarrassingly heated, with admirals and generals making public claims and counter-claims. When the USAF posited that the B-36 flew at altitudes unattainable by fighters, the navy flew a F2H-1 to 52,000 feet (15,850 m).

A new SECDEF canceled the FDSC in April 1949, prompting the secretary of the navy (SECNAV) to resign. Other carrier construction was curtailed, three mothballed, and the navy budget cut further while B-36 funding was expanded. This caused such a row that Congress investigated via hearings while admirals and generals traded sharp words about undermining national security. The legislators found value in both arguments, restoring the FDSC and the continued upgrade of existing carriers to support jet operations, which began in 1947 as Project SBC 27A. The new SECNAV was so perturbed over the "Revolt of the Admirals" that he compelled the chief of naval operations to resign and disciplined other officers.

The advent of the Korean Conflict little more than a year later, with the continuous need for carrier-based aviation, showed the fallacy of cutting the navy so deeply. Their policies shown to be gravely shortsighted, the SECDEF and SECNAV resigned. The service then possessed fifteen operational carriers, and the three preserved ships were soon reactivated. Even as vessels were pulled from mothballs and put to sea, they could be manned and equipped only by drawing on the naval reserves.

Changes were occurring in the carrier environment that affected aircraft and operations. The length of the wartime carriers was judged too short for jet combat aircraft. Catapult assist became common to improve safety as aircraft weight increased. Escort carriers (CVE) were just 512 feet (156 m) long and 63 feet (19 m) across and could generally barely manage 19 knots compared with 33 knots for the Essex-class ships. The service took great interest in the British steam catapult, angled deck, and mirror landing system developments as a more practical means of launching jet aircraft. Steam catapults could propel the jets with enough speed to permit full combat loads while the hydraulic "cats," even at full pressure, did not permit this. However, this also brought new concerns with engine response to steam ingestion. Shore testing was underway in 1953. The angled deck permitted simultaneous launch and recovery ops, especially bolters, without risking collision with aircraft positioned ahead. The mirror or optical landing system (OLS) was a system of lights allowing the pilot to judge a glide path rather than a landing signals officer waving flags.

The Project 27A changes included reinforced deck and elevators to take 40,000-lb (18,144-kg) aircraft, jet blast deflectors, higher capacity hydraulic catapults, more fuel bunkers, and additional deck space with a revised island, plus the elimination of gun platforms. Beyond the nine 27A carriers were six 27Cs that added more capable arrestment and barrier systems, steam catapults, the angled deck, and other improvements. The carriers were also given nuclear weapon storage with dedicated elevators. The SCB 110 modifications further strengthened decks and elevators of Essex hulls to allow them to take aboard the projected A3D bombers (see page 165). The USS *Antietam* (CVA-36, Essex class) was fitted with a "canted" deck and began sea trials in early 1953.

This turbulent period made for a shockingly high accident rate of about fifty-one aircraft per 100,000 flying hours by 1950. In 1954, at fifty-three per 100,000 hours, this amounted to a shocking 776 machines destroyed.[2] Without the angled deck that

Although seeking to exploit the speed benefits of the jet engine, the first generation of combat aircraft had straight wings. This is typified by the F9F-2 (123575) on an elevator of the USS *Bon Homme Richard* (CVA-31) on November 29, 1952. The wingtip tanks were also emblematic of this period. (*National Archives*)

| As Built | SCB-27A | SBC-27C | Angled Deck |

This composite image shows *Essex* class carrier modernization from 1944 as the vessel was adapted to jet aircraft. Externally, the changes are mostly altered elevators and reduced number of gun installations. The angled deck, first introduced in early 1953, was the most significant in reducing mishaps and increasing the tempo of flight operations. (*National Archives*)

was soon to be introduced, ready aircraft were placed in the path of landing airplanes. If the trap went wrong and the barriers failed to halt the aircraft, a pile-up or other damage was likely. Many barrier encounters ended with some damage to at least the engaging aircraft. If all cables were missed, the aircraft went into the barrier of two steel cables stretched across the deck at about 3-foot height to keep the aircraft from barreling into parked aircraft and personnel. In a tricycle gear aircraft, the first cable could shear off the nose gear and the second shear off the canopy and pilot's head, or the propellers cut the cable. The Davis barrier was developed that had canvas straps above the deck that, when engaged by the initial part of the aircraft, lifted the cable from the deck to engage the main landing gear struts. Barriers were rigged depending on the nature of the aircraft coming aboard.

It was probably only the Korean Conflict that kept naval aviation alive long enough to survive those tough times. The accident rate declined after the war with angled deck carriers, steam catapults, and OLS.

The navy's efforts to define unique naval missions, contributing to power-projection and nuclear strike, in a bid to remain relevant and so sustained by the defense budget, found expression in several new aircraft programs and unique applications of airpower. Carrier-based bombers capable of carrying the first generation of atomic bombs to meaningful distances were one such challenging effort. The resulting aircraft were cumbersome to operate aboard ship, especially with existing deck lengths. The size and weight of nuclear weapons steadily decreased to the point where more typical naval jets could deploy them. Unmanned aircraft—cruise missiles—were another. Projects to launch ballistic missiles from ships found this to be most problematic. A captured V-2 rocket was fired off USS *Midway* in October 1947, and there were concepts for carriers converted to such a role, possible with atomic warheads.

The aerial minelaying mission gained traction in budget battles as a relatively inexpensive sea control measure, uniquely navy. Mines could isolate a shoreline

An F9F-2 (123494) takes the barrier aboard USS *Midway* (CVB-41) on November 11, 1951, but then breaks through to barrel into a parked aircraft at the bow. Conducting launch and recovery operations aboard the veteran carriers possessing a single deck with ready aircraft created conditions conducive to such accidents. With the introduction of heavy jets, the accident rates soared to dismaying levels, demanding changes to carrier decks. (*National Archives*)

and waterway, if not an entire nation, and so significantly influence a conflict. The department also saw it as an avenue for the service to develop aircraft capable of being armed with "nukes" as well. Particularly flying boat bombers might be made to safely land in the open ocean and be refueled from tenders or even submarines. They also conceived a vertical take-off or landing (VTOL) fighter that could operate from small decks on numerous surface ships for fleet air defense rather than rely on the few and potentially vulnerable carriers. Anti-aircraft missiles were also pursued with vigor.

In the late 1940s, the navy promulgated the Mobile Base Concept (MBC) by which seaplanes would quickly establish a presence in suitably sheltered waters after which vessels would bring in heavy freight and many more personnel. These would be offloading to a floating dock to be assembled in place. To explore this potential, the service planned to develop a heavy and fast flying boat transport.

Expanding on the MBC was the Seaplane Strike Force (SSF). This would be made up of striking, service, and defensive units. The striking unit was High-Speed Minelaying jet-powered flying boats tended by the service unit of seaplane tenders, ammunition ships, tankers, and oilers. Apart from nuclear weapon delivery, the airplane would perform conventional bombing, mining, and reconnaissance missions. The defensive unit would be composed of a jet seaplane fighter, similarly supported at sea. Most of these elements would normally be dispersed, coming together only when necessary to support operations in the open sea and so generating a low signature for detection and engagement. Extensive work in a floating dry dock was expected to be conducted in protected waters such as a lagoon.

Studies begun in 1949 suggested these capabilities were within reach. Work began to explore the concepts with demonstrations, ship modifications, and new aircraft development. This extended into the late 1950s and was clearly going to be a long-term and costly realignment of service resources for which the whole-hearted dedication of leadership was uncertain.

Development Resources

Even more than the last war, the next was expected to be waged in the laboratory well before the first shots were fired. It was clear to all that technology could make a war of shorter duration and fewer friendly personnel loses, though destruction could be vast with the advent of atomic weapons. Airpower was expected to be even more dominant. Hence, despite the postwar contraction, more capabilities were built for R&D.

The National Advisory Committee for Aeronautics (NACA) quickly refocused on research rather than directly assisting aircraft development teams. The wartime restrictions on information dissemination were eased, and NACA technical conferences were resumed. However, as the confrontation with the USSR deepened and the Korean Conflict emerged, classification and control on research results began to be reasserted.

New test cells were designed and built at all the NACA centers to meet the demands of the programs emerging in the military and commercial fields, substantially pushing the state-of-the-art. Among the new resources were the first computers. The problem

Above: The navy paid scant attention to helicopters during the war, leaving the coast guard to explore their search and rescue potential. They finally turned their attention to rotorcraft in summer 1946 to seek machines suitable for naval applications and supporting Marine Corps missions. They put together their first helicopter squadron in summer 1946 to assist during Operation Crossroads, the atomic bomb tests at Bikini Atoll, in the Pacific. This HOS-1 (Army R-6) hovers above the USS *Saidor* (CVE-117) on June 3, 1946, during that endeavor. It has features of the wartime YR-6C with added external fuel cells, a rescue hoist, and an entrance step bar. (*National Museum of Naval Aviation*)

Below: The NACA wind tunnels, among their many other test cells, were invaluable national assets. In particular, the very large full-scale tunnels at Langley and Ames were not duplicated elsewhere in the country. The Langley tunnel is shown with the Custer CCW-2 Channel Wing (dressed with fabric covering) mounted. (*National Aeronautics and Space Administration*)

of the transonic wind tunnel, with choking and reflected shocks, was finally overcome with the advent of the slotted throat developed at NACA Langley. New airfoils were created and performance documented supporting high-speed flight.

It was clear that turbojet engines still lacked thrust to push aircraft supersonic through the drag rise in level flight, and rockets remained questionable for combat aircraft (see later). Overall drag reduction to facilitate transonic flight was investigated extensively. Consequently, the NACA devised the area rule. This sought a uniform longitudinal distribution of airplane cross-sectional area from the nose to the tail to discourage shock formation and so drag rise. Opposite the wing, a reduction in fuselage area would be necessary, producing a "coke bottle" appearance. First presented in September 1952, area rule was initially derived analytically, checked in the Langley wind tunnel, and then via rocket-launched models at their Wallops Island station.

The next challenge was the heating effects of supersonic flight, making the cockpit uncomfortable, undermining subsystem functions, and risking loss of structural strength. This was soon addressed with new or revised facilities. Flight testing continued at all its center, but the NACA also established a High Speed Flight Research Station at their facility at Muroc Army Air Base (AAB, soon AFB).

The course of USAF materiel investment to ensure the superiority of its arsenal was guided by advice from various bodies. The USAAF/USAF began working to the recommendations of the Scientific Advisor Group (later Scientific Advisor Board) that followed the end of the war. The recommendations were guided, in part, by a study, published immediately following the war, laying out a weapons technology R&D path. Among the advice, backed by the outgoing chief of staff, General Arnold, was the establishment of an air force R&D center. This emerged in 1949 as the Air Engineering Development Center (later Arnold Engineering Development Center) in Tullahoma, Tennessee. It included new wind tunnels and engine test cells. Many other resources were being created. Eglin AFB, Florida, built a climatic test hangar, with the temperature ranging from -65 to 165 °F (-54 to 74°C).

A more intensive regimen of testing had been imposed during the later years of the war, and this was further codified. Particularly hazardous air force flight testing continued at the remote Muroc, on the edge of Rogers Dry Lake. This was renamed Edwards AFB in December 1949 in honor of a test pilot killed performing such duties. After Howard Hughes' XF-11 crash into a residential area (see page 387), the air force insisted that all initial flight tests of new designs be conducted at the desert base. The base also came to include rocket test stands as the Rocket Propulsion Laboratory.

As before, naval aircraft development was guided by the Bureau of Aeronautics (BuAer). Also, the Office of Naval Research (ONR) was under the assistant secretary of the navy for air as an independent body. Naval test installations were derived from those emerging from the war. The principal navy aircraft testing site was the Naval Air Test Center (NATC) at Naval Air Station (NAS) Patuxent River ("Pax"), Maryland. The Naval Air Modification Unit (NAMU) at Johnsville, Pennsylvania, became the Naval Air Development Station in 1947 and later Naval Air Development Center (NADC). All were initially associated with the Naval Aircraft Factory (NAF) in Philadelphia, Pennsylvania. Air-launched ordnance tests were usually conducted on the California desert range around NAS China Lake, the Naval Ordnance Test Station (NOTS), and the pilotless aircraft unit at nearby Marine Corps Air Station at Mojave, California.

The growth of missile testing, especially as long-range and exceptionally high-altitude missiles were sought, demanded new test ranges. The army expanded its White Sands Proving Grounds in New Mexico into a missile range. The USAF created the Long Range Proving Ground at Cape Canaveral, Florida, in 1950, but renamed it the Air Force Missile Test Center, Patrick AFB, in 1951. The navy employed NAS Point Mugu on the southern California coast, becoming the Naval Air Missile Test Center in October 1946. The NACA further developed Wallops Island for missile testing, becoming the Pilotless Aircraft Research Division. Many of its rockets carried aerodynamic shapes for data collection or tested rocket and ramjet propulsion units.

A side note to development resources was personnel. With indisputable evidence that the Germans had made significant progress in several areas of aeronautics and propulsion, the U.S. government moved to exploit this knowledge. At the end of the war in Europe, German R&D centers were occupied and materials were gathered. Personnel were interviewed and paid to assist in collating documents and record their past work. Thousands of tons of hardware and paper were shipped to the U.S. for closer study and dissemination. This included entire wind tunnels, aircraft, and

Initially lacking suitable wind tunnels to collect clean transonic data, other methods were employed. Among these was launching a model aboard a rocket, usually from NACA's Wallops Island, Virginia, to collect data via telemetry or recorded onboard to be dug up after the model impacted the tidal mud. This image shows a model of the Convair XFY-1 atop a rocket being prepared for launch from Wallops. (*National Aeronautics and Space Administration*)

engines. To benefit more fully from the associated personnel, the government recruited approximately 1,600 German and Austrian engineers, scientists, and technicians who otherwise would be little employed in the postwar European economy. They began laboring at U.S. government facilities, but they soon moved out to industry. Their contributions to better focusing and accelerating American progress are notable. The USSR undertook similar activities, though as a forced or coerced activity.

Programs Come and Go

The new weapons emerging from the war and those evolving against new or altering requirements kept aeronautical technology and manufacturing moving ahead. From the immediate postwar slowdown, with companies idling or closing shop awaiting new contracts to the high volume and urgent work for another war, the "feast or famine" nature of military aircraft development and manufacturing remained unchanged. Yet aircraft technology advanced at an astonishing clip, sustaining a continual pace of experimentation and testing. The "state-of-the-art" was pressed ahead at such a fast rate that the obsolescence of military aircraft and their systems could be measured in just a few years for fighters.

All services, but especially the air force, wished to have more than a single program in development against a requirement in the event one stumbled or came up short. Budget realities generally denied this approach. Yet the next, more capable model of a new type was being designed as the current one entered production. In some cases, two models were in production simultaneously. Additionally, the practice of placing production orders for aircraft still in development, even if not having flown or undergone operational suitability evaluations, persisted—although questioned by lawmakers as a peacetime practice. When it came to "urgent requirements," the services were still able to press for such authorization. Some contracts were allowed without the competition normally required by law.

The adoption of jet engines was rapid, ensuring a comparatively quick turnover in inventory from the war. Exploiting the airspeed enabled meant design changes to avoid compressibility effects that undermined performance and safety. The weight of armament increased for lethality and as new aircraft weapons were introduced. For the bomber, accommodating atomic bombs was a persistent requirement. Where older aircraft had to be retained, modifications to more modern standards were commonplace.

Dealing with the new jet engine was also a learning process. The high fuel consumption rate of the early turbojets meant a tremendous increase in fuel volume to meet practical range and endurance requirements. The "jets" would be larger and heavier than their World War Two predecessors. For example, the North American P-51D of 1944 had an internal fuel capacity of 269 gal (1,018 l) and could fly 950 miles (1,529 km) at cruise altitude, clean-wing (3.5 miles per gallon). The selected replacement, the Northrop F-89D, had 2,434 gal (9,214 l) internal to bring it to 764 miles (1,230 km) in combat range (0.3 miles per gallon). The 9,386-lb (4,257-kg) gross

The jet engine was still maturing when pressed into use on military aircraft, but that created the impetus for progress. Reliability, time between overhauls, and efficiency, all improved rapidly, although some aircraft projects floundered given undelivered or poorly performing powerplants. This image shows General Electric J47s removed from air force B-45A bombers. (*San Diego Air & Space Museum*)

weight (GW) Grumman F8F-1 carried 183 gal (693 l) of fuel internally (13 percent fuel fraction), while the 14,235-lb (6,457-kg) F9F-2 had 683 gal (4,128 l) internally (33 percent fuel fraction) for around 3,400 lb (1,542 kg) additional fuel weight.

In another dimension, stall airspeeds (and so landing speeds) went up for these heavier aircraft with thinner airfoils. For example, the P-51D landed at 100 mph (161 kph) while the F-100A stalled at 159 mph (256 kph). High landing speeds also demanded higher-capability wheel braking or arrestment systems. For naval aircraft, this meant a tremendous change in weight from take-off to landing just from fuel burn, and so a change in stall speeds. The disparity eventually led to the adoption of angle of attack gages in the cockpit.

Many other design aspects were evolving as well. Ensuring suitable stability and control (S&C) plus handling qualities required the continuing growth of autopilot and stability augmentation systems. Autopilots were also enablers for unmanned missiles for which increasing reliability was a constant imperative.[3] Pressurization and ejection seats were becoming common features. The demand for greater operational safety saw growth in the application of such systems as fire suppression, anti-ice/de-ice systems, wheel brakes with anti-skid, and improved instruments. Both weapon delivery and intercept required an unending advance in radar, navigation, and communication systems such that the avionics content rose. The addition of more powered systems, some flight-critical, meant a growth of hydraulic, electrical, pneumatic, and cooling systems with greater redundancy. Electronic content grew steadily, but failure rates were high and the services had to greatly expand their electronics maintenance and repair capacity and expertise. Aircraft became more complex and heavier, yet operators demanded greater reliability. The rapidly changing requirements and equipment content of each new aircraft also made estimating design weight most difficult.

Non-combat aircraft were also moving ahead as a more operational capability was sought. Helicopters advanced at an almost dizzying pace. Transports likewise grew in performance and the tactical/assault transport came into its own. The mammoth war effort had seen hundreds of airfields created all over the world, including in formerly remote areas. The flying boat was no longer essential in reaching such locales. Yet, the navy continued to develop such warplanes for special purposes and buy them in modest quantities. The dedicated reconnaissance platforms in development at the end of the war were passed over owing to the budget crunch while fleet aircraft were adapted to the role.

Tremendous resources were expended while attempting to create intercontinental airplanes and cruise missiles. This was generally unsuccessful except for making aerial refueling an operationally practical capability. With the perceived threat from the Soviets increasing, the ballistic missile was given more emphasis—that story is beyond the scope of this book. Only in 1954 were those programs accelerated, and systems were initially deployed in 1959. However, test results appeared so promising that wing-borne counterparts were being canceled well short of those achievements. There was also throughout the period a dispute between the army and the air force over ownership of the mission for delivering long-range strikes via missiles. The more they looked like artillery shells, the more they appeared to belong to the army. Hence, the airmen worked for missiles with wings and air-breathing engines. The navy suffered less confrontation with such systems, provided they remained at sea.

As the new aircraft and systems grew in complexity, refined manufacturing techniques had to be brought to bear. This meant that the time to produce each new generation of aircraft increased markedly. For example, the B-17 bomber had required 200,000 labor hours to produce while the B-29 and B-36 each required about 3,000,000 hours. The XB-52 would require 7,000,000.[4] Costs of aircraft also rose with the never-ending demand for greater performance, mission effectiveness, and safety. The price of constructing a pound of aircraft ran $10–15 during the war, but $22–25 by 1950.[5]

Engine Woes

The war had fostered the new turbine engine to replace reciprocating engines for propulsion on at least some aircraft. Free of propellers with tip speed and efficiency limitations, turbojets offered greater airspeed—and speed is survival, reducing vulnerability. They are also less complex and give greater altitude performance. The jet engine generally has superior power:weight ratios compared to high-performance military recips. As one example, the Pratt & Whitney R-4360 had a dry weight of roughly 3,500 lb (1,588 kg), not counting any turbosuperchargers and intercoolers or the propeller. The unaugmented General Electric J33 was 1,750 lb (794 kg), discounting the inlets and ducting. The piston aero engine was clearly at its limits while turbine engines had tremendous growth potential.

The new engines engender operational adjustments. The early propensity for fires on startup, usually from excessive fuel in the combustor and exhaust, were so prevalent that a "fire guard" with an extinguisher was commonly standing beside the aircraft during engine starts. Some engines had to be run up before take-off brake release to allow internal conditions to stabilize. Others had low engine air inlets, and so foreign object damage (FOD) became a hazard that required careful clearing of aprons, taxiways, and runways of debris. The services introduced standard jet fuels, meaning a separate fuel supply at bases with mixed airplanes.[6] The new jets did not slow down as quickly as "prop jobs" when the throttle was pulled. Consequently, it was difficult to use power to adjust a flight path on landing approach given the slow response to throttle. It became necessary to change drag instantly via speedbrakes, which became commonplace.

The early engines had a low rotational acceleration, and the throttle often had to be advanced slowly to avoid compressor stalls and flameouts. These factors and the heavier aircraft summed to longer take-off runs. Whereas previously runways of 1,200 to 2,500 feet (366 to 762 m) in length were suitable, 6,000 to 7,000 feet (1,829 to 2,134 m) were required for turbine-powered fighters, and sometimes more for bombers. Many runways had to be lengthened.

Short-burning rocket motors began to be used more frequently to enhance take-off thrust. The solid-propellant Jet-Assisted Take-Off (JATO) rocket bottles from the war, manufactured by Aerojet, became more prevalent. They had to be used at the right moment of the take-off to be effective, and the bottles then dropped. They raised enormous and lingering dust and smoke clouds that impeded operations such as interval take-offs. Yet, use was becoming so accepted that the navy permitted Grumman to use the boost to meet take-off distance requirements for the new S2F anti-submarine aircraft, and its consideration may have been permitted in meeting the take-off specifications for other aircraft.

There was no end of new service issues to address as well. In particular, turbine blades were subject to cracking and failure due to manufacturing flaws, metallic impurities, and extreme operating conditions fatiguing the material. Turbine failures took their toll. For example, at least 14 percent of the B-45 fleet was lost to engine failures.[7] Finding metals more suitable for the high temperatures and pressures was a persistent undertaking, as were the non-destructive inspection techniques to find tiny cracks. A crack leading to a sudden fracture could send a blade out through the case or precipitate cascading destruction of the entire stage.

There was much to learn about jet engines by developers. It was difficult to maintain stable operation in the presence of altering pressure distribution across the face of the compressor, rapid throttle movements, and inertial loading during maneuvering, plus power extraction via accessories and bleed air. Compressor stalls, surges, and flameouts were all too common. The engine needed to be "babied" at certain conditions on throttle advance to avoid these problems. Successful airstarts at high altitude after combustor blowouts were challenging. The time between overhauls was

Above: The Boeing B-50s were upgraded B-29 bombers that featured Pratt & Whitney R-4360 engines, shown here being installed in the production line in 1949. Of the high-performance aero-engines emerging from the war, this powerplant lasted the longest and was installed on new types for years after. (*National Museum of the United States Air Force*)

Below left: An eight-blade contra-rotating propeller turned by an R-4360 engine is prepared for a run in a test cell on June 16, 1950. The NACA, service labs, and individual manufacturers all conducted such installed tests to collect system data for optimization prior to flight tests. The contra-rotating propeller held appeal for converting the higher power output of the final generation of reciprocating aero engines to thrust, but they were heavy and complex. (*National Archives*)

Below right: Particularly for the heavy jet aircraft of the era, the Americans employed JATO booster rockets more frequently than at any other time. Ignited electrically during take-off, they added thrust and could then be jettisoned when exhausted. Seamen are seen installing JATO bottles on a ski-equipped P2V-2N in Point Barrow, Alaska, during March 1952, showing the mount, electrical connection, igniter, and exhaust, plus an impression of the weight of the bottles (likely 1,000 lbf units). (*National Archives*)

initially measured in dozens of operating hours and service life disappointingly short, greatly frustrating operators. Extending these were a priority, but it was several years and much effort just to raise them to a tolerable few hundred hours.[8]

Much work focused on improving existing model engines by addressing deficiencies and taking advantage of steady progress in the technology. It was desirable to run the turbine as hot as practical for work extraction and thrust generation. This required improved materials, working these in new ways, and blade cooling. Design teams were always seeking more effective combustors to improve fuel economy. Generating higher pressure ratios and air mass flow for thrust generation required an unending chase after efficiencies, especially in optimizing the compressor/turbine pair on the same shaft. An innovation introduced nearly concurrently by the British was the twin-spool engine. Pratt & Whitney built the first American twin-spool turbojet in the J57, earning it very favorable characteristics to include being identified as the first turbojet to generate more than 10,000-lbf (44.5-kN) thrust. Similar gains were expected from variable incidence inlet guide vanes or stators being pursued. Electronic engine controls were another means of efficiency and operability gains, though the vacuum tube electronics of the period challenged reliability given their fragility.

There was steady work early on to adopt axial flow designs to replace the centrifugal compressor. The navy especially championed axial flow engines to reduce diameter and aircraft dimensions for lower drag. Likewise, moving away from combustor "cans" to an open combustor stage was another early goal.

The thrust output of the first generation of engines was comparatively low, usually demanding two engines for fighters and four for bombers. Augmenting the thrust with water injection, afterburning (AB or reheat), and variable exit area nozzles were solutions pursued, potentially eliminating JATO, but their introduction required careful integration. At the end of the review period, the services and NACA were also planning thrust reverser tests to include inflight use.

Afterburners had been devised during the war, but they had much fundamental design work remaining to be done. They are not a simple addition to an engine. Its airflow, pressure, and heat also affect the engine core forward, and so considerable design and experimentation were necessary to ensure harmonious and reliable operation. It also increases fuel consumption by a factor of two to three and so was used for only brief periods. New and more powerful engines, or at least older ones fitted with afterburners, were going to be vital in achieving supersonic flight, pushing the aircraft past the transonic drag rise. Airframers initially developed afterburners themselves, though sometimes with the assistance of a vendor, before the engine companies focused on the requirement. With the aid of AB, Allison worked the J35 into a 9,000-lbf (40.0-kN) unit while GE had an afterburner for the J47 promising 13,000 lbf (57.8 kN), and P&W the J57 with 15,000 lbf (66.7 kN) in reheat.[9]

A measure of progress was the ability to squeeze significantly more thrust from the same basic engine via upgrades. The I-40, derived from a British World War Two engine and among the very first production turbojets, was eventually produced in large numbers by GE and Allison as the J33. In the Lockheed P-80 application, it initially delivered 3,850 lbf (17.1 kN), but was quickly revised for 4,000 lbf (17.8 kN) and then 5,400 lbf

Early jet engines had the option of a centrifugal-flow compressor or axial flow. The Pratt & Whitney J42 is shown at left in a F9F-2 (during a maintenance engine run at NAS Patuxent River on August 3, 1950). The centrifugal-flow compressor design gives a high diameter compared with the axial-flow Westinghouse J34 at right from a F2H-1 (May 23, 1949, photo). The J42 features the then-typical "cannular" combustor design whereas the J34 has the open combustion stage common in the next generation of engines. (*National Archives*)

(24.0 kN). The GE (then Allison) J35 saw similar evolution from 3,750 lbf (16.7 kN) to 5,600 lbf (24.9 kN). As important were improvements in serviceability that saw time between overhauls increase from an initial forty hours to more practical values.

Delivering a favorable pressure distribution across the face of the compressor via an efficient inlet and duct design, and retaining favorable pressure recovery, was a persistent design imperative. Vortices generated from the inlet lip during attitude changes and other separated and unsteady flow, work against the ideal pressure distribution. Ingesting the thick boundary layer from surfaces ahead of the inlet was likewise detrimental to high-pressure recovery. Consequently, diverters beneath splitter plates at the base of the inlet, stood off from the fuselage, were being adopted. The initial wing root inlets were inadequate as higher thrust engines emerged, demanding greater air mass flow. The common supersonic inlet design usually has to facilitate the creation of a standing normal shock to drop intake airspeed to less than Mach 1 to avoid engine damage. The effects of icing shed from the inlet was also subject to testing for development of design guidance leading to mitigation efforts.

One of the problems impeding progress was that there was little exchange of information and experience between the competing engine developers. The NACA came to serve as that conduit and the source of important design information. Engine-related materials collected in Germany were compiled at the NACA's Aircraft Engine Research Laboratory in Cleveland, Ohio—renamed the Flight Propulsion Research Laboratory in 1947 and then the Lewis Flight Propulsion Laboratory the next year. The NACA and military labs concluded early on that turbojets would consume the majority of its engine work, and they began to plan resource allocations appropriately. Likewise, rocket engines were bound to grow in importance. The services were then developing rocket motors likely suitable for manned flight that

Rocket motors as a principal propulsion system for manned aircraft was not roundly considered practical, or even safe, although they could supplement turbojet thrust. For research aircraft, it had value in pushing the airplane supersonic, but it soon faded in even this role. The Curtiss-Wright XLR-25 motor is seen during a ground test run at Edwards AFB, installed in the Bell X-2 with both combustion chambers burning. (*National Archives*)

would deliver tremendous thrust, albeit for a short period. Rockets were more likely to see use in missiles.

The ramjet held the promise of pushing aircraft to very high speeds, and so their development was pursued with vigor. This engine needs considerable forward flight speed to achieve suitable compression for efficient combustion. Then, the faster the engine is pushed, the greater the thrust produced and so more acceleration to speeds initially unachievable by turbojets. However, the ramjet was deceptively simple. Efficiency across flight conditions was a consistent objective and durability always challenging given the very stressful internal operating conditions. Regardless, ramjets were more widely used during this period than any other, especially for missiles.

The Ford copy of the Argus-Schmidt AA 109-014 pulsejet engine (a.k.a. intermittent ramjet) from the German V-1 missile, was designated PJ31. It powered the Republic JB-2 (see page 436) but was explored for other applications. Several other pulsejets were developed and some produced. These were usually smaller than the 900 lbf (4 kN) PJ31 with its 21.5-inch (55-cm) combustion chamber.

The industry leader in ramjets was Marquardt Aircraft founded by Roy Marquardt in 1944 to pursue ramjets. Eventually settling at the Van Nuys Airport, California, the firm began delivery of experimental units in 1946. They were soon producing units for the military and its contractors; they had their first supersonic engine by 1949. Many of the ramjets manufactured during this period were for drones that were launched to operating speeds. Consequently, these were on the scale of 7 to 14 inches (18 to 36 cm) and producing a few hundred pounds of thrust. Among others producing ramjets given military designations were Curtiss-Wright, McDonnell Aircraft ("McAir"), Continental, Solar, and Giannini (an Italian-American automaker). The navy also built a 14-inch pulsejet and NACA Cleveland a 20-inch (51-cm) model.

An Aerojet pulsejet undergoes chamber testing in this image, showing the inlet shutters. A variant of the ramjet and a very simple jet engine, it was made operational by the Germans in the V-1 cruise missile. The Americans gave pulsejets a thorough testing, also aiming only for missiles given its severe operating parameters and a practical service life of a few hours. It saw only limited production applications for targets. (*Air Force Test Center*)

Many projects still demanded high-performance reciprocating aero engines where propellers held a performance advantage, such as transport and patrol aircraft cruise. The principal manufacturers continued to develop new models for those customers as well as seeking performance improvements. However, no entirely new engine types were introduced. One significant innovation was the introduction of the turbo-compound engine in which exhaust gasses spin turbines coupled to the crankshaft. This exploited turbine technology, especially the turbosupercharger matured during the war. The work was funded by the navy to deliver more power for its twin-engine flying boats, but other programs adopted the turbo-compound as well. In the U.S., only Wright Aeronautical worked up a turbo-compound aero engine with their R-3350 Turbo-Cyclone possessing three turbines that each added 180 hp (134 kW) or approximately 15 percent of the total power. The specific fuel consumption (SFC, fuel consumed to produce a unit of thrust) was possibly the lowest of any reciprocating aero engine.[10]

The variable discharge turbine (VDT) passed the turbosupercharger exhaust through a nozzle of variable exit area for optimal thrust production based on ambient atmospheric pressure. The VDT was to be mated to the P&W R-4360 and Wright R-3350, but the teams could not overcome the technical challenges. Although slated for use on various military programs, all found alternative powerplants.

The work on turbines also supported an engine focused on generating shaft torque power to spin a propeller. This turboprop, then known as the propeller-turbine, has the advantages of generating more power at a higher operating altitude and at a lighter weight than reciprocating engines while enjoying a bit better fuel economy than turbojets. A gearbox is necessary, however (though not uncommon in recips), adding weight and complexity. The propeller has to convert more power to thrust than with piston engines, and this exacerbates the blade tip speed issue, with supersonic flow resulting in a great loss of efficiency and thrust. Transonic aircraft speed is not practical. Yet, there were hopes turboprops could stretch bomber range and offer greater efficiency for transports and patrol aircraft. Similar is the turboshaft that was sought for helicopter applications.

The propeller still held value in that blade pitch change produced a near-instantaneous change in thrust, in addition to prop reversing to assist in deceleration or backing. The engine could also be run at a steady throttle setting or rpm while prop setting (coarsening pitch or making it finer) created the thrust adjustments to rapidly correct landing approach flight path. The initial turbojets' slow response to throttle made them a marginal choice for carrier ops given poor bolter performance, and crashes were occurring. Consequently, the navy particularly pressed for turboprops and this led them in the meantime to explore hybrids with a turbojet in the aft fuselage and a recip in the nose that was driving a propeller.

The Americans had been working to find a suitable turboprop since 1941, with both the air force and navy providing funding. Six firms worked on eleven designs, none of which can be considered to have reached maturity during the period under review. This led to the downfall of several programs that attempted to adopt them. Only two of these turboprops would go on to resounding success. Another was adopted as a turboshaft engine.

As with recips, turbine engine development ran longer than airframe development, and creating a truly successful powerplant was an elusive endeavor. The work was slow in converging on truly reliable designs, and some never reached a satisfactory stage. Many aircraft programs that had started with one engine had to select another because the manufacturer could not deliver on time or their product was disappointing. Other programs foundered entirely owing to engines that failed to measure up to promises made at the outset. Engine programs themselves failed or yielded hardware that found few applications. The technology was still maturing and there was much still to learn. Even those that made it into service were often hamstrung with a low mean time between failures (MTBF) and short periods between overhauls until maturing. The British were then producing the best engines in terms of performance and reliability, and several were manufactured under license in the U.S. to power American airplanes. The almost-disastrous engine development problems were one cause for the USAF to create ARDC.

Some engines became so important that manufacturing teams were formed to increase production volume. The J47 was one example, used in the B-47 and F-86, with Allison, Packard, and Studebaker contributing. Peak production rate was 975 per month. A total of 36,500 were manufactured by the end of 1956 as the most produced engine to that time. A shuttered navy plant in Kansas City, Missouri, was reopened to produce the Westinghouse 24C (J34). Ford and P&W also built the engine, and elements were manufactured in Columbus, Ohio. The new business brought fresh competitors into the field, some with less institutional inertia for moving in new directions, and so encouraging innovation. Winning a production contract for GE's J33, Allison contributed to improvements such that the engine became quite reliable and was produced through 1959 by Allison in numbers exceeding 15,000. Allison worked hard to establish its turbine engine development capabilities, to include applying water injection and afterburners to existing designs, and soon became a significant competitor. It improved the J35 (also manufactured by Chevrolet), used in many aircraft, but frustrating in its high number of failures and other maladies. Its initial operational time between overhauls was just twenty hours. Allison toiled to correct these and then evolved it into the superior J71. Yet, they still stumbled badly with the T38 and T40 turboprops.

Structures

High-operating speeds, greater maneuvering inertia and airloads on the airframe, and never-ending demands for reduced weight continued driving advances in aircraft structures. Jet engine installations also required the ability to survive high temperatures, pressures, and sonic overpressure. More aluminum, steel, and titanium alloys were introduced, along with primers and paints to resist corrosion. Forgings, machining, and mechanical assembly continued to advance with finer tolerances required by newer designs. The use of fiberglass for secondary structures (not primary load-bearing) also expanded. It was clear that the age of fabric surfaces was nearing its end. Retained well into the metal airplane era, they had been meant to keep the surfaces light and avoid flutter.[11] Yet there were other solutions readily adopted and fabric disappeared from new designs.

Vought still employed its Metalite process with a layer of balsa wood between metal sheets for stiffening rather than heavier ribs and stringer. The Glenn L. Martin Company had its Marbond honeycomb composite to stiffen structures without the usually semi-monocoque construction with riveting. Welding of titanium was a challenge confronted and solved by several firms. As an experiment, an F-80C (47-171) was constructed entirely of magnesium.[12] The magnesium that was used in the B-36 and other aircraft for weight savings proved especially hazardous during ground fires or crashes as it burned furiously and conventional extinguishing methods were ineffective.

Laminar flow airfoils, pressurization, and flush riveting became commonplace, and so will not be specifically mentioned in the text to follow. Swept wings were recognized as essential for achieving greater airspeeds even before the war had ended. Especially after examining German aircraft and research, there was clearly no reason to continue holding back. Nearly all high-speed aircraft projects from that point had a swept wing and tail surfaces. However, these introduced structural design plus S&C challenges. Especially at wing stall, lateral control is compromised and promotes a destabilizing pitch up. The trend to thin wings was increasing the tendency for flutter. The thin swept wings tended to twist more than earlier structures, promoting roll reversal. This drove the use of inboard ailerons at high speed or even resorting to spoilers. Additionally, the wings tended to stall suddenly due to abrupt flow separation at the leading edges. This could and did lead to sudden loss of lift on the final approach, which began to cost lives. Aircraft such as the B-47 (see page 241) also had long and flexible fuselages that contributed to aeroelastic modes of the airframe and their potential consequences. All this required more focused attention on analytical and test techniques by NACA, academia, and others.

Nuclear Dimension

The thinking regarding the employment of nuclear weapons was varied in the early years following the war. While some regarded them as revolutionizing warfare, engendering changes in bomb delivery systems plus tactics, others saw them as just another item of ordnance to be used in much the same manner as earlier weapons. They were seen as both a weapon of last resort and as one to be employed as necessary to destroy the enemy's warfighting capacity. Targets would predominately be population and industrial centers. Initial planning made it clear that there were insufficient weapons for this task—namely, targeting the USSR—through to 1951, and the existing bombs were cumbersome. There was pressure to develop new A-bombs, more powerful and operationally flexible, and stockpile a meaningful number. The vastness of the Soviet Union and the existing forces confounded planning in the early postwar period. In particular, the introduction of atomic weapons by the Soviets energized the work.

The nation's atomic weapons were developed and controlled by a government agency outside the Department of Defense. The Atomic Energy Commission (AEC) released weapon assemblies to the Armed Services Special Weapons Project for delivery to combat units. While responsive to the military as its principal "customer," the AEC did not initially allow routine access to the bombs and warheads. Even physical specifications were rarely available to aircraft design teams and fleet operators. Coordination between these parties was often frustrating, especially given the added complexity of security clearances and document control. With the usual uncertainty in any development effort, airframers frequently found it necessary to adjust their design to match the weapons once specifics became available.

Initially, it was not permitted to cache American atomic weapons outside of U.S. territory. Only in 1950 was this eased to permit all but the fissile core to be kept at foreign bases. The cores would have to be brought in from the U.S., with the weapon elements collected together before any potential use. Navy vessels, considered sovereign U.S. territory, could carry fully assembled weapons. This would appear to give the USN an advantage in claiming some portion of the nuclear strike role, if they just had the means to exploit it.

Most or all the weapons were improved or altered for various operational uses via "Mods" (modifications). An effort was initially expended on improving the ballistics of the early bombs to enhance accuracy. In the atomic physics, work was done to improve the efficiency and yield of the fission weapons, reducing the quantity of the rare fissile material required. Production of the material was also improved and expanded. An enormous industry and various government organs grew from the exceptionally costly undertaking. After the USSR detonated its first nuclear device and fostered communist confrontation against Western aims, efforts were redoubled. Additional weapons development programs were launched or accelerated, with production ramped up markedly to stockpile hundreds and then thousands of weapons, while delivery systems also proliferated. Work began in a concerted way to develop the fusion bombs (hydrogen or thermonuclear).

Delivery was just as important as the stockpile. When the Soviets appeared on the verge of "overrunning Europe" in the summer of 1948, there were just thirty-two B-29s configured for a nuclear strike. Strategic Air Command readiness was low, and the wisdom of placing all of one's eggs in one basket was questioned. Since war plans for an offensive against the USSR rested largely on the use of the A-bomb, the USAF was given priority. New combat-capable B-50s and B-36s were only just being delivered to operational squadrons that had to work up to mission-readiness. A crash program was launched to prepare 225 bombers and support aircraft to deliver atomic weapons by the end of 1948, if called. Many of the aircraft were "winterized" for deployment to Alaska and some given aerial refueling capabilities.[13] Weapons and delivery capacity grew rapidly from that point.

At the time, a vigorous nuclear testing program was underway with dozens of atmospheric detonations. Some were dropped by bombers. These tests were largely conducted in remote deserts of western America or on small and isolated islands in the Pacific. Weapons integration, test, and operational development were conducted at the remote Wendover AFB, Utah, for the USAF. It created Special Weapons Command in December 1949 to address all matters associated with atomic strike missions.

The two bombs dropped on Japan at the end of the war were the sole weapon designs in the immediate postwar period. The Little Boy became the Mk I, but only five were built to serve into January 1951. It had a yield of approximately 15 kilotons (kton), which is the same destructive potential as an equivalent weight of TNT. It weighed 8,900 lb (4,037 kg), was 2.3 feet (0.7 m) in diameter, and 10.5 feet (3.2 m) long. The 21-kton Fat Man was refined to become the Mk III and was stockpiled beginning in April 1947 until retiring in December 1950 after around 120 were assembled. It weighed 10,300 lb (4,672 kg), was 5 feet (1.5 m) in diameter, and 10.7 feet (3.3 m) long.

Operations with these early weapons were burdensome and time-consuming. The bombs had to be accessed in flight for final assembly and preparation for drop. This required an individual to crawl into the bomb bay to perform the tasks or disarm if the drop was aborted. The bombs needed to become more serviceable and reliable, with stockpiling requiring much less attention. The imperatives were addressed in the Mk 4 as the first standard weapon design; a productionized Fat Man introduced in March 1949. The U.S. built around 550 Mk 4s, which served until May 1953. The design was improved further with the Mk 6 that weighed 8,500 lb (3,856 kg). Although of similar dimensions to the early Fat Man designs, the weight reduction allowed more mission alternatives in fuel or defensive armament. Accuracy was improved with

The dawn of the Nuclear Age was cause for much fundamental rethinking of modern warfare and the associated weapon systems. Particularly offensive aircraft would need to be adjusted to support the changes in tactics. This Operation Crossroads detonation in Bikini Atoll, with many warships positioned in the impact area, was confirmation of the worst potential outcome for naval operations. Shown is the air burst explosion on July 1, 1946, named Able, of a 23-kton plutonium Mk III implosion device, dropped from a B-29. (*National Archives*)

circumferential spoiler rings around the body. The Mk 6 offered operational flexibility via surface or air burst, various fusing means, and a variety of cores yielding from 30 to 60 kton. These weapons were available from April 1952 with approximately 1,100 assembled until 1955.

A concerted effort began in 1948 to reduce the size of weapons and so increase the number of delivery platforms and their range. The services began developing such platforms in anticipation. Such was of greater interest to the navy than the air force who emphasized yield, and so there was a struggle over priorities. The work brought the Mk 5 at 3,175 lb (1,440 kg) with 3.7 feet (1.1 m) in diameter and 11.0 foot (3.4 m) in length. From May 1952, 140 of the bombs with a roughly 80-kton yield were produced. The explosive heart became the W-5 warhead introduced in July 1954, employed in many other weapons to include cruise missiles.

The 1,700-lb (771-kg) Mk 7 Thor was small enough to be deployed by fighter-bombers and so could be considered the first tactical "nuke." Such use negated the assembly of the weapon in flight. This meant the aircraft took off with an armed nuclear device and a crash could result in detonation—a problem that was being worked on with remote arming but did not inhibit immediate deployment of such weapons. The bomb was in conceptual design in 1949 and the Korean Conflict accelerated development. It was 2.5 feet (0.8 m) in diameter and 15.3 feet (4.7 m) long—too long for B-29 and B-50 bays. The explosive heart became the W-7 warhead adopted for many other systems to include rockets, missiles, and torpedoes.

It had many configurations for variable yield up to 70 kton and a variety of fusing options. The early bomb cases were intended only for subsonic employment. They had airbrakes to slow descent, permitting the delivery aircraft to escape the blast zone since fighter-bombers generally did not operate at the high altitudes of bombers.

Nearly concurrent with the Mk 7 was the Mk 8, which used a gun-type fission warhead design (versus implosion) that rendered it long and narrow. The design was less efficient, with lower yield, and used more fissionable material, yet lent itself to a more practical external store for aircraft carriage and missile warhead. The Mk 8 was intended for penetration to destroy buried or hardened targets, or create an "earthquake" effect. This also required the internal mechanisms to withstand the penetration shock plus delay detonation to permit the delivery aircraft to escape. While the navy welcomed the design, the USAF opposed it such that another controversy ensued. Nonetheless, the first weapons were available in April 1952. It weighed 3,250 lb (1,474 kg) and was 11.0 feet (3.4 m) long with a streamlined penetrator nose, plus fins spanning 2.1 feet (0.6 m) though the case was only 1.2 feet (0.4 m) in diameter.

The issue of fighter-bomber escape prompted the navy to begin work on a rocket-boosted store fired in a lofting manner for ballistic arc delivery. The requirement was approved in fall 1952 and work began at China Lake on the Bureau of Ordnance Atomic Rocket. Field testing of at least some of the components began in June 1953. With a W-7 warhead and solid-fuel motor, the rocket was expected to weigh 2,000 lb (907 kg) and have a range of 7.5 miles (12.1 km).

The first large-scale test detonation of a fusion device occurred in November 1952, but even the crudest "emergency capability" deliverable weapons remained a few years in the future. The yield of these weapons was an order of magnitude greater than the fission devices, measured in megatons of TNT. It was clear these would initially even be larger weapons than the original fission devices. The USSR detonated their first H-bomb in August 1953. A new and very hazardous period for humankind had dawned.

2

Flight Research

Continuation of much of the research from the war was guided by pushing on with that underway and that projected as achievable. The latter was informed by German experience and navy eagerness to establish unique capabilities, augmented by responding to perceived Soviet advances. The goal, as with any such research, was to establish the possible and the practical, and provide data to development teams.

New Shapes

New designs striving for new performance limits demanded research and test resources. The NACA, military laboratories, academia, and individual companies provided these when suitably funded. The first few years after the war were lean, but the situation soon improved. This was timely in that designs with radical new shapes were demanding analysis and data.

An example of these new shapes for high-performance aircraft was V-tails. Data had been collected on these "butterfly" tails during the war with a modified P-63 and AT-10. However, several postwar jet designs incorporated the feature in initial design proposals. The attraction was reduced in weight, drag, and construction time, and potentially less interference from flow off the wings upstream that might improve stall behavior. Prior results showed the V-tails, with control surfaces serving rudder and elevator functions, seldom gave the same control authority and fidelity of a conventional tail, and so it was always discarded during final design choices. Data from more representative subjects were sought.

Republic Aviation, of Farmingdale, New York, temporarily installed a V-tail on the second prototype XF-91 (see page 210) at air force insistence. The team found the mixed results expected, and there was no follow-up on a program fated to death. No other team adopted the feature because of the maneuverability compromises.

New aircraft shapes and performance stretch the ability to design in natural S&C, plus favorable handling qualities. Automatic flight control and autopilots were turned to more frequently to provide compensation. In researching ideal handling,

Already dizzyingly radical, the Republic XF-91 could not be any worse off with a "butterfly" V-tail. This was installed temporarily on one of the two prototypes (46-681) to check test results against predictions. These were confirmed, detractors outweighing advantages, and so there was no production follow-up. (*Air Force Test Center via Tony Landis*)

the NACA had modified a F6F-3 (bureau number 42874) in 1948 so directional and lateral stability parameters could be altered in flight.[1] A stability augmentation system adjusted control linkages to produce the desired changes, representing the stability and associated responses of different aircraft or configuration changes, though still providing the pilot with conventional control. This was the first such variable stability research aircraft and, apart from studying basic aircraft stability, allowed pilots to explore the handling of new aircraft before they were ready for testing. The USAF began conceiving their own variable stability testbed in 1953. They would soon issue a contract to Cornell Aeronautical Laboratory to modify a TF-33A with a long F-94A nose for the added electronics.

An autopilot for helicopters was developed in a navy lab and test flown in 1950 on a HO3S-1. Others were doing similar work.

While still struggling to develop wind tunnels for transonic airspeed investigation, the measures used during the war persisted. These included dropping aero shapes from a high altitude for brief data collection before ground impact. While telemetry transmission was being matured, many test programs used photography of instruments within their vehicle, the film then having to be recovered (hopefully intact) from the wreckage. Flying the model atop a small rocket was a similar technique, with NACA providing this from Wallops Island. Drops also permitted scale models to be "flown," either autonomously or remotely, before parachute recovery. This supported subsonic data collection filling gaps where tunnel data were unavailable or inadequate. The

Above: Initially still struggling to collect transonic data given wind tunnel limitations, the NACA continued its drop test of shapes from a high altitude. The Ames Aeronautical Laboratory adopted a Northrop F-15A (45-59300) with supercharged engines that permitted the aircraft to reach 42,000 feet altitude, though stressing the pilot who lacked cockpit pressurization. The aircraft is here seen carrying a large shape with highly swept aero surfaces of a high-aspect ratio. (*Gerald Balzer collection*)

Right: Lockheed found value in supplementing wind tunnel data with that gleaned from scale models flown captive beneath an airplane or dropped for free-flight. For some of these tests, they used their P-38E aircraft with its lengthened fuselage for a second cockpit usually occupied by a flight test engineer looking after the test subject. These images show the aircraft with models of the company's XF-90 and X-7 products. (*Jay Miller collection*)

NACA's Ames Aeronautical Laboratory at Moffett Field, Sunnyvale, California, adopting a Northrop F-15A (serial number 45-59300) and a P-61C for this purpose, while Lockheed Aircraft of Burbank, California, used their highly modified P-38E 41-2048.

Sweeping Advances

Investigations to alleviate compressibility problems progressed apace to include more suitable airfoils. One key to high airspeeds with less hazard of compressibility effects were swept aero surfaces, and there was much clamor for associated information. The reports from German research were quickly exhausted, but unique new work was underway.

Swept wings promote spanwise airflow on the surface at elevated angles of attack (AoA) that undermined lateral control approaching or at stall. This was combated to some extent with the use of upper surface fences. Such wings have the notorious problem of tip stall before the root during high AoA maneuvering. Tip stall shifts the center of lift inboard and gives an abrupt pitch-up, destabilizing as it deepens the stall and can promote unsuitable spin characteristics. It was learned that swept wings made the aircraft prone to a combined pitch-yaw oscillation called Dutch Roll. Any abrupt roll, pitch control input, or gust can excite the oscillation that spoils bomb delivery and gunnery accuracy, or diverge and cause destructive structural loads. Yaw dampers became common, especially in bombers, to combat the oscillations.

Flying a landing approach at a safe airspeed meant long runway rolls. These speeds could be unacceptable for carrier landings owing to high arrestment energy or too little time for a wave-off. For a heavy fighter with high wing loading, the danger was even greater. These detractors were further exacerbated by the thin airfoils used to reduce drag.

The navy was particularly keen to ensure safe low-speed handling qualities with swept wings and selected Bell to create an experimental aircraft to explore this potential. The company converted two P-63As with 35-degree swept wings, one with leading-edge slats creating slots and the other without. The aft fuselage was also extended, with ventral surface added, to ensure suitable control given the large aft shift in the center-of-gravity (CG). These L-39s began flying in April 1946 and focused on less than 200 mph (322 kph)—especially as the wing lacked wells for main gear retraction and so were fixed down.[2] The aircraft without wing slots had unsafe stall characteristics, breaking without warning and losing considerable altitude during recovery. Slots of 40 to 60 percent span offered docile stalls. The aircraft were also flown by test pilots of programs featuring swept wings to become familiar with the expected handling.

Contemplation of transonic S&C problems led to consideration of tailless designs. Examples of the Messerschmitt Me 163 and de Havilland DH 108 suggested that this layout held promise for ameliorating some of the issues associated with wing/ tail interaction in the presence of shocks. Wing trailing-edge control surfaces have to serve both longitudinal and lateral axes. To explore this beyond the wind tunnel, the

Under navy sponsorship, Bell Aircraft modified two P-63 King Cobras with swept wings to collect fundamental data on stability and control of such designs. Flight testing during 1946 showed the efficacy of leading-edge slats to ensure safe low-speed handling. This example of the L-39 lacks the slats and has yarn tufts on the wings to permit visualization of airflow across the surfaces. (*Jay Miller collection*)

Of the aircraft collected from former adversaries at the end of the war was the unusual Me 163. The "tailless" design with sharply swept wings held interest, particularly as the design team contemplated transonic flight. Testing in the U.S. was performed by towing to altitude by a B-29 (shown), release for test maneuvers, and landing on the Muroc lakebed. The buffeting behind the B-29 caused the wooden wing to delaminate and so testing was brief. (*National Archives*)

USAAF contracted with Northrop Aircraft in June 1946 to build two X-4 research vehicles (originally XS-4). Northrop had built a number of such designs seeking drag and weight reduction, along with the ongoing B-35 and ill-fated wartime XP-79B, and so was granted the contract without competition.

Built to the purpose, the X-4 Bantam was tiny and compact. It spanned 26.8 feet (8.2 m) and grossed 7,820 lb (3,547 kg). It used two Westinghouse 1,600-lbf (7.1-kN) J30 engines fed by wing root inlets possessing bypass slots. The wings had magnesium skin—a Northrop specialty. The flaps could split, with segments moving up and down, as very effective speedbrakes. Outboard were boosted elevons. The X-4 was also equipped with an early ejection seat.

The first flight was in December 1948. Stability and control testing by both the USAF and NACA were the priority, with modifications as indicated by the data. Flying through July 1953, the aircraft was taken to Mach 0.94. The program yielded data directly contributing to military aircraft development.

The ultimate in swept wing was the delta with a high degree of leading-edge sweep that permitted the elimination of the horizontal tail. While this looks attractive as a weight-saving measure, the delta has characteristics that make its application challenging. At low airspeeds, such as landing approach, the wing has to be flown to a high AoA where it can approach stall, and lateral control is difficult, in addition to poor forward view for the pilot. German research was examined and a captured Lippisch experimental glider was used to collect test data. Alexander Lippisch, employed at Wright Field following the war, was consulted.

The first American-powered delta-winged aircraft to reach flight was the Convair XF-92A. This was a demonstrator for the supersonic XP-92 rocket/ramjet point-defense interceptor (see page 208). That project represented considerable technical risk even without the delta; it was eventually terminated. However, the delta-winged demonstrator element of the contract was carried forward for research purposes.

The single-engine XF-92A had a delta with a 60-degree sweep and included an exceptionally large triangular vertical tail. To contain costs, elements of other aircraft were employed in the assembly and the design was kept simple. It was powered by a water-injected J33 fed by an annular inlet. All control surfaces were boosted and the pilot provided artificial feel. A Convair ejection seat was installed. After time in Ames' full-scale tunnel, the first flight was in September 1948 at Muroc. Valuable data were collected. The jet was later fitted with reheat, requiring the aft end of the airplane to be extended. It began flying in this configuration in July 1951j, although the afterburner was troublesome and offered meager performance gain. The USAF and NACA shared the flying with Convair during testing in late 1953 at Muroc. The aircraft, as designed and powered, could not reach supersonic airspeed in level flight, though Mach 1.1 was achieved once in a dive. Some handling deficiencies were uncovered, notably sharp pitch-ups during turns at high g that drove the installation of wing fences. These would be adopted on later delta-wing designs. The research results informed designs that followed, including Convair's own F-102.

The potential that a tailless design held advantages in the presence of compressibility, the air force had Northrop develop the X-4 research aircraft. The USAF and NACA tested the small, twin-engined jet for four and a half years. The data directly contributed to ongoing military aircraft development programs. (*National Archives*)

The Lippisch DM-1 was a delta-wing glider intended for researching the merits of the layout in Germany, during the war. It never flew but was captured after the German defeat (as shown in this image) and transported to the U.S. for wind tunnel evaluation. NACA published the data that was then exploited by design teams. (*Jay Miller collection*)

Convair's solitary XF-92A inaugurated delta-wing flight-testing in the U.S. in 1948. Seen during an early sortie from Muroc Army Air Base with the J33 engine lacking afterburner, the tail cone is not as long as it would later become. The design was quickly determined to be suitable for research only. (*San Diego Air & Space Museum*)

Variable Geometry

The detrimental aerodynamic and stability effects of thin, swept wings were proving dangerous. One solution to this was to use a variable-sweep wing that would be moved to a low sweep for take-off and landing and to elevated sweep for high-speed operation. Just sweeping the wings from one constant pivot point or line promised severe static longitudinal stability consequences given that the center of lift on the wing moves aft with sweep to decrease the static margin and potentially even negative. It would be necessary to move the entire wing assembly forward with an aft sweep change, and *vice versa*. Yet this moved the CG as well, and so the design would require great care. This suggested a complex and heavy mechanism.

A number of experimenters had collected data on variable sweep designs, though none at a high flight speed. Messerschmitt had designed the P.1101 jet with such a design and had begun building a prototype during the war. The company had intended for the wings to be adjusted in flight over a large range, but the initial article had ground adjustment only to 30, 40, and 45 degrees, without translation, for optimizing the design through flight test. The project was largely a failure and had been canceled. The incomplete and cheaply built airframe was collected by the Allies and studied by several bodies, including Bell Aircraft with the aid of the principal designer, Woldemar Voigt, who had been brought to the U.S. Bell made a proposal in 1948 to complete and fly the P.1101, seeing this as a shortcut to collecting desired data. However, it was more practical to design a similar airplane; this was funded under a February 1949 contract from the USAF and NACA for two research vehicles. They bore a resemblance to the P.1101, but they were an entirely new design—larger and heavier.

The X-5s grossed 9,875 lb (4,479 kg) and were powered by a single 4,900-lbf (21.8-kN) J35, which was unaugmented. The wings swept from 20 to 60 degrees, pivoting on hinges just outboard of the fuselage. This was done with electric motors driving jackscrews. As they swept aft, the wing translated forward on rails and was locked in any selected position with disk brakes. The full motion was 2.3 feet (0.7 m), requiring twenty seconds. There was a hand crank to sweep the wing manually in an emergency because the aircraft could not be landed safely with the wings aft of 40 degrees. A fillet fared the forward root leading edge of the wing to the fuselage throughout the sweep action. Designing this fairing was difficult and delayed the program. The wings had leading-edge slats, trailing-edge flaps, and ailerons. The flaps began outboard of the fuselage such that none of their area fell within the fuselage when swept fully aft, and so could be used at any sweep angle. Speedbrake panels were placed on the forward fuselage. A cartridge-fired ejection seat was included.

The X-5 first flew in June 1951, soon becoming the world's first manned aircraft to sweep its wings in flight. One X-5 was lost in a fatal crash in October 1953 owing to an unrecoverable spin. The second continued trials into 1955. The design was not intended to be supersonic and no attempt the fly to such speeds was made.

The X-5 collected invaluable data to inform projects to follow, although the next was nearly concurrent. Grumman set out to design a swept-wing version of the F9F. This eventually departed so far from the Panther that it was designated F10F. The appearance of the MiG-15 prompted the shorter-term redesign of the F9F Panther into the swept-wing Cougar (see page 191), and so the F10F work was temporarily suspended.

The Bell X-5 tested variable wing sweep on a small and lightweight experimental airplane. The idea had been well-discussed in aerodynamic circles, but the airplane design was inspired by a German wartime project that never reached fruition. All testing was at Muroc (January 3, 1953, image), with the USAF and NASA participating. (*National Archives*)

By 1949, the F10F had progressed through many evolutions to a variable-sweep design with a T-tail. This offered good handling and speed compatibility for carrier ops while also accommodating level-flight transonic airspeeds. A formal development contract came in December 1950 for a dozen XF10F-1s. This was followed in February 1951 with an order that eventually reached more than 100 jets. For such a radical design, this was premature, but such was the navy's faith in Grumman. The armament was to be four 20-mm cannon and rocket packs.

The XF10F-1's wings could be varied from 13.5 to 42.5 degrees of sweep while also translating along the longitudinal axis of the fuselage, all under the power of a single hydraulic actuator.[3] The wing variable geometry mechanism was designed to withstand full 7-g fighter maneuvering. However, it also added approximately 1,500 lb (6,804 kg) to the airplane. Grumman did not bother fairing the leading-edge root, accepting drag from the gap between the slats and fuselage side. However, they did have sliding panels to seal the slots along the fuselage. The moving wings also contained fuel that was pumped across the fuselage interface. The external store mounts also swiveled to remain aligned with incident airflow. The wings had full-span automatic (aerodynamic) slats, Fowler flaps extending over 80 percent of the semi-span, and small ailerons. Lateral control was initially to rely upon eight spoiler paddles that pivoted out of the wings—four up and four down. The ailerons were intended only to provide the pilot feel. A delta horizontal stabilizer without elevators was mounted atop the vertical with a large bullet fairing that enclosed the trim actuator. A smaller delta at the front of the fairing was actuated by the pilot as a servo surface moving the larger surface aft. This was done because it was feared shocks at transonic airspeeds would render a more conventional tail ineffective.

The Jaguar weighed 20,468 lb (9,284 kg) empty and 35,370 lb (16,044 kg) at maximum take-off with two 300-gal (1,136-l) external tanks. It was powered by a Westinghouse J40 axial-flow turbojet offering 10,900 lbf (48.9 kN) with reheat, fed by "cheek" inlets allowing for a radar radome. This engine was noted for being among the first with electronic fuel controls and had inlet de-ice via hot air bleed plus, for the XF10F-1, a clamshell exhaust nozzle. The augmented engine variant was not immediately available, so the 7,310-lbf (32.5-kW) version without afterburner was installed for taxi work.

The first aircraft was completed in early 1952 and, following taxi tests, was shipped to Edwards for the first flight in May. From first ground movement to last flight, the XF10F-1 suffered grave S&C issues. Grumman did their usual analytical predictions and wind tunnel testing, as well as flying a scale model. They also simulated the design in flight with Ames' F6F-3 variable-stability airplane. All results indicated inadequate longitudinal stability and very poor lateral-directional stability.[4] However, Grumman did not believe the results, much to its grief. Attempting to size controls for both the low-speed/low-sweep angle regime and the high-speed/high-sweep example was not successful, yielding unsuitable control and pilot forces.

Many significant changes were made to the airplane over nearly a year of testing, seeking a safe and controllable airplane, much less an effective combat jet. Directional stability was deficient given what was discovered to be an undersized rudder. Two small ventral horizontals, or "horsals," were fitted at the end of the fuselage. The delta horizontal was quickly shown to provide inadequate longitudinal stability as the aircraft approached stall and was otherwise simply dangerously inadequate for control. It was replaced with surfaces of a more common high aspect ratio from the F9F-6, but even these were too small. Stall was still unsatisfactory in aft sweep, as were control forces. Flap extension generated unacceptable trim change. The spoiler roll control promoted flutter. The airflow through the spoiler paddle slots in the wing degraded lateral-directional stability and were sealed. The spoilers were then deactivated after a time. The small ailerons alone were used, though with excruciatingly slow roll rate. Speedbrakes needed to be added. The wing slats deployed erratically to degrade control, as did control cable stretch. The aircraft featured an electronic fuel balancing system, but lateral balance was poor and also undermined control.

The afterburner was never fitted to the J40 that produced just 6,800 lbf (30.2 kN). Consequently, the aircraft was underpowered and engine acceleration was desperately slow.[5] Grumman added a diffuser at the end of the engine under a boat tail shroud that reduced drag and improved engine thrust. However, closing down the exhaust nozzle caused some flow to impinge on the base for the rudder with violent yawing motion resulting. A deflection plate had to be added at the projecting base of the vertical tail.

On the bright side, the XF10F-1's wing sweep feature proved trouble-free and was not the source of the myriad problems. The testing showed that the center of pressure (CP) moved very little during sweep change, and the stab was adequate to correct trim. The aircraft reached Mach 0.86 and touched 0.975 in a steep dive.

The program wrapped in 1953 with only a single pilot ever flying the one aircraft. This was due to the failure of the J40 program and a rare "miss" by Grumman's design team. The eventful testing saw numerous changes to the aircraft in addressing

The Grumman XF10F-1 was a bid to improve the swept-wing stability and control issues by introducing variable wing sweep. Grumman found the first attempt at translating this into a combat aircraft a trying experience. A year of testing in 1952 and 1953 showed the aircraft to be unacceptable and none of the "cures" entirely effective. The program, with standing production orders, was canceled. (*Air Force Test Center*)

the defects. While it was impressive to see Grumman respond so swiftly with revised hardware, they were indicative of a design that was gravely flawed from the beginning. While many of the prototypes of the period that did not proceed to production were worthy, this cannot be said of the Jaguar. The thirty-two flights amounted to just shy of twenty hours for $30 million spent. All prototype and production orders were dropped as the swept-wing F3H Demon and F9F-6 were meeting requirements suitably with much less complexity, though the Demon's landing approach airspeed was approximately 23 mph (37 kph) faster than the XF10F-1's.

Supersonic Reach

In the final year of the war, the army, navy, and NACA had begun collaborating on the development of heavily instrumented research aircraft aimed at exploring transonic flight. The data collected would fill gaps unavailable from wind tunnels of the period and support analytical derivations. The results would then support practical applications for military and commercial aircraft. In this way, design teams could proceed with more confidence dealing with the drag rise, shocks, and stability challenges of flight near the speed of sound. These programs proceeded cautiously and methodically.

The army championed the straight-wing Bell XS-1 (soon X-1) that used rocket propulsion, an exceptionally strong airframe, and an all-moving horizontal tail with an elevator to push beyond Mach 1. The weight of the aircraft and short rocket burn time compelled the selection of air launch from beneath a B-29. The X-1 was loaded into the modified B-29 from a pit, or the bomber could be jacked via lifts built into the apron on which each gear rested, allowing the test aircraft to be rolled under. The design emulated that of a .50-cal bullet that was known to exceed the speed of sound. Wings of 10 and 8 percent thickness:chord ratio sections were constructed. Three X-1s were built, each spanning 31.9 feet (9.7 m) and grossing between 12,000 and 14,751 lb (6,691 kg). With rocket engine ignition following drop and a brief burn, a deadstick landing was mandated.

The 6,000-lbf (27-kN) Reaction Motors XLR11 rocket motor was chosen. This weighed 345 lb (157 kg) dry and had four selectable combustion chambers for throttling. Endurance was just sufficient to meet the specific mission objectives. The ethyl alcohol and liquid oxygen (LOX) were stored within the fuselage, the spherical tanks dictating fuselage diameter. The ethyl alcohol was diluted with water before being circulated in a cooling jacket around the combustion chamber (regenerative cooling) and then injected into the chamber. A stream of fuels was ignited by a spark plug before full fuel flow was established. The fuels, in a dozen small spherical tanks, were moved via 4,500-psi (311-bar) nitrogen. Regulating this pressure to each propellant tank with cockpit controls was another means of varying thrust. The pressure also provided motive power for moving control surfaces and lowering landing gear (with gravity assist).

Testing began in January 1946 with glides following drops from the B-29. Powered flights at Edwards began in April 1947, and it was taken supersonic in October—the first for a manned aircraft.[6] This was to be kept secret but leaked in December. The craft eventually reached Mach 1.45 and 71,902 feet (21,916 m). The third aircraft and the "mother ship" were lost in November 1951 when a rocket motor exploded during ground defueling.

Back in 1945, the navy had pushed for a Douglas Aircraft Company (DAC) design, the D-558, propelled by the most powerful turbojet engine then available, the General Electric TG-180 (soon J35), with hopes of a combat aircraft spin-off. Douglas adopted a nose annular inlet to simplify the challenges of supersonic flow into the intake. The aircraft retained straight aero surfaces to avoid excessive technological risk. The airframe was built to exceptionally high strength requirements to ensure it would hold together under emergency recovery loads. Yet, the aero surfaces were comparatively thin and had magnesium skin. It used a trimming horizontal tail, with elevators, to ensure suitable control authority in the presence of compressibility effects. Douglas also added speedbrakes. Emergency egress from the X-1 was bailing out the side entry door while the entire nose section of the D-558 separated to decelerate to a safe bail-out speed.

Three of the Skystreaks were assembled. They grossed 9,750 lb (4,423 kg) and spanned 25 feet (7.6 m). First flying in April 1947, it went on to reach Mach 0.99 in a dive, collecting invaluable data while testing multiple small configuration changes. The trials continued through June 1953, though with one ship lost to an engine failure with the NACA test pilot killed. Both the Bell and DAC airplanes set new if short-lived speed records.

In April 1948, the air force contracted with Bell for operational and maintenance improvements to the basic X-1 to include a proper canopy, improved cockpit with pressurization, additional fuel capacity, and engine revisions. These aircraft were about 5 feet (1.5 m) longer and weighed about 4,250 lb (1,928 kg) more than the baseline. All three of the aircraft looked similar but with internal differences to meet test objectives. The X-1A, X-1B, and X-1D were built (one each) while the X-1C was canceled.

The X-1D first flew free in July 1951, but it was destroyed a month later when an inflight fire was the cause to jettison the craft from the B-29.[7] One outcome of the incident was the decision to retrofit a Bell-developed ejection seat to the remaining vehicles. The X-1A conducted its first powered flight in February 1953. This "rocket plane" would soon be pushed to Mach 2.4, topping 90,400 feet (27,554 m).

Like other supersonic testbeds of the period, the X-1 experienced a roll, or inertia, coupling that was a new phenomenon aircraft developers had to contend with. This is experienced by aircraft with short span, low-density wings such as the research aircraft and first generation of high-speed swept-wing fighters. An abrupt roll may generate large angles and rates in all axes of motion given the inertia of the comparatively high-density fuselage. Inadequate roll authority and stabilizing surface areas may make it impossible to arrest the motion, leading to the loss of control and structural failure. The research vehicles were important assets in understanding this coupling.

The X-1A was also lost in summer 1954 when it had to be jettisoned after an inflight explosion. The X-1B was delivered in 1954 to a fruitful test career. The second X-1

Supersonic research with manned aircraft was an immediate priority following World War Two, with the U.S. Army, Navy, and the NACA collaborating. Bell built the XS-1, powered by a rocket motor, for an assault on Mach 1, which it achieved in October 1947. The aircraft was air-launched from a modified B-29, with loading as shown at Muroc AAB. (*Jay Miller collection*)

Soon redesignated X-1, the research craft is seen in powered flight over the California desert. This aircraft inaugurated a series of experimental machines in a period of rapid aeronautical advancement to gather data informing designers of production aircraft serving the U.S. armed forces. Rocket propulsion was initially the norm for supersonic research because of the low performance of the first generation turbojet engines, and straight aero surfaces soon gave way to swept. (*National Archives*)

The U.S. Navy and NACA sponsored the Douglas D-558's contemporary of the X-1. Propelled by the most powerful turbojet then available, it was intended to explore transonic conditions just short of supersonic. It was launched and recovered in the usual manner from the ground and had straight aero surfaces like the X-1. (*Tony Landis collection*)

was destined to be modified into the X-1E with a 4 percent wing and a turbopump to move the fuel. It flew at the end of 1955.

Almost concurrent with the XS-1 and D-558 was another USAAF project intended to push well into the supersonic realm for sustained flight greater than Mach 1. The contract went to DAC and this became the X-3. As it evolved into 1949, the exceptionally sleek design still had straight wings, but of short span and thin section at 4.5 percent with leading-edge slats. This was matched to comparatively small tail surfaces. The horizontal tail was placed at the base of the vertical to avoid the issues encountered on the D-558-2 (see later). Two Westinghouse 24C-10 (J46) engines were selected, the inlets with boundary layer bypass. Aiming at Mach 2, airframe heating became an issue, limiting time at that condition without suitable measures. This prompted the use of chilled fuel as a heatsink. With studies showing that pilots could withstand forces from downward ejection, this was chosen to simplify some design problems. Cockpit entry was then from the bottom, the pilot mounting the lowered Douglas ejection seat to be drawn into the interior.

Delays with the J46 forced the temporary installation of axial flow J34s, leaving the Stiletto underpowered. The AB boosted thrust from 3,000 lbf (13.4 kN) to 4,900 lbf (21.8 kN). The delay also resulted in the construction of the second aircraft being suspended. By fall 1951, it was clear that the J46 was in serious trouble and likely years from delivery. Alternatives to boost performance, including substituting a rocket and adopting air launch, were considered but rejected. This meant the aircraft would not meet the program objectives and likely never go supersonic in level flight. The program moved ahead to collect low-speed data, and the second aircraft was canceled. The X-1 and D-558 projects had already delivered suitable results.

The X-1 evolved to a more mature design of which three were built, designated X-1A, X-1B, and X-1D. As seen here with the X-1B, they had a more usual canopy and soon an ejection seat, plus additional rocket fuel capacity. They carried on the supersonic research, reaching Mach 2.5 even with their straight aero surfaces. (*Jay Miller collection*)

The X-3 flew in October 1952 and reached low supersonic speeds in a dive, Handling was unimpressive and take-off rolls exceptionally long. A titanium shield had to be added aft of the engines to prevent overheating during AB operation.

The navy and NACA had planned a follow-on D-558-2 Skyrocket with swept surfaces and a rocket motor supplementing the turbojet for a brief dash to supersonic speed. The wing was swept to 35 degrees and the horizontal to 40, ensuring that each would not achieve critical Mach simultaneously. In addition to wind tunnel tests, models were boosted aloft on rockets. The J34 was fed by rectangular flush inlets installed in the lower quadrant of the forward fuselage, without boundary layer bleed, and the jet exhaust also below the fuselage. This proved less than efficient, and JATO bottles came to routinely assist take-off. The Reaction Motors LR8-RM-5 rocket, for supersonic speeds, expelled on the centerline under the tail. The aircraft also featured automatic leading-edge flaps. Three aircraft were built, each grossing 10,572 lb (4,795 kg) and spanning 25 feet (7.6 m).

The maiden flight was in February 1948. Dutch Roll was uncovered and addressed via an extension to the vertical tail. The horizontal placement mid-tail was found to be a poor choice given wing blanking during high-g turns. This finding would influence ongoing fighter designs.

After a brief period, given poor turbojet performance and rocket motor issues, the team chose to adopt air-launch in meeting their goals. This allowed the J35 to be eliminated from two of the aircraft while rocket fuel volume was increased. All this drove weight up about 5,000 lb (2,268 kg). A B-29 had to be dedicated to the project given the extensive modifications. Loading was with the bomber raised on long maintenance jacks or the pavement jacks, as with the X-1.

The next evolution of the supersonic research aircraft was the sleek Douglas X-3, though still with straight wings. This aircraft was to be powered by a new turbojet engine from Westinghouse, but this was seriously delayed. The alternative afterburning engines left the craft underpowered and it never lived up to expectations. (*Lloyd Jones collection*)

Drops resumed in the fall of 1950. In time, dives were being made from 63,000 feet (19,202 m), the pilot clad in a partial-pressure suit, in pushing to Mach 2 and 80,000 feet (24,384 m).

The exploration of supersonic flight with swept aero surfaces was also the goal of the X-2 program, with the aircraft contract awarded to Bell. The contract was signed in December 1945 for two airplanes. An evolution of the X-1 (though a new airframe), it had 40-degree swept surfaces. Measuring aerodynamic heating of the structure was another primary goal. The wing used a bi-convex section (circular arcs) with leading and trailing-edge flaps. Low-speed handling with this airfoil was evaluated with the second L-39 by gluing wooden leading-edge shapes to the wings.

Each X-2 spanned 37.8 feet (11.5 m) and grossed 24,910 lb (11,299 kg). The main gear were skids since lakebed landings at Edwards were sure to be common. A Curtiss-Wright XLR25 two-chamber rocket was adopted, rated to 15,000 lbf (66.7 kN) with water-alcohol and LOX fuel. This was throttleable, featured a turbopump, and employed regenerative cooling. The nose capsule separation system for emergency egress was adopted, and the system was tested atop a German V-2 rocket launched from White Sands, with jettison at 150,000 feet (45,720 m) and 200 fps (61 mps). The high airframe temperatures and loads expected, plus the corrosive effects of the propellants, led to the selection of K-monel and stainless steel alloys as the principal materials, with spot welding.

A B-50 was modified to carry and release the X-2. The pair began flying in July 1951, with glide flights commencing in June 1952. Waiting for the delivery of the rocket motor greatly delayed progress. During a captive flight with fuel transfer to one of the X-2s, the test craft exploded, killing the pilot and an observer. This further delayed the program. Glide tests resumed in 1955 and uncovered an instability during a landing roll that thrice damaged the aircraft. Powered flights finally got underway

The U.S. finally moved to swept surfaces for their supersonic research aircraft with the navy-sponsored Douglas D-558-2. Initially with a combined turbojet and rocket propulsion system, and ground-launched, this soon gave way to air-launch with pure rocket propulsion—the two images showing these configurations, with and without the inlets and turbojet engine exhaust. The D-558-2 went on to collect invaluable data supporting the development of supersonic military aircraft. (*National Archives*)

The air force sponsored the Bell X-2 with swept surfaces and a new rocket motor. The latter delayed the program, and only glide flights from the modified B-50 occurred during the period under review. It would go on to push the supersonic flight speeds beyond Mach 3. (*San Diego Air & Space Museum*)

late that year, three years behind schedule. It eventually achieved Mach 3.2 and 126,200 feet (38,466 m). The ship and test pilot were lost in 1956 on its thirteenth powered flight owing to roll coupling instability.

In June 1952, the NACA identified the need for a test vehicle to explore hypersonic flight—Mach 4 to 10—and the edges of space. This would challenge construction due to the very high temperatures and control in the almost complete absence of atmosphere, plus reentry into the atmosphere. Years of studies and experiments resulted in specifications at the end of 1954. A contract was let to NAA for what became the X-15 program. Flight testing began in 1959.

Engine Work

The challenges of the new propulsion systems required extensive ground and flight testing. New test cells had to be built or the old modified to accommodate turbine engines. Flight trials usually required dedicated test aircraft as modifications of existing airframes, and with the test subject as an added article or replacing one of two of more existing engines. This ensured safety, particularly airstarts that were initially a challenge for the turbojets. Especially when pressing a developmental powerplant design to maturity for integration into a prototype aircraft or resolving fleet operator problems, the work was persistent if not urgent. See Chapter 6 for discussion of aircraft rocket propulsion tests.

Given the heavy investment in turboprops, an aircraft for safe and thorough testing was needed. The first was likely a TG-100 (T31) installed on the starboard firewall of C-46G 44-78945 by Curtiss, becoming the XC-113. General Electric had been working on this engine since 1941. During initial taxi tests in October 1946, the different torque and throttle response of the two very different engines on either side of the airplane proved too much. After a ground mishap prior to flight, the project ended. The Convair CV-240-21, built as a prototype turboprop airliner (see page 84), was subsequently employed to test turboprops in support of company programs, with the subject powerplant replacing one of the two standard engines.

With the services still needing to conduct turboprop flight tests, Boeing was contracted to modify two B-17Gs (44-85734 and 44-85813) for the role from 1947–1948. Identified as Model 299-Z, the fifth engine was mounted in the nose. To ensure suitable CG, the flight deck was moved aft approximately 4 feet (1.8 m). One of these EB-17Gs was bailed to Wright for their T35 Typhoon testing and the other to P&W for the T34. The latter was operated in flight for the first time in August 1950. Both aircraft and a third B-17 continued in the role for many years, testing turboprops plus the R-3350 turbo-compound.

The most immediate jet bomber experience was with the hybrid XA-26F. This was an A-26B (44-34586) with a 1,600 lbf (7.1 kN) GE J31 installed in the aft fuselage, exhausting out the rear and the intake on the spine. The kerosene fuel was drawn from a bomb bay tank, allowing just twenty minutes of operation. With turrets deleted and a tank in the bomb bay, it would not have been much of a bomber. This was more of a demonstration.

Instead of a nose mount, the air forces and Curtiss chose to place the experimental TG-100 turboprop on the starboard firewall of a C-46G. Despite what calculations may have predicted, the torque and response to throttle asymmetry made for hazardous ground operations. This XC-113 never flew following a ground operation accident. (*The Peter M. Bowers Collection/ The Museum of Flight*)

The Pratt & Whitney XT34 turboprop got its first inflight exposure via one of three Boeing-modified B-17G engine testbeds (44-85734 with civil registration). The spinner has been removed for the test shown in this September 7, 1950, photograph. Intake and exhaust are visible beneath the nose. (*National Archives*)

The modification by DAC began in July 1945, and the jet was initially operated in flight during October 1945. It added just 32 mph (52 kph) compared with the top speed of an A-26D. There was also a tuck-under tendency at high speed that was attributed to the influence of flow off the inlet impinging the tail. As a jet booster for the Intruder, for which production had been halted, it was not worth the effort. Although there were plans to substitute a GE J39, that engine was canceled.

In the same vein, the two 1,600-lbf (7.1-kN) J30s in nacelles were "scabbed" onto each wing of the first Douglas XB-42 (43-50224). The flaps had to be rebuilt, segmenting and notching them behind the engines, owing to the heat and pressure from the jet blast. While the J30s burned the same 100-octane as the recips in the aft fuselage, dedicated fuel, oil, and fire suppressant lines had to be run out to the turbojets. The landing gear was also strengthened for the nearly 4,000 lb (1,814 kg) increase in empty weight, even with the armament removed.

This XB-42A came under contract in April 1945 and, delayed by engine availability, first flew in May 1947. The team measured a peak of 473 mph (761 kph), compared with an expected 488 mph (758 kph), with the range decremented by 550 miles (885km). The only bright spots were that the take-off distance nearly halved and the ceiling increased over 6,000 feet (1,829 m). This could not hope to save the pusher light bomber that had already been left behind, and so was just another effort to gain experience with jets.

At least four B-24s were modified to test turbojet engines mounted inside and fed via an S-duct from an inlet above the wing. General Electric was operating their J33 inside a B-24H (42-95100, in single-tail J configuration) from the end of the war. Another had twin tails and features of the C-87 transport version of the bomber. By 1946, Consolidated had another B-24J (42-73215) for J35 work that possessed an oval intake. During the same period, NACA Lewis took up a B-24M (44-41986), which had a rectangular inlet. Later, Lewis used the same airplane with the engine suspended from a pylon inboard of the number 3 engine. The axial flow J34 was among its first subjects.

One of Lewis' principal tests was the effects of inlet icing, with at least some of the trials likely conducted at the Icing Research Base at Wold-Chamberlain Field in Minneapolis, Minnesota. The initial configuration of 44-41986 had a water droplet spray rig mounted on the aircraft's spine upstream of the dorsal intake. The underwing pylon-mounted engine allowed the testing of bleed air inlet deicing, apparently collected via natural inflight icing conditions. Inlet deicing abruptly became a priority after eight Republic F-84s in a flight of thirty-four were lost during June 1951, with aircrew deaths, following engine failures in ice. It had already been receiving attention in the Lewis icing test cells and flight tests. Soon, ice accumulation on radomes, degrading radar performance at a minimum, became the next issue to be addressed. So, NACA's odd B-24M was given a substantial nose modification to take a fighter-like radome for icing trials, while also used for continuing windshield deicing work.

Pratt & Whitney acquired a B-29B (44-84043) in 1947 to test its J42 and then J48. The J42 was a Rolls-Royce Nene that P&W reluctantly agreed to produce for Grumman, with navy funding. Redesignated as the sole XB-29G, the engine was on

Douglas installed a J31, the earliest turbojet engine available to the Americans, into the aft fuselage of an A-26B to explore the potential for a jet booster. Flying initially in October 1945 as the XA-26F, the benefits were too meager to justify the modifications, but valuable experience was gained. This image of the aircraft, probably near the end of its flying career in 1949, shows the jet exhaust at the end of the fuselage and the spine inlet. (*National Archives*)

The Douglas XB-42A hybrid makes a low pass at Muroc AFB during a test mission. The J30 turbojets are encapsulated in neat pods under the wing. Although they burned the same fuel as the Allisons in the rear, other accommodations helped add to a significant weight growth, and performance was not what had been hoped for. Yet the experience was valuable for Douglas and the young air force. (*Gerald Balzer collection*)

Several B-24s were modified for use as turbojet engine testbeds. These were typically characterized by an inlet above the wing to the engine mounted internally with its exhaust under the tail. This example was being employed by General Electric and has the features of a C-87 version of the Liberator with "solid" nose and cargo doors. (*National Museum of the United States Air Force*)

a pantograph rig in the forward bomb bay. Partially retracted into the bay on the ground, it was extended in flight for operation. The aircraft was also used to test GE engines, including the J35, J47, and J73. The NACA acquired a B-29A for jet engine trials from 1946–1948.[8] Pratt & Whitney later substituted a B-50A (46-036) to test the J57. As with the B-17 testbeds, the test engine was usually more powerful than the four production powerplants together. Occasionally, the crew would shut down the production engines to fly only on the test unit.

It was important to test turbojets at speeds that were representative of jet aircraft flight, not achievable with prop-driven testbeds. It was unusual for single-engine aircraft to be used for this work given the flight safety concerns. Yet the single-engine P-80A (44-85214) was converted to test the J42, though by that time there was confidence in the powerplant. The navy especially facilitated the development of the afterburner, and an early example was tested on an F6U's J34 during 1948 before it became the production configuration (see page 145). More common were multi-engine testbeds, and the second Douglas XB-43 (44-61509, see page 231) was among the first of these. Its operations included flying with a J47 replacing one of its two J35s. The airplane was flown until late 1953 in this role, partially sustained by parts from its grounded sibling.

A B-45A (47-049), two B-45Cs (48-002 and -009), and an RB-45C (48-017) were also adapted as engine testbeds. The turbojet could be retracted into the bomb bay for ground clearance and then extended for operation in flight. The engine still extended below the bottom of the aircraft when retracted, and so the bay doors were cut for clearance. Engines tested on these Tornados included the J35, J40, J71, and the General Electric J57.

Above: The testing of powerful turbojet engines required safe flight trials, preferably on an existing, proven aircraft rather than a new developmental aircraft. General Electric modified a B-29B for the task with the engine extended from a bomb bay in flight—shown here with the J42. Later, they adapted a B-50A for the role, seen with the J57 operating and the production engines all shutdown with props feathered. (*Jay Miller collection and National Archives*)

Below: Three B-45s were modified to test jet engines, with the powerplant partially retracted into the bomb bay for take-off and landing, but extended for inflight operation. Particularly when running in afterburner, the test unit could induce a pitching moment on the jet. This B-45C (48-009) is testing the General Electric J79 and so becoming the JB-45C in an image that post-dates the period under review but illustrates the common test installation. (*San Diego Air & Space Museum*)

To test the J57 at high airspeeds, a B-47B (49-2643) was modified to carry one of these powerplants at each outboard station in place of the J47s.

With the promise of ramjets and pulsejets and their potential applications for high speed, these were also tested. Lewis employed the North American XP-82 44-83887 and an F-82B (44-65168), plus P-61B (42-39754) for such trials. A NACA-built ramjet was unique in being flattened to an airfoil shape. Another testbed was an A-26C (JD-1) for navy ramjet testing in late 1946 supporting their drone work. The navy also used an F7F in 1946 with a 20-inch Marquardt ramjet weighing just 100 lb (45 kg). Early work was also done with Marquardt 20-inch (51-cm) XRJ30-MA ramjets applied to the wingtips of a P-51D, also reported as German motors.

To thoroughly test a ramjet, it had to be pushed to ignition speeds of at least 300 mph (483 kph), and this could be challenging for prop-driven airplanes. In 1946, the initial XP-83 prototype was put to this task with a Marquardt RJ30 ramjet under each wing and an engineer station slipped in behind the pilot seat. One of the ramjets caught fire and exploded during the first test on September 4, 1946. Both men bailed out and the airplane was lost. Two P-80As were also employed in the work with Marquardt units, with the first inflight operation in March 1947. Aircraft 44-85214 got 30-inch (76-cm) units at the wingtips and fuel pumps added within the wings. The test engines burned the same fuel as the J33. Aircraft 44-85042 had 20-inch (51-cm) units. The work was intended to test the throttling of the ramjets, performance, plus develop the test instrumentation and methodologies supporting more dynamic trials. Fuel consumption during ramjet operation was so great that runs were brief. The main powerplant was set to idle during ramjet operation, but the aircraft were still pushed to their maximum airspeed. In June 1948, the J33 was shut down for the first flight of a manned airplane powered solely by ramjets.[9]

During a test flight in August 1948, the starboard ramjet on the P-51 exploded and the pilot had to abandon the aircraft. The accident was attributed to a ruptured fuel line and a pump not being flash-proof. This poor engineering was reflected in the P-80 modifications as well as it was admitted that a single ramjet flameout at maximum Mach would likely see the tail separate from the jet.[10] The testing was wrapped up soon after this revelation.

Testing ramjets as "scab on" to a manned aircraft was limited by the aerodynamics of the host. Pushing the ramjet to the highest speeds permitted by the materials of the time, as fast as Mach 3, in a manned aircraft during these years was not achievable. An unmanned vehicle, more like a missile, to boost the ramjet to operating speed and then accelerate out, appeared desirable. This would also permit data to be collected on the aero surfaces that allowed the missile to fly like an airplane.

The navy converted the canceled Martin Gorgon IV missile (see page 434) to a propulsion test vehicle fitted with a 1,500-lbf (6.7-kN) Marquardt RJ30 ramjet. This aircraft had swept surfaces, roll control via spoilers, and speedbrakes were needed to prevent the craft from accelerating past the engine's operating limit. The 1,600-lb (726-kg) missile was 21.7 feet (6.6 m) long and spanned 10 feet (3.1 m). This combination became the first solely ramjet-powered craft flown in the U.S., launched from two Navy P-61Cs (F2T-1) and recovered by parachute. Testing began in 1947 and Mach 0.85 was achieved, with much higher speeds likely possible.

The navy used one of their JD-1s (A-26C 44-35572) to test ramjet engines in support of their drone programs. Here it operates a pulsejet beneath the bomb bay. The length of the supports in the insert image compared with those in flight suggest it was lowered further than wheel level for operation. (*Air Force Test Center and Jay Miller collection*)

Early testing of ramjets was performed on a P-51D to develop test methodologies. The Marquardt XRJ30-MA ramjets are shown mounted in a June 11, 1947, ground photograph and in operation. (*National Archives*)

Above: The first XP-83 (44-84990) prototype was put to use as among the earliest inflight testbed for ramjet engines. Trials began in 1946 and ended quickly for the Bell jet on the first ignition when one of the ramjets exploded, causing loss of aircraft. Note the cameras mounted under the starboard wingtip. (*Jay Miller collection*)

Below: Ramjets were also tested on two P-80As in preparation for tests on high-speed platforms. To the best of the author's knowledge, the flights did not include the underwing tanks because of buffet concerns at high speed. (*National Archives*)

This work was done at Point Mugu and the Naval Aviation Ordnance Test Station at Chincoteague, Virginia, wrapping up in 1949.

Towards the end of 1946, the AAF sought a similar vehicle with a sustained flight of Mach 1.7 to 3 at up to 80,000 feet (24,384 m). They gave this X-7 contract to Lockheed. The brief was to develop a reusable craft to be dropped from a mothership and then boosted with a rocket to ramjet-operating speed for efficient data collection at low cost. The main, cylindrical airframe contained only avionics, flight controls, and the ramjet's fuel. The ramjet to be tested, and power the craft, was affixed below. Wings and tails of various types could also be attached to the airframe. Thusly, all these elements could be easily swapped. The X-7 had a spike in the front and a recovery parachute in the rear. At the end of the mission, the chute was deployed to

The navy employed a Martin-built drone to test the Marquardt RJ30 ramjet. First launched from an airplane in 1947, this was the first solely ramjet-powered craft flown in the U.S. and soon clocked Mach 0.85. This example is the KDM-1 Plover target version. (*National Museum of Naval Aviation*)

lower the vehicle nose-first to impale the spike into the ground. The missile would project above the ground without damage and for relatively easy recovery.

The X-7 was built mostly of steel. The 4-percent-thick wing was straight, though tapered and with sharply swept leading and trailing edges. Small ailerons and an all-moving stab were the only control surfaces. A split dive brake was installed at the base of the vertical. Lockheed adopted a Lear flight control system.

The X-7 air launch was off a trapeze beneath the port wing of a B-29 or B-50. Its motor was ignited as the craft was pushed to operating speed with a booster. The initial booster configuration was a solid rocket motor, with three stabilizing fins, attached to the tail of the X-7. This was a 105,000-lbf (467-kN) unit from Allegheny Ballistic Laboratory weighing 3,650 lb (1,656 kg). It burned for about five seconds and detached at propellant exhaustion to leave the vehicle to accelerate out under ramjet power. A second configuration had two Thiokol motors under the wings, each delivering 50,000 lbf (222 kN) and weighing 1,700 lb (771 kg). These also permitted the drop from the bomb bay of the bomber, plus ground launch.

The initial X-7A-1 was 32.8 feet (10 m) long, spanned 12 feet (3.7 m), and grossed 8,000–8,300 lb (3,629–3,765 kg). It flew up to 100,000 feet (30,480 m) and out to more than 100 miles (161 km) at more than 2,000 mph (3,219 kph). Flown at Holloman, the first launch was in 1951, though it took most of that year and several launches to achieve a safe and effective flight. By spring 1953, the X-7 had pushed out to Mach 2.6. Many missions followed through 1959 with twenty-seven vehicles built. Apart from the two basic configurations, other changes extended the fuselage or employed different aero surfaces. Many different ramjets were tested, including

The Lockheed X-7 was principally a testbed for ramjet engines, but flight to as much as Mach 3 also facilitated supersonic aero surface testing. The initial configuration is shown here with a detachable booster rocket attached to the tail, with large fins, and the entire missile on a trapeze launcher under the left wing of this B-50. At the end of the flight, the missile descended nose-first under a parachute to impale itself into the desert and protect all the craft aft. (*National Archives*)

various models of the Wright XRJ47 and Marquardt XRJ43, along with different propellants or additives. The work contributed directly to ensuring engine suitability for the BOMARC missile (see page 445).

The revelation of the tremendous power unleashed in a nuclear reaction brought forth innumerable notions of how to harness the energy for all manner of applications. Atomic energy was seen as potentially holding the key as a future power source for everything from powering a city to powering a vehicle.

The concept presented such a tantalizing promise that the USAAF began the Nuclear Energy for the Propulsion of Aircraft (NEPA) program in 1946 and gave the first study contract to Fairchild Aircraft. The AEC took over direction of NEPA in 1949. Another contributing entity was the Joint Committee on Atomic Energy that sought to provide guiding advice on progress. These bodies and the JCS generated an "Aircraft Nuclear Propulsion" requirement in March 1951. The USAF followed with contracts to GE and P&W to develop prototype engines while Convair was to prepare a B-36 to serve as a testbed. The expected first flight was 1956 or 1957. The navy contracted with Allison and Wright to study nuclear propulsion while Convair and Martin looked at naval aircraft applications. The idea of a hybrid nuclear engine burning conventional fuels for certain phases of a flight was also examined.

There were two schemes for a nuclear-powered turbine aero engine. The direct-cycle approach would send compressor air through a reactor core to be heated without burning fossil fuels—except to initially spin up the equipment—while also cooling the reactor. The air then passed through the turbine and out the nozzle. The indirect cycle passed the air through a heat exchanger containing a working medium like sodium or water used to conduct the reactor heat. The nuclear fuel would last far beyond any practical mission duration. Nuclear rockets and ramjets were also being pursued.

General Electric worked on the direct-cycle engine to the point of adopting a J47 turbojet to the technology and conducting bench tests. The best design approached hardware that could have been flown but remained to be optimized. Pratt & Whitney worked on the indirect-cycle engine and did not progress as far as GE owing to greater technological challenges.

In 1951, GE was contracted to assemble a flight-worthy engine adopting its XJ53, to be integrated by Convair into two aircraft. The engine was not expected before 1954 and the flight vehicle in 1956. Convair envisioned the latter X-6 as four turbojets protruding under the belly of a B-36 with the reactor above in a bomb bay. The entire assembly, with radiation shielding, was expected to weight 140,000–165,000 lb (63,503–74,843 kg). The crew would be confined to the flight deck that would be heavily shielded.

By summer 1953, a reactor capable of being taken airborne was being devised. The sole X-6 came together in 1955 as the nuclear test aircraft, an extensively modified B-36H. The 1,000-kW air-cooled, 35,000-lb (15,876-kg) reactor was secured in the aft bomb bay and provided no power at all to the aircraft for the trials. Intake and exhaust ducts accommodated cooling air. Literally tons of lead and water shielding were added to protect the aircrew of five isolated in a compartment inserted into the greatly modified nose. While the tests showed a reactor could be operated in flight, the radiation hazard was great. It would be a decade and many millions of dollars before the official government efforts were shelved.

Prop and Rotor Spin

The new turboprop engines were driving a further evolution of propellers. Exploring the potential for flight with much of the prop in a supersonic state was felt necessary. By 1951, the Propeller Laboratory at "Wright-Patt" wanted to collect test data in flight to supplement wind tunnel and analytical results, and so a suitable platform was sought. The RF-84F appeared a good candidate for modification with a turboprop, and Republic was duly placed on contract. Initially, three aircraft were to be modified, including one for the navy. However, the USN pulled out of the project when turbojet performance improved and turboprop application for fighters appeared unnecessary. Consequently, only two of the testbeds were completed. The Curtiss-Wright J65 was initially selected, but replaced with the Allison T40.

The Allison engine derived from a 1945 contract. It joined two T38 axial flow turboprops to a common reduction gearbox via two long power shafts. Rated at 2,250 hp (1,677 kW), the T38 first ran in May 1947 and then flew on the B-17G testbed, nicknamed the "Anudderone," in April 1949. It was adopted for the Convair CV-240-21 Turboliner twin, the prototype flying at the end of 1950 as the first turboprop airline in the U.S. However, the engine proved so troublesome that the program was dropped entirely. All other T38 applications were experimental. The T40 ran on a test stand for the first time in June 1948. The coupled 2,500-lb (1,134-kg) powerplant was initially expected to deliver 5,100 hp (3,803 kW) and 830 lbf (3.7 kN) of thrust. It potentially had 20 percent greater fuel economy than single-engine turboprops. The design included a means of declutching a failed unit so it would not drag down the entire engine's power output. At cruise, it was thought possible to decouple and shut down one unit for additional fuel economy. However, the T40 was a complex product and Allison struggled with numerous issues.

The T40's gearbox in all other applications drove a contra-rotating propeller. The lab decided that, for clean data, they wanted a single propeller of three or four blades. The three principal high-performance propeller manufacturers in the country—Aeroproducts, Curtiss Electric, and Hamilton Standard—were contracted to deliver products for evaluation.

Republic's greatly modified airplane was initially denoted the XF-106, but later the XF-84H. Instead of adding a turboprop in the jet's long nose, the T40 was in the aft fuselage and the power shafts extended a remarkable 18 feet (5.5 m) to the gearbox in the nose. A governor controlled the engine speed to 14,300 rpm for a constant propeller rpm of 2,103, such that the throttle controlled only propeller pitch. Prop reversal would facilitate landing rollout deceleration. Additional rudder deflection and directional trim were provided to counteract prop torque. For the test aircraft application, the engine exhausts were joined to a common afterburner created by Republic. Hence, the 5,332 hp (3,976 kW) was augmented by 1,296 lbf (5.8 kN) of jet thrust.

The aircraft were relatively slow coming together. A T-tail was fitted to move the horizontal stabilizer and elevators out of the propwash. A "takeoff fin" or "vortex gate" was added aft of the canopy to further assist in counteracting propeller torque. This could be retracted in flight but extended for take-off and landing. The fuselage panels on either side of the exhaust could be deflected forward as speedbrakes. A ram air turbine was automatically deployed to provide additional electrical power and hydraulic pressure with the gear down.[11] Republic hoped to derive a production fighter from the project, and so included provisions for a 0.60-cal T-45 Gatling gun with 1,200 rounds and the usual load of underwing stores. Initially, a three-blade, 12-foot (3.7-m) diameter, hydraulically controlled Aeroproducts prop was fitted, fated to be the only operated.

From a December 1952 contract, the maiden flight was expected in spring 1953. However, the first example was only completed in February 1954 and did not fly until July 1955. Only a handful of flights were completed on each machine, all but one ending in a precautionary or emergency landing. The engine was especially balky. The maximum speed of 680 mph (1,094 kph) was never achieved, touching only 450 mph (724 kph). This was due to power shaft vibration and governor surging, the latter producing violent rolls. The afterburner was never lit in flight. The outer 1–1.5 feet (0.3–0.5 m) of the propeller blades were supersonic at all times. The supersonic props were so excruciatingly noisy during ground runs that personnel were numbed and hearing loss was surely suffered. Even operating 1 mile away, tower personnel had to wear ear defenders and covered their radios with a blanket to help attenuate the vibration of the sensitive vacuum tubes. The aircraft could be heard 20 miles (32 km) away. At a certain power setting, the acoustic waves produced acute nausea in bystanders. The program was canceled on its lack of merit, but also because there was an alternative.

Frustrated by the delays in the XF-84H, the USAF had McDonnell commit one of the XF-88s to modification with a 2,650-hp (1,976-kW) T38 in the nose and gearbox for three prop speeds. Ballast was added in the tail to compensate and fuel volume was surrendered to instrumentation. The nose gear was offset 18 inches (46 cm). Given that the aircraft retained its original engines, the turboprop did not need to be run for take-off and landing. This reduced noise complaints. Although work began in 1949, the sole XF-88B did not fly with the turboprop operating until April 1953. Testing involved the propellers from the three manufacturers slated for the XF-84H. The NACA performed most of the trials, collecting the desired supersonic propeller data. The XF-88B flew to Mach 1.12 in a dive powered only by the turboprop—a notable feat for a propeller-driven aircraft.

Several production aircraft or company ground test rigs were employed in optimizing helicopter rotor designs. Rotors were a limitation for all-weather operation. Rain erosion of blade material was rapid and deicing seemed impractical. Some work was also done to address erosion with leading-edge strips. Construction material went from wood with metal spars to all metal. There is evidence of experimentation with some hot air anti-ice, but no practical operational applications emerged.

The XF-88B takes flight for the first time at St. Louis' Lambert Field in March 1953 with the McDonnell plant as a backdrop. One of the stored XF-88s from the late 1940s was modified with a turboprop in the nose to collect data on supersonic prop operation—here with a feathered four-blade unit. This aircraft aptly supported such work over several years, operated by the NACA. (*Jay Miller collection*)

This XH-5 appears to be fitted with a hot-air rotor blade anti-ice system. The image dates from March 30, 1950, and shows a ram air intake with air passing into a turbine and likely combustion heater, and then ducted to the rotor hub where there appear to be hoses into the root of each blade. The effectiveness of this system is uncertain, but it was not adopted operationally. (*National Archives*)

Testing of rotor systems generally began with a ground whirl stand and then proceeded to flight testing. In some cases, this last was performed with an unmanned scaled vehicle. The practice is illustrated by the rig identified as the Firestone HM-1, photographed on October 6, 1948. It is testing a coaxial rotor system and is prepared for tethered, remote control trials. (*National Archives*)

Seaplane Stretch

Combat seaplanes were a unique "species" among the services that the navy sought to exploit in ensuring they retained important aviation missions in the new postwar milieu. Several new ways of employing flying boats were conceived, and BuAer was encouraged to maintain a lead in the field with technology development and innovation. In particular, new hull design efforts continued beyond the 6:1 length:beam design for the Martin Marlin (see later). Efforts were also sought to bring seaplane performance closer to landplane performance.

Research soon hit on a 15:1 hull that was tested on a Grumman J4F-2 that was modified by EDO Aircraft, manufacturer of almost all aircraft float and ski equipment during and after the war. The airplane tested various hull designs, at about one-third scale, attached to the fuselage. Funded by BuAer and NACA, the testbed first flew for trials in 1948 and provided data for years. When Convair ran into some issues with the XP5Y-1 (see page 367), with undesirable spray patterns and some handling deficiencies, the J4F was modified to represent that hull for additional research. This suggested additional length to the hull would be beneficial for the follow-on R3Y (see page 311), but this was not adopted.[12] This suggested similar trials in the future needed to be conducted at full scale.

The Marlin's 8.6:1 hull was based on research seeking reduced porpoising tendency on the water and lower aerodynamic drag. It was similar to the successful German Blohm und Voss BV 222 and Kawanishi H8K Emily flying boats from the war, both tested by the U.S. The American hull had a single V-shaped step and was wetted all the way to the tail rather than the aft fuselage sweeping up from the water. This also had the advantage of greater usable fuselage volume. To prove the suitability of the significant changes, Martin was contracted in 1946 to build a demonstrator like the J4F-1. Based on a heavily modified PBM-5 (98616), this XP5M-1 retained the Mariner's tip floats and wings—though with fixed leading-edge slats added—and the upper forward portion of the fuselage. All the rest was built new. Incorporated were R-3350s turning reversible props to greatly improve maneuvering on the surface as well as cut the landing run. The vertical tail was apparently taken from the P4M (see page 373).

First flying in May 1948, the XP5M-1 was very successful, permitting innovative aspects of the Marlin to be optimized and lend confidence to the production decision. Martin took the same approach for the P6M (see page 271) in 1951, with the XP5M-1 serving as testbed for the new 15:1 hull. Redesignated the M-270, the boat was stretched with 6-foot (1-m) additions ahead and behind the wing. The new hull was built over the original and R-3350-30 engines mounted. The hydroflaps planned for the P6M were installed, enhancing surface maneuvering, but also serving as airbrakes. Testing proceeded from 1952 into 1955.

Much work was done to show that planing skis, much like personal water skis, would generate sufficient hydrodynamic lift to raise the aircraft on the water such that wing lift would pull it clear sooner. Research into these "hydro-skis" by BuAer, NACA, and the Stevens Institute of Technology, in New Jersey, saw testing from water basins

Right: A J4F-2 Widgeon (32976), *Petulant Porpoise*, was extensively modified to be a testbed for new seaplane hull designs and given a new retractable undercarriage to retain amphibious operation. These three images show three different hulls on this airplane. In the bottom view, note the window aft of the step to permit observation of water flow. (*Jay Miller collection and National Archives*)

Below: This highly modified PBM was used to model the hull for the P5M and then the P6M. This last (shown) gave the aircraft the title M-270 and was photographed here on June 8, 1952, during initial testing. (*National Archives*)

Water tow tanks were one means of collecting scale data on the performance of "hydro-skis" added to aircraft for sea operation. In this case, a D-558-2 model has been fitted with simple dual skis for testing in a NACA tow tank during 1952. (*National Archives*)

An SNJ-5C (51925) fitted with skis is seen taking off from a beach in Wilmington, Delaware, on June 8, 1950. The skis are clearly evident, but they appear to be attached to the main gear and tail wheel struts and are usually broad for the former. As a side note, the SNJ-5C was among a handful converted for deck landing training. (*National Archives*)

This JRF-5 (708747) was used for hydro-ski by EDO for navy full-scale testing of the concept. Photographed on January 30, 1952, the airplane is on a special and exceptionally tall beaching gear that permitted ready access to the test article. Instead of a planing ski, the centerline article is actually a hydrofoil that produces lift in the water. (*Naval Aviation Archives*)

to flight trials to a progressively larger scale. This started with operations in shallows using a Piper Cub from All American Airways and moved to a North American SNJ. Following were sea trails with a JRF-5 handled by EDO. This began with a single ski under the keel and later two skis attached at the fuselage/keel joint on either side of centerline. In designing the skis for the XF2Y-1 fighter (see page 211), Convair had performed scale aircraft tests and an instrumented article cantilevered off the side of a speedboat, while BuAer conducted water tank trials. The F2Y experience showed that all this work and analysis still failed to reveal the detrimental vibration issue with the hydro-ski.

Short Work

The conventional means for facilitating short take-off or landing (STOL) with high-lift wing surfaces was well understood and documented. Other work along these lines included further boundary layer control (BLC) research. Such efforts had been performed during the war, but at low priority. There was a desire to build on those results for potential production applications. Yet no great effort at additional BLC research was made during this period. The Lockheed T2V-1 design (see page 404) did incorporate bled compressor air blown through slots in the top of the slats. This would become the first production application of such systems with a contract in 1954.

There was a follow-up on Willard R. Custer's channel wing concept, evaluated during and immediately after the war with wind tunnel tests and fight trials of his twin-engine CCW-1. His design had the lower half of the propeller arcs passing through the aft end of half-barrel channels that were major elements of the wing. The airflow entrained into the propellers was accelerated across the channel inner airfoil surfaces to create lift even at zero forward velocity. This was demonstrated to provide sufficient lift to allow flight with no take-off roll. Since the aircraft lacked attitude control at zero airspeed, the goal was exceptional STOL performance without complex flap systems. The testing showed that the aircraft did take-off in a remarkably short distance, but it had to be rotated within a narrow speed range and then climb out at a very steep angle that would challenge vision over the nose in most conventional aircraft. The configuration also produced more drag, and wing structural complexity added weight. Low-speed single-engine-out scenarios could be more hazardous than with conventional twins. The conclusion then was that the benefits of the channel wing did not outweigh the negatives.

Custer and his National Aircraft Corporation (later Custer Channel Wing Corporation) built a follow-on CCW-2 testbed at Hagerstown, Pennsylvania, on the uncovered fuselage, empennage, and tail wheel of a Taylorcraft BC-12. A center-section truss linked the channels. There were short straight wing elements outboard of the channels with ailerons and slats—reportedly at the insistence of the Civil Aeronautics Authority (CAA), though it flew using only asymmetric throttle for roll.[13] Beneath the truss elements at the top of the channels were hung Lycoming engines with two-blade props. The main gear wheels were affixed beneath the channels. There was also a nose wheel that only touched the ground with the pilot aboard.

The CCW-2 was flown by Willard's son, Harold, from first flight in summer 1948 into the 1950s, demonstrating take-off in 45–65 feet (14–20 m). In a headwind, the aircraft lifted off the ground at zero airspeed while tethered. The NACA took notice and the craft was transported to Langley for NACA evaluation in the tunnel (where

The skeletal Custer Channel Wing CCW-2 was built and tested at the Hagerstown Airport, Pennsylvania, but also spent time at NACA Langley. They tested the channel wing concept by which air was induced into the channel wing elements by the propellers to create lift at low or zero airspeed. The NACA testing in 1953 did not lead to further government interest in the concept. (*The Museum of Flight*)

fabric was applied) and flight. As before, an aircraft with simple flaps and a bit more power could achieve all the channel wing could do. There was no further government interest in channel wings.

Convertible Airplanes

The ability for an aircraft to take off and land vertically held many tactical advantages. However, helicopters were naturally limited in airspeed, range, and endurance by their fundamental design. Inherent retreating blade stall effectively limits helicopter flight to about 230 mph (370 kph), though not approaching even that speed through 1953. Seeking greater airspeed while retaining VTOL advantages, many schemes were proposed for such convertible aircraft (a.k.a. "convert-o-planes" or "convertiplanes"). A decade later, these would be known by the acronym VSTOL (vertical/short take-off and landing). Even if a supplemental propulsions means for forward flight was added with wings for high flight speed—the compound helicopter concept—stability of the rotor blades was a concern. The rotor had to be allowed to spin unpowered and off-loaded. Whatever the means, the conversion from vertical to forward flight and back again, suggesting two propulsion and lift-generating modes, was a particularly challenging engineering undertaking for suitable stability, control, and handling.

The USAF had seen the vulnerability of airfields and runways during the war. The navy realized it had just so many aircraft carriers for a worldwide mission, and these were perhaps more vulnerable with the advent of nuclear weapons. That service would benefit from aircraft that could be launched and recovered from surfaces so small that each sizeable vessel could carry its air defense fighter. A joint navy/air force design study named Project Hummingbird was initiated in 1947. The various concepts and their potential were explored during a December 1949 First Convertible Aircraft Congress in Philadelphia—a locale that was proving a nexus of much innovative rotorcraft development. The congress was partially sponsored by the U.S. military and NACA, with subsequent meetings and correspondence. The conclusion was that a convertible aircraft was possible and that various avenues to reach the goal lay open, provided resources were directed to solving the development problems in a methodical manner. This suggested investment in R&D with flight research vehicles. The USAF and army subsequently initiated the Convertible Aircraft Program in 1950 and, in 1951, funded three projects. While experimental platforms, these were sized for an observation/reconnaissance mission. With concurrent NACA and navy efforts, this began a decades-long attempt to develop technology for fieldable military VSTOL aircraft.

Rotorcraft work at McDonnell Aircraft, in St. Louis, Missouri, had continued in 1949 with the ONR-sponsored study of a compound helicopter employing tip burning (see page 340). The results were then ready when the USAF/army held a convertible aircraft design competition in 1950, and an army project for a convertiplane employed the technology. This was among the first VSTOL efforts seeking to gain speeds beyond that achievable by a helicopter. The aircraft would take off and land via the rotor and, once in forward flight above the stall speed of the wings, use a pusher propeller for propulsion while the rotor was allowed to spin freely. The use of rotor blade tip propulsion was advantageous in that the burning could be easily discontinued and restarted.

The USAF/army project began as the XL-25 in summer 1951, and the first of two test aircraft was completed in September 1953. In the meantime, the aircraft had become the XH-35 and then the XV-1. It was powered by a Continental R-975 radial at 525 hp (391 kW) turning a two-blade propeller. The 31-foot (9.5-m) diameter three-blade rotor had burners with fuel and air pumped to tip burners. McDonnell developed a governor that maintained a constant rotor rpm via blade incidence during unloaded forward flight for static stability. A good deal of work was performed reducing drag at the rotor pylon and hub. The tail booms extended to twin tails and an elevator, and the wings were fitted with ailerons. The vehicle seated two pilots and had a small cabin used for test equipment, but capable of seating two persons or taking two stretchers.

The XV-1 flew tethered in February 1954 and free in July. The first conversion from rotor to wing-borne came in April 1955, and the machine reached 200 mph (322 kph) the next year—a speed then unachievable by conventional helicopter.

The Sikorsky Model S-57 (soon XV-2) was to use a turbojet engine, but either diverted the exhaust to a blade tip nozzle for cold-cycle tip propulsion or for forward flight. The rotor was a single counter-balanced blade that could be stopped in trail and aligned with the fuselage then to be stowed in the fuselage during forward flight. The wing was to be either a highly swept delta or straight. This concept had low

The path to a "convertible airplane" was energized in a 1950 air force/army program to build experimental VSTOL aircraft. Among these was the XV-1. McDonnell won the contract for a compound helicopter with tip burning to spin the rotor. The XV-1 was in the process of being completed in summer 1953, the first of the two prototypes (53-4016) seen in St. Louis. (*Jay Miller collection*)

potential for success given the challenges of stopping a rotor in flight during transition to wing-borne flight while also transitioning the engine to axial flow—provided that could be achieved. Regardless, Sikorsky did not get deep into the design phase before withdrawing from the program owing to the press of other work during the first year of the Korean Conflict.

The Bell Aircraft project was to be a tiltrotor aircraft. Using lateral-tandem, counter-rotating rotors at the tips of a wing, the aircraft would take off vertically then transition to forward flight by tilting the rotor shafts forward through 90 degrees such that the blades served as propellers, with rotor hub control then serving as prop feathering control, while the wing generated lift. The conversion had to be done judiciously such that the rotor collective and cyclic control remained effective until the wing passed through its stall airspeed. In forward flight, relatively conventional wing and empennage control surfaces provided altitude control. Conversion back to "helicopter mode" from "airplane modes" confronted the same challenges in reverse. Limitations were also the rotor downwash on the wing that robbed it of lift plus the greatly varying forces and structural dynamics during transition. Cross-shafting between the tip rotors, if driven off separate engines, was crucial to ensure suitable side-to-side control in the event of engine failure.

Among the first to make a determined engineering assault on the profound tiltrotor challenges was the tiny Transcendental Aircraft Corporation of New Castle, Delaware, and later Glen Riddle, Pennsylvania. This was another of the many rotorcraft teams formed in the few years following the war, Transcendental incorporating in 1947. They undertook a private effort to build the first tiltrotor testbed as the Transcendental 1-G. This was a small, single-seat machine of 19.7 feet (6 m) in length and just 1,450 lb (658 kg) empty weight, with a hovering maximum of 1,750 lb (794 kg). The three-blade rotors were 17 feet (5.2 m) in diameter. A single 160-hp (119-kW) Lycoming O-290 drove the rotor shafts via a two-speed reduction gearbox—lower rotation rate for airplane mode. Small electric motors worked the tilting axis at a very slow three minutes for the full 84-degree motion, with cross-shaft ensuring an identical angle side-to-side.

The 1-G ground testing began in 1951 and proceeded slowly as problems were confronted and resolved. This was aided in 1952 and 1953 with funding from WADC. However, the first flight was still a year beyond the end of Korean fighting, and it was 1955 before a near-full conversion was performed.[14]

Bell undertook a tiltrotor design initially as the XH-33 and then the XV-3. This began, as do all aircraft projects, with deep analysis, design informed by wind tunnel and laboratory test results, and ground trials. The greatest challenge was phasing in or out of the rotor control of the blades during conversion, whereas the wing and tail control surfaces were functional throughout. Keeping the blades dynamically stable during the process was another major engineering challenge. The envisioned four-place aircraft was to be roughly 3,500 lb (1,588 kg) powered by a single, fan-cooled, 450-hp (336-kW) P&W R-985 driving the three-blade "proprotors" via cross-shafting through the wing. The power transmission gearbox had a two-speed reduction feature to step down the rate for airplane mode cruise. Electric motors at

Tiny Transcendental Aircraft developed the 1-G tiltrotor testbed as a private venture, but they received air force money to help bring it to fruition. This image shows the small aircraft undergoing ground runs on a test stand. A very marginal machine, it demonstrated the feasibility of this VSTOL approach. (*Author's collection*)

the wingtips drove electro-mechanical actuators to tilt the transmissions to the rotor masts. This tilt axis was also interconnected via cross-shafting to ensure against any variation in the tilt axis even if one actuator failed.

As with the XV-1, the Bell project moved safely and methodically, with the complex aircraft years coming to fruition. Construction began in January 1952 and continued for two years. The first ground run was in June 1955, initial hover in August 1955, the first cautionary rotor tilt in July 1956, and finally a full conversion/reconversion in December 1958. It proved to be woefully underpowered.

American VSTOL work was not restricted to the USAF/army program. In their 1950 proposal for the navy's HR2S, Sikorsky had offered a compound helicopter version with the engines driving the propellers as well as the rotor. The navy passed on this option. Hiller explored adapting their HJ-1 ramjet-powered rotor helicopter as a compound aircraft. One of the prototypes was modified in 1953 with a 65-hp (49-kW) engine in front driving a propeller with the idea the ramjets could be shut down for autorotation in forward flight as an autogyro. The drag of the non-operating ramjets compromised the rotor autorotation and so conversion was not attempted.

Aside from the experimentals, the Navy Department sought a heavy-lift helicopter for USMC operations. Its base was to be a new class of carrier intended for troop helicopters devoted to marine assault, the first being the repurposed USS *Commencement Bay* (CVHE-105). This required the helicopter to fit onto a 42 × 44-foot (12.8 × 13.4-m) elevator. The mission profile was a 115-mile (185-km) flight to shore with thirty marines, then return to the ship for refueling. Two jeeps or

Another of the convertible aircraft research projects was the Bell XV-3 tiltrotor to further develop the tiltrotor concept. Probably photographed in June 1952 at Buffalo, New York, the mock-up shows fairings for retraction of the skid landing gear, though the feature was eventually deleted. Only the rotor hubs are installed, lacking "proprotor" blades. (*Jay Miller collection*)

twenty-four litters could also be accommodated. Sling loads up to 11,518 lb (5,225 kg) were to be hauled.

McDonnell answered the 1950 request for proposals (RFP), and their Model 78 won the bid to develop the XHRH. Settling on a large compound helicopter, the contact for three XHRH-1s was issued in spring 1951. A mock-up was inspected in October 1952. A pair of 3,507-hp (2,615-kW) Allison T56 turboprops—derived from the T38 and still developmental—were to be mounted under wings on either side of the large fuselage to propel the aircraft in forward flight. For vertical lift, the engines powered compressors to feed 1,600-lbf (7.1-kN) McDonnell 12JP20 "pressure jets" (understood to be burners) at the tips of the three-blade, 65.9-foot (20.1-m) diameter, free-spinning rotor. Loading of vehicles or other wheeled cargo was via a drop-down nose ramp. The wings, empennage, and rotor blades folded for shipboard storage. Empty weight was projected at 19,169 lb (8.695 kg) and maximum 36,000 lb (16,329 kg). The firm predicted a top speed of 276 mph (444 kph).

The T56 was taking a long time to emerge, ultimately not flying until 1954. The pressure jet rotor power had also been shown through multiple other projects to hold little true operational value. These and other design issues caused the HRH to lose out during the budget struggles following the end of the Korean Conflict. The program was canceled in spring 1954.[15]

Using jet engine efflux directly for vertical lift was also being explored. Ryan Aeronautical and BuAer had begun conceptualizing VTOL in 1947 with a turbojet oriented vertically for more than 1:1 thrust:weight ratio and reaction control. Funded by the navy, the company began hardware tests by the end of 1948, mounting a J33 on a horizontal stand and diverting compressor air to jet nozzles that might serve attitude control. This progressed to a vertical rig with three-axis control, and then a pilot station added, for tethered trials checking control suitability. This rig flew free, though with an umbilical, in May 1951 as the first hovering jet-powered craft.

After summer 1953, the effort was funded by the air force. A contract was let in 1954 for two research vehicles to demonstrate the concept. These X-13 "tailsitters" began flying at the end of 1955, with hover and transitions in 1956. Unlike the navy's XFV-1 and XFY-1 (see page 216), with vertical take-off and landing from the ground, the X-13 was to engage a bar atop a raised platform that proved more practical. It demonstrated the first-ever full vertical take-off, conversion, and reconversion, then vertical landing (via hook-up) in 1957.

Bell was developing a rudimentary Air Test Vehicle (ATV) with a pivoting Fairchild J44 on either side of the fuselage. A turbo-compressor supplied air for attitude jets. This would come together only beyond the review period.

Exploring lift from jet engine thrust directly, and using bleed air for reaction control jets, Ryan built a test rig. This initially had the J33 restrained in a vertical orientation, and then with some translation freedom (seen at left in January 1951). Eventually, a pilot station was added as shown (right) for an almost free flight with a limited range of motion. These tests led to the X-13 research VTOL vehicle in the late 1950s. (*Jay Miller collection*)

3

Mission Imperatives

Much experimentation was driven by urgent mission needs. Especially with the advent of jet engines and the duty to project military power over large portions of the globe, much innovation was applied. Of greatest importance was a credible means of executing bombing missions against the USSR. In 1947, the air force was seriously expecting to execute one-way bombing missions and had units trained to recover aircrew who had abandoned their fuel-exhausted aircraft over Soviet territory.[1] Alternatives had to be devised straightaway.

Undercarriage

The faster landings of heavy jet aircraft were requiring longer runways and demanding better wheel brakes than previously. Stacked steel disk brakes began to be adopted, but even these could be inadequate. Deceleration or drag parachutes were adopted for many, to be deployed on landing. Testing these at Wright-Patt saw an A-26B (44-34137), shorn of its outer wing panels to permit rapid acceleration, used as a testbed with a parachute canister under the aft fuselage.

There is always demand to operate tactical transports on unpaved or semi-prepared surfaces to support troops. The Korean Conflict gave impetus to take the Fairchild C-119 into and out of forward bases with soft and rough surfaces. Development of a tandem gear truck began in 1951 as a means of increasing the ground footprint. A new main gear truck was devised with two smaller wheels ahead of the standard pair and with a separate shock strut attached to the post. The gear doors were cut to permit the tires to partially protrude with gear retracted. Flight testing was performed, but nothing more came of the option.

Track-laying "tread" landing gear tests had been performed during the war on A-20s. Postwar, A-20H trials continued while adding other transport and bombers as subjects. This was seen as a means of extending bomber range by operating from semi-prepared surfaces, particularly in the Arctic. The bombers would be supported by transports, namely the Fairchild C-82, delivering fuel, oil, and maintenance assets. The weapons

Desiring to operate the C-119 at forward bases, Fairchild was tasked with developing a "rough field" landing gear for the airplane. The solution was a main gear truck with two pairs of wheels and a revised shock strut arrangement. Shown during testing on C-119C 50-139, but also known to have been mounted on 50-135, the tandem gear was not produced for fleet deployment. (*National Archives*)

and associated personnel were to be delivered by Boeing C-97s likewise equipped with track gear.[2] In this way, SAC would ensure mission accomplishment while awaiting the development of aerial refueling, and that command was the major motivator of the continuing tracked undercarriage program. The challenge was always to maintain tension on the endless track throughout the great speed range of ground operations and also to retain the track during side loading such as taxi turns and crosswind landings.

For the Fairchild aircraft, the track was designed and constructed in-house with rudder belt treads. The main gear fit into the gear wells with no alterations to even the doors. For the nose gear, the opening had to be lengthened, but this was minor sheet metal work and the doors were not altered. There were disc brakes within the sprocket wheels tied to the aircraft hydraulic braking system. Even the nose unit had brakes. From a contract in spring 1946, the modified aircraft was ready two years later. It operated throughout 1948, and the system did well. Fairchild was contracted to modify a further eighteen packets.

Operation of the initial modified C-82As began to encounter problems during 1949. When tested on soft fields, the equipment quickly became fouled with mud and sod. The tread could also be blown off the sprocket wheels when landing in a crosswind owing to the side loads. Consequently, only twelve more modifications were completed in 1949, then reworked back to standard gear when the configuration was set aside.

A B-50B was modified for tracked gear by Boeing, in Seattle, for testing in 1949. All three units were retractable. Apart from camera installations, there was also a wheel added on struts below the belly of the bomber for independent ground speed measurement.

For an even heavier testbed, the idle XB-36 was selected. The tread gear would certainly distribute the enormous weight of the XB-36 bomber and potentially permit

The first C-82A to be modified with the caterpillar track gear, 45-57746, is seen during ground operations. Lights had been installed on the belly of the ship to illuminate the track for high-speed photography. The track-laying gear initially looked practical, and so a further eighteen aircraft were being modified before problems cropped up and the program was dropped. (*National Archives*)

operation on additional runways. Goodyear track-laying bogies were created for main and nose gears. All units had two parallel tracks, and brakes were enclosed in the forward rollers of the main gear. None could be retracted. The modification in early 1950 added approximately 5,000 lb (2,268 kg) to the bomber.[3] The installation was assembled and tested in Fort Worth throughout March 1950. The gear issued a screeching noise during one brief flight and the mechanism began to break up during landing. No production application was seriously considered.

Presumably to provide fighter cover for SAC's arctic force, tread gear for a P-80 was also developed. The comparatively small "Auto Crawl" units appear to have been attached to each of the three wheels of P-80C (47-171) as "boots" to permit towing and taxi across soft or rough surfaces.

Skis and floats continued to be fitted to transport and liaison aircraft that might need to operate on snow and ice. The "Sliding on Ice and Snow" project that had started in 1950 established equipment characteristics and aircraft performance. The YC-125Bs (see page 300) were also turned to this service, though the only difference from the A-model, which also could be fitted with skis and floats, was additional radios. Likewise, the L-13 and L-15 (see pages 404–407) were initially designed for skis and floats. Fifteen Cessna 195s were fitted with amphibian floats or skis as the LC-126. Among nonstandard configurations via modification was a C-82A on skis. Two P2V-2s were given with retractable skis in 1949, to become P2V-2Ns that included other scientific instruments to support polar exploration efforts. When an F-80 executed a forced landing in the Alaskan tundra, the unit built skis for the jet so it could be flown out. The same was repeated in February 1951 with F-80C 49-429. The mechanics had examples of existing installations for other aircraft to guide their work.

Above left: The SAC concept of extending a bomber's range with operations on semi-prepared fields led to the modification of the first B-50B (47-118) with a tracked landing gear. These units were fully retractable (note camera installation for testing). The tracked gear had its issues, but the remote field operational concept was itself fraught with difficulties and ultimately scraped as aerial refueling answered the range challenge. (*National Archives*)

Above right: The idle XB-36 offered the opportunity to test the Goodyear tread gear on a super heavy airplane. The tread gear had parallel tracks and made an unnerving screeching sound in flight. The tread also began to disintegrate during landing. There were no serious plans to adopt such gear for the bomber—though creating a lighter "footprint" for the Peacemaker would have been a worthy goal. (*National Archives*)

Below: Tread gear was also fitted to a P-80C fighter, presumably to offer fighter support for the deployed SAC force. With a light footprint, the "Auto Crawl" track units were relatively small. They appear to be attached directly to the wheels on each strut. (*National Museum of the United States Air Force*)

A C-82A (44-23004) is seen on March 24, 1948, with skis installed. The skis are raised to permit operations on the wheels. The units on the main gear have a sizable aerodynamic surface. (*National Archives and Jay Miller collection*)

Above: Two P2V-2Ns were created in 1949 by installing retractable skis and scientific instruments supporting polar exploration. The nose ski has a shock-absorbing strut at the front and restraining cable at the rear, while the main gear skis have this arrangement reversed. Note that all armament has been removed and a projecting tail probe is installed to measure magnetic fields. (*American Aviation Historical Society*)

Below: A P-80C was fitted with non-retractable and improvised skis for recovery, with the assistance of JATO, following a forced landing in the Alaskan tundra. Some of the ground material is still clinging to the nose after return to base. The shock-absorbing feature appears to be via bungees. This event was repeated with another P-80C in 1951 and different skis. (*American Aviation Historical Society*)

Fighter Carry-Along

Fighter escort for the B-36 appeared well-nigh impossible given mission duration beyond a day and up to a 9,000-mile (14,484-km) range. Yet, from the experience of the war, an escort was considered essential and so options were explored. Apart from very large jet fighters with enormous fuel quantities presented elsewhere in this volume, other means of bringing the escort along unpowered were explored.

During the war, the army and navy conducted tests towing airplanes to explore the potential for moving aircraft with unserviceable engines to a location for repair, or recovering ships that had made forced landings in locations where they could not fly out. This involved the passing tug ship "snatching" the towrope and unpowered airplane from the ground by a technique perfected for recovering combat gliders. Snatching and towing jet fighters could be important considering the high fuel consumption rate of turbojets.

When in 1947 Wright-Patterson's aircraft laboratory explored the potential for a bomber towing its escort fighter, they faced a far more complex scenario than normal snatch and tow. The fighter would need to power essential aircraft systems with the engine secured and without draining the battery. The bomber would have to supply power via the towline. Past experience using the common nylon lines with an interphone cable running its length was that the typical line stretch caused the cable to break. Consequently, a conducting steel cable towline would be used. Lacking the elasticity of nylon, snatch would be impractical owing to shock loads, and other means of absorbing cable tension than nylon stretch would be necessary. The fighter would have to hook the cable in flight. This had been demonstrated during the war with Douglas C-47s snagging towlines in flight with wingtips that had worked well, and a P-38 snagging a fuel tank towed by a B-24 that had not gone at all well. For a practical application, the fighter would have to join up with the bomber, snag the tow cable, shut down the engine until required to start up, release and fight, then join up again until releasing to land. This was a considerable extension of the experimental systems and experience at that time.

The demonstration involved a B-29 modified to tow the 500-lb (227-kg) steel cable and passing auxiliary power unit (APU) electricity down the length to a modified P-80 (44-84995) with towing mods and electrical system interface. The nature of the P-80 cable capture system and tension relief is unclear, but it may have involved the common tow jaws, at the end of a tube projecting from the fighter's nose, to close over a loop of cable trailing from a boom beneath the bomber standing the cable clear of the belly.

The first hook-up attempt was in September 1947. The team quickly learned that a successful hook-up was only possible with the right cable length and fighter position. Too close and the fighter's "bow wave" disturbed the bomber and cable. Too far back and the cable danced around too much. Finally joining up, the P-80 was towed at idle power for about ten minutes. The pilot then found the release mechanism would not function. Jettisoning the cable would surely be catastrophic for the P-80, and the pilot might not escape. The pilot finally broke free by overstressing the attached hardware by maneuvering into harsh buffet beneath the B-29. This damaged both the fighter and bomber, who made emergency landings. Whether the project continued after this outcome is unclear, but the scheme was not adopted operationally.[4]

The parasite fighter program initiated during the war was also carried forward. With wings folded, the McDonnell XP-85 (redesignated XF-85) was designed in early 1945 to fit inside the bomb bays of the B-36 and B-35. The dimensions made for a tiny airplane with a 37-degree-wing leading-edge sweep and multiple tail surfaces of small dimensions, seeking suitable stability. The V-tails were fitted with ruddervators. There was also a pilot height limit of 5 feet 8 inches (1.7 m). It was powered by a J34 and armed with four .50-cal machine guns. Given the small fuel volume, combat endurance of the fighter was just twenty minutes. The cockpit was pressurized and equipped with a simple powder-charge ejection seat. A perforated speedbrake extended beneath the belly.

The prominent feature was a large retractable "skyhook" on the nose of the fighter with which the pilot was to engage a "trapeze" crossbar extended about an aircraft length beneath the bomber. The front of the trapeze had an articulated "horse collar" that rested on the fighter's nose to stabilize the aircraft securely. The fighter pilot could then shut down his aircraft, which was lifted into the bay where he could dismount. The launch was the reverse of this process. Launch or recovery was to be performed in 2.5 minutes. A radar beacon was to permit the fighter to rapidly locate the bomber. The bomber was to contain fuel and ammunition to replenish the fighter, permitting two missions. The total added weight of the fighter and accouterments was 5 tons.

The practicality of conducting such operations while in combat was no doubt the subject of heated debate. If the bomber were lost, the fighter would be marooned over

The potential for a bomber towing its jet fighter escort was explored in 1947 as a means of overcoming the range deficiency of the jets. For the test, a B-29A (42-93921) towed a P-80A (44-84995) that snagged the tow cable in flight. The means for snagging the cable, held clear of the bomber's belly via a stiff boom, is unclear, but the cable is held at the end. The first hook-up ended with a very dangerous situation that probably saw the end of the project. (*National Museum of the United States Air Force*)

enemy territory. If unable to hook-up or if exhausting fuel, a forced belly landing was the only alternative to ejection as the fighter had no conventional undercarriage. The belly would be fitted with a retractable skid, and steel bars were to be placed under the wingtips.

Two aircraft were constructed without the guns or wing fold. The first was damaged during wind tunnels tests at NACA Ames when it was dropped from 40 feet (12 m). That testing showed the need for more vertical surface area and so centerline dorsal and ventral fins were added to the craft. For flight test, the fighter was loaded onto the extended trapeze from a pit beneath the B-29B—a B-36 being unavailable. It could be retracted only up to the wings, though this was sufficient for safe take-off and landing. For initial trials, a hoop of metal was fitted under the inlet to keep the nose up on a dry lakebed landing to avoid dirt ingestion.

Proximity flights were performed with a P-80 beneath the B-29, the fighter with a tall "wand" projecting above to indicate the distance the XF-85 would experience on the trapeze. Aircraft handling was found to be good. Captive carriage flight with the XF-85 began in summer 1948 at Muroc. An initial flight saw the XF-85 lowered on the trapeze, the engine started, the horse collar raised, and the aircraft flown just within the confines of the hook diameter. The aircraft was very difficult to handle and was damaged in recapture. The first free-flight event was also far from promising. Although successfully launched, reengagement proved exceptionally difficult given the adverse airflow beneath the B-29 and challenging flight control. There was also an optical illusion making the trapeze appear closer than actuality. The fighter hit the trapeze, smashing the canopy and tearing away the test pilot's helmet and oxygen mask. He was able to put the craft down on the lakebed with no further damage or injury.

Testing continued for a total of seven free flights, but only three enjoyed successful engagements. Tests with the skyhook well open degraded control. During one flight, the hook was damaged, while on others, the hook-up simply could not be accomplished in the brief flight time following multiple attempts. Additional vertical surface area was created via winglets, rudder trim authority increased, and fairings added around the skyhook well. However, the engagements continued to be quite difficult and, in another event, the trapeze was damaged. Most flights ended with a belly landing, including the first jet that had joined the program in April 1949 for a single flight. To that point, there had been a total of 2.3 hours of flight time accumulated over nine months.

McDonnell XF-85 Characteristics (Some Figures Estimates)

span, spread	21.1 feet (6.4 m)	weight empty	3,984 lb (1,807 kg)
folded	5.4 feet (1.7 m)	loaded	5,600 lb (2,540 kg)
length	14.8 feet (4.5 m)	speed, max. (sea level)	648 mph (1,043 kph)
height	8.3 feet (2.5 m)	endurance, cruise	32 minutes
wing area	100.5 feet² (9.3 m²)	combat	20 minutes
fuel	115-201 gal (435-761 l)		
service ceiling	48,000 feet (14,630 m)		
climb rate, initial	12,500 fpm (3,810 mpm)		

It was evident that the average fleet pilot would find the fine control necessary to engage consistently the trapeze far too difficult. The capture mechanism could have to be moved much farther beneath the bomber. The XF-85 was also too limited as a fighter by 1949. The .50-cals were no longer very lethal and maneuverability too limited to fight well against likely opponents. Given the shortage of development funds in the latter half of 1949, the program was canceled in October after expending $3.1 million. The USAF was already having second thoughts about the concept. Although they had contemplated an initial purchase of thirty F-85 Goblins, this was set aside even before the flight tests. Several early B-36s may have had fittings for the trapeze, and operational concepts of carrying one to three fighters were considered.

Still seeking some fighter escort solution, it was surmised that a standard fighter might be better behaved beneath a B-36 than the diminutive XF-85. Thus the Fighter Conveyor (FICON) program that examined the carriage of an F-84 only partially retracted into the bomb bays was born. All four bays were effectively devoted to the test operation.

The operational concept was similar to the F-85. An H-shaped cradle was created with the hook-up bar between two long beams. Once the F-84 was attached, the

The diminutive McDonnell XF-85 (shown in the loading pit undergoing final checks and in flight test on the trapeze) was designed, with wings folded, to fit in a bomb bay of the B-36 bomber. The "parasite fighter" was to be carried into battle by the bomber, released, and recovered in flight, as the only practical escort fighter concept for the intercontinental B-36. However, tests with a B-29A showed the airplane to be exceptionally limited and the operation so difficult as to be hazardous. (*National Archives*)

cradle would rotate such that the rear ends of the beams engaged fittings on the fuselage of the fighter aft of the cockpit to stabilize the airplane for shutdown and retraction.

The operation was flight tested from January 1952 into 1953 with a modified RB-36F and straight-wing F-84E. All bay doors were removed for the tests that also required the aft upper gun bay doors to be open throughout the flight to prevent them from being blown off by ram pressure. For the initial trials, a funnel at the forward end of the cradle accepted a probe extending ahead of the fighter's nose inlet to simplify engagement. Early results found room for system improvement. The initial hook-up was very difficult, with much uncommanded motion, and the test pilot backed away without engaging. On the next attempt, the hook-up was made, but the aircraft was becoming so uncontrollable that the pilot attempted to release it. Failing this, the crew had to resort to emergency explosive bolts to separate the airplanes.

The cradle was reworked to alter dimensions and make the extension boom more rigid. Another hook was added just ahead of the cockpit in seeking the ideal location. Yet, on the next hook-up attempt, one of the locking pins at the aft end of one beam sheared while the cradle was being retracted, and the hook-up was aborted. Unfortunately, this occurred at low speed after the engine had been secured, so the dive and restart was exciting. More system changes were made to ease the operation. The first complete recovery and launch cycle was accomplished in April 1952. Eventually, the team concluded that safe and practical hardware and techniques had been devised.

Follow-up later in 1953 was no longer focused on the escort. Effectively giving up all bombing capability to carry the fighter, with several bombers in a formation likely so encumbered, was undesirable. Night, inclement weather, and the mutual defense with the guns seemed the better options. Additionally, aerial refueling was rendering the capability superfluous. However, a lone reconnaissance airplane seeking clear images might have none of these advantages except perhaps darkness. An RB-36 could bring a short-range recce fighter the long distance to just outside the threat zone where it could be launched to make the dash over the objective. The fighter could then be recovered for the return home. Consequently, FICON became an RF-84F carried by an RB-36 for a great increase in effective photoreconnaissance (PR or "recce") range.

The selected swept-wing YRF-84F and the RB-36F required some changes to the cradle and hook equipment, and both were heavily modified. All bay doors were again removed for the trials. The high-set horizontal tails of the fighter had to be given a pronounced anhedral for suitable stowage in the bomber. Loading was again via the pit. For the testing that began in May 1953, the operation proved much easier and safer than with the F-84E.

The decision was made in 1954 to make FICON operational. The USAF committed ten RB-36Ds and twenty-five RF-84Fs (becoming RF-84Ks) for the capability. The bombers had doors modified to enclose the bays and seal around the fighter, albeit without pressurization and so limiting operations to about 25,000 feet (7,620 m). The aft bulkhead in the bomber's camera compartment had a window and trapeze controls. The rear-most bay had to be sacrificed and so the electronic countermeasures (ECM) equipment (previously radio countermeasures or RCM) was moved to the

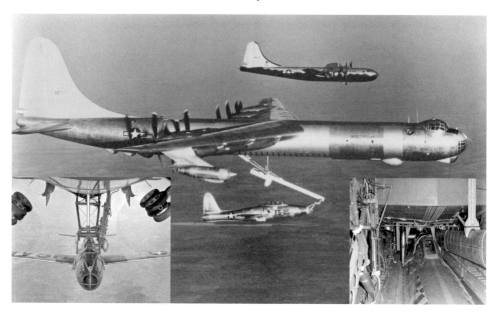

Further parasite fighter trials used Republic F-84s and a Convair B-36 under the FICON program. The first iteration used this straight-wing F-84E (49-2115) and RB-36F (49-2707)—initially with a hook-up probe ahead of the nose and then just ahead of the windscreen. The images show the attempt with just the nose engagement probe, then (insert left) a hook-up with the aft probe, and (insert right) the fighter raised into the bomb bay (B-36 wing center section overhead). (*National Archives and National Museum of the United States Air Force*)

The next FICON trials focused on carrying a swept-wing reconnaissance aircraft, and so a YRF-84F was tested with the RB-36F. Leveraging off the prior work, some changes to the system were still required. Shown is the YRF-84F (49-2430), with a horizontal tail anhedral, engaging the trapeze with its mid-nose hook and the RB-36F with bay doors removed for test. After much work, a safe and practical system was devised that was used operationally only to a limited extent. (*National Museum of the United States Air Force*)

aft pressurized space. The fighter pilot could dismount for most of the mission, only deploying for the flight over the target. There was a tank of JP-4 in the bay to refuel the jet. The B-36 could collect the fighter inflight or load on the ground. A pit could be used or the bomber positioned on ramps to raise its aft end to admit the RF-84 that was rolled forward on a low trolley, with the gear retracted and vertical tail temporarily removed. FICON became operational in 1956, but the program was shut down after just a few months owing to several mishaps.

While still looking at parasite escort fighters, the USAF examined means to keep the bays clear for weapons. A potential was seen in the concept of a Douglas C-54 with flying wingtip tanks pursued during the war, but not advancing to the flight test stage. The winged tanks and transport were hinged wingtip-to-wingtip such that the tanks flew via their own lift without adding to the wing loading of the C-54, yet were coupled for fuel transfer. The Germans had conducted similar research during the war, and two of the engineers involved were employed at Wright-Patt. The approach was felt to have the potential for flying fighters attached at a bomber's wingtips where they could sail power-off, and possibly hands-off, in the uplift. The effective addition to the bomber's wingspan (increasing effective aspect ratio) reduced drag for improved performance.

The initial Project Tip Tow trials used a Culver PQ-14B optionally piloted drone and a Douglas C-47A. The coupling gear was little more than a ring on a short boom projecting from the starboard wingtip of the transport. The light-plane had a "lance" pointing aft from its port wingtip. The Culver pilot was to line up just ahead of the C-47 wingtip then slow to engage the ring with the lance. The coupler permitted limited motion in all three axes such that the light-plane could fly with power reduced and hands-free. Since the PQ-14 was not locked into place, being pulled along, decoupling was simply a matter of advancing the throttle to pull away. However, the C-47 crew could jettison the ring in an emergency.

Flying out of Wright-Patterson, the initial flights in August 1949 found that the approach and hook-up were difficult given interaction with the transport's wingtip vortices.[5] Flying at 8,000 feet (2,438 m) also left little margin for maneuver for the low-powered light-plane. However, a hook-up was achieved only to have the Culver roll to 90 degrees below the Skytrain wing followed by immediate disengagement by the pilot. The ring, just 3 inches (67 mm) from the transport's wingtip, was moved out 19 inches (0.5 m) on a longer arm to hopefully move the PQ-14 out to a weaker vortex effect. Successful engagements were made in October. The Culver pilot's workload once coupled, with C-47 maneuvering, was modest. The PQ-14's ailerons were largely ineffective, but the elevator also gave roll control. A total of 231 couplings with 28.5 hours tow time, the longest 4.1 hours, were recorded. These were made with many pilots from fighter to transport backgrounds. The hook-up task became so routine for the skilled test pilot that it was also demonstrated at night and with the original ring arm length.

The next step for Tip Tow had already begun by this time. This involved F-84Ds attaching to a B-29A's wingtips. The coupling mechanism was more complex, but still notionally simple. The lance faced forward to simplify the joining, especially for a jet

In 1949, the USAF explored the advantages of towing an aircraft attached at the wingtip of a larger craft. The Tip Tow project began with a Culver PQ-14B (44-68334) coupling with a C-47A (42-23918) in the simplest possible manner. This showed the concept to be feasible, though the initial hook-up could be challenging or even hazardous given the smaller airplane's encounter with wingtip airflow vortices. (*National Archives*)

with a slow throttle response. There was a locking mechanism limiting fighter motion once coupled. Either pilot could command a disconnect with explosive bolts. Rubber strips sought to seal around the fighter/bomber interface. Once the wings were locked together, the fighter could be powered down.

Join-up in turbulence was particularly difficult given the B-29 wing oscillations, but it was again demonstrated as feasible. The first coupling was in July 1950, and dual hook-ups in September. A dual tow of 2.5 hours was flown, and at certain flight profiles, the combination was more efficient than the B-29 cruising alone.

The team then introduced a hydro-mechanical connection between the lance movement and the F-84's roll control system in an effort to provide auto-stabilization on tow and permit the pilot to relax. Once locked together, the use of the elevator could twist the B-29's wing. Consequently, a rolling arc "flapping" was the only large motion permitted, though if the limits were exceeded the bolts fired automatically. The pilot could override these inputs or disconnect. Among the first tests of this, in April 1953, the fighter pilot hooked up and then activated the automatic system. The fighter immediately rolled over the top of the wing and struck with catastrophic results. Both aircraft went down with all aircrew lost.

Despite the tragic outcome of Tip Tow, the USAF was contemplating extending the concept to the B-36. If not fighters, jettisonable fuel panels could be adopted, as considered for the C-54 during the war. It became a pure research effort after

The Tip Tow project continued with a B-29A (44-62093) and two F-84Ds (48-661 and -641) in late 1950. Although hook-up was challenging, the system was shown feasible with the fighter pilots continuing to control their aircraft while on tow. A hydro-mechanical interface between the fighter roll control and motion at the interface between the aircraft offered auto-stabilization on tow, but on the first attempt, the F-84 rolled over to smash into the B-29 wing and both aircraft went down with all aboard killed. (*The Museum of Flight*)

SAC withdrew its support. Aerial refueling offered a much safer alternative to range extension while long-range bomber escort had been largely abandoned.

The project was kicked off in 1954 with a RB-36F and two RF-84Fs. The coupler devices were more elaborate, with an extending retriever arm on the bomber and a claw capture device on the fighter. Once coupled, the fighter would be drawn in to lock to the bomber's wingtip. Electrical, interphone, conditioned air, plus pneumatic and hydraulic pressure, would then be passed to the fighter. A production application was expected to also pass fuel. The testing proceeded very slowly and cautiously, with the RF-84 pilots finding the joining task very challenging in the presence of wingtip vortices. Multiple couplings for extended periods were performed, including a three-ship. During a September 1956 test, a violent roll oscillation of the coupled fighter exceeded 30 degrees, and separation damaged both airplanes, ending the program.

Aerial Refueling

A B-29B set several speed/distance records in\ November and December 1945. The aircraft (44-84061, *Pacusan Dreamboat*) was stripped of all non-essential gear and fuel cells filled the bomb bays. Designated the B-29L, this airplane showed the avowed capabilities of America's strategic bomber force and taught some things about very long flights. It otherwise was not indicative of actual bombing operations. The weight of heavy bombers, along with multiple refueling bases that could be withdrawn by host nations, emphasized the great difficulty of translating such performance to a true combat means.

The global strike mission demanded much from the veteran B-29s, with the B-50s soon to follow. Turbojet-propelled escorts would never go the distance with them. The world situation in the immediate postwar period left the United States in favorable circumstances with respect to airbases across the globe. However, although SAC could move bombers to locations under U.S. dominion, these still did not permit B-29s to reach many priority targets in the USSR without assistance. This prompted the addition of external fuel tanks and such ideas as semi-prepared field operations in the Arctic with a tracked undercarriage (see earlier). Operating from Alaskan bases year-round saw the aircraft confront cold-weather ops. The B-29 had not had to meet such demands during the war, and so six Superfortresses were tested with winterization gear as B-29Fs.

The initial intercontinental range objective of the piston-powered B-36 was a staggering 12,500 miles (20,117 km), the approximate mission distance of a B-36 flying from Fort Worth to Vladivostok, USSR. However, this was redefined as a 4,350-mile (12,875-km) radius in November 1947, perhaps not coincidentally equal to the performance of the B-36B expected to be delivered soon and the approximate distance from Okinawa to Moscow.[6] Yet the development of the aircraft was long, and its weight continued to increase at the expense of range such that even the latest objective became problematic. Many senior officers did not see the enormous and slow B-36 as practical in any event.

Jet-powered bombers were sought for speed to potentially leave enemy intercept as a tail chase in which only a tail gun would be necessary for defense, greatly reducing weight and crew size. No escort might be needed. However, the high fuel consumption of turbojets shrank its range, and the B-47 was not expected to be mission-ready before 1951. It was unclear if the future XB-52 (see page 260) would have the solution with its proposed turboprops that were still experimental. The same concerns applied to jet fighters that were expected to assume the fighter-bomber mantle. More fuel volume only went so far in balancing weight and performance.

Discussions during 1946 and 1947 concluded that aerial refueling (AR) should be pursued with vigor in answering the range imperative.[7] It could also allow lighter weight take-offs from runways not stressed to higher loads or just too short, and possibly answer the seemingly unreachable escort fighter capability. The notion of two squadrons required to do the role of one (tanker and bombardment or fighter-bomber), which had previously caused rolled eyes, disappeared with the advent of atomic weapons. If delivering a single bomb could prevent or end a war, every effort to deliver that weapon was justifiable.

The success with an inflight refueling experiment during the war was looked at as a possible solution. A B-24 tanker had refueled a B-17 via a trailing, looped-hose system developed by the U.K. firm Flight Refueling Limited (FRL). Under a November 1947 air force contract, Boeing prepared studies of this and other options. A high-priority development program was begun in late February 1948. Then, in March, Secretary of the Air Force Stuart Symington bragged before a Senate committee of the ability to reach any point on the planet with a USAF bomber and return to American soil by use of aerial refueling. This created an urgency to prove it true, and air force development personnel moved into high gear.

The service had been made aware of continued FRL progress by former general and aviation hero Jimmy Doolittle. In short order, officers traveled to the U.K. to observe the latest work. Flight Refueling Limited was the world leader in AR systems and experience. It had continued the refinement of their system postwar, aimed at commercial use. This had been placed into operation on a small scale and was shown as safe and practical.

The FRL system involved both aircraft trailing weighted cables from chutes under their aft fuselages. By positioning the aircraft suitably, the lines crossed and rode down until end grapples engaged. The tanker, flying above and slightly ahead, reeled in the cables to a point at which the grapples were manually removed and the receiver's line attached to a hose with end nozzle. The tanker then allowed the hose to unwind as the receiver winched in its line. The hose nozzle was ultimately seated in a coupling at the base of the chute and held by latches. The aircraft were then linked by some 200–250 feet (61–76 m) of looped hose trailing behind. Valves opened and fuel flowed via a tanker pump and gravity. Once refueling was complete, the latches were released and the tanker reeled in its hose to the point where a weak link in the receiver's line broke under high tension as the aircraft moved apart. There was, of course, a good deal more complexity to the system and operation to include inerting of hoses, electrical and hydraulic power, modifications, control for hardware, and fuel system changes. The receiver had several hundred pounds of added gear while the tanker had about 1,000 pounds.

The USAF personnel were impressed by this and immediately acquired two sets of aircraft hardware, contracted for forty more, obtained manufacturing rights to the system, and arranged for a year of technical support.[8] Boeing used the two systems brought to the U.S. in March 1948 to modify two B-29s at their Wichita, Kansas, plant. This was accomplished in thirty days and testing began in May. The tanker carried a jettisonable 2,300-gal (8,706-l) fuel tank in each bomb bay while the hose reel and associated equipment were in the aft fuselage. The system was cumbersome and imposed speed limitations owing to drag on the hose. Yet it functioned and was urgently needed.

The USAF decided to modify eighty Superfortresses into pairs of receivers (atomic bombers) and tankers to be known as B-29MR and KB-29M, respectively. Given the urgency, Boeing was selected as the sole source. Flight Refueling could not meet the desired delivery schedule, so American suppliers were sought to manufacture the hardware. Refinements like greater flow rate, low-temperature operation, and higher airspeed were set aside in the interest of the earliest operational capability. Deliveries of the revised bombers commenced in June. Ninety-two tankers and seventy-four receivers were ultimately completed.

The USAF directed in June 1948 that all new B-50Bs were to be equipped as receivers using the FRL system while those already manufactured would be retrofitted. The airplanes' fuel system would be reworked for single-point pressure refueling.[9] The partially shuttered Wichita plant was restored to full operation to handle this workload. Time was found for the refinements previously held back.

By the end of 1948, SAC had two AR squadrons with about forty tankers. A demonstration of the new capability was conducted in December with a B-50A flying from Fort Worth (Carswell AFB) to Hawaii to drop a dummy bomb load and return over the 9,400 miles (15,128 km). This was accomplished in three refuelings by KB-29Ms, though not without drama given unexpected headwinds and system failures. A few months later, another B-50A (46-10, *Lucky Lady II*) flew around the globe nonstop, refueled by four pairs of KB-29Ms along the 24,452-mile (37,742-km), ninety-four-hour journey. This took considerable effort, but confidence was growing in the system and crews, and the ability of the USAF to deliver an atomic weapon anywhere in the world.

The USAF began standing up additional refueling squadrons. By the end of 1950, there were a dozen operating 126 KB-29Ms.[10] That summer, SAC felt that it could make a number of round trip missions to the USSR, though it had an emergency capability much earlier.

The looped-hose refueling was clearly a stopgap. Under its 1947 contract, Boeing had conceptually explored many alternatives. Based on this research, the company conceived a telescoping "flying boom" on a universal joint at the aft end of the tanker. An operator guided the boom visually via a pair of "ruddervators." The receiver pilot would fly in a suitable contact "box" as guided by alignment marks and lights on the bottom of the tanker, as well as radio communication. The boom had a telescoping tube through which the fuel was pumped to a nozzle at the tip. The "boomer" was to guide the nozzle into a receptacle on the receiver airplane flying close behind. When the nozzle was seated into the receptacle, valves were opened and fuel flowed. The fuel delivery rate would be much greater and the entire process faster and less awkward than the looped-hose method.

Boeing began developing the boom on their own initiative since the USAF was slow giving them a contract owing to fiscal limitations. The company assembled the first system in four months. The assets were ready by June 1948 when the company finally got government funding. Boeing and Wright-Patt had conducted proximity flight profiles with B-29s during May to determine mutual influences and the best positioning of the aircraft pair facilitating safe and efficient refueling in close proximity, this also determining required boom length. They then proceeded with modifying two RB-29Js as YKB-29Js. Funding was so short that the effort was delayed a year while Boeing continued integration design work on their own. Along with necessary system changes, the tanker had a boom operator in the former rear turret and gunner volume,

Two B-29s engage in the earliest operational aerial refueling system fielded by the USAF (note the proximity of the aircraft). A spin-off of the British system tested by the Americans during World War Two, it involved the inflight linking of trailing cables followed by the receiver pulling in the tanker's hose through which fuel then flowed. Boeing converted bombers as the ninety-two KB-29M tankers and seventy-four B-29MR receivers for operational employment. (*San Diego Air & Space Museum*)

behind a transparent dome. The boom locked up in trail to a truss extending from the aft fuselage. The receiver was given a receptacle in the crown of the forward fuselage, enclosed by doors to eliminate added drag.

Evaluations with the YKB-29Js finally got underway in April 1949 with ground tests, then "dry" flight trials, followed by complete refueling cycles. The autumn 1949 flight trials were relatively successful, with poor low-temperature operation as one complaint. The enthusiastic USAF had decided in May to go operational with the flying boom system at the earliest opportunity. It directed that an initial forty B-29s be modified with the boom as KB-29Ps in the reopened Renton, Washington, plant. New B-50Ds were to be delivered with receptacles recessed above the flight deck, ahead of the upper forward turret that would be rotated to place the barrels to the side during AR. The receptacle was enclosed by doors that swung aside to serve as boom guides while also possessing embedded lights to illuminate the slipway for night refueling. Lead-in lines were painted ahead of the slipway for boomer reference. With B-50s by then on force in large numbers, the B-29 was turned from bombing to this vital support role. The first of 116 KB-29Ps reached SAC squadrons in September 1950 and all were delivered by the end of 1951.

The first boom refueling of a jet aircraft was conducted in the fall of 1950 with a KB-29P passing gas to an RB-45C, and the first jet bomber in June 1951 with a KB-29P and B-45. The Tornado was the first to be routinely boom-refueled in fleet service. The B-45A was known as a bomber with such short legs that it could not fly to Hawaii and its benefit to SAC, apart from recce, was minor. Aerial refueling showed how the equation could be altered when, in July 1952, an RB-45C flew from Elmendorf AFB, Alaska, to Yokota AB, Japan, non-stop with the aid of two tanker contacts.

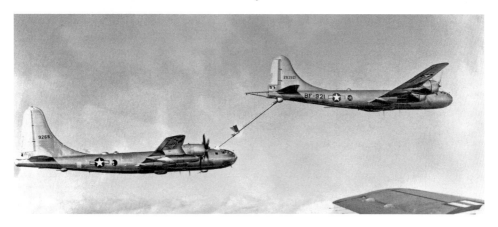

A KB-29P (42-93921, a former B-29A) employs its flying boom to refuel a B-50D (49-265). Boeing developed the boom system after a study of alternative aerial refueling methods. It would modify 116 B-29s to the role in 1950 and 1951 while B-50s were built with the receptacles for the boom fuel nozzle. (*San Diego Air & Space Museum*)

Despite the large commitment to the KB-29P, the decision had already been taken to make the C-97 the primary boom tanker. This aircraft had a speed advantage on the B-29 tankers and could deliver more fuel via four tanks on the cargo deck with a total capacity of 7,200 gal (27,255 l). Modification of three C-97As with booms began in June 1949, and they were under test by September. The "boomer" station was below the boom pivot point and accessible through a floor opening. The man visually guided the operation through windows in a bubble added to the outer moldline of the belly. The results were so positive that the USAF directed that all future production 97s be convertible tanker-transports.

The KC-97As became prototypes of the KC-97E, of which sixty were built in Renton from July 1951 to 1952. These could be converted from tanker to transport—though not quickly—by removing the boom, boomer pod, and cargo floor tanks. The F-model introduced a more powerful R-4360 variant plus instrumentation improvements, and 159 of these were built, with the first delivered in April 1952. These were followed by KC-97Gs, which allowed unimpeded cargo operations with AR tanks moved to the lower deck and two 700-gal (2,650-l) underwing tanks from the B-50D. They could thus deploy with the bomber while carrying personnel, maintenance kits, and parts. Boom changes were also introduced; the boomer lay prone instead of sitting upright, and the radio operator was eliminated given advances in communications technology.

The KC-97G became the standard tanker model with a $1.22 million per unit cost and deliveries beginning in May 1953. It was also the end of the line, short of future upgrades, with 592 built of the 888 representing the entire Stratofreighter production through 1956.

The tanker and bomber units continued to build operational procedures to include rendezvous and closing to contact, flying refueling tracks, emergency breakaway, and experience to include night AR. During 1952, war plans began to reflect AR in meeting operational commitments. By 1953, there were thirty squadrons with 502 tankers, dominated by the new KC-97s, and that year, SAC pumped 11.5 million gal (43.5 million l) to receivers.[11] Bomber and fighter units began to perform rotations to Europe via AR.

The new-built KC-97s were a great improvement over KB-29 tankers. However, they were still prop-driven and so continued to present a speed disparity with the "fast movers." In particular, the B-47 found refueling from the 97s to be challenging, and *vice versa*. The bomber had to descend to the 97's operating altitude, and both had to enter a shallow dive ("toboggan") for a compatible AR airspeed. The 97 also delivered just a fraction of the bomber's total fuel load. The bomber then burned half the fuel it just took on to get back to its operating altitude. Yet in March 1952, KC-97Es refueled a B-47 that completed a 12,000-mile (19,312-km) flight.

Two jet engines were added under the KC-97's wings in later years to help keep up, but this would not be enough for the B-52 and advanced fighters on the horizon. Strategic Air Command began to lust after a turbojet-powered tanker that could also deliver more fuel. Boeing's proposals to put turboprops and even a swept wing on the KC-97, and the Douglas XC-132 program (see page 286), were more half-measures that did not spark enthusiasm. In 1952, Boeing began developing an airplane with four turbojets on a swept wing that could serve as the basis for both an airliner and a tanker. They began work on a prototype Model 367-80 in 1952, and it flew in 1954 to become the 707 and KC-135. There was little USAF money in the initial effort. The KC-135s began displacing KC-97s in the late 1950s.

Flight-refueling tactical aircraft could be just as important as SAC requirements, as the Korean emergency soon demonstrated. The looped-hose technique was impractical for fighter and attack machines, but FRL was working on a solution. During spring 1949, they began flight testing their new hose and drogue system. A 100-foot (31-m) refueling hose was trailed behind the tanker from a reel, stabilized with wire and canvas basket. The receiver was fitted with a probe, a fuel nozzle at the end, projecting a short distance ahead of a portion of the aircraft. The pilot flew this probe into the basket that guided the two to seating the nozzle into a valve at the base of the basket. This action and tension relief on the hose caused it to reel in a bit and allowed fuel to begin flowing. They had reduced the system to a point it could be fitted into a tanker underwing pod, which the company also built. A British Meteor jet was refueled in this way during April 1949, remaining aloft for twelve hours. The USAF took immediate notice.

The air force promptly dispatched four B-29s and two F-84Es to the U.K. for modification to employ FRL's "probe-and-drogue" system. Two of the bombers were fitted with probes projecting from the brow of the nose, above the flight deck. The second pair were fitted with a hose reel in their aft fuselages. One of the last was also given two hose reels within wingtip pods, permitting it to refuel three fighters simultaneously. This three-point tanker was designated YKB-29T (45-21734) and was tested with two Royal Air Force (RAF) Meteors. Two of the F-84s had their fuel systems modified for single-point refueling and an AR probe attached to each port wing's leading edge. These airplanes were flown back to the States in September 1950 with the aid of AR from a British Lancaster tanker. One of the F-84s did not make

The Boeing C-97 production was almost entirely devoted to the flying boom tanker-transport configuration supporting SAC. Although possessing more fuel to offload compared with the KB-29P, the KC-97G (52-2790 shown with underwing tanks) still had a significant performance disparity when compared with new jet bombers like the RB-47E (51-15838) shown. Note the high deck angle and deployed split flaps of the swept-wing bomber as it flies at the slow AR airspeed. (*National Archives*)

it owing to damage sustained to the probe during an AR contact. The pilot had to abandon the jet, but it was rescued. The other fighter completed a ten-hour non-stop crossing that would normally take that number of days with multiple stops and awaiting suitable weather.

Tactical Air Command began taking a serious interest in tankers and routine AR. Wright Air Development Center fitted probes projecting from various fighters to test with the probe-and-drogue system. The "production" design of the B-29 hose and drogue had the reel in the aft fuselage and fuel tanks in the bomb bays. Tests were also performed with a boom receptacle in the nose of an F-86A, displacing the ranging radar. However, the speed of the B-29 was not compatible with many jet-powered receivers, forcing more toboggan maneuvers. A KC-97F (51-322) was fitted with a hose-reel in place of the boom in 1953 for tests as the sole KC-97H, but this was not adopted as a fleet option.

Wright-Patt modified a B-47 with a probe projecting from its nose as a YB-47F and another as a tanker (YB-47G) with an FRL hose-reel in the bomb bay along with a long-range fuel cell. The modifications were performed in the first half of 1953, and the first all-jet refueling action was conducted in September of that year.[12] Strategic Air Command remained unimpressed. The boom offloaded faster, left most of the work to the enlisted boomer, and did not use a bomber as a tanker.

Although the B-36 never got any AR receiver kit, it was considered as a tanker. Strategic Air Command was seeking an aircraft suitable for refueling jet bombers at a high altitude. An FRL hose reel system was adapted to fit in the aft bomb bay of

The special YKB-29T (45-21734) tanker with wingtip AR pods, in addition to the centerline hose, is seen refueling a probe equipped B-29 (44-87763). This was not adopted as a bomber AR method, but it served as the basis for refueling fighters equipped with single-point refueling systems and probes. (*National Archives*)

In an effort to answer the marginal compatibility between the recip-powered tankers and the turbojet B-47, an experiment was performed with a Stratojet equipped as a tanker. The hose-and-drogue system saw a B-47B (50-40) modified with a British hose reel in the bomb bay to become the sole YB-47G tanker and another B-47B (50-009, though often reported as 50-069) modified with a AR probe to become the only YB-47F receiver. The testing showed the scheme as feasible, but SAC chose to retain the B-47 as a bomber and await a turbojet-powered tanker. (*San Diego Air & Space Museum*)

a B-36H. This had a wind turbine to pressurize the pumps and a retractable boom extending the hose well clear of the bottom of the bomber once the bomb bay doors were opened. Long-range jet fuel cells filled the other three bays; these totaled nearly 16,000 gal (60,567 l) to be passed at up to 600 gal (2,271 l) per minute. The AR system in the aft bay was designed for installation and removal in 12 hours, but the tanks were permanent installations. While the B-36 could reach the high altitude of the B-47, the speed incompatibility was still a great impediment. This scheme was not carried forward.

The air force also tested an alternate system with an extendable probe projecting from a fairing on the nose of B-29A 44-61651 "PA." The pilot guided the nozzle at the end of the probe into a receptacle within a fairing added beneath the rear fuselage of B-29 44-27352 "MA." While this author found little information on the system, it was clearly not adopted. Precisely maneuvering a large airplane, even in smooth air, could be challenging, and the probe did not have the range of motion of the boom.

The advantages and disadvantages of the boom versus probe-and-drogue were debated, and SAC conducted a "fly-off" between the two systems in February 1951. Bomber crews preferred the boom rather than chasing a basket with their slow-responding machine, while fighter pilots liked the probe. Hence, both survived for different applications. The service would soon introduce a boom-to-drogue adapter, with a short length of hose and the drogue replacing the boom nozzle.

Aerial refueling began to be used in Korea during summer 1951 (see pages 453–454) and left a positive impression on TAC. They began insisting on single-point fuel systems and probes on new aircraft plus advocating for dedicated tankers. Efforts were made, but no fleet-wide solution emerged during the period under review. The suitability of the probe-and-drogue system was tested with the KC-97H. The B-36 tanker system was tested against an F-84 receiver in March through May 1953, but it encountered many technical problems. Correcting the issues was not approved. Besides this, the slow speed of the bomber and its greater value as a bomber meant that there was little eagerness for the capability. The project was shelved, but the USAF was committed to finding a suitable tactical aircraft AR solution.

Range was also a hindrance for the navy in acquiring the nuclear delivery capability they saw as vital to sustaining naval aviation. Like the air force, they also felt the mission impact of turbojet fuel consumption on their fighter-attack fleet. The two services discussed ongoing AR work beginning in 1948 to ensure against duplication of effort, and so the navy knew of FRL's work. The USN approached the company about a system more suitable for shipboard aircraft. With probe-and-drogue development already underway, this was demonstrated to the naval fliers.

The new P2V anti-submarine patrol aircraft (see page 265) held some promise for nuclear weapon delivery, but it still fell short on range when launched from either ship or land bases. In 1948, the navy explored using the FRL system to refuel the *Neptune* from PB4Y tankers—although the Convair airplane would likely present a speed incompatibility. Contracts were let to modify one of each, but only the tanker made good progress before the project was dropped in 1949 due to lack of funds.[13]

Another tanker-receiver AR method explored by the USAF was the system depicted by these images of two modified Superforts (B-29A 44-61651 and B-29 44-27352). The telescoping probe with tip fuel nozzle is flown into a receptacle at the aft end of the tanker. Such fine maneuvering of heavy aircraft is not so easy, especially in the presence of turbulence, and the method was not adopted. (*National Museum of the United States Air Force and San Diego Air & Space Museum*)

The hose-and-drogue refueling method held value for fighters. Although evaluated and adopted after modest use in Korea, it was only in the late 1950s that it became available for routine employment. Here an unmarked F-84 (probably one of the F-84Es modified in the U.K. with a probe on the port wing's leading edge) has engaged the drogue from a similarly anonymous KB-29 during 1950. (*National Museum of the United States Air Force*)

The department negotiated with FRL for the modification of their stable of fighter-attack jets as receivers and B-29s (P2Bs) or P2Vs as tankers. They also considered flying boats as tankers, but their obvious speed and basing limitations spoke against this. Since a large flying boom on a carrier-based aircraft was impractical, probe-and-drogue held appeal. As the USN wanted any such work to be performed in the U.S., FRL established an American subsidiary, Flight Refueling Incorporated (FRI), in Danbury, Connecticut. Under contract, FRI developed an electrical hose reel system that could fit in the bomb bays of the larger naval aircraft and even be jettisoned. The fuel system changes and operator accommodations were considerable. The probes and fuel interfaces on receivers were also no mean task.

The navy continued to move slowly owing to the press of other obligations. Patuxent River modified the surviving XAJ-1 (see page 267) as a tanker. The hose reel was mounted in the aft fuselage, displacing the jet engine, and the hose with basket exited the former jet exhaust opening. Tests commenced in March 1952, and receivers included a F9F-5 fitted with an AR probe projecting from the nose. The trials in summer 1952 were generally favorable, giving the navy confidence in the system. However, they still moved ahead leisurely. It was 1954 before they emphatically committed to probe-and-drogue, all future fighter and attack aircraft to be suitably equipped, and then 1956 before they had an operational capability. When the AJ became the first shipboard tanker in 1955, the jet engine was retained. The hose reel was placed in the bomb bay with the hose emerging from a mast extending beneath the bay doors. By that time, the USAF had taken an interest in the navy's probe-and-drogue progress, and there was joint work on standardizing the equipment.

Douglas also developed the D-704 "buddy refueling" pod for the navy. First appearing in 1953, it was aimed at use under the belly of the developmental A4D (see

The surviving North American XAJ-1 (121460) was modified for Navy aerial refueling trials. Employing the probe and drogue system, the results are evident in this August 28, 1952, image of the Savage refueling a F9F Panther, both aircraft out of NAS Patuxent River. In these trials, the hose reel replaced the XAJ-1's jet engine, while in later iterations, the hose reel was placed in the bomb bay. (*National Archives*)

page 198). The system was all self-contained with the hose reel, fuel and hydraulic pumps, a ram air turbine generator (small propeller on the nose), and 300 gal (1,136 l) of fuel, all contained in a store like an underwing drop tank. It would see its first use under a Douglas AD. The Skyraider was clearly an interim solution given the small fuel quantity available for a receiver, having to segregate the jet fuel from its own, and speed incompatibility with the vast majority of a carrier air wing's aircraft.

Snatch and Tow

Trials towing "crippled" aircraft continued for a time after the war. A P-59 was towed behind a C-47 until the latter encountered engine troubles in instrument conditions and had to cut the fighter free. The fighter pilot was then forced to bail out.[14] Snatch and tow of a T-33 was done by a B-50. With the same motivations to towing airplanes, towing a helicopter was explored. A C-47 towed a Sikorsky R-5, presumably in autorotation. One attachment design for the helicopter was a bifurcated fitting with a line to rigs on either side of the nose. The other was to a bar attached at the nose. For the snatch, some means of spinning up the rotor before pickup must have been introduced.

Having investigated German glider experience during the war, the U.S. Army learned of the use of a rigid tow bar in place of the long rope. Some work along these lines had also been also been performed in the U.S., and the decision was made to conduct follow-up. The Third Air Force's Airborne Division conducted field trials with such an arrangement, and this stimulated Wright-Patt into action during May 1946. Equipment fabrication was underway in November 1946, apparently following a pattern established by the navy during similar wartime work.

At the tug end was a ball and socket. At the glider end was a standard tow fitting, but on a universal joint. The bar was 4 feet (1.2 m) long and weighed approximately 100 lb (45 kg). It had a spring-loaded telescoping section with 4 inches (10 cm) of travel for damping longitudinal motion and stress relief. Position lights were added to the horizontal stabilizer of the tug to help the glider pilot maintain position during night ops.

Flight trials in June–October 1947 employed Waco CG-15As and CG-4As behind C-47A, Curtiss C-46F, and C-82A tugs. In this last case, the bar was at the apex of a triangular truss attached to the end of each of the transport's tail booms. Test results were favorable. Flight in weather and turbulence did not prove any more fatiguing than in a twin-engined trainer. The tug could tow the glider down on a night or instrument approach and release it at about 50 feet (15 m) above the runway. The glider could then land on the sod beside the runway as the tug landed on the pavement. Alternatively, the glider could make S-turns to kill speed and land behind the tug on the hard surface. The combination could even taxi together, including negotiating turns. Additionally, the rigid bar provided a more reliable interphone connection between the two aircraft than a cable along the rope.

The tow bar design was not without some concerns. The CG-4A behind the C-46 was not as good a combination because the glider's roll response was too slow during

Above: The ability to snatch and tow aloft airplanes with crippled engines continued for a time after the war. Here a B-50D (49-307) snatches a T-33 from the Muroc lakebed. The matter of tow cable attachment to the trainer is unclear, but definitely not that seen with the P-80 shown previously with a tube projecting from the nose. (*Air Force Test Center*)

Right: Towing an unpowered helicopter had to require that the rotor be initially spun up for autorotation. Ensuring a stable tow within the control margins of the helicopter would also be important, and these images show two tow line attachment methods—one to booms extending off each side of the nose of an H-5D for a bifurcated line and with explosive releases, and the other a vertical bar on the nose of an H-5H that allowed the line to ride up and down. A C-82A is shown towing the H-5D off on August 3, 1948. (*National Archives*)

Following up on work in the United States and Germany conducted during the war, the U.S. Army performed comprehensive work on rigid tow of gliders behind tugs. Eliminating the long tow rope hoped to permit safer towing, and this was tested with CG-4 and CG-15 gliders behind the common tugs. This combination is a CG-15A (45-55276) with heater "hump" above the cabin, behind a C-47A (42-23918) on a 4-foot bar over Ohio during 1947. (*National Museum of the United States Air Force*)

take-off, in addition to other undesirable characteristics. Unlike common practice with a towline, if the glider lifted off before the tow plane, it would lift the tug's tail wheel off the ground and produce directional instability. So, while promising, the rigid tow system was not adopted as standard.

Eject Option

Ejection seats were in their infancy at the end of the war. Research and laboratory work was underway in the U.S. and U.K. while the Germans had working if rudimentary seats that had at least sixty successful combat egresses to their record. The British continued to lead postwar, and the U.S. Navy favored their Martin-Baker seats. However, American work closed the gap rapidly. While service labs developed design standards via analysis and tests, the aircraft manufacturers were already being challenged to include ejection seats in new models. They had to design and test the units themselves that were incorporated in new designs emerging during and soon after the war. Douglas would become the American production leader in ejection seats for a time through this process. While this situation engendered much original thinking and a great deal of learning, it was inefficient and sometimes saddled a type with a poor egress system for its entire service life.

The initial seats had narrow operational envelopes, with zero-altitude/zero-airspeed a distant goal. The ejection sequence was largely manual at the start until automation was introduced over time. The catapult systems used a variety of compressed gases, rockets, and explosive charge to propel the seat out and clear of the aircraft. The early explosive charges had such a high initial impulse that many of the pilots suffered back injuries. When it came to very high-speed ejections, the designs had to deal with inadvertent flailing of pilot limbs that could produce dislocations and breaks. Supersonic ejections were going to be particularly challenging. Among the solutions were face curtains and leg stirrups. More novel approaches were explored to include separating the entire cockpit as a capsule.

The seat designs were demonstrated through static ground testing, then at various speeds on a sled track, and on to flight testing with dummies and then live individuals. Northrop was contracted to design and build a 2,000-foot (610-m) sled track at Muroc that became operational in late 1947. It used rocket motors to propel the rig containing the seat, sometimes in a mocked-up aircraft forebody. These tests initially employed an anthropomorphic dummy before people. The USAAF/USAF employed a Lockheed T-33A and a P-61B modified to fire seats in flight, while NACA used a P-61 and the navy a Douglas JD-1 (A-26). All required a dedicated station for the test seat while the safety pilot continued to fly the aircraft without adverse impact of the ejection. The downward trajectory ejection seats featured in some aircraft were also analyzed and tested, as were all other egress methods.

The ejection seat from a German He 162, which used an explosive cartridge, was acquired by the Ordnance Department and installed in a P-80 for testing soon after the war. This seat was not satisfactory and a new catapult system was created for the Frankfort Arsenal T-2 seat propelled by a 37-mm cannon shell. This was testing in the USAAF's P-61 "Jack-in-the-Box," from the reworked gunner's compartment, by the

Ejection seats became an essential element of high-performance aircraft in the postwar period, and they advanced rapidly in capabilities and sophistication. The F-86A seat (a manual system) is shown in a systems familiarization trainer. Testing the designs were essential, beginning with static trials and then progressing to sled tracks as shown by this 1951 F-102 test at Edwards AFB. (*National Museum of the United States Air Force and Air Force Test Center*)

Flight testing of ejection seats required dedicated testbeds. Among these was the TF-80C (later T-33A, 48-357) shown on March 23, 1948, with a camera in a fairing on the nose viewing backward, a cut-down canopy for a clear seat path, and a line to help guide the seat away from the tail. An actual seat test is illustrated by the navy JD-1 (A-26C) modified with a fighter cockpit windscreen and "pit" in the former gunner and turret station. (*National Archives*)

end of 1945. Flying out of Patterson AFB, the first live-subject ejection test in the U.S. was conducted in August 1946. Enlisted personnel rode the shots. The T-4 followed, with testing moved to Muroc. The P-80 was used for ejection seat demonstrations to skeptical aircrew until true emergency separations experiences were shared.[15] The first live jump for the navy, from the JD-1, was in November 1946 in a Martin-Baker seat.

Miscellany

Much analysis, lab tests, and flight trials took place supporting the rapid advance of flight sciences and avionics during the period. Some carried forward from the war while others trod new ground as fundamental research or supporting the warfighter directly. Several can be examined to highlight the scope of this work.

Prone pilot position research continued postwar with a couch and controls developed at Wright-Patt. The feet were for braking only; all other controls were via the two arms and hands. An electric sidestick controller was employed. Head support was also incorporated. After lab work to include centrifuge trials, the system was installed in the nose of B-17G 44-85570 with the ability to fly the bomber from that station. Next, the system was installed in an extended nose of P-80A 44-85044 with basic flight controls. Stanley Aviation of Buffalo, New York, executed this installation. The prone pilot could withstand more g than the safety pilot. However, head support remained problematic, vision to the rear would be dependent upon mirrors, the normal parachute weighed uncomfortably on the back, alternative ejection methods would be required, and vertigo was more likely depending on pilot location forward of the CG. Otherwise, little more was learned than from previous attempts.[16]

The physiological effects of flight at the conditions becoming attainable had to be understood for suitable aircraft design and support system construction. Garments such as G-suits and partial-pressure suits were already in use, and full-pressure suits were anticipated as required eventually. Flight conditions included exposure to windblast and extreme deceleration effects during high-speed ejection, high altitude unpressurized flight, and radiation. Both services had aeromedical labs that sought the data. Windblast and deceleration effects were investigated with centrifuges and the Muroc sled track, plus a 3,500-foot (1,067-m) track erected at Holloman AFB, New Mexico, also by Northrop. Pressure chambers offered additional data, along with animals and instruments sent aloft in rockets and gas balloons.

Instruments carried aboard aircraft such as B-29s collected data on the upper atmosphere. The navy leveraged off its lighter-than-air aircraft experience for this research. New plastics, including very thin polyethylene film, could contain the helium or hydrogen released from pressure cylinders before launch. The ONR launched gas balloons carrying instruments to altitudes unreachable by airplanes. More than 1,500 such ascensions took place. The gas composition of the atmosphere, temperatures, and radiation were all measured in anticipation of manned flight to those altitudes. That day was not long in coming as the program to carry men to these unheard off altitudes via balloons started in the mid-1950s with the navy and USAF again competing.

Efforts to develop true all-weather aircraft prompted the establishment of the All-Weather Flight Test Center at Clinton County AFB, Ohio. Among their projects were penetrating thunderstorms to record their characteristics. This was performed off the Florida coast, from Pinecastle AFB and the All-Weather Flying Center, in Ohio, from 1946–1947. The team flew P-61Cs and an F-15A for these missions where they were struck by lightning and hail as well as subjected to tremendous turbulence and up/downdrafts. The service also funded the Minneapolis Lightning and Transients Research Institute where an F-15 was subjected to artificial lighting using a huge Tesla coil generating a 3-million Volt discharge.

Two Pratt, Reed TG-32 (LNE-1) gliders were employed in mountain wave and jet stream research. Given oxygen systems in addition to scientific instrumentation, they flew to a record-setting 40,000 feet (12,192 m).

The keen interest in safe ditching procedures and potential design practices for these continued following the war. The NACA carried on with the investigation of water impact characteristics, principally in their water tanks at Langley. As with the B-24 ditching test performed during the war, a B-17 was intentionally landing in water to check the best configuration and conditions for the safest practical ditching. Unlike the wartime test that had a crew of two pilots, this was performed under remote control. The NACA also took on crash fire research to inform safer designs. This led to planned crashes of remotely controlled aircraft to study fire origins and determine mitigations.

During the war, the navy had delivered army land planes to distant combat zones aboard aircraft carriers. Instead of the laborious task of offloading the aircraft shore,

Above: The prone pilot orientation had attracted experimentation with flight testing for years given the potential for greater g-tolerance and lower drag of the cockpit installation. This was attempted again with a P-80A (44-85044) given a second pilot station in an extended nose. In this case, the added canopy for the prone pilot in the nose is not of a notably lower profile than the standard installation retained for the safety pilot. (*National Museum of the United States Air Force*)

Left: The navy's first practical full-pressure flying suit is shown under test in a pressure chamber at 70,000 feet "altitude" on February 18, 1953. Commander Harry Peck is wearing the BFGoodrich ensemble intended to give the wearer enough freedom of movement to operate an aircraft. As aircraft were being developed to fly to greater and greater altitudes, with potentially unreliable pressurized cabin systems, such approaches were pursued by all services. (*National Archives*)

The USS *Norton Sound* (AVM-1) is seen launching a gas balloon on March 31, 1949, to carry instruments to the upper atmosphere for cosmic ray research as part of the Operation Skyhook series of ascensions. The balloons initially appeared under-inflated, but the gas expanded in volume as outside pressure fell with altitude increase to the full diameter of about 30 feet (9.1 m). The navy and air force both conducted such work to collect data on the upper atmosphere and gain insights into the possible physiological effects of flight at such altitudes. (*National Archives*)

they were catapulted off the deck—excepting light-planes that could fly off unaided. This required little pilot instruction and no flight training to be accomplished safely. Returning to the ship, however, was impractical. Enabling the catapult entailed a program of developing, for each suitable army type, the bridle attachment and holdback cable fitting, then testing these with a shore "cat." This effort continued for a time postwar, including jet aircraft. No sea trials or operational employment is known to have occurred.

As the weight of combat aircraft increased, the risk of overrunning the runway in emergency scenarios increased. Gross weight initially outpaced the energy-absorbing capacity of wheel braking systems, and there was little willingness to sacrifice weight in fighter-bombers to drag chutes. The services had to develop land barriers to help stop the aircraft. While carrier-based naval aircraft had arresting hooks, other machines, especially with the air force, lacked these during the period. Consequently, barriers to engage the undercarriage without risking the aircraft were the focus, and then means of dissipating the energy in bringing the aircraft to a stop. Teams began experimenting with arresting hooks with less damage potential.

Still anticipating delivery of army and air force aircraft aboard its carriers, the navy continued postwar the program of developing catapult equipment for new types. This F-84B (46-657) is positioned on the NAS Patuxent River H-4 catapult on October 13, 1949, for testing. The holdback cable and shuttle bridle attachments are all on an added belly installation. (*National Archives*)

The services had to develop runway arrestment systems to help stop the heavy jet fighter-bombers when system failures or combat damage precluded normal wheel braking. An F-86A (48-257) engages such an arrestment barrier at a base in Japan during June 1953. This system used netting to capture the aircraft that then dragged very heavy chains across the ground to dissipate the energy and bring the aircraft to a stop. (*National Archives*)

4

Fighters Evolve

The fighter story is characterized by adapting the old and growing the new. The multitude of late-war fighter projects were trimmed only a little despite the meager budgets, and more still added, given their importance. No missions were neglected, though some morphed. All services were eager for jets and their high speed, but the change had to be paced for a variety of reasons. The limitations of first-generation turbine-powered fighters were principally range and take-off distance, leading to tip tanks and JATO. The tip tanks became widely used despite the drag because it did not consume internal volume for the fuel, did not occupy an underwing station, improved airflow about the wingtip for some reduction in drag, and also improved wing stresses for positive-g maneuvers. However, the added tip mass slowed the initial roll rate. These factors and simply building up the fleet were reasons to maintain prop planes for a while longer. Compressibility continued to be a constraint until research determined how to build airplanes suitably and safely. Speed was also limited by straight wings for the first generation of jet fighters before teams were ready to undertake swept wing designs. The early engines were balky, but the second generation offered more flexibility. All the new aircraft emphasized the growing importance of radar and electronic warfare (EW), pressurization, and ejection seats.

Recips Carry On

The USAF was determined to move firmly to jets, continuing the fighter-bomber evolution, and not build further prop fighters. However, the North American P-82 Twin Mustang continued into production and even set a distance record. It was suitable for escorting bombers and reconnaissance (see later). Others types carried on until the jet force grew and matured were P-51s and P-47s. The USN was even more circumspect, needing to ensure immediate power was available for wave-off and bolter during carrier ops. The turbine-powered airplanes emerging from the war could not deliver this. Carrier decks also needed to be adapted to jets at a suitable pace, and the early jets were poor ground attack and night fighters. Consequently, the best of the World War Two developments continued to serve, though some moved down to equip reserve units. The Grumman F7F Tigercat, F8F Bearcat, and Vought F4U Corsairs were the principals continuing to fill carrier air wings in the interim.

Towards the end of the war, the navy was emphasizing multi-role airplanes, as demonstrated by the excellent F4U that was superior air-to-air and delivered well in ground support. The shortest path, then, was to hold the remaining 1,912 F4U-4s built near the war's end, serving the navy and marines. Vought continued to roll out new F4U-4s for a time longer while other production lines were closed. When it became clear the path to carrier-based jets would be lengthy, the Corsair was extended. However, the advanced models being developed at the end of the war, such as with turbosupercharger, bubble canopy, and substituting the R-4360, were not adopted.

The F4U-5 had been conceived in 1944 and approved for production in 1945, but with the war winding down these plans were shelved. Once committed to extending production postwar, time was taken to improve the wartime design evolved under the relentless pressure of combat. Prototypes were flown in 1946, and production of 223 F4U-5s for the USN and marines ran from 1947 through 1948.

The "dash 5" was equipped with an uprated 2,459-hp (1,834-kW) R-2800 engine with water injection and an improved supercharger for operation up to 45,000 feet (13,716 m). This required the already notoriously long nose to be lengthened and widened. The engine was also angled down to lower the deck angle—improving longitudinal stability—and the canopy raised, both recovering some of the degraded pilot's view of the deck during carrier landings.[1] The cockpit was improved and many operability features were added for reduced workload. For the first time, the tailwheel well was fully enclosed by doors with gear retracted. All fabric on aero surfaces was replaced with metal covering, cutting drag. Vought used their Metalite aluminum/balsa sandwich in the horizontal stabilizer to give suitable rigidity for reduced weight. The only nod to all-weather ops was heated cannon and pitot tube, plus windscreen defrost.

While the F4U-5 was the fastest of the family at 470 mph (756 kph), it had many features improving its air-to-ground mission capability. Four 20-mm cannon replaced the six 0.50-cal MGs in the wings. A gyroscopic lead-computing gunsight was included. Added hardpoints or weight capacity increased external stores and fuel, including eight 5-inch High Velocity Aircraft Rockets (HVAR).

Korean combat experience emphasized that jets dominated air-to-air combat while their short endurance and comparatively modest weapons carriage made them less desirable for ground attack. The Corsair was performing superbly in the latter role and production of the type was continued into 1952 with 111 examples optimized for ground attack. The model was initially to be the F4U-6 but soon redesignated AU-1, indicating "attack." These had a further-improved R-2800 at 2,800 hp (2,088 kW) with a simplified supercharger—entirely adequate to the role. A change permitted the cannon to be fired all four together or one on each wing as a pair, helping reduce rounds expenditure. Five fixed weapon pylons per wing mounted rockets or up to 4,600 lb (2,087 kg) of weapons. The discouraging evidence of P-51D vulnerability to ground fire in low-level attack compelled the adoption of 378 lb (173 kg) of armor beneath the engine accessories, fuel tanks, and cockpit. The oil coolers were also moved from the stub wing leading edges to the wing roots, rotated to face to the

With the slow maturation of the new jet fighters and their questionable suitability for ground attack, the navy continued the production and service of several prop fighters from the war. This included the Corsair, with a new model, the F4U-5 introduced. As shown here, this was characterized by the two "cheek" scoops in the cowl lip. This F4U-5 is seen on display at the NAS Patuxent River with rockets and bombs loaded and the four cannon ports evident. (*Naval Aviation Archives*)

side instead of forward, and protected by armor. The added weight did not adversely impact mission performance.

Vought AU-1 Characteristics

span, spread	41 feet (12.5 m)	weight empty	9,835 lb (4,461 kg)
length (2-point att.)	34.5 feet (10.5 m)	gross	18,979 lb (8,609 kg)
height	14.8 feet (4.5 m)	max. take-off	19,398 lb (8,799 kg)
wing area	314 feet² (29 m²)	speed, max. (14,000 feet)	389 mph (626 kph)
fuel, int.+ext.	234+300 gal (886+1,136 l)	cruise	184 mph (296 kph)
service ceiling	28,800 feet (8,778 m)	range, ten rockets	1,277 miles (2,055 km)
climb rate, max.	4,620 fpm (1,408 mpm)	4,600 lb bombs	484 miles (779 km)

A version of the AU-1, the F4U-7 with another iteration of 2800 and supercharger, was built for France in 1952–1953. These ninety-four airplanes were the last prop-driven fighters produced in the U.S.A.; the Corsair had been in production for longer than any other.

The navy had begun a program during the war seeking a purpose-built fighter-bomber. Among the competitors evaluated beyond VJ-Day were a few Boeing XF8B-1s and Curtiss XBTC-2s, but quickly set aside. The Martin BTM was worthy enough to have the wartime production contract sustained at ninety-nine, and even increased by fifty, with deliveries from December 1945 through November 1949. This had a 2,975-hp (2,219-kN) R-4360 and four 20-mm cannon. The wings and fuselage had fifteen hardpoints for approximately 4,500 lb (2,041 kg) of weapons. The flaps split open as dive brakes, supplemented with a fuselage "Swiss-cheese" perforated dive flap. Ailerons were supplemented with spoilers for a suitable roll rate with less adverse yaw.

Upon entering service with the new AM-1 designation, lengthy refinements were necessary and so the aircraft grew heavier and more complex. It was met with mixed reviews from operators given the idiosyncrasies. The Mauler was moved to the reserves in 1950 and retired in 1953.

Martin AM-1 Characteristics

span, spread	50.1 feet (15.3 m)	weight empty	15,100 lb (6,849 kg)
length	41.3 feet (12.6 m)	combat	20,083 lb (9,110 kg)
height	11.8 feet (3.6 m)	max. take-off	25,000 lb (11,340 kg)
wing area	496 feet² (46 m²)	speed, max. (11,600 feet)	367 mph (591 kph)
fuel, int.+ext.	510+450 gal (1,931+1,703 l)	cruise	189 mph (304 kph)
service ceiling	25,630 feet (7,812 m)	range, attack	1,324 miles (2,131 km)
climb rate, initial	3,310 fpm (1,009 mpm)	combat	1,800 miles (2,897 km)

Douglas had brought forth the XBT2D-1 against the navy fighter-bomber requirement. It featured fifteen weapons stations under the wings and fuselage, eschewing a weapons bay, for 6,000 lb (2,722 kg) of ordnance, in addition to a pair of 20-mm cannon. The 2,300-hp (1,715-kN) R-3350 with supercharger turning a 13.5-foot (4.1-m) four-bladed prop. The simplicity of the design was reflected in all internal fuel contained in one fuselage tank and the gear remaining partially exposed upon retraction. Three large dive

Near the end of the war, the navy had worked to obtain a fighter-bomber and several companies offered solutions. One that saw modest postwar production was the Martin AM-1 with impressive payload capacity and performance. However, it struggled with problems and the competing Douglas AD was better liked, so the Mauler saw only brief service. (*Naval Aviation Archives*)

brakes folded out of the unusually faceted aft fuselage sides. A bubble canopy covered the cockpit, which included 208 lb (94 kg) of armor.

Cessation of hostilities saw production trimmed to 277; still, a large order given the numerous programs axed outright. Testing revealed problems that required remedy, yet the aircraft was shown as rugged and reliable. Pilots had to be cautious not to add too much power for a wave-off or the powerful propeller torque would roll them over into the deck or "drink." Regardless, it was less troublesome and better liked than the more expensive Mauler, with greater growth potential. Readily adaptable, production as the AD carried on to numerous models and sub-models. These addressed issues, made improvements, and added external tanks on two wing stations and centerline.

In Korea, additional armor was added to the Skyraider to reduce ground fire losses. That war also ensured continued production, with the -5 model seeing the fuselage widened for line-abreast seating of pilot and assistant plus two additional seats behind. This required a compensating increase in length and vertical tail area, with fuselage dive brakes deleted. From the first flight in August 1951, the usual variety of sub-variants followed. A total of 3,180 Skyraiders were pushed out through 1957, including export, and served for decades with the USN, USMC, and USAF.

Douglas AD-2 Characteristics

span, spread	50 feet (15.3 m)	weight empty	10,546 lb (4,784 kg)
length (ground)	38.2 feet (11.6 m)	loaded	16,268 lb (7,379 kg)
height (ground)	15.6 feet (4.8 m)	maximum	18,263 lb (8,284 kg)
wing area	400 feet² (37 m²)	speed, max. (18,300 feet)	321 mph (517 kph)
fuel, int.+ext.	380+750 gal (1,439+2,839 l)	cruise	198 mph (319 kph)
service ceiling	32,700 feet (9,967 m)	range, normal	915 miles (1,473 km)
climb rate, initial	2,800 fpm (853 mpm)	combat	1,386 miles (2,231 km)

Another of the lingering piston aircraft projects from the war was the all-wing Vought XF5U-1 that depended upon a complex propulsion system and stability augmentation for its beneficial features. When its development dragged on, termination in March 1947 was an easy decision.

Air Force Press

Most of the early jet models faded quickly given the poor performance of the initial crop of turbojet engines. Those that did survive usually did so with the substitution of a more mature engine for production and other improvements.

Out of the wartime programs were a few fighters that either died or persisted to some value in the immediate postwar period. Bell's few YP-59A Airacomets were poor performers and fighters, serving for a brief time only for jet familiarization.

The Lockheed P-80A was ordered in the thousands during the war. With the end of hostilities, the orders were greatly truncated to 525 delivered from December 1945

The Douglas AD-1 became legendary for its ruggedness, adaptability, and performance. Built in the thousands with a remarkable number of variants for numerous roles, the Skyraider was operated by many users for decades. Shown are EW variant AD-2Qs in August 1950. (*National Archives*)

The Chance Vought XF5U-1 "Flying Flapjack" used powered lift from the large propellers blowing over a near-circular, low-aspect-ratio wing to give impressive low-speed flight matched with high-speed owing to low drag. Problems with the teetering prop blades, gearboxes for cross-shafting, and developmental stability augmentation all meant such a long gestation that its benefits were moot beside the emerging jet fighters. The two 1,350-hp P&W R-2000s were almost certainly going to render it underpowered and so re-engining was assured. (*Naval Aviation Archives*)

The Bell P-59 was the American's first jet fighter—or jet aircraft of any kind. It was a disappointment and served only as an introductory type for training. This example, YP-59A 54108 on July 19, 1947, was employed by the Naval Air Test Center for this purpose. (*Tony Landis collection*)

through December 1946. Each was armed with six .50-cal MGs and eight 5-inch underwing rockets or two 1,000-lb (434-kg) bombs. The boundary layer bleed ducts in the engine inlets would soon become standard features on a number of jets. Dive brakes beneath the fuselage allowed steep dives without exceeding critical Mach, but they also served as speedbrakes. The wingtip drop tanks were among the first. The Shooting Star was clearly an introductory model, and so early operations were inundated with problems. Especially engine failures claimed many airplanes and lives. Mishap rates ran to twice that of the piston fighters at sixty-one lost per 100,000 flying hours, and the jet was grounded for several months. These problems were slowly overcome, mostly via pilot training. A "souped-up" P-80A with NACA flush inlets broke a speed record in June 1947 at 624 mph (1,004 kph). Transcontinental flight records were also set.

The type was liked, performing well and reliably enough to see 240 P-80Bs procured through March 1948. Internal fuel capacity was sacrificed to water-alcohol tanks for J33 injection, with JATO provisions added. Also new was a Lockheed ejection seat and upgraded guns. The A-models were retrofitted with P-80B features, and some Bs and As were winterized with canopy defrost and cold-tolerant materials.

Combating the 1,000 lb (454 kg) or so added with the "B" features, the F-80Cs gained more power from an uprated J33. Higher capacity tip tanks were also introduced, projecting from the tip rather than hanging beneath. The wings were strengthened to carry additional rockets for a total of sixteen, or an added pair of pylons for bombs. It also incorporated the first explosive canopy jettison feature for ejection. From October 1948 to June 1950, Lockheed produced 670 of these jets, and many As and Bs were similarly upgraded. The Shooting Star flew until 1958 in U.S. service, though mostly as a fighter pilot trainer. Its range was acceptable with tip tanks, as demonstrated by it performing the first non-stop transcontinental jet flight.

Lockheed F-80C Characteristics

span	38.8 feet (27.4 m)	weight empty	8,240 lb (3,738 kg)
length	34.4 feet (10.5 m)	combat	12,330 lb (5,593 kg)
height	11.3 feet (3.4 m)	maximum	16,856 lb (7,646 kg)
wing area	238 feet² (22 m²)	speed, max. (7,000 feet)	580 mph (933 kph)
fuel, int.+ext.	425+520 gal (1,609+1,968 l)	cruise	439 mph (707 kph)
service ceiling	42,750 feet (13,030 m)	range, normal	825 miles (1,328 km)
climb rate, max.	6,870 fpm (2,094 mpm)	maximum	1,380 miles (2,221 km)

Designed as the smallest airframe capable of being wrapped around the axial-flow TG-180 engine (J35), the Republic XP-84 Thunderjet had an annular inlet and long tailpipe. The goals were 600 mph (966 kph) and 850-mile (1,368 km) radius of action with eight MGs. Its initial flight was in February 1946—the first aircraft powered into flight by the J35—after being transported from New York to Muroc in the new XC-97. The second prototype was "slicked-up" to break a speed record in September 1946 with 611 mph (983 kph).

Matters were initially paced by slow engine progress, and there were a few design problems to iron out. The fifteen pre-production YP-84As had the 3,750-lbf (16.7-kN) Allison version of the engine, could mount wingtip tanks, and had four guns in the nose and one in each wing to shave weight. The USAAF also accepted a 705-mile (1,135-km) combat radius. The initial production example, the P-84B (soon F-84B), was powered by a 4,000-lbf (17.8-kN) J35, possessed an ejection seat, a dive brake beneath the fuselage, substituted upgraded guns, and had retractable mounts for eight underwing rockets. Republic built 228 of these jets, initially becoming operational in December 1947.

The Lockheed Shooting Star matured to the P-80C as a respectable introductory jet fighter for American pilots. They remained a goodly portion of the fighter clan into the Korean Conflict but turned to ground attack (like this F-80C) as swept-wing jets were introduced. (*National Museum of the United States Air Force*)

The F-84s were suffering many maintenance headaches and were grounded for a period awaiting long-term fixes. Readiness was suffering. Among the issues were skin wrinkles at high speed and poor maintenance access. Everyone was learning how to build successful jet aircraft. An $8 million rework effort had to be instigated. This brought the program close to cancelation and Republic struggled financially in bringing the F-84 to fruition. The government had to assist to keep the contractor and the program alive.

About half the production contract was turned to follow-on models owing to the bad reputation of the F-84Bs that were phased out as quickly as practical. The 191 P-84Cs had a revised electrical system and a sequencing bomb release, but also many minor changes to answer maintenance complaints. However, it too had to undergo many modifications to correct deficiencies. The ejection seat was not cleared for use in any of these early models. The number of aircraft on contract was reduced to divert funds to the P-80. Accidents with wing failures saw the jet placarded to 0.8 Mach and 5.5 g. It was learned that, at high speed, airflow about the tip tanks twisted the wing and contributed to structural failures. A fin was added to the tanks to cure the problem and allow flight to the maximum Mach 0.82.

It was hoped that the 154 D-models would be more successful, with heavier-gauge wing and aileron skin plus a winterized fuel system. The ejection seat was finally cleared for use. Yet as these aircraft were being initially delivered in late 1948, the USAF contemplated canceling the program entirely owing to disenchantment with the Thunderjet and uncertainty it could perform the assigned missions. A thorough evaluation of the F-84D was conducted, including a comparison with the F-80, and was judged suitable. This airplane served until 1957, while the earlier models disappeared by 1953.

The 843 F-84Es, delivered through summer 1951 (100 to allies), had a foot of length added to improve cockpit comfort and increase fuel volume, and introduced revised tip tanks. It also had two wing root hardpoints for 1,000-lb (454-kg) bombs, 11.75-inch

Republic's Thunderjet proved a very worthy combat aircraft after a period of maturation. The F-84B was the first production example, though with numerous maintenance complaints. The order was not completed and Republic struggled financially correcting the deficiencies for the following models. (*National Museum of the United States Air Force*)

(30-cm) diameter Tiny Tim rockets, or drop tanks. The engine thrust had been upped to 5,000 lbf (22.2 kN) to compensate for the ever-increasing GW. Provisions for JATO bottles on the aft fuselage, via retractable mounts, permitted take-off weight to be pushed up. The model also included a small Sperry APG-30 radar above the intake that calculated range and closure rate on a target, automatically computing the lead so that the pilot needed only steer the pipper to the target and fire when in range. These aircraft were running about $212,000 apiece and served until 1959.

Republic F-84E Characteristics

span	36.4 feet (11.1 m)	weight empty	10,205 lb (4,629 kg)
length	38.5 feet (11.7 m)	combat	14,850 lb (6,736 kg)
height	12.6 feet (3.8 m)	max. take-off	22,463 lb (10,189 kg)
wing area	260 feet² (24.2 m²)	speed, max. (sea level)	613 mph (987 kph)
fuel, int.+ext.	452+920 gal (1,711+3,483 l)	cruise	481 mph (774 kph)
service ceiling	43,220 feet (13,173 m)	range, combat	1,485 miles (2,390 km)
climb rate, max.	6,061 fpm (1,847 mpm)	maximum	1,950 miles (3,138 km)

The F-84G was developed as the first American fighter-bomber to carry the first tactical nuclear weapons, the Mk 7. Initially delivered to operational units in November 1951, service commenced the following year. This had a single-point refueling system with an AR receptacle in the leading edge of the port wing to accept a tanker boom nozzle. The 4,000 lb (1,814 kg) of external stores demanded the added power of a 5,600-lbf (24.9-kN) J35. Two blow-in doors had to be added in the forward fuselage to provide sufficient airflow for ground operations. The Low Altitude Bombing System (LABS) was also developed in 1952. This permitted a 1,000-foot (305-m) ingress to a target area and pull-up to a half-loop to release the bomb, with the fighter then rolling upright to escape the blast zone. The jet also received an autopilot and instrument landing system. Republic produced 3,025 G-models (only 789 going to the USAF), the final example delivered in July 1953. The last left USAF service into the early 1960s as its final straight-wing jet fighter. The aircraft that was initially troubled ended up being produced in larger numbers than any other U.S. combat jet during this period.

The F-84G was the first American fighter-bomber fitted for AR in production. The receptacle in the port wing was covered by two small doors that, when snapped open, guided the boom nozzle. The USAF demonstrated the Thunderjet's new AR capability in September 1950 with a non-stop flight of two Thunderjet's across the Atlantic. Its ability to end sea shipment of aircraft to distant theaters was realized in 1952 when wings of aircraft deployed across both oceans non-stop. Aerial refueling was becoming routine.

Escort Pursuit

The unusual Twin Mustang had been conceived during the war as a B-29 escort. The contract for 500 was reduced to twenty P-82Bs with the end of hostilities, and two of these were converted as prototype night-fighters. One of the P-82Bs, with extra fuel, flew from Hawaii to New York non-stop in 1946, setting a record. The production contract was renegotiated and included 100 bomber escort P-82Es followed by 150 night fighters. The USAAF also insisted that North America use surplus V-1710 engines, with flame-dampened exhausts, instead of the Packard Merlins that had powered the legendary P-51Ds during the war. This greatly slowed the program since Allison had difficulty producing the engine in a reliable form. Much effort was required to resolve all of the "bugs" and deliveries were stymied for nearly two years as airplanes were stored outside in southern California. The P-82Es finally began filling squadrons in May 1948. The escorts served about two years in SAC before being replaced.

North American F-82E Characteristics

span	51.3 feet (15.6 m)	weight empty	14,914 lb (6,765 kg)
length	39.1 feet (11.9 m)	combat	20,741 lb (9,408 kg)
height	13.8 feet (4.2 m)	max. take-off	24,864 lb (11,278 kg)
wing area	417 feet² (38.7 m²)	speed, max. (21,000 feet)	465 mph (748 kph)
fuel, int.+ext.	576+620 gal (2,180+2,347 l)	cruise	304 mph (489 kph)
service ceiling	29,800 feet (9,083 m)	range, normal	2,504 miles (4,030 km)
climb rate, max.	4,020 fpm (1,225 mpm)	ferry	2,708 miles (4,358 km)

With adversary jet interceptors certain to appear soon, jet fighter escorts had to have superior maneuverability as well as at long range. Bell was put on contract in 1944 for two XP-83s to meet the escort requirement. This appeared very much a growth of their

North American Aviation's Twin Mustang from the war was revitalized and matured. The P-82E (46-268 shown) performed fine supporting the fighter escort mission. However, their service in the role was briefing before jets began to displace such assets. (*National Museum of the United States Air Force*)

The officers standing beside one of the prototypes suggest the enormous size of the Bell XP-83. For the bomber escort mission to be executed by twin-engine jet fighters demanded a prodigious quantity of fuel given the consumption rate of the first generation of turbojet engines. This made the Bell airplane a virtual flying fuel tank with modest performance. It did not proceed to production. (*National Museum of the United States Air Force*)

XP-59A to encompass a great deal more fuel to go the distance with bombers. The first jet flew in February 1945, but it was overweight and the engines did not perform to promised performance. The two 4,000-lbf (17.8-kN) J33s were inadequate to pushing the heavy machine, at 24,090 lb (10,927 kg) gross, to the desired airspeed. Performance was barely above prop-jobs at 522 mph (840 kph) and maneuverability was uninspiring.

The parasite fighter concepts (see page 105) were too exploratory to count on. The XP-85 program moved slowly and remained experimental. The more practical programs pursued transonic performance with wing sweep; they are dealt with in the next chapter.

Navy Day Jets

During the war, the navy had issued three contracts for carrier-based jet fighters. They knew these would be tricycle-gear airplanes to avoid the hot jet exhaust impinging on the wooden decks and the high-velocity ground flow endangering deck crew. As an added measure, they desired the airplanes to "kneel" by retracting the nose gear but leaving small dolly-like wheels to angle the exhaust up. This would also allow tighter arrangements of airplanes below deck. When swept-wing designs began to emerge at the end of the war, the navy hesitated to adopt the feature owing to potentially hazardous low-speed handling on landing approach to the carrier. Consequently, these initial naval jets were cautionary designs with modest order sizes reduced even further postwar.

The single-engine Vought F6U used the 4,100-lbf (18.2-kN) J34 turbojet. This proved inadequate for the aircraft that ended up heavy at a 12,874-lb (5,840-kg) take-off weight, even with the addition of the first American afterburner on a production aircraft. A short production run for jet familiarization platforms was delivered in 1949–1950. Their performance was so poor that they were disposed of by the end of 1950 following a series of mishaps. The aircraft was notable for a pressurized cockpit, automated dive brakes to avoid Mach buffet, the kneeling nose gear, and one of the first airplanes with wingtip tanks. Vought itself apparently developed the "jettison seat" that employed an explosive charge and a drogue parachute. It had leg braces and stirrups to prevent flailing, and the face curtain initiated the jettison sequence. All these aspects would become common for many seats to follow.

Vought F6U-1 Characteristics

span	31.8 feet (10 m)	weight empty	7,320 lb (3,320 kg)
length	37.7 feet (11.5 m)	combat	11,060 lb (5,017 kg)
height	12.9 feet (3.9 m)	max. take-off	12,900 lb (5,851 kg)
wing area	204 feet² (19 m²)	speed, max. (sea level)	596 mph (959 kph)
fuel, int.+ext.	420+280 gal (1,590+1,060 l)	cruise	432 mph (695 kph)
combat ceiling, best	46,300 feet (14,112 m)	range, combat	900 miles (1,448 km)
climb rate, sea level	8,060 fpm (2,457 mpm)	maximum	1,150 miles (1,851 km)

Among the U.S. Navy's first jet fighters was the Vought F6U-1 with the Westinghouse J34 turbojet. Even with one of the first afterburners, the Pirate was such a marginal performer that the thirty aircraft, delivered in 1949 and 1950, were considered unsuitable even for familiarization training. They were set aside unceremoniously. (*National Archives*)

Another wartime project was the North American FJ-1, which was powered by the 3,820-lbf (17-kN) TG-180 fed by a nose intake. Although the aircraft was similar to the swept-wing F-86 that was being developed in late 1945 by NAA for the air force, the navy stuck with the conventional design. Pitch and roll axes were boosted. There was no ejection seat, and the cockpit was neither pressurized nor heated. The aircraft had six .50-cal guns arranged around the nose, and there were no provisions for underwing stores. Dive brakes rose vertically out of the wings, and jettisonable tip tanks were also featured. The kneeling feature was enabled with the attachment of dual wheels close to the top of the nose strut, with the nose gear then retracted with a hand pump. Kneeling had the added benefit of allowing for stowage below deck without a wing fold.

The first of three XFJ-1s flew in fall 1946 and did well enough to justify the start of production. These FJ-1s were powered by the 4,000-lb (17.8-kN) J35. Changes from the prototypes were the extension of the wing root leading edges forward with a fillet and moving of the speedbrakes from the wings to the aft fuselage. The first Fury was delivered in October 1947, and carrier suitability trials followed in March 1948. The nose gear had to be beefed-up but still appeared understrength.

Just thirty FJ-1s were built, with the last delivered in April 1948. Although it set some speed records, such straight-wing designs were not going to be the future of naval fleet defense fighters. Its stall speed was uncomfortably high and the .50-cals antiquated—it became the last new naval aircraft with MGs. In March 1948, the sole Fury squadron took their jets to sea for routine carrier ops, becoming the first to do so. All launches were via catapult with the notable exception of one flying off unaided. However, the time aboard was not a happy one. They suffered several barrier crashes and a hard landing tore away a wing and collapsed the nose gear, with the rest of mishap machines ending off the side. These and other events reduced the squadron to no serviceable airplanes within just two days. The engine required frequent removal for inspections and overhaul, and NAA had designed it to be removed through the top of the fuselage with a crane—a frustrating exercise aboard ship. Overhaul was then every thirty-five hours, up from an initial ten, and mandating the aircraft be towed to the end of the runway when operating from land to save operating time. A shortage of spares was another headache. The kneeling feature proved of little real value. So, while the pilots liked the airplane, it was unpopular with the maintainers. The FJ-1s were passed to reservists after little more than fourteen months.

North American FJ-1 Characteristics

span (tip tanks)	38.2 feet (11.6 m)	weight empty	8,843 lb (4,011 kg)
length	34.4 feet (10.5 m)	combat	12,824 lb (5,817 kg)
height	14.8 feet (4.5 m)	max. take-off	15,600 lb (7,076 kg)
wing area	221 feet² (20.5 m²)	speed, max. (sea level)	587 mph (945 kph)
fuel, int.+ext.	465+340 gal (1,760+1,287 l)	cruise	432 mph (695 kph)
service ceiling	38,000 feet (11,582 m)	range, combat	1,220 miles (1,963 km)
climb rate, max.	5,660 fpm (1,725 mpm)	maximum	1,496 miles (2,408 km)

This August 16, 1950, image shows a trio of portly FJ-1s in reserve service after a very short frontline fleet period. The North American aircraft was one of a trio of initial naval jet fighters sought during the war and flying during a period of rapid change in aviation technology. This left the straight-wing Fury as presenting too limited and displaying immature features. (*National Archives*)

The McDonnell FD twin was designed during the war with two of the 19-inch (48 cm) diameter J30 axial-flow engines. Initially with a meager 1,165-lbf (5.2 kN), these were placed in the wing roots. The engine exhausts were angled slightly outboard to keep the jet efflux clear of the aft fuselage, and the horizontal tails were mounted mid-tail with dihedral owing to the same concern. McDonnell added a butterfly value in each inlet to shut off flow through the engine in engine-out conditions to cut drag. The airplane was otherwise quite conventional to include split flaps and wing top speedbrakes. A 1,000-lbf (4.5-kN) JATO bottle could be attached to assist take-off. A flush belly tank could be fitted, the wing fold was hydraulically powered, and the aircraft lacked an ejection seat. There were four .50-cal nose guns and provisions for eight underwing rockets.

The type had barely begun flight test when the war wrapped up. Progress continued until the XFD-1 Phantom made the navy's first jet carrier cycles in July 1946. These were without catapult assist and included a wave-off at 95 mph (153 kph). McDonnell produced sixty FH-1s (USN redesignation of McDonnell). Beginning in July 1947, the navy equipped their first jet fighter squadron—and the first shipboard jet aircraft unit in the world—and one USMC outfit. These were powered by 1,600-lbf (7.1-kN) production J30s.

McDonnell FH-1 Characteristics

span	40.8 feet (12.4 m)	weight empty	6,683 lb (3,031 kg)
length	38.8 feet (11.8 m)	gross	10,035 lb (4,552 kg)
height	14.2 feet (4.3 m)	maximum	12,035 lb (5,459 kg)
wing area	276 feet² (25.6 m²)	speed, max. (sea level)	479 mph (771 kph)
fuel, int.+ext.	375+295 gal (1,420+1,117 l)	cruise	248 mph (399 kph)
combat ceiling, best	41,100 feet (12,527 m)	range, normal	695 miles (1,119 km)
climb rate, sea level	4,230 fpm (1,289 mpm)	maximum	980 miles (1,577 km)

The U.S. Navy's first jet fighter in fleet service, and first to operate from an aircraft carrier, was the McDonnell FH-1. Only sixty of these twin-jet aircraft were built, operated initially by a navy and a marine squadron in the late 1940s. An exceedingly conventional and modestly powered aircraft, the Phantom was clearly a transitional type and so had a brief service career. Aircraft 111789 of VF-17A is shown aboard *Coral Sea* (CVA-43) on May 18, 1948. (*National Archives*)

The FH-1s were clearly a transitional aircraft as its speed and ceiling only made it competitive against prop aircraft. More powerful types were emerging (especially in the air force) in the fast-evolving fighter technology field. The Phantoms were passed to reservists in 1949 and ended service in 1954. However, the type still held promise as an attack aircraft where the high speed permitted by swept surfaces was not as vital. So, even as McAir was completing tests on the FD-1 and preparing for production, the navy asked them to develop a more capable spin-off powered by the J34 at 3,000 lbf (13.3 kN) and with considerable fuel capacity increase. The inlet butterfly valves were retained. The wing area was enlarged and the section thinned. Speedbrakes lifted vertically out the top of the wings. Weapons were also changed to four 20-mm cannon matched to a small ranging radar in the nose. The weapons were moved to the bottom quarter of the nose to avoid blinding the pilot on firing. An ejection seat of McDonnell design was featured.[2] Although retaining the appearance of the Phantom, the new airframe was slightly larger and entirely redesigned. The main gear retracted outboard instead of inboard with the FH-1. There was a small wheel under the nose that could be extended for kneeling with the nose gear retraction. The F2D-1 Banshee first flew in January 1947 and a production contract soon followed as the few issues were corrected.

Deliveries of the F2H-1s (redesignation, again) began in August 1948 with fifty-six produced through August 1949. Fleet service commenced in March 1949. The F2H-2 was under development while the -1 model was being manufactured. This had an engine uprated to 3,250 lbf (14.6 kN) and extended fuel capacity within a lengthened fuselage plus wingtip tanks. The beefed-up wing structure also accommodated two 500-lb (227-kg) bombs or six rockets under each wing. This model seemed the optimal Banshee and 364 were ultimately manufactured for the navy and marines. The Banshee had very respectable range and endurance for an early jet. To further extend the endurance, fleet operators would shut down an engine while cruising, fly at optimal altitude, and use the Jet Stream. The kneeling feature was rarely used and soon eliminated from production. The type set unofficial speed and distance records.

McDonnell F2H-2 Characteristics

span (tip tanks)	44.9 feet (13.7 m)	weight empty	11,146 lb (5,056 kg)
length	40.2 feet (12.2 m)	design	17,742 lb (8,048 kg)
height	14.5 feet (4.4 m)	maximum	22,312 lb (10,121 kg)
wing area	294 feet² (27.3 m²)	speed, max. (sea level)	582 mph (937 kph)
fuel, int.+ext.	877+400 gal (3,320+1,514 l)	cruise	501 mph (806 kph)
service ceiling	44,800 feet (13,655 m)	range, normal	1,200 miles (1,931 km)
climb rate, average	5,950 fpm (1,814 mpm)	maximum	1,475 miles (2,374 km)

To deliver the new small tactical nuclear rounds, the navy had twenty-seven F2H-2 Banshees modified as F2H-2Bs with a hardpoint under the port inboard wing segment for a 3,000-lb (1,361-kg) store. These first went to sea in August 1952. The Banshee stable grew even further with night fighter, reconnaissance, and all-weather fighter versions, as detailed elsewhere in this volume.

A spin-off of the wartime FH-1, the F2H-2 Banshee, was a good, solid performer and was ordered in much larger numbers. This became the first widely used Navy shipboard jet fighter with several associated sub-variants. This example (123222) is out of NAS Patuxent River and the Naval Air Test Center's Tactical Test Division. (*National Archives*)

Along with the wartime jet fighter contracts, the Navy also sought more mature designs with more mature engines. These remained straight-wing airplanes aimed at fleet defense. It was only well after the war that Grumman felt engines had reached this stage and they would not be burdened with all the delays and uncertainties other firms had struggled with. The company had been working on conceptual designs and so was ready when the navy engaged them on the XF9F-1 night-fighter (see later). In this case, the service pushed a poor choice of engine and the project was aborted. Grumman urged the adoption of the centrifugal-flow 5,750-lbf (25.6-kN) wet Rolls-Royce Nene for a single-engine daylight aircraft. The BuAer chose to proceed with this via a contract change in October 1946 for three prototypes, paying all development and licensing fees to the Nene (not then in British production).

Congress had dictated that no foreign-produced engines would be used in American warplanes. So, licensed production was mandatory and the USN convinced a reluctant P&W to take on the program as the J42. Among other adjustments, this required redesign for American accessories. Despite the challenge, the company had production engines ready in seventeen months. This also helped spur competition between American engine manufacturers. However, the navy had been worried about the ability of P&W to meet schedule and so hedged its bets by specifying that the third aircraft be powered by a 4,600-lbf (20.5-kN) dry J33. This hesitancy was carried into production with initial modest-sized orders for forty-nine Nene-powered F9F-2 and fifty-four Allison-powered F9F-3.

Named the Panther, the Grumman used wing root intakes supplemented with blow-in doors on the spine. There were fuselage split flaps as well as wing flaps, leading-edge "droop snoot" flaps working simultaneously, plus twin speedbrakes beneath the forward fuselage. The wing fold was hydraulic and a Grumman ejection seat was fitted. The jet was armed with four 20-mm cannon in the nose joined by an APG-30 ranging radar. Well into testing, the navy determined that the airplane did not have sufficient endurance to permit deck crews to reconfigure for traps after a squadron launch, and asked that tip tanks be adopted.[3] This was accomplished with little difficulty. Instead of tank jettison, a fuel dump was employed.

Like almost all new jet airplanes of the era, the Panther's maiden flight was delayed awaiting engines. It finally took to the air in November 1947 and the XF9F-3 in August 1948. The design was sound apart from lateral snaking motion and a longitudinal instability at low airspeeds. The snaking was largely due to fuel slosh in belly tanks and corrected with baffles. The instability was cured with some increase in the vertical tail and rudder area. The aft fuselage had to be strengthened after one of the airplanes suffered a separated tail during the initial arrested landing at Pax. Although stall speeds were still a bit high despite the leading-edge flaps, the margins were considered suitable. Grumman had a solid performer and a step ahead of those that preceded it.

The first production aircraft began appearing in November 1948. Slow delivery of the J42s meant that the F9F-3s entered service first. The first Panther unit went to sea in September 1949. More were to follow, plus USMC outfits. All fifty-four F9F-3s were later converted to F9F-2s with a change to the J42, and the F9F-2 production was greatly extended. This made for a total of 564 Panthers by August 1951.

North American F9F-2 Characteristics

span (tip tanks)	38 feet (11.6 m)	weight empty	9,303 lb (4,220 kg)
length	37.8 feet (11.5 m)	combat	14,235 lb (6,457 kg)
height	11.3 feet (3.5 m)	max. take-off	19,494 lb (8,842 kg)
wing area	250 feet² (23.2 m²)	speed, max. (sea level)	575 mph (925 kph)
fuel, int.+ext.	683+240 gal (2,585+909 l)	cruise	487 mph (784 kph)
service ceiling	44,600 feet (13,594 m)	range, combat	1,353 miles (2,177 km)
climb rate, initial	6,000 fpm (1,829 mpm)		

During the production run, in January 1950, Grumman was given a high-priority project to introduce underwing weapon stations to the production line as F9F-2Bs. These were soon retrofitted to earlier aircraft such that the suffix eventually disappeared. Two inboard stations could accommodate 1,000-lb (454-kg) weapons or 150-gal (568-l) drop tanks, while six outboard stations could take 250-lb (113-kg) bombs or rockets, for a total capacity of 3,000 lb (1,361 kg).

The next models also had two engine choices initially. The F9F-4 featured an uprated J33 at 6,950 lbf (30.9 kN) wet while the F9F-5 had a 7,000-lbf (31.1-kN) J48 with water injection. This P&W engine was a licensed production of the Rolls-Royce Tay, and the Panther was its first application. Prototypes, created from modified F9F-2s, flew between December 1949 and July 1950. Production deliveries commenced in November

An F9F-2 (123434) is raised to the flight deck of the USS *Philippine Sea* (CV-47) on September 18, 1950. The first Grumman jet was more successful than its naval brethren of the period in that it was bought in greater quantity and equipped more squadrons. Initially just a fleet defense fighter, it was soon equipped with underwing pylons for attack missions. (*National Archives*)

1950 for both models. Given that the J33 proved less reliable and delivered slightly less thrust, most of the F9F-4s were completed with the P&W J48 or modified with that engine. Initial deliveries were slow, and then there was an early spate of fatal accidents owning to burn-through of burner cans that had to be corrected. The availability of J33s to sustain Korean Conflict production deliveries saved the day and allowed the navy to build up its jet fighter force at a goodly pace, with Grummans leading in numbers.

These new jets required a lengthened fuselage for greater fuel volume and the vertical tail height was extended. A new wing was thinner in a bid for a higher critical Mach number. This was found to have unacceptable torsional deformation at high-g that had to be corrected. These aircraft had the same underwing store arrangement as the F9F-2s except that the outboard stations could carry up to 500 lb (227 kg) of weapons for a total of 3,465 lb (1,572 kg). During the production run, a fence was installed at the wing leading edge, just outboard of the inlets, to correct flow separation. This and other wing aerodynamic cleanup gained a 12 mph (19 kph) decrease in landing speed that the fleet judged to be urgent. The fences were also added to earlier models.

Grumman pushed out 109 F9F-4s and 616 F9F-5s with deliveries through January 1953. Some of these advanced models flew combat sorties over Korea.

North American F9F-5 Characteristics

span	38 feet (11.6 m)	weight empty	10,147 lb (4,603 kg)
length	38.9 feet (11.9 m)	combat	15,359 lb (6,967 kg)
height	12.3 feet (3.7 m)	max. take-off	21,245 lb (9,637 kg)
wing area	250 feet² (23.2 m²)	speed, max. (sea level)	604 mph (972 kph)
fuel, int.+ext.	1,003 gal (3,797 l)	cruise	481 mph (774 kph)
service ceiling	42,800 feet (13,045 m)	range, combat	1,300 miles (2,092 km)
climb rate, initial	6,000 fpm (1,829 mpm)		

Night and All-Weather

Night fighters continued to be specialized models during this period and became all-weather machines. Improved onboard radar and a better understanding of weather effects on aircraft permitted the penetration of inclement weather, in addition to darkness, to intercept enemy formations and pursue fighters. The radar was a substantial weight and electrical burden on the aircraft, and usually with the need for a second crewman to operate the equipment optimally. The hoped-for jet all-weather fighters were long in appearing and so the prop machines continued for a time.

There were a series of high-level goals at the end of the war that drove the fighter development objectives for the USAAF, and then USAF. In September 1945, the air force set out to acquire, with an RFP, penetration fighters for long-range escort of bombers (yielding the McDonnell XF-88 and Lockheed XF-90, Chapter 5), interceptors (Republic XF-91 and Convair XF-92, Chapter 6), and the all-weather

A F9F-5 (125644) of VF-111 is seen over Korea on May 15, 1953. A more powerful engine and additional fuel capacity gave continued life to the Panther and its Grumman production line during the war. The tail hook and tail skid are extended while the wing fence just outboard of the inlet is visible. (*National Archives*)

fighter (Curtiss-Wright XF-87 and Northrop XF-89, see later). As will be seen, only the F-89 was carried to production owing partially to the immaturity of supporting technology and also to the rapid advance of those technologies. With the emergence of the Tu-4 in 1947, the USAF formed a board to examine potential responding defensive fighters. These had to be aircraft devoted to bomber intercept, with rapid climb and high speed to catch the enemy, possibly finding the bomber at night via radar, and carrying armament offering near certainty of destroying the prey. Meeting at Muroc beginning in October 1947, they chose to pursue a trio of interceptors. These became the F-89A, Lockheed F-94A, and North American F-86D, though largely as stopgaps. The board continued to meet through May 1949 to assess and recommend options. They then proposed pursuing supersonic interceptors to be fielded by 1954—the 1954 Interceptor. This led to the Convair F-102 (see pages 184–186).

The wartime Northrop P-61 Black Widow (soon F-81) continued to be counted on to 1950 when age and lack of spares spelled its end. This aircraft had no airframe, anti-ice, or de-ice features.

The P-82 was adapted to the all-weather fighter role with 150 night fighters given a large radar pod hung off the wing center segment and the radar operator in the right cockpit. Manufactured from February 1948 to March 1949 at $215,154 each, ninety-one were fitted with the new AN/APG-28 radar as P-82Fs while forty-five P-82Gs got surplus SCR-720C units from P-61 production. It was not an ideal adaptation, but the aircraft were intended as a stopgap awaiting a jet solution. These were the last prop-driven plus "tail-dragging" fighter bought by the USAF.

The P-82's armament was still six .50 cals, but it also carried drop tanks and bombs or rockets, for 4,000 lb (1,814 kg) of stores. The airplanes were modernized to an extent with jettisonable canopies, boosted controls, climate-controlled cockpits, autopilot, and accommodations for G-suits. Importantly for the all-weather mission,

From World War Two night fighters, the USAF carried on with the Northrop Black Widow. This image of an F-61C (43-8333) shows the complex layout with a pilot, radar operator, and gunner. It could not be considered "all-weather," and the new USAF was eager to move to jet-powered aircraft for the mission. This example lacks a top turret because it was being used as a night fighter trainer for F-82 crews, but shows the fairing on the cowling bottoms for the turbosupercharger common with this model of which just forty-one were completed. (*National Archives*)

internally heated surfaces gave an anti-ice capability. The ability to detect weather at night with the radar meant that it could be avoided if necessary. Fourteen fitted with winterization gear became P-82Hs for service in Alaska.

North American F-82F Characteristics

span	51.6 feet (15.7 m)	weight empty	16,309 lb (7,398 kg)
length	42.2 feet (12.9 m)	combat	21,116 lb (9,578 kg)
height	13.8 feet (4.2 m)	max. take-off	26,208 lb (11,888 kg)
wing area	417 feet² (38.7 m²)	speed, max. (21,000 feet)	460 mph (740 kph)
fuel, int.+ext.	576+620 gal (2,180+2,347 l)	cruise	288 mph (463 kph)
service ceiling	38,700 feet (11,796 m)	range, combat	2,200 miles (3,541 km)
climb rate, max.	3,690 fpm (1,125 mpm)	ferry	2,400 miles (3,862 km)

In pursuing a jet night and inclement weather interceptor, the USAF needed a system that permitted the engagement of an unseen target. In June 1948, the service chose to adopt elements of the General Electric APG-3 tail gun-laying radar from the B-36, a Hughes APG-33 X-band fire control radar, and Sperry A-1C gunsight. Integration was via Hughes as the E-1 fire control system (FCS). The radar antenna lay behind a dielectric dome developed by Lockheed ("Lock-foam") that had to remain unpainted.

Though already considered obsolete, this F-82G (46-376) awaits a mission in Korea, dressed for all-weather night fighting. Along with the P-82F and P-82H, these Twin Mustangs were fitted with the prominent radar pod shown and the operator in the starboard cockpit. Under-wing tanks, rockets (rails carried on this machine), and bombs allowed the aircraft to support other missions. (*National Museum of the United States Air Force*)

This FCS would continue to evolve over the years, seeking greater capability in deriving intercept engagement solutions and especially improved hardware reliability. The initial system would require a dedicated crewmember to operate, and so a two-seat aircraft would still be required.

The USAAF issued an August 1945 requirement for the All-Weather (Night) Interceptor. As defined in November, it called for 525 mph (845 kph) at 35,000 feet (10.668 m), a 550-mph (885-kph) top speed at sea level—600 mph/966 kph was frequently mentioned as desired—plus 600-miles (966-km) combat radius at 10,000 feet (3,048 m) and 1,000 miles (1,609 km) at best-range altitude. Climb to 35,000 feet was to be achieved in twelve minutes. The aircraft was to be capable of air-to-ground ordnance delivery via a bomb bay as well as intercept. This program soon saw Curtiss-Wright and Northrop placed on contract. In the meantime, the North American F-93 (see page 180) appeared suitable for the night-fighter role as well and the air forces ordered a single example equipped for the mission. However, the collapse of the Penetration Fighter program (see page 181) also affected this effort and the NAA airplane was never completed.

The short path to the capability appeared to be repurposing the wartime Curtiss-Wright XA-43 design. A contract was issued in December 1945 for this XP-87. The four 3,000-lbf (13.3-kN) J34s were in twin pods integral with the wings. The nacelles had been designed by NACA for drag equivalent to a single-engine enclosure. Side-by-side seating of the two crewmen, in Curtiss-designed ejection seats, helped to increase the size of the machine. It possessed dive brakes but no nose wheel steering. Four 20-mm cannon and twin .50-cal tail guns in a remote-controlled nose turret were envisioned, though where that placed the radar is unclear—a radar for the night and all-weather aircraft being notably absent from accounts of the project. A Martin FCS was to drive the turret manually or via an APG-3 gun-laying radar. Given night operation and low probability of rear intercept, aft armament and considerable armor were eventually eliminated. Large tip tanks helped meet the ambitious range requirements.

Only one prototype XP-87 was completed, without radar or armament, as costs had escalated. After taxi tests in Columbus, Ohio, the aircraft was trucked to Muroc, though not without two highway accidents and aircraft damage along the way. With the initial flight in March 1948, several problems were soon revealed. These included buffeting, sometimes heavy, at both low speed during maneuvering and high speed with transonic effects on the tail. A bullet fairing was added at the interface of the vertical and horizontal tails—a solution attempted by several teams of the period—although the buffet persisted. Approach airspeed was uncomfortably high. The J34s were anemic, at 250-lbf (1.1-kN) less thrust each than promised, while the airframe was also overweight by thousands of pounds. Performance suffered, falling short of the desired 600 mph. Although the airplane met or exceeded most other specifications, some were by then considered marginal or merely inadequate. At maximum speeds, the aircraft had run out of trim; there were marked trim changes with flap extension, and buffeting remained unacceptable.

It was felt that substitution of two J33s and increasing wing area by 23 percent would cure many F-87 ills of what was then the F-87. The second prototype was modified to take the GE engines. An order for fifty-eight F-87A fighters and thirty photorecce models was placed in March 1948. Clearly, the development would be extended even further while the all-weather missions continued to be poorly served. An evaluation against the F-89 and F3D (see later) in October 1948 found the XF-87 inferior in many respects. Predicted performance with the alterations was still felt to leave the Blackhawk behind the F-89. Given very tight budgets, it was decided in October 1948 to drop the F-87 and focus the remaining funds on the Northrop design. This cancelation was the death knell for Curtiss-Wright as well, which was unable to compete adequately in the postwar period.

Curtiss-Wright XF-87 Characteristics

span	60 feet (18.3 m)	weight empty	27,935 lb (12,671 kg)
length	62.8 feet (19.2 m)	gross	39,874 lb (18,087 kg)
height	20.4 feet (6.2 m)	maximum	49,900 (22,634 kg)
wing area	600 feet² (56 m²)	speed, max. (8,500 feet)	572 mph (921 kph)
fuel, int.+ext.	1,380+1,200 gal (5,224+4,543 l)	range, tip tanks	1,891 miles (3,043 km)
service ceiling	45,000 feet (13,716 m)	ferry	2,175 miles (3,500 km)
climb rate, max.	5,500 fpm (1,676 mpm)		

The competition was Northrop, who received a contract in June 1946 for two XP-89s based on a December 1945 proposal. This was a straight-wing, two engines design with two tandem Northrop ejection seats. The wing was of a high aspect ratio for a good high-altitude cruise. The straight wing and good slow-speed flight stability were

Among the last airplanes built by Curtiss-Wright was the F-87 all-weather night fighter. The four-engined jet, built on World War Two technology, took few risks and was not liked. It was dropped in favor of the F-89, and Curtiss subsequently shut its doors. (*San Diego Air & Space Museum*)

considered essential for safe approach and landing in weather. Placement of the J35s at the base of the fuselage allowed for short intakes and exhausts for lower drag and weight. It also avoided disturbing the optimal wing root profile with embedded inlets as was then the common layout. Reheat was added with the second prototype. Exhaust efflux on the fuselage aft of the engines, with heating and acoustic stress concerns, was reduced by designing as much physical separation as practical. The horizontal tail was placed mid-span on the vertical to be well clear and avoid blanking by flow off the wings at high AoA. However, the leading edge of the horizontal was placed ahead of the vertical's leading edge to circumvent adverse aerodynamic influences degrading control surface effectiveness. Ailerons could split open as airbrakes or "decelerons." These drooped with the double-slotted Fowler flaps. All surfaces were hydraulically powered, with artificial feel, and the rudder featured a yaw damper. Wingtip tanks were standard. With thin wings, the desired location of the cannon was in the nose. Yet the radar placement at the apex of the nose ensured the largest unobstructed scan angles. Nose guns in proximity to the vacuum-tube avionics of the period were not conducive to long periods of effective operation.

The initial flight of the first XF-89 was in August 1948, six months behind schedule. The airplane was clearly underpowered and did not seem destined to meet the desired performance given then state-of-the-art. Since development appeared to be protracted, the USAF had to seek alternatives that might be fielded in a shorter time span. It authorized the development of F-80 and F-86 derivatives as all-weather fighters, designated F-94 and F-86D, respectively. It also funded Republic to modify one of the XF-91 prototypes from the Penetration Fighter competition with a chin inlet below a radome. Though flown, this last option drew no appeal. Lockheed offered a revised XP-90 while DAC pointed to the F3D they were developing for navy carrier-based

The difficult and lengthy path to a night/all-weather fighter included many offerings by the nation's airframers. Republic modified the first of two XF-91s (46-680) with a nose radome, squeezing the annular inlet into a chin scoop. The air force was as unmoved by this potential as by the others. (*Air Force Test Center via Tony Landis*)

night fighting. The USAF evaluated the XF3D-1, with a suggestion to add afterburning, but was unmoved. This was an ironic move since the design had been offered in the USAF competition but rejected. However, this ultimately went nowhere.

Regardless of all the options, the air force decided in September 1948 to proceed with the F-89, with production orders placed in October while the flight test was still in early stages. All these moves indicated what was perceived as a dire need demanding the earliest fielding as possible of some capability, plus acknowledged limitations of then-present technology making multiple approaches advisable. The service was already looking ahead to the next interceptor integrating many technologies then maturing. Hence, the three all-weather interceptor projects were considered "gap-fillers." Once the Korean Conflict began and ADC lost squadrons to the Far East Air Force, more interceptors had to be procured for national defense. So, even marginal equipment was bought to bolster wings as quickly as practical.

The initial examples of the F-89 were fitted with six 20-mm cannon, the notional turrets dropped, and wing stations for a 1,600-lb (726-kg) store per wing. Inlet boundary layer bypass and auxiliary blow-in doors were added. Deliveries began in the summer of 1951. With multiple design changes in early production, only eleven F-89As and thirty-seven Bs were accepted. The C-model introduced the fixes to the production line. Equipment changes added inlet deicing from an alcohol tank and retractable inlet screens for FOD. Uprated engines with AB were installed. The long nose was lengthened further. This enclosed added equipment to support all-weather capabilities. Included were a Lear L-5 autopilot, marker beacon receiver for Instrument Landing System, and suitable cockpit lighting. The Sperry Zero Reader flight computer indicator (referencing a flight plan) combined attitude, altitude, direction, and radio steering plus glide slope guidance into a single unit. Many of these systems were new and developed with military funding.

The F-89 testing and early service revealed grave deficiencies. A fatal accident was chalked up to tail flutter, induced by engine exhaust pattern interaction with the tail structure for what was termed "shimmy." Balance weights were added to the tail surfaces and the exhausts were redirected. Engine failures brought a grounding during upgrades. Worse was six accidents, some fatal, from wing failures. One of these occurred at an airshow, with photographs of the mishap circulated. Although aggressive maneuvering was partially to blame, the wings were twisting under maneuver loads and attach fittings cracking. While more restrictive operating limits were imposed, the fleet was soon grounded for more than a year and production suspended. A major rework and test period was imposed. Wing attach fittings were redesigned, and fins were added to the tip tanks for more favorable wing loads. Nearly 200 airplanes were subjected to the major structural modifications at the Hawthorne, California, factory and nearby Ontario during 1952. This was a crisis for Northrop who, with the cancelation of their flying wing bombers, had the F-89 as their sole production program.

The 164 F-89Cs cost nearly $800,000 each, but served only briefly. They were followed by F-89Ds that became the standard Scorpion with 682 delivered. This configuration was first flown in 1951 and deliveries began in June 1952. However, with fleet groundings and production suspension, manufacturing did not resume a good clip until November 1953 and actual combat service in January 1954.

For the F-89D, initially delivered in June 1952, the nose was enlarged for the APG-40 radar, the cannon removed, and the Hughes E-6 FCS adopted. Also featured were further upgraded engines, additional internal and external fuel, plus additional external wing stations for more rockets. Particularly introduced were large wingtip pods with fuel at the aft end and fifty-two air-to-air rockets at the front. The Folding-Fin Aircraft Rockets (FFAR) were the NAA 2.75-inch Mighty Mouse projectile developed with the USN. It was 4 feet (1.2 m) long, weighed 18.5 lb (8.4 kg), had a 7.6-lb (3.4-kg) warhead with a variety of fuses, and flew at 2,500 fps (762 mps) at motor burnout for a range of 13,500 feet (4,115 m). This meant a greater engagement range than the 20-mm cannon, and fired from beyond the range of a bomber's defensive guns, with more potential damage from a hit. Given that the interceptor pilot might not actually see the little-maneuvering bomber, a spread of rockets fired from 1,500 feet (457 m) approximately abeam would likely ensure that the target would be brought down. Fired in large numbers, the rockets fanned out in overlapping patterns to saturate an area the size of a football field.

With deliveries of F-89s so late, it was already being eclipsed by the more capable F-94 and F-86D. Production did not approach that of the F-86D, ADC's preferred interceptor, and fielding was limited to just a few wings. While the Scorpion's structural defects were cured, a reputation was earned that was hard to live down. Engine improvements never kept up with the weight growth. Despite the two engines, climb and acceleration was uninspiring. It had also developed into a heavy aircraft lacking superior maneuverability or speed, not suitable for mixing it up with other fighters. The low-set engine inlets promoted FOD damage without the inlet screens, and the engines themselves had a discouragingly high number of breakdowns. The jet also had the highest accident rate of its contemporaries at 383 per 100,000 flight hours.[4]

All this left the Scorpion third in this field of rocket-firing all-weather bomber interceptors. Despite the criticisms and straight wing, it was still a worthy weapon system, with respectable range. The airplane was advertised as the most heavily armed jet fighter in the world, possessing an awesome "Sunday Punch" with all its rockets. It was especially appreciated at the edges of the air defense network in Alaska and Greenland. It was suitable for intercepting and engaging bombers—though the coming jet bombers might present a challenge. Its *raison d'etre*, with rockets in heavy and draggy pods to shoot down bombers, lasted but a short time. Advanced models with more rockets and more powerful engines did not proceed beyond the initial design.

Northrop F-89D Characteristics

span	59.7 feet (18.2 m)	weight empty	25,194 lb (11,478 kg)
length	53.8 feet (16.4 m)	gross (tip fuel)	42,214 lb (19,148 kg)
height	17.5 feet (5.3 m)	max. take-off	46,614 lb (21,144 kg)
wing area	606 feet² (56 m²)	speed, max. (sea level)	630 mph (296 kph)
fuel, int.+ext.	2,434+400 gal (9,214+1,514 l)	cruise	467 mph (752 kph)
service ceiling	49,200 feet (14,996 m)	range, combat	764 miles (1,230 km)
climb rate, initial	8,360 fpm (2,548 mpm)	ferry	1,367 miles (2,200 km)

At the behest of the air force, Lockheed began in March 1948 to rework the F-80 into an all-weather fighter targeting production by the end of 1949. Lockheed had twice before suggested the potential for such a design. This would use the two-seat T-33 trainer airframe (see page 402), a spin-off of the P-80C, to accommodate an operator for the APG-33 radar. An extended nose would encompass the radar, a Hughes E-1 FCS, and four .50-cal guns. Two 1,000-lb (454-kg) bombs could be delivered in night strikes. Tail surfaces were enlarged and ejection seats were installed. An afterburning J33 was created as a cooperative "crash" effort with Allison, bringing 4,400 lbf (19.6 kN) dry and 6,000 lbf (26.7 kN) wet, with an anti-ice system added. Accommodating this powerplant required lengthening the fuselage and enlarging the inlets. The AB initially proved problematic, with flameouts and reluctant relights. Eventually, Lockheed, Allison, and Solar Aircraft jointly devised flame-holders that solved the problem and these became an industry standard.

The cancelation of the F-87 helped fund F-94 development. With a prototype, derived from a T-33A, initially flying in April 1949, the jet went promptly into production. The first F-94A was accepted in December and the type was operational by May 1950. Lockheed manufactured 109 within a year as America's first jet all-weather interceptor and first production aircraft with AB. They replaced the F-82 and remain alone in the role through 1953. The F-94B had larger tip tanks on the

Northrop's F-89 was slow-maturing as an all-weather interceptor, suffering a litany of in-service crashes, groundings, and fixes that marred its reputation. When finally fielded in significant numbers, with the F-89D shown the principal model, the type was being eclipsed by swept-wing fighters and jet bombers were sure to appear soon to render the Scorpion too slow. The characteristic long nose with tip radome, wingtip rocket pods, and large straight wing are evident in this formation. (*National Archives*)

wing centerline, a revised hydraulic system, windscreen deicing and defog, and the Sperry Zero Reader. First flying in September 1950, the production of 357 ran from January 1951 to January 1953. They began reaching the fleet in April 1951. However, the F-94s suffered problems with engines and electronics, taking a long time to achieve tolerable maturity. The cockpit was also too narrow for consistently safe ejections. The straight-wing airplane was clearly the stopgap intended.

Lockheed F-94B Characteristics

span (tip tanks)	38.9 feet (11.9 m)	weight empty	10,064 lb (4,565 kg)
length	40.1 feet (40.1 m)	loaded	13,474 lb (6,112 kg)
height	12.7 feet (3.9 m)	max. take-off	16,844 lb (7,640 kg)
wing area	235 feet² (21.8 m²)	speed, max. (sea level)	588 mph (946 kph)
fuel, int.+ext.	318+465 gal (1,204+1,760 l)	cruise	452 mph (727 kph)
service ceiling	47,260 feet (14,405 m)	range, normal	664 miles (1,069 km)
climb rate, initial	6,850 fpm (2,088 mpm)	maximum	905 miles (1,457 km)

An F-94A (49-2520) sits alert at a very cold Ladd AFB, Alaska, in about April 1952, waiting to be launched in response to radar detection of intruders—with Soviet bombers the principal threat. Derived from the T-33A trainer and given all-weather interceptor gear, the Lockheed jet was the first successful such system to be fielded. Although quickly dated with inadequate armament, the Starfire served as a worthy gap filler. (*National Archives*)

North American had offered in March 1949 to rework the swept-wing F-86A into an all-weather interceptor, and the air force bit. The NAA design placed an APG-36 radar antenna in the nose to necessitate a chin inlet. This radar had a 30-mile (48-km) target acquisition range. The Hughes E4 FCS was incorporated to ease radar intercept tasks that, along with the autopilot and electronic engine controls, made a second crewman unnecessary. After being vectored by ground control, the fire control system would guide the pilot to a lead-collision intercept at right angles to the target vice the pursuit-curve intercept from the rear. After the pilot centered the target on the radar scope, the FCS flew the aircraft to an optimal solution and automatically fired weapons. This "single man interceptor" concept, the first in the world, permitted the pilot alone to handle the tasks even at night. It was, however, reliant on much more electronic content than previously common. The fuselage was extended and fattened to take the J47 with AB for a marked improvement in performance. General Electric had worked with NAA to develop a single-lever control for the engine employing an electronic fuel selector to greatly ease the pilot's engine operation tasks while also providing rapid and efficient engine response. The powerplant also had a clamshell variable-area exhaust nozzle for optimal exit area. The AB demanded additional fuel volume and so the self-sealing tank feature was deleted. Bleed air deicing was beneficial to the mission. Full hydraulic controls were employed and stabs substituted. A redesigned NAA ejection seat possessed automatic features.

Adopting the 2.75-inch Mighty Mouse armament from the F-89, a retractable tray of twenty-four projectiles was nestled in the belly. Rapidly extended, all twenty-four rockets could be salvoed in a fraction of a second and the tray retracted, all within a few seconds, or fired in groups. When first launched from the F-86D in February 1951, the FFAR became the first such weapon fired for intercept by the Americans.

The company was given a June 1950 contract for two YF-86Ds (converted F-86As) and 153 F-86Ds. The aircraft was soon designated F-95A, but realizing that lawmakers were more likely to fund an upgrade than a new airplane, the service reverted to the F-86D. The "upgrade" retained only 25 percent of the original Sabre in the wings and undercarriage, yet with a unit cost averaging $343,839 versus $178,408 for an F-86A.[5] The first flight was in December 1949 and initial production aircraft were accepted in March 1951. Although 2,500 lb (1,134 kg) heavier than the F-86A, the Sabre Dog's performance was exemplary with the J47. Initially at 5,435 lbf (24.2 kN) dry and 7,500 lbf (33.4 kN) augmented, it was improved to 5,550 lbf (24.7 kN) and 7,660 lbf (34.1 kN), respectively. The USAF demonstrated the performance by twice breaking world speed records, the second time in July 1953 by clocking 716 mph (1,152 kph) at near sea level.

Although deliveries of near full-up jets began in July 1952, many capabilities reliant upon electronics were faulty or remained to be installed. After a time, more than 320 newly manufactured aircraft were sitting at Inglewood awaiting radar, fire control, or engine control systems. Even when pressed into service in April 1953, the systems were still suffering "teething" problems. Many modifications were necessary throughout the course of production and service via Block upgrades. Air Defense Command just could not wait.

Initially, a lower-power radar and the E3 fire control system (not supporting lead-collision intercept) were installed until the final systems were ready. Among airframe improvements was a powered rudder design that eliminated trim tabs. There were initially stability issues, with the potential for pilot-induced oscillation, until a suitable empennage design was devised through multiple tests. Changes included single-point refueling, drop tanks, fuel filter deicing system, and Sperry Zero Reader auto-coupled approaches to landing. A drag chute helped keep landing distance within reasonable limits, especially on wet or ice surfaces, given the thin wing and high approach speeds.

Northrop F-86D-1 Characteristics

span	37.1 feet (11.3 m)	weight empty	13,518 lb (6,132 kg)
length	40.3 feet (12.3 m)	combat	16,068 lb (7,288 kg)
height	15 feet (4.6 m)	cross	18,183 lb (8,248 kg)
wing area	288 feet² (26.8 m²)	maximum	19,975 lb (9,061 kg)
fuel, int.+ext.	608+240 gal (2,302+908 l)	speed, max. (sea level)	692 mph (1,114 kph)
service ceiling	49,750 feet (15,164 m)	max. (40,000 feet)	612 mph (985 kph)
climb rate, initial	12,150 fpm (3,703 mpm)	cruise	550 mph (885 kph)
		range, combat	554 miles (892 km)
		ferry	769 miles (1,238 km)

One of the earliest North American Aviation F-86Ds (50-574) displays the retractable rocket tray beneath the forward fuselage and 2.75-inch projectiles leaving their tubes. The Sabre Dog was a substantial growth of the F-86 in many ways, but most noticeably with the nose altered for an intercept radar. It was an early and very successful all-weather interceptor, with hundreds operated by the USAF and foreign air arms. (*National Museum of the United States Air Force*)

The extensive avionics content of the F-86D reflected a general trend. While enhancing mission effectiveness, the vacuum tube technology of the period has not terribly reliable. The mission was very demanding of the pilots who required more training than was common. Yet the F-86D was successful and popular, standing well above all other all-weather interceptor entrants. The "gap-filler" became the standard for many years. Eventually, hundreds were built through 1955 for the USAF, outfitting two-thirds of ADC units, and more still for allies. Various models of the Sabre were exported and built under license to a total of twenty-five countries—the most numerous American type in foreign operator hands of the period.

The navy carried on with F7F night fighters after the war and even had a brief affair with a dozen P-61Bs as F2T-1Ns for radar operator training. Vought built 315 new Corsair night fighters, more than the baseline aircraft. This began in 1948 with 214 F4U-5Ns. These had the AN/APS-19 air intercept radar embedded in the starboard wing's leading edge and scope in the middle of the instrument panel. This radar had been introduced near the end of the war and permitted acquisition/intercept at 20 miles (32 km) and gunfire at 1,500 yards (1,372 m). Also featured were an autopilot, radar altimeter, flash suppression of the cannon, and flame masking of the exhaust. The experience of operating in winter in the Sea of Japan, with snow on carrier decks and icing aloft, compelled some accommodation for safe and effective operations. Vought responded to an urgent USN request in September 1950 and began delivering seventy-two winterized F4U-5NLs within two months, twenty-nine more from converted F4U-5s. These had leading-edge deicing boots on the flying surface, and glycol for propeller blades and windscreen deicing.

The Korean Conflict accelerated the U.S. Navy's progress towards an all-weather fighter. The F4U-5N, with its podded APS-19 radar integral with the starboard wing, was produced in larger numbers than the baseline design without the radar. A "winterized" model, the F4U-5NL with leading-edge de-icing boots were manufactured in short order to answer an urgent wartime need. The boot on the vertical stabilizer is evident in this image of 124672. (*San Diego Air & Space Museum*)

Near the end of the war, the USN anticipated Japan operating aircraft employing Germany's jet engines. This could mean high and fast bombers engaging ships from altitudes that were unattainable by the piston fighters, especially at night. In August 1945, the service defined a requirement for a jet night fighter that could reach 40,000 feet (12,192 m), achieve 500 mph (805 kph), and detect enemy aircraft at 125 miles (201 km). Douglas won the bid with an April 1946 contract for three XF3D-1s.

The Skyknight had a crew of two seated line abreast in the pressurized cockpit. Ejection seats were considered too heavy, and so bail-out was via a chute out the bottom of the aircraft. The jet carried the 1,000-lb (454-kg) Westinghouse APQ-35 with a large radar antenna in the nose that essentially sized the airplane. This was the first track-while-scan unit, permitting intercept while continuing to scan for additional targets. The large airplane was powered by two 3,000-lbf (13.4-kN) J34s in fuselage nacelles in the lower hemisphere, allowing ready access by the ground crew. The layout was otherwise conventional save for two speedbrakes in the aft fuselage. There was no nose wheel steering and a retractable tailwheel was included in the event of over-rotation. Armament was four 20-mm cannon, and there were hardpoints beneath the wings for two tanks or 2,000-lb (907-kg) bombs. Also integrated was the power generation capacity for the radar and other systems, such as navigation gear and de-ice systems, plus tail warning radar.

The maiden flight was in March 1948, and a production order for twenty-eight examples followed in May. Deliveries began in February 1950 as the introductory F3D-1. This was followed by the F3D-2 powered by the 4,600-lbf (20.5-kN) J46. This model also got additional armor, an improved cockpit air conditioner, an autopilot and other electronic gear, windshield wipers, and wing spoilers for greater roll rate. When the J46 failed to materialize, the jets retained the J34s. The nacelles, enlarged for the J46, always looked too big for these smaller engines. Although engine power was pushed up to 3,400 lbf (15.1 kN), the aircraft had put on more than 5,000 lb (2,268 kg) and so was sadly underpowered, especially as engines deteriorated over time. Douglas pushed out 237 Dash-2s between February 1951 and October 1953.

Douglas F3D-2 Characteristics

span	50 feet (15.2 m)	weight empty	18,160 lb (8,237 kg)
length	45.4 feet (13.8 m)	loaded	23,575 lb (10,693 kg)
height	16.1 feet (4.9 m)	max. take-off	28,800 lb (13,263 kg)
wing area	400 feet² (37.2 m²)	speed, max. (sea level)	549 mph (884 kph)
fuel, int.+ext.	1,350+300 gal (5,110+1,136 l)	cruise	463 mph (745 kph)
service ceiling	38,200 feet (11,643 m)	range, clean	1,150 miles (1,851 km)
climb rate, initial	4,430 fpm (1,350 mpm)	maximum	1,540 miles (2,479 km)

The Corsair and Tigercat night fighters began to be replaced with the F3D-2s beginning in November 1952. However, as the weight grew, the Skyknight seldom went to sea. Only one squadron took their airplanes on a cruise. The navy employed the aircraft in shore-based training and experimental efforts and, much later, EW tasks. The marines alone continued operational service with the night fighter, all ashore.

Concurrent with the DAC work, Grumman was approached for their response to the requirements. Unfortunately, the service stepped out on the wrong foot with the April 1946 contract by insisting Grumman use the J30 for a dual-seat night fighter. At just 1,500 lbf (6.7 kN), powering the heavy airframe meant using four of these turbojets.[6] While the designers came up with a layout that had two turbojets paired in underwing nacelles, this XF9F-1 was quite impractical as a naval fighter. With the twin-engine Skyknight making encouraging progress, the Grumman project was dropped.

A more practical shipboard jet night-fighter was derived from the first practical naval jet fighter, the F2H-2. This was turned to night fighting with the addition of a Sperry AN/APS-19 radar in the apex of an extended nose with the four cannon distributed behind. The model first flew in February 1950 and a total of fourteen were built. The F2H-2N was the navy's first single-seat jet night fighter and was considered all-weather.

The navy judged they could squeeze a bit more life from the straight-wing Banshee and so had McDonnell develop the F2H-3 with Westinghouse AN/APQ-41. This model got another uprating of the J34 at 3,250 lbf (14.5 kN) that, with the addition to greater fuel capacity, roughly retrained the performance of the baseline F2H despite the weight increase that demanded the undercarriage be strengthened. An aerial refueling probe could be installed in place of one of the nose cannon. This model was another step towards making such equipment as radar common in a single-seat machine (no "N" suffix), the dedicated night fighter seeing its days numbered. It had four hardpoints under the wings for weapons from rockets to 500-lb (227-kg) bombs. A single heavy "special weapon" (nuclear) could be fitted under the port wing on an inboard hardpoint as with the F2H-2B.

One of the Douglas F3D-1s shows off the original small engine nacelles during September 1950. The Skyknight was about as big an aircraft as could be accommodated on the decks of the carriers that the navy was then putting to sea. However, the type seldom operated from ships, and in Korea, the marines employed them in combat from land bases. (*National Archives*)

The horizontal tails were moved down to the fuselage and further aft. During development, this suffered flutter issues that were successfully addressed by adding a stiffening brace to each side, between the surface and fuselage, covered by sheet metal as "horsal" fairings. First flying in March 1952, 250 F2H-3s were built through October 1953.

McDonnell F2H-3 Characteristics

span (tip tanks)	45 feet (13.7 m)	weight empty	13,183 lb (5,980 kg)
length	48.2 feet (14.7 m)	combat	18,367 lb (8,331 kg)
height	14.5 feet (4.4 m)	maximum	25,214 lb (11,437 kg)
wing area	294 feet² (27.3 m²)	speed, max. (sea level)	580 mph (933 kph)
fuel, int.+ext.	1,102+340 gal (4,172+1,287 l)	cruise	495 mph (797 kph)
service ceiling	46,600 feet (14,204 m)	range, normal	1,170 mi (1,883 km)
climb rate, sea level	5,900 fpm (1,798 mpm)	maximum	1,716 miles (2,762 km)

Even while the F2H-3s were working their way through the production line in St. Louis, the F2H-4s had begun to be assembled. These featured yet another model of the

This flight test F2H-3, taking the wire coming aboard USS *Antietam* (CVA-36) on January 14, 1953, shows the large radome for the nose radar antenna, marking it as an "all-weather" fighter. Several underwing pylons could be installed as well as wingtip tanks (lacking here). The split flaps, one under the fuselage, are deployed. The cannon ports are notable farther aft than for earlier Banshee models; the top one on the shown side could be replaced with an aerial refueling probe. (*National Archives*)

J34 with 3,600 lbf (15,994 kN) and a change to the Hughes AN/APG-37 radar. The added power pushed the top speed to 610 mph (982 kph), upped the ceiling to 56,000 feet (17,069 m), and pushed the maximum range out to 2,000 miles (3,219 km). This model totaled 150 articles through September 1953, even before the last F2H-3 was handed over. It became the USMC's only all-weather Banshee.

These aircraft had cockpit lighting for night ops, autopilots, and a good suite of navigation instruments. However, apart from the usual assortment of rain removal and heated pitot plus AoA probes, they lacked de-ice and anti-ice systems. This would become the norm for "all-weather fighters" in all services.

Ground Attack

A contract was let to Lockheed in January 1951 for 113 examples of a ground attack version of the F-94C (see page 170). These were to be single-seat variants and with a new wing adding half-again as much area. External munitions went up to 4,000 lb (1,814 kg). The wing permitted markedly more fuel in addition to external tankage and volume in place of the rear seat. The nose grew even longer to house eight 0.50-cal guns and a ranging radar, plus a retractable AR probe. Lockheed had completed the conversion of two F-94Bs—with only the revised nose and short of the full eight MGs—that had begun as YF-94Ds when the project was dropped in October 1951. The USAF felt that the company needed to focus on solving the problems hamstringing the F-94C.

This was essentially the USAF's last attempt at a dedicated air-to-ground jet for many years. F-type fighters were expected to suitably fill the role. The navy had such a machine under design in a few years, apart from a turboprop, both addressed in later chapters.

5

Second Generation Fighters

It was recognized early on in the adoption of jet engines to fighter aircraft that straight aero surfaces would impede high speeds owing to compressibility effects. In particular, the wartime example of Germany swept-wing combat aircraft had demonstrated the benefits of this speed advantage. Straight wings were initially retained in America because of familiarity, avoiding added technical risk, and because they still permitted the airspeeds initially sought. Dive brakes helped protect against Mach tuck and other compressibility effects. However, what was sought continued to advance, as had happened continuously in military aircraft evolution since the beginning. It was not long before the challenges of practical swept-wing applications had to be confronted. The services began with swept-wing versions of existing aircraft for expediency while also undertaking "clean-sheet" designs. As the USSR was especially expected to introduce such jets, with a marked increase in airspeed, the U.S. had to be ready to meet them. There was also a dimension of competition between the navy and air force, though the naval teams had to move more cautiously to ensure the safety of shipboard landings.

By the end of the 1940s, the services were ready to try for aircraft capable of supersonic airspeed in level flight. Most of the early jets could pass Mach 1 in dives—barely. However, a great reduction in drag and use of an afterburner would be required to achieve this in level flight. All continued to be hamstrung by poor predictive airflow and drag data given the continuing limited wind tunnel data. The NACA had worked these problems diligently and had potential solutions. As already described, the experience with afterburners was not deep and had usually been pursued at the instigation of the airframe developer. Thanks to nearly a decade of turbojet engine maturation, aerodynamic lessons learned, and the motivation of another war, the developers were finally going to get the performance and reliability they had sought since World War Two.

By this juncture, it was clear that jet fighters could perform all the roles attributed to fighters or fighter-bombers of the past. While design concessions were made for specific mission requirements, no great distinction was made—all-weather, in the sense of a capable radar and suitable navigation equipment, with the pilot as the sole operator, was generally a given.

Air Force Leads

Republic began exploring a swept-wing and tail F-84 in 1949 that retained some 60 percent of the baseline aircraft. Although facing budget shortages, the USAF funded a prototype as the YF-96A, via modification of an F-84E, with surfaces swept 38.5 degrees. Flying in June 1950 after the airlift to Edwards, performance was uninspiring. With the Korean Conflict opening coffers, the service asked Republic to prepare a second prototype with the 7,200-lbf (32.0-kN) Wright J65—a licensed production of the Armstrong-Siddeley Sapphire. Many changes to the engine were required for the application. It also made it necessary to greatly alter the airframe that grew larger and fatter—becoming the F-84F to allow the use of F-84 program funds. The intake and canopy were redesigned as were the speedbrakes, plus the addition of a braking parachute, as just the more obvious alterations. Also, the horizontal tails were moved higher which necessitated introducing anhedral to the wings. Aircraft Mechanics provided the ejection seat. By that point, only 15 percent of the straight-wing F-84 was retained.

Owing to the added complexity of a new engine and the swept surfaces, the initial pre-production YF-84F did not fly until February 1951, and with a J35. Production contracts soon followed, including General Motors manufacturing the aircraft at a former NAA plant in Kansas City, Kansas. It was still a long road to a suitable aircraft such that the first Thunderstreak flew only in November 1952. It would go supersonic only in a steep dive. Deliveries began early the next year. The long gestation period made it necessary to fund F-84G production (see page 142). The F-model still had many problems, including S&C issues at high speed plus engine faults, which delayed fleet introduction. Among the changes was the introduction of stabs. Another year passed before the type was considered operational. Production of 2,713 continued through 1957.

The J65 problems prompted plans in 1953 for the substitution of General Electric J73 engines. The XF-84J flew in 1954, but the budget scuttled the project.

Lockheed had made developing and producing all-weather jets look easy. They hoped to extend their success with the growth of the F-94, which might match the faster jet bomber adversaries that were bound to be introduced eventually. However, the next iteration met with more difficulty, and the F-94B purchase was to become an interim fill via half measures.

The penultimate F-94 began as an unsolicited Lockheed proposal in July 1948 to deliver better performance and upgraded avionics. While the USAF prevaricated, the company converted an F-94A during 1949 and flew it in January 1950. Soon after, facing continuing delays with the F-89 and F-86D, the air force ordered a full prototype, followed by a production contract before testing was complete. Initially designated the F-97, this soon reverted to F-94C.

The new model used the J48 at 8,750 lbf (38.9 kN) wet fed by revised intakes. A thinner wing with greater dihedral and dive flaps, plus deicing boots, was matched to a swept horizontal tail for a critical Mach number moved from 0.80 to 0.85. This produced an odd appearance with a swept horizontal tail but straight vertical and

Republic offered, and the USAF accepted, a proposal to sweep the surfaces on the F-84 to improved transonic performance. However, the air force went further and asked for an engine swap among other very extensive changes. The new aircraft (YF-84F 49-2430 shown in test) took years to come together as a reliable combat system, but it went on to a respectable career. (*National Museum of the United States Air Force*)

wings. The fuel system was greatly altered to include underwing drop tanks and revised tip tanks. The APG-40 radar was substituted, flight data computer added along with an autopilot, and switch to the Hughes E5 FCS. Other features included new ejection seats, altered speedbrakes, and a drag chute. Armament became twenty-four rockets in a ring around the nose, behind four snap-action doors. A pod for a dozen more rockets could be added on the leading edge of each wing, introduced with the 100th production article and retrofitted to early examples. The aerodynamic nose of the pod was frangible, blown off with the first rocket launch.

The first production F-94C was handed over in July 1951. However, deliveries were slowed owing to rework resolving numerous design problems. The vertical tail and rudder were extended in area for improved directional stability. Eliminating aileron buzz led to dampers added to those surfaces and spoilers installed for more positive roll control. Firing a salvo of rockets above 25,000 feet (7,620 m) caused the engine to flame out. The AB suffered development difficulties of its own, but it did enable the jet to become the first twin-seat aircraft to go supersonic (in a dive). The drag chute proved surprisingly challenging, and the autopilot was unreliable. Poor weatherproofing allowed moisture to intrude into the cockpit, shorting out avionics. The solutions drove modifications to aircraft already delivered. Although the USAF considered canceling the program, superior products to fill operational needs remained just out of reach. Yet fleet introduction had been delayed until March 1953 by which time the design was being eclipsed and adversary bombers were expected to soon be too fast for the Starfire, each costing $1,068,246. Production was cut back with 387 ultimately delivered, serving to 1958.

Lockheed F-94C Characteristics

span, over tanks	42.4 feet (12.9 m)	weight empty	12,708 lb (5,764 kg)
length	44.6 feet (13.6 m)	gross	18,300 lb (8,301 kg)
height	14.9 feet (4.6 m)	max. take-off	24,184 lb (10,970 kg)
wing area	233 feet² (21.6 m²)	speed, max. (sea level)	556 mph (895 kph)
fuel, int.+ext.	566+960 gal (2,143+3,634 l)	cruise	493 mph (793 kph)
service ceiling	51,400 feet (15,667 m)	range, combat	805 miles (1,296 km)
climb rate, initial	7,980 fpm (2,432 mpm)	ferry	1,275 miles (2,052 km)

What has been considered the standout success in American jet fighters of the period was the North American Aviation F-86. It was impressive with its swept wing and met the Soviet swept-wing MiG-15 on equal or superior terms in Korea. It was best air-to-air, leaving ground attack to its straight-wing brethren, and so held a more glamorous role. Yet its birth was paced by new technology, as were all the others.

The Sabre emerged from a wartime contract for a jet fighter reaching 600 mph (966 kph). North American initially proposed an aircraft like its XFJ-1 with straight wings and tail surfaces. By summer 1945, it was clear from growing transonic aerodynamic research that this had little hope of meeting the speed goal. Given access to German records on swept wings, NAA was able to rework the design in fall 1945 with a 35-degree sweep, and the USAAF gave the go-ahead for prototypes. As with all who approached swept wings, NAA had to deal with the tip stall phenomenon and dangerously degraded low-speed roll

Lockheed's F-94C was a bid to rapidly add performance to the all-weather interceptor with swept surfaces (horizontal tail only) and stabs matched with a more powerful engine plus improved avionics. Quick-acting doors cover a ring of rocket tubes just aft of the nose radome, and a dozen more missiles were contained in each leading edge pod with cover blown off with the first rockets fired. Unlike its earlier efforts, the company ran into difficulties with the F-94C (51-5592 shown), this photo displaying the extended vertical tail and rudder areas as one of the "fixes." (*National Archives*)

control. The team chose the leading-edge slats solution many others adopted, basing the initial design on that from the Me 262. Just designing the structure for transonic airloads was a challenging, driving adoption of milled skins and other departures from convention. All controls were boosted and with trimming horizontal tail. Despite the technical risks, the USAAF ordered production examples before the aircraft flew.

The complexity of the swept-wing airplane and new 4,000-lbf (17.8-kN) J35 meant it was October 1947 before the first XP-86 took off at Muroc. There were still hurdles to overcome, including optimizing the slat operation, but the aircraft held definite promise.[1] The drop tank was causing transonic buffeting and had to be redesigned so it could be retained into a fight. The 5,200-lbf (23.1-kN) J47 was installed in the production articles, but it was still suffering teething problems that drove frequent engine changes. An icing issue was addressed by bleed air passed through hollow inlet guide vanes. The fighter had six .50-cals in the nose, could accommodate sixteen rockets under the wings, and 1,000-lb (454-kg) bombs could replace the external tanks. Quick-acting gun doors were eventually deleted. A radar rangefinder was installed at the tip of the nose above the annular inlet. There was a speedbrake on both sides of the aft fuselage, initially hinged at the aft end, and an NAA ejection seat. Antennae were embedded within the structure behind fiberglass panels—which would become a common practice.

The F-86A was first delivered in May 1948. Proud of their first swept-wing fighter, the USAF had one break the speed record again in September 1948 with 671 mph (1,080 kph). In total, 554 F-86As were produced through December 1950, with its fleet introduction in spring 1949. As with most new aircraft with fairly youthful engines, parts supply and system immaturities meant the Sabre was unfit to be deployed overseas until December 1950.

The F-86B was to have the fuselage widened to accommodate larger tires and brakes for rough field ops, but this was ultimately judged unnecessary given improvements in that equipment. The F-86C and F-86D are discussed elsewhere. The 336 F-86Es were taken up between February 1951 and July 1952. These reflected many small improvements, some introduced over the production run via Block upgrades, to keep the Sabre at the front of the daylight fighter pack. Controls (save the rudder) were fully powered versus merely boosted, requiring pilot artificial feel. The powered ailerons combated transonic sluggishness and stabs replaced the trimming stabilizer but with geared elevators. The USAF bought sixty more Es produced under license by Canadair to meet urgent war needs.

North American F-86E Characteristics

span	37.1 feet (11.3 m)	weight empty	10,555 lb (4,788 kg)
length	37.5 feet (11.4 m)	combat	14,255 lb (6,466 kg)
height	14.8 feet (4.5 m)	gross	16,346 lb (7,414 kg)
wing area	288 feet² (26.8 m²)	speed, max. (sea level)	679 mph (1,093 kph)
fuel, int.+ext.	435+240 gal (1,647+909 l)	cruise	537 mph (864 kph)
service ceiling	47,200 feet (14,387 m)	range, normal	642 miles (1,033 km)
climb rate, max.	7,250 fpm (2,210 mpm)	ferry	1,022 miles (1,645 km)

North American Aviation's F-86 Sabre led the USAF fighter ensemble at the beginning of the Korean Conflict, and upgrades made it the best fighter in the world. The F-86Es (shown) were introduced just before the outbreak of combat and featured fully powered controls and stabilators replacing elevators. The F-model saw the most alterations and fought in the last year of the war. (*National Archives*)

The F-86F strengthened the wing for additional store capacity, upping drop tank capacity to increase intercept loiter time or range for strike missions, improved hydraulic system combat survivability, and changed the gunsight; the uprated J47 gave 5,910 lbf (26.3 kN). This model took flight initially in March 1952. Among the Block changes was the "6-3" wing that eliminated the slats that had tended to open in high-g maneuvers, slightly extended the leading edges that also increased sweep to 35.7 degrees and area by 5 percent, and added wing fences. Allowable load factor was increased for tighter turns at high altitudes and Mach numbers while delaying transonic buffeting. The loss of slats meant a 16-mph (26-kph) increase in stall speed and so higher approach speeds, with greater take-off and landing distances. Ultimately, 1,159 F-86Fs were built.

Improvement in the Sabre continued beyond Korea and several international partners manufactured the type. The F-86H was in advanced development as a fighter-bomber, given a larger intake and longer fuselage for the 8,920-lbf (39.7-kN) J73, additional fuel capacity, LABS for nuclear weapon delivery, and cannon with some Blocks. The first flight was in June 1953, and it went into production the following year as the last model delivered to American forces.

The final new model Saber built for the U.S. armed forces was the F-86H. It included features to enhance its role as a fighter-bomber. Evident here with the YF-86H is the enlarged intake and fuselage to accommodate the powerful J73 engines. (*National Archives*)

The Penetration Fighter program, which dated from 1945, offered another opportunity for the air force to attain its long-desired jet escort fighter. Yet, to get the most from the effort, the USAF soon changed the requirement to include a strike mission as well—sort of a modern-day P-51 that could escort as well as serve a fighter-bomber role. This meant that the aircraft would need the performance and maneuverability for air combat, the strength for dive pullouts, as well as fuel volume for long-range flights. These goals worked against each other in aircraft design that was also paced by available powerplants.

The initial requirements called for a swept-wing aircraft with two engines, a 600-mph (966-kph) top airspeed, ten-minute climb to 35,000 feet (10,668 m), and a 900-mile (1,449-km) combat radius. Ordnance was to include four to six 20-mm cannon, bombs, and external tanks. In short order, the performance was upped to a 1,500-mile (2,414-km) range and five minutes to 50,000 feet (15,240 m). Then the combat radius was reduced to 600 miles (966 km). The service also hinted that they would prefer an upper GW of 15,000 lb (6,804 kg). These dramatic swings were the source of consternation for the design teams.

Of the design submittals for the Penetration Fighter, two were selected in early 1946. McDonnell was to develop the XP-88 and Lockheed the XP-90 (later XF-88 and XF-90). Convair was initially selected instead of Lockheed, but the Pentagon voided the decision. That firm had also won an interceptor competition and was working the lucrative B-36. The DoD wished to spread the contracts around the field of airframers to sustain capabilities.[2]

McDonnell began working on a detailed design in June 1946 to continue into detailed design, then a contract in February 1947 for two prototypes with their first flight pegged for April 1948. When the strike mission was added, it was too late to redesign for a stronger structure and the prototypes were limited to 6 g.

McDonnell offered a sleek airplane with wing root intakes and an aft fuselage swept up above and behind the engine exhausts to a V-tail. Lacking much data of their own or from NACA on swept wings, the designers studied the translated German documents made available by the government. This led them to choose a 35-degree sweep angle.[3] The wing was unusually thin at 7.9 percent. As with many others, fences were added to discourage spanwise flow undermining desirable stall and longitudinal stability. Leading-edge flaps and split trailing-edge flaps were featured. The butterfly tails were abandoned when it was found they compromised stability. The flight controls were among the first fully powered and entirely irreversible systems in an American aircraft. All control "feel" was artificial. This included bungees and springs, but also bellows that provided resistance as a function of flight speed. The hydraulic actuators added stiffness to the control axes and so reduced the potential for buzz. Although McAir designed large 350-gal (1,325-l) tip tanks for their jet, these reduced the flutter speed unacceptably on the thin wing. McDonnell also developed a loader that quickly fed the cannon shells into the ammunition boxes, integral with the airframe.

The XF-88 was to be a big and heavy airplane to accommodate the large fuel volume, radar, and FCS, plus other systems the USAF insisted were necessary. Ensuring sufficient power from engines available in 1947 was challenging. The selected J34 was still evolving, so McAir designed their jet to take any of the engines in development. One of the prototypes was designated XF-88 to carry a J34 lacking reheat, and the second the XF-88A with an afterburner. The baseline J34 was to generate 3,200 lbf (14.2 kN), but reheat added 1,000 lbf (4.5 kN).

Not finding vendors willing to undertake the design and construction of an afterburner just 2.5 feet (0.8 m) long to ensure ground clearance in take-off attitude, McAir had to do this themselves. An F2H-1 was used to test the unit. They also designed and built the first automatically controlled iris nozzle for a turbojet, this changing exit diameter in a smooth manner. Placement of the engine pair near the CG with an up-swept aft fuselage made for short inlet ducts, short exhausts, and low heating of the airframe, making for overall weight savings. They chose a short ramp on the fuselage leading to the inlet as opposed to moving plates and boundary layer bleeds. The inlet itself was unusually swept 40 degrees to increase its critical Mach. Ease of engine access and removal was an admiral feature of the installation.

The XF-88 was taken up on its maiden flight at Muroc in October 1948. The second Voodoo was initially flown without the afterburner and was equipped with six cannon and a variable incident horizontal stabilizer. The jet was clearly underpowered without augmentation, but even when both jets were so fitted, they could not be pushed supersonic in level flight. The aircraft reached Mach 1.175 in a split-S dive, reaching a 67,600-fpm (20,604-mpm) rate of descent and consuming 24,000 feet (7,315 m). The maximum level flight speed of 641 mph (1,032 kph) was comparatively unimpressive. The most immediate problem was inadequate take-off power owing to the choking of the flow in the inlet duct that was optimally sized for high-speed flight. This was resolved with sprung blow-in doors added to the duct segment within the gear wells. The flight controls performed quite favorably. However, the team experienced a Dutch Roll that complicated fine control for gun tracking, yet defied any aerodynamic correction. This compelled McAir to adopt a yaw damper acting via the rudder. The large speedbrakes installed in the aft fuselage were hinged at the rear for ease of opening, although that meant a hydraulic failure could leave them open. Regardless, the buffet they induced was only moderated by drilling many holes into them and lowering the open angle, reducing their effectiveness.

The McDonnell airplane came in well beyond the desired GW. Although they did find room in the wings for 100 gal (379 l) of additional fuel, the inability to incorporate the tip tanks reduced range and endurance even further. The McDonnell jet was otherwise quite trouble-free despite all the advanced features.

McDonnell XF-88A Characteristics

span	39.7 feet (12.1 m)	weight empty	12,140 lb (5,507 kg)
length	54.1 feet (16.5 m)	gross	18,500 lb (8,392 kg)
height	17.3 feet (5.3 m)	maximum	23,100 lb (10,478 kg)
wing area	350 feet² (33 m²)	speed, max. (level)	641 mph (1,032 kph)
fuel	834 gal (3,157 l)	diving	Mach 1.175
service ceiling	36,000 feet (10,973 m)	cruise	527 mph (848 kph)
climb rate, max.	2,414 fpm (736 mpm)	range	1,737 miles (2,795 km)

This photograph of the McDonnell XF-88A Voodoo was taken on October 10, 1948, over the desert near Muroc AFB. The slick lines of the design and inlet ramp are evident. The short afterburner section and airbrakes opening to the rear are also seen. (*National Archives*)

The Lockheed entry was ordered in June 1949 as the XF-90 with an afterburner. The firm had begun with the results of a broad jet fighter design study following the war and with reference to German material. Among their offerings for the Penetration Fighter was a 60-degree swept delta-wing design with pivoting wingtips for trimming. Both twin vertical tails and T-tail designs were investigated. They proceeded far enough with the delta-wing design that parts were being fabricated before they concluded that it would have stability challenges, plus being too heavy and draggy. A quick redesign adopted a more conventional layout with a V-tail considered but rejected. The delta-wing detour had cost the project precious time. However, it meant that their design could respond to the structural strength demands of the strike mission. Aerodynamic tests included a 890-lb (404-kg), 9.4-foot (2.9-m) long, one-sixth-scale free flight model dropped from Lockheed's highly modified P-38E testbed.

The XF-90 had an exciting look with a needle nose, swept side inlets with boundary layer bleed, and all aero surfaces sharply swept, the thin wing at 35.3 degrees. Concerned with S&C at supersonic speeds, the horizontal tail incidence angle could be adjusted by changing the sweep angle of the entire vertical tail up to 8 degrees. An electric actuator tilted the vertical tail about a pivot on the forward spar. All control surfaces had electrically operated trim tabs. Only the ailerons were boosted. Lockheed chose to employ dive flaps. Leading-edge slats were actuated, and slotted Fowler flaps were included. To help meet the fuel demands, the tip tank design of the P-80 was adopted—rare if not unique for a swept-wing airplane. To meet the structural strength required for maneuvering demanded by the strike mission, the team adopted stout frames along with 75ST aluminum that was some 25 percent stronger than the more common 24ST but also lighter. The aft fuselage, enclosing the engines, was steel. All this made the XF-90 the largest and heaviest of the competitors. The compressed nitrogen catapult ejection seat was a Lockheed development.

By the time of flight testing at Edwards, the Lockheed team found the J34s some 20 percent short of the guaranteed performance. Initially lacking AB, the airplane was dreadfully underpowered. For some flights at elevated weight or air temperatures, they added four 1,000-lbf JATO bottles just to get the jet airborne. The first take-off was in June 1949. The burner was a co-development of Lockheed and Westinghouse; it was initially tested on a modified XP-80A fitted with the J34. It added approximately 25 percent more thrust for a 50 percent higher fuel consumption. Although not mature when added in May 1950, results were encouraging. The AB and variable geometry "eyelid" nozzles permitted touching Mach 1.12 in a steep dive. Other difficulties involved empennage buffet that prompted many minor changes seeking a remedy.

Lockheed XF-90A Characteristics

span	40 feet (12.2 m)	weight empty	18,050 lb (8,187 kg)
length	56.2 feet (17.1 m)	loaded	27,200 lb (12,338 kg)
height	15.8 feet (4.8 m)	maximum	31,060 lb (14,089 kg)
wing area	345 feet² (32.1 m²)	speed, max. (level)	668 mph (1,075 kph)
fuel, int.+ext.	1,225+440 gal (4,637+1,666 l)	diving	Mach 1.12
service ceiling	39,000 feet (11,887 m)	cruise	473 mph (761 kph)
climb rate, max.	556 fpm (1,693 mpm)	range, normal	1,050 miles (1,690 km)
		maximum	2,300 miles (3,702 km)

North American decided to enter the Penetration Fighter fray with a reworked P-86, and so with just a single engine. This was a much smaller airframe than the competition despite adopting the centrifugal-flow J48 with a much larger diameter than the axial-flow engines. With reheat and clamshell nozzle, this was to deliver 8,000 lbf (35.6 kN). With comparatively more power, less weight, and lower fuel consumption than a pair of J34s, it held the promise of meeting the requirements. Seeking to keep down drag, NAA chose to use NACA-designed flush inlets on either side of the fuselage and leave the nose free for six 20-mm cannon and "black boxes." Other armaments were to be two 1,000-lb (434-kg) bombs or eight rockets. Automatic wing slats were also introduced. Some 50 percent heavier than the standard Sabre, the jet also required dual main-gear wheels on each strut. A radar installation could make the jet suitable for the All-Weather (Night) Interceptor mission as well.

The design was pitched to AMC in September 1947 as the P-86C, suggesting commonality with the earlier Sabres. This was misleading as, of the major assemblies,

The competition for a Penetration Fighter supporting bomber escort yielded the attractive Lockheed XF-90. This first example (46-687) lacked an afterburner but featured the wingtip tanks. The two under-performing engines could not push the heavy fighter fast enough to suit the air force. (*Air Force Test Center*)

only the tail was common.[4] The USAF responded in December with a contract for two YP-93 prototypes, and 118 production P-93s were ordered in June 1948. This undermined efforts by Lockheed and McDonnell, who were instructed in December 1948 to cease any work towards production designs. This was a tacit cancelation of the program.

The "Sabre Cat" first flew in January 1950 and flight testing quickly found that the NACA inlets provided insufficient airflow to the engine, especially at elevated AoA, resulting in compressor stalls and flameouts. The second jet was fitted with protruding "cheek" inlets more suitable for the J48. The jet reached Mach 1.05 in a dive. The first aircraft was gravely damaged by an engine explosion.

North American YF-93A Characteristics

span	38.9 feet (11.9 m)	weight empty	14,035 lb (6,366 kg)
length	44.1 feet (13.4 m)	loaded/combat	21,610 lb (9,802 kg)
height	15.7 feet (4.8 m)	maximum	25,516 lb (11,574 kg)
wing area	306 feet² (28.4 m²)	speed, max. (sea level)	708 mph (1,139 kph)
fuel	1,581 gal (5,985 l)	diving	Mach 1.05
service ceiling	46,800 feet (14,265 m)	cruise	534 mph (859 kph)
climb rate, max.	11,960 fpm (3,645 mpm)	range	1,967 miles (3,166 km)

North American's entry in the Penetration Fighter skirmish was a growth of the Sabre with a large engine fed by bifurcated inlets to allow for the nose radomes—initially with the flush intakes shown and then cheek inlets. The YF-93 did not perform as well as the competition, but the air force had already placed a production order by the time the results were available. Regardless, the budget did not support moving forward and the contract was canceled. (*National Archives and Air Force Test Center*)

There was a "fly-off" between the three Penetration Fighter competitors in summer 1950—for a program that had already been canceled. All of the aircraft fell short of the performance requirements owing to poorly performing engines, weight, and fuel quantity. They offered little that extant fighters did not already possess. For what it was worth, the F-93 placed last, and the F-88 was identified as the best. The continuing evolution of the F-86 with the J47 (see F-86D, page 163) gave a respectable performance, with the P-86A exceeding the speed performance of some of the Penetration Fighter competitors. This and the budget squeeze meant that the USAF also had to drop F-93 production in February 1949. There was also a reduced budget for 1950, with most USAF development funds going to bombers and interceptors. Then the Korean Conflict began, and emphasis was placed on the production of existing types with bombing and attack the order of the day. Furthermore, the speed of the B-47 was making escort unnecessary.

The advent of the Korean Conflict, with combat more like World War Two than the quick atomic strikes anticipated, forced the USAF to return to the Penetration Fighter requirement. At the beginning of 1950, none of the existing fighters (principally the F-84E) could escort the B-29s and meet the MiG-15 on superior terms. The coming F-84F was expected to answer the immediate need, but it could not escort the B-36 throughout its envisioned extra-long range mission. For this, a requirement was released in February 1951. The need was considered urgent and so all proposals were for versions of existing designs. The decision came quickly, and in May, the McDonnell growth of the F-88 was selected. However, working up the specs and going through the preliminary design became a protracted affair, especially when the nuclear strike mission was added. Consequently, it was January 1953 before a letter of intent for the F-101A was approved, and a production order followed in May.

Given that this was just a development of McDonnell's F-88, it was felt that prototypes were not needed. However, this was a generous simplification of the design challenges. The decision was partially motivated by the Korean Conflict, but with its end later in 1953, the program was slowed to a moderate pace. Two J57s, each delivering 15,000 lbf (66.7 kN) in reheat, were to power the F-101. One of the F-88 prototypes served as a testbed for the installation of the new engine and aerial refueling tests. For the 101, the airframe had to be extended to accommodate the powerplants and even more fuel. The inlets were also enlarged, the area of the thinner wing expanded, the ailerons moved inboard, and the all-moving horizontal tail moved to near the top of the vertical. The MA-7 FCS was incorporated for the four 20-mm cannon. The jet was shaping up as around 67 feet (20 m) in length and 48,000 lb (12,700 kg) in loaded weight.

The F-101A flew in September 1954 and had its share of design changes prompted by flight test results. The gravest was the horizontal tail being blanked by separated flow off the wing at high AoA. This caused the aircraft to pitch up violently and depart into a spin. The chosen solution was a warning system for the pilot to avoid the condition. There were hundreds of other changes to be made, and the initial machines had to be restricted in normal load factor. The first production aircraft were so flawed that manufacturing was suspended for a time, delaying service introduction. Advertised as the first "1,000-mile per hour fighter," it did set new records.

Strategic Air Command dropped its requirement for the F-101 soon after its first flight. It was the largest and heaviest single-seat aircraft at the time, and battling nimble interceptors was not an enviable mission. Even with 3,150 gallons (11,924 l) of internal and external fuel, the Voodoo's range was just 1,350 miles (2,180 km). The command finally admitted, after nearly a decade of effort and many programs, that an escort for the B-36 was not practical. However, the F-101 was saved somewhat reluctantly by TAC, using its centerline hardpoint for a nuclear weapon or large conventional bomb. The LABS permitted low-level and all-weather delivery—a valuable capability in Europe.

The USAF was clearly seeking heavy and powerful jet fighters reaching for supersonic speeds in level flight. Observing this trend, NAA began with another upgraded F-86 before moving to a "clean sheet" design. Their May 1951 proposal featured a single J57 fed by an oval annular inlet with very thin lips and using an iris exhaust with overlapping leaves that would become the standard. This engine was powerful enough to push the aircraft through the transonic drag rise and so area ruling was unnecessary. The 45-degree swept surfaces were so unusually thin at 7 percent that there was concern with roll reversal. Consequently, the ailerons were moved inboard. For high lift, only slats were employed. With these features, North American willingly guaranteed Mach 1.3 at 35,000 feet (10,668 m) in level flight. As was becoming common, a belly speedbrake panel helped in slowing the aircraft, but along with the

The Korean Conflict, and prospects from similar conflicts elsewhere, revived the perceived need for a long-range bomber escort with respectable aerial combat capabilities. The basic McDonnell F-88 design was resurrected to be given much more powerful engines. This F-101A is shown during early 1953 in mock-up form, and the actual aircraft would enjoy a maiden flight in September 1954. (*National Archives*)

slats, it also helped in tightening turns. The horizontal tails were stabs placed low on the fuselage to remain clear of wing turbulence during high-AoA flight and avoid pitch up in stall. It had the typical 20-mm cannon, but also underwing hardpoints for potential air-to-ground ordnance given the experience in Korea showing all fighters should contribute to that mission. Survivability considerations dictated the separation of the redundant hydraulic system elements for the irreversible controls.

The NAA design won a November 1951 contract for the F-100A. The air force was so eager for the new fighter, and had such confidence in NAA, that it placed a production order while still an early design. A notable feature of the construction was the extensive use of titanium, with its good heat resistance but lightweight benefits. However, this and the extensive use of new and advanced manufacturing techniques drove up costs. There was also a new NAA automatic ejection seat and drag chute.

The initial aircraft actually had preproduction "Y" prefixes. The YF-100A flew in May 1953, during which it exceeded Mach 1 in level flight—the first aircraft bound or production to achieve this goal, much less on a first flight. The testing found few complaints, though the vertical tail and rudder were eventually shortened and broadened. Production yielded the first article in October 1953, the same month the jet set a new speed record of 755 mph (1,215 kph). It soon demonstrated the guaranteed Mach 1.3 in level flight. However, a rework of the vertical tail was necessary owing to inadequate directional stability, leading to a loss of control via inertia coupling and subsequent structural failure, which claimed several aircraft and lives. Rudder flutter demanded a damper. The type still initially suffered a high accident rate, though seen as the cost of adopting supersonic fighters. One cause was the high stall speed of required care on landing approach given the thin wing. However, the Super Sabre went on to a respectable career in several models and roles.

North American F-100A Characteristics

span	38.8 feet (11.8 m)	weight empty	18,185 lb (8,249 kg)
length	47.4 feet (14.5 m)	combat	24,996 lb (11,338 kg)
height	15.5 feet (4.7 m)	max. take-off	28,971 lb (13,141 kg)
wing area	385 feet² (35.8 m²)	speed, max. (35,000 feet)	852 mph (1,371 kph)
fuel, int.+ext.	744+550 gal (2,816+2,082 l)	cruise	589 mph (948 kph)
service ceiling	44,900 feet (13,686 m)	range, normal	716 miles (1,152 km)
climb rate, max.	23,800 fpm (7,254 mpm)	ferry	1,294 miles (2,083 km)

The growing confrontation with the USSR and the emergence of their long-range bombers led to the air force issuing an Advanced Development Objective in January 1949. With the detonation of the first Soviet atomic bomb later in the year and intelligence warning about A-bomb-equipped bombers soon to be expected, the USAF established the year 1954 as the goal of several projects. The "1954 Interceptor" would integrate many new technologies and be the superior aircraft when initially operational in 1954. This would bring many new technologies together to make an integrated weapon system.

North American created the first supersonic fighter bound for production. The initial article was the YF-100A that flew in May 1953 and went supersonic on its first flight. The vertical tail would undergo changes, but production aircraft were emerging before the end of the year. (*National Archives*)

A conference in May 1949 explored defense options and invited the aircraft and electronics industry to propose solutions. For air defense, this became Weapon System WS201A, combining an airframe with an FCS and missiles. Only the engine was left to the airframer, though this would change in the future. An RFP for the all-weather aircraft portion was released in June 1950 with initial goals to fly supersonically in level flight (700 mph/1,127 kph identified) and climb to 50,000 feet (15,240 m) in four minutes. Convair, Lockheed, and Republic were given development contracts for the airframe portion. The Hughes MA-1 fire control system and Hughes Falcon air-to-air missile (AAM, see page 430) were chosen in May 1951.

Convair was selected in July 1951, and the contract for YF-102 prototypes followed in September. Their interceptor would carry six Falcons in a belly and two side weapon bays. These were on "trapeze" launchers that extended to fire. Four of the six fast-acting bay doors would also contain twenty-four 2.75-inch FFAR.[5] Convair's design leveraged off the XF-92A (see page 60) delta wing experience with a 60-degree sweep and similar vertical tail. Pre-production articles were ordered during design development with the expectation that any changes identified during flight testing could be incorporated while flight experience was gained. The jet was initially to be powered by the Wright J67—license-built Bristol Olympus—and equipped with the MA-1 FCS, but these were not coming together soon enough. The J40 and Hughes E-9 (a modified E-4 later redesignated the MG-3 and upgraded to the MG-10) were substituted in the F-102A "Interim Fighter" to bridge the gap between the F-86D and the F-102B "Ultimate Fighter" with the final system and powerplant. Even as this plan was adopted, the delayed J40 was dropped in favor of the J57.

The first application of the weapon system development concept was not going well. Furthermore, reflecting the urgency to field the capability, production F-102As were ordered while the prototypes were still in design. This reflected a USAF policy adopted in 1953 to accelerate the fielding of combat aircraft by initiating production as soon as practical such that the fleet could at least begin gaining operational experience. It was recognized that the aircraft would likely require modifications to bring them to final production standards, and the design matured through flight testing and service trials. Still, it was hoped that a year could be shaved off the development–fielding timeline.

The F-102 shaped up as a heavy aircraft with more than 1,000 lb (454 kg) of fuel in the wings, nearly 1,200 lb (544 kg) of ordnance, and about 2,000 lb (907 kg) of electronic components in the fuselage. The MG-10 alone came in at 1,425 lb (646 kg) and consumed 24.6 feet^3 (0.7 m^3).[6] The wing was to encompass about 660 feet^2 (61.3 m^2) with a 37-foot (11.3-m) span. Empty weight was projected at around 18,000 lb (8,165 kg) and gross about 26,000 lb (11,793 kg). The final production airplane would cost more than $1 million each.

The first YF-102 flew in October 1953. It was quickly evident that the aerodynamic design would not permit the available engine thrust to push the airplane through the transonic drag rise. Wind tunnel and Wallops Island rocket-launched shapes had presaged this. Directional stability deficiencies and buffeting were additional issues. Short-term measures were considered including added wing camber and upturned tips, shifting the wing and vertical tail, and tapering the fuselage via a lengthening, but all to no avail—apart from adding 3,500 lb (1,588 kg). Tunnel and rocket tests showed that these would be inadequate.

With urgency by then for the capability represented by the promised fighter, the aircraft was famously redesigned and another prototype was built in seven months with the area-ruled "coke bottle" waist. Design studies along this line had been underway before the first YF-102 had flown. The fuselage was also lengthened and the forebody was made longer and narrower plus angled down, the canopy reworked, the inlets redesigned to include splitter plates, the wing camber adjusted, another wing fence added, the vertical tail area increased, and fairings added on the aft fuselage to meet area rule guidelines. The greatly altered airplane eventually met expectations. The avionics had also continued to evolve with shifting USAF requirements and delays of various elements. The ten production machines, built prior to the redesign, were essentially a waste of tens of millions of dollars.

The Delta Dagger reached the fleet in spring 1956, some three years behind schedule. This was the first all-weather supersonic interceptor, the first delta-winged jet to become operational, and the first USAF fighter armed only with missiles. The "Ultimate Fighter" emerged in 1956 as the F-106 project, the same year the Falcon AAM finally became operational with the envision FCS capabilities. Unfortunately, performance was found to be poor. Everyone had badly misjudged how long it would take to mature the originally envisioned technologies.

Republic's XF-103 reached for Mach 3 and 80,000 feet (24,384 m) with delta surfaces and an afterburning J67 matched with a ramjet for operation at high speed. Seeking to reduce drag, the cockpit and canopy were conformal with the smooth

The first Convair YF-102 (52-7994) rests on the Edwards AFB lakebed in preparation for a test event—the maiden mission in October 1953. Developed in response to a USAF need for a supersonic interceptor, the thin and highly swept surfaces plus inlet, and the wing fences are evident here. The jet fell well short of supersonic airspeed in level flight and required a considerable redesign. (*National Museum of the United States Air Force*)

forward fuselage making a periscope necessary for pilot vision.[7] A jettisonable capsule was also envisioned. The high flight speed would heat the airframe materials to such an extent that only titanium was judged suitable. Like the F-102, a weapon bay would house Falcons and FFARs. This design was finally ordered into prototype development in July 1954, but it pressed the limits of technology so much that it became a protracted effort. It was canceled in 1957 without the flying prototype being built.

The Lockheed effort was to be powered by as J53 with 15,000 lbf (66.7 kN) in reheat and carrying half a dozen Falcons in a weapon bay also fitting twenty FFARs. The aircraft was unusual in having the inlet on the spine and using straight, low-aspect-ratio wings. During detailed design, the weight progressively increased until it was agreed it was best to begin anew. The contract was canceled in January 1951 owing to funding constraints of the Korean Conflict. The J53 also never emerged as an installed powerplant. Lockheed employed some features of this aircraft and data from the straight-wing X-3 research craft with its long slender body to conceive another design that diverged in moving back to a relatively simple and lightweight

Republic assembled this mock-up of their radical XF-103 proposal seeking Mach 3 or faster. It rested on a low-drag design with delta wings and an advanced turbo-ramjet engine fed by the ventral intake. A conventional pilot canopy was abandoned in favor of a periscope and side windows, with ejection via the capsule shown. Weapons were to be mounted in weapons bays. (*Lloyd Jones collection*)

fighter. In forsaking the Falcons and heavy electronic content, it relied instead on very high speed matched with GE's new 20-mm, five-barrel Gatling gun to catch and destroy its quarry.

The new Lockheed design sought to be the first to use a new GE afterburning turbojet that would become the J79, but matched to minimal systems in a narrow fuselage and thin, low-aspect-ratio straight wings for Mach 2 speed. The inlets initially had ramps for shock positioning throughout the speed range. The ejection seat was to fire downward. Surprisingly, Lockheed's unsolicited proposal won a prototype order for the F-104 in March 1953, which first flew in March 1954.

A less radical Republic F-105 effort was a Mach 2 strike jet for TAC, possessing a bomb bay for a nuclear weapon. Powered by a J57, the airframe would be stressed for low-altitude, high-speed operation. Electronic content would be the latest navigation and targeting systems. Offered in spring 1952, the USAF gave the firm a development contract in September. Although flying initially in October 1955, a change in engine matched to inlet ramps, and an area-ruled fuselage meant new prototypes. So, it was years more before the introduction of the F-105.

Among this flurry of fighter programs was the growth of the F-100 as a Mach 2 all-weather fighter-bomber. This was initiated in June 1953 by diverting Super Sabre funds, and the project was initially referred to as the YF-100B. In the beginning, it had a chin inlet beneath a nose radome before adopting a spine intake feeding a new P&W

A new fighter was conceived as forsaking the complexity of rockets and missiles for a powerful airplane propelled by the new afterburning J79 turbojet matched with a multi-barrel 20-mm cannon. The supersonic Lockheed design leveraged off the sleek airframe of the X-3 research aircraft and with a small, straight wing. This XF-104 concept is shown in a summer 1953 drawing. (*National Archives*)

The notional Republic YF-105 tactical fighter is shown as concept art (design AP-63) from which the development diverged a bit by the time of flight. Most noteworthy would be forward-swept intake lips. Powered by the J57, it was to have an internal weapon bay for a nuclear weapon. (*National Archives*)

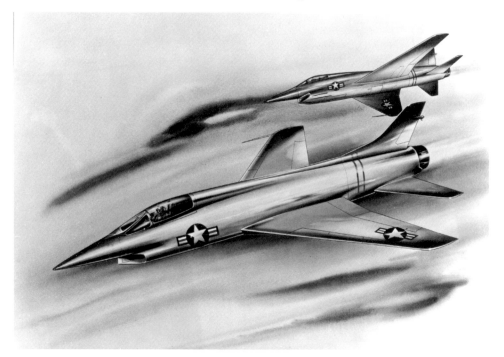

A growth of the F-100 to a Mach 2 all-weather interceptor was initiated in summer 1953, requiring the intake to be moved to allow for a nose radome. The initial concept was a chin inlet with ramps to position supersonic shocks, as seen in this concept art of the North American F-107. This variable air inlet duct would be important in the next generations of fighter aircraft, though the XF-107 did not progress beyond the prototype stage. (*National Archives*)

afterburning turbojet, the J75 promising 15,000 lbf (66.7 kN) or more. The intake featured adjustable ramps to position the supersonic shocks for optimal flow into the engine. This variable air inlet duct was the latest innovation for supersonic flight and would become common in the next two generations of fighters. The duct fairing atop the jet would feature area ruling. Flaps were adopted while roll would use spoilers on both the upper and lower wing surfaces. The first YF-107A flew in 1956, but it was denied production in favor of the F-105.

Navy Sweep

In 1947, the navy began exploring options for the second generation of jets with a step up in performance. This principally meant swept surfaces to increase the critical Mach number. The central concerns remained higher approach and launch speeds to compensate for the low-speed handling and high stall speed hazards of the thin, swept wings and the implications this had for carrier suitability employing war-era vessels. Much research was necessary before designers would make confident proposals. Especially with a conflict raging in the Far East and American aircraft confronting the MiG-15, some quick solutions were sought along with more paced efforts. These included converting successful straight-wing designs to swept and adopting an air force airplane.

It was noticed that the F-86A flew patterns and landing approaches at speeds less than for the straight-wing F9F-2. Hence, the navy turned to NAA for a "navalized" Sabre. Given the tenuous ancestral connection with the FJ-1, this was designated the FJ-2.

The three XFJ-2 prototypes were essentially modified F-86Es, ordered in March 1951 during the defense surge compelled by Korea. One, the XFJ-2B, had four 20-mm cannon replacing the machine guns while the others got all the carrier operation accouterments plus a lengthened nose strut to increase the AoA for deck launches. The first of these airplanes flew in December 1951 and those properly equipped went to sea for "carrier suit" trials at the end of 1952. These did not earn high marks, with some structural deficiencies and a concern with its adaptability to the new steam catapults.

An order for 300 FJ-2s had been placed in February 1951, to be built in the Columbus plant. These were powered by a 6,000-lbf (26.7-kN) J47 and featured folding wings plus other minor adjustments that included eliminating the horizontal tail dihedral. Initial delivery was in November 1952, but progress was slowed by the higher-priority F-86 such that only a handful were completed by the end of the Far East war. Given the desultory sea trial results and expected mediocre performance, the order was cut to 200. The 1,200 lb (544 kg) of added weight compared with the F-86E was quite unfavorable. So, the aircraft were destined for the mrines and land-based operations. Although some carrier deployments were performed, the FJ-2 was marginal when departing and coming aboard the boat. Its endurance made it marginal again with carrier cycle time for the Combat Air Patrol mission. The experience started the USN maxim that no air force aircraft was ever going to be suitable as a naval aircraft.

North American FJ-2 Characteristics

span	37.1 feet (11.3 m)	weight empty	11,802 lb (5,353 kg)
length	37.6 feet (11.5 m)	combat	16,122 lb (7,313 kg)
height	13.6 feet (14.1 m)	max. take-off	18,791 lb (8,524 kg)
wing area	288 feet² (26.8 m²)	speed, max. (sea level)	676 mph (1,088 kph)
fuel, int.+ext.	435+400 gal (1,647+1,514 l)	cruise	518 mph (834 kph)
combat ceiling	43,000 feet (13,106 m)	range, combat	622 miles (1,001 km)
climb rate, initial	7,230 fpm (2,204 mpm)	maximum	990 miles (1,593 km)

Hope was placed in the FJ-3 that was already in advanced development. This had the 7,650-lbf (34-kN) J65 matched to a larger intake, larger wings, and added underwing store stations. Two of these stations would be taken up with external tanks to extend endurance. The FJ-3 flew in December 1953, and additional models would follow with the Fury enjoying a respectable naval career.

Douglas hoped the ultimate T40 turboprop, potentially delivering 7,100 hp (5,295 kW), could push up the A2D Skyshark's (see page 205) top speed, necessitating a modest wing sweep to avoid compressibility effects. The contra-rotating propellers

The navy was slow adopting swept-wing fighters and, given the impetus of war, sought a converted F-86 for the role. Shown is the third prototype FJ-2 (XFJ-2B) featuring the four 20-mm cannon in the nose that would be adopted for the production airplanes. The production Furys looked the same except for a wing fold line mid-span. The FJ-2 went to the marines because it did not do well in carrier operations and the better performing FJ-3 was around the corner. (*National Archives*)

also eliminated torque effects on the airplane and promised a uniform slipstream. However, the engine was not going to mature and the entire program died before such ambitions could be realized. In 1951, DAC also proposed a swept aero surface F3D-3 with the then still-promised J46s. The demise of that powerplant, with no suitable alternative, spelled the end of this effort as well. A production order was dropped in February 1952.[8]

The original October 1946 contract for the Grumman F9F included a provision for the firm to explore a swept-wing variant. Neither the company nor the navy was ready for this at the time when the design had to move rapidly to meet urgent fleet requirements. However, research continued to the point in 1950 when both felt that they could move confidently to a swept-wing version of the Panther. A new contract in March 1951 for three prototypes derived from F9F-5s that flew little more than six months later.

The F9F-6 Cougar had 35-degree swept wings and a horizontal tail. The wing had an increased area in the interest of lower stall speed. The area of the flaps and hydraulically powered slats were also increased. Spoiler panels lay ahead of the flaps to augment aileron roll control. The belly split flaps were also increased in area and an aft portion hinged to serve as additional speedbrakes, though locked out for landings. This helped slow the aircraft that gained speed rapidly by virtue of reduced drag and added power from a 7,250-lbf (32.2-kN) version of the J48. Water injection was eliminated. The fuselage was also lengthened to expand fuel volume, and bladders were added to the wings. Tip tanks would have placed too much mass aft of the CG and so were eliminated. The two-segment rudder of the Panther was altered with the bottom enlarged and the upper actuated by a yaw damper mandated by the reduced stability in turbulence offered with the swept wing. Armament remained unchanged. A Grumman-developed ejection seat was installed in the Cougar prototype, but Martin-Bakers were procured for production.

Despite the underlying research and extensive design engineering, there was still work to do optimizing the swept-wing airplane. Flight testing found poor control in some regimes. The trimming tail with elevators became all-moving stabs. A sharp junction of the wings and inlets was smoothed with fillets. At transonic speeds, the ailerons floated to various angles to spoil fine tracking for gunfire. So, the ailerons were eliminated and the flaps extended to the tips. The port flap included a small trimming surface. Roll was via spoilers, called "flaperons," with the trailing portion separately actuated as "flaperettes." These last were on a second hydraulic system and only employed on landings in the event of a single hydraulic system failure rendering the flaperons inoperable. In the event of a total hydraulic system failure, the flaperettes could be actuated ten times via a pneumatic bottle to ensure suitable lateral control for landing. Wing fences were also added to discourage spanwise flow. That all these changes could be implemented within months while still moving smartly to production is a testament to Grumman's capabilities and the nature of the airplanes of the period.

The F9F-6 first flew in September 1951, with initial delivery following in November. As before, a version with a 6,350-lbf (28.3-kN) J33 was produced as the F9F-7, although many were finished or later modified with J48s. The Cougar demonstrated better carrier compatibility than its predecessor. Overall, the swept surfaces raised the critical Mach number from 0.79 to 0.86 at sea level. The initial Cougar unit took up its airplanes in November 1952, and the type became the first naval swept-wing jet to go to sea. It was very successful. Hundreds of Cougars were built and additional models followed, to include a trainer, with production rolling into the second half of the 1950s. The F9F line ultimately numbered nearly 2,000 aircraft.

Grumman F9F-6 Characteristics

span	34.5 feet (10.5 m)	weight empty	11,255 lb (5,105 kg)
length	40.9 feet (12.5 m)	combat	16,244 lb (7,368 kg)
height	12.3 feet (3.8 m)	max. take-off	21,000 lb (9,525 kg)
wing area	300 feet² (27.9 m²)	speed, max. (sea level)	654 mph (1,053 kph)
fuel, int.+ext.	919+300 gal (3,479+1,136 l)	cruise	541 mph (871 kph)
service ceiling	44,600 feet (13,594 m)	range, combat	932 miles (1,500 km)
climb rate, initial	6,750 fpm (2,057 mpm)		

The first swept-wing Grumman Cougar prototype (XF9F-6 126670), created from converting an F9F-2, is seen on February 15, 1952, with a flight test nose boom and before installation of wing fences. The F9F-6 made many fundamental changes to the baseline aircraft that would typically have resulted in a new type designation. (*National Archives*)

Simultaneous with initial efforts, the service issued an RFP in May 1948 for a swept-wing naval fighter via new, second-generation designs. From this, BuAer initiated four programs, giving contracts without competition. These were the Douglas F4D, Vought F7U, Grumman F10F, and McDonnell F3H. The service dictated the use of the axial-flow J40 and J46 turbojets. Unfortunately, the J40 never shaped up suitably, with or without reheat. The aircraft employing it, the F3D and F3H, all had to be re-engined with great delays. The F10F (see page 64) failed for a multitude of reasons. Consequently, the navy continued to lag behind the air force. The projects did support the evolution of more successful designs.

From McDonnell, the navy ordered two F3H prototypes in September 1949. This was a single-seat, single-engine day fighter with 45-degree swept surfaces. The layout was similar to the USAF F-88 with low wing and upswept aft fuselage to the empennage. The wing had slats and a fence, and there were a pair of aft fuselage speedbrakes. The armament was the then-common four 20-mm cannon. A McDonnell-designed ejection seat was featured. The company integrated the mandated J40 with a new afterburner, fed by tall and narrow cheek inlets, with a planned 9,200 lbf (40.9 kN)—markedly more than any other engine employed by the USN.

Delayed by engine availability, flying began in August 1951 without the afterburner that did not appear until January 1953. By that time, the navy had decided the Demon would be an all-weather fighter. Hence, production aircraft needed an enlarged nose for the APG-30 radar, added avionics such as autopilot, and the fuel capacity upped by 24 percent. All this increased the weight by 31 percent. Production was to be expedited by a second line operated by Temco. There was also a need to improve pilot visibility on approach and landing via a rework to tilt the forward fuselage 5 degrees nose down, and the nose gear was shortened. Roll rate and lateral stability were improved with the ailerons moved inboard at the sacrifice of flap area and the wing fences were removed. Excessive wing twist then compelled the adoption of inboard spoilers. The trailing edge root fillet was eliminated by extending the trailing edge straight to the fuselage with a 17 percent increase in area.

When the first of the F3H-1Ns flew in December 1953, it was expected that an uprated J40 would compensate for the weight growth. However, this was asking too much of the powerplant and Westinghouse. Although the Demon flew very well, the unreliable J40 was its Achilles' heel, with many failures leading to accidents. The engine was abandoned and, of the fifty-six completed machines, twenty-nine were re-engined as F3H-2Ns while twenty-one were used as ground static trainers or scrapped at a loss of some $198 million. The Allison J71 was substituted, though still delivering short of the desired thrust and requiring rework of the inlet ducts. The F3F-2 finally reached operational service in 1956. It went on to a useful career as a missile carrier.

McDonnell F3H-1N Characteristics

span	35.3 feet (10.8 m)	weight empty	18,691 lb (8,478 kg)
length	59 feet (18 m)	combat	26,085 lb (11,832 kg)
height	14.6 feet (4.5 m)	maximum	29,998 lb (13,607 kg)
wing area	442 feet² (41.1 m²)	speed, max. (sea level)	616 mph (991 kph)
fuel	1,506 gal (5,701 l)	cruise	553 mph (890 kph)
combat ceiling	44,000 feet (13,411 m)	range, normal	1,130 miles (1,819 km)
climb rate, initial	10,900 fpm (3,322 mpm)		

Chance Vought began investigating advanced jet fighter designs in June 1945 in response to a navy exploratory requirement for a 600-mph (966-kph) day fighter that could operate to 40,000 feet (12,192 m). This would require measures combating compressibility effects, with shock impingement on the tail surfaces one of the principal problems. Addressing these while also seeking reduced drag, Vought's tailless design had wings swept 38 degrees and two verticals mid-span with rudders. The wings featured trailing edge "ailervators" plus root clamshell speedbrakes while leading-edge slats moved in concert with the undercarriage. The layout, with a very low aspect ratio of 3:1, was favorably compact with wing fold. It also gave a generous volume for wing fuel cells. An automatic fuel transfer system maintained the CG within the narrow limits mandate by the tailless layout. An astonishing nose-high deck angle for wing AoA on take-off and landing was necessary. By the time BuAer examined the design in October 1945, the efficacy of the approach was strengthened by German wartime documents of research on similar designs.

The navy was ready to proceed with their new jets in January 1946 and issued a solicitation for a daylight naval fighter. Despite the uncertainties of the design, the navy took a chance and funded three XF7U-1 prototypes in June 1946. Power would come from two J34s fitted with afterburners yet to be developed.

The second XF3H-1 (125445) is seen on August 11, 1953, late in the test program, with an afterburner. While it still has the wing fences, the inboard ailerons have been adopted with their own temporary fences. These changes were among others for the production F3H-1Ns, but the engine proved so recalcitrant that the model was abandoned entirely with twenty-one struck off. The follow-on F3H-2 was then late joining the fleet and a disappointing performer. (*National Archives*)

As the XF7U-1s came together, there many atypical features. A Vought ejection seat and cockpit pressurization were to be incorporated. Its nose wheel steering was still uncommon. The extended main gear had two positions: aft for landings and forward for take-off with a higher nose attitude. More radical still was that all controls were fully boosted with only an artificial "feel" for the pilot. The airframe used a good deal of magnesium and Vought's Metalite composite.

The prototypes began flying in September 1948, but the Solar afterburners were delayed. The verticals were lengthened to correct poor directional stability manifested by nose "hunting." Nose wheel spin-up reduced landing loads and strut extension for take-off reduced a sink tendency after launch. Fourteen production examples had been ordered in July 1948, but progress was slowed by Vought's move to Dallas. The first flew in March 1950. By that point, it was clear the design had an impressive performance, but it required multiple revisions before it could enter fleet service, especially owing to poor pilot visibility and other carrier operations deficiencies. There were also several accidents. All three prototypes and two production jets had crashed, with three Vought test pilots killed. None of the Dash-1s were fielded.

The September 1949 contract for eighty-eight F7U-2s was canceled when it became clear the J34 was never going to mature suitably. War in Asia was soon the motivation to persevere, and so the F7U-3 model was ordered in August 1950, substituting J46s promising 7,000-lbf (31.1-kN), or 10,000-lbf (44.5-kN) with reheat.

These heavier airframes featured a revised nose to give the pilot greater forward vision on approach and landing, further enlarged verticals, a longer and stronger nose gear strut with dual wheels, rare dual-redundant 3,000-psi (20,684-kPa) hydraulic system, and additional fuel capacity. Initially, only one rudder moved depending on which pedal was pressed, but this was altered to both deflecting, and the airplane still needed a yaw damper. Weapons included four 20-mm cannon plus underwing stores, to include tanks. An optional belly pack for thirty-two Mighty Mouse rockets was also devised. The aircraft may have been amongst the first with pressure refueling. Testing included supersonic store separation as another "first."

The first F7U-3 Cutlass flew in December 1951, but initially with non-afterburning J35s in place of the delayed J46s that did not appear until 1953. Still, the design continued to be optimized. It was May 1953 before the aircraft flew with J46s, and fated to be the only production type to do so. The powerplant was progressively derated to an eventually 4,800 lbf (21.4 kN) dry and 6,500 lbf (28.9 kN) wet in an effort to preserve engine life and delay heavy maintenance. Westinghouse had failed the navy again, but there was no suitable replacement powerplant for the Cutlass. Aircraft were initially parked after manufacturing awaiting engines before the line was slowed and personnel laid off. The type finally entered fleet service in 1954. Yet production quantity was fairly low, with the engines literally deafening, performance marginal, mishap rates atrocious, and service short. The airframe was strong and the jet flew nicely, but these attributes alone did not make a successful naval fighter.

Chance Vought F7U-3 Characteristics

span	39.8 feet (12.1 m)	weight empty	18,210 lb (5,550 kg)
length	43.2 feet (13.2 m)	combat	23,672 lb (10,737 kg)
height	14.5 feet (4.4 m)	max. take-off	32,500 lb (14,742 kg)
wing area	535 feet² (49.7 m²)	speed, max. (sea level)	696 mph (1,120 kph)
fuel, int.+ext.	1,320+500 gal (4,997+1,893 l)	cruise	518 mph (834 kph)
service ceiling	40,600 feet (12,375 m)	range, normal	696 miles (1,120 km)
climb rate, initial	11,150 fpm (3,399 mpm)	maximum	817 miles (1,315 km)

Douglas had been researching delta-winged craft and consulting German data. The USN gave them funding for the preliminary design of a naval fighter based on the tailless configuration. This evolved into a single-engine airframe with a rounded-delta planform and wing root inlets. Outer wing panels folded up for storage. A Douglas-developed ejection seat, a Westinghouse APQ-50 intercept radar, and an autopilot were featured. Four 20-mm cannon were positioned in the wings that also had seven hardpoints under the fuselage and wings for a wide variety of tanks and weapons. The navy directed the use of the J40. The anticipated output of this powerplant was expected to give impressive climb rates for rapid intercept plus possible supersonic speeds in level flight.

In December 1948, DAC won a contract to build two XF4D-1 prototypes. The unusual design required a longer detailed design phase than was common, and so it was January 1951 before the first jet flew. The J40 was still lagging and so the J35 had been substituted for initial testing. Even when the J40 could be installed, these were early models, initially without AB, performing short of the promised final equipment. It was 1953 before the representative engine was available, and sea trials could be

While it had inspiring clean-airplane performance, the unusual Cutlass struggled to measure up to expectations. The first image shows one of the XF7U-1 prototypes during 1948 in its original and very deficient form followed by the greatly revised F7U-3 (128464) photographed on May 9, 1953, revealing very significant external changes. Even the latter early production airframe has small intakes and the J35 engines, all to be replaced. It was a challenging airplane to operate and came late to the fleet when better aircraft were already emerging. (*Vought Aircraft Heritage Foundation and National Archives*)

undertaken. It then allowed the Skyray to break an absolute speed record at 753 mph (1,212 kph), the first for a carrier-based airplane.

The challenging tailless layout of the F4D-1 compelled the adoption of features that were a step toward increasing complexity. Primary flight control was via nearly full-span elevons (crossing the wing fold line) and the rudder. Unpowered slats spanned the wing's leading edges. There were speedbrakes that extended above and below each wing. Two redundant 3,000-psi (20,684-kPa) hydraulic systems powered the elevons and speedbrakes. Manual flight control was quite difficult above 200 mph (325 kph), and the control column could be lengthened to add mechanical advantage. Inboard of the elevons, and adjacent to the aft fuselage, were pitch trim wedge surfaces driven by electrical jackscrews. The airplane required an electro-mechanical pitch trim change compensator, but this was only the best compromise between Mach tuck and pitch-up during rapid deceleration required some pilot adjustment. When the compensator failed, the aircraft became a handful. The lower rudder segment was moved directly by the pilot while the upper was moved by a yaw damper. The aircraft experienced a good deal of yaw during rolls, though the rolls could reach a remarkable rate. The aircraft developed a sink below 115 mph (185 kph), as it got on the backside of the power curve, which could require maximum thrust to overcome. Tail buzz was experienced, which drove many configuration changes around the exhaust until a suitable configuration was found. The tricycle undercarriage was supplemented with a retractable tailwheel, given the high deck angles for many launches and recovery ops mandated by the tailless design. Like many jets of the period, the aircraft lacked nose wheel steering.

The troubled J40 was canceled and Douglas had to adapt their jet for the J57 delivering 9,700 lbf (43.2 kN) dry and 14,800 lbf (65.8 kN) wet. This required the redesign of the inlet ducts that, given the limitations of the existing airframe, could not provide optimal airflow and so thrust production suffered. As the USAF was then dominating J57 production, there was a delay outfitting the DAC jets. All this meant that the type did not become operational as a fleet asset until 1956. The F4D-1 spanned 33.6 feet (10.2 m) with 557 feet² (51.8 m²) wing area, had an empty weight of 16,024 lb (7,268 kg) and gross of 27,116 lb (12,300 kg), with a maximum 722 mph (1,162 m) and initial rate of climb of 18,300 fpm (5,578 mpm). It was built in the hundreds and served honorably for many years.

The long gestation of the Skyray gave the designers time to contemplate test results and conceive an improved all-weather variant. Initially identified as the F4D-2N, this was eventually designated the F5D-1 Skylancer. This was to encompass the same engine, but with thinner wings, a lengthened forebody for added fuel volume, an extended tail cone, and many aerodynamic refinements for greater performance. Systems would be the latest generation autopilot, flight data computer, gunsight, FCS, and ballistic computer for bomb delivery. The preliminary design was underway in late 1953, and so this development lies beyond the scope of this volume.

The growing weight and complexity of naval fighters was a concern to some. Especially with their failed turboprop A2D (see page 205) as an example, Douglas undertook design studies, seeking solutions. Their preliminary single-engine jet design had a marked reduction in empty weight and dimensions, allowed by the delta wing augmented with a tail, that did not require any folding. With pure jet fighters then considered suitable for the attack mission, the navy bought into the concept and gave the firm a June 1952 contract for two A4D-1 prototypes and nineteen pre-production examples.

The empty weight was to be on the order of 8,000 lb (3,629 kg), wing area around 250 feet² (23.2 m²), and top speed over 600 mph (966 kph). The 7,200-lbf (32-kN) J65 was the identified powerplant. There were to be two 20-mm cannon in the wing roots and four underwing store stations for 5,000 lb (2,268 kg) of external weapons and fuel. One of its principal missions was delivery the new generation of tactical nukes. The A4D-1 first flew in 1954 and so is left for other sources to detail. Suffice to say the Skyhawk (as the A-4) had a remarkable decades-long career through many variants and operators, as well as a couple of wars.

The navy's solicitation went out in August 1952 for the supersonic day fighter. They awarded an April 1953 contract to Grumman for a spin-off of the F9F series, though it shared nothing in common. Initially the F9F-9, this eventually became the F11F-1 Tiger powered by the proven J65 with AB addition. It was the smallest airframe that could engulf the engine fed by side inlets, initially without boundary layer diverters. The fuselage would employ area ruling to cut transonic drag—the first aircraft designed from concept with the feature. There were belly speedbrakes at the front and mid-fuselage. To ensure a very thin wing of sufficient structural strength, the skins were milled from aluminum planks with integral stiffeners. Slats were joined by full-span flaps and roll spoilers.

The YF11F-1 flew in July 1954, but it had to await the afterburner, which proved problematic. Inlet splitters had to be added and the vertical tail redesigned. Even with

This June 31, 1953, image shows one of the two XF4D-1 Skyrays (124586) at NAS Patuxent River during flight testing in which solutions to tail buzz were being explored. The construct around the engine exhaust was one such modification subjected to flight testing. The rounded delta wing with trailing edge root pitch trim wedges and wheel embedded in the tailhook fairing are seen to advantage. One of the more streamlined external tanks that had begun to appear is also evident, and cameras have been placed on the tail and beneath the fuselage in preparation for tank separation trials. (*National Archives*)

With jets shown to be effective in the ground attack mission during the Korean Conflict, the need for turboprop attackers like the failed A2D Skyshark became anachronistic. Douglas offered a compact and relatively simple design that sparked the USN's interest. The company soon had a development contract for the A4D-1, with the work falling predominantly beyond 1953. (*National Archives*)

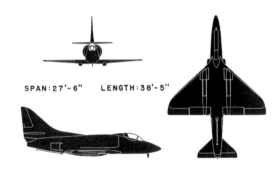

By 1952, the state-of-the-art and practical experience had reached a stage where powerful and reliable jet engines with afterburners could push appropriately designed jet fighters to supersonic airspeeds in level flight. For the navy, they gave a contract to Vought in summer 1953 for the XF8U-1 Crusader. The design extended beyond the scope of this book, but the aircraft became legendary and served a long career. (*National Archives*)

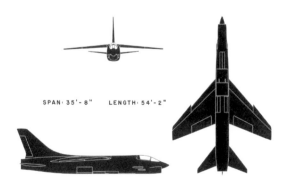

AB, the thrust was always short of expectations and the engine was troublesome. Although carried to production as the navy's first supersonic fighter, the F11F-1 was built in few numbers owing to the disappointing powerplant. A later model substituted another engine, but by then, the design faded in the shadow of the more capable F8U-1.

The USN also gave a contract to Vought in June 1953 for three XF8U-1s, each to be powered by a single J57 at 10,200-lbf (45.4-kN) military power and 16,000-lbf (71.2-kN) maximum power. The company's innovation was a low deck angle for pilot vision during low-speed carrier approach and landing achieved by tilting the wing up 7 degrees with two hydraulic actuators. They also used stabilators and a chin inlet for low drag. Area ruling would help reduce transonic drag to permit supersonic flight. The jet would make extensive use of magnesium and titanium plus wet wings. The aircraft first flew in 1955, and the Crusader was very successful.

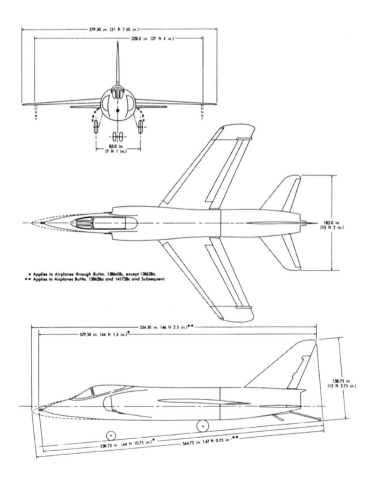

This period drawing of the F11F-1 shows the original nose dimensions as well as a later lengthened nose plus later intake diverter. The AR probe at the apex of the nose is also a later addition. The drawing reveals the area-ruled pinched waist of the aircraft and the swept-wing control surfaces of full-span flaps and roll spoilers plus leading-edge slats. (*Author's collection*)

6

Deviant Fighters

The struggle for greater fighter performance and operational flexibility compelled services to pursue design options well off the common path. There was much to be learned about building successful turbine-powered fighters. Yet while much was gathered from these programs during a time when many aircraft configurations were being experimented with seeking superiority, many poor products also emerged. Considerable resources were expended that could have been put to better use. A more considered approach was advisable. Yet many felt that a "race" for capabilities in a competition between services and with the Soviets was justified.

Hybrids

The cautionary propeller recip-jet hybrids did not last long after the war. These had been born from concern over the slow throttle response and high fuel consumption of the early turbojets. Particularly for carrier operations, jets were considered marginally safe. That these were also tricycle gear designs was further cause for naval service pause that was only just accommodating to this feature.

From the war was the Curtiss XF15C-1, which had a J36 in back, fed by wing root inlets, and a R-2800 in front. Tested through 1946, the tail had to be redesigned, and one of the three prototypes was lost in an accident, along with the test pilot. The aircraft was judged as too short of requirements and dropped in 1947. There was an alternative in the Ryan FR-1. Using a 1,610-lbf (7.2-kN) J31, with wing root inlets, and a 1,350-hp (1,007-kW) Wright R-1820, the development encountered similar pitfalls. The war urgency had the aircraft in production by the end of hostilities, only to be truncated to sixty-six delivered in 1945. In fleet service, the Fireball had excellent maneuverability, but it proved too lightly built for carrier work and was withdrawn in 1947.

The Curtiss XF15C-1 dated from the war and represented the navy's caution in moving to jets. It had a J36 in the aft fuselage and an R-2800 in the nose to help ensure carrier suitability and mission endurance, using the jet principally for a high-speed dash. This photograph dates from December 3, 1946, with the revised empennage and after the program had been terminated. (*Naval Aviation Archives*)

Ryan FR-1 Characteristics

span	40 feet (12.2 m)	weight empty	7,689 lb (3,488 kg)
length	32.3 feet (9.9 m)	gross	9,958 lb (4,517 kg)
height	13.9 feet (4.2 m)	maximum	11,652 lb (5,285 kg)
wing area	275 feet² (25.6 m²)	speed, max. (17,800 feet)	404 mph (650 kph)
fuel, int.+ext.	180+200 gal (681+757 l)	recip. only (sea level)	287 mph (462 kph)
service ceiling	43,100 feet (13,137 m)	cruise	160 mph (258 kph)
climb rate, initial	4,650 fpm (1,417 mpm)	range, normal	930 miles (1,497 km)
		maximum	1,620 miles (2,607 km)

The experimental XFR-2 had a more powerful R-1820.[1] Substituting the J39 was proposed for the XFR-3, but it was dropped when the engine was canceled.

In answer to a navy requirement for a turboprop-turbojet mix, a FR-1 was retrofitted with a 1,700-hp (1,268-kW) General Electric TG-100 "prop-jet" (T31); this also delivered 550 lbf (2.5 kN) of jet thrust. The dorsal extension of the vertical had to be expanded to compensate for the added torque from the four-blade 11-foot (3.4-m) Hamilton Standard prop plus turbine disk. The blade pitch could be flattened during the landing approach to steepen the glide path via drag for a shorter landing. Then, when the weight-on-wheels signal came, the blades went into reverse.

This XF2R-1 was first flown in 1946 as the USN's first turboprop to fly. While being more than 1,000 lb (436 kg) heavier than the FR-1, even with all naval features like the arresting hook and the folding wing removed, it still possessed an impressive climb rate, setting a world altitude record. Yet the T31 was still immature, and the jet fighters on the

As another expression of initial apprehension regarding jet fighter suitability for naval operations, the navy created a few hybrids such as this Ryan FR-1 with a turbojet in the aft fuselage and a reciprocating engine in the nose. It had too little to recommend it when the jets began operating from carrier decks and so were built in small numbers for a brief service life. (*San Diego Air & Space Museum*)

horizon were seen as rendering the Darkshark obsolete before it reached the fleet. The USAF considered a XF2R-2 version, switching to the 4,200-lbf (18.7-kN) J34. To test this installation, a Fireball was modified with an extended aft fuselage. The wing root inlets were replaced with NACA flush inlets on the fuselage side. These could be closed via electrical doors to cut drag when the turbojet was not operating. While this XFR-4 had a 100-mph (161-kph) advantage on the FR-1, the XF2R-2 did not advance beyond the mock-up stage because it promised less than the turbojets just around the corner.

In August 1943, the USAAF had reached for what many must have thought to be "unobtianium" with a high-speed, single-seat, long-range bomber escort matching the extraordinary range of the B-29. The air force was hoping for a 500-mph (805-kph) top speed—dictating a turbojet—with 250-mph (402-kph) cruise matched with a 1,250-mile (2,012-km) range. The high fuel burn rate of the early turbojets suggested that it would only be used for bursts of speed. This brought forth the concept of a hybrid. Convair was placed on contract in February 1944 for an airplane with a J33 in the rear and T31 in front—the aircraft becoming the first aircraft to fly the T31. The aircraft had a loaded weight of 19,500 lb (8,845 kg), spanned 50.5 feet (4.7 m), and was to have either half a dozen 20-mm cannon or .50-cal MGs.

With the "propeller turbine" slow emerging from the test cell, the XP-81 ran late. It was December 1945 before the twin-turbine configuration flew, but both powerplants performed below expectations and the T31 was troublesome to boot. Speed fell short of specs and mechanical problems were discouraging. By 1946, the desire was for pure jets, and the XP-81 was allowed to fade. It may have had the first American ejection seat, likely developed by Convair itself.

Ryan's XF2R-1 Darkshark was captured over the California desert in this January 20, 1947, image, emphasizing the turbojet engine exhaust under the tail and turboprop in the nose. Although possessing a record-setting climb rate, the aircraft was not going to compete with the jets on the way. (*National Archives*)

The XFR-4 (39665) was a testbed for the turbojet installation planned for an air force version of the Fireball, the XF2R-2, which never flew. The XFR-4 substituted a J34 in an extended fuselage and eliminated the wing root inlets for flush NACA designs with ramps that could be closed when the jet engine was secured. The XF2R-2 mock-up shows the NACA inlets in the closed position, a taller vertical stabilizer, a bubble canopy, and four 20-mm cannon matched with rockets. (*Jay Miller collection*)

Convair's XP-81 44-91000 (fitted with wing slipper tanks) runs up the turboprop at Edwards AFB in preparation for a test flight. Dating from the war, the aircraft only got its turboprop after and flight testing ran through 1947. Convair built the XP-81 for a bomber escort contract in which the USAAF sought not only long-range but also high speed. The thought was that a turbojet in the tail could provide the airspeed boost while a turboprop in the nose was more efficient for cruise. The General Electric powerplants were slow coming and then performed below expectations, and so the XP-81 withered. (*Tony Landis collection*)

Turboprops Disappoint

In the early postwar period, the navy was seeking the next generation of attacker. There was concern at the time about fast jet fighters filling the role suitably. Yet any prop-driven aircraft had to be as fast as possible to stay clear of any such enemy interceptors. With reciprocating engines at the limit of their potential, the service considered turboprops as offering the marked increase in power and contra-rotating props best converting the power to thrust. These were also less of a "gas hog" compared with the turbojets and the prop controls allowed more rapid response to throttle. The first requirement for a turbine-powered naval attacker was expressed in June 1945.

Douglas was placed on contract to perform design studies and wind tunnel tests to inform decisions along this path. Although the results were reported in 1946, it was another year before the navy had a turboprop engine ready for application and the new attack program could move forward. The developmental T40 appeared to have more than adequate power, as delivered by the contra-rotating propellers. The requirement called for an aircraft capable of operating from the short-deck escort carriers with a 600-mile (966-km) radius of action and 438 mph (705 kph) top speed.

Douglas won again with a June 1947 preliminary contract, followed in September by an order for two XA2D-1 prototypes. The Skyshark was a conventional straight-wing evolution of the AD. The high speed compelled the adoption of a comparatively thin 12 percent wing, challenging the ability to stow the main landing gear. A large-paneled speedbrake lay in the belly. Dual inlets for the engine were placed in the nose and large exhausts in the fuselage's sides. Douglas designed the engine installation for simplified removal by sliding the entire assembly, with nose mounts, forward on rails to expose hoist points. Blown plexiglass canopies were not then suitable for the expected high speed of the A2D, and so single-curvature glass panels were used in a framed enclosure. A Douglas cartridge-powered ejection seat was fitted, designed leveraging data from German wartime seats. Four 20-mm cannon were placed in the wings and external weapon stations included three primary and eight secondary stations for a full 8,000-lb (3,629-kg) loadout. All manner of stores were expected to be carried with individual weapons up to 2,000 lb (907 kg) plus a 300-gal (1,136-l) drop tank. An AN/APS-19A radar antenna was to be placed in the propeller spinner.

Allison was late delivering T40s, with its 14-foot (4.3-m) diameter, six-blade Aeroproducts propeller, and so the completed DAC airframe waited a year for an engine. The first powerplant was provided with severe interim operational limitation, but it allowed flight testing to begin in March 1950. The breakout of the Korean Conflict added urgency to moving the program ahead. During 1950, Douglas began to receive production orders for the airplane. However, the T40 remained the pacing item—at a sluggish pace. An unusual aspect of the very noisy engine was that the acoustic waves produced by the propeller as it went through various speed ranges had deleterious effects on personnel nearby, including vibrating joints and producing nausea. The navy considered substituting the 5,700-hp (4,251-kW) T34, but P&W could not commit to a rapid development of a version geared for the contra-prop that was seen as essential in avoiding the powerful torque of the thrust generation.[2]

Douglas XA2D-1 Characteristics

span	50 feet (15.2 m)	weight empty	14,139 lb (6,413 kg)
length	41.4 feet (12.6 m)	combat	18,720 lb (8,491 kg)
height	18.9 feet (5.8 m)	gross	22,966 lb (10,417 kg)
wing area	400 feet² (37 m²)	speed, max. (25,000 feet)	501 mph (806 kph)
fuel, int.+ext.	500+300 gal (1,893+1,136 l)	cruise	286 mph (460 kph)
combat ceiling	48,400 feet (14,752 m)	range, combat	1,708 miles (2,749 km)
climb rate, max.	7,290 fpm (2,222 mpm)		

By December 1950, the XA2D-1 had made sufficient progress to permit initial navy evaluations. During one of these flights, one of the twin engines failed and the pilot failed to declutch it from the gearbox. With greatly degraded power, the aircraft came down to a fatal impact. Subsequently, Allison began developing an auto-decouple feature while adding improved failure indications to the cockpit. Flight of the second prototype was delayed until spring 1952 by engine issues. The aircraft eventually flew with a T40 that was more representative of the production design, but this too suffered numerous failures and limitations. This airplane also featured a new canopy with double-curved plexiglass.

Douglas envisioned the A2D assuming all the myriad roles serviced by the AD. However, the Allison was so troubled that even the baseline model had to be

Planning to replace the Douglas AD Skyraider with a faster mount, the navy tasked the same airframer with the task. The first XA2D-1 runs its turboprop engine with contra-rotating propeller. The nearby personnel show the scale of the large attack aircraft. (*San Diego Air & Space Museum*)

abandoned. By that time, the Korean Conflict had shown that jets could perform the attack mission suitably and the Skyraider was more than satisfactory. Skyshark production plans were dropped during 1952, although ten were finished and six flown. Persistent engine glitches led to another crash. The remaining prototype and two of the production examples were passed to Allison for continued engine work. Although navy and DAC flight testing ended in 1955, Allison pressed on for a few more years.

Rocket Addition

One of the earliest postwar programs was to develop a jet interceptor with tremendous performance. This was to defend point targets from enemy bombers that, it was presumed, would soon become jet-powered, high-speed craft armed with A-bombs. The delivery of just one weapon could be devastating, and so the fighter had to get to the bomber's altitude in as brief a time as possible and execute the intercept just as quickly. The tentative USAAF requirement of August 1945 sought a daylight supersonic airplane reaching 50,000 feet (15,240 m) in four minutes with a top speed of 700 mph (1,127 kph) at altitude. Armament was projected to be 20-mm cannon and Falcon AAM. The requirement of September 1947 sought to climb to 47,500 feet (14,478 m) in 2.5 minutes and 790 mph (1,271 kph) cruise.

Republic and Convair won the competition in spring 1946 for the XP-91 and XP-92, respectively. Development then moved slowly given the postwar cutbacks and preliminary design challenges. These were the first American contracts seeking the production of supersonic aircraft. The extraordinary requirements compelled the designers to reach for some equally innovative solutions. Swept wings were certainly going to be required to push out the critical Mach number.

At the time, only rocket motors were expected to boost the aircraft to altitude in the required time. The air force had several under development, of various propellant types and thrust ratings, aimed at manned flight applications. Some were referred to as turborockets because of turbo pumps delivering the propellants to the combustion chamber. Curtiss-Wright and Reaction Motors were among the contractors. The top speed was also unlikely to be reached by the jet engines of the time, suggesting some exotic propulsion systems like ramjets or supplemental rocket motors. The high speed suggested supersonic flight, with high transonic drag to overcome. Such had yet to be achieved, and for which wind tunnels were still lacking, so design guidelines were few.

Convair's XP-92 design was an odd ducted rocket/ramjet with a couple of external booster rockets, a V-tail, and thin 35-degree swept wings. The external rockets would push the craft to ramjet operating speed while more than a dozen low thrust internal rockets also served as the flame-holder for ramjet combustion. The rockets would power the take-off from a cart, which also contained fuel cells, and would be left behind on the runway. A J30 also served as auxiliary propulsion to support a low-speed return to land on lightweight tricycle undercarriage. Mission duration might be just thirty minutes.

The wind tunnel test results did not bode well for the aerodynamic layout and so the team leaned toward a 60-degree sweep "tailless" delta wing with symmetric airfoils. The flight controls were fully boosted and with artificial feel. Convair consulted NACA plus Lippisch and other Germans working in the states who had conducted research on deltas. Apart from wind tunnel tests, delta shapes were also launched on rockets at Wallops to collect aerodynamic data. Avoiding a canopy to cut drag, the cockpit was to be in the inlet diffuser cone. Ejection at high speed would be unsafe and so the entire forward section of the aircraft would separate and be decelerated by parachute to a speed at which the pilot could bail out. The turbojet was deleted in favor of an APU—a racecar engine aspirated with vaporized LOX—to provide power for accessories. During take-off and climb, the thirsty rocket motors were fed via drop tanks.

In fall 1947, two prototypes had been added to the Convair contract along with a delta-wing demonstrator. However, it would be fair to say that there were few easy aspects of XP-92 development. The propulsion system remained in flux, given the infant state of the rocket motors and even the propellants to be used. Throttling of such a system was not as reliable as for a jet engine and mission flexibility was meager, with the entire concept of marginal practicality. The first prototype would not fly until the summer of 1949, at the earliest, and fielding likely years beyond that. The aircraft was essentially a recoverable manned missile at a time expendable unmanned missile looked to be close to fruition. In summer 1948, the Convair design was assessed as too risky and the program canceled after the expenditure of some $3.4 million. The contract was reduced to the delta wing research aircraft as the XF-92A (see page 60).

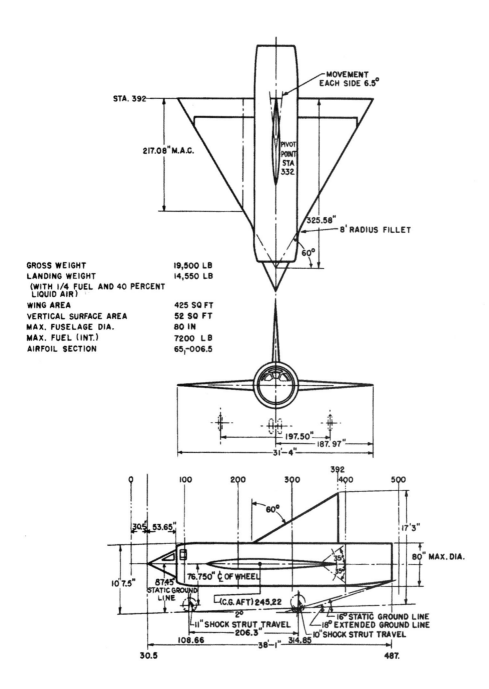

GROSS WEIGHT — 19,500 LB
LANDING WEIGHT — 14,550 LB
(WITH 1/4 FUEL AND 40 PERCENT
LIQUID AIR)
WING AREA — 425 SQ FT
VERTICAL SURFACE AREA — 52 SQ FT
MAX. FUSELAGE DIA. — 80 IN
MAX. FUEL (INT.) — 7200 LB
AIRFOIL SECTION — 65₁-006.5

In 1947, the concept of an interceptor to climb to 50,000 feet in minutes and accelerate to beyond the speed of sound looked like this. Convair's design for the XP-92 was to employ a ramjet supplemented by rocket motors and with the aerodynamic innovation of a delta planform. After years of work, the design was considered to encompass too great a technological risk and was set aside. (*National Museum of the United States Air Force*)

The Republic XF-91 was initially powered by the 5,200-lbf (23.1-kN) J47 turbojet (unaugmented) fed by an annular inlet. For take-off and climb, this was to be supplemented by a Curtiss-Wright XLR27-CW1 rocket motor with an expected 16,000 lbf (71.2 kN) of thrust divided among four combustion chambers for 90 seconds of operation. Pairs of chambers were optimized for ideal performance at different operating altitudes, producing varying thrust during a climb or operation at altitude. Two chambers were to be placed above and two below the turbojet engine nozzle. The lower housing for the chambers doubled as a ventral surface for flight stability. The LOX and water-denatured ethyl alcohol (WALC) propellants were to be carried internally as well as in two large external tanks. The WALC regeneratively cooled the thrust chambers before being injected for combustion. The propellants tanks were pressurized by helium gas that also purged the motor after firing. With the turbojet in reheat and all four rocket thrust chambers burning, the aircraft was expected to have a 40,000-fpm (12,192-mpm) climb rate or Mach 2 dash.

The Thunderceptor's thin, 35-degree sweep wings precluded typical landing gear stowage within the wing. Consequently, Republic used two narrow wheels per side that were mounted in tandem on the trucks. The wing had an inverse thickness taper such that the slatted wings were thicker at the tip to accommodate the stowage of the gear and the covering door. Republic also worked to avoid the notorious swept-wing problems of tip stall before the root during high angle of attack maneuvering. The designers chose an inverse chord taper for a wider wing chord at the tip than the root. This would also have the less desirable effect of moving the center of lift outboard for greater root bending loads. Designing the structure to support such loads meant heavier assemblies, but Republic judged this an acceptable trade-off. In addition to all this, the incidence of the entire wing could be raised as much as 6-degree leading-edge-up for safer take-off and landing via a larger margin on stall. It could be rotated down as much as 2 degrees for a more efficient cruise. The motion was accomplished via two actuators. It was thought that the use of the feature in combat might add to agility. Lending even more to the odd appearance of the airplane, the horizontal tails lacked chord taper.

The aircraft incorporated cockpit pressurization and a catapult seat apparently developed by Republic itself. The two very large underwing tanks had three cells separating the three fuels. These tanks could be jettisoned via pneumatic pistons to push the units clear of the aircraft. A belly panel speedbrake was also featured. The aircraft grossed 28,300 lb (12,837 kg).

From a May 1946 contract award, it was three years before the aircraft flew in May 1949 without the delayed rocket motor. The wing design and leading-edge slats were shown to give the XF-91 very good low-speed maneuverability. The second ship was fitted with an afterburner for 7,500-lbf (33.4-kN) of thrust. The USAF eventually gave up on the Curtiss motor and had a four-chamber 6,000-lbf (26.7-kN) Reaction Motors XLR-11 modified for installation in the XF-91's enlarged ventral housing. The rocket was first fired in flight during December 1952 and the aircraft reached Mach 1.07 under 11,200 lbf (49.8 kN) of combined thrust. It also climbed to 45,000 feet (13,716 m) in 2.5 minutes. This was the first developmental aircraft (not research) that had gone supersonic in level flight, and the only "rocket fighter" to be demonstrated in the U.S.

The XF-91 remained experimental, with the weapons never fitted. It was not going to sustain supersonic flight with just the J47 given its aerodynamic design, and the rocket was cumbersome. Area defense had become the goal during 1951. By 1953, projected aircraft with newer engines were expected to come suitably close to the initial bomber interceptor requirements. Time had run out for the rocket fighter.

The solid propellant JATO booster motors were the most common, but a liquid propellant alternative was created for the air force that burned JP-4 and nitric acid. While the 23,300-lbf (104-kN) Aerojet LR63-AJ-1 was technically successful, being lighter than the bottles and permitting shutdown instead of just burnout, servicing hazardous nitric acid was a minus. Yet with the F-86A a near match for the MiG-15 in Korea, the USAF considered adding the rocket motor for combat enhancement. The motor was tested under the aft fuselage of an F-84G during 1952. A few additional tests on USAF and navy fighters continued into the late 1950s.[3]

Seaplane Fighter

As part of the USN's SSF concept, a transonic jet fighter was to provide protection for the SSF. A small fighter capable of operating in the open sea, something even huge flying boats found hazardous, initially appeared impractical. Yet concepts began to be explored in 1948. Convair proposed a blended wing-body "Skate" seaplane with a swept wing and retractable hull step that was more compatible with supersonic flight. This won a preliminary design contract in 1949 as the Y2-1. However, the research work on the hydro-ski (see pages 88–91) showed a possible solution in that the classic features of the seaplane hull could be eliminated with more aerodynamic shaping adopted. Concepts were explored via powerboat-towed models and radio-controlled scale airplanes. BuAer converged on a twin-engine fighter incorporating the hydro-ski, for which a specification was issued in October 1950. Combining the new delta wing with a watertight fuselage for floatation, hydro-skis, and reach for supersonic airspeeds held much design risk. Convair accepted the challenge in January 1951 with a contract for two XF2Y-1s.

The SeaDart was initially to be powered by two afterburning J46s at 6,100 lbf (27 kN) each, but this engine fell behind schedule and the non-afterburning J34 at 3,400 lbf (15 kN) was substituted temporarily. The engines were mounted above the wings to be clear of spray. Auxiliary blow-in doors aft of the intakes supplemented airflow during low-speed operation. The end of the fuselage had speedbrake panels that also served as water rudders. The initial configuration used two skis extending from the belly of the fighter via individual forward and aft oleo struts. These had wheels with brakes at their aft end and a castoring wheel was in a keel at the extreme aft end of the fuselage. These permitted the fighter to be taxied into and out of the water via a seaplane ramp. It placed the jet in an exceedingly nose-high attitude while also aiming the engines' exhaust onto the surface. The wing was swept 60 degrees with

Left: Republic XF-91 Thunderceptor had a turbojet engine supplemented with a rocket booster. The fairings above and below the exhaust were for the four thrust chambers. The twin tandem main gear wheels were narrow to retract outboard completely into the wings that had unique inverse thickness taper. They also had inverse chord taper to combat adverse stall characteristics of the swept surfaces. (*National Archives*)

Below: An F-84G takes off from Edwards AFB assisted by a rocket below the engine exhaust, though intended for intercept engagement of another fast jet. This was the Aerojet XLR63-AJ-1 generating 23,300 lbf (104 kN). The rocket fuels are likely in the under-wing tanks—though there appear to be other small cells under the aft fuselage. (*National Museum of the United States Air Force*)

a symmetrical airfoil, and Mach 1.4 was sought. Flight controls were fully powered. A Convair ejection seat and a radar were fitted. The suggested armament was four 20-mm cannon and forty-eight 2.75-inch rockets in two mid-body pop-out doors.[4]

Following only the mock-up inspection, a contract for twelve production F2Y-1s powered by the J46 was signed in August 1952. Although later amended to include preproduction YF2Y-1s, this was still an extraordinary move given the experimental nature of the program that had yet to demonstrate the most fundamental of its exotic operations.[5]

The XF2Y-1 first operated on the water in December 1952 immediately encountered severe airframe vibrations that affected the pilot's ability to function, suggesting a very short airframe life plus high equipment failure rates. The blunt aft end of the skis passing over waves combined with ski flexing was the culprit. The design of the fuselage itself created a resonance that amplified the "ski-pounding" further. This grew so severe near liftoff speed that pilots reported a total loss of vision. At some point, the flight test nose boom broke away owing to the extreme vibrations. Solving the problem proved a protracted exercise such that the first flight did not occur until April 1953.

The first YF2Y-1 to reach test began operating in summer 1954. However, the J46 was revealed to be plagued with problems and generated only 5,725 lbf (25 kN), although it permitted the high-speed flight tests the J34 denied. While the aircraft did exceed the speed of sound in a dive (a unique achievement for a seaplane), this could not be achieved in level flight without such drag-reducing measures as area-ruling.[6] Wing fences were added to discourage spanwise airflow.

Among the changes to combat the ski-pounding were revisions to their aft end, altering the shock-absorbing characteristics of the forward struts, and extending the aft end of the fuselage with exhaust scoops. For a time, the ski wheels were deleted, mandating the use of beaching gear. Some attenuation was achieved, but a complete solution remained elusive. Alterations continued as the central focus of the program. One such was the adoption of a wider and more rigid single ski. This was not fully retractable and so precluded high-speed flight. However, S&C on the water was greatly compromised, especially in a crosswind. A revised twin-ski design was then substituted and progress was made.

At the beginning of a take-off run, the skis were fully extended and broke the surface at about 8–10 knots (9–12 mph/15–19 kph). Above about 15–20 knots (17–23 mph/28–37 kph), the elevons provided directional control. The ski oleos were in an intermediate position until between 40–60 knots (46–69 mph/74–111 kph), and then extended to full length for the remaining run to liftoff with rotation at 125 knots (144 mph/232 kph). The thin, symmetrical delta wing required a high nose attitude of 17–19 degrees to become airborne. The skis were retracted after take-off to permit high-speed flight. Time for a take-off run averaged thirty-five seconds. A take-off and landing in 10–12-foot (3–4-m) seas was successful but very hazardous.

Convair YF2Y-1 Characteristics (Some Figures Estimates)

span	33.7 feet (10.38 m)	weight empty	12,652 lb (5,739 kg)
length	52.6 feet (16 m)	loaded	16,725 lb (7,586 kg)
height, beaching gear	16.2 feet (4.9 m)	max. take-off	21,500 lb (9,752 kg)
wing area	568 feet² (53 m²)	speed, max. (35,000 feet)	825 mph (1.328 kph)
fuel	615 gal (2,328 l)	max. level	Mach 0.99
service ceiling	54,800 feet (16,703 m)	range (estimated)	513 miles (826 km)
climb rate, initial	17,100 fpm (5,212 mpm)		

One feature of the J46 was that starting required an external compressed air source such that a restart in flight was not possible and even a restart on the water would require a boat with the air cart. Salt accumulation on the engine blades caused a deterioration of performance after just a short time operating on the water. This could be resolved with freshwater sprayed into the inlet with the engine rotating. A 20-gal (76-l) water tank and spay lines were added to the aircraft to permit this to be performed by the pilot, but it represented yet another impediment to routine ops.

Operationally, a production F2Y seemed a very limited combat aircraft. How the fighter might be serviced and maintained under the MBC was explored. Recovery trials with a Landing Ship, Dock (LSD) were performed. It was found impractical given that the jet could not taxi into the well. After engine shutdown, it had to be winched in with care to avoid damage to the wings. Under even moderate winds and sea, this was too fraught. Perhaps a larger ship would have been satisfactory. One concept of seabasing that was not tested was a modified CVE with a recovery ramp at the stern.[7]

By March 1954, the USN had lost hope for a production run of the fighter, and with no operational requirement ever having been approved, the F2Y-1 order was reduced to four YF2Y-1s. Only two were ever fitted with engines and operated. In November 1954, the initial YF2Y-1 and test pilot was lost in an inflight breakup during a low-altitude, high-speed pass, owing to a divergent pitch oscillation. This was in front of the press and navy "brass" during a demonstration of MBC. Testing continued, focused on gaining the most data from the ski configurations, abandoning flight trails altogether apart from take-off and landings. The navy worked with a PBM fitted with a single ski seeking solutions, but those only showed a similar detrimental vibration. The next YF2F-1 began operating in 1955 with further revised twin skis and wheels restored. The XF2Y-1, which was also fitted with J46s and the aft fuselage modification, got a much smaller single ski. This produced such severe pounding that the aircraft never exceeded 50–60 knots. Tests with JATO were also conducted. Although trials continued into 1957, the airframe vibrations and abuse of the pilot remained unacceptable for safe and routine operation. It was a unique experiment, but this approach to jet fighter sea operations appeared a dead-end.

With the Regulus cruise missile (see page 440) operating from several modified submarines, the navy explored a manned aircraft launched from the same hull hangar. The service tasked Douglas with the design, and in 1952, the company offered the Model 640. Even at 32 feet (9.8 m) in length and 25 feet (7.6 m) in span, plus 7,800

This photo of YF2Y-1 135762 was taken on November 4, 1954, in San Diego on the occasion of the navy's MBC demonstration for which the R3Y in the background was included. The SeaDart broke up in flight, and the pilot was killed shortly after this photo was taken. The aircraft shows the twin ski configuration without aft wheels, accounting for the beaching gear installation. (*Jay Miller collection*)

lb (3,538 kg) normal GW, the small airplane would fit in the hangar only by folding the nose and vertical tail in addition to the wings. The jet was to be rail-launched and, lacking undercarriage, would land on its belly ashore or ditch beside a vessel. Drawings appear to show the aircraft carrying a centerline Mk 7 tactical nuclear store.[8] By the time this design emerged, it was looking like carrier-based fighters could perform the nuclear strike mission and submarines would become ballistic missile platforms. The Model 640 did not move forward.

Vertical Dimension

In another effort by the U.S. Navy to adapt to the new dimensions of airpower, they sought a defense fighter that could take off and land vertically. Launched on radar warning of a threat, it would hold back the attackers until carrier aviation was in range to respond. From the joint VSTOL study begun in 1947 (see page 93), the navy began a more determined study of a naval VTOL fighter the next year. It appeared that turbine engines had achieved the ability the deliver more than 1:1 thrust:weight ratio and so facilitate such vertical take-off and landing of a fighter. The service envisioned operations from a deck of the barest dimensions. This pad could be placed on individual ships of a convoy or many varieties of naval vessels and so would carry their air defense with them rather than rely on a carrier air wing. This suggested a "tail sitter"-type aircraft that would convert to forward flight after taking off vertically, and then revert to vertical flight for a backward landing on the tiny pad aboard a moving vessel at sea. The aircraft would be housed inside a "tepee"-like shelter that would swing aside to expose the aircraft ready to launch.

BuAer sought the assistance of NACA in 1949 to help in focusing on a solution. The effects of jet blast or propeller downwash on the tiny flight deck and surroundings had to be considered. The assumed powerplant became the T40 driving contra-rotating propellers for a lower velocity of downwash than a jet plume. The NACA tested their model of a likely aircraft with 2-foot (0.6-m) diameter props driven by a 5-hp (3.7-kW) electric motor. Encouraged by the outcome, the USN sought bids from the industry in September 1950. The mission clearly presented very great challenges, but the USN found willing bidders. It awarded two prototype contracts in May 1951. This was unusual for the period, but it reflected the great technical risk and the desire to have two separate teams attacking the problems with possibly different solutions.

Convair and Lockheed were each to build two tailsitting VSTOL aircraft powered by the 5,850-hp (4,362-kW) T40. A production example of the Allison was expected to deliver 7,100 hp (5,295 kW). Curtiss-Wright turboelectric contra-rotating propellers would convert the power to thrust. This had six blades with 16-foot (4.9-m) diameter. The proposed armament was two or four 20-mm cannon and forty-eight rockets; the rockets to be carried in wingtip pods.

Convair's XFY-1 had delta wings plus identical ventral and dorsal fins, creating a cruciform arrangement of aft edges. Swiveling wheels shock-mounted at the tip of these surfaces facilitated motion on the ground. The wings had elevons and the smaller surfaces rudders. The delta has superior lift characteristics at extreme angles of attack than a straight wing and so was felt to be more suitable for the conversion and reconversion phases of flight. A large spinner ahead of the propellers enclosed a parachute that was to be shot out and inflated clear of the props. This, it was hoped, could allow an emergency recovery of the aircraft in the event of an engine failure— the Convair ejection seat a hopeful second option. The aircraft spanned 27.7 feet (8.4 m), stood 32.3 feet (9.8 m), and had a combat weight of 13,250 lb (6,010 kg). The top speed was expected to be 489 mph (222 kph).

Lockheed's XFV-1 was more like the NACA model with straight wings and cruciform tail surfaces. Only the four tails had control surfaces and trim tabs. These also had the shock-mounted castoring wheels at the tips. The aircraft's projected combat weight was 15,000 lb (6,804 kg), initial rate of climb 10,820 fpm (3,298 mpm), and maximum speed 595 mph (958 kph). The wing spanned 27.4 feet (8.3 m), and the airplane stood 37.5 feet (11.4 m). It featured a Lockheed ejection seat. Both contractors assembled special transporter/erector rigs to move their aircraft in a horizontal orientation and then place it vertically for flight. Special ladders also had to be constructed to allow the pilot to enter the cockpit high above the ground.

As the contractors performed detailed design studies, the profound challenges of this configuration of VTOL aircraft became clearer. Take-off and transition to forward flight by pushing over to level was a fairly straightforward proposition. Transitioning back to vertical flight would pose the problem of getting through wing stall and arresting both forward and upward velocity. This reconversion would be a pull-up at idle power followed by a rapid increase in power at just the right moment to establish a hover. The power would then be modulated to affect the slow and controlled descent to a vertical landing.

Lacking references, a pilot would have difficulty judging altitude and rate of descent beyond just one or two aircraft lengths. Engine control had to be fine and respond immediately to adjust vertical velocity. Likewise for aerodynamic control of attitude. This derived from propwash over the surfaces, and so effectiveness varied with throttle movement controlling the rate of descent. The control strategy would not have the conventional sense, with the aircraft neutrally stable in this mode and flying backward. Once near the landing surface, the propwash is reflected back onto the aircraft to alter control behavior again.

A seat orientation suitable for forward flight would have the pilot fall away from the controls lying backward with the aircraft vertical. So, a dual-orientation seat was necessary, being adjustable in flight. Adjusting the seat while also transitioning to vertical flight appeared a fraught exercise. The pilot also had arms and legs extended up to the controls, and this would be quite tiring. These projects came before the age of digital fly-by-wire, and so all control was mechanical (save for electronic prop control). The pilot looking over a shoulder while backing down to a spot landing would find the effort exhausting and precision nearly impossibly.

Ensuring that the aircraft was perfectly vertical such that it would not topple over upon touchdown and throttle idle would be exceptionally difficult. The wheels at the end of this tall aircraft had to swivel given how it might drift under power, especially on landing until power was cut to "press" the aircraft down. Yet this also meant that wind could move the aircraft across the surface or even topple it.

To say such an operation, with multiple piloting techniques and changing control sensitivity, was a very difficult piloting task would be an understatement.

The program was delayed by the late arrival of engines. Allison could deliver only one article with the special lubrication system permitting extended operation in a vertical orientation. The second would be much delayed, and ultimately, this was cause to cancel the second prototype from each contractor. The XFV-1 design, with its cruciform tails oriented off the plane of the wings, could accommodate flight test landing gear permitting horizontal take-off and landing. Consequently, Lockheed received a T40 not cleared for vertical operation to permit flight testing to begin. Stopping after landing was afforded by a drag chute.

The Lockheed team built a quarter-scale flying model of their aircraft for operation in the Ames 40 × 80-foot wind tunnel. This was powered by two 38-hp (28-kW) electric motors. It lent insight into control effectiveness and strategies for safe operation. The Convair test pilot practiced the take-off and landing of helicopters while lying on his back. The company also built a vertical engine test rig with propellers and a simple cockpit. This was operated in the first half of 1954. By the end of the period under study, the two VSTOL fighters were preparing for flight testing.

Convair conducted vertical flight trials tethered from the ceiling of the 195-foot (59-m) tall dirigible hangar at Moffett Field in an effort to train their test pilot for the very difficult vertical take-off and landing task. It was found that the powerful ground wash from the propeller slipstream reflected off the interior walls, creating complicated

Above: The Lockheed XFV-1 was envisioned as a "tailsitter" VTOL aircraft filling a navy mission. For testing, it was fated to fly with conventional take-off and landing using the improvised undercarriage shown because an engine suitable for vertical operation was not delivered. The aircraft is shown at Edwards AFB where testing was conducted. (*Jay Miller collection*)

Left: Convair built a competing VTOL fighter and was fortunate to receive the only engine suitable for vertical operation. The XFY-1 went on to set records as the first "tailsitter" to perform complete conversion and reconversion. However, the vertical operations were exceptionally difficult piloting tasks, and the single prototype had a short career. (*Naval Aviation Archives*)

turbulence patterns that further confounded control. Moving outside, successful vertical take-off, hover, and vertical landings were performed in August 1954—the first for such an airplane. The equally notable first conversion and reconversion were conducted in November 1954. Lockheed began flight testing at the end of 1953 and during the next year demonstrated conversion and reconversions well clear of the ground, but only brief hovers were permitted. When the test pilot attempted to begin a vertical descent, the aircraft tended to lean over and was recovered by adding power.

The projects moved at a very slow pace given the hazards and engineering challenges. By the end of 1954, the T40 was clearly a lost cause. For a time, the navy pinned its hopes on the Allison T54, adequate to lift a useful load, but this engine was also abandoned. The dismal engine situation and flight test results were cause to cancel the program. The XFV-1 never got a suitable engine and so could not conduct VTOL operations. It completed just twenty-seven flights. The experimental aircraft were configured only for testing, lacking any armament or mission systems, and so operational suitability could only be surmised. Regardless, an examination of the test results could only lead to the conclusion of the basic fallacy of the concept. There were jet fighter and missile projects in work that promised capabilities that made the VTOL approach appear unnecessary.

The tailsitting VTOL fighter operation, with a near-prone pilot, was so difficult as to be hazardous. Only the one Convair test pilot that had participated in the Moffett Field tethered training could perform the XFY-1's vertical landing feat. When a second pilot attempted to fly the XFY-1, it ended in a hard landing.[9] Convair and Lockheed both adopted a Doppler system of reflected sound waves to help the pilot determine the rate of descent. Convair used this to illuminate director lights on a wingtip while Lockheed had it provide audio cues in the pilot's earphones. Lockheed ultimately installed a mechanical device at one wingtip that indicated up or down motion via a flopping vane that also rose or dropped along a pole to indicate the very slow vertical velocities. The T40 was so powerful, even with the throttle at idle, that it was difficult to slow the aircraft. The engine and prop controls were "touchy" and still had "teething" problems. The electro-mechanical engine-prop control used vacuum tubes that were prone to failure in the stressful environment. The engine was very sensitive to altitude and ambient temperatures, losing power at elevated temperatures. Testing was only conducted in cool morning air. After just a few dozen operating hours, the XFY-1's engine was showing the deterioration of the gearbox and in need of an overhaul.

Even if these aircraft could have been made practical with a suitable engine, the operational concept appeared impractical. Aboard a vessel, the ground plume would be reflections off nearby vertical ship structure to further complicate the landing task. Adding winds to this would have further stressed the task-saturated pilot. The XFY-1 was only flown in calm winds. Furthermore, ejection seats of the period would not have permitted safe egress at the low altitudes of this hazardous operation and seat orientation. The engine exhaust and propwash created a very powerful ground plume that kicked up any surrounding material. This, in addition to the excessive engine noise, would have made ground support personnel jobs unpleasant duty. In short, there was no hope of a suitable fleet application of the aircraft at that stage or any envisioned with extant technology.

7

Bombers Transform

World War Two had demonstrated the important role of bombing in both tactical and strategic realms for prosecuting a modern war. The delivery of atomic weapons became especially vital. While the war left the American armed forces with considerable superior equipment, these had to be sustained and modernized even as the force was drastically downsized and many types retired. Most bomber/attacker development projects from the war carried forward to continue growing capabilities and to advance the technology. Money was tight and schedules were stretched out, but notable accomplishments were achieved. Bombers were costly, and so new types bought in large numbers were not common. Given the rapid advance of the enabling technology, progressive models of the new types helped to make the bomber more effective while the next generation was in development. The general theme was uprated engines, expanding avionics and ECM content, plus a reduction in defensive armament and so aircrew. By intent, the speed of the new jet bombers grew, setting records, such that even escort appear anachronistic.

The initial turbojet engines produced such modest thrust that JATO rockets were ordinarily needed to get a heavy bomber off in a practical field length. The range was also greatly degraded by the high fuel consumption rate of the engines. These factors and the promise offered by the still-to-emerge turboprops caused a conundrum. While the services sought a speed that the propellers could not support, the turboprops were looked at as potentially rivaling turbojets in fuel consumption. Consequently, AMC pushed studies of these alternatives until about 1949. Some development programs emerged with turboprops during that period. A half-measure was turbine-augmented reciprocating engines that also saw some attention. However, turbojet technology advanced rapidly and kept pushing rivals aside.

Mission separation agreements left land-based bombers as the domain of the new USAF. Yet the navy won some measures that led them to develop quite capable ship-based bombers.

The very large intercontinental bombers became the new heavy bomber while the heavy bombers from the war, namely the B-29, became a medium bomber and the A-26 was rendered a light bomber. For the USAF, the Attack designation fell by the wayside, leaving fighter-bombers to service such missions. When the new jet bombers emerged, the USAF redefined the class by combat radius. The light bomber had a 1,000-mile (1,609-km) range radius, the heavy 2,500 miles (4,023 km), and in between the mediums. For the navy, heavy shipboard bombers retained the Attack designation and shore-based aircraft with bombing capability were "Patrol."

Although in the immediate postwar period it was expected that the number of atomic weapons would be few and their use rare, it was necessary that delivery means be maintained. Atomic weapon development continued and enjoyed success, reducing bomb size only late in the period. The Mk 7 weapon weighed just 1,680 lb (762 kg) and so could be carried by a tactical aircraft. In general, bombs in service were quite large with few suitable delivery platforms, and some potential types were rejected because their bomb bays were too small.

The Elderly

As with all other categories of combat aircraft, the best World War Two bombers were carried forward, generally late-war types, while struggling to bring forward the new. The Douglas A-26 (B-26 with the advent of the USAF) was one such, still relatively new at the end of the war though seeing respectable action and no additional production beyond summer 1945.[1] These were B- and C-model aircraft—with many Bs upgraded to C- standard that permitted an interchangeable nose. They otherwise retained their wartime equipment and supercharged R-2800 engines, though with upgrades such as water injection.

Douglas B-26B Characteristics

span	70 feet (21.3 m)	weight empty	22,370 lb (10,147 kg)
length	50 feet (15.2 m)	design gross	27,600 lb (12,519 kg)
height	18.5 feet (5.6 m)	max. gross	35,000 lb (15,876 kg)
wing area	540.5 feet² (50.2 m²)	speed, max. (15,000 feet)	355 mph (571 kph)
fuel, max. (built-in)	924-2,025 gal (3,498-7,666 l)	cruise	284 mph (457 kph)
service ceiling	22,100 feet (6,736 m)	range, 4,000-lb bombs	1,400 miles (2,253 km)
climb rate, 35,000 lb	1,235 fpm (376 mpm)	ferry	3,200 miles (5,150 km)

The B-29 was the USAAF's principal heavy bomber in the immediate postwar period. The type was retained while B-17s, B-24s, and B-32s were all retired but for special uses. Production of Superfortresses that had been in advanced assembly in August 1945 was allowed to continue to completion, with the last delivered in June 1946. Each had cost approximately $0.6 million. More B-29s were drawn from storage to be reconditioned and placed into service as the U.S. judged it required more military power to respond to potential contingencies. Strategic Air Command had approximately 148 B-29s on force at the end of 1946, 319 by December 1947, and 486 by 1949, although many of these last were being employed as tankers. Aircraft were deployed abroad in what became routine rotations.

The Douglas A-26 from the war was relabeled B-26 and sustained into the next war. Here, a B-26B (44-34331) of the 3rd Bombardment Group, Far East Air Force, is seen in flight over Korea during February 1951 with external rockets and drop tanks. Many of the type were extracted from storage and restored for operations on the peninsula. (*National Archives*)

The B-29s were standardized with the most advanced equipment emerging from the war and then upgraded further to improve mission effectiveness. About six B-29s were modified with the "Andy Gump" cowlings plus fuel-injected engines, with both features tested during the war. The cowling features were not adopted, and these YB-29Js were used for other activities.

At the beginning of the Korean Conflict, the USAF had 1,787 Superfortresses and 162 RB-29s on the books, though most were in storage. The demands of the Asian war, plus combat attrition, meant many of the B-29s in outdoor dry storage were refurbished and upgraded by contractors and government depots, then placed into service. Likewise, Superforts in heavy use in the theater were returned stateside for overhaul and further upgrades.

The initial war plans from October 1946 allowed for striking the Soviet Union with twenty to thirty atomic weapons. This would have stressed the existing B-29 special weapons team. By the end of 1947, the USAF still had only thirty-two B-29s configured for the mission, and these were growing long in the tooth. The efforts to create more A-bombs and a more normalized force moved slowly. An additional 180 B-29s were eventually converted for A-bomb delivery. By the start of 1949, there were 124 Superforts appropriately configured and fifty-six Mk III bombs stockpiled. Still more B-29s were converted for the mission, and all were maintained with the best equipment. They had to be repeatedly modified as new bomb types emerged.

There were 147 B-29 A-bombers active in December 1952, 179 more as tankers, and more as conventional platforms. From that point, the B-50 began taking over the missions. However, these and the B-36 did not emerge fast enough to meet the need for additional nuclear delivery means as the Korean Conflict heated the confrontation with the USSR. The Superfortress only began to be withdrawn from the nuclear mission in 1952. Still, the B-29 lingered longer than expected, finally retiring from frontline bomber duty in 1954.

Boeing B-29B Characteristics

span	141.3 feet (43.1 m)	weight empty	69,000 lb (31,298 kg)
length	99 feet (30.2 m)	gross	110,000 lb (49,895 kg)
height	27.6 feet (8.4 m)	maximum	137,500 lb (62,369 kg)
wing area	1,736 feet² (161 m²)	speed, max. (25,000 feet)	367 mph (591 kph)
fuel, int.+bay	5,566+2,560 gal (21,070+9,691 l)	cruise	228 mph (367 kph)
service ceiling	32,000 feet (9,754 m)	range, 18,000-lb bombs	3,875 miles (6,236 km)
climb rate, average	526 fpm (160 mpm)	ferry	5,725 miles (9,214 km)

The Boeing B-29 ended World War Two as the most outstanding bomber, with tremendous capacity and high-altitude operations via pressurization. Although being eclipsed by its descendant, the B-50, it was the heart of the strategic bombing missions during the Korean Conflict where 42-65357 is shown in flight. They became vulnerable when the MiG-15 was introduced and moved to night operations. (*National Archives*)

Carryovers

The war ended while several advanced bombers equipped with reciprocating engines were in development. These designs included pressurization, de-icing equipment, radar-directed tail guns, early ECM equipment, and the like. Although the USAAF anticipated jet bombers to displace all "prop jobs" eventually, this would not be quick and much maturation could be expected. Consequently, some of the piston-engined projects moved forward.

During the war, a B-29A had been modified with R-4360 engines. An initial order was placed in July 1945 for 200 equivalent B-29Ds, but this was reduced to sixty at the war's end. With severe budget cuts, the USAAF had to fight to retain even this number. The service felt strongly that it needed additional Superfortresses, especially with atomic weapons emerging as a deterrent. However, the hastily introduced B-29s had many deficiencies the D-model addressed, not the least of which being the R-3350 engines. Still, given that there were hundreds of new bombers in storage, it was an uphill battle with lawmakers to grow the Boeing production contract. Consequently, it became expedient to change the designation to B-50A.[2]

The B-50s moved at a slow pace through the much diminished Boeing capacity in the Puget Sound area, Washington. The USAF insisted that these were 75 percent new airplanes—at least structurally. These included the use of new aluminum alloys for added strength but reduced weight. The forward fuselage had jacking points that permitted the nose to be raised for the large atomic weapons to be rolled under to the bays without the use of a loading pit. The more powerful R-4360 engines permitted the bomber to execute long-range, heavy missions with the full complement of defensive weapons. A taller tail gave enhanced directional stability for such portions of the mission profile as landing with wind gusts, and could be folded down to fit into hangars. Also featured were thermal anti-ice via combustion heaters, reversible props, hydraulic system alterations that would provide rudder boost, enlarged flaps, revised landing gear for the higher GW, and nose-wheel steering. The bomber carried a 28,000-lb (12,701-kg) payload.

These airplanes began flying in June 1947 with delivery following in February 1948. They became the first new type to join SAC's ranks. The initial unit ready to deliver atomic weapons was mission-ready at the end of 1948.

Ultimately, seventy-nine B-50As were produced, before moving to an order for forty-five B-model airplanes. These last possessed structural alteration to bring GW capability up 18 percent. Most of the aircraft were soon modified as RB-50Bs (see page 388). The first B-50B flew in January 1949, and that same year, the next model also emerged. The B-50D became the definitive model and was most distinguishable by the addition of external tanks, a new top forward turret, and molded plexiglass nose transparency. Less evident was single-point refueling, many internal equipment changes, bomb bay alterations accommodating the latest series of atomic weapons, and a small GW increase. A 4,000-lb (1,814-kg) bomb could be substituted for the underwing tanks. They also had provisions to add a receptacle for boom refueling. The growing confrontation with the USSR led to orders extending to 222 examples.

The final model was the twenty-four unarmed TB-50H trainers, handed over in early 1953. These had the B-47 bombing radar and navigation system, with a good deal of the associated electronics in the aft bomb bay. In total, Boeing manufactured 371 B-50s with the unit cost running from $1.1 to 1.5 million.

The slow introduction and capability growth of jet bombers made modifying Superfortresses to extend their utility the order of the day. Before the new B-50As could be combat-ready, they needed modifications to operate in arctic conditions and for the forward bomb bay to take the latest Mk 4 A-bomb. Throughout the years, bomb bays were upgraded to carry new atomic weapons. Fifty-seven B-50As were fitted out in Wichita for the earliest hose refueling system. It was 1951 before the B-50 fully replaced the B-29 in the nuclear strike mission. Eleven TB-50A and eleven TB-50D conversions, without armament or other operational accouterments, were trainers for B-36 aircrew.

Boeing B-50D Characteristics

span	141.3 feet (43.1 m)	weight empty	80,609 lb (36,564 kg)
length	99 feet (30.2 m)	combat	121,850 lb (55,270 kg)
height	32.7 feet (10 m)	gross	173,000 lb (78,471 kg)
wing area	1,720 feet² (160 m²)	speed, max. (30,500 feet)	347 mph (558 kph)
fuel, int.+ext.	10,301+1,384 gal (38,994+5,239 l)	cruise (combat)	248 mph (399 kph)
service ceiling	40,150 feet (12,238 m)	range, basic combat	4,492 miles (7,229 km)
climb rate, initial	2,165 fpm (660 mpm)	ferry	4,801 miles (7,727 km)

A measure to stretch the capability of the B-50 was to add the variable discharge turbine to the R-4360 engines. The sixtieth B-50A began to be built as the YB-50C with these powerplants. This became the XB-54A featuring a span extended by 19.9 feet (6.1 m) owing to an expected maximum take-off GW increase by some 61,500 lb (27,900 kg). This would have required the addition of outrigger gear under the outboard wings and some taxiways were eyed to be widened. Larger external tanks would assist in growing range to 9,300 miles (1,497 km). Fuselage length was to be enlarged by 12 feet (3.7 m) that accommodated a larger, unitary bomb bay. Maximum speed was predicted to be 430 mph (692 kph) and cruise 305mph (491 kph).

The project was begun in 1947 with contracts let in May 1948 for fourteen B-54A and twenty-nine RB-54As. However, the VDT ran into trouble and, with the extensive airframe changes causing disquiet, the B-54 was dropped in April 1949 to help fund B-36Ds. Piston-powered bombers had clearly reached their zenith while jet bombers were rapidly establishing themselves. Yet the slow introduction of jets meant that B-50s continued in the nuclear strike role until 1955.

Northrop's B-35 was still to fly at the end of the war. The "flying wing," with aft-mounted pusher engines, inspired wonder and excitement, but there were doubts about its military utility. The company originally targeted 10,000 lb (4,536 kg) payload to 10,000 miles (16,093 km) and 40,000 feet (12,192-m) ceiling, but this appeared dubious soon after detailed design began.

Boeing built a close relative of the B-29 after the war in the B-50 Superfortress. The most evident feature of these bombers was the revised cowlings enclosing R-4360 engines and taller vertical tail. This B-50D (48-096) shows off the under-wing tanks, the molded nose transparencies, and a new top forward turret, as the most obvious characteristics of the model. (*San Diego Air & Space Museum*)

The USAF eyed a growth of the B-50 by adding variable discharge turbines to its R-4360 engines plus installing very large external fuel tanks. The gross weight would be substantially boosted, requiring a wingspan increase. The Boeing B-54 won a production contract, but the program was canceled in 1949 because the engine ran into trouble and the airframe changes were too extensive for an aircraft clearly at the end of the prop-driven era. (*Author's collection*)

The lift:drag and gross:payload benefits of the all-wing design, plus generous internal volume across the span, were well appreciated. The simpler structure could be less costly to build. However, lacking a tail made providing suitable S&C challenging. It could mean pitch sensitivity and a higher speed take-off and landing for longer runway distances. The CG travel is also less than a conventional airplane layout. For static stability, the B-35 had a swept wing with the leading edge at 27 degrees. Northrop planned to ameliorate some of the deleterious effects by accepting reduced stability, a tenth or twentieth less than a conventional airplane. This was felt justified because destabilizing influences of a fuselage, engine nacelles, and propwash were eliminated.

The B-35's primary control surfaces were inboard split landing flaps, mid-span elevons, and wingtip-split drag rudders hinged to trim flaps. The trim flaps were for both pitch and roll while the neutral position of the elevons could also be biased as elevator trim. Outboard leading-edge slots opened automatic below 140 mph (225 kph) and when the gear was extended. All hydraulically driven controls were "fully boosted"—the first on an American airplane—and so featured artificial feel in all axes. There were still many articles powered electrically, demanding two APUs that also served as emergency power sources for the hydraulic motor, especially for the elevon actuators. Production airplanes were expected to have thermal leading edge de-ice.

Testbed data did suggest low dynamic stability damping that could reduce the B-35's value as a bombing platform and complicate formation flying. With the assistance of USAAF laboratories, Northrop began working to acquire an artificial yaw damping system that would use rate gyro feedback to automatically command drag rudder motion countering the oscillations. A modified C-1 autopilot had four servomotors instead of the common three. Instead of simply relieving pilot workload during extended cruise flight, the C-1 was to be used nearly full-time to damp undesirable aircraft oscillations. This was one of the first such uses of stability augmentation. Hydraulic brakes were backed up by an emergency pneumatic system.

A pusher propulsion layout was considered ideal in eliminating the drag of propwash while the propeller shaft housings above the tapered aft portion of the airfoil contributed directional stability. However, cooling the buried engines was challenging, and long power extension shafts were historically prone to high stresses and vibration. Cooling and induction air to the four 3,000-hp (2,237-kW) R-4360s were drawn in at wing leading edge then accelerated into a shroud around the engine by a variable-speed, engine-driven fan. The engines drove contra-rotating propellers with de-icing. The reduction and dual-rotation gearboxes were at the end of the power shafts.

The central portion of the wing contained the pressurized zones for the crew of nine with a relief of six more. The flight deck had the pilot elevated to see out of a bubble canopy, the co-pilot lower to see out windows in the leading edge, and the bombardier sighting through lower windows. A flight engineer and navigator sat to the rear. A gunner perched on an elevated platform behind the pilot to see out the same canopy. The rear gunner sat farther back in the center-section, and the tail gunner was at the aft end of the pressurized compartments. Armament consisted of twenty .50-cal guns in seven GE remote turrets and directed by their FCS. The three gunners controlled the turrets via periscope sighting stations. There were eight bomb bays across the span, each with a flexible door that rolled onto a drum at the aft end of the bay.

Northrop had a contract for two XB-35s and thirteen YB-35 service-test examples while Martin was to build 200 B-35 production airplanes at its Baltimore, Maryland, plant. By the end of the war, disquieting design changes and workload imbalances had driven enormous schedule slips and ballooning budget. Adding weight growth and diminishing performance projections, the production order had been dropped. Any hopes that the airplane would be "intercontinental" faded, as did the motivation to build another piston bomber.

The service was already looking ahead to jet bombers and survivable combat airspeeds the Northrop aircraft would never meet. The USAAF began to "fiddle" with the equipment content, schedule, and objectives for the X- and Y-planes in an effort to fly early and gain operational insight quickly. Yet it was clear the airplanes would be experimental with little chance of production. Then, the decision to build two of the YB-35s as jet-powered YB-49s (see page 235) further eroded enthusiasm. Apart from the B-50, it was doubtful that the air force would carry two prop-driven bombers to production following the war, and the B-36 appeared to have decisive advantages.

The first XB-35 finally flew in June 1946, the second a year later, and the only YB-35 to be finished nearly a year beyond that. A noteworthy feature of the testing was the use of television to record flight instruments. A "chase plane" P-61 received the images that were then photographed with a movie camera for later visual data tabulation. The trials revealed S&C deficiencies that made the airplane a poor bombing platform, with little hope of remedy. This emphasized the importance of the artificial damping, which was then in development, but it could not save the B-35. The gearboxes and dual-rotation propellers were fraught with difficulties, including speed-governor "hunting" and "creep," which caused wide airspeed variations. The engine cooling fans suffering fatigue cracks and the exhaust ducting demanded excessive maintenance. Propeller vibration was also a problem, with the props beginning to show cracks suggesting their service life would be as little as eighty hours. Consequently, serviceability was atrocious, with very high maintenance hours per flight hour.

The two XB-35s were flown eighteen times through August 1948 when they were grounded to substitute single-rotation gearboxes and props. This eliminated the most complex and troublesome features of the original gearboxes. In this guise, testing resumed in February 1948, and the YB-35 flew only in that configuration. However, the change degraded power extraction and so performance, while there were also worrying vibrations. If the B-35 were to proceed, the dual-rotation propellers would be essential.

Ship No. 1 ultimately flew only nineteen times for fewer than twenty-four hours before journeying back to Hawthorne in October 1948 to be scrapped. Ship No. 2 accumulated about a dozen hours over eight flights, and then it followed to an identical fate in August 1949. The YB-35 was flown to Edwards, but then returned to Hawthorne just three months later, never to fly again. The entire endeavor had consumed $66.1 million.

Northrop XB-35 Characteristics
(Some Performance Numbers Estimates)

span	172 feet (52.4 m)	weight empty	89,560 lb (40,624 kg)
length	53.1 feet (16.2 m)	gross	162,000 lb (73,482 kg)
height	20.1 feet (6.1 m)	maximum	209,000 lb (94,801 kg)
wing area	4,000 feet² (372 m²)	speed, max. (35,000 feet)	391 mph (630 kph)
fuel	5,000 gal (18,927 l)	cruise	183 mph (295 kph)
service ceiling	39,700 feet (12,101 m)	range *	1,440 miles (2,318 km)
climb rate, average	614 fpm (187 mpm)	maximum	7,500 miles (12,070 km)

* Determined from a stated 720 miles (presumably mission radius) with 51,070-lb weapons load. Many such range values were calculated as combat radius, assuming a bomb load delivered midway through the mission.

The first Northrop XB-35 (42-13603) is seen in flight over Southern California with a P-61 chase plane. The image shows the powerplant installation, canopy plus leading-edge windows, and dummy gun turrets. The buried R-4360 engines with contra-rotating propellers proved to be an enormous challenge for the design that yielded to a jet-powered model. (*Air Force Test Center*)

Experimentals

In order to stay ahead of the jet fighters sure to emerge, the army had initiated a program to develop jet bombers during the war. They envisioned machines from 80,000–200,000 lb (36,287–90,718 kg) across a number of projects. The effort seeking a medium bomber of 90,000 lb (40,823 kg) began in spring 1944 with axial-flow turbojets appearing more suitable for a multi-engine, podded installation. These were J35s with 4,000 lbf (17.8 kN) thrust or the still developing J47 of 3,745 lbf (16.7 kN). The envisioned aircraft would operate up to 40,000 feet (12,192 m) and 500 mph (805 kph) with a 1,000-mile (1,609-km) range. Radar and visual bombing for the 8,000-lb (3,629-kg) load would be necessary. The requirements continued to evolve such that by the time the invitation to bid went out in August, the requirements had been upped to 550 mph (885 kph), 45,000 feet (13,716 m), and 3,500 miles (5,633 km) with a 16,500-lb (7,484-kg) payload. The giant British Tallboy and T-14 Grand Slam weapons, at 22,000 lb (9,979 kg), were to be accommodated, perhaps to ensure the bombers could also carry the large atomic bombs being developed but which remained top secret.

Given the uncertainty associated with the new technologies and performance goals, four contractors were selected. North American was to develop the B-45, Convair the XB-46, Boeing the B-47, and Martin the B-48. A later addition was the B-49, the jet-powered version of the B-35, though not necessarily competing with the others. Work on all was much slowed as a result of the end of the war and trickle of engine production. Given the technological challenges and the slim potential that all four competitors could be taken to prototype, much less production, the development proceeded in phases with contract amendments funding successive steps. Ultimately, given the desire to field a jet bomber as early as practical, all were taken to prototype rather than make an early down-select. By summer 1946, the service was seeing the B-45 as the most likely to proceed quickly to a combat-suitable design. In August, they negotiated a production contract with NAA before the company's airplane had flown, yet all the other projects were permitted to proceed.

The 500–550 mph speed goals would just be touching compressibility effects. Yet the aircraft might be fairly conventional apart from the jet engines. Given their modest thrust and slow throttle response, JATO could assist take-off. It was also expected that the top speed goal, if achieved, would reduce most fighter intercepts to tail chases such that only an aft gun might be necessary. The intercept might be long enough to permit a radar-directed, remote control gun turret to be suitable. Hence, most turrets, gunners, and sighting stations were eliminated. Radar for blind bombing was already in use, plus pressurization for high altitude, and more EW systems always being added. Still, the industry had much to learn about integrating jet engines into airframes and building the same for high-speed flight.

An interloper in the jet bomber program was offered by DAC. When B-42 prospects had grown bleak, the company had proposed converting the aircraft to jet engines as a short path to a light jet bomber. Two J35s were to be placed in the aft fuselage, exhausting under the tail, flush inlets ahead of the wings, and empennage revisions.

These represented tolerable changes, leaving the great majority of the airframe unaltered. The XB-43 was born via a January 1944 amendment to the existing XB-42 contract for two aircraft.

The baseline airframe grew 2,000 lb (907 kg), but also 4,500 lb (2,041 kg) in maximum GW. Close placement of the engines reduced the controllability issues associated with single-engine flight. The inlets had boundary layer bleed slots. Bay tanks and drop tanks were to help retain favorable range despite the guzzling turbojets. There were also provisions for JATO bottles under the wings that should cut take-off distance by 40 percent. The bomb load was 8,000 lb (3,629 kg), but only provisions for this were included in the prototypes. A radar-directed rear gun turret and radar bombing systems were also left for later integration.

As the new bomber came together at the end of 1944, the air forces had enough confidence to contemplate a production contract and make the B-43 its first, but likely transitional, jet bomber or alternative attacker. Although progress was made on the effort, the end of the war stretched things out and other developmental bombers possessed projected capabilities closer to evolving requirements—especially payload capacity. By summer 1945, the production options were shelved. Douglas was also struggling a bit with the new turbojets, both because of powerplant immaturity and just lack of experience. The engines were late because of technical difficulties, but also labor disputes at G.E. Even pressurization was such a challenge that it was set aside temporarily to move the aircraft to flight. During a ground engine run in October, an engine shed a compressor blade that caused catastrophic failure and damage to the aircraft, plus injuring a ground crewman. All these factors delayed the first flight until May 1946 as the first American jet bomber to achieve the goal.

The XB-43s had the usual development issues uncovered during testing. However, all performance objectives were achieved except take-off distance—earning it a reputation of being underpowered. The craft continued to be flown to collect experimental data. The first jet was grounded after damage in February 1951, and the second was turned to engine testing.

Douglas XB-43 Characteristics

span	71.2 feet (21.7 m)	weight empty	22,890 lb (10,383 kg)
length	51.3 feet (15.7 m)	combat	35,900 lb (16,284 kg)
height	24.3 feet (7.4 m)	gross	39,533 lb (17,932 kg)
wing area	563 feet² (52.3 m²)	speed, max. (sea level)	507 mph (815 kph)
fuel, int.+ext.	1,209+900 gal (4,577+3,407 l)	cruise	420 mph (676 kph)
service ceiling	38,200 feet (11,643 m)	range, normal	1,000 miles (1,609 km)
climb rate	2,470 fpm (753 mpm)	ferry	2,840 miles (4,571 km)

The Convair XB-46 paired its four engines in pods under the straight wing. The nacelles closely followed the design offered by NACA for low drag but made room for the main landing gear. The fuselage was long and slender, containing all the fuel cells and with an Emerson Electric remote tail turret for twin .50s. The co-pilot/gunner/

The first Douglas XB-43, jet conversion of the XB-42, sits on the tarmac at Muroc AAB awaiting another test mission. The boundary layer bleed slot in the inlet is visible as is one of the engine exhausts under the empennage, and the twin "bug-eyed" canopies that were replaced on the second airplane with a more conventional flight deck cover planned for production. The bomber did much of what was sought, though possessing a long take-off distance, but air force sights had already passed beyond to more capable jet bombers on the horizon. (*National Archives*)

radio operator sat behind the pilot under a bubble canopy, and the bombardier/ navigator was in the nose. Convair built the aircraft fairly conventionally, though using magnesium and the first to employ pneumatics for rapid actuation of bay doors, landing gear, and wheel brakes. The 90-percent span Fowler flaps were electrically operated. The small ailerons served primarily for pilot feel while spoilers provided the lion's share of the roll authority.[3] This avoided potential role reversal at high speed with the slender and thin wings. The wing and empennage hot air de-icing system used ram air heated in the engine exhaust.

The postwar fiscal constraints brought the threat of cancelations, but Convair won a continuation by reducing the effort to a single stripped-down airplane, eliminating related research efforts, while funds were diverted from the XA-44 (see page 245). The de-icing system was deferred in this process along with all the military equipment and ejection seats, and metal tanks without self-sealing features were installed. In this way, the team proceeded to the first flight with the sole XB-46 in April 1947. During testing, they had to deal with a resonance between the spoilers and wings at high speed that produced heavy and hazardous wing oscillations. There was also a good deal of fuselage bending in turbulence or if the pilot oscillated the longitudinal controls. Lateral control forces could be heavy.

Convair XB-46 Characteristics

span	113 feet (34.4 m)	weight empty	48,018 lb (21,781 kg)
length	105.8 feet (32.2 m)	combat	75,200 lb (34,110 kg)
height	27.9 feet (8.5 m)	max. take-off	94,400 lb (42,819 kg)
wing area	1,285 feet² (119 m²)	speed, max. (sea level)	545 mph (877 kph)
fuel, int.+bay	4,280+2,408 gal (16,202+9,115 l)	cruise	439 mph (707 kph)
service ceiling	36,500 feet (11,125 m)	range, 8,000-lb bombs	1,388 miles (2,234 km)
climb rate, sea level	2,400 fpm (732 mpm)	ferry	2,870 miles (4,619 km)

Although Convair worked through the problems and had a respectable product, NAA's B-45 had already been selected for production and the Boeing B-47 was sure to out-perform its competition. The USAF also could not afford to place another bomber into production. The $4.9 million program was shut down in August 1947, though the aircraft continued research flights into 1950.

The Martin bomber fared no better. The design had six J35s, three in individual nacelles closely spaced under each wing. The narrow "bypass ducts" between the engines were expected to reduce drag and weight while enhancing lift.[4] The crew was to be three with the pilot and co-pilot under a top canopy and the bombardier in the nose. A radar-controlled tail turret with twin .50s was planned. The airplane also featured a bicycle undercarriage with twin-wheel trucks supporting the fuselage, the front steerable, and the wings supported by light outriggers retracting into the outboard engine pods. Brakes were pneumatic. The arrangement had been tested on a modified Marauder, the XB-26H. It allowed the wings to remain thin and not have to accommodate retracted undercarriage elements. Fuel was in the fuselage and inboard wing segments. Double-slotted flaps ran nearly full span. At the tips were small "feeler" ailerons while spoilers lent most of the roll power. Engine bleed air heated aero surfaces in one prototype while the other used electrical heating leading-edge "blankets." Martin built a mock-up of a "horizontal bomb bay" in which a carrier loaded with bombs apart from the aircraft was wheeled under the bay and hoisted up. This promised to greatly speed the weapons' loading process, especially between sorties. The bay doors were pneumatically operated for rapid action. These retracted into the fuselage to reduce drag in flight while permitting easier access for personnel on the ground.

The first XB-48 flew in June 1947. The second went up in October 1948, by which time the project was moribund. There were a few anomalies to resolve, among them buffeting with the bay doors open. Crosswind landings on the bicycle gear were problem-prone; the airplane was heeling over into the wind, the lightly loaded downwind tires slipped and the upwind could blow with brake application. A master throttle to control all six engines simultaneously was of little use as each needed to be adjusted separately. The major problem was its poor performance, falling well below requirements, guarantees, and predictions. This can largely be blamed on a 24-percent weight growth and the nacelle arrangement with the channels generating high drag.

The XB-46 is seen over the California high desert during flight testing in August or September 1947. The elegant-looking, four-engined bomber was just an aerodynamic and systems test ship without mission equipment. By the time of testing, the competition had already won a production contract and so there was no future for the Convair aircraft. (*Gerald Balzer collection*)

Martin's choice of the unusual bicycle undercarriage for the XB-48 compelled them to conduct testing with the configuration as part of the design effort. They modified one of their B-26s into the XB-26H "Middle River Puddle Jumper" with two tandem main gear within the fuselage and outriggers within the engine nacelles. This image from January 20, 1947, shows that the fuselage required additional strengthening via external stringers. (*National Museum of the United States Air Force*)

Martin XB-48 Characteristics

span	108.3 feet (33 m)	weight empty	58,500 lb (26,535 kg)
length	85.7 feet (26.1 m)	combat	92,600 lb (42,003 kg)
height	26.5 feet (8.1 m)	gross	102,600 lb (46,539 kg)
wing area	1,330 feet² (123 m²)	speed, max. (20,000 feet)	516 mph (830 kph)
fuel, int.+bay	4,150+818 gal (15,709+3,097 l)	cruise	453 mph (729 kph)
service ceiling	39,200 feet (11,948 m)	range, 8,000-lb bombs	1,340 miles (2,157 km)
climb rate	3,250 fpm (991 mpm)		

By the end of the war, Northrop already had a contract for two jet-powered versions of their B-35. These YB-49s would eliminate propeller torque that might contribute to the S&C issues, hopefully improve serviceability, and increase speed. It was expected to fly some 100 mph (161 kph) faster than the B-35, seeking 500 mph (805 kph), but to less than half the range. Just creating the jet from the earlier airframe eliminated the potential for design optimization and so performance was expected to suffer a bit more. The empty weight was predicted to be comparable to the YB-35, although gross would increase by about 30,000 lb (13,608 kg) and bomb capacity was cut by about 5,000 lb (2,268 kg). Air force efforts to "modernize" Northrop's airplanes included adding radar, jettisonable fuel tanks, and all-weather gear. None of these got far into the design and so was never installed in either type.

The original six 3,750-lbf (16.7-kN) J35 turbojets became eight during detailed design. Air entered through leading-edge intakes and passed via long ducts to the engines that had extended tailpipes to the trailing edge. The outboard bomb bays were sacrificed to engines and additional fuel tanks. This left the airplane with six bays

The first Martin XB-48 rests on the apron near the Baltimore plant. The bicycle undercarriage and channel between the engine nacelles are evident. The aircraft fell short on performance and could not compete with others in production or imminent. (*San Diego Air & Space Museum*)

and the ability to carry a dozen 1,000-lb (454-kg) bombs. A new fire-extinguishing system also had to be installed. The elimination of the stabilizing influence of the XB-35's propeller shaft housings required the addition of four vertical stabilizers above and below the wings. These were placed near the trailing edge and at the end of "separator" fences that discouraged detrimental spanwise airflow owing to wing sweep. Defensive weapons were reduced to just the tail turret of four .50s that was never fitted. With this and the greatly reduced endurance, the crew dropped to six.

The YB-49 effort slipped badly and costs ran well beyond allocation. The first example flew in October 1947 and the second three months later. The YB-49s had many fewer mechanical problems compared with the XB-35s. They were extensively tested by comparison to their antecedents, accumulating approximately 330 hours over seventy flights to include service evaluations. In a February 1949 air force trial, the aircraft was flown from Edwards to Andrews AFB, Maryland, in 4.5 hours at an average speed of 511 mph (822 kph).

Specific data on the aircraft's suitability as a bomber was discouraging. The YB-49 was simply not stable enough, frustrating the pilots' ability to hold a steady course, airspeed, and altitude. It would take four minutes or more to accurately line up for a bombing run while the B-29 achieved this in under forty-five seconds. Bombing accuracy would be half that of the Superfortress. In an effort to improve yaw damping, Northrop engaged Minneapolis Honeywell to develop a full-time electronic yaw stabilization system. It improved matters but did not solve them. Continuing problems with operating power generators off the J35s meant reliance on the APUs.

Even had the B-49 approached an operationally representative state, the air forces considered the aircraft to have inadequate bomb capacity. The 16,000-lb (7,257-kg) maximum was less than the B-29, and no single weapon could be larger than the standard 4,000-lb (1,814-kg) weapon due to bomb bay dimensions. The bays were certainly too small for the atomic bombs of the day—though this was revealed to few. At best, the shape could be carried semi-submerged and so the added drag would cut range by 10 percent and maximum airspeed by 6 percent.[5] Aircrew arrangement was judged poor and six persons excessive. Also, the bomber was likely to be very expensive to procure. Even before the first flight, the YB-49s were considered experimental subjects only.

There was simply too little to recommend the B-49 over other choices extant or emerging in a tight budget environment. The second YB-49 crashed in June 1948, with five fatalities, after suffering wing structural failure due to an overload—the cause of which was never determined. This fueled speculation of mysterious controllability "gremlins." The first YB-49 was destroyed in March 1950 when its nose gear collapsed during taxi tests, the airplane flipping over and burning. The program was canceled on that day.

Northrop YB-49 Characteristics

span	172 feet (52.4 m)	weight empty	88,442 lb (40,117 kg)
length	53.1 feet (16.2 m)	combat	133,569 lb (60,586 kg)
height	15.2 feet (4.6 m)	gross	193,938 lb (87,969 kg)
wing area	4,000 feet² (372 m²)	speed, max. (20,800 feet)	493 mph (793 kph)
fuel	12,752-14,542 gal (48,272-55,047 l)	cruise	420 mph (676 kph)
service ceiling	40,700 feet (12,405 m)	range, 10,000-lb load	3,229 miles (5,197 km)
climb rate, sea level	1,780 fpm (543 mpm)	ferry	3,575 miles (5,753 km)

In an effort to salvage something from the enormous time and fiscal investment in the flying wings, the USAF decided in summer 1948 to have thirty of the aircraft built as an eight-engine RB-49A reconnaissance variant. The USAF continued to have doubts about Northrop's ability to produce reliably exceptionally large airplanes on cost and also on schedule. Its wartime work had been respectable, but it was not on the scale of the big bomber. As a consequence, an arrangement was made for Northrop—who only reluctantly agreed—to build one example while Convair were responsible for the remainder in Fort Worth.

The USAF soon thought better of the arrangement. It later decided to have the remaining ten idle YB-35 airframes remanufactured into another reconnaissance variant, the six-engine RB-49B. A testbed for these was another YB-35 airframe remanufactured as the YRB-49A. By fall 1948, the service reconsidered these plans as well because the potential delivery dates and performance of the aircraft did not meet the need. The decision also freed funds for B-36 and B-50 modifications. Formal cancelation followed in January 1949, though flight testing of the YRB-49A was salvaged.

The YRB-49A model had only four internally mounted J35s, generating 5,600 lbf (24.9 kN), and another pair in underwing nacelles. The change permitted additional fuel volume for an extended range. A protruding fairing was added to the belly for a radar. The airplane flew in May 1950, and testing included bombing trials. It was marginally lighter than the YB-49, but also approximately 100 mph (161 kph) slower. What made the flying wing a poor bomber also made it a poor photography platform. After thirteen test flights through April 1951, the airplane was retired.

Fifteen Northrop flying wing airframes had been assembled to various states, and six were flown. The programs had spanned nearly a decade with $83.9 million expended and nothing close to an operationally suitable bomber as a result.

First Fleet Jets

The B-45 proved the more practical of the first competition and went into production as America's first fielded jet bomber. North American achieved this by not pushing the technological bounds too far, as endorsed by its customer. A clean, light design was counted on to enable the 500-mph goal.

The two YB-49 jet-powered versions of Northrop's flying wing were built from modified YB-35s. The first (42-102367) is shown in test over the California high desert. The eight-engined airplane had speed and serviceability advantages over the reciprocating version, but the range was sacrificed. It was a poor bombing platform, and bomb capacity was deficient. (*Gerald Balzer collection*)

In another bid to glean something from the large investment in the Northrop flying wings, a six-engine reconnaissance version was funded. This was soon reconsidered, but the one prototype, derived from a YB-35, was tested. This YRB-49A is shown taking off from the company's Hawthorne facility. (*San Diego Air & Space Museum*)

Four J35s were paired in underwing pods and the horizontal tails were given dihedral to keep them clear of the jet exhaust. The nacelles were designed with knowledge of the NACA layout, but it was otherwise an NAA inspiration. The centerline of each pod was made a hardpoint to carry a 214-gal (810-l) tank of water and alcohol for water injection, JATO rockets, or chaff dispensers. The 14-percent wing was thick enough to contain fuel cells and the main gear, with single, thin wheels. Internal fuel, in wings and fuselage, amounted to 3,400 gal (12,870 l). Refueling was via a single point accessible from ground level—an innovation introduced before AR demanded it. All controls were boosted with a 3,000-psi (20.7-kPa) hydraulic system, with hydraulic system and possessed electric trim tabs. Single-slotted Fowler flaps were featured.[6] Anti-ice derived from engine bleed air passed through insulated ducts to the aero surfaces' leading edges.

The crew was four with two pilots under a fixed canopy, a bombardier in the nose, and a gunner in the tail station with a pair of .50-cals. There were initially no ejection seats. A radar-directed Emerson Electric remote turret with fire control system had been planned, but this failed to measure up and was abandoned in the interest of schedule. The gunner was isolated unless the aircraft was depressurized, the bay doors closed, and the bay empty. The bombardier's nose station was equipped with a Norden bombsight plus APQ-24 radar. The radar was in the lower nose instead of a bottom blister, and this was criticized as reducing the field of vision. The conventional bomb bay could contain a variety of weapons up to a single 22,000-lb (9,979-kg) T-14 Grand Slam. A kit for bomb bay door reinforcement was carried to be installed in anticipation of a ditching to help ensure survivability.

The first of three XB-45s flew in March 1947. The team had to work through some problems, but the aircraft met expectations. A standing USAF order for ninety-six B-45As had funded early production line erection. These airplanes were built at the Douglas plant in Long Beach, California, owing to the scope of F-86 work in Inglewood. Changes included dual nose wheels of smaller diameter and the nose redesigned. Internal fuel capacity was increased, 500-gal (1,893-l) external tanks included, and two 1,200-gal (4,543-l) bay tanks could be installed.

The first B-45A emerged in February 1948, but deliveries were paced by engine availability—the F-86 having priority. Radar and other mission avionics were also in short supply. With the small defense budgets of the period, many bombers were stored for a time after delivery. The first Tornado squadron went operational in November 1948, displacing B-26s, but suffered so many issues with the aircraft and parts shortages that they would have been hard-pressed to go to war. Initial operations found numerous structural and mechanical problems, unreliable engines, and an excessive take-off distance for a heavy airplane. No Tornado unit could be deployed until the engines were more mature, with up to 100 hours between overhauls, and there were enough in the supply chain to support routine ops, plus mission avionics available for all aircraft. These conditions were not expected to be met for at least another year.

A fatal accident with one of the prototypes compelled the installation of a jettisonable canopy and catapult ejection seats for the two pilots. Deflectors ahead of the forward and aft hatches would ease bombardier and gunner bail-out. The mishap suggested that the aircraft lacked sufficient longitudinal control. Instead of redesigning the empennage, the aft fuselage was angled up via a wedge on a frame aft of the bomb bay. This lowered the incidence of the horizontal tail and so increase download. After twenty-two production examples, the 5,200-lbf (23.1-kN) J47 was substituted. The last B-45A was delivered in March 1950, each costing about $1 million.

Being an introductory model that looked antiquated when fielded, with the B-47 on the horizon, leadership had decided in May 1948 that B-45A production would not be expanded. However, a small follow-up order was approved. A B-variant was planned with improved FCS and radar but passed over for the B-45C. Airframe structure was strengthened, the horizontal tail area increased, boom AR capability installed, an autopilot and instrument landing system added, and 600-gal (2,271-l) jettisonable tip tanks accommodated. Weapon load was increased by 2,000 lb (907 kg) while GW went up 20,000 lb (9,072 kg). The initial B-45C flew in May 1949 and delivered the same month to SAC. Yet only ten of these jets were completed through April 1950 while some B-45As were upgraded to the standard. Thirty-three RB-45Cs were delivered. Air force chiefs were still convinced that the Tornado held little real combat value and canceled two B-45Cs and forty-nine RB-45Cs on contract.

The B-45 had not been designed from the outset as a nuclear bomber given the secrecy surrounding the weapons at the end of the war. The layout of the bomb bay made it impossible to accommodate the early weapons. The jet's range was also inadequate for strategic missions. Given the growing confrontation with the Soviet Union, TAC was granted a nuclear strike role in November 1950. This brought renewed interest in the Tornado, and forty B-45As were upgraded to deploy the Mk 7. They all finally got their APQ-24 radar, though some were fitted with the Short Range Navigation (SHORAN) system as an interim capability, and additional fuel capacity was found.[7] This program of extensive modifications was a high-priority, fast-paced effort that was completed only thirty days behind schedule. The first examples went to Europe initially in May 1952, and the last was delivered in March 1954.

As expected, the B-45 design was quickly eclipsed by newer airplanes with swept wings and more reliable plus powerful engines. Yet it served its purpose into the late 1950s as a transitional machine. The aircraft was also adapted to many ancillary roles. It became the first jet bomber to drop a nuclear weapon—in testing.

North American B-45C Characteristics

span (tip tanks)	96 feet (29.3 m)	weight empty	48,969 lb (22,212 kg)
length	75.3 feet (23 m)	combat	73,715 lb (33,437 kg)
height	25.2 feet (7.7 m)	max. take-off	112,952 lb (51,234 kg)
wing area	1,175 feet² (109 m²)	speed, max. (sea level)	573 mph (922 kph)
fuel, int.+bay+ext.	6,933+2,400+1,200 gal (26,244+9,085+4,543 l)	cruise	466 mph (750 kph)
service ceiling	41,250 feet (12,573 m)	range, 10,000-lb load	1,100 miles (1,770 km)
climb rate, max.	4,550 fpm (1,387 mpm)	ferry	2,426 miles (3,904 km)

The four-engine North American B-45A (47-091) reveals the tail gunner's sight in the bulged window and the slotted flaps. Forty Tornados were upgraded in the early 1950s to become TAC's first nuclear bomber, the bomb bay modified and additional mission avionics installed. Regardless, the type was bought in low numbers as an introductory jet bomber with the expectation that it would be quickly displaced by more capable types. (*San Diego Air & Space Museum*)

The Boeing B-47 embraced 35-degree swept aero surfaces early in the conceptual design phase based on examinations of German research. The team also adopted twin-engine pods inboard and single-engine pods outboard, all on forward-jutting pylons. One advantage of the arrangement is that catastrophic failures and engine fires would less likely risk the entire aircraft. The thin wings would not accommodate retracted undercarriage. Consequently, Boeing adopted a bicycle gear retracting onto the fuselage, and outriggers retracting into the inboard nacelles. A B-50B (47-118) was modified to test this arrangement. All of these features made the Stratojet the most technologically risky of the original four competitors, and the air force sustained the effort acknowledging this.

The wing was so thin and flexible that it had anhedral on the ground just from static bending under its own weight, but it flexed up under airloads. All controls were boosted, and with particular attention to maintaining directional control with engine-out or Dutch Roll yaw-damping scenarios. With hydraulic failures, the pilots could fly in manual reversion, aided by trim tabs. As an added measure to reduce engine wind-milling drag on early aircraft, in an engine-out event—apparently anticipated to be a relatively common event—doors on the inlet cones could close off the intake. Later engines had integral brakes.

The wings had long and narrow ailerons, eschewing the spoilers used by other design teams, yet narrowly managing to avoid aileron reversal—though roll authority was marginal at the edge of the airspeed range. At low speeds, with the flaps extended, flaperons augmented roll authority. All flap surfaces were Fowlers. The aero surface leading edges and nacelle struts also contained hot air anti-ice ducts, the air bled from the engines. Late in the airplane's service, it was concluded that the system was unnecessary.

The pilot and co-pilot sat in tandem under the canopy while the bombardier/ navigator/radar operator/radio operator was in the nose. All aircrew had Republic ejection seats. The radar antenna was in a fairing beneath the nose. The bomb bay could take sixteen 1,000-lb (454-kg) bombs or the defined 22,000-lb weapon standing in for the nuclear device. When the bay doors were opened, three spoiler panels deployed at the forward end of the bay to prevent adverse airflow causing the bombs to hang up in the airstream, bumping other bombs, and even impacting the aircraft before falling away, as was observed in early testing. The bombing system consisted of the autopilot, radar, computer, and bombsight. As a measure of the complexity, this consisted of forty-one major elements containing approximately 370 vacuum tubes and weighing hundreds of pounds.[8] The initial tail armament was two .50-cal with an Emerson system, tested initially by GE on a modified B-24L (44-49916 becoming the solitary XB-24Q). This could be directed automatically via radar or from the cockpit by the co-pilot who could swivel his seat around to view the radar screen. With the production of fully combat-capable models, ECM gear was added and underwent progressive updates. This included receivers, jammers, and chaff dispensers.

Apart from underwing drop tanks, all fuel was in the fuselage, ahead of and behind the bomb bay. However, with the fuselage so long, it was vital that the fuel be managed properly to maintain a safe CG location. The aircraft also featured a single-point refueling system to aid rapid turns between missions. As with the XB-48, the landing gear was jigged to take-off and landing attitude such that rotation was unnecessary, if not impractical. The gear was extended in flight to serve as an airbrake—and quite effective as it increased overall drag by 100 percent. At least later models of the bomber had an anti-skid system—this being rare at the time.

Even six J47s were not expected to get a fully loaded B-47 off in a reasonable field length. Like other early jets, the XB-47 suffered an exceptionally long runway required for a refused take-off—twice that of the B-29—and denying a great many airfields to Stratojet operations. Consequently, provisions were made for nine 1,000-lbf (4.5-kN) JATO bottles on each side of the aft fuselage. These could reduce a 9,100-foot (2,774-m) take-off roll to 7,200 feet (2,195 m) and more comfortably clear obstacles in the take-off path. The bottles were fitted into cavities and so were retained throughout the flight. For heavy-weight landings, a 32-foot (9.8-m) diameter ribbon braking parachute was developed following the example of German units from the war.

The slow response of the engines also made go-arounds hazardous, and so a 16-foot (4.9-m) approach chute was carried to be deployed on approach, as high as 230 mph (370 kph). This allowed the engines to be held at higher power settings facilitating a go-around after the chute was jettisoned. Otherwise, the chute was retained throughout the landing. Even on a good approach, the main chute came to be deployed on short final. The B-47 still had unique hazards that claimed some airplanes and lives. Landing on the bicycle undercarriage required care, with errors leading to porpoising and accidents. An outboard engine failure on take-off left little room for safe yaw recovery. At high altitude, the wing stall speed and high-speed buffet onset coincided into a "coffin corner" from which normal recovery only exacerbated the phenomenon.

With suitable design development, the USAAF ordered prototypes in April 1946. The first of these flew in December 1947 with J35s. The second was powered by J47s when it lifted off initially in July 1948, and the other was soon re-engined. The flight test quickly showed the Stratojet to be the fastest bomber in the world, with its speed exceeding 600 mph (966 kph). The sleek, silver B-47, taking off with a deafening roar on a trail of black smoke, was a sensational example of American prowess. However, while the B-47 could cover the operating radius of a B-29 in a fraction of the time, it required twice the fuel. Just building such an advanced aircraft demanded improved construction methodologies that challenged the "state of the art."

The first production order was placed in September 1948 for only ten B-47A service-test machines, again reflecting the USAF's caution. Although the XB-47s were born in Seattle, production was in Wichita. The first flight was in June 1950, followed by initial delivery in December. These airplanes grossed 151,324-lb (68,639-kg) maximum take-off weight compared with the 125,000-lb (56,699-kg) normal GW of the prototypes. Mission equipment included the bombing radar and an FCS for the Emerson tail turret matched to a tail warning radar.

The operationally suitable model was the B-47B that first flew in Wichita in April 1951. The aircraft grew again, to 180,000-lb (81,647-kg) gross. The newer atomic weapons allowed the bomb bay length to be reduced by adding a fuel tank and installing shorter bay doors. The aircraft could be reconfigured from short to long bay with a day of effort. Only a small number of the bombers were configured for conventional weapon delivery.

The first B-47Bs were delivered to SAC in October 1951, but units spent a year working up to operational readiness. Although the initial order was for eighty-seven aircraft, Korea propelled an increase to 399, each costing about $2.5 million. These included ten built by DAC in Tulsa, Oklahoma, and eight by Lockheed in Marietta, Georgia, from Boeing assemblies. The arrangement allowed the bombers to be delivered by June 1953. However, the first squadrons were barely operational by the end of the Korean Conflict.

The YB-47C (initially XB-56) was to be powered by four J35s with reheat. When these engines became a "long-pole," the J71 was swapped. First proposed in January 1950, the program was dropped in December 1952 when it became clear the J71 would also be much delayed and the B-52 was imminent. The two XB-47D were B-47Bs with the inboard engine pods replaced by Curtiss-Wright T49 turboprops delivering 9,710 hp (7,241 kW).[9] These did not fly until 1955 and remained experimental. The focus was instead on a much-improved model that proved the definitive Stratojet. The first B-47E was delivered in January 1953, and 1,241 would be assembled through 1957 with Tulsa and Marietta again contributing.

The B-47E grossed 230,000 lb (104,326 kg), requiring a structural beef-up and higher capacity tires. It had a lower fuel capacity, but the J47s were uprated to 7,200 lbf (32 kN) with water injection. Instead of the internally mounted JATO bottles of

The first combat-worthy high-speed jet bomber for the USAF was the Boeing B-47B (51-2212 shown). Given the low-performance engines of the period, the JATO tubes at the rear of the craft and the drag chute were important features. Also noteworthy are the bicycle undercarriage, tail guns, bombardier windows in the nose behind projecting periscope, and radar radome under the forward fuselage. (*National Museum of the United States Air Force*)

the earlier models, an external rack for thirty to thirty-three 1,000-lbf JATO bottles—nearly doubling the take-off thrust—could be fastened beneath the rear fuselage and jettisoned after take-off. This cut take-off roll to 5,400 feet (1,646 m) and clearing a 50-foot (15-m) obstacle at 6,750 feet (2,057 m). A take-off corridor for s safe drop of the rack was cleared off the end of runways. However, the use of either the water or JATO had to be performed at the right moment of the take-off to achieve the best, or any, benefit from the added thrust.

The bomb bay could take 18,000 lb (8,165 kg) of weapons, and 845 lb (383 kg) of chaff was also carried. The original tail armament system had been found unsatisfactory and was changed to twin 20-mm cannon and new gun-laying radar with a GE fire control system. The bombardier's upward-firing Republic ejection seat had proven unsatisfactory and was replaced with a downward-firing Stanley seat. Pilot seats became Weber units. The nose was noticeably altered for these seats, there were fewer bombardier windows, and an AR receptacle was added. The receptacle was accessed with a drop-down door that also served to guide the flying boom nozzle. Matched with KC-97s, the B-47E became an intercontinental bomber and rendered the B-36 anachronistic. Routine boom refueling made it practical for the bomber to depart with reduced fuel for improved take-off performance, and then refuel to maximum capacity.

Boeing B-47E Characteristics

span	116 feet (35.4 m)	weight empty	78,620 lb (35,661 kg)
length	107.1 feet (32.6 m)	combat	123,080 lb (55,828 kg)
height	28 feet (8.5 m)	max. take-off	200,000 lb (90,718 kg)
wing area	1,428 feet² (133 m²)	speed, max. (16,300 feet)	607 mph (977 kph)
fuel, int.+ext.	14,610+3,390 gal (55,305+12,833 l)	cruise	498 mph (802 kph)
service ceiling	40,500 feet (12,344 m)	range, 10,845-lb bombs	4,020 miles (6,470 km)
climb rate, initial (water)	4,660 fpm (1,420 mpm)	ferry	4,035 miles (6,494 km)

Production of the B-47 continued into 1957 with nearly 2,000 airframes—more than any other postwar American multi-engine bomber.

The Replacements

The USAAF explored the potential for a light jet bomber for the attack mission, replacing what devolved to just the B-26 (originally A-26), as soon as jet engines were becoming available. This became a convoluted and multi-year effort with disputed results.

Curtiss-Wright was working on the XA-43 since accepting a November 1944 contract. By February 1945, this had gelled into a conventional-looking four-engine, straight wing design powered by J35s in twin-engine NACA nacelles. The requirement continued to be revised, and new characteristics emerged in July 1945 that left the Curtiss airplane deficient. The project was closed in September, although the company carried much of the work into its XP-87 all-weather fighter (see page 155).

With technology evolving rapidly, the service struggled to arrive at a stable requirements list. The next set was issued in February 1946. The basic requirements included 8,000 lb (3,629 kg) of bombs carried 800 miles (1,288 km). When the requirements were issued in August, it attracted a rework of a wartime proposal from Convair. Becoming the XA-44, this was a forward-swept wing "tailless" design with three J35s in the fuselage and a tall vertical tail. The wingtips were to have variable incidence. The tight budgetary environment required the shuffling of funds to allow a contract for two prototypes. The mission evolved through light bombardment in 1947 to a jet bomber in 1948 as the XB-53. However, this led nowhere and was canceled in December 1946, partly because postwar, there were too many programs to sustain.

Against that 1946 requirement, a contract was also sent to Martin for the XA-45. This was to be a straight-wing hybrid with a pair of turboprops matched with turbojets and a crew of six owing to the many defensive weapons. At a projected 70,000 lb (31,751 kg), such a large machine did not seem to be the best path to a ground-attack aircraft. However, the air forces soon dropped the attack class, all being recognized as bombers and sought more speed for survivability. The new spring 1946 requirement was 4,000 lb (1,814 kg) to 600 miles (966 km) and a top speed of 640 mph (1,030 kph). This last

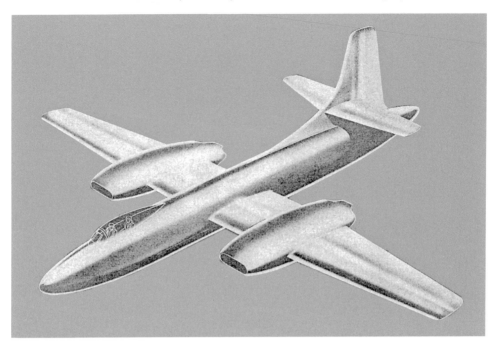

In reaching for its first jet bombers, the USAF offered designers the J35 turbojet that delivered modest power and so four were required to achieve the speed and weapon delivery capacity desired. Curtiss conceived the XA-43 as a fairly conventional airplane of the period. This progressed to an initial design with a mock-up before evolving requirements rendered it unsuitable. (*American Aviation Historical Society*)

Another early jet bomber design was offered by Convair, yet it was far from conventional. In a bid to reduce drag, the team adopted a "tailless" layout with a forward-swept wing and three J35s within the fuselage. The XA-44 moved slowly from its 1945 origin to a name change to B-53 in 1953, but it was ultimately set aside. (*National Museum of the United States Air Force*)

made propellers unsuitable, and the redesignated XB-51 became a three-engine machine with swept wings. This brought a May 1946 letter contract, but the requirements were significantly revised again. Design alterations were offered in February 1947, and a letter contract for two prototypes was approved in April. Once accepted, the development, held up for a year, moved ahead. The formal contract was only inked in November 1949, probably because of the fear more requirement mutations would occur.

Martin's XB-51 looked excitingly innovative in 1947. To achieve the high speed demanded, the wings were clean and thin, with no fuel tanks within. Like the horizontal tail atop the vertical, the wings were swept 35 degrees. The bicycle undercarriage was adopted. The wings had marked 6 degrees anhedral to combat Dutch Roll, but also got the tips, with outrigger gear, near the pavement while on the ground. The long, slender fuselage had a fighter-like bubble canopy covering the pilot only. The crew of two, in Martin ejection seats, included a bombardier/navigator/radio operator. The "nav" was below and behind the pilot with a skylight window in the overhead escape hatch and side "portholes." Operating the SHORAN was a primary task of this crewman. To get the most from the extant engines, two were hung off the forward fuselage in pods and a third under the tail, fed by an S-duct with inlet on the jet's spine.

The 5,200-lbf (23.1-kN) J47s were water-injected. They also had two-piece "eyelid" variable exit area nozzles. The aft engine would be shut down during cruise and the inlet sealed via a clamshell that rotated across from within the fuselage. There were accommodations for four JATO bottles on the aft fuselage. There was an optional bomb bay ferry tank, with refueling via a single point. The horizontal stabilizer was trimmable, and the wing incidence would also be adjusted automatically with flap extension in a 2–7.5-degree range. Hydraulic jackscrews at the front spar pivoted the wing about the aft spar. This accommodated an acceptable take-off distance given that the bicycle gear did not permit the normal rotation to take-off attitude. It also maintained pilot visibility over the nose during landing in a flat attitude for the touchdown on both gear trucks. If too fast, the jet touched down on the nose gear with a risk of overstress. If too slow, the jet touched down on the aft gear first and caused an abrupt derotation to again strike the nose down too hard. Each gear truck could be pivoted to align with the ground track during a crabbed landing in a crosswind. The wing's leading edges had slats and hot air anti-ice inside. At the trailing edge were single-slotted flaps. Roll was via spoilers, leaving the tip ailerons for pilot feel alone. There were speedbrakes in the aft fuselage, a braking parachute, and anti-skid tested initially on the XB-26H.

Eight 20-mm cannon were to be placed in the nose. This could be swapped with a bombing nose containing the associated avionics, or a camera nose. The bomb bay was to accommodate up to 10,495 lb (4,761 kg) of weapons. Martin had to address the challenges of high-speed, LABS. As the speed had been pushed up, the classical bomb bay and pedal doors were becoming unsuitable, or the aircraft would have to slow for delivery and increase exposure to ground fire. High-velocity airflow would buffet the doors and create adverse flow through the bay, preventing clean store separation. Spoiler panels deploying at the front of the bay as the doors opened were being added to designs to combat the issue.

Martin's solution was a rotary bomb bay door in which bombs were loaded onto the inside of the single door that rotated 180 degrees to stow the weapons inside and place the outer surface flush with the exterior. This required a large empty interior volume for the door edge to swing through. The door could be detached from the aircraft for loading, then wheeled to the aircraft and hoisted into place for attachment to the pivots while the wheels were removed. Separate doors could be prepared while the aircraft was on a mission, then quickly swapped with the on-jet door to reduce bomb upload to just nine minutes—although it took fifteen minutes to reload cannon shells. The outside surface of the door had mounts for two 2,000-lb (907-kg) bombs to be drop first before rotating the door. A 4,000-lb (1,814-kg) bomb fit in a door that was bulged to accommodate its large diameter, and so did not allow for external bombs. This door also permitted a Mk 5 "special weapon" to be carried. The design had store ejectors—twin pneumatic pistons for each bomb shackle—to push bombs clear of the aircraft rather than rely solely on gravity.[10]

The first flight of the two XB-51 prototypes was in October 1949. During testing, it was found necessary to add a bullet fairing at the juncture of the horizontal and vertical tails to reduce buffeting at high speed. The feel ailerons were eliminated as unnecessary and because they were suffering reversal due to wing torsional deformation. The design had high wing loading as it had been designed for speed and not maneuverability. It was so fast during flight test that it ran away from F-80 and F-84 safety chase airplanes. Control changes were necessary to reduce some handling deficiencies. The aircraft otherwise flew quite well. Some of the challenges were the narrow take-off and landing speeds to ensure against excessive drag on take-off to permit climb and the proper landing attitude to set down on both trucks simultaneously and avoid overloading the nose gear. Several landing mishaps were credited to pilot error in this regard.

Martin XB-51 Characteristics

span	53.1 feet (16.2 m)	weight empty	29,584 lb (13,419 kg)
length	85.1 feet (25.9 m)	combat	41,457 lb (18,805 kg)
height	17.3 feet (5.3 m)	maximum	62,452 lb (28,328 kg)
wing area	548 feet² (50.9 m²)	speed, max. (sea level)	645 mph (1,038 kph)
fuel, built-in+bay	2,835+700 gal (10,732+2,650 l)	cruise	532 mph (856 kph)
service ceiling	41,400 feet (12,619 m)	range, 4,000-lb bombs	870 miles (1,400 km)
climb rate, max.	6,980 fpm (2,128 mpm)	ferry	1,613 miles (2,596 km)

The Korean Conflict began while the B-26 replacements were still in development. Combat quickly showed the veteran to be deficient in speed and payload for the circumstances, especially for the night intruder mission. A jet-powered equivalent, with modern systems, was urgently needed. The USAF set up a committee in 1950 to consider alternatives from existing airframes that might be quickly fielded. The goals were an all-weather tactical bomber able to operate from unimproved fields, possessing 630-mph (1,019-kph) top speed, 40,000-foot (12,191-m) ceiling, and 1,150-miles (1,852-km) range.

The unusual three-engine Martin XB-51 shows its lines during a test flight over the test range near Edwards AFB. The centerline engine could be shut down for cruise and the top inlet closed via a cover that rotated up from within the fuselage. This first prototype has already been modified with a bullet fairing ahead of the horizontal tail. (*San Diego Air & Space Museum*)

The XB-51, then in flight testing, had been intended to replace the B-26. However, requirements had evolved again such that it might not be the best choice. Adopting the B-45 and North American AJ-1 (see page 266) were looked at. The committee's view also extended internationally with consideration of the U.K.'s English Electric Canberra B.2 and the Avro Canada CF-100 Canuck.

The Canberra had left strong impressions during public displays, and the USAF personnel took a closer look during visits to the island in August and September 1950. A fly-off of the contenders occurred in February 1951 at Andrews AFB after a Canberra prototype was flown across the "pond" non-stop.

The B-45 was clearly too heavy and under-performing, and most had been reworked to carry nukes or would otherwise require modifications for the tactical mission. The AJ-1 was too slow, appeared vulnerable, and did not possess forward-firing guns. The Canuck had too light a payload. The B-51 was not sufficiently maneuverable owing to normal load factor limits and had too short a range. Although designed for high-altitude radar bombing, the British machine, with its low wing loading—less than half that of the XB-51—was easily the standout performer in maneuverability. Additionally, the British aircraft could loiter for 2.5 hours over a target 900 miles (1,448 km) from base whereas the Martin jet could do just one hour at 400 miles (644 km). The Canberra was selected to fill the requirement as the B-57A.

The B-51 was canceled in November 1951 after expending $12.6 million. The relentless USAF push for high speed, even for a TAC bomber, had again failed to meet the actual need of the battlefield in which the aircraft had to circle at modest speed to locate targets and roll in on them for direct attack, especially at night. A high-speed dash across a previously identified target, using SHORAN with a 200-mile (322-km) range, was not the tactical mission the USAF struggled with in Korea. Given the multiple changes to requirements before the definitized contract was signed, it is perhaps no surprise that it changed again by the time of flight evaluation. The high cost of producing the B-51 was also a consideration in the choice of the Canberra.[11] The XB-51s continued under test until both were wrecked in fatal accidents.

British production could not accommodate American needs—the RAF coming first—and so a U.S. manufacturer was sought. Given that the B-51 was not going into production and Martin needed a contract, the firm was chosen. They were to deliver 250 Canberras between November 1952 and October 1953, with a peak of fifty per month. This was to be achieved by subcontracting out 60 percent of the work. After a March 1951 contract, an agreement with English Electric was concluded in April, and in June, two DC-4s carried Canberra B.2 drawings to Baltimore. The process of converting these to American standards, substituting locally available materials, and accommodating U.S. gear, was thought to be well understood. One British-built airplane was kept as a pattern aircraft, but this broke up in flight owing to an operational error. A second jet was then supplied.

Since the Canberra was considered good enough for the RAF, the U.S. Air Force leadership was initially of the opinion that the aircraft would be suitable with minimal changes and fielding would be rapid. However, those in operational and developmental agencies lobbied for changes to optimize the jet for the mission, and they won the day. Their focus was operational safety, mission utility, and maintainability. They pointed out that the RAF was seeking similar design refinements, where it was only just entering service. Just creating a logistics "tail" of British Standard piece-parts would be complicated and costly. The crash of the pattern aircraft and the death of one of the crewmembers brought forth even further revisions.

The decreed adjustments included the substitution of American avionics, the addition of wingtip tanks, canopy revisions for better visibility, the cockpit rearranged for more room and a crew station eliminated by combining bombardier and navigation functions, plus addition of airframe and engine anti-ice. More significant was the replacement of the two Rolls-Royce Avons with the more powerful J65 at 7,220 lbf (32.1 kN). This engine was only just being assembled and it was encountering difficulties. The demand for more rapid production had Buick Motors spun up as a second supplier. This ultimately did not pan out as the Buick engines were found deficient. Wright had to meet full production quantity on its own. Consequently, deliveries were delayed and slow. Suffice to say that all these factors lengthen the path to airplane production and fielding by years. Weight grew and performance suffered.

Additional changes, some proposed by Martin, were left to a B-model. Most evident was a tandem cockpit with a conventional canopy, Martin ejection seats, fuselage speedbrakes, eight .50-cal guns installed in the wings, underwing hardpoints, and the adoption of a detachable rotary bomb bay door. The eight external hardpoints accommodated 3,000 lb (1,361 kg) of stores.

The first B-57A flew in July 1953, a week before Korean combat ended. It could carry 4,000 lb (1,814 kg) of weapons internally and 3,000 lb (1,361 kg) externally.

Ultimately, only eight of these aircraft were completed, at a cost of $9.3 million per jet, and not expected to ever serve as bombers.[12] The rest of the initial production of sixty-seven machines were built as RB-57A photoreconnaissance variants. Early service had its usual share of problems to be resolved. The air force waited for the B-57B that served both bomber and recce roles. With 407 Canberras completed through 1957, the type served for decades in these roles plus EW.

Martin B-57A Characteristics

span	64 feet (19.5 m)	weight empty	29,241 lb (13,263 kg)
length	65.8 feet (20.1 m)	loaded	48,421 lb (21,963 kg)
height	15.3 feet (4.7 m)	max. take-off	51,547 lb (23,381 kg)
wing area	960 feet² (89.2 m²)	speed, max. (4,500 feet)	609 mph (980 kph)
fuel, int.+ext.	2,252+640 gal (8.525+2,423 l)	cruise	495 mph (797 kph)
service ceiling	51,400 feet (15,667 m)	range, combat	1,524 miles (2,453km)
climb rate, max.	5,700 fpm (1,737 mpm)	ferry	2,568 miles (4,133 km)

The delays in the B-57 prompted the USAF to look at the Douglas A3D bomber (see pagge 269) under advanced development for the navy and yet to fly. It was ordered as the B-66 Destroyer in February 1952 to be built in Long Beach and Tulsa. The contract called for five preproduction machines in recce configurations. Again, the need was considered urgent and the intent was to adopt the jet quickly with minimal changes. However, the same pattern of altered requirements was experienced with

Martin was selected to manufacture an Americanized version of the English Electric Canberra bomber. What was supposed to be a rapid step to U.S. production to meet an urgent operational need was greatly lengthened by changes introduced by the USAF and Martin. The Baltimore production line for the B-57A and RB-57A is shown with tip tanks fitted to some aircraft as one of the changes to the baseline British airplane. (*National Museum of the United States Air Force*)

a combination of those perceived as essential for safety and mission suitability, and those pushed as important for enhancing mission effectiveness. The service wanted a 1,150-mile (1,852-km) radius of action and carrying 10,000 lb (4,536 kg) of ordnance. Consequently, this program also ran late and so the B-57 program was sustained.

All the A3D naval accouterments were removed, including swapping to an undercarriage more appropriate to the mission and with larger tires for softer surfaces. The flight deck was rearranged under a canopy that permitted ejection seats. New navigation and bombing radars were installed (the former with a much larger antenna), a thermal de-icing system introduced, and a remotely controlled GE tail turret with twin 20-mm cannon added. The latest ECM and electronic counter-countermeasures (ECCM) were to be integrated. The air force disliked the hydraulic and fuel systems, wanting to add a fuel purge feature. The wing was revised to include altering the planform, the thickness:chord ratio, and the incidence was reduced 2 degrees for greater stability. Justification for these was ensuring suitability of the structure to carry the buffeting stresses associated with the low-altitude, high-speed mission profile. The flaps and ailerons were revised, with spoilers added. Pratt & Whitney J57s, at 9,700 lbf (43.1 kN), was wisely chosen to replace the troubled J40, although the P&W was itself still immature.

It was more than two years before the first flight of the B-66 in June 1954, and a year into flight testing before the engine swap could be made. The jets would span 72.5 feet (22.1 m), were 75.2 feet (22.9 m) in length, and weighed 42,549 lb (19,300 kg) empty and 57,800 lb (26,218 kg) loaded. Their top speed was 631 mph (1,016 kph), had a service ceiling of 39,400 feet (12,009 m), and a combat range of 1,800 miles (2,897 km). Building preproduction B-66As proved a wise choice as there were numerous significant deficiencies. Among these were grave controllability issues, flight control system reliability problems, heavy wing buffet, and poor visibility from the cockpit. Consequently, the production B-66B aircraft did not emerge until 1955. These added an AR receptacle and twin hardpoints for external tanks, among the many changes to correct the deficiencies.

The air force continued to pump money into the Destroyer and it eventually came together. The B-66B finally went operational in 1956. Ultimately, 249 airplanes were completed through 1958. The career of the B-66 was similar to the B-57 in that they came to focus on PR and then EW missions.

The USAF was working on a purpose-built bomber to assume the role the interim B-57 and B-66 were intended to fill. Although a TAC bomber, the requirements evolved to a long-range, nuclear-armed, twin-engined, two-place jet with supersonic dash at 50,000–60,000 feet (15,240–18,288-m). A highly accurate inertial navigation and bombing system was to permit bomb delivery at high speed and low altitude. Radar would allow terrain avoidance for low-level night operations. Proposals were entertained in 1952, but a decision was not made immediately, and refreshed proposals were assessed in 1954. Martin was selected to proceed with the B-68, but the contract for the prototypes was not signed until 1956, with service entry aimed at 1962. The avionics ran into severe development delays such that it looked like the aircraft would not emerge until 1963. By 1957, the air force had higher priorities in a constrained fiscal environment and so closed the overly ambitious program.

This concept art shows the air force's adaptation of the navy's A3D as the B-66A, as initiated in early 1952. Although the design was initially to be minimally altered to allow rapid move to production meeting an urgent requirement, very significant changes crept in to greatly delay the effort. The drawing does not depict the final flight deck enclosure, but it does illustrate the remotely controlled tail turret. (*United States Air Force*)

Intercontinental

Although the United States had been able to secure bases from which strategic bombers could reach enemy territory during the war, this might not be so in the future. Seizing the Pacific bases for the bombing campaign against Japan had been bloody affairs no one wanted to repeat. The air force remained eager for a true intercontinental bomber. Holding atomic bombs as a deterrent to foreign aggressors threatening the homeland or American interests abroad would be bolstered by the ability to deliver such weapons anywhere on the globe, from American soil, within a day or so.

The Convair B-36 Peacemaker program started in 1941, but it was moved down in priority in the late years of the war. Postwar, with the growing hostility of the Soviet Union, the program was sustained. However, the technological hurdles were high and the program to build two prototypes and 100 production articles moved slowly. The normal problems of weight and drag were a constant battle. New materials and construction techniques were adopted to combat these trends. The customer contributed to delays by revising requirements that included adding nose defensive armament, which forced the flight deck to be raised, plus radar and other evolving avionics. The performance goals vacillated but were generally around a 10,000-mile (16,093-km) range, a 40,000-foot (12,192-m) ceiling, and up to 300 mph (483 kph) top speed.

The bomber was characterized by six piston engines in a pusher configuration to eliminate propwash across the wing that would disturb the laminar flow. Inlets for cooling and carburetor air were in the wing leading edges with ducting running back to the

3,000-hp (2,237-kW), supercharged R-4360 engines embedded in the aft portion of the wing. Instead of cowl flaps, a translating annular "air plug" altered the area between the cowling and spinner. The Curtiss-Wright 19-foot (5.8-m) diameter props were automatically synchronized and reversible. The wing was so thick (7.5 feet/2.3 m at the root) that the engines were accessed in flight for minor servicing. Three slotted Fowler flaps were found per side. There was hot air de-ice for the propellers and aero surface leading edges anti-ice.

Forward and aft pressurized crew compartments were joined by a 2.1-foot (0.6-m) diameter "communication tube" running 80 feet (24 m) near the base of the bomb bays. The crewman lay on a cart moving on rails and pulled along by hand. The nominal crew was fifteen men. Flight controls were unpowered, instead moved by free-floating servo tabs in the surfaces, with some tabs electrically driven. To provide force feel to the pilot, a double-acting spring-piston in each surface compressed whenever the tab was deflected. In addition, the spring produced a dampening effect when the main surface was deflected by turbulence.

Four bomb bays, with a 72,000-lb (32,659-kg) total capacity, were enclosed by flush doors that slid up the side of the aircraft. Weapons included as many as seventy-two 1,000-lb (454-kg) bombs and up to the 22,000-lb (9,979-kg) T-14 Grand Slam. Standard bombs were loaded via an electric winch positioned atop the aircraft with its cables extending through holes into each bay. Exceptionally large weapons were lifted into the bay via hydraulic loaders. A 3,000-gal (11,356-lit) jettisonable auxiliary fuel tank could be carried in one bay. A total of eight gun turrets, each with two 20-mm cannon, defended the bomber. Paired gun turrets were retractable into bays enclosed by sliding doors; these were found at the top front of the bomber, with top and bottom behind the wing. Gunners with electronic fire controls sat before blister sighting stations. The tail guns were matched with a radar, while the nose gun was handled via a periscope sight. The aft upper gun doors had to be opened whenever a bomb bay door was opened owing to ram pressure.

The nose landing gear was hydraulically steerable via a wheel on the console to the left of the port-seat pilot. This tiller would become common in later transports and bombers where rudder pedal deflection alone did not provide sufficient steering fidelity during taxi. Despite lessons of the past, single main landing gear wheels and tires of an extraordinary 9.2-foot (2.8-m) diameter and 3.8-foot (1.2-m) width were chosen so that they could fit in the wing when retracted. The largest tires ever fitted to an airplane, alone weighing 1,475 lb (669 kg), they generated enormous surface pressure and the USAAF expressed concern for aircraft safety if one of the tires blew out on take-off or landing. There were initially only three runways in the country stressed to take the load of the bomber, including Carswell AFB neighboring the production plant in Fort Worth where an acceptable runway was built of 1.8-feet (0.6-m) thick concrete.

Given the weight of the aircraft, the six engines still gave little performance margin, and braking likewise contributed to an accelerate/stop distance so great as to require a minimum 8,000-foot (2,438-m) runway. The climb gradient of the airplane could be so low that an unobstructed departure path extending 5 miles (8 km) beyond the departure end was necessary.[13] Trees were cut down in this zone as necessary.

The XB-36 finally flew in August 1946, but changes were already in work. The team struggled with engine cooling and propeller vibration, which threatened to rapidly fatigue the blades; also, the wing flaps had to be redesigned. Cooling fan changes and revised construction techniques addressed these issues. The revised flight deck and nose for the forward turret windows were featured on the second aircraft, flown initially in December 1947 as the YB-36. New four-wheel main gear trucks were also tested that permitted the aircraft to operate from any field supporting the B-50, or just 1.1-foot (0.3-m) thick concrete. The change also cut 2,600 lb (1,179 kg) of weight, though accommodating the trucks within the wings meant accepting bulged doors.

The aircraft was so tall that few hangars could accommodate it. Typical movement in and out of the Fort Worth hangars had the main gear on rollers to permit sideways movement and the nose raised on rolling jacks to lower the tail nearly to the ground. The aircraft was then inched in or out at an angle.

The first of twenty-two preproduction B-36As flew in August 1947, with delivery to the Carswell squadron between May and September 1948. These machines lacked the ability to deploy nuclear weapons because the necessary top-secret data had not been provided to Convair. They also had aluminum electrical wiring for weight savings that proved an unfortunate choice given how readily it broke under tension from airframe flexure and vibration, causing all manner of systems faults. Consequently, the B-36As were used for general training.

The initial combat-capable B-36Bs flew in July 1948 and began arriving in squadrons during November. These sixty-two airplanes had the full defense armament and a newer bomb-nav radar. Power output of the R-4360 was upped by 500 hp (373 kW) with water injection; this helped recover performance lost to weight and drag growth. Each bomb bay was equipped to carry a 10,800-lb (4,899-kg) Mk 4 atomic bomb or two 43,000-lb (19,504-kg) T-12 Grand Slams could be accommodated. Delivering a single Mk 4 permitted a 4,300-mile (6,920 km) radius and a 28,500-foot (8,687-m) combat ceiling, at nearly 42.5 hours of mission time. These aircraft averaged around $4.7 million each. At peak production, the bombers were being turned out at a rate of one per week.

In December 1948, a B-36B flew from Carswell to Hawaii and dropped 10,000-lb (4,536-kg) of inert bombs before returning home. It covered the 8,100 miles (13,036 km) without refueling during the 35.5-hour mission (an average of 228 mph/367 kph). In March 1949, a distance record of 9,600 miles (15,450 km) was set during a 43.6-hour flight. A flight carrying two 42,000-lb (19,051-kg) T-12s was also demonstrated.

Convair B-36B Characteristics

span	230 feet (70.1 m)	weight empty	140,640 lb (637,932 kg)
length	162.2 feet (49.4 m)	combat	227,700 lb (103,282 kg)
height	46.8 feet (14.3 m)	gross	328,000 lb (148,778 kg)
wing area	4,772 feet² (433 m²)	speed, max. (34,500 feet)	381 mph (613 kph)
fuel, max.	26,217 gal (99,242 l)	cruise	203 mph (327 kph)
service ceiling	42,500 feet (12,954 m)	range, 10,000-lb bombs	8,600 miles (13,840 km)
climb rate, sea level	500 fpm (152 mpm)	ferry	8,174 miles (13,155 km)

The earliest combat-ready Convair Peacemaker was the B-36B (44-92038 shown). The nose and tail turret doors are seen as well as the lines of the top forward and aft turret doors. Reaching relevant numbers in USAF squadrons during 1949, they could each carry an A-bomb 4,300 miles and return. (*San Diego Air & Space Museum*)

The upper aft pair of cannon turrets of the B-36 is shown retracted and with doors open. Remotely controlled and joined by two other pairs of such turrets plus nose and tail turrets, the arrangement suggests an evolution of the defensive armament of World War Two bombers. With the introduction of jet bombers, this was all rendered anachronistic. (*National Archives*)

The speed and altitude performance of the B-36 in the dawning of the "jet age" was a concern. Even sixteen 20-mm cannon with 9,200 rounds might not be enough to ensure survivability and so represent a convincing deterrent. An 8,000-foot (2,438-m) take-off run was also barely tolerable. With the U.S. military presence around the world, it appeared the faster B-50 would be sufficient until jet bombers were on force with routine aerial refueling support. The future of the B-36 was clouded.

One solution appeared to be adopting the variable discharge turbine engines for the last thirty-four aircraft of the Peacemaker program as B-36Cs. This was to boost top speed by more than 50 mph (81 kph) to 410 mph (660 kph). However, the VDT jet exhaust would be at the wing's trailing edge and the propellers moved to the leading edge turned via long extension shafts after turning the engine around. These major alterations were worrisome, requiring an almost entirely new wing. With the future of the bomber in doubt, this was too great an investment. When propulsion system challenges proved too daunting, heat dissipation the greatest obstacle, the VDT fell by the wayside. The Soviet blockade of Berlin was then an incentive to sustain the B-36 program. The C-model order became additional B-model machines. However, performance remained to be addressed.

In 1948, Convair proposed adding turbojet engines to supplement the recips and increase airspeed. The twin-engine pods of the B-47 were to be adapted to the airplane, mounted outboard of the R-4360s. These could be used for take-off and dash aloft, but otherwise shut down and the inlets shuttered. The J47s were modified to burn avgas rather than jet fuel, slightly degrading their performance. This configuration first flew in June 1949. It added an average of 50 mph (81 kph) to the top speed and 25 mph (40 kph) to cruise, plus nearly 3,000 feet (914 m) to the ceiling—bringing the latter to over 45,000 feet (13,716 m)—although it cost a bit in range. At its combat altitude, it was expected that extant interceptors could barely manage a tail chase with little or no maneuver margin—although interceptor performance was increasing rapidly. Payload also went up 12,000 lb (5,443 kg) to 84,000 lb (38,102 kg). A remarkable 30 percent was shaved off the take-off distance. However, the pods further complicate crosswind landings in the large-span airplane with the risk of pavement strike during a wing-low touchdown.

The jet units were adopted for the B-36D for which the first was delivered in August 1950. These ten-engined bombers also featured more capable bomb-nav radar that permitted the bombardier to handle navigation radar functions instead of two men performing the role; a new tail gun radar; two-segment "snap-action" bomb bay doors replacing the slow and draggy original doors; and metal replacing the control surface fabric. The bays were further modified to take the newest assortment of atomic bombs. Weight was driven up some 20,000 lb (9,072 kg) by these improvements. Mission radius decayed to 3,530 miles (5,681 km) with the 10,000-lb bomb load and a combat ceiling of 33,100 feet (10,089 m). This undermined the "intercontinental" claim of the bomber as no potential adversaries lay within that radius without deploying the bombers to an overseas base on foreign soil.

All but twenty-two of the B-36Ds and RB-36Ds (see page 390) were created by modification of B-36Bs such that ultimately, there were eighty-six and twenty-four, respectively. Some were being modified as other new B-36Bs were still being delivered. The rework cost about $1.6 million per aircraft. The E-model was a reconnaissance variant. The B-36F brought an additional 300 hp (224 kW) per Wasp Major, a newer radar bombing system, an uprated tail radar that required two radomes permitting simultaneous search and track, and "Ferret" ECM improvements that included adding a chaff dispenser in the aft fuselage. Thirty-four of these bombers and twenty-four recce equivalents were delivered in March through December 1951. The G-model became the YB-60 (see page 262).

The B-36H was already being built as the last F-models were being turned out. Eighty-three bombers and seventy-three recon variants were delivered from December 1952 to September 1953. This revised the flight deck arrangement for a second engineer, substituted yet another tail radar that permitted simultaneous search and engagement, upped chaff capacity to 1,400 lb (635 kg), and installed additional fuel cells in the outboard wing volume. The mission radius was then down to 3,110 miles (5,005 km) with a combat ceiling of 33,000 feet (10,058 m). However, it also resolved many of the annoying mechanical issues that had made the Peacemaker such a handful to maintain and operate. Among these, some elements of the radar bombing system were relocated to the pressurized compartment where they could be serviced in flight. The guns had not been fully functional before 1953.

The last model, the B-36J, was already being developed by the end of the period under review. These featured additional outer wing panel fuel volume, for an additional 2,770 gal (10,486 l), and strengthened undercarriage for higher take-off GW. Thirty-three would be built through mid-1954 to bring total production to 385 airplanes, with many redelivered after extensive upgrades that altered their original designations. Also, in January 1954, the "Featherweight" program was initiated that reduced weight to improve performance and stay ahead of interceptor advancements. Many of the crew comfort features were removed as were all but the tail cannon. The aircrew was thusly brought down to thirteen. It was concluded that the lighter aircraft would operate at such a high altitude that no interceptor could reach it. This proved true at least through the rest of the decade, though darkness and inclement weather were always the bomber's best defense. The weight reduction restored mission radius to 3,990 miles (6,421 km) with a combat ceiling of 27,400 feet (8,352 m) for the J-models.[14]

Convair B-36H Characteristics

span	230 feet (70.1 m)	weight empty	168,487 lb (76,424 kg)
length	162.2 feet (49.4 m)	combat	253,900 lb (115,167 kg)
height	46.8 feet (14.3 m)	gross	370,000 lb (167,829 kg)
wing area	4,772 feet² (433 m²)	speed, max. (36,700 feet)	416 mph (670 kph)
fuel, max.	33,626 gal (127,288 l)	cruise	234 mph (377 kph)
service ceiling	44,000 feet (13,411 m)	range, 10,000-lb bombs	6,220 miles (10,010 km)
climb rate, sea level	920 fpm (628 mpm)	ferry	7,690 miles (12,376 km)

Answering the need for more speed in response to jet fighter advances, and safer take-off, the Peacemaker was made a ten-engine bomber with the addition of jet engine nacelles from the B-47. This configuration is shown by RB-36E 44-9012 taxiing at Ramey AFB, Puerto Rico. The aircraft has one of its forward turrets deployed. (*National Archives*)

Although there was discussion of employing the Peacemaker in Korea, this never occurred because of the escalatory message it would send, and its greater value as a strategic deterrent force. Some also believed that the USAF would not risk losing one of the bombers in the warzone because it would undermine the indomitable character the service was promoting for the B-36. However, its limitations and tremendous resource demands were readily evident. It was a complicated and maintenance-intensive beastie that, during 1952, was suffering a dismal accident rate of twenty-three per 100,000 flying hours. Yet, crews practiced the daylong missions to targets in the USSR, deploying to such locales as North Africa to be within range, and the bomber was suitably reliable. The B-36 was the only bomber capable of carrying the first hydrogen bomb and so its service was extended further. The type was withdrawn in 1959 after barely ten years of active service as jet bombers and aerial refueling became more common. However, during most of that time, the Convair airplane was the sole means of delivering nuclear weapons across ocean distances and so the principal deterrent force. It remains the largest aircraft ever operated by the air force at the time of writing.

The air force had begun seeking an all-jet replacement for the B-36 in January 1946. The initial requirement was carrying a 10,000-lb (4,536-kg) bomb load to a 5,000-mile (8,047-km) mission radius at 300 mph (483 kph) and 34,000 feet (10,363 m). The outrageous fuel consumption of the early turbojets did not bode well for achieving the range, but turboprops—yet to emerge as practical powerplants—might hold the key. Design teams still struggled to meet the range and speed desired, the latter continuing to grow.

The USAAF initially funded a Boeing project with six Wright T35 turboprops on a straight wing. The Typhoon was an adaptation of the hardware developed for the Lockheed L-1000 turbojet, dating from the war, which had been slow coming together. Eventually known as the J37, only three were built and offered nothing that other turbojets were not already producing. Ultimately, the turboprop bomber was passed up. The T35 failed to find other applications and the project was closed out in

1953. To draw some value from the $4.5 million already spent, the engine hardware and all data were made available to others in the industry.

A contract for two XB-52s was promulgated in 1948. By that point, the design had evolved to four turboprops on a 20-degree swept wing with a goal of 445 mph (716 kph). One candidate was the Northrop Turbodyne Corporation (a Northrop subsidiary) T37. This engine gave very promising ground test results and a YB-35 was intended as a testbed for flight trials. However, based on the early success of the B-47, Boeing proposed switching to turbojets and the bomber armed with only a tail turret. By the end of 1948, the design was sporting eight J57s in four twin-engined underwing nacelles on a 35-degree swept wing. Consequently, there were no perspective operational platforms for the Turbodyne, and the effort was shelved in 1950. All materials were passed to G.E. The switch to turbojets was to ensure the highest practical airspeed. The J57 was an effort to develop a high-thrust turbojet with more moderate fuel consumption. By the time of flight testing, it was delivering 9,000 lbf (40 kN) with an amazing 0.82 SFC. Such characteristics might support reaching 500 mph (805 kph) and a range of 5,000 miles, with more offered by aerial refueling.

The notional XB-52 would carry a prodigious quantity of fuel, and also burn it at a tremendous rate. Consequently, the high cruise speed came with a short range. The service was working hard on creating a practical AR capability to support the intercontinental mission, but this would take time and was not guaranteed to be successful. With USAF urging, Boeing offered an alternative that the service funded as the XB-55. This had four T35s on a modestly swept wing. The range improvement was, as expected, offset by a slow cruise speed that the service found unacceptable. This and the insupportable costs of developing two large bombers simultaneously led to the XB-55 being dropped.

Proceeding with the turbojet-powered design, the wing was swept 36.5 degrees. The aero surfaces were large and long, with high taper ratios. Large Fowler flaps were joined by inboard flaperons and outboard servotab-driven ailerons. Spoilers augmented drag on landing approach, eliminating the chute the B-47 had needed. Pitch was via all-moving stabs, eschewing elevators. All controls were hydraulically boosted. Four turbines were driven by bleed air to turn alternators in meeting the high electrical power demands. Two pairs of two-wheel trucks were in staggered pairs ahead and behind the bomb bays. This quadricycle landing gear was less cumbersome than the B-47, though all the mains were still stowed in the long and narrow fuselage. The gear normally mandated a level take-off and landing. Take-off distances were great, but JATO was not incorporated. The long wings still required outriggers near the tips, especially for full wing fuel when the tips drooped so much that ground contact was risked during taxi. Over half the take-off weight consisted of fuel. A braking parachute was included. Dealing with the same problem of the very tall B-36 fitting in hangars, the vertical tail was designed to fold.

The pilot and co-pilot were seated in tandem under a canopy much like the B-47. The navigator and bombardier were below in the same pressurized compartment. The radar was in the nose. The gunner was in a small compartment in the tail. Four .50-cals guns in the tail turret were directed either visually or automatically by radar. During turbulence, the ride in the tail station would be quite wild given fuselage bending motion. Bomb bays were proportionally smaller than the B-36 because of the evolving size of nuclear weapons. Yet capacity was 72,000 lb (32,659 kg).

The first of two B-52 prototypes (the second, designated YB-52) was taken up in April 1952. While there were problems to overcome—particularly control forces and handling—the type showed immediate promise. The USAF had given Boeing a contract for thirteen B-52As in February 1951 at a then-breathtaking $29 million each. Changes were already being designed as SAC demanded line-abreast seating with a conventional transport-like windscreen. This was felt essential for the co-pilot to assist the pilot in the absence of a flight engineer. The crew became six, the forward-placed personnel on either upward or downward ejecting seats. Chaff dispensers were also added. The J57s were upgraded with water injection to aid heavyweight take-off. There would also be provisions for boom AR plus external tanks. The bomber would still require unusually long runways, and the few bases that had these may not also have long crosswind runways. Consequently, the gear was designed to pivot when down to permit the aircraft to land in a crab, the fuselage aligned with the wind while the trucks remained aligned with the approach ground track and runway. Another motivation for this was the blown tires suffered in crosswind landings with the prototypes given side-loading from drift with the slab-sided airplane. It was also discovered that, at high speed, aileron effectiveness fell off owing to wing twist. Spoilers had to be used to ensure suitable roll rates. The USAF also insisted on thorough systems testing before integration in an effort to avoid the pitfalls of the B-47.

The first B-52A emerged in summer 1954, but the B-52B was the initial model to be fielded. It was 1955 before combat units began receiving these, and more before they were truly combat-capable. It was also clear that the aircraft would be upgraded with evolving technology, but the baseline airplane had to be placed into production expeditiously to represent a convincing deterrent given world events of the mid-1950s.

Boeing XB-52 and YB-52 Characteristics

span	185 feet (56.4 m)	weight empty	155,200 lb (70,398 kg)
length	152.8 feet (46.5 m)	combat	256,800 lb (116,482 kg)
height (21.5 feet folded)	48.3 feet (14.7 m)	gross	390,000 lb (176,900 kg)
wing area	4,000 feet² (372 m²)	speed, max. (20,000 feet)	611 mph (1,132 kph)
fuel, int.+ext.	36,540+2,000 gal (13,832+7,571 l)	cruise	519 mph (835 kph)
combat ceiling	46,500 feet (14,173 m)	range, 10,000-lb bombs	5,200 miles (8,369 km)
climb rate, initial	4,550 fpm (1,387 mpm)	ferry	7,015 miles (11,290 km)

The Stratofortress would remain in production through 1962, serving through the height of the Cold War and into the complexities of twenty-first-century threats. At the time of writing, it was expected to serve until 2030. Upgrades and reconditioning were necessary to achieve this, but replacement costs were very high and the capabilities met the evolving mission profiles.

Although SAC was fully behind the B-52, AMC had funded a similar aircraft in the event the technically risky design ran into serious trouble—although there was no

Relying upon aerial refueling and high subsonic airspeed with turbojet engines for an intercontinental bombing capability led to a new airplane by 1952. One of the prototype Boeing Stratofortresses, the YB-52s (49-231) is seen on take-off during May 1952 emphasizing the unusual main gear layout, slab-sided fuselage, and generous aero surface area. The engine nacelles and flight deck would undergo changes—note the tandem-seating cockpit—but the layout would survive through decades of production and generations of operation. (*National Archives*)

official competition. This was a revised B-36 with swept surfaces and eight turbojets. Convair had initially proposed such an evolution in August 1950 with Pratt & Whitney T57s, but the design had evolved to 8,700-lbf (38.7-kN) J57s by the time of contracting in March 1951. However, there was a continuing discussion of replacing the jets with six turboprops.

The YB-60 began as the YB-36G with two to be built new, although based on B-36F fuselages off the production line. The inboard wing box from the standard B-36 was retained, and 37.9-degree sweep outboard panels were added to this. Fuel capacity was increased. Convair was permitted to use the nacelle design for the B-52. All but the tail guns were deleted from the prototypes. The company envisioned new turrets that retracted into the fuselage without the use of doors. A steerable tail wheel on a long strut was added owing to the aft shift in the CG, making tipping a possibility for some fuel and payload conditions, and because full power for take-off tended to produce a tail-down pitching moment. However, the tail gear was retracted during the take-off roll to permit rotation and extended after the tricycle gear was securely on the ground during a landing roll.[15] A braking parachute was also added. The nose profile was altered to add volume for a search radar. Convair initially envisioned a crew of five only in the forward compartment. The engineer was eliminated and the co-pilot's seat could slide aft to the engineer station. However, the USAF insisted it needed a crew of nine to include ECM operators. The addition of an AR probe was also envisioned.

Given 72 percent commonality with the B-36, the first YB-60 was completed in just eight months. The program was then delayed awaiting engines for which the B-52 had priority. The maiden flight was in April 1952. It was soon evident that the YB-52 was more than 100 mph (161 kph) faster than the YB-60 that displayed control and flutter issues. With sixty-six hours logged, the airplane was parked and the second never received its engines. The program was canceled in August 1952. By that time, the use of turboprops was nixed. Some $14.4 million had been expended on the effort.

Convair YB-60 Characteristics

span	206.4 feet (62.9 m)	weight empty	153,016 lb (69,407 kg)
length	175.2 feet (53.4 m)	combat	260,250 lb (118,047 kg)
height	60.4 feet (18.4 m)	gross	410,000 lb (185,972 kg)
wing area	5,239 feet² (487 m²)	speed, max. (39,250 feet)	508 mph (818 kph)
fuel	42,106 gal (159,388 l)	cruise	467 mph (752 kph)
combat ceiling	44,650 feet (13,609 m)	range, 10,000-lb bombs	5,840 miles (9,399 km)
		ferry	6,192 miles (9,965 km)

The USAAF, and then USAF, worked closely with design teams exploring technologies and concepts seeking solutions to emerging operational needs. For bombers, this process was a series of efforts named "Generalized Bomber Study" for which conceptual design contracts were let. Of these, an informal requirement for a supersonic bomber was first documented in 1945. This was well before the true implications of supersonic flight were fully understood, and so the work continued to evolve. By 1951, the concept had come to focus on a delta-wing airplane, a single remote-controlled turret, and a crew of three including the pilot, bombardier/ navigator, and defensive systems operator.

Boeing's offering, the B-59, was an area-ruled design with four podded J73s grossing 148,300 lb (76,268 kg). By the end of 1952, Convair's delta-wing B-58 concept was selected and design work became more focused. Building on their recent experience, they converged on an area-ruled fuselage with four then-notional J79s in individual underwing nacelles. Seeking Mach 2, surface heating had to be addressed. A large, jettisonable belly pod was envisioned containing fuel and a nuclear-armed missile or bomb. The ambitious B-58 flew in 1956 and deliveries to combat units followed in 1960.

Navy Plays

The navy did not completely abandon the bomber field to the air force. They had traditionally employed patrol-bomber flying boats. The bombing aspects of these aircraft had lost significance as they focused on anti-submarine warfare (ASW) and principally deploying only sonobuoys. By the end of the war, the "B" in the "PB" designation had been dropped, and long-endurance land-based patrol aircraft were being built and deployed with weapons bays supporting the ASW mission. Under postwar roles and responsibilities considerations, these had to be clearly distinguished

In seeking their all-jet intercontinental bomber, the air force funded a proposal by Convair for a swept-wing and re-engine B-36. Eventually emerging as the YB-60, it retained most of the fuselage of the B-36F and the inboard wing box with the main landing gear. Built and flown in a relatively short time, the bomber came up short in comparison to the prototype Boeing B-52, and so the two prototypes were scrapped. (*National Archives*)

Building on their delta wing experience, Convair offered a supersonic bomber with such a layout. The air force placed the firm on contract for the B-58. This 1953 art shows paired engine nacelles that were eventually rejected in favor of four separate nacelles. It also shows a concept for a detachable belly missile, but tanks and bomb dispensers were also considered, compensating for the small interior volume of the area-ruled fuselage. (*National Archives*)

from "bombers." However, seeking a means to deliver nuclear weapons from aircraft carriers, the USN had sought naval airplanes capable of delivering the enormous nuclear weapons then being assembled. When the USS *United States* class super carrier had been canceled, this task became more difficult. The service looked again at seaplanes for a bomber capability that would be divorced from land bases.

Within a month of the end of the war, the navy had begun exploring how they could contribute to the atomic bomb delivery mission. They started growing the organizational and equipment basis for such capabilities, in addition to challenging the USAAF (and later USAF) dominance of the field from within the political arena. Given the enormous size and weight of the bombs as they then existed, flying them off carriers was going to be an exceptionally difficult task. It meant the redirection of significant fiscal resources at a time these were painfully slender. Yet it appeared that unless naval airpower could take on the mission, carriers were going to be sidelined.

While working to develop suitable new aircraft, the navy sought to demonstrate the potential to the politicians. It worked to adapt the land-based P2V patrol aircraft to the role. Flying the large and heavy aircraft from a carrier would be very challenging, if possible at all. A team set out in early 1947 to make it happen. The bay could take the narrower Mk I Little Boy bomb, and the navy petitioned the AEC to retain the weapon. With the bomb and full fuel onboard, the aircraft would weigh 70,000 lb (31,751 kg) and, on a Midway-class carrier, clear the island by a few feet. Instead of a catapult, eight JATO rockets added 8,000 lbf (35.6 kN) of thrust to shorten the take-off roll. The team also explored returning to the ship via arrestment or barrier. Tests ashore showed arrestment was possible with a very skilled pilot as demonstrated once. A second try by a less skilled aviator resulted in severe structural damage. So return, other than ditching beside the carrier, was off the table.

By April 1948, the nuclear-powered Neptune was ready for sea trails aboard the three Midway carriers—*Midway* CVA-41, *Franklin D. Roosevelt* CVA-42, and the *Coral Sea* CVA-43—with their strengthened decks. A standard P2V-2 and P2V-3 were lifted aboard the USS *Coral Sea* dockside in Norfolk, Virginia. Once at sea, both aircraft were flown off with JATO assist, blanketing the flight deck with dense smoke.

While this work was underway, Lockheed worked to convert a P2V-2 and eleven P2V-3s for the mission under a classified contract. This included removing non-essential external protuberances to cut drag and internal equipment to shave weight. The tail guns were retained and "high altitude" engines were installed.[16] Fuel tanks were added ahead of and behind the bomb bay that was altered to carry the weapon. The radar bombing system was revised for high altitude delivery and a single versus the normal two operators. Based upon NACA advice informed by laboratory testing, a "hydroflap" was added beneath the belly, deployed by a hydraulic actuator. Extended prior to ditching, this prevented the nose digging in on touchdown and so was hoped to make the event more survivable. The modified P2V-3s became P2V-3Cs.

The P2V-3Cs were delivered between September 1948 and August 1949. The first of these was launched from the *Coral Sea*, off the Virginia Capes, in March 1949. Weighing 74,000 lb (33,566 kg) at take-off, the aircraft went on to fly across the country to drop the dummy bomb on the Muroc range and then fly back to land at

Pax River. In September 1948, the navy's first atomic strike unit was in business and performed occasional shipboard launches, in addition to shore-based operations, to remain proficient. The maximum range was 5,060 miles (8,143 km) on a flight of nearly twenty-six hours. The Neptunes continued to be operated into the mid-1950s when a suitable number of the purpose-built AJ-1s (see later) were on force.

The U.S. Navy had kicked off a design competition in August 1945 to carry an 8,000-lb (3,629-kg) bomb load.[17] However, this was soon changed to a requirement to accommodate one of the 10,000-lb A-bombs in a carrier-based aircraft. An RFP was issued in January 1946, and the service selected North American under a June contract. The mission was for low and fast ingress then climbing to 30,000 feet (9,144 m) or more for weapon drop, followed by a dash egress. Given wing and vertical tail fold, plus other accouterments of carrier compatibility, there was no weight allowed for defensive armament. This was a sharp contrast to the USAF philosophy of the time of high and slow with many defensive guns.

The AJ-1 used two 2,400-hp (1,790-kW) R-2800s in wing nacelles and a centerline 4,600-lbf (20.5-kN) J33. The turbojet was fed by a NACA inlet atop the spine, ahead of the tail, and the exhaust was beneath the tail. The inlet was closed when the jet was not operating to reduce drag. The Allison would be operated during heavyweight take-off from the ship, for high-speed dash over the target or to evade, and in the event of a

A U.S. Navy P2V-3C performs a JATO-assisted take-off from the USS *Midway*. Although stripped of non-essentials, the aircraft was still very heavy, especially for launch from a carrier deck to that time. Yet the marginal capability allowed the USN to assume some nuclear delivery role carrying a single 8,900-lb Mk I Little Boy weapon. (*National Archive*)

recip failure. All burned the same avgas. The aircraft otherwise looked like a World War Two medium bomber with a large bomb bay under the shoulder-mounted straight wing.

An APS-31 radar, with antenna under the nose radome, supported navigation and target location. The crew of three sat in a pressurized flight deck. Bail-out was through the crew entrance door. They also had a hatch into the bomb bay where the weapon had to be armed manually. The bomb bay was sized for the 10,800-lb (4,899-kg) Mk 3 Fat Man uranium fission bomb. When the production Mk 4 weapon emerged during the aircraft's detailed design, it became the focus of the bay layout. However, the bay could also be fitted out for six 1,600-lb (726-kg) conventional bombs and mines.

The first of the three XAJ-1 prototypes was taken up for its maiden flight in July 1948. Production of fifty-five Savages had already been ordered based solely on inspection of the mock-up, with a request that the first dozen be delivered by July 1947. This was not to be, given that two of the prototypes crashed from structural failures. Considerable review and remedial actions stretched out the march to production.

The first production AJ-1 took off in May 1949. These had a greater fuel volume via the addition of tip tanks, plus strengthened and fixed canopy. Deliveries ran from August 1949 through to January 1952. Sea trials took place during mid-1950 and the first squadrons went to sea in 1951 aboard the Project 27A carriers. Originally, there were only the three Midway-class ships capable of taking the Savage. The revised Essex-class vessels began to emerge in 1950.

The navy had fifty-five AJ-2s built, these a spin-off of the AJ-2P camera ship (see page 391) featuring improved engines, greater fuel volume, the problem-plagued hydraulic system revised, eliminated the horizontal tail dihedral and aft fuselage strakes, while the vertical tail and rudder were extended 1 foot. From its first flight in February 1953, production rolled into 1954. The earlier AJ-1s were upgraded to this standard. A new bombing director system came with the 8,500-lb (3,856-kg) Mk 6 and 3,250-lb (1,474-kg) Mk 8 weapons.

North American AJ-1 Characteristics

span	75.2 feet (22 m)	weight empty	30,776 lb (13,960 kg)
length	63.1 feet (19.2 m)	combat	46,352 lb (21,025 kg)
height	21.4 feet (6.5 m)	maximum	54,000 lb (24,494 kg)
wing area	836 feet² (77.7 m²)	speed, max. (sea level)	471 mph (758 kph)
fuel, int.+ext.	1,217+1,240 gal (4,607+4,694 l)	cruise	270 mph (435 kph)
service ceiling	40,800 feet (12,436 m)	range, combat	1,732 miles (2,787 km)
climb rate	2,900 fpm (884 mpm)	ferry	2,993 miles (4,817 km)

The relative haste with which the Savage was developed, produced, and fielded was soon evident in many maintenance challenges, mishaps, and occasional groundings as the aircraft matured in service. The big airplane was not so welcome aboard the ship, despite the importance of its mission. Aside from leaking hydraulic fluid and requiring many sailors to manually fold the wings and tail, then move the airplane, it was difficult to integrate into the carrier air wing's fighter operations. It was usually the first launched and the last recovered. Only a few were typically carried aboard a carrier at any one time.

A North American AJ-1 (122590) navy bomber is photographed in flight on December 8, 1949, while another (122597) is shown folded and with the bomb bay doors open on December 14, 1949, both at NAS Patuxent River. The rear image reveals the turbojet engine exhaust while the inflight shot shows the closed inlet on the spine. The Savage gave the service a shipboard nuclear strike capability, from suitably modified carriers, in 1951. (*National Archives*)

With the advent of tactical nukes, the fighters in the air wing could ensure the continuation of the navy's nuclear mission while the new A3D-1 jet (see page 269) found its way aboard. The Savages were left ashore for other duties. The Douglas AD-4 was the first adapted to carry the new tactical nukes with an "over the shoulder" bomb toss delivery technique planned to permit the aircraft to escape the bomb blast radius. Initially, twenty-eight were suitably modified, the structure strengthened to carry the very heavy "special weapon" beneath the center fuselage. These were followed by 165 of the AD-4Bs built new. The external evidence was a recess in the belly to clear the bomb's fin. The aircraft flew common attack missions in service, though ready to be redirected to special weapon delivery if necessary. The 1,600-lb (726-kg) Mk 7 weapon, first available in 1952, was the initial intended store.

Desiring the speed and potentially greater carrying capacity of turbine engines, the navy directed NAA to replace the recips on the Savage with T40 turboprops and contra-rotating propellers. This request was made before the first AJ was even delivered. The redesign required a much larger vertical tail swept back dramatically and folded down for carrier stowage, and the forward fuselage redesigned. Twin nose wheels were introduced, and twin 20-mm cannon in a remotely controlled tail turret were planned. Initiated in October 1948, the first of the two XA2J-1 prototypes flew in January 1952 and were hounded by engine problems.

As related elsewhere, the Allison engine was plagued with issues and eventually canceled, dragging down many projects including the Super Savage. However, the airplane was heavy—empty weight going up by 1,388 lb (630 kg). It achieved little beyond the baseline airplane, as demonstrated during the short test program. Those results and the failing engine project saw the effort terminated before the second prototype was completed.

With the navy's Super Carrier expected to enter service after 1950, the service sought a more capable bomber to match the large deck. Within days of the USS *United States* being order in August 1948, BuAer put out an RFP for the carrier-capable aircraft carrying the enormous A-bombs. At the time, the service foresaw a 100,000-lb (45,359-kg) aircraft powered by two turbojets and capable of transonic

The XA2J-1 Super Savage also fell prey to the Allison T40 that killed all programs for which it was adopted. However, the multiple changes besides the engine, such as the vertical tail, forward fuselage alterations, and dual nose wheels, added to weight that compromised the expected performance gain. Provisions for the tail turret and associated radar are evident. (*San Diego Air & Space Museum*)

flight via swept aero surfaces. It was to carry the 10,000-lb (4,536-kg) bomb 1,150 miles (1,850 km) and return to the ship. Douglas was selected to develop the jet with a March 1949 contract for two XA3D-1s. When the new aircraft carrier was canceled in April, the company pivoted with a revised design cutting weight to a level suitable for Midway-class vessels and even the Essex hulls (with JATO assist, if necessary) subjected to the Project 27 upgrades. Then, in July 1951 when the USS *Forrestal* (CVA-59) was approved—essentially, the super carrier resurrected—the design had room to grow.

All surfaces of the A3D were swept, the wings at 36 degrees. Both wings and the vertical tail folded. Trailing edge single-slotted flaps and unpowered leading-edge slats constituted the high lift configuration. All controls were hydraulically boosted and the horizontal stabilizer was trimmable. The nose wheel was steerable. The aircraft had three hydraulic systems, one 3,000 psi (20,684 kPa) and two 2,000 psi (13,790 kPa). The design also used engine compressor bleed air to drive pneumatic air turbine motors that powered the hydraulic pumps and electrical generators as the first example of a design that would become common. The engines were in underwing nacelles, initially with doors to close off the inlets during inflight shutdown to reduce drag. Up to a dozen 4,500-lbf (20-kN) JATO bottles could be mounted on the aft fuselage and jettisoned when expended. Aft fuselage speedbrakes supported rapid changes in airspeed while also permitting a landing approach to be flown while carrying power for a wave-off or bolter. This compensated for the slow spool-up of the engines.

The crew of three sat in a pressurized flight deck. Instead of heavy ejection seats, the bail-out was via a chute out the belly of the airplane. Armor was also eliminated as a weight savings measure. An ASB-1 radar bombing system was featured, with an antenna in the nose radome. A barbette with two 20-mm cannon in the tail was remotely controlled and automatically aimed via an aft fuselage radar. Initially configured for the earliest very large and heavy nuclear devices, the weapon bay could also be configured for conventional ordnance to include four 2,000-lb (907-kg) bombs or mines.

The first XA3D-1 flight occurred in October 1952, powered by two J40s. The team dealt with a number of problems, as is common during development flight testing. Tire ruptures led to the adoption of the first anti-skid system, called Hytrol, from Hydro-Air Company. The repeated overheating of brakes led to the adoption of a drag chute. Roll rate at high speed was reduced by wing torsion induced by aileron action. This was cured with the addition of inboard spoilers to assist roll. The bomb bay doors suffered from buffeting, and the bombs would not separate cleanly owing to adverse airflow in the bay. An air deflector had to be added at the forward end of the bay to cure this problem. However, there was a more fundamental issue plaguing the development. The J40 was supposed to deliver 10,000 lbf (44.5 kN) at the pinnacle of its development, but it never matured and the program was canceled. Douglas had already begun work to substitute the J57 that delivered the required thrust. The nacelle inlet doors were eventually eliminated. Likewise, a forward slant of the inlet face at the top, intended to ensure suitable flow even at high angles of attack, was found unnecessary and redesigned.

The Skywarrior spanned 72.5 feet (22.1 m), had a wing area of 779 feet (72.4 m), weighed 35,900 lb (16,284 kg) empty and 70,000 lb (31,751 kg) gross, and reached 620 mph (998 kph) at sea level. An order for a dozen A3D-1s was placed in October 1952, and the first of these left the ground in September 1953. However, the air force had already spoken for the lion's share of J57 production. Delivery of the by-then fifty aircraft backlog was paced by the engine such that only twenty airplanes had been completed by the end of 1955, and another two years elapsed before an operational squadron deployed the jet aboard ship.

The DAC jet went on to a long career with several variants and rework for alternative missions. It was the largest aircraft routinely operated aboard an aircraft carrier.

The navy's SSF concept was to include a very fast flying boat designed as the bomber segment. However, to avoid conflict with the USAF, this was to fill the High-Speed Minelayer role as the stated principal mission. A nuclear strike was certainly an implied capability, with the delivery of a very heavy "special weapon" included in the requirements. The aircraft was commonly referred to as a bomber. The requirement included up to 30,000-lb (13,608-kg) payload, missions to 750 miles (1,207 km) in radius, and a top speed of 691 mph (1,111 kph) at sea level, though revised to 633 mph (1,019 kph). These requirements were unheard of for a flying boat and experience with proposed design solutions relatively low.

Specifications and a RFP were issued in July 1951 with only Convair and Martin participating. Neither saw the hydro-ski that BuAer had expended so many resources developing (see pages 88–91) as practical given the great weight and complexity of the feature for such a large and heavy seaplane. Both offerings appeared to have clear deficiencies. Consequently, the service allowed the competitors to revise and resubmit their proposals. Both had merit, and ultimately, it appeared that Martin was selected

Douglas developed the A3D-1 beginning in 1948 (a XA3D-1 shown on its first flight test on November 5, 1952) in answer to a U.S. Navy request for a transonic jet bomber to carry the heavy nuclear bombs of the period of America's aircraft carriers. This was a demanding requirement that took time to meet, but the program was further delayed by a change of engines. Consequently, the Skywarrior went to sea operationally for the first time only in 1957. (*Air Force Test Center*)

to ensure seaplane manufacturing included two companies, given that Convair was working on both the F2Y and R3Y at that time.[18] The October 1952 contract called for building two XP6M-1. Soon, contracts were let for six YP6M-1 and two dozen P6M-2 airplanes. There were hopes for as many as 100 airplanes.

To meet the high-speed requirement, Martin adopted a wing swept 40 degrees and four afterburning J35s (later redesignated J71). The turbojets were placed in two nacelles above the wings, clear of water spray. Instead of retractable floats, the aircraft was to have a shoulder-mounted wing with enough anhedral to place wingtips, with integral fiberglass floats, into the water. This also assisted in operating in open seas—defined as Sea State 3, or 6–8-foot (1.8–2.4-m) waves. The hull was the new 15:1 length:beam design developed as described on page 88. Hydroflaps were to assist surface movement, as with the Marlin, although also serving in flight as airbrakes. The horizontal stabilizer was atop the vertical with stab trimming and a marked dihedral. The occupied spaces were pressurized for the five crewmen that included two pilots, a navigator/bombardier, radio operator, and gunner. Self-defense was provided by two 20-mm cannon in a remotely controlled tail turret with a search and track gun-laying radar. Also, 1,079 lb (489 kg) of armor was to be fitted.

The SeaMaster incorporated a new and advanced minelaying and navigation system. The bomb bay was a detachable segment of the hull that could be loaded separately and then installed in the aircraft. Made watertight with an inflatable seal, it rotated 180 degrees to dispense the weapons. Up to fifteen of the more common mines could be carried as well as twenty-seven of the typical Mk 82 500-lb bombs, but only two Mk 84 2,000-lb bombs, and one or two nukes. To reload at sea, a fuselage crown hatch with crane, aft of the wing, was conceived. Stores would be lowered into the loading compartment and then moved forward to the rotary bay on a dolly track then a hoist on overhead rails. This was a laborious process requiring calm seas.

Lifting the P6M onto a tender was impractical given its great weight. Consequently, LSDs were to be modified to permit the aircraft to be winched into its partially submerged dock. Once inside and on beaching gear, the ramp was to be raised and the well pumped out.

The first SeaMaster rolled out at the end of 1954 and flew the following year. It grossed 167,000 lb (75,750 kg) and spanned 102.6 feet (31.3 m). It achieved 646 mph (1,040 kph) in level flight at 5,000 feet (1,524 m) and Mach 0.95 in a dive at optimal altitude. The afterburners were found to excessively heat and cause sonic resonance of the aft fuselage that could rapidly fatigue the structure. Consequently, the inboard afterburners could not be used. This impacted performance. For the YP6M-1 airplanes, the nacelles were canted outboard 5 degrees and the aft fuselage structure altered. Despite incorporating bypass doors, there were also problems with water ingestion, and so the inlet face was moved farther back from the wing leading edge. Yet, there was still water ingestion, power loss, and flameouts.

The navy invested in many other aspects of their SSF concept to include a beaching vehicle for the P6M. Once the pilot taxied into the floating device, a crewman manually connected it to the aircraft's pneumatic systems via a hatch such that the pilots could apply brakes after moving up the ramp onto land. Vessels were also modified to demonstrate the SSF concept. All was for naught.

One aircraft was lost to a stab actuator failure and the second to an overloaded horizontal tail owing to design errors. The preproduction aircraft were built and performed mission-representative tests including dispensing simulated nuclear bombs. A change from the troublesome Allison to the J75 gave more thrust for a higher GW and eliminated afterburning. However, the weight guarantee was exceeded. Sitting lower in the water, the wing anhedral was eliminated. Some changes to the aft hull were also made to correct hydrodynamic deficiencies. This aircraft demonstrated aerial tanking with a hose reel kit in the rotary bomb bay. The program fell behind schedule and overran the budget—an all too common occurrence. Only four of these aircraft were completed and flown before the program was canceled in summer 1959, largely for budgetary reasons. Six years was a comparatively long development in the period where aircraft obsolescence was measured in about that duration, and other naval armaments were evolving rapidly. Even atomic bombs had shrunk in size, allowing aircraft with a much smaller operational "footprint" than a flying boat to deliver such weapons. The SeaMaster was the navy's last new seaplane and Martin's last aircraft.

This artist's concept of the Martin XP6M-1 SeaMaster shows the radical design features for a flying boat. The highly swept wing, turbojet engines, and high-mounted wing with anhedral to eliminate wing floats were all remarkable at the time, and even today. It would be the fastest such aircraft at over 600 mph. It was the end of an era. (*Author's collection*)

8

Transport and Assault

As during the war, transports remained of medium priority and so funding postwar was initially difficult to come by. Much was carried forward, especially with the navy and marines. The Military Air Transport Service handled non-tactical freight and passenger obligations. Troop Carrier continued for the tactical.

When the Soviets cut off America, British, and French access to their zones in Berlin in June 1948, a massive airlift was put into motion to supply the city. Across 462 days (through to September 1949), more than 300 American and 101 British transports airlifted over 1,500,000 tons of freight during nearly 190,000 flights. Most of the participating aircraft were of World War Two origin. The western allies even built Berlin Tegel Airport to ease congestion at Tempelhof. The runway was completed in just ninety days. The Soviets, seeing the futility of their move, lifted the blockade. The value of military transport was reaffirmed.

Carried Forward

The Curtiss C-46 was retained given its high capacity. It appeared that the smaller Douglas C-47 (naval R4D) would serve endlessly. However, that fleet was attrited over time and the desire for better performance grew. When DAC improved on the C-47 design to match commercial competition and new federal air regulations, the military took notice while the civil market did not. The remanufactured aircraft had a lengthened and strengthened fuselage for greater passenger volume, more powerful engines in the R-1820 for single-engine safety, revised nacelles to fully enclose the landing gear, and greater stability via expanded wing and empennage areas. The air force evaluated one of the prototypes in 1950 as the YC-129 (later YC-47F), testing dual main-gear trucks, but chose to go with a modern Convair for its twin-prop needs. The navy took it up as the R4D-8X and subsequently had 100 wartime R4Ds upgraded to Super DC-3s (DC-3S) standard in 1951–1953. These R4D-8s remained in service for another forty years.

The Berlin Airlift was the largest sustained air transport challenge since the war and met largely with transports from that conflict. The C-54 is one such, derived from a commercial aircraft and so not optimized for military freight operations given its high cargo door not aligned with the long axis of the cargo deck as shown in this image with the need for a forklift during offloading at Tempelhof. While the airlift was successful, the need for improved military transport types was emphasized. (*National Archives*)

Just another navy gooney bird? Look again. The longer and square-tipped wings and tails identify it as a Super DC-3 or R4D-8. There is also a different engine under the cowling. However, all 100 of these Super Gooneys were created by remanufacturing World War Two R4Ds. The upgrade allowed the type to serve more safely and effectively for more decades. (*National Archives*)

The pressurized Lockheed C-69 Constellation (Lockheed L-49), built in few numbers for personnel transport on a wartime contract, were let go in 1946 and 1947 to reduce costly support for disparate types. However, in 1948, the USAF picked up ten L-749s, with greater fuel capacity, as C-121s, for long VIP trips with MATS. Several designation suffixes reflected different combinations of internal passenger and cargo configurations with a side freight door. Then, after the outbreak of war in Korea, thirty-three larger and more economical L-1049 Super Constellations were purchased as C-121Cs. These featured the turbo-compound version of the R-3350 and the freight door. The navy acquired fifty of the same model in 1952 for its contribution to the MATS mission. These were initially R7O-1s, but soon revised to R7V-1s. Additional Constellations were acquired for special missions or converted from these transports, and they served for decades.

At the end of the war, Douglas developed a pressurized C-54 Skymaster with 2,500-hp (1,864-kW) R-2800 engines and lengthened fuselage. This YC-112A was completed and enjoyed a maiden flight in February 1946. It was operated for a time until sold. Maturation and production of this configuration were continued by DAC as the commercial DC-6, and the further lengthened DC-6A freighter with a forward cargo door. Confronted with demands of the Korean Conflict, the latter was picked up as the C-118A and Navy R6D Liftmaster, with windows added. It could accommodate seventy-four passengers or sixty litters, or 27,000-lb (12,247-kg) of freight in the cargo configuration. The air force procured 101 from 1951 through 1955 and the navy sixty-one R6D-1s delivered between 1950 and 1952, plus three VIP R6D-1Zs in 1953.

Another Skymaster upgrade project involved finding additional power by substituting inline engines. Four 1,620-hp (1,208-kW) V-1710s replaced 1450-hp (1,081-kW) P&W R-2000s on a C-54G (45-874) to create the XC-114. The fuselage was also lengthened 6.8 feet (2.1 m). The Americans did not follow up, but the Canadians produced the configuration as the DC-4M (or C-54GM) with the Rolls-Royce equivalent engine. The similar XC-116 used 45-875 to test a thermal anti-ice system in place of de-icing boots. This idea of placing inline engines on the DAC airframe was continued with the XC-115 using V-1650s, but the project did not move to the hardware stage.

Growing Up

All new transport aircraft projects started during the war only bore fruit after, and some of the fruit was bitter. These supplemented the wartime transports as the backbone of airlift capabilities by the time of the Korean Conflict.

The war ended with the Douglas C-74 just a month from its first flight. This was the largest landplane transport in production at the time, with a flight crew of five. A 48,150-lb (21,840-kg) payload on a 75-foot (23-m) long cargo deck could allow for a wide range of heavy military equipment, 125 troops, or up to 115 litters with attendants. Two overhead traveling hoists could bring cargo into the aircraft as well as move it within the cabin. One hoist could be positioned to raise and lower a rear platform that dropped down through fuselage pedal doors. A hoist could also be

Both the USAF and USN began acquiring versions of the commercial Super Constellation beginning in 1948. These pressurized, long-range aircraft principally supported passenger transport, but the freight door also permitted some cargo missions. This navy R7V-1 (equivalent to the air force C-121C) is seen on delivery in 1953. (*National Archives*)

A MATS C-118A (51-3827) shows off its forward and aft freight doors while taxiing on September 25, 1952. The militarized version of the Douglas DC-6, also acquired by the navy as the R6D-1 Liftmaster, offered a pressurized cabin and a long range. They were easily procured and reliable, serving well while more purpose-built (and more costly) military transports were being developed. (*National Archives*)

swung out of a forward cargo door opening. Loading was laborious, but labor was plentiful and cheap at the time the aircraft was built.

The wings had full-span Fowler flaps, with double-slotted inboard segments and triple-slotted outboard, augmented with a split-flap segment under the fuselage. The outboard segments were ailerons that operated as "flaperons" in the high-lift configuration. The large, fabric-covered control surfaces were operated via flying tabs. However, the flaperons were hydraulically boosted. These could operate in manual reversion mode, although accompanied by very high control forces and risked overloading the outer wing.

The four R-4360s were matched with reversible Curtiss Electric props that were automatically synchronized. Thirteen combustion heaters, using engine fuel, warmed the cabin as well as the leading edges for anti-icing. Propeller anti-icing was via an alcohol pumping system for fluid migration along the blades. The ability to back up, and an APU powering electrical equipment, gave the aircraft a self-sustaining capability at forward airfields.

Save for lack of pressurization and tank inerting, the C-74 was a thoroughly advanced aircraft. Yet some of its innovations were not well-liked. The unusual double-bubble "bug-eye" canopies did improve all-around visibility. However, it was met with widespread disdain by pilots who could not easily communicate and coordinate without being able to make eye contact. They could not easily pass items across the cockpit without ducking their heads inside. A modification program installed a conventional windscreen arrangement.

The very worthy Globemaster arrived at the wrong time and a high unit cost, and could not survive in the early postwar fiscal environment. Just fourteen were completed, with eleven entering squadron service. A Globemaster became the first aircraft to cross the Atlantic with more than 100 people aboard. They contributed very well during the Berlin Airlift, setting some airlift records, though their heavy weight limited the runways available. They also served through the Korean Conflict before parts shortages and wear limited their life. The airplanes were retired in 1954.

Douglas C-74 Characteristics

span	173.3 feet (52.8 m)	weight empty	83,000 lb (37,648 kg)
length	124.3 feet (37.9 m)	gross	145,000 lb (65,771 kg)
height	43.9 feet (13.4 m)	maximum	172,000 lb (78,018 kg)
wing area	2,510 feet² (233 m²)	speed, max. (16,400 feet)	300 mph (483 kph)
fuel	11,000 gal (41,640 l)	cruise (10,000 feet)	214 mph (344 kph)
service ceiling	22,000 feet (671 m)	range, normal (200 mph)	3,400 miles (5,472 km)
climb rate, initial	2,605 fpm (794 mpm)	ferry (198 mph)	7,000 miles (11,265 km)

The type with the longest duration in service and greatest utility was the Boeing C-97 spin-off of the B-29 bomber. However, this product was slow in reaching meaningful fleet numbers in a practical guise. The first of three XC-97s had flown in November 1944. The design featured a twin-lobe fuselage that was an expedient but also permitted more floor area and simplified design for pressurization stresses. The lower

The Douglas C-74 was the largest landplane transport in production at the end of the war and had many unique features as shown by the image of 42-65414 at Gatgow during the Berlin Airlift with its forward cargo door open and freight being offloaded from the lift lowered through the aft doors. These features gave the Globemaster comparatively high utility for a strategic transport, but it was a costly airplane and only a handful were operated for less than a decade. Aircraft 42-65408 is seen inflight with the conventional windscreen that replaced the original "bug eye" canopies seen on 42-65409 beyond. (*National Archives*)

lobe had the diameter of the B-29 fuselage while the upper was more capacious—a total of 6,140 feet^3 (174 m^3) volume available. The pressurized upper deck was principally for the 36,000-lb (16,329-kg) useful load with the 74-foot (22.6-m) length allowing alternately 142 troops, eighty-five casualties with four attendants, three loaded 1.5-ton trucks, or two light tanks. Vehicles were loaded via a steep ramp lowered through clamshell doors in the aft fuselage. The ramp was two joined segments folding in half and raised above the level of the doors for flight. Other items could be hoisted up and moved forward using an overhead traveling hoist running on a rail the length of the cabin. The hoist could also winch articles up the ramps. The lower hold was split into two volumes by the wing box and loaded via a pair of doors. Ladders permitted inflight movement between the two decks. A crew of five was common. The aircraft mounted the B-29s R-3350 turbosupercharged engines. The bomber's wings came with the standard Fowler flaps. Complex and heavy hydraulics were avoided by the use of flying tabs and many electric motors.

In the last days of the war, ten more aircraft were ordered and began flying in March 1947. The first six became YC-97s that were similar to the prototypes except for the adoption of "Andy Gump" cowlings, added fuel, and greater capacity electrical system. The remaining four airplanes were completed with features of the B-50 that included R-4360 engines, extended vertical stabilizer with fold-aside capability, 75ST aluminum, thermal de-ice replacing the boots, hydraulic rudder boost, and nose wheel steering. Three of these machines became YC-97As fitted out as troop carriers while the last was a YC-97B with airline accouterments. These aircraft began flying in January 1948. Fleet operations with Stratofreighters had begun in October 1947 and contributed to the Berlin Airlift with one YC-97A flying a1 million lb of freight into the city over twenty-seven missions in May 1949.

The C-97A entered production under a March 1947 contract with each aircraft costing $1.2 million. It introduced the weather radar in a chin radome and additional wing fuel cells. This type could carry up to 52,800 lb (23,950 kg) or 134 troops and introduced a forward starboard side cargo door. Also featured was airdrop of up to 25,500 lb (11,567 kg) off the overhead rail through the aft cargo doors. Deliveries of these fifty airplanes commenced in October 1949. Fourteen C-97Cs, equipped for medical airlift with, among other small changes, a strengthened fuselage, began being taken up in 1951. Five YC-97As and the YC-97B were converted for passenger flight as C-97Ds, and three of these were subsequently reworked as VC-97D flying command posts with external tanks. The earlier aircraft were brought up to production standards and continued in service.

The rest of the C-97 production focused on tanker-transports, as previously described. The side freight door remained free, though fuel tanks on the deck restricted cargo volume. The boom and operator bubble could be removed to permit the aft cargo doors to be installed. As mentioned, the evolution ended in May 1953 with the KC-97G that had changes easing the complexity of cargo ops, with up to ninety-six troops or sixty-nine litters. This was quite useful and, after its tanker career end, the C-97 served on in cargo-hauling jobs and special missions until the 1970s.

Boeing KC-97G Characteristics

span	141.3 feet (43.1 m)	weight empty	82,500 lb (37,421 kg)
length (with boom)	117.4 feet (35.8 m)	loaded	153,000 lb (69,400 kg)
height	38.3 feet (11.7 m)	max. take-off	175,000 lb (79,379 kg)
wing area	1,769 feet² (164 m²)	speed, max.	375 mph (604 kph)
fuel	9,000 gal (34,069 l)	cruise	300 mph (483 kph)
service ceiling	35,000 feet (10,668 m)	range, normal	4,300 miles (6,920 km)
climb rate, average	400 fpm (122 mpm)	ferry	5,760 miles (9,270 km)

The Boing Stratofreighter is shown to good advantage by C-97A 48-399 bearing a weather radar in a chin installation. The adjoining image shows a YC-97 (48-419) with its tail being folded down and the cargo doors open with the stowed wheel ramps visible—a capability still possible with the KC-97 once the boomer pod was removed. These aircraft were very worthy transports, but the type had a more urgent mission to fulfill as a tanker and so the greatest portion of the production was devoted to the KC-97s. (*National Archives*)

Strategic Lifters

The lack of roll-on/roll-off loading capability of the C-74 limited the cargo size that the air force wanted addressed in the next strategic transport. The Berlin Airlift experience also suggested more payload could be added to the C-74 with little degradation in performance, for short ranges at least. The program that sprung from these considerations near the end of 1947 became the C-124. Loaded weight rose by approximately 20,000 lb (9,072 kg).

Douglas designed a voluminous double-deck fuselage with clamshell nose doors for roll-on/roll-off cargo across steep wheel ramps. The hoist could assist in drawing in the load. The aft bottom hatch and loading platform were retained. Nearly all army equipment could be transported. Fold-down panels could create an upper deck for light freight such as the crews and baggage associated with the cargo. The cargo compartments could also be configured solely for passengers and fit 200 fully equipped soldiers. Alternatively, 123 litters, forty-five ambulatory patients, and fifteen attendants could be accommodated.

The fifth C-74 was modified as the YC-124 that flew in November 1949. The testing went smoothly and production of the C-124A commenced promptly. Of these, 204 were built, with initial deliveries in May 1950. Over time, the engines were improved, a weather radar added in a "thimble" attached to the nose, and combustion heaters were moved to wingtip fairings. Production continued through May 1955 with 243 C-124Cs that featured all the upgrades plus additional fuel capacity and a 10,000-lb (4,536-kg) hike in operating weight. The C-124B is discussed on page 308.

Douglas C-124C Characteristics

span	174.1 feet (53.1 m)	weight empty	101,165 lb (45,888 kg)
length	130.4 feet (39.8 m)	loaded	185,000 lb (83,915 kg)
height	48.3 feet (14.7 m)	maximum	194,500 lb (88,224 kg)
wing area	2,506 feet² (233 m²)	speed, max. (20,800 feet)	304 mph (489 kph)
fuel	11,058 gal (41,859 l)	cruise (10,000 feet)	230 mph (370 kph)
service ceiling	21,800 feet (6,645 m)	range, 26,375-lb freight	4,030 miles (6,486 km)
climb rate, normal	707 fpm (216 mpm)	maximum	6,820 miles (10,976 km)

The Globemaster IIs served for twenty-five years. Their early service was tragically marked by two crashes that set new records for the number killed in single accidents, the worse being 129 individuals. However, in general, the aircraft performed with distinction until replaced with jet-powered airplanes possessing much lower cargo decks.

The Lockheed R6O had been conceived during the war to serve the navy's transoceanic heavy transport needs. It accommodated 168 passengers and a crew of twelve on the upper deck and considerable cargo volume on the lower deck. Both decks were pressurized. Cargo could be hoisted in through side doors. The aircraft was powered by four turbosupercharged R-4360s, with water injection, turning reversible Curtiss Electric props, and flight controls that were fully boosted. The wings

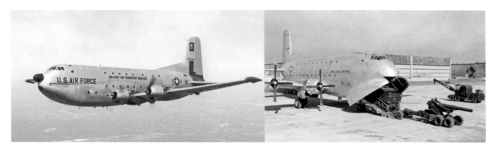

The C-74 was revised by Douglas with a larger capacity fuselage possessing nose doors to take larger payloads up wheel ramps. The C-124 was built in respectable numbers and served for twenty-five years. Shown is a C-124 52-1035 with weather radar nose "thimble" and anti-ice combustion heaters at the wingtips, and tactical equipment loading across nose ramps through the cargo doors. (*National Archives*)

and Fowler flaps were commonplace by that time. Leading edges were heated by exhaust gases for anti-icing. The main landing gear had two tandem two-wheel struts interconnected by links to act as one, and with electric motors spinning the wheels up to about 80 mph (129 kph) to reduce strut drag loads upon touchdown.

War priorities left the completion of the two R6O prototypes until after hostilities, with the maiden flight in November 1946. By this point, with low postwar funding and heated arguments with the emergent air force over roles and missions, no production beyond the prototypes was undertaken. The airplane fell short of the desired range, partially because of the cooling demands of the R-4360s, an issue that afflicted the powerplant throughout its existence. The pair of Constitutions began serving in 1949 and were giant wonders of U.S. Navy audacity. They were flown until willingness to operate just two airplanes of a type faded by the end of 1953.

Lockheed R6O Characteristics

span	189.1 feet (57.6 m)	weight empty	114,575 lb (51,970 kg)
length	156.1 feet (47.6 m)	max. take-off	184,000 lb (83,461 kg)
height	50.7 feet (15.4 m)	speed, max. (20,000 feet)	303 mph (488 kph)
wing area	3,610 feet² (335 m²)	cruise	269 mph (433 kph)
fuel	9,600 gal (36,340 l)	range, max. (no load)	6,300 miles (10,139 km)
service ceiling	27,600 feet (8,431 m)		
climb rate, initial	1,100 fpm (305 mpm)		

The air force had its own "white elephant." As part of the original contracts for the B-36 bomber was the provision for developing a transport version of the aircraft for $4.7 million. The project was intended to incentivize vendors in support of the primary bomber program given potential commercial sales. This would also position Convair for the expected postwar commercial transport surge. The double-deck fuselage could carry 100,000 lb (45,359 kg) of freight. By intent, XC-99 development was always a step behind the bomber.

The Lockheed R6O was developed during and immediately after World War Two to equip the Naval Air Transport Service in flying its transoceanic routes. It was a most impressive airplane with tremendous capacity and performance. However, funding for production beyond the two prototypes could not be found, and this would have been opposed as an intrusion on the missions of the USAF. (*Air Force Test Center*)

Assembled in the San Diego plant, aluminum was substituted for much of the magnesium present on the B-36 in the interest of construction simplicity. The prototype was unpressurized and so normally did not exceed 10,000 feet (3,048 m) flight altitude. Due to this, leading edges were heated for anti-ice. The fuel tanks were inerted. The transport had a crew of eight and like relief.

The 16,000 feet³ (371 m³) loadable volume in a double-deck fuselage accommodated 400 troop seats, or 305 litter patients with thirty-five attendants, or 5 tons of freight including vehicles. The two decks were connected via staircases at the forward and aft ends. The lower deck was divided by the wing center box beam into two 40-foot (12.2-m) long loading zones, each with a hatch in the floor to the exterior. Two bottom cargo doors were located along the centerline of the airplane, one forward of the wing box and the other at the aft end of the fuselage. These doors slid forward along the outside skin of the airplane. Two pair of clamshell cargo doors were installed immediately aft of the rear sliding cargo door to provide clearance for rolling vehicles aboard. A pair of cargo hatches in the upper deck floor was positioned over the lower deck cargo doors. Cargo was loaded, unloaded, or shifted within the compartments by means of four electrical hoists, two on each deck, which ran on overhead rails. The two hoists in the lower compartment were designed to permit airdrops in flight through the opening made by the sliding doors.

The aircraft's maiden flight was in November 1947, after a more than $6 million overrun. The USAF decided to put the unusual aircraft into service. The aircraft got the four-gear trucks in 1949 and a nose radar in 1950, among other improvements. While it made useful cargo runs, mostly from Texas to California, it was seldom filled because so much materiel had to be positioned at its departure location via other lifts, or the C-99 had to make multiple short hops. The cost per ton-miles was the lowest of other heavy transports, but this could not be exploited effectively. The XC-99 was operated until 1957 when it was withdrawn with the expiration of airframe life. It remains the largest piston-powered transport ever flown and the largest operational airplane in existence, setting unofficial payload records.

The C-99 was demonstrably impractical. Even with the impressive attributes, the aircraft did not fit any mission requirement. The enormous size and footprint of the airplane, even with four-wheel truck main gear, greatly limited the airfields from which it could operate. Like the XB-36, at its heaviest, the airplane needed a minimum 8,000-foot (2,438-m) runway for safe accelerate-stop distance and an unobstructed departure path of several miles because of the very low climb gradient. From these fields, the cargo would have to be redistributed for further transport. The excruciatingly slow cruise and day or more flight time may have been tolerable if the aircraft were otherwise more useful. While it could carry the load of several then-extant air force cargo airplanes, those aircraft could be loaded and unloaded more easily, access more fields, and get there faster.

A commercial market for such an aircraft never developed, and the military was then not convinced a giant airlifter was required. Such an aircraft would have needed a pressurized upper deck. One concept was for nose and tail vehicle loading ramps, though the lower deck remained obstructed by the wing box. Besides, the military wanted to focus on turboprops.

Convair XC-99 Characteristics

span	230 feet (70.1 m)	weight empty	135,914 lb (61,650 kg)
length	182.5 feet (55.6 m)	normal gross	265,000 lb (120,201 kg)
height	57.2 feet (17.4 m)	overload gross	295,000 lb (133,809 kg)
wing area	4,772 feet² (443 m²)	speed, max. (30,000 feet)	335 mph (539 kph)
fuel	21,116 gal (79,933 l)	cruise (10,000 feet)	180 mph (290 kph)
service ceiling	30,000 feet (9,144 m)	range, max. (10,000 lb)	8,100 miles (13,036 km)
climb rate, sea level	700 fpm (213 mpm)	100,000-lb freight	1,720 miles (2,768 km)
		ferry (173 mph)	9,400 miles (15,128 km)

Exercises had made clear that the existing slow piston-engine transports, plus lengthy onload and offload periods, would be unable to adequately support the army in worldwide high-intensity conflicts. Likewise, logistics support during the first year of the Korean Conflict emphasized the cumbersome operation of existing transports. Flying a transport from the U.S. mainland to Korea, or even Japan, with any significant load was well-nigh impossible in the early 1950s. Aircraft with modern turbine propulsion, increased cargo capacity with dimensions matched to army equipment, and lower operating costs were going to be essential in the future. After the outbreak of war in Korea and the potential for a wider conflict with the Eastern Bloc, Congress was prepared to provide the funding for new airlifters.

Applying the Weapons System process for the Logistics Carrier Support System SS-400L, the USAF simultaneously sought a tactical transport, a strategic airlifter, and a very large tanker-transport for outsized freight—wider than about 9–10 feet (2.7–3.1

The sole XC-99 is seen wearing the markings of the San Antonio Air Depot, Kelly AFB, and with bottom loading doors open. The men beneath the aircraft and the open emergency exits give scale to the transport derived from the B-36 bomber. The giant airplane was impressive but largely impractical given its size and performance. (*Jay Miller collection*)

m). The T34 turboprop was mandated for all. The P&W/Allison powerplant first flew in September 1950 on the nose of the B-17 engine testbed. It entered production in 1951 and with water injection in 1953. However, years more were required before adopted to power an airplane.

The axial-flow T34 had been in development since 1945, initially under a navy contract, and expected to deliver 6,000 hp (4,475 kW). This engine developed 20 percent of its thrust from the jet exhaust. Initially rated at 5,500 hp (16,405 kW) compared with the 3,250 hp (2,424 kW) of the R-4360s, it was much lighter and expected to demand less maintenance. If these benefits were actually realized in fleet-deployed applications, a marked improvement in performance, mission turnaround time, and support costs were likely. The air force was eager to transition to the turboprop, and it promulgated a policy in January 1951 to adopt these powerplants.

The requirements for the strategic lifter were issued in 1952, and a DAC design was selected. Under contract, the company began a detailed design of the XC-133 in February 1953. This was to have a straight wing with four turboprops. The main gear would be in side sponsons and the wing atop the fuselage so to leave the cargo volume unobstructed. There was the by-then typical cargo door and ramp in the upswept aft fuselage and a freight door in the forward side. The body sat low for truck-bed freight transfer and ease of roll-on loading/unloading. This layout would become classical for military cargo transport in the future.

With the specified T34, the new strategic airlifter was to carry nearly twice the cargo weight of the C-124, perform cargo operations much faster, fly substantially farther at higher speed, and operate at higher altitude. Based on DAC's expertise and the perceived nature of the design being well within established technology, no prototypes were built. Instead, the contract called for a dozen production aircraft, with seventeen more authorized before the aircraft flew.

The Cargomaster was to be about 158 feet (48.2 m) long, with a span of around 180 feet (54.9 m), and possess an operating weight of approximately 119,000 lb (5,398 kg). Cruise airspeed was anticipated at 310 mph (500 kph). The pressurized cargo compartment was designed with a 90-foot (27.4-m) length, 11.8-foot (3.6-m) width, and 13.3-foot (4-m) height. Like the C-124, the new airplane was to carry large or "outsized" cargo that could not be loaded aboard standard freighters. Some 96 percent of all existing U.S. Army field equipment, including M-41 tanks, was to be loadable without disassembly. The ramp and cargo floor could be fitted with trays of rollers to facilitate the movement of freight packed onto pallets, and such gear would become standard in future cargo transports. Advertised performance was 50,000 lb (22,680 kg) to 4,000 miles (6,437 km) at 310 mph (499 kph), or 1,300 miles (2,090 km) with 100,000 lb (45,360 kg). It was expected to get off in less than 6,500 feet (1,980 m) at high GW and climb at up to 1,500 fpm (7.6 mps). Significant advances were anti-skid, the inclusion of two gas turbine APUs, and single-point pressure refueling.

The first C-133 flew in 1956 and entered service the following year. The airplane proved a disappointment in many respects, and only fifty were built. The Cargomaster was the first and only aircraft produced with the T34 that accounted for some of the maturation difficulties encountered later. It ultimately provided less power than originally promised and aircraft performance suffered. Structural degradation under the acoustic pounding of the propellers, with sonic tip speeds, was rapid and the

As part of a three-aircraft Weapon System development program, Douglas was to develop a high-capacity cargo transport called the C-133. The aircraft (summer 1953 concept art shown) was designed with the advantageous features explored to that point to include a low cargo deck, rear loading door and ramp, and forward side freight door. Ordered in 1952, the aircraft first flew in 1956, but it had several grave deficiencies to include the turboprop engines. (*National Archives*)

cargo compartment interior noise level was unbearable. Maintenance demands were atrocious. Stall behavior was wicked and contributed to several fatal accidents until addressed.

From the design studies during 1951 for the "XC-Heavy" portion of SS-400L, DAC was chosen to continue more focused analysis. Many configurations were proffered, including adding J57 engines to the wings to boost speed for refueling fast-movers. Likewise, the combination and placement options of flying booms or hose reel systems were many. A swept wing was planned from the first to increase critical Mach. From the two years of work emerged a December 1952 contact to begin detailed design of the XC-132 Logistic Transport and Inflight Refueler. Separate aircraft built with considerable commonality would serve the two missions. Along with booms and hose reels, fuel tanks would dominate the tanker's freight deck. Cargo compartment dimensions for the transport were planned at 16.5 feet (5 m) wide and 12.5 feet (3.8 m) high—accommodating almost all army equipment.

The Douglas heavy was to be powered by four of the 15,000-hp (11,186-kW) T57s, a turboprop spin-off of the J57 ordered in 1953. A growth version was expected to

The CX-Heavy tanker-transport was another part of the Weapon System effort with Douglas getting the contract to develop the XC-132—the early 1953 concept art showing tip pods potentially for AR hose reels. Two purpose-built aircraft would serve the twin missions separately, though with much commonality, rather than one reconfigurable airframe. The design rested on a developmental engine and the effort ran so long that potential refueling receivers became incompatible with the prop-driven "KC-132," and delivery of the first transport would be about when turbojet counterparts would be possible. (*National Archives*)

deliver 20,000 hp (14,914 kW). Cargo ops were supported by a cargo door and ramp in the back and a side freight door in the front. An upper fuselage lobe was pressurized ahead of the wing box, but there was no deck aft. The airplane was expected to be approximately 184 feet (56.1 m) long and span 187 feet (57 m), with a baseline crew of five. Maximum GW in the transport configuration was projected to be 390,000 lb (176,900 kg) with 137,000 lb (62,142 kg) of payload. As a tanker, the airplane was to gross 470,000 lb (213,188 kg) with 19,500 gal (73,816 l) of fuel to transfer. Cruise speed was projected at 435 mph (700 kph) for the cargo carrier with range calculated to be 2,500 miles (4,023 km) with 100,000 lb (45,359 kg) payload and 6,000 miles (9,656 km) carrying 75,000 lb (1,207 kg). The designers aimed for 480 mph (773 kph) for the tanker.

This enormous aircraft underwent years of design with much development difficulty. The T57 was flown on the nose of a C-124 in 1956. The tanker version of the C-132 was abandoned as the design had taken so long to mature that receiver airspeed were running ahead—the B-58 would be most problematic—and turbojets for tankers were then practical. It appeared that the transporter would not likely move the new Atlas ballistic missile, and integration of an upper deck for troops was going to be protracted. The engine development was not encouraging—it never came together as a production article—and fleet entry would probably be in the mid-1960s. The ax finally fell in 1957 owing to these issues and budget cuts.

Going Tactical

The war had been fought largely with transports derived from commercial airplanes. The primary ersatz tactical transport was the Douglas C-47 with its sloped deck and cumbersome loading through a side cargo door. The airdrop was out a troop door within that cargo door. Several projects were set into motion during the war to produce a more suitable airplane with ready loading through nose or aft fuselage doors with the cargo deck at truck bed height to allow quicker and easier onload and offload. Wheel ramps could allow vehicles and wheeled equipment to be brought aboard, with the assist of a winch if necessary, then quickly rolled off. The programs yielded one very worthy product meeting these requirements.

The war ended with Fairchild having delivered a handful of C-82As from its Hagerstown, Maryland, plant. North American was working production in Fort Worth and Kansas City, Kansas, and delivered three C-82Ns. The contracts were reduced to just Fairchild, who manufactured 220 C-82As through September 1948. It had twin booms with a podded fuselage that facilitated loading through aft clamshell cargo doors, the wood-covered cargo deck at truck bed height and with wheel ramps. This accommodated a wide variety of equipment.

The principal loadable volume was roughly 8 × 8 feet (2.4 × 2.4 m) and 28 feet (11.6 m) long and was essentially the same 2,598 feet³ (81 m³) as a railroad boxcar— hence the "flying boxcar" moniker. This could take most of the army's wheeled vehicles and field guns, forty-two troops, or thirty-four litters. Paratroops could jump from the troop doors in each cargo door. However, the C-82 was also designed to drop up to fifteen 350-lb (159-kg) parapacks hung from an overhead rail and sequentially positioned over "paratainer" hatches in the cargo floor for drop. With troops jumping from two doors and weapon packs being dropped simultaneously, the team and their weapons could be on the ground in a potentially concentrated area with a single pass.

The fuselage hung from an inverted gull wing selected only to allow for shorter main landing gear struts. The nose gear was not steerable. The slotted flaps had segments both inboard and outboard of the booms. Aileron segments inboard of the wingtips drooped with flap extension to enhance low-speed lift. All control surfaces were fabric-covered. Hot air de-icing was provided to leading edges by combustion heaters. The supercharged 2,100-hp (1,566-kW) R-2800s turned three-blade, Hamilton Standard quick-feathering Hydromatic propellers, also equipped for de-icing. All heavy equipment was motivated electrically; hydraulics were reserved for brakes. The crew of five was made up of two pilots, navigator, radio operator, and crew chief.

The C-82s performed acceptably, though it had its challenges. It was underpowered in single-engine out scenarios and with deficient lateral stability, and this contributed to mishaps. The construction, under war limitations, did not mean a rugged airplane or a long service life. There were gear collapses and boom failures. The flight deck position was so high that the runway sometimes disappeared from view on landings. It also did not provide a view of a drop zone. Regardless, the aircraft contributed to the growth of tactical airlift with the development of airborne and airdrop tactics. During the Berlin Airlift, five were contributed to lift large cargo, particularly vehicles. They especially delivered earth-moving equipment for the construction of the Tegel Airport runway. The C-82A set the standard for tactical transports that followed and was retired in 1954 as these more advanced machines displaced them.

Fairchild C-82A Characteristics

span	106.5 feet (32.5 m)	weight empty	29,800 lb (13,517 kg)
length	77.1 feet (15.6 m)	gross (max. landing)	42,000 lb (19,051 kg)
height	26.4 feet (8 m)	ferry (max. take-off)	50,000 lb (22,680 kg)
wing area	1,400 feet² (130 m²)	speed, max. (45,000 lb)	248 mph (399 kph)
fuel, max.	2,834 gal (10,728 l)	cruise	218 mph (351 kph)
service ceiling	21,200 feet (6,462 m)	range, 210 mph	2,390 miles (3,846 km)
climb rate, initial	620 fpm (189 mpm)	best time (225 mph)	1,075 miles (1,730 km)
		ferry (183 mph)	3,875 miles (6,236 km)

Note: Some variation with serial number Blocks

One of those advanced machines was a development of the Packet. A C-82A was modified in 1947 to move the flight deck lower and forward on a more streamlined nose, eliminate the ventral tail extensions, and substitute 2,650-hp (1,976-kW) R-4360s. The engine provided a larger power margin, but it also turned four-blade reversible-pitch props. The cockpit relocation, with the addition of side down-view

The Fairchild C-82A was developed during World War Two as a purpose-built cargo transport with ease of freight onload and offload its hallmark. This image of 44-23037 shows the rear cargo doors with inset troop doors—here seen trailing parachute deployment bags following a paratrooper jump. The Packet served as a good introductory airlifter, but it was quickly eclipsed by the C-119 spin-off. (*National Archives*)

windows, assisted in landing vision and maintaining sight of drop zones. It also eliminated the lower ceiling at the forward end of the cargo compartment. Flying in December 1947, this XC-82B became the C-119A. For production as the C-119B Flying Boxcar, the fuselage was widened 14 inches (0.4 m), the wing was strengthened and span increased to allow greater GW, and troop capacity was upped to sixty-two.

Fairchild began delivering fifty-four C-119Bs in December 1948, and the first squadron was operational in early 1950. The C-model added water injection for 3,500 hp (2,610 kW), installed dorsal extension to the verticals, and removed the horizontal projections outboard of the booms. Over the course of manufacturing, the electrically operated elements, carried over from the C-82, gave way to hydraulics. The paratainer capability was raised to twenty packs of up to 500 lb (227 kg), dropped at eight-second intervals. The navigator was usually only taken on over-water flights or those where the aircraft was the lead in a formation. Airdrop usually demanded a second loadmaster.

With C-119C deliveries nearly coincident with the start of the Far East war, Fairchild expanded its plant to meet production demands. Kaiser-Fraiser Corporation was contracted to produce the airplane in Willow Run, Michigan. Ultimately, 303 of the machines were turned out, with forty-one from Kaiser-Fraiser. All B-models were soon upgraded to the C-standard. The D-model and E-model are discussed later.

Answering the deficiencies evident in Korea, and dissatisfaction with the P&W product, a change to 3,500-hp R-3350s turbo-compound marked the C-119F along with another GW rise. Kaiser-Fraiser manufactured seventy-one alongside Fairchild's

139. Ventral extensions for the verticals were reintroduced as a later modification—still chasing the ideal lateral stability. Fairchild built 396 of the final model, the C-119G, that substituted Aeroproducts props, while Kaiser-Fraiser contributed eighty-eight. The latter had been building the aircraft for about $1.3 million per unit against Fairchild's $260,000. By June 1953, the urgency was passed and the contract was canceled. Eventually, all F-models were upgraded to G-standard.

Fairchild C-119G Characteristics

span	109.3 feet (33.3 m)	weight empty	40,758 lb (18,488 kg)
length	86.5 feet (26.4 m)	design gross	64,000 lb (29,039 kg)
height	26.5 feet (8.1 m)	max. take-off	72,700 lb (32,976 kg)
wing area	1,447 feet² (134 m²)	speed, max. (17,900 feet)	253 mph (407 kph)
fuel, int.+aux.	2,590+2,024 gal (9,804+7,662 l)	cruise (5,000 feet)	162 mph (261 kph)
service ceiling	21,580 feet (6,578 m)	range	1,415 miles (2,277 km)
climb rate, initial	852 fpm (260 mpm)		

The marines acquired forty-two C-119Cs as R4Q-1s in 1950 with few changes. These were displaced beginning in 1952 with fifty-eight R4Q-2s, similar to C-119Fs, and were operated by both USMC and USN units. A radar in a prominent proboscis characterized the R4Q-2s. Eighty-eight more C-119Gs were built for allies. The line ended in late 1955 with 1,185 Flying Boxcars. The airplanes served into the 1970s.

The C-119 was the ultimate expression of Fairchild's "flying boxcar" concept and addressing C-82A deficiencies, with 1,185 built from 1947 through 1955. The flight deck was moved lower on a more streamlined nose for better vision, further enhanced with down-view windows, the engines were changed for more power, and lateral stability improved with dorsal extensions (lacking on the model shown). This C-119B (49-147) is configured for airdrop during a mission over Korea in July 1952. (*National Archives*)

Airdrop Progress

The flying boxcars became the most numerous transports in MATS and Troop Carrier squadrons within TAC. However, they were not intended for fields other than paved or at least surfaces covered with pierced steel planking. They facilitated further development of airdrop by pallets sliding out the back of the aircraft for parachute descend. The cargo doors were left on the ground for such ops. As an alternative, a horizontally oriented C-119 "beaver tail," hinged at the top, allowing a door to be raised for airdrop. A loading ramp was also incorporated. The tail proved successful in testing and was subsequently retrofitted to sixty-eight C-119Fs and G-models in 1955.

Very heavy equipment could be delivered by this means to rapidly enforce paratroop assaults. However, despite these resources, the army had still to develop airdrop techniques after the end of the war. The earliest extraction methods were improvised. For the C-82 and C-119, the run-in to the drop saw the loadmaster removing all the restraints on the pallet except one strap that was routed over a knife edge. On the green light, a 6.5-lb (3-kg) beanbag at the end of the floor sill was released via a cable from the flight deck. This deployed a pilot parachute that pulled out an extraction chute that also drew the strap taut over the knife-edge such that it was cut and the equipment roll out the back of the airplane. A static line attached to the airplane then pulled out the descent parachute(s). A chain of platforms could also be extracted in this manner.

Experimentation and training raised the airdrop experience level rapidly. Supporting this soon became a requirement for new tactical transports.

The removal of the C-119 cargo doors to facilitate airdrop greatly increased drag. With the type sustained in service, an upgrade was introduced called the "beaver tail" that permitted the fairing to be retained, though rotated up and the integral door raised to allow airdrop. This C-119G has been fitted with the door for Fairchild flight trials, and sixty-eight F- and G-models would be upgraded to become C-119Js in 1955. (*National Archives*)

A C-82A (44-22987) performs a logistics airdrop in this composite photo produced by the air force at the time of early airdrop techniques development. A gun is shown secured to a pallet resting on roller trays inside the Packet. The extraction parachute (seen packed in the upper right photo) pulls the load from the airplane and the static line to the descent chute on the load is growing taut (lower photo). (*San Diego Air & Space Museum*)

Gliders Sail Away

What would come to be known as "airland" techniques were pioneered during the war. The goal was to establish "air heads" by landing assault troops to secure a landing zone for other personnel and equipment to be air-landed. The primary means of performing the role during the war was to land assault troops in inexpensive gliders. The gliders too often became disposable, and towing them required a great many transport airplanes. Although generally assessed as successful, recreating the mass glider assault postwar was problematic.

It was clear that true high-utility assault transports, capable of operating from unprepared fields, coupled with advanced airdrop techniques and helicopters, were the way of the future. However, it would take years to develop these assets. In the meantime, combat gliders would have to remain one means of inserting airborne troops. Although some types produced during the war were carried over, their limitations and discouraging operational safety were stark.

The assault gliders were maintained in modest numbers. The expectation was that these simple aircraft could be built *en masse* if needed. Most numerous were the Waco

CG-4A (G-4A after 1947) and the similar CG-15A (G-15A). Some others survived a while but were considered unsupportable given deterioration owing to the wood, fabric, and glue elements. The army's Airborne troops suspected the USAF fliers just lacked enthusiasm for powerless aircraft.

Some efforts to improve operational safety did occur. Amongst these were continuing investigation of rapid deceleration means employed once the glider was on the ground to prevent barreling into obstacles at the end of the selected landing field. These included spikes fired into the ground and attached to the glider via an elastic rope, plow blades rotating down from the bottom of the aircraft, and retro rockets. The spike testing was preceded by tests with a Piper Cub firing the projectile while still above the surface.

Money was found to explore the next generation of combat gliders that were to be more rugged and durable to avoid the extraordinary hazards and waste of World War Two airborne operations. All-metal designs would be sought, with APUs to operate hydraulic systems and radios. Higher tow speeds than the war-period gliders would reduce risk and enhance stability for a lower pilot workload on tow. The notion was that the aircraft would serve as a glider for initial assaults, and then be fitted with engines to fly materiel into a seized airhead.

Air Materiel Command's Engineering Division prepared representative model specifications for two envisioned gliders of 8,000-lb (3,629-kg) and 16,000-lb (7,258-kg) capacity. The clear intent was for a tricycle undercarriage and a lifting aft fuselage with a drop-down ramp. This last was considered more favorable than the upward opening nose designs of war gliders wherein rough landings could jam the nose closed and prevent the removal of large articles. The aircraft would be capable of being broken down for shipment. Provisions would be included for acceleration and deceleration devices. Characteristics were also published for a powered version of these gliders, with conversion in eight hours. The engine nacelles were to contain

In continuing tests from the war seeking to stop rapidly a glider after touchdown, follow-up work was conducted firing a spike into the ground that was on a nylon rope attached to the aircraft. Apart from the CG-15 tests shown in preparation at right during 1948, some tests were performed with a Piper Cub and the spike fired while still airborne, the rope then paying out behind. The Cub tests were conducted at NAS Patuxent River on July 30, 1947, using an All American Aviation aircraft and shows the spike impact and initial arrestment rope deploying from a device presumably inside the fuselage. (*National Archives*)

fuel tanks, supplemented with a cabin tank and jettisonable external tanks supporting ferry ops.

Specs for the 8,000 lb glider were released and initial bids were welcomed. Of the three submittals, Douglas was selected to prepare the XCG-19.

The USAAF urged Douglas to adopt the upward swinging tail in place of their proposed swing-aside design. Troop Carrier (Third Air Force) passed along word that they strongly felt both features were tactical non-starters and recommended clamshell-type doors in the aft fuselage like the C-82 airlifter. Additionally, Engineering Division's Glider Branch championed a system that eliminated the clamshells, instead featuring an upper door opening into the aft fuselage overhead and an adjacent drop-down ramp hinged to the cargo floor, creating an opening with good overhead clearance. During a June 1946 meeting, it was decided that the most expedient and practical design was folding doors opening down and out from the bottom of the fuselage. However, the USAF had already contracted for the Chase XCG-18 (see later) that had an upward swinging tail for a 7.7 × 6.5-foot (2.4 × 2-m) opening, and Engineering Division recommended revising that design. Iterations on that glider converged to the simple cargo door and ramp configuration.

Douglas' 8,000-lb all-metal glider got a contract in January 1946. The XCG-19 had the appearance of a conventional, tricycle-gear tactical airlifter with slotted flaps, save for the lack of engines. In the detailed design, DAC adopted doors opening out and down from the aft fuselage, and a loading ramp offering 6.8 feet (2.1 m) of additional cargo floor length. Landing distance with normal braking was projected to be 298 feet (91 m).

By the end of 1946, Douglas had the mock-up well along, and its first flight was anticipated in December. However, air force budget limitations compelled the service to down-select in December 1946 to either the XCG-18 or XCG-19, and the latter got the ax after the new year.

In initially contemplating the growth of assault gliders at the end of the war, Engineering Division had considered yet another evolution of the Chase Aircraft gliders. Chase was one of the tiny firms that had emerged during the war to meet the high demand for materiel. Founded by Michael Stroukoff who was also chief engineer, the New York City firm had shallow experience and no production capacity. Yet it built the XCG-14, a wood and fabric 4,000-lb (1,814-kg) useful load assault glider. It was aerodynamically clean and efficient, allowing a higher tow speed. They also built the 5,000-lb (2,268-kg) class XCG-14A with welded steel tubing covered with wood for greater crashworthiness. This had a tricycle undercarriage and a lifting tail with a cargo ramp dropped down, accompanied by stabilizing jacks.

The XCG-14A first flew in October 1945, and testing continued following the war. At AAF encouragement, Chase made an offer to convert the aircraft to a metal airframe XCG-14B. When a formal program to develop metal gliders was kicked off, Chase submitted proposals in December 1945. Arriving before the release of the characteristics, the notional design did not match the requirements of the 8,000-lb glider. Regardless, Chase was given a January 1946 contract for a XCG-18 even before formal bids had been received from other competitors.

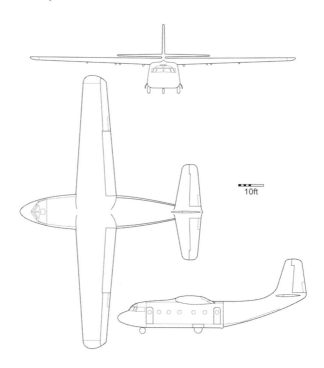

In meeting the 8,000-lb capacity combat glider requirement, Douglas Aircraft conceived this all-metal XCG-19. It had the appearance of a modern tactical airlifter but for lack of engines—although these were supposed to be attachable. Particularly noteworthy were the twin cargo doors and loading ramp at the rear that would be adopted for military transports to follow. (*Author*)

During the war, the start-up Chase Aircraft built the sole XCG-14A (44-90990) aerodynamically clean assault glider for the U.S. Army. This flew only after the war and offered the upward-opening aft fuselage with a drop-down loading ramp. This glider was the basis for postwar all-metal experimental gliders also built by Chase. (*National Archives*)

Later in 1946, Chase got a new contract driving the design to the 8,000-lb specification for two XCG-18A gliders. Consequently, the first flight slipped to December 1947. This saw the modestly redesigned XCG-14B become an entirely new, larger, and heavier aircraft. Towing speed dropped and landing distance increased. Chase relocated to larger facilities at the Mercer County Airport in Ewing Township (West Trenton), New Jersey, during late 1946 to build its aircraft. Recommendations to acquire thirteen of the CG-18s for service trials could not be borne by the meager defense budgets.

The XCG-18A became the world's first all-metal transport glider. It retained the welded steel tube fuselage structure, but with duralumin sheeting skin. The nose featured down-view windows at the pilots' knees. The wings had Fowler flaps and spoilers. The main landing gear, with hydraulic brakes, was fixed but for the electrically retractable nose gear. This could be retracted on the ground if desirable to change the slope of the cargo floor. Twin skids under the nose protected the fuselage during a nose-gear up landing or should the gear fail. An APU was located under the cockpit for electrical power and battery charging, particularly powering the flaps and gear. Cabin dimensions were, in feet, 22.4 long × 7.7 wide × 6.5 height (6.8 × 2.4 × 2 m). There was a troop door forward of the ramp on both sides of the fuselage. The loading ramp and cargo door were interlocking and hydraulically operated in the up-swept aft fuselage. Support jacks ahead of each corner of the loading ramp stabilized the fuselage for heavy equipment onload/offload. A total of thirty troops could be seated in the cabin or twenty-four litters accommodated. A third row of seats could be erected on the centerline.

The first XCG-18A finally flew in December 1947 behind a C-46E. The two prototypes were supplemented in March 1948 with a contract for five slightly altered YCG-18As for further evaluation, soon becoming YG-18As. These had a larger wing for more ready conversion with engines. The first of these flew in June 1948. The 1948 defense budget had funding for 147 CG-18s, but fiscal battles left these as casualties. Flight trials and evaluations continued into 1949 and were generally favorable. The biggest criticisms were inadequate rate of descent, suggesting a need for greater spoiler dimensions, and excessive landing ground roll unless very heavy braking was applied. With only differential braking for landing directional control, deceleration was inadequate. In general, the YG-18A was suitable for the tactical air assault missions and much superior to prior combat gliders.

Chase YG-18A Characteristics

span	95.7 feet (29.2 m)	weight empty	7,500 lb (3,402 kg)
length	61.7 feet (18.8 m)	loaded	16,000 lb (7,258 kg)
height	22.2 feet (6.8 m)	max. gross	16,900 lb (7,666 kg)
wing area	706 feet² (66 m²)	speed, max. tow/dive	216 mph (348 kph)
sink speed, max.	1,500 fpm (457 mpm)	stall (flaps)	62 mph (100 kph)

The second Chase XG-18A (46-067) shows the all-metal glider's low-slung fuselage with the fixed main gear. The nose gear was retractable, even on the ground, though the doors appear likely to be damaged. At the aft end, under the tail, was a cargo door and ramp for rapid onload and offload of troops and freight. (*National Archives*)

The Engineering Division also prepared a concept representing the 16,000-lb capacity glider with folding doors opening down and out from the bottom of the fuselage plus a loading ramp. The representative specification mentioned retractable undercarriage and the ability to land gear-up on skids. Provisions for the powered variant were identical in concept to the smaller aircraft. Four firms responded to the solicitation, and Chase was selected to pursue the XCG-20. The June 1946 contract allowed for one test article with its first flight planned for June 1947.

The contract to Chase for the heavy glider was held up by congressional appropriations questions. It was finally issued in April 1947 for two XCG-20 gliders. As before, eagerness to assess the design gave birth to proposals to acquire Y-prefix birds, but caution prevailed and this was set aside. A March 1948 revision reflected one prototype of the glider and added a XC-123-powered variant. The XC-123 specification stated the airplane should be capable of being towed as well as towing. Deliveries were delayed as new ideas intruded that grew size and weight.

Built entirely of metal with conventional construction, eschewing welded steel tubes, the XG-20 was a substantial aircraft so far removed from the World War Two combat gliders that a crew chief had to be added to the complement. The nose was reinforced with steel tubing and down-view windows were installed. It featured hydraulically actuated slotted flaps, spoilers, and fully retractable landing gear with differential braking. The hydraulic pump was electrically powered via an APU that also supplied electrical power in addition to a battery. The nose gear, with dual wheels, was steerable. A pad under the nose, aft of the nose gear well, served as a skid for landing with the nose gear up. Instead of nose gear doors that opened to the sides that could be easily damaged, the XG-20 had a door that slid aft along the belly.

The fuselage was set low to the ground and the up-turned aft fuselage allowed for the same cargo door and ramp arrangement adopted for the XG-18A. Cabin dimensions, in feet, were 35 long × 9.2 wide × 8.2 height (10.7 × 2.8 × 2.5 m). A pulley at the forward end of the cargo compartment allowed assistance in pulling loads aboard by a truck, the cable or chain running out the back of the aircraft or through a nose opening. Aft troop doors were placed on both sides of the fuselage. The glider could accommodate sixty fully equipped troops in sidewall and optional centerline tube and canvas seats. It could operate up to a maximum GW of 70,000 lb (31,751 kg). However, no tow plane existed that could haul such a load aloft. Consequently, the aircraft was limited to 40,000 lb (18,144 kg) as a glider. Not surprisingly, the aerial pickup was not intended.

The XCG-20 was developed coincident with the XCG-18, both under Chase's moniker Avitruck. Construction ran six months longer than the powered XC-123. This reflected both Chase's inexperience and dwindling interest in gliders. Its first flight followed in April 1950. The thorough flight evaluation during that summer was brief, as the focus had turned to the XC-123 that was already flying.

Chase XG-20 Characteristics

span	110 feet (33.5 m)	weight empty	17,495 lb (7,936 kg)
length	77.1 feet (23.5 m)	loaded	33,495 lb (15,193 kg)
height	32.6 feet (9.9 m)	overload *	70,000 lb (31,751 kg)
wing area	1,223 feet² (114 m²)	speed, max. tow/dive	190 mph (306 kph)
sink speed, max.	1,500 fpm (457 mpm)	stall (flaps)	65 mph (105 kph)

* impractical

The fact that the XCG-20 was beaten into the air by the powered counterpart highlighted the low priority of the gliders. There was no production of either Chase glider after expending more than $10 million on the postwar glider effort.

The sole Chase XG-20 (47-787) is seen under tow by a C-54 during its brief flight test campaign. An all-metal glider of advanced design, it was eclipsed by the powered version of the aircraft and the general advance of airlift technology. The undercarriage was retractable, and a cargo door plus ramp were featured in the aft fuselage. (*San Diego Air & Space Museum*)

A months-long assault transport evaluation during 1951 at Eglin AFB tested the G-18A, XG-20, and transports C-82, C-122, C-123, and C-125 (see later). The evaluators had to conclude that the glider was no longer useful enough to accept the operational safety issues of their employment. The emergent tactical transports employing new airdrop techniques, alongside the growing capabilities of helicopters, made these better choices. Military exercises and Korean airborne operations further accentuated these conclusions. The direct and relatively precise insertion of troops and heavy weapons into unprepared fields via gliders was achieved at great risk, plus tying up a valuable transport or bomber as a tug. Hundreds were required that were demonstrably one-use operations, and then only in favorable weather. This was no longer judged justifiable. The airlifters could also self-deploy whereas gliders had to be broken down and transported into the theater via sea transport. By fall 1950, the army agreed that the glider was obsolete and all were soon discarded.

Assault

With the glider fading from practical application, and helicopters still maturing, the army and air force focused on powered aircraft to perform the assault landings that were the fastest means of inserting airborne troops and their equipment. The obvious advantage was more flexibility on choosing a landing site and the ability to readily fly out, and repeat the operation multiple times during an operation. It would also have more flexibility in affecting rescues and evacuating casualties. It was a demanding mission, however, requiring rugged construction and landing gear. High lift devices would be important for short-field ops, but JATO could assist. Cargo had to be offloaded rapidly to reduce exposure to enemy fire.

By the end of 1947, the USAF became serious about exploring the powered option for the XCG-18A all-metal glider as an experimental assault transport. After some back-and-forth during the first half of 1948, a contract was signed in June. One of the YG-18As was converted to the YC-122 powered by a pair of 1,100-hp (820-kW) R-2000s. This first flew in November 1948. The twin made a nice companion to its glider counterparts, which it could tow. The air force had two more built entirely new in 1949 as YC-122As using 1,300-hp (969-kW) versions of the R-2000. Although these were initially conceived as gliders with rapidly installed or removed power "packages," the design eventually evolved to meeting all the standards of a purpose-built airplane.

One of the YC-122As was soon re-engined with 1,450-hp (1,081-kW) R-1820 and the fuselage stretched 3.6 feet (1.1 m). This also had more wing and tail area, and horizontal stabilizer dihedral. The same year, 1949, this configuration entered limited production with nine built as the YC-122C. These aircraft were operated by TAC for a few years. Their performance was marginal, particularly with a single engine-out, but they were good introductory assault transports.

Chase YC-122C Characteristics

span	95.7 feet (29.2 m)	weight empty	19,000 lb (8,619 kg)
length	61.6 feet (18.8 m)	design gross	32,750 lb (14,855 kg)
height	24.6 feet (7.5 m)	maximum	36,000 lb (16,329 kg)
wing area	813 feet² (76 m²)	speed, max.	220 mph (354 kph)
service ceiling	29,100 feet (8,870 m)	cruise	175 mph (282 kph)
climb rate	1,340 fpm (408 mpm)	range, normal	2,900 miles (4,667 km)
		max. payload	875 miles (1,408 km)

The XC-123 flew during October 1949 powered by two 2,100-hp (1,566-kW) R-2800. Its cargo capacity was 21,000 lb (9,525 kg) for a design GW of 44,500 lb (20,185 kg). It still used the design philosophy of the powerplant being a "button-on" arrangement. This included the ability to jettison the fuel cell at the aft end of the engine fairing. The design at least allowed for an engine change in about forty-five minutes. The XC-123 was subjected to extensive testing and evaluation.

The aircraft participated in the 1951 assault transport trials at Eglin AFB discussed earlier. The G-18A and XG-20 gliders, and C-82, C-122, C-123, and C-125 transports, were all subjected to grueling off-field operations; all suffered damage. Yet the XC-123 was revealed as possessing the highest potential value as an assault transport. The air force moved to buy a goodly quantity.

Chase won a March 1951 contract to build five pre-production C-123Bs, and with plans for many more. The C-123A is discussed later. However, the little company struggled to position itself for large-scale production. Industrialist Henry Kaiser, who had dabbled in aircraft development and production during the war, bought 49 percent of Chase's stock and prepared for C-123B manufacturing in Willow Run with a 300-aircraft order on the books. By summer 1953, Kaiser-Fraiser's cost overruns on the C-119 work and slow progress on the C-123 had soured the air force to the arrangement. Only two airplanes had been assembled in Trenton, and three more in Michigan. Additionally, another Kaiser subsidiary had purchased the remaining interest in Chase, but also leased the Willow Run plant to General Motors for automobile production.

With Kaiser effectively abandoning the C-123 and Stroukoff starting a new company, the USAF sought another manufacturer. In September 1953, they selected Fairchild who took over testing the five C-123Bs—that resulted in dorsal extension of the vertical tail—while preparing production in Hagerstown of 250 airplanes. Owing to these machinations, the first Fairchild production aircraft did not fly until September 1954, and entry into fleet service was in July 1955. It ultimately built 302 airplanes, which were very successful.

A determined early effort at creating a STOL assault transport saw Northrop engaged in March 1948 to create a spin-off of the commercially unsuccessful N-23 Pioneer. The USAF contracted for twenty-three YC-125s. Thirteen were standard YC-125As while ten were YC-125Bs intended for rescue ops with a larger suite of communications and navigation radios. Other than the basic layout, little remained the same from the Pioneer.

The XCG-18A glider was fitted with engines to create the USAF's first assault transport, and more of these airplanes were built. They went through several engine changes and slight dimensional adjustments. This YC-122B shows off the loading ramp and door that was becoming the standard configuration for assault transports. (*National Archives*)

The powered version of the XG-20 glider was the Chase XC-123 with more round engines from the past war. The aircraft was a standout success as an assault transport, and production was pursued beginning in 1951. However, industrial machinations meant that the path to manufacturing was slow and the operational capability was not introduced until 1955. (*National Archives*)

The fuselage was enlarged with a loading ramp in the rear. A hatch within the ramp permitted airdrop of paratroops or packs. The tail wheel strut could be extended to change the deck angle and support the aft fuselage during loading/offloading. A hatch under the nose permitted exceptionally long items like lumber to be inserted into the cargo compartment. The cargo floor had the by-then common tie-down rings. It could take thirty-two troopers or 12,000 lb (5,443 kg) of freight. Combustion heaters de-iced the leading edges and windscreen, plus warming the interior. The three 1,200-hp (895-kN) R-1820s turned featherable and reversible propellers. Many airframe parts were interchangeable, and ease of maintenance was a key design point.

For STOL, the wing had nearly full-span double-slotted Fowler flaps, spoilers, and feeler ailerons. There were also fittings on the belly for six 1,000-lbf JATO units. The aircraft could get off in 500 feet (152 m), clearing a 50-foot obstacle in 1,000 feet (305 m), and land in 330 feet (101 m). The gear was designed for operations on rough fields. The tail strut featured twin wheels, and the main gear could have an axle extension installed for second wheels to reduce ground footprint. Fittings on the gear posts support airborne towing by a suitable tug.

The aircraft first flew in August 1949 and deliveries ran throughout 1950. However, the Raider proved underpowered. During the 1951 Eglin assault transport trials, two of the machines were badly damaged in rough field landings. The YC-125 was assessed as essentially valueless. The alternative 1,525-hp (1,137-kN) R-1810 was apparently never tried, and how the conclusion was reached is unclear. The YC-125s were disposed of embarrassingly quickly, some apparently going directly to the mechanics' school as instructional articles—a discouraging waste of $5.5 million in a period of tight budgets.

Douglas C-125A/B Characteristics

span	86.5 feet (26.3 m)	weight empty	21,760 lb (9,870 kg)
length	67.1 feet (20.5 m)	maximum	40,900 lb (18,552 kg)
height	23.1 feet (7 m)	speed, max.	207 mph (333 kph)
wing area	1,131 feet² (105 m²)	cruise	171 mph (275 kph)
fuel	1,800 gal (6,814 l)	range	1,856 miles (2,987 km)
service ceiling	12,200 feet (3,719 m)		

The initial year of Korean Conflict experience emphasized the need for an improved tactical airlifter and assault transport. This was developed under the Weapons System Logistics Carrier Support System and, in concert with heavy lifters, with turboprop engines. Working with the army to define the requirements for the Medium Cargo Support System contact (XC-Medium), the USAF asked for an assault transport capable of lifting seventy-two troops 2,000 miles (3,219 km) or 30,000 lb (13,608 kg) of materiel over a shorter distance. The cargo compartment cross-section would need to be a minimum of 24 feet long and 10 feet on the sides (7.3 × 3.1 m). The cargo deck had to be at truck-bed height, accessible via a side door and ramp, and support airdrop operations. A side freight door was not included. It was to operate from

Working to replace World War Two gliders with a powered aircraft of comparable off-field capabilities, the USAF contracted with Northrop to adapt a commercial utility airplane to the mission. The YC-125 held great promise given its rugged design, simplicity of operation, and tactical airlifter features like the cargo ramp. Unfortunately, even three of the R-1820 engines did not provide enough performance, and it failed an important comparative evaluation. The thirteen machines (arctic rescue YC-125B 48-620 pictured) were set aside with embarrassing haste. (*National Archives*)

short and unprepared surfaces and perform assault landings. Performance demanding STOL technology was not an overt objective. The T34 (later evolving to the T56) was specified.

With a solicitation in March 1951, the XC-Medium contract went to Lockheed in July. It called for two YC-130s; it was followed in September 1952 by the first production contract though the aircraft was far from flight. This reflected confidence that the underlying technology was well in hand, that Lockheed was well placed to perform, and that the capabilities were urgently needed. The firm's design offered a 42.4-foot (12.9-m) compartment, 10.3 wide and 9.2 high (3.1 × 2.8 m). They aimed at a maximum take-off weight of 113,000 lb (51,256 kg) and a payload of 23,700 lb (10,750 kg). The aircraft had four of the turboprops on a high wing with slotted Fowler flaps. Two tandem wheels per side, in sponsons to minimize cargo compartment intrusion, were matched with a dual wheel nose gear. The wing box, however, did introduce an overhead limitation.

The first Hercules flew in 1954 and fleet service began at the end of 1956. This became the first turbine-powered transport airplane to reach production in the U.S. The type went on to a sterling career running to production in the thousands and service in dozens of countries, still underway at the time of writing.

A substantially capable assault transport was sought via a contract awarded to Lockheed and yielded the turboprop YC-130 as shown in this early 1953 model. Although not STOL, the field length performance was expected to be very good and matched with the ability to operate on unimproved fields. The Hercules became a legendary airlifter, with production continuing to the date of writing. (*National Archives*)

Specialized

Apart from assault landings, arctic operations were another specialized mission for transport types. Arctic rescues during the war had been exceptionally difficult. Persistent operations over the North Atlantic and over remoted Alaska to the far east of the Soviet Union via the Bering Sea persisted in placing American aircraft at risk of going down in harsh arctic conditions of snow, ice, and rough terrain with hidden crevasses. This continued to demand modified aircraft, special gear, and continuous training. Apart from searching for missing aircraft and dropping supplies, affecting a rescue by landing to retrieve personnel and then taking off again were very demanding tasks. Aircraft equipped with skis were generally necessary, and the ability to maneuver on the surface with the skis. Keeping an aircraft system operating in extreme cold was an enduring challenge.

The work to adapt skis to many aircraft types that could be of assistance continued after the war (see page 101). Even the navy participated given its missions in such environments. Ski-equipped C-47s were vital for the mission. The gliders had high potential as rescue aircraft, getting into difficult areas and then extracted by snatch (see page 104). Some remaining G-15s were fitted with skis and given heaters atop the cabin.

Arctic rescue became a growing priority with continuing flights to and from Europe and reconnaissance approaching the USSR, across far northern routes, and Alaska. Gliders were employed for a few years after the war for arctic rescue and resupply, but the mission became a specialty for airplanes and helicopters. This CG-15A and C-47B have been fitted with a ski undercarriage, both main and tail. (*National Museum of the United States Air Force*)

Experiments

In particular, the pressure to develop more efficient tactical and assault transports was motivation for continuous analysis and development supporting these goals. Several experimental efforts were undertaken and explored the practical in the possible.

The YC-119H sought to improve the safety and utility of the Flying Boxcar. The modifications included a 40 percent larger wing spanning 148 feet (45 m), the introduction of slotted flaps, boosted ailerons, and all fuel was in external tanks for a dry wing. The booms were extended, the vertical tail area increased, and the horizontal expanded in span plus attached directly to the verticals. Gross weight was pushed to 80,870 lb (36,682 kg) and R-3350s installed. The landing gear was reworked for greater rough-field capability, and provisions made to test a dual-tandem truck design.[1] Lower wing loading was the primary intent of the wing changes, but reduced take-off and landing airspeeds for safety, plus shorter field length, would be realized.

Fairchild first flew the YC-119H Skyvan in May 1952 and realized the intended benefits. The USAF was already planning C-119H production, but a closer look at the results suggested higher weight than anticipated, undesirable nominal CG, and a 12-percent loss in cruise speed. By January 1953, the USAF had decided that the C-119 had run its course and was looking ahead to newer designs.

A more radical approach was an airplane delivering a container or very heavy equipment slung beneath, to be lowered to the ground after landing or recovered by the reverse means. This would save the time for offloading or, if the loaded container was ready to attach to the airplane, the time for loading. As first conceived, this was to be either the C-119D with R-4360s or the C-119E with R-3350s. These were later given preliminary designations C-128A and C-128B, respectively. They were to have

Seeking to resolve lingering undesirable characteristics of the Flying Boxcar, Fairchild won a contract for an airframe reflecting significant changes. The most evident revisions to the YC-119H were the much-expanded wing with all fuel in underwing tanks and expanded tail area with the surfaces moved aft on extended booms. Along with the improvements were detractors, and the air force decided that the basic design had reached its limits. (*National Archives*)

the fuselage cutout behind the flight deck and under the wing center section, though some fuselage extension above and aft of the wing would be made for equipment. The "pack" would slide in under all this and be secured in place.

To demonstrate the feasibility, Fairchild built a prototype of the aircraft as the XC-120 Packplane. A new fuselage was built, all above the wing save for the flat lower surface where the pod matted or equipment was slung. The wings and tail were those of the C-119B, though additional landing gear had to be added to the forward end of the booms to support the airplane in the absence of the nose gear. Although flying in August 1950 and doing well, there was no follow-up. Advanced aircraft coming along were more affordable and apparently more practical if conceivably less flexible.

Although recognizing that jet engines would greatly detract from transport aircraft range, the USAF explored creating a turbine-powered modification of the XG-20. The initial thought was turboprops, but these remained immature and Chase quoted an unacceptable bid. A quicker and less expensive choice was adopting a pair of 5,200-lbf (23.1-kN) J47-equipped twin turbojet engine pods from the B-36D. It flew in this form, as the XC-123A, in April 1951 to become the USAF's first jet transport. A brief test program was well underway when the piston-powered XC-123 crashed and operations stood down. The jet was fast at 500 mph (805 kph) maximum, cruising at 400 mph (644 kph). The full payload was 33,200 lb (15,059 kg) and had a design GW of 67,000 lb (30.391 kg). However, there was no future in the configuration owing to the high fuel consumption and the propensity for the engine to become easily damaged by foreign objects when operating off-field.

The navy was as eager as the air force to realize the benefits of turboprops. They contracted with Lockheed in February 1951 to convert four R7V-1s to R7V-2s with P&W T34s. The change was expected to yield a 20,000-lb (907-kg) increase in GW

The idea of a transport with a detachable cargo pod was given a proof-of-concept test with the XC-120, which contained elements of a C-119B. Fairchild had won USAF interest in a C-119 variant with such a feature that would greatly speed turnaround time with shortened onload/offload cycles. However, less radical and costly approaches carried the day. (*National Archives*)

The first jet-powered transport for the USAF was a modification of the XG-20 glider. The XC-123A was fitted with J47 engine pods derived from the B-36D bomber and subjected to test and evaluation—here on its first flight from Mercer County Airport in Trenton, New Jersey, on April 21, 1951. The jets sucked fuel at a prodigious rate and the engines sucked ground material when operated off-field, so the idea was set aside. (*National Archives*)

and about 180 mph (290 kph) rise in cruise speed. Such benefits were worth the long wait and much effort to mature the turboprops. The R7V-2 did not fly until September 1954, and the USAF evaluated two as YC-121Fs. The air force had its own program to experiment with T34s on two KC-97Gs, becoming YC-97Js after initially being YC-137s. These aircraft flew in 1955.

Seeking the advantages of turboprops on the C-124s, the USAF responded positively to a 1951 proposal from Douglas to substitute T34s, anointing it as C-127.[2] A boost in cruise performance and ceiling was anticipated, though the aircraft still lacked pressurization. Douglas hoped that this would make a tanker variant more suitable for jet-powered receivers. One C-124A (51-074) was converted to become the YC-124B that first flew in February 1954. Before this event, the air force had already committed to using C-97 as their tankers, and so the YC-124B became a testbed for the P&W propeller turbine.

Uniquely Navy

The navy's transport squadrons had a diverse fleet of aircraft to draw upon. Several transport squadrons remained. The service retired its utility seaplanes—the JRF Gooses and J4F Widgeons—soon after the war. Grumman had Columbia Aircraft carry on with its G-42 design for a monoplane follow-up to the popular J2F Duck. The XJL-1 featured an R-1820, accommodated four to six passengers, and had an overhead trolley in the cargo/passenger space to move heavy freight. It was a large airplane with a 50-foot (15.2-m) wingspan, 16-foot (4.9-m) height, and weighing 13,000 lb (5,897 kg) loaded. It gave 2,070 miles (3,332 km) range, albeit at a dismal 119 mph (192 kph). The more practical Grumman Albatross (see later) took on the mission. The interior of the UF-1 could seat ten passengers comfortably and twenty-two uncomfortably on canvas benches. Up to 5,000 lb (2,268 kg) of freight could be loaded through a top hatch. The airplane flew soon after the war, but it was then abandoned.

Rapid transport of men and materiel to, from, and between carriers was always desired, but it was always a matter of squeezing aboard aircraft flying under normal ops. The great increase in the number of flat tops and available aircraft made this a bit more predictable. The Grumman Avenger torpedo bombers were capacious enough to take up to seven personnel in the top crew stations and within the fuselage, with cargo stuffed into these spaces or suspended in the bomb bay within a wire mesh basket or hinged bin. After the war, some General Motors-built aircraft (Eastern Aircraft) were converted for the role as TBM-3Rs via the conversion of TBM-3Es. Armor, weapons, and weapon equipment were all removed, and the canopy extended aft over the turret location. One high-priority task was carrying nuclear bomb components out to the ships. With operations beginning in 1951, the TBM-3R became the first Carrier Onboard Delivery (COD) aircraft that would not see a purpose-built type developed until beyond the period under review.[3] Others were general utility aircraft, designated TBM-3U. These even carried wounded personnel out of forward airstrips in Korea.

Above left: The utility floatplane mission was carried on for a few years following the war. This is typified by the Grumman J4F-2 Widgeon (32976) seen in the San Francisco Bay. The mission could be suitably served by other types that did not require the additional complexities of operating a seaplane. (*Naval Aviation Archives*)

Above right: One of two Columbia XJL-1 prototypes was photographed on September 17, 1948. The ultimate utility floatplane, its advanced features would have greatly improved the contributions of such aircraft. Though flying postwar, it did not survive the funding struggles and with a mission fading away—Columbia also folding shop. (*Naval Aviation Archives*)

Above left: Built principally as a search and rescue aircraft for the air force, the U.S. Navy also acquired ninety-four UF-1 variants for transport duties. The design dated from World War Two and employed engines even older, which would be operated for decades to come. Distributed to stations for utility runs, the Grumman was a fine airplane that served the service well. (*San Diego Air & Space Museum*)

Above right: Some TBM-3s were retained following the war to support on-ship delivery of personnel and light freight. These were given the suffix "R." This photo from July 6, 1951, shows sailors boarding a TBM at NAS Norfolk with the weapons bay open for potential cargo loading. (*National Archives*)

The final wartime production variant of the Mariner, the PBM-5, was employed principally as a transport both during the war and after. However, they were not designated with the "R" suffix. Admiring the success of the amphibious Catalina, the PBY-5A, Martin was asked to do the same with the Mariner. A PBM-5 (59349) was converted as the XPBM-5A and evaluated by the navy in 1946. While four were created via conversion, thirty-six PBM-5As were built new from 1948 to 1949, these also getting Curtiss Electric reversing props. The amphibians were initially intended for armed patrol, but the weight of the undercarriage (2,300 lb/1,043 kg) and displaced fuel volume (600 gal/2,271 l) detracted too much from endurance and range (430 miles/195 km). They were turned to transport.

On an even larger scale, the big flying boat transports of the war had lost importance as seen by the order for twenty giant Martin JRM variants of the canceled PB2M Mars being reduced to six postwar. The transports moved to a single vertical tail, improved R-3350 engines, rearranged interior, and large cargo doors under the wings and in the aft fuselage. An overhead electric hoist, running on rails within the wing undersurface, could lift heavy cargo and move it inside through the wing root doors. There were fittings under the wings for JATO bottles. The standard crew was eleven. Arranged for maximum personnel transport on canvas seats, the aircraft could accommodate 133. Freight for the JRM-1 could reach 35,000 lb (15,876 kg). However, freight onload and offload pier-side was cumbersome and labor-intensive.

The first JRM flew in summer 1945, but it was soon lost in an accident. Of the five remaining Mars, the last built was a JRM-2. This adopted R-4360 engines that lent 2,400 hp (447 kW) more power, raising maximum GW by 20,000 lb (9,072 kg). The JRM-1s brought up to -2 standards became JRM-3s. They were all impressive

Martin had a postwar go at creating an amphibious Mariner. Although mechanically successful, the PBM-5A's empty weight rose to such an extent that its value as a patrol aircraft was compromised and production was limited to just thirty-six seaplanes—and stretching Mariner production to twelve years—devoted principally to transport duty. (*San Diego Air & Space Museum*)

machines that broke some records, serving for ten years. While they showed better economy in ton-miles than landplanes, the boats were much slower and suffered more limited operations. They were complex and challenging to maintain. Their importance for sea communications via air was fading; they were retired in 1956.

Martin JRM-1 Characteristics

span	200 feet (61 m)	weight empty	75,000 lb (34,019 kg)
length	120.3 feet (36.7 m)	gross	145,000 lb (65,771 kg)
height	44.6 feet (13.6 m)	speed, max.	222 mph (357 kph)
wing area	13,220 feet² (1,228 m²)	cruise	158 mph (254 kph)
fuel	2,400 gal (9,085 l)	range, max. passengers	2,150 miles (3,460 km)
service ceiling	17,400 feet (5,304 m)	5,129 lb freight	3,185 miles (5,126 km)
climb rate, initial	633 fpm (193 mpm)		

During the protracted and troubled development of the Convair XP5Y-1 (see pages 367–369), the decision was made to create a transport aircraft based on the design to replace the Mars. The R3Y Tradewind was placed on contract in August 1950 for six airplanes, soon raised to eleven via a February 1951 change. The R3Y-1 had a side cargo door like the JRM. However, answering the USMC desire for a seaplane addition to amphibious landing capabilities and contributing to MBC, the R3Y-2 had bow onload/offload via a raised nose door and wheel ramps. For both of these variants, considerable redesign was necessary. The hull was lengthened and the interior greatly altered for unobstructed cargo movement. The space was also soundproofed,

One of the few Martin JRM flying boats to be built was JRM-1 76820 *Philippine Mars*. This shot from December 13, 1945, suggests the enormous dimensions of the airplane and reveals the cargo doors under the wing and in the aft fuselage. (*National Museum of Naval Aviation*)

air-conditioned, and pressurized. Externally, the vertical tail was altered and the dihedral in the horizontals eliminated, and armament was removed. Additional fuel was added in the wings and the float mounting strengthened. Answering some of the complaints with the P5Y's powerplant installation, upgraded 5,332-hp (3,976-kW) T40 engines were repositioned above the wings and with shorter power extension shafts to eliminate the difficulties encountered with wing flexure altering thrust axes. All this drove substantial changes to the wing structure. The crew consisted of seven persons.

For the R3Y-1, a large cargo door was installed behind the wing on the port side. A platform and hoist could be erected in the opening to assist heavy cargo movement. Eighty troops or seventy-two litters could be accommodated, or a payload of 48,000 lb (21,772 kg). The last six airplanes were built as R3Y-2s with the flight deck raised to allow an unobstructed cargo volume of 9-foot (2.7-m) width and to accommodate an upward-opening bow loading door to permit roll-on/roll-off of vehicles from a dock or beach. With a payload of 44,480 lb (20,176 kg), one of these aircraft could carry three 2.5-ton trucks, four 155-mm howitzers, or six jeeps. The personnel load rose to 103 seated or ninety-two litters.

The Tradewind development also ran long with the first flight of the R3Y-1 in February 1954, almost a year late. The initial R3Y-2 flew in October of that year and soon demonstrated the amphibious potential. The "bowloader" would taxi towards the beech, open the door and deploy the powered ramps, dropping a stern anchor at the opportune point, power up onto the shallows, fully lower the ramp, then begin cargo operations. The crew would keep the two outboard engines running to hold tension on the anchor cable and stabilize the craft. However, the nose rose as the boat rode higher in the water with weight offload, causing the aircraft to inch up the beach and shove the ramp forward. The craft would also settle off level with one float in the water. The crew was never able to winch themselves off the beach via the anchor cable, as intended. They instead had to use reverse thrust that created a sandstorm tormenting those ashore.[4]

There was no follow-up production and only seven Tradewinds were placed into fleet service beginning in 1956. They immediately set new records given their remarkable speed for a flying boat. Four of the airplanes were eventually converted to four-point hose reel tankers. However, the powerplant continued to give fits, and after two hull losses, the aircraft were withdrawn in 1958. There had also been corrosion of the aluminum in some portions of the aircraft.[5] The R3Y marked another protracted and costly large flying boat program that contributed little to navy operational capabilities, and another marker along the road to the demise of such warplanes.

Convair also created a motorized beaching cradle for the Tradewind to ensure that the hull remained clean of any beaching gear attachments. This enormous device, with two pontoons and eight wells, would be positioned under its own power into the shallows to allow the pilot to taxi into the cradle, capturing it as the hull contacted the rudder wheel guides, and power onto the sea ramp and stop with engine power alone. Launching was the reverse of this. The navy was so pleased with the cradle that they contracted with Convair to adapt it for the PBMs and P5Ms.[6]

Right: These flight manual drawings show the basic aspects of the Tradewind plus the differences between the R3Y-1 and R3Y-2, derived from the XP5Y-1. Both variants were still under construction at the end of the period being reviewed. (*Author's collection*)

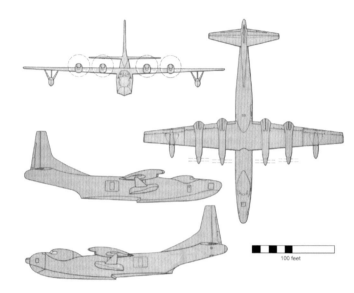

100 feet

Below: A trio of PBMs gathers around a tender. This is indicative of the added resources required to sustain large seaplanes and which became burdensome in the postwar years. The flying boat fleet continued to shrink, and the missions were assumed by less resource-intensive platforms. (*Naval Aviation Archives*)

9

Helicopters Ascend

In the recent war, the USAAF had used helicopters to rescue downed aircrew as well as for general liaison and urgent parts delivery. They wished to continue this with more efficient machines. The USAF formed the Air Rescue Service (ARS) for which helicopters were procured. The Army Ground Forces wanted to extend the liaison capabilities and seek a troop transport to replace the inefficient gliders from the war, but also offering rapid repositioning of squads to critical points. The marines saw the potential for vertical envelopment using helicopters to augment amphibious landings. Battlefield replenishment and casualty evacuation (casevac) were equally vital roles for both land combat arms. The U.S. Coast Guard (USCG) had pioneered air-sea rescue (ASR) with helicopters to show the potential if exploited, but the navy was not prepared during the war to give this much attention. The USN's wartime hesitation slowly dissipated as they foresaw the use of helicopters for plane-guard duty, supply transfer between ships at sea, and general transport. However, integrating USN or USMC helos into carrier operations would require time and operational experimentation. All these military helicopters required aircrew instruction via trainers. In fall 1945, and even through 1949, most of these ambitions were "pie-in-the-sky" as the available rotorcraft possessed very limited performance and durability. However, the services pressed to bring the technology along and develop ever more capable machines.

After decades of research and development, mostly as private endeavors, a few helicopters had flown under fine control just before World War Two. It took the conflict to push this the next step to practical vehicles. The U.S.A. was the standout leader in this enterprise, building more types and a higher quantity of truly effective helicopters than all other country combined. As a consequence, a new industry had been fostered. The appeal of entering the military and civilian markets, which appeared inevitably to grow after the war, brought many aspirants. As many as 300 new rotorcraft enterprises emerged in the country. With a fair number of both government and civil projects, there were many examples being evaluated and design problems being overcome, with experience building rapidly. Safety and efficiency grew apace with customer input, with mission effectiveness coming along as an outcome.

With turboprop engine development lagging, and so too the associated turboshaft that might provide turbine power for helicopters, these aircraft were confined to using the fine piston aero engines emerging from the war. These were usually air-cooled radials, but even the opposed or inlines were employed. Buried in the fuselage and so not normally exposed to passing air for cooling, fans were commonly added to encourage airflow through the engine compartment and baffles. Still, powerplant temperatures usually ran on the high side for long periods.[1] Additionally, rotorcraft application was a demanding installation for piston engines, with power:weight ratios disadvantageous for vertical lift machines where engine weight as a fraction of gross weight is even more critical than for an airplane. The recips were also commonly run at near full power all the time at low altitudes where air temperatures are greatest and at much lower (or no) airspeed than typical airplane applications. Consequently, maintenance demands were high and failure rates discouraging.

The army had already experienced the benefits of military helicopters, but also the limitations of the early types. They were eager to foster further development of the technology. Despite the postwar budget cuts, the services—the USAAF/USAF then also acting on behalf of the army and the navy for the marines—consistently found money for experimentation and prototyping. Funding such work from within the new industry was beyond the means of private or even public companies given the small return on investment, especially from the initially almost non-existent commercial market. The Pentagon was also able to buy small production lots permitting in-service evaluation and to build experience while sustaining the struggling manufacturing base. Budget limitations aside, there was hesitation to buy large quantities given the continuing immaturity yet rapid progress being made. The exposure continued to demonstrate the helicopter's limitations and engineering difficulties in meeting military requirements. This prompted a 1952 decision for the NACA to form a Subcommittee on Helicopters and for Sikorsky to establish a research department.[2]

The USN finally turned its attention to examining the naval applications of helicopters in mid-1946. As suggested by many advocates, this included ASW, ASR and plane-guard, scout and observation duties from surface combatants—replacing catapult floatplanes—transport and liaison between ships and to shore, general utility tasks, supporting amphibious landings with scouting, observing/reporting, and artillery spotting. The service formed VX-3 to explore these potentials. The unit operated from NAS Lakehurst in New Jersey and began by flying the wartime Sikorskys adopted by the coast guard—the HNS (R-4), HOS (R-6), and HO3S (R-5). Added to these were the new Bell HTL-1 trainer and Piasecki HRP-1s—all to be introduced below.

By most measures, military helicopters saw remarkable technological advances and capability growth through 1953. Operational expertise grew rapidly. The services shared in this effort, contributing to developments benefitting all alike while also sharing testbeds and buying helicopters developed by a sister air arm.[3] So Pentagon money was crucial to growing the industry and the capabilities of the helicopter for military exploitation while greatly benefitting the commercial market as a by-product. All of this work was rewarded with rapid maturation such that when war came again, just five years after the last, some worthy rotorcraft were available that offered the capabilities well beyond that existing at the end of World War Two. The helicopters had grown more capable and safe, but also heavier and more complex. Yet the S-56 experience (see page 339) made it clear that design challenges pressed the limits of available know-how and technology, presenting limitations such that especially practical troop transports remained just beyond reach. It took the availability of turboshaft engines, just a few years beyond Korea, to transform the helicopter into a truly efficient military aircraft.

Light Machines

All the World War Two helicopters that entered production were lightweight by any measure. Such machines were suitable for scouting, liaison, casevac, and urgent supply delivery, all as demonstrated during the war. All those helicopters continued operating beyond the immediate end of the war, though production was cut off. All of the development efforts already underway were allowed to run their course.

The principal wartime supplier, Sikorsky Aircraft, consolidated operations in Bridgeport, Connecticut, with additional development and production space while it sought further military contracts and hoped-for commercial sales. Civil orders proved slow to emerge. The company's two-place R-5 survived well into postwar service as a training and light observation helicopter. In development at the end of the war, the R-5D continued to be refined but did not go into production. Instead, twenty-one R-5As were modified to the "D" standard. This had a nose wheel, widened cabin for two seats in the rear and the pilot moved to the single forward seat. A sliding side door was featured on the port side and a hydraulic rescue hoist was added above it. Gross was increased 200 lb (91 kg) to 5,100 lb (2,313 kg). Five YR-5As were also modified with dual controls as R-5Es.

Sikorsky had developed the four-place Model S-51 as a growth of the R-5D, initially flying in February 1946. It became the first helicopter in commercial service. This had a more sophisticated fully articulated rotor, a bungee trim system to ease pilot fatigue, plus all-metal blades. With a 1-foot (0.3-m) diameter rotor growth and GW rising a few hundred pounds, it was designed to appeal to a hoped-for emerging market. Commercial sales were, however, anemic given size and price. Thankfully, in 1947, the army purchased eleven as R-5Fs (H-5F after June 1948) with the addition of a rescue hoist. They followed with thirty-nine R-5Gs in 1948 and sixteen R-5Hs in 1949 with optional pontoon gear and GW raised by 1,000 lb (454 kg). These had a pan on each side of the fuselage into which the litter and casualty were placed and then a cover with a window above the head at the front.

Eager to show the naval potential of the type, Sikorsky operated a single S-51 from the *Franklin D. Roosevelt* (CV-42) for weeks at its own expense during 1947. It performed well, executing six actual rescues. The navy, suitably impressed, placed an order for at least eighty-eight HO3S-1 with folding blades. Most went to the USMC as its first helicopter in any substantial numbers. The marines found the HO3S-1s to have good utility in many roles. It proved to be rugged and required only modest maintenance. The "O" for observation belied the many roles the helicopter filled, especially in Korea, where it was used for SAR, reconnaissance, and liaison. However, the high stance and tricycle gear made it unsuitable on sloping ground, the engine was difficult to access, the controls were heavy, it was generally unsuitable for night ops, and it was not configured for medivac.

Sikorsky HO3S-1 and H-5F Characteristics

rotor diameter	48 feet (14.6 m)	weight empty	3,975 lb (1,803 kg)
rotor blades	3	loaded gross	5,500 lb (2,495 kg)
length, fuselage	57.7 feet (17.6 m)	climb rate	1,000 fpm (305 mpm)
height overall	12.7 feet (3.9 m)	ceiling, absolute	13,500 feet (4,115 m)
rotor area	1,810 feet² (168 m²)	speed, max. (sea level)	103 mph (166 kph)
fuel	108 gal (409 l)	cruise	85 mph (137 kph)
		range, combat	260 miles (418 km)

The Firestone Aircraft XR-9B program from the war continued for a time. This was a rework of the earlier XR-9 with controls at two tandem seats, though just one forward instrument panel. Advanced features included an electro-hydraulic governor that maintained constant rotor speed with automatic blade pitch control regardless of power setting. The rotor hub was gimbal-mounted to reduce the magnitude of blade flapping and so vibration. It did fly smoothly and even hands-off, and could climb or descend with a change in throttle alone. The XR-9B (later H-9) was to lock out the gimbal feature and added offset flapping hinges. It grossed 1,380 lb (626 kg) and was powered by a 134-hp (100-kW) Lycoming O-290 driving a 28-foot (8.5-m) three-blade rotor. First flying in October 1945, it was evaluated by the AAF. However, there was low interest in the type and little funding in any event. It was allowed to wither, and attempts to find customers for a commercial variant, which was flown, did not succeed.

The XR-11 (H-11) was a tandem twin-rotor design from Rotor-Craft Corporation of Los Angeles, California. Their innovation was overlapping rigid wooden blades, lacking flapping and lead-lag hinges. The control links were within the hollow torque shafts to give a comparatively low-profile arrangement. Expected to gross 1,100 lb (499 kg), the two-place XR-11 was powered by a 110-hp (82-kW) Continental A100 four-cylinder flat engine. The experimental craft flew in 1947, and testing found considerable technical issues with the rotor system. Army funding expired, as did official interest.

Seeking a replacement for the early Sikorskys as trainers, all services took up Bell's new commercial rotorcraft. This employed the rotor system developed by Arthur Young during the war and patented by Bell Aircraft. It was a two-blade, semi-rigid rotor linked to a perpendicular cross-beam gyro-stabilizer bar with tip weights, all on a universal joint as a self-stabilized teetering arrangement. If the rotor was disturbed, tilting the bar, it caused the blade angle to change and right the unit. Bell's three experimental Model 30s were flown through the end of the war. The

A HO3S-1 (equivalent to the army H-5F) returns a pilot to the deck of the USS *Leyte* after a take-off mishap on November 7, 1950. The helicopter is equipped with the rescue hoist so vital to extracting survivors from the sea during plane guard duty. Several additional models of the S-51 design were produced in modest numbers after the war, generally representing equipment changes for mission effectiveness, but also introducing a fully articulated rotor system. (*National Archives*)

The Firestone XR-9B was a further development of a World War Two project. It was a worthy two-place helicopter, but AAF interest lay elsewhere during the early postwar period of austerity. (*National Archives*)

The XR-11 had some interesting features worth pursuing as a research effort, but the Rotor-Craft testbed remained just that. It had no production future, and there was no funding follow-up after flight in 1947. (*National Archives*)

commercial Model 47 first flew in December 1945. This helicopter went through some evolution as produced for commercial and military customers, but was basically the same power and rotor system in a welded steel tube frame. The engine was the six-cylinder opposed, air-cooled Franklin O-335 with fuel tanks mounted above. The blades were laminated wood with a steel leading edge. The Model 47 was granted the first helicopter commercial type certificate in May 1946, and the first customer took delivery that December. The 1,000th example was delivered in April 1953, with no end in sight. A 47D set a distance record for straight-line flight for its class at 1,217 miles (1,959 km) in twelve hours fifty-seven minutes in September 1952.

The U.S. military took an immediate interest in Bell's light helicopter. Bought in the hundreds and frequently paralleling commercial models, use went beyond training to liaison, utility, observation, reconnaissance, radio relay, rescue, and casevac—roles ably demonstrated in Korea. The navy and marines acquired them as HTLs. These were ordered beginning in June 1946 and delivered from February 1947. The air force and army began acquiring the type in April 1947 as R-13s (H-13 Sioux).

Purchases by all services continued over many years with details of the machines varying over time as distinguished by model letters or numbers. After beginning with a quadricycle-wheeled undercarriage, they were usually seen with landing skids—a Bell innovation—but floats could be substituted. Casualty evacuation was enabled by extended skids permitting litters to be attached behind a wind deflector. The cockpit was initial two seats with dual controls, but it evolved to a three-seat bench with one set of controls removable. In place of passengers, 500 lb (227 kg) of cargo could be carried. The enclosure was usually a bubble with the doors removable, although some were more elaborate. Various models of the O-335, from 175 to 220 hp (131 to 154 kW), were substituted with minor increases in performance. Likewise, fuel tanks saw some variation in design, placement, and quantity. An elevator was added in 1949 that deflected in concert with rotor tilt to improve stability and CG range.

Bell H-13D Characteristics

rotor diameter	35.1 feet (10.7 m)	weight empty	1,380 lb (626 kg)
rotor blades	2	design gross	1,969 lb (893 kg)
length overall	41.4 feet (12.6 m)	climb rate (sea level)	1,025 fpm (312 mpm)
height overall	8.7 feet (2.7 m)	service ceiling	13,000 feet (3,962 m)
rotor area	965 feet² (90 m²)	speed, max. (sea level)	98 mph (158 kph)
fuel	19 gal (109.8 l)	cruise, max.	78 mph (126 kph)
endurance	2.3 hours	range, best	164 miles (264 km)

Seeking to extend the H-13 to greater value, the USAAF funded the development of a larger helicopter based on the design. The mission was general liaison and light cargo. They exploited the initial development of Bell's Model 42 accommodating two pilots and three passengers in a comely cabin. Bell's rotor system was scaled up to 58.8 feet (17.9 m), and the P&W R-1340 at 540 hp (403 kW) was selected. Two XR-12s were ordered in 1946 in addition to a static test article, and delivery commenced in May 1948. Although initial production of thirty-four R-12As was planned in 1947, this was dropped in favor of exploring the enlarged R-12B (see page 325).

Pursuing a more suitable observation and liaison machine for both the air forces and Army Ground Forces, the USAAF began procurement action in February 1946 for a two-place single-rotor helicopter of approximately 3,000 lb (1,360 kg) with a supercharged engine of modest power. Firestone Aircraft won a contract for a trio of four-place XR-14s with a 100-hp (205-kW) Continental A100. Derived from the XR-9, it was all-metal and planned to have two tail rotors. However, the service thought better of the program in light of changing requirements, and the helicopters were never built.

Under the same program as the XR-14, Bell was funded in mid-1946 for the XR-15s (H-15). This four-place helicopter also employed the H-13's rotor system turned by a Continental O-470 at 275 hp (205 kW). A fully enclosed cabin and tail boom were matched to a quadricycle landing gear, later changed to skids. The 37.3-foot (11.4-m) diameter rotor lifted the helicopter with a loaded weight of 2,777 lb (1,260 kg). The three prototypes were delivered but, again, there was no production follow-up and the effort was terminated in 1950.

For a dedicated casevac helicopter, the army turned to the competing Hiller product. Stanley Hiller had developed a coaxial, rigid rotor light helicopter during the war that flew quite well. He also worked on a two-place machine with the conventional layout using some navy funding, but the end of the war saw this fade away. Hiller, based in Palo Alto, California, was determined to survive as a helicopter manufacturer. The

Above: The Bell Model 47 was one of the original commercial light helicopters and so successful that the military took notice, procuring it in several forms. This HTL-2 (left, 122954), photographed at NAS Patuxent River on June 14, 1948, was one form with an enclosed cabin and tail boom, as well as a wheel undercarriage. The H-13D (right), seen performing casevac in Korea during June 1952, became the more common configuration. (*National Archives*)

Below: The XR-12 was a scale-up of the Bell R-13 with a practical cabin for a trio of passengers. Delivered in 1948, the two machines (46-215 shown on pontoons) did well enough and production was planned as the R-12A. However, attention had turned to a larger helicopter. (*National Archives*)

company developed a light commercial helicopter with simplified controls dubbed Rotomatic. Initially a cyclic hung from above, the pilot directly moving "control rotors" or paddles at the end of a cross-beam that then adjusted the rotor head and so blade pitch. This was later revised to a conventional cyclic stick. If the rotor was disturbed, it displaced this servo-rotor as well with a concurrent change in paddle incidence and so a correcting change to the blades for a self-stabilizing system. This permitted hands-free flight. The first machine featuring the Rotomatic was the Model 360 that first flew in 1947 and received certification in 1948 as the UH-12.

The U.S. Army acquired the 360 as a single YH-23A Raven beginning in 1950 for evaluation, then followed with its largest order for helicopters yet at 100 H-23As set for initial delivery in early 1951. Most had enclosed skid panniers for stretchers. The USAF evaluated five of the type as well. The navy took forty-one as the HTE for training. Versions substituted other models of the Franklin O-335 with additional

Above: In 1946, the AAF sought a more capable liaison and observation helicopter, contracting two companies to include Firestone Aircraft that had developed the XR-9 helicopter. The design employed the rotor system of that earlier machine, but with an airplane-like fuselage for the two-place machine. This mock-up of the XR-14 also reveals that the team planned to have two tail rotors, one on either side of the tail, and positioned quite low. (*National Archives*)

Below: Another 1946 project was adapting the H-13 rotor system to an enclosed-cabin machine with four seats. This example of the three Bell XH-15s, 46-530, has the tricycle undercarriage that was later replaced with skids. The army chose not to take the helicopter to production. (*National Archives*)

horsepower (178 to 200 hp/133 to 149 kW), some changing from skids to wheels, a larger cabin, and adoption of the floor-mounted cyclic. The Hiller proved to be underpowered during Korean operations, but the service bought hundreds more, with horsepower incrementally increased, for training and general utility.

Hiller H-23B and HTE-2 Characteristics

rotor diameter	35.4 feet (10.8 m)	weight empty	1,816 lb (824 kg)
rotor blades	2	gross	2,700 lb (1,225 kg)
length, fuselage	27.8 feet (8.5 m)	climb rate, initial	770 fpm (235 mpm)
height overall	9.8 feet (3 m)	service ceiling	13,200 feet (4,023 m)
rotor area	984 feet² (92 m²)	speed, max. (sea level)	84 mph (153 kph)
fuel	28 gal (106 l)	cruise, max.	76 mph (132 kph)
		range	197 miles (317 km)

The army also evaluated the very minimal Seibel S-4A Skyhawk helicopter. Charles Seibel came from the Bell team to create his own company in 1947. His team's helicopter was very simple and easy to maintain. The open frame could have a fabric and plastic covering installed over the pilot and passenger volumes during inclement weather. The innovation was that the rotor hub lacked bearings, hinges, and dampers because the blades were attached via a simple "blade attaching angle" that twisted elastically for blade angle change. Attitude control was via CG shift created by displacing the stick, which caused the pilot station to shift longitudinally. Heading changes were, presumably, just with the pedals and the tail rotor. Seibel's first helicopter, the single-seat S-3, was flown in 1947 and the S-4 received civil certification in 1950. The USAF bought two of the slightly larger and more powerful S-4As in 1951 as the YH-24 for army evaluation. The 125-hp (93-kW) Lycoming O-290 drove the two-blade rotor and the machine had an empty weight of 960 lb (435 kg). It topped out at 65 mph (105 km) at a range of 98 miles (158 km). One of the machines was modified to shorten and widen the craft so that the passenger was moved up beside the pilot. Although the helicopter was indeed simple, the service judged it to be of too little utility.

The services explored another tandem rotor with the two-place, all-metal McCulloch MC-4 helicopters. McCulloch Aircraft was a division of McCulloch Motors, an engine manufacturer, and their helicopter was initially developed as the JOV-3 by Drago Jovanovich while he was employed by the Helicopter Engineering and Research Corporation. First flying in 1948, the tiny helicopter was enlarged as the MC-4 that flew in 1951. The navy evaluated this machine and also the later MC-4A, two of which were designated XHUM-1. The larger-still MC-4C was the first tandem-rotor helicopter to be certified in the U.S. for commercial operations. Powered by a 200-hp (149-kW) Franklin O-335, it possessed 22-foot (6.7 m) three-blade rotors that overlapped and had a 2,000-lb (907-kg) gross weight. It flew to 200 miles (322 km) with a 105-mph (169-kph) top speed. This was the configuration of the three YH-30s that were evaluated by the army in 1952. They proved to be underpowered and the drive system judged too complex.

Competing with Bell in the light helicopter market was the Hiller 360, also known commercially as the UH-12. This was also adopted by the military for rotorcraft training. The photo is of a Navy HTE-1 (128637) from August 23, 1951, taken at NAS Patuxent River. Evident is the Rotomatic control with paddles at the end of a crossbeam. (*Naval Aviation Archives*)

The minimalist Seibel helicopter had some unique features the Army chose to explore via two YH-24 prototypes. Blade angle change was purely elastic. Attitude change was via the pilot shifting his weight by moving his seat forward and aft with the cyclic and deflecting the tail rotor pedals. The construction was very light and airspeed low, so the army judged the design to have too little utility. (*Naval Aviation Archives*)

Another small firm, among many dozens of others, to undertake helicopter development in postwar America was McCulloch Aircraft. Their tandem-rotor MC-4 (Al Bayer at the controls in this image) was the first such design to gain commercial certification as the improved MC-4C. The navy explored the potential of the intermediate MC-4B and the army looked at the MC-4C, but neither found enough to recommend a large purchase. (*Naval Aviation Archives*)

More Utility

Moving on from the light helicopter introduced engineering difficulties, but the development teams were eager to engage the challenges. There were always more powerful engines. Yet these remained recips that grew in weight and cooling demands with the greater horsepower. The addition of freight and passengers also meant the need for broader CG travel. As with all things aeronautical, progress was incremental and with as many or more failures than successes.

The Bell XR-12A (see page 320) was dropped in favor of a model enlarged to ten passengers—a squad of soldiers. The XR-12B was satisfactory and so ten service-test YR-12Bs (YH-12B) were manufactured with a 600-hp (447-kW) variant of the R-1340. The helicopter weighed 6,600 lb (2,994 kg) loaded. However, serious development issues were encountered with the much-enlarged rotor that required assistance from Wright Field's Propeller Laboratory. By the time the helicopters were delivered for evaluation, starting in 1949, interest had waned given more attractive alternatives, and there was no follow-up.

In the same vein, the army—prior to the arrangement of USAF procurement for the ground forces—contracted Sikorsky to create a military helicopter from their commercial S-52 that had set three speed and altitude records. This two-place machine improved on its wartime rotor, adding offset flapping hinges and substituting metal blades. However, it had found no commercial customers after its 1947 certification. It was then enlarged with two additional seats and a more powerful engine, and it was this S-52-2 that attracted army interest. The four XH-18As delivered in 1951 used

The Bell XR-12 was grown in order to transport ten passengers or a squad of soldiers. This was asking a great deal of the enlarged rotor system and engineering problems were encountered. Evaluation of the ten YR-12Bs (46-217 seen in hover) was so delayed that, during a period of rapid helicopter technological advancement, more attractive alternatives had emerged. (*National Archives*)

the Franklin O-425 at 245 hp (183 kW). Although the army passed up production, the navy placed an order as the HO5S to replace the HO3S. Delivered from March 1952, the HO5S came at a time of urgent need in Korea and so more were procured for marine operation. The naval arm ultimately took seventy-nine.

Sikorsky HO5S-1 Characteristics

rotor diameter	33 feet (10.1 m)	weight empty	1,650 lb (748 kg)
rotor blades	3	gross	2,700 lb (1,225 kg)
span	33 feet (10.1 m)	service ceiling	15,800 feet (4,816 m)
length overall	28.8 feet (8.8 m)	speed, max.	110 mph (177 kph)
height overall	8.7 feet (2.6 m)	cruise	92 mph (148 kph)
rotor area	855 feet² (79 m²)	range	290 miles (467 km)

Charles Kaman, formerly of Hamilton Standard, formed Kaman Aircraft in Connecticut during December 1945. He focused on two-blade, contra-rotating intermeshed rotors. Blade pitch change was via small servo-flaps placed at about the three-quarters span. These acted like tabs controlled by the pilot via pushrods running out through the leading edge of the blades, twisting the spruce blades via aerodynamic forces for both collective and cyclic pitch change. The helicopters commonly had large vertical tails, some with rudders. Kaman's first experimental machine flew in January 1947. That same year, the navy contracted with them to provide a rotor for NACA evaluation. Another engineering contract in 1948 provided data on their "synchrocopter" layout. A

The Sikorsky S-52 was aimed at the commercial market, but the army and navy evaluated it for potential military application. Four XH-18A prototypes (49-2888 shown on February 8, 1952) were evaluated. The navy ultimately acquired a large number as the HO5S-1 for work in Korea. (*National Archives*)

commercial two-place K-225 took flight in December 1948. Two of a refined cabin-class version, the K-240 with the 240-hp (179-kW) Lycoming O-435, were sold to the navy in 1950 as the XHTK-1 for evaluation. Demonstrations by a company pilot included what was reported to be the first loop ever performed by a helicopter.[4] A horizontal tail was geared with collective pitch control. A litter could be installed in place of the co-pilot and passenger, the nose plex swinging aside to admit this.

A 1950 design competition for a marine observation helicopter, also serving utility and rescue roles, was won by Kaman's K-600. Redesigning the helicopter to a military specification and then putting it into production demanded capital Kaman lacked. The navy helped by giving the firm an order for twenty-nine three-place HTK-1s. These were delivered between 1951 and 1953. The first of two XHOK-1s underwent its maiden flight in April 1953. These and the eighty-one HOK-1s substituted an R-1340 at 600 hp (447 kW) with closer rotor heads, 6-feet (1.8-m) larger rotor diameter, and additional empennage area. The loaded weight rose by about 2,500 lb (1,134 kg) and range by about 100 miles (161 km). Many more were built in later years for navy and air force missions.

Kaman HTK-1 Characteristics

rotor diameter, each	41 feet (12.5 m)	weight empty	2,300 lb (1,043 kg)
rotor blades	2 each	normal gross	2,880 lb (1,306 kg)
span	45 feet (13.7 m)	max. gross	3,000 lb (1,361 kg)
length overall	41 feet (12.5 m)	climb rate	938 fpm (286 mpm)
height overall	12.3 feet (3.7 m)	absolute ceiling	10,000 feet (3,048 m)
rotor area, total	1,320 feet² (123 m²)	speed, max.	92 mph (148 kph)
fuel (usable)	40 gal (151.4 l)	cruise	70 mph (113 kph)
endurance, max.	2 hours	range	125 miles (201 km)

Kaman Aircraft developed a rotorcraft featuring the contra-rotating, intermeshed rotor layout that eliminated the tail rotor. The design won a competition for a marine observation helicopter, but Kaman needed working capital to proceed. Consequently, the service bought a modest number of the design used for the evaluation. The HTK-1, shown here, displays considerable clear surfaces supporting the observation mission. (*American Aviation Historical Society*)

The refined Kaman HOK-1 had closer rotor heads, the shafts and supporting rods enclosed, and an additional vertical tail area. The revised exhaust testifies to the change in engine. Only the prototypes emerged during the period under review. (*National Archives*)

In the tandem-rotor field, Piasecki Helicopter continued the development of the XHRP-1 from the war at its Sharon Hill, Pennsylvania, site. This navy program was intended for coast guard SAR and sought a remarkable 1,800-lb (817-kg) useful load with seating for ten apart from the two pilots arranged in tandem. The longitudinal tandem-rotor layout held promise for generous CG travel while achieving a necessary disk area for the aircraft GW without an exceptionally large single diameter. As with the intermeshed rotor, ditching the tail rotor meant that all power was employed in creating lift instead of some diverted to countering torque. It had its aerodynamic idiosyncrasies, but no more than other layouts. Powered initially by the Wright 450-hp (335-kW) R-975 and then the 600-hp (447-kW) R-1340, the fuselage swept up to the rear rotor to place it above the front for a "flying banana" appearance. Construction was primarily welded steel frame with wooden ribs and stringers, the whole wrapped in fabric. The company made good progress with the design, demonstrating the required payload and being the first U.S. helicopter to carry a sling load.

The wartime Piasecki XHRP-1 matured to the production HRP-1 and for a time could carry the heaviest load of any helicopter. Developed for coast guard SAR, the marines took interest in the odd-looking machine to explore its potential in supporting its missions. The USS *Palau* (CVE-122) has eight HRP-1s on its deck for marine assault exercises in 1949. The helicopter was marginal for the USMC mission, yet it was a start that eventually yielded a new dimension to amphibious warfare. (*National Archives*)

Piasecki's hard work was rewarded with two contracts, in June 1946 and April 1947, for twenty HRP-1 Rescuers. This compelled a move to a new factory in Morton, Pennsylvania. The most capacious helicopters when delivered, the minor changes included a new empennage for added stability. The first was taken up in late summer 1947 and deliveries ran into 1949. They served for experimentation by the marines, who practiced operating them from ships for amphibious assault. In all, this was a fruitful experience, both for the military and Piasecki, demonstrating that there remained much to learn about building reliable military helicopters. The HRPs struggled with inconsistencies between individual aircraft, serviceability problems, and vibration.

A greatly reworked all-metal HRP-2, though still wood blades with steel spar, was ordered in 1948 for the coast guard. These had line-abreast pilot seating and fourteen troops or twelve litters. Ultimately, only five were completed as the design was becoming dated. However, it was also adopted by the USAF as the H-21 Work Horse. Eighteen YH-21s were ordered in 1949 and delivered from April 1952. It was a much heavier machine than its navy antecedent and so had a larger rotor diameter and the supercharged 1,250-hp (932-kW) R-1820, though down-rated to 1,150 hp (858 kW).

Piasecki YH-21 Characteristics

rotor diameter, each	44.5 feet (13.6 m)	weight empty	8,000 lb (3,629 kg)
rotor blades	3 each	fully loaded	11,500 lb (5,216 kg)
span	44.5 feet (13.6 m)	gross	13,300 lb (6,033 kg)
length overall	86.4 feet (26.3 m)	climb rate, initial	1,080 fpm (329 mpm)
height overall	16 feet (4.9 m)	absolute ceiling	9,450 feet (2,880 m)
rotor area, total	1,555 feet² (145 m²)	speed, max. (sea level)	131 mph (211 kph)
fuel	304 gal (1,151 l)	cruise (sea level)	98 mph (158 kph)
endurance, typical	4.4 hours	range, typical	500 miles (805 km)

The service found the YH-21s satisfactory and ordered thirty-two H-21As for the ARS. An Arctic Rescue Helicopter Board also evaluated the McDonnell XHJD-1 (see page 336) as a potential candidate, but chose the H-21.[5] Aimed primarily at arctic operation and so "winterized," this required extensive cold-weather testing. Inflatable "doughnut" floats around the tires improved floatation on snow. The helicopter had a capacity of a dozen litters or fourteen troops. The first was delivered in October 1953 and set speed and altitude records. The service went on to fund further development of the design for itself and the army, with hundreds of these follow-on models manufactured.

Finally ready to attempt shipboard ops and seeking a more mature utility rotorcraft, the navy specified the use of the 525-hp (391-kW) R-975—supported by Continental postwar—that was believed to be easier to cool. After issuing requirements in 1945 and ordering prototypes in 1946, they evaluated two Sikorsky XHJS-1 single-rotor helicopters after the first flew in September 1947. This S-53 was another iteration of the S-51 with folding metal blades and the tail rotor raised above head height. Grossing 5,300 lb (2,404 kg), the landing gear was strengthened while the cabin accommodated three and the pilot. It was equipped for night ops. The unacceptable fault was that CG travel was marginal

An all-metal HRP-2 caught the attention of the USAF that acquired eighteen examples as the YH-21 for the MATS Air Rescue Service. It would be principally for arctic rescue, as depicted in this image of 50-1238. This gave birth to a modest production run of the helicopter for the USAF mission, but many more for the army vertical envelopment mission. (*National Archives*)

Sikorsky suffered one of its few misses when competing for the navy's first shipboard utility helicopter. The HJS-1 was a try at developing a cabin-class helicopter using the same engine and rotor layout as World War Two types, but this left too small a CG travel. (*San Diego Air & Space Museum*)

given the layout with the engine and rotor behind the cabin and so degraded controllability. First flying in September 1947, the helicopters were assessed and then set aside.

BuAer was still convinced tandem rotors were favorable for their missions and chose another Piasecki design. The first of the XHJP-1 prototypes flew in March 1948. Deliveries of thirty-two HUP-1 Retrievers ("U" for utility instead of "J") commenced in February 1949, though fleet service did not begin until January 1951. A clear descendent of the HRP-2 but much shorter to fit on a carrier elevator, the banana shape was "bent" with an aft pylon to the rotor. For the first time, the fore and aft rotor disks overlapped and the blade fold was unnecessary. This left a cabin able to accommodate just four seats or three stretchers. Early blades still had wooden elements and the cargo floor was wood, but the helicopter was otherwise all metal. A 1,500-lb (680-kg) sling load could be carried.

The HUP-1s were followed by 165 HUP-2s, with 25 hp (19 kW) more powered, that entered service in 1952. The first production helicopter to be equipped with an autopilot—derived from a World War Two Sperry unit—and eliminating the tail surfaces, this permitted flight in instrument conditions and hands-free hover.[6] Eventually, 166 of this model were procured. In a change the navy had insisted upon, it was also the first Piasecki with all-metal blades.

After a few years of technological maturation, the navy was convinced the helicopter could serve on a carrier deck fulfilling utility roles. They remained certain that the tandem-rotor layout was best for their applications, and Piasecki won a production order for the HUP-1. One feature of the Piasecki aircraft was the rescue hoist being internal, personnel and cargo pulled in through a hatch below the co-pilot station as shown here in a February 1952 picture. (*National Archives*)

The HUP is noteworthy as the navy's first routinely ship-based helicopter. Duties were liaison, including moving personnel and cargo between ships, and plane-guard aboard carriers. They had a quicker response time for plane-guard than the nearby destroyers, though they did not fly at night.[7] They were also employed by the marines. There was a hydraulic hoist to bring up personnel, stretchers, and up to 400 lb (181 kg) or cargo through a door below the co-pilot seat that could be folded aside. The pilot could easily see the operation and hover with precision. Given the tandem-rotor helicopter's propensity for flying sideways, some pilots would fly in this orientation beside the ship underway so that they could keep an eye on the flight operations without always having to turn their head. The machine was fast, unofficially breaking the helicopter speed record with a 131-mph (211-kph) trial. It was also allegedly the first helicopter to fly a loop.[8] The autopilot proved unreliable, with hard-over failures contributing to several crashes, and was eventually removed. The engine also gave fits, with a dismaying number of failures and hull losses. This led to the engine being initially derated and aircraft GW reduced until R-975 improvements were introduced.[9] Further versions of the HUP were manufactured beyond 1953.

Piasecki HUP-2 Characteristics

rotor diameter, each	35 feet (10.7 m)	weight empty	4,300 lb (1,950 kg)
rotor blades	3 each	fully loaded	5,750 lb (2,608 kg)
span	35 feet (10.7 m)	overload	6,100 lb (2,767 kg)
length overall	56.9 feet (17.3 m)	climb rate (sea level)	1,000 fpm (305 mpm)
height overall	13.2 feet (4 m)	absolute ceiling	10,000 feet (3,048 m)
rotor area, total	962 feet² (293 m²)	speed, max.	100 mph (161 kph)
fuel	150 gal (569 l)	cruise	75 mph (121 kph)
endurance, typical	4 hours	range, combat	400 miles (641 km)

The HUP-2 was also produced for the army as seventy H-25A Mules that began entering service in early 1953. Changes included hydraulically boosted flight controls, altered doors, and strengthened floor with cargo tie-down rings. Although utility was comparatively low for army missions, helicopters were urgently needed given the Korean emergency.

The high-utility ASW Bell HSL tandem-rotor (overlapping) helicopter is covered in the next chapter.

Doman Helicopters also produced a hinge-less rotor helicopter that was evaluated by the U.S. Army. The firm was established in 1945 to exploit the patents of Glidden Doman, who worked as an engineer for Sikorsky. His four-blade rotor was gimbaled at the hub and so dispensed with flapping and lead-lag hinges or dampers. The hub was enclosed within a housing to avoid damage. The rotor was first flight-tested in 1947 on a Sikorsky R-6 lent to Doman by the USAF. Flying in 1950, the results were very favorable. A prototype of a cabin-class helicopter incorporating the hinge-less rotor, the LZ-4, was tested from 1950.

The army contracted Doman, of Danbury, Connecticut, for two production-representative versions of the LZ-4 as YH-31. It was powered by an eight-cylinder

The rare Doman YH-31 is seen in U.S. Army colors. The layout with the engine in the nose, pilots above, and rotor above the cabin proved successful for Sikorsky, but Doman was not given a production contract. (*American Aviation Historical Society*)

Lycoming SO-580-D at 400 hp (298 kW), fuel-injected and supercharged, and cooled by exhaust ejectors. The layout had the two-place pilot station above the engine in the nose and the rotor above the cabin behind. The cabin accommodated six passengers or four stretchers. The first of these flew in April 1953, and both were delivered by 1955. There was no subsequent order for the type.

The USAF finally hit on a winning solution with the Sikorsky S-55, designed during 1948. Like the Doman machine, it placed the engine in the nose and rotor above the cabin for respectable CG options and pilots above the engine for good visibility. The engine was readily accessible for maintenance via two doors. Intrigued, the USAF ordered five YH-19s for evaluation, the first flying in November 1949. Bought as the H-19A, with a fillet added in the step from the fuselage to the tail boom, this used a 600-hp (447 kW) R-1340. The air force moved in 1951 to acquire fifty production H-19As that added fins to the tail boom. It followed with 250 H-19Bs that had the tail boom angled down, a reduced diameter tail rotor atop a wider vertical, and revised horizontals. The army bought seventy-two of the -19As as the H-19C beginning in 1951 for Korean operation as the service's first true assault helicopter. They followed with 338 H-19Ds equivalent to the -19Bs, delivered to 1959.

The helicopter had respectable lifting capacity in a spacious cabin seating ten and was a good performer, though it could struggle in hot temperatures. Yet the marines turned to it as well with an August 1950 order for sixty HRS-1s that introduced self-sealing tanks. The first was handed over in April 1951, followed by ninety-one HRS-2s with minor differences. A final order was eighty-nine HRS-3s with another model of Wright R-1300.

This H-19A (51-3858) of the 3rd Air Rescue Group within MATS was photographed in Korea during June 1953 demonstrating the hydraulic hoist above the cabin door. The type would come to be identified as SH-19s owing to their initial devotion to the rescue role. In one year of Korean duty, the H-19s were credited with evacuating 2,000 wounded and rescuing 500 soldiers and seamen. (*National Archives*)

Sikorsky H-19A and HRS-1 and HO4S-1 Characteristics

rotor diameter	53 feet (16.2 m)	weight empty	4,550 lb (2,064 kg)
rotor blades	3	fully loaded	6,835 lb (3,100 kg)
span	53 feet (16.2 m)	overload	7,900 lb (3,583 kg)
length overall	42.2 feet (12.9 m)	climb rate (sea level)	1,100 fpm (335 mpm)
height overall	14.7 feet (4.5 m)	absolute ceiling	10,500 feet (3,200 m)
rotor area	8,825 feet² (820 m²)	speed, max. (level)	112 mph (180 kph)
fuel	190 gal (719 l)	cruise	86 mph (138 kph)
		range	470 miles (756 km)

Twins

The USAAF flew its first helicopter in 1941 and placed three types into production by 1944. These were all two-seaters and the service was eager to move to machines with more capacity. With power still limited, the greatest value of the helicopter seemed to be casevac and rescue. Consequently, in summer 1944, it sought a helicopter capable of accommodating at least four litters—soon growing to ten passengers along the sidewalls or six litter patients—or other freight and passengers. The anticipated gross weight suggested possibly twin rotors and two engines. Winning the contract was Kellett Aircraft, of Camden, New Jersey, with an enlarged version of their wartime XR-8 Synchrocopter with intermeshed rotors and a single engine. That project had run into serious problems but showed promise. The new XR-10 would have two engines to meet the power demands, becoming the largest helicopter the U.S. Army had under development during the war.

The two pilots sat line-abreast and shared the same collective lever between the seats.[10] A 2,200-lb (998-kg) useful load was predicted. Each 525-hp (392-kW) Continental R-975 engine was in a side nacelle to leave the cabin free and ease CG concerns. These were cooled by engine exhaust directed into steel venturi-shaped ducts that drew outside air through the nacelles. Power shafts ran externally from the nacelles to the rotor gearbox above the cabin. A cross-shaft between the rotor gearboxes ensured safe single-engine operation. Kellett expected operation at up to 4,600 feet (1,402 m) at normal GW on a single engine. The blades were a steel spar and wooden ribs wrapped with metal sheeting spot-welded into place. Each 65-foot (19.8-m) diameter rotor had three blades. The fuselage was entirely metal employing common aircraft semi-monocoque construction. Just behind the cabin was a hoist over an opening in the deck to raise and lower cargo or personnel. The center of the three vertical stabilizers was fitted with a rudder. The wheels had taxi and parking brakes.

Redesignated the XH-10, Kellett's design was slowly coming together. Scheduled for a November 1945 flight, this was finally accomplished in April 1947. Weight grew to a discouraging 7,555 lb (3,427 kg) empty, as did contract over-runs to the tune of more than $1 million or one hundred percent. Although the performance was good at 90 mph (145 kph) cruise, with a range of 160 miles (258 km) and a three-hour endurance given 180-gal (681-l) fuel, including single-engine operation, occasional blade-on-blade contact were alarming occurrences. The air force lost interest and cut the second of the two prototypes as well as dropping a preliminary production order. The single prototype, lacking any cabin doors, was delivered to the USAF in June 1948 and set aside.

The navy also decided to have a go at the lateral tandem layout that had not helped the army's unsuccessful Platt-LePage XR-1 during the war. The USN had concluded this was a favorable configuration for a naval helicopter with the safety of two engines. McDonnell Aircraft had helped finance Platt-LePage and had personnel working with that firm to learn about rotorcraft. McDonnell took up a preliminary design for a twin-engine growth of the XR-1 from Platt-LePage and offered it to the navy. With all but Piasecki already working under contract with the army, BuAer chose to gamble on the young firm. McDonnell got a contract in March 1945 for a single XHJD-1 as America's first twin-engine helicopter. Its first flight was in April 1946.

Carrying up to ten occupants, the XHJD-1 was powered by a 450-hp (336-kW) R-985 in each outboard nacelle. Empty weight was on the order of 8,000 lb (3,629 kg) and loaded was 11,000 lb (4,990 kg). It could touch 120 mph (193 kph) and a range of 300 miles (485 km). The pylons to the rotors constituted wings that generated about 10 percent of the lift during cruise flight and up to 30 percent during

A twin-engine SAR helicopter capable of transporting markedly more personnel was sought during the war and the Kellett program was continued after. The XR-10 had the recip engines in nacelles to either side of the cabin, the exhaust used to draw in air for cooling. Note the exposed power shafts running from the nacelles to the internal rotor gearbox and the rudder on the center of the three vertical tails. Only one of the helicopters was built and no production followed. (*National Archives*)

What interest the navy did show in helicopters during World War Two were usually stretches of the infant technology and directed to new firms. An example was a twin-engine aircraft contract won by McDonnell Aircraft. The XHJD-1 (later HJH-1) flew after the war and employed the lateral tandem-rotor layout. It served as a testbed with no production follow-up. (*Naval Aviation Archives*)

engine-out autorotation. Cross-shafting passed through the wings such that one engine could drive both rotors with enough lift to sustain level flight at maximum gross weight. Downwash on the wings from the rotors somewhat compromised hover performance. Despite its advantages, the sole Whirlaway served research purposes only. Experiments included reversing the rotation direction of the rotors, altering rotor diameter, and working on vibration suppression.

The USAAF had confidence in the future of the helicopter and continued pushing the technology. However, their 1946 requirement for a long-range rotorcraft capable of rescuing the large crew of a downed strategic bomber was very ambitious. A specified 1,400-mile (2,253-km) range demanded a large quantity of fuel. They awarded a contract to Piasecki in June 1948 to develop the XR-16 Transporter (soon XH-16). This enormous machine, the interior equal to the volume of a C-54 four-engine airplane, demanded two engines. It flew in October 1953 as the largest helicopter to that time at 134 feet (40.8 m) in length and two overlapping 82-foot (25-m) diameter, three-blade rotors. It had a 32,000 lb (14,515 kg) empty weight with 14,000-lb (6,350-kg) useful load, cruising at 110 mph (177 kph). A drop-down ramp in the rear facilitated rapid loading/unloading. The tall undercarriage and flat bottom of the fuselage allowed for an envisioned detachable cargo pannier beneath.

The perceived utility of the XH-16 brought army interest, seeing up to forty infantryman or thirty-two litters, or three jeeps, being carried. Their participation brought another redesignated as the YH-16, though it remained a very experimental effort. However, the two P&W R-2180 at 1,650 hp (1,230 kW) each were found

The Piasecki XH-16 was on an initial ground test at the end of the period under review. Designed for a long-range air force rescue mission, the high fuel volume ensured it was the largest helicopter in the world at the time and equipped with two reciprocating engines delivering inadequate power. The large size and rear loading ramp are evident. (*National Archives*)

inadequate for the task during initial testing. A YH-16 was re-engined in 1955 with two T38 turbines—becoming the first twin-turbine helicopter—significantly dropping the empty weight. This was briefly designated the YH-27 before becoming the YH-16A. However, a fatal crash eventually ended the program.

The marines pressed BuAer to seek an assault rotorcraft of suitable capacity—a squad with their weapons, replenishment cargo, or delivery of heavy weapons. They initially explored a 3,500-lb (1,588-kg) capacity machine. In July 1947, the commandant specified a 5,000-lb (2,268-kg) capacity helicopter, with no requirement to fit below the carrier flight deck, as meeting these extrapolated needs. The USMC created an experimental squadron in December 1947 to begin trials of potential tactics, and the two services stood up the Helicopter and Transport Seaplane Board to develop heliborne amphibious assault doctrine. The YH-16 attracted BuAer's interest, especially as it was underway and so would save development time. However, slow progress on projects like the YH-16 only emphasized the continuing limitations of the technology, with much maturation and growth still ahead to meet the demanding requirements levied by the USMC. Even if not required to fit on an elevator, aircraft like the YH-16 appeared unsuitable for operations from the small amphibious assault ships being envisioned.

The Korean Conflict showed both the value of the helicopter and the deficiencies of the existing types and so added a new impetus to finding a suitable marine assault helicopter. All services were eager to push the technology, especially to carry heavier loads, such as a squad of infantrymen, farther and faster. A March 1950 helicopter conference discussed these factors and concluded that a large helicopter might still be within reach. The naval arms suggested the USAF and army abandon the YH-16 and join this effort. A subsequent navy requirement the same year went out for a rotorcraft capable of deploying twenty-six troops, vehicles, and heavy equipment. A contract was issued in May 1951 for four Sikorsky S-56s as the XHR2S-1.

The HR2S-1 would become the largest helicopter under development in America during the period, four times larger than anything Sikorsky had attempted. Gross weight was to be 30,000 lb (13,608 kg), length 64 feet (19.5 m), and height 22 feet (6.7 m). It was to have two 1,900-hp (1,417-kW) R-2800 engines, each in a nacelle under stub wings off the top of the fuselage. Power shafts ran through the wings into the rotor gearbox. The main landing gear would retract into these nacelles. Fuel was contained in the wings and nacelles. The horizontal stabilizer would pivot freely until becoming fixed in cruise flight. Rather than twin rotors, an enormous 68-foot (20.7-m) diameter unit with five all-metal blades was positioned above the cabin in typical Sikorsky fashion. With a requirement to fit on an elevator, the rotor would have an automatic blade fold and the tail, with an anti-torque rotor, was also to fold forward. The stub wings provided lift in forward flight, unloading the rotor to delay blade stall. The flight deck was above a nose with side-opening doors and a fold-down ramp for roll-on/roll-off of vehicles and wheeled equipment like field guns. There were also to be large doors on the starboard side of the fuselage. The cabin seated thirty-six fully equipped marines or took twenty-four litters. A 2,000-lb (907-kg) capacity electric cargo hoist would run on rails in the ceiling of the cabin.

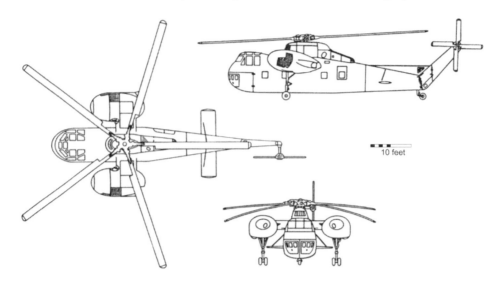

10 feet

The HR2S-1 was a serious attempt at creating a heavy-lift helicopter for the Marine Corps. Still tied to recip engines, the engineering challenges were enormous and it took years to design and then perfect the machine. Contracted in May 1951, the aircraft flew in December 1953, and years more were required before delivery of production articles. (*Author's collection*)

Powering this and starting the engines demanded an APU. The external sling load was to be 10,000 lb (4,536 kg). The navy sought cruise as high as 160 mph (260 kph). Automatic Stabilization Equipment was to permit hands-free flight at night and under instrument conditions.

The first XHR2S-1 flew in December 1953, but the type took until 1955 to perfect owing to multiple engineering challenges. Weight grew by 1,000 lb (454 kg), driving rotor diameter to 72 feet (21.9 m) and speed fell well short of requirements—generally below 130 mph (208 kph). Two jettisonable external fuel tanks were ultimately added and a 2,100-hp (1,566-kW) version of the R-2800 was substituted. During that time, the U.S. Army became interested in the aircraft and placed its own production order for the H-37 Mojave. The S-56 would be the largest piston-powered helicopter.

Tip Propulsion

One solution to both the limitations of the piston engines and rotor torque was to eliminate the engine altogether. The alternative was using jet propulsion units at the tips of the blades to turn the free-spinning rotor. Many teams worked on this, mostly by ducting high-pressure air and fuel through the rotor hub and out through the blades to tip combustors and nozzles. Centrifugal acceleration would help feed the fuel out to the tips once pumped up to the rotor hub. An alternative was to use the passing air from the spinning of the rotor to provide the oxygen for combustion such that only fuel had to be passed to the tip. These options were the hot-cycle solution while pumping compressed air alone was the cold-cycle approach. The latter had few adherents until the advent of the jet engine that could generate copious volumes of high-pressure flow. The hot-cycle approach required a motor to compress air and possibly also pump this and the fuel. All eliminated an engine with power shaft turning the rotor and potentially the tail rotor. The free-spinning main rotor then lacked any significant torque reaction. A tail rotor was usually still required for directional control.

The first to be successful with the hot-flow technique was Austrian Friedrich von Doblhoff with his WN 342. First flying in fall 1943, Doblhoff's technology demonstrator had a motor to pump the fuel-air mixture through the rotor hub and out the blades to combustors at the tips where the mixture was ignited with an electric spark. It also had a pusher propeller making the machine an autogyro when tip burning was discontinued in cruise flight. Doblhoff made certain he and his team, with their helicopters, were in the Allied zone of occupation at war's end. General Electric ultimately examined the equipment at their Schenectady, New York, facility. It was clearly a marginal machine, but the WN 342 did offer some insights during initial design studies for the XH-17 (see page 344), while Doblhoff came to work for McDonnell on the XH-20 (see below).

Of several tip jet projects underway in the U.S. after the war, most focused on some manner of fuel-air combustors. Tip propulsion researchers included Marquardt, McDonnell, Hughes, Hiller, Kellett, and American Helicopter. Tip propulsion especially appeared as a solution for powering giant "flying crane" helicopters, lifting tens of thousands of pounds of payload. For such machines, the weight of powerplants with gearboxes appeared prohibitive by period calculations.

McDonnell explored hot-flow technology independently and then approached the AAF with an unsolicited proposal. This won them a July 1946 contract with enough funding for two experimental testbeds. They developed the 8RJ4 (or M-38) ramjet of 7.2-inch (18.4-cm) diameter weighing 10 lb (4.5 kg), generating about 30 hp (22 kW). McDonnell built a simple flying rig for testing—the XH-20 they dubbed *Little Henry*. The two-blade, 18-foot (32.9-m) diameter teetering rotor had ramjets at the tips burning propane. The 285-lb (129-kg) empty weight rig was hardly an aircraft, but it got the job done. It had a rudder at the far end controlled by pedals. The rotor cyclic lever from overhead had a twist grip for fuel flow. The welded tube frame seated a pilot and held tanks for the fuel that was preheated before being fed through the blades.

The initial of two XH-20s flew in mid-1947, claiming to be the first manned aircraft powered by ramjets. Testing continued for four years, though the USAF ended its participation in 1951. It had considered a two-seat derivative, the H-29, but this was not consummated.[11] Fuel was changed to gasoline, and one of the rigs was given a second seat. The basic principles were shown sound as well as the very significant detractors. The ramjets, providing 640 rpm, were very loud, burned fuel at a phenomenal rate, and autorotation performance bordered on hazardous owing to the drag of air flowing through the ramjet nacelles slowing rpm of the naturally low-inertia rotor.

Above: Many of the aircraft captured following the defeat of Germany were quickly set aside following the war. However, the Doblhoff WN 342 autogyro, with rotor blade tip propulsion, was extensively evaluated and then modified while in the care of General Electric. Here the aircraft is undergoing tethered hover trials, likely at Wright Field. (*National Archives*)

Left: Many organizations were exploring the potential for building a "flying crane" helicopter of large proportions able to lift very heavy loads. Kellett, like others, felt that rotor blade tip propulsion was the key, and they generated this simple drawing to conceptualize the idea. It shows some manner of gas generator delivering air or fuel-air vapor to the rotor hub and then out to the blade tips for burning. (*Author's collection*)

McDonnell undertook tip propulsion research and constructed the XH-20 testbed as a simple means to flight-test the ramjets and overall concept. The fuel line to the rotor hub is visible. (*National Archives*)

McDonnell continued its tip propulsion research, though it was unable to attract further military funding. It built a larger, more substantial testbed in the Model 79 *Big Henry* aimed at the agricultural market. This first flew in March 1952, though with all the limitations of the technology, it failed to find customers. Their XV-1 experimental entrant in the convertible aircraft contest (see page 94) also used tip propulsion.

General Electric had become interested in helicopters during 1945 and began serious experimental research at their Schenectady test facility.[12] The principal researcher was Igor Bensen, a Russian immigrant and engineer who was enthusiastic about rotorcraft. The team also established a working relationship with Kellett to benefit from their rotorcraft experience. The engine company's primary interest was the application of jet propulsion with tip-mounted ramjets developed in Schenectady, occasionally referred to as "Athodyds." Some of the work had army funding via the Hermes rocket program. Apart from a whirl stand, GE was able to borrow two autogyros from the Army for possible flight testing. The Kellett XR-3 and YO-60 were primarily used for static ground testing and underwent many modifications. The YO-60 was damaged early on but demonstrated tip ramjet operation on the ground. The army also lent GE the WN 342 and a single-seat autorotation "kite" by Raoul Hafner called the H.8 Rotachute borrowed from the U.K. The Doblhoff machine was eventually destroyed in a ground-resonance mishap that also injured Bensen.[13] The German Focke-Achgelis Fa 330-towed autogyro, used during the war for U-boat observation, was also tested in the U.S. for insight.

The opportunity to apply tip propulsion to a "sky crane" arrived with a January 1946 AAF solicitation. It was to haul a 10,000-lb (4,536-kg) container of 8 × 8 × 20

Among the foreign equipment from the war evaluated afterward by the Americans was the Focke Achgelis Fa 330 towed autogyro. This had been used sporadically by U-boat crews for observation and was a simple device from which little was learned. It is seen under test at Wright Field on April 31, 1946. (*National Archives*)

feet (2.4 × 2.4 × 6.1 m) at up to 65 mph (105 kph). It was to have an endurance of thirty minutes, a 100-mile (161-km) flight radius, and hover at up to 3,000 feet (914 m). Kellett had worked on cold-flow during the war and was awarded a May 1946 contract for the initial design phase. They envisioned a giant helicopter with four long gear posts that straddled the cargo pod. After a year, their research had revealed great difficulty in meeting the requirements. They proposed a machine with two turbojets providing the compressed air for tip burning in an enormous two-blade rotor unlike anything attempted previously. It was hoped that in cruise flight the burning could be curtailed for cold-flow only.[14] There was a considerable technical risk in the effort. Yet AMC chose to move to the hardware phase with an August 1947 contract for a single XR-17 (XH-17) prototype. This was initially to be a ground test rig but with an option to fly it if the service agreed.

Kellett found itself in grave financial straits and, as part of a bankruptcy settlement, decided to sell the XH-17 project. With USAF approval, Hughes Aircraft bought the research and all resources. Nine engineers and the partially completed rotor blades were moved to Culver City, California, in March 1949. Howard Hughes applied considerable resources to the development and hired talented engineers away from other firms with the allure of high salaries. Schenectady was central to the continuing project in designing and fabricating the burners and blade tip segments, and conducting ground tests.

The XH-17 had two J35s modified by GE as gas generators. The last few compressor stages were replaced with a scroll duct to divert the bleed air to feed into the rotor blade along with fuel. These were mixed and combusted in four General Electric pressure-jet burners exhausting at the tips of each blade. Each blade was a remarkable

Tip propulsion appeared the best path to a super large "flying crane" heavy-lift helicopter. Kellett began developing such a machine with research into the tip-burning rotor blades. Hughes bought the project and brought it to flight in Culver City, California, where it is seen in this image. The insert is one of the tip burner installations for ground testing. The XH-17 was shown to be impractical as the basis for a fleet aircraft. (*National Archives*)

12 inches (30.5 cm) thick and 58 inches (147.3 cm) wide, weighing 5,000 lb (2,268 kg). Without burning, the blades produced 1,000 hp (746 kW) and with burning, 3,480 hp (2,595 kW).[15] The test rig began ground tests in December 1949 and uncovered numerous issues that the team worked to overcome. It was badly damaged in June 1950 when a cyclic gear failed. However, in October of the preceding year, the program had chosen to proceed to flight. So, repair work was undertaken along with work to turn the rig into an aircraft—the world's largest helicopter. A dual hydraulic system was added, servo controls refined, and a tail boom installed supporting a horizontal stabilizer and a tail rotor driven off the main rotor for yaw authority. To save costs, many components from other aircraft were employed. Its empty weight was 28,562 lb (12,956 kg) and it carried 636 gal (2,408 l) of fuel. The modifications proceeded at a modest pace such that testing did not resume until 1952, with its first flight in September.

The flight trials uncovered more engineering deficiencies that were worked out. Ultimately, the helicopter handled well enough for its limited mission. The 130-foot (40-m) diameter rotor's operating speed was just 88 rpm, and the tip jets made a deafening noise. However, high blade stresses from vibratory loads yielded a short fatigue life of the preliminary design. It was flown to 80 mph (129 kph) and 50,000 lb (22,680 kg), lifting an 8,000-lb (3,629-kg) trailer. However, fuel consumption was extraordinarily high and made the range requirement unattainable, possessing only 30 to 40 miles (48 to 64 km).

Hughes proposed a production version of the XH-17, but with four rotor blades and two turboprop engines as shown in the conceptual art. Cargo would be suspended between the long gear posts, or on a platform likewise suspended. The air force initially endorsed the approach and endowed it with the designation XH-28, but the XH-17 results demonstrated the low potential and funds were short, so the program was dropped. (*National Archives*)

This was most significant as the helicopter was too large to be airlifted into its operating area and so needed to self-deploy or be virtually constructed onsite. One had to conclude the aircraft was impractical as a fleet article. The XH-17 itself only flew up and down the Culver City runway and accumulated ten hours over thirty-three flights in three years.

Development of a production example of the giant hauler rotorcraft had begun in January 1951. This was to carry 50,000 lb (22,680 kg) on top of its 52,000-lb (23,587-kg) empty weight. It was to be powered by two T40 turboprop engines to provide compressed air. Hughes built a mock-up that had four blades, the hub encased in fairings. Cargo would hang between the four stilted gear posts and a hanging platform was devised onto which vehicles could roll on and off. Plans for a XH-28 prototype were abandoned given the XH-17 results and funding limitations for such projects as the Korean Conflict wound down. When the design life of the blades was expended at the end of 1955, the XH-17 program was ended.

Stanley Hiller had worked on the tip propulsion problem since 1945 in his aspiration to build flying crane helicopters. His first success with a ground rig had the combustion within the blades and exhausted at the tip through a nozzle turned 90 degrees. The "Hiller Powerblades" were tested with navy funding and produced 14–30 lbf (62–133 N) of thrust each. Challenges included deformation of the blades due to the thermal gradients.

Seeking an air-breathing motor at the tips, Hiller at first experimented with a pulsejet with an inlet shutter valve, but the forces imparted by the centripetal acceleration at the tip interfered with the mechanical operation. Instead, Hiller's team focused on using ramjets that had no moving parts. This approach was derided by NACA, who predicted uneven combustion from the fuel being accelerated to the outboard side of the combustion chamber, eventually leading to engine failure, and the fouled air from the prior blade's exhaust also greatly undermining efficiency. Convinced these conclusions were wrong, Hiller had to work all the harder to attract funding, and the navy stuck with him. The testing proved NACA's predictions false. Hiller's ultimate goal was some manner of turbine engine placed at the blade tips, but developing such a powerplant was beyond the capabilities of the company, and engine manufacturers saw too little market to undertake such work.

Hiller eventually devised a simple 8-inch (20-cm) diameter ramjet, the 12.7-lb (5.8-kg) 8RJ2B, producing 38 lbf (169 N) of thrust. These could burn just about any liquid fuel, though some performed better than others. The lower thrust on the retreating blade engine, by virtue of the lower inlet velocity in forward flight, was actually beneficial for load balancing at the hub.[16] Hiller flew its first HJ-1 Hornet helicopter powered by this technique in August 1950. The firm continued its research and developed more refined ramjets for the application.

The rotor of the HJ-1, equipped with the 8RJ2B, was spun up to about 50 rpm by a 1-hp gasoline engine to support ramjet ignition. No anti-torque device was required for this low rate other than the resistance offered by the landing skids. For suitable yaw control, it had a rudder automatically deflected with lateral displacement of the collective lever—pedals having been eliminated. Rotor control was via Hiller's Rotomatic method with overhead cyclic. The blades had aluminum leading edges and magnesium aft fairings. The tiny two-place machine was exceptionally simple with fiberglass and reinforced plastic laminate over a steel tube frame. This was advertised as marking the first use of fiberglass as an aircraft structural component.[17]

The navy ordered five HJ-1s in June 1952 for evaluation as the HOE-1 to meet a marine requirement for a very light scout. Two would go to the army as YH-32s for evaluation against their observation mission. These had a counter-balanced single-blade

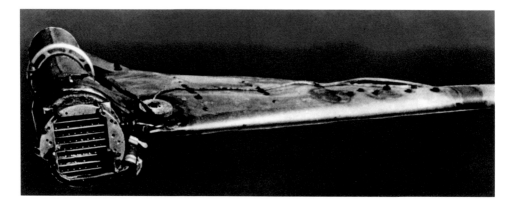

This July 19, 1952, image shows a small pulsejet engine at the tip of a test rotor blade. The inlet shutters are evident. The hardware was built by the Naval Research Laboratory and ran for over 200 hours on a whirl stand at an average of 150 mph. (*National Archives*)

tail rotor and pedals for more positive directional control, and a floor-mounted cyclic. They were also heavier than the HJ-1, with empty weight growing from 356 to 536 lb (162 to 243 kg), and performance suffering as a consequence. They substituted an electric motor to spin the rotor to 150 rpm for ramjets ignition. Those engines proved to be inefficient at the subsonic rotation speeds of the rotor of 450–500 rpm. Fuel flow was high, making for a very limited range. The ramjets were also exceptionally loud and at night the blue halo they inscribe around the helicopter was visible for a long distance. Autorotation required a jaw-clenching 3,500-fpm (1,067-mpm) descent rate and skill to arrest this for a safe landing.

Hiller HOE and XH-32 Characteristics

rotor diameter	23 feet (7 m)	weight empty	536 lb (243 kg)
rotor blades	2	gross	1,080 lb (490 kg)
span	23 feet (7 m)	climb rate, best	700 fpm (213 mpm)
length, fuselage	11.3 feet (3.5 m)	absolute ceiling	6,900 feet (2,103 m)
height overall	8 feet (2.4 m)	speed, max.	80 mph (129 kph)
rotor area	416 feet² (39 m²)	cruise	69 mph (111 kph)
fuel	52 gal (197 l)	range, combat	28 miles (45 km)
endurance	0.5 hours		

Hiller YHJ-1 was a commercial precursor to the military HOE and H-32 helicopters that apparently tested the features of the military example. The design used ramjets at the tips of the blades to rotate the free-spinning rotor controlled with the company's Rotomatic system. The man beside the tiny aircraft appears to be starting a small motor to spin up the rotor once coupled to the attachment projecting from the side of the machine. (*Naval Aviation Archives*)

The first helicopter was flying in September 1953, but none were delivered until late 1954 owing to the military decision to accept commercial certification and the CAA taking time to define certification regulations for the unusual type. It then certified the machine for military application only, considering the autorotations too dicey. Although Hiller devised a means to close the ramjet nacelles to improve the "auto" performance, the military would not add this to the specification and so the CAA would not consider it in the civil certification. Twelve more YH-32s would go to the army in 1956, these with just small stabilizers at the end of the tail boom replacing the tail rotor.

A virtually identical machine was built by American Helicopter Company of Manhattan Beach, California, with the inspiration of C. D. Denny, who established the firm in 1947. He focused on pulsejet-powered rotors, developing the equipment in-house. Their first experimental aircraft flew in 1949 and attracted the attention of the military. The USAF contributed to the next machine that flew in 1951. The single-seat XA-8 was then developed with Army and USAF funding, the June 1951 contract calling for a collapsible ultra-light airframe that could be airdropped to serve as an easy-to-fly rescue craft or observation platform. Fabricated mostly of aluminum and fiberglass, the first XH-26 Jet Jeep flew a year later, powered by two XPJ49-AH-3 (or AJ 8.5) pulsejet engines of 31 lbf (0.1 kN). The engine was 6.8-inches (17.1 cm) in diameter, weighed 16 lb (7.3 kg), and burned just about any fuel. A 2.2-foot (0.7 m) single wooden blade tail rotor operated at the end of a thin tubular tail boom also mounting a V-tail. Both skid and wheeled undercarriage were tested. The helicopter could be packed into a 5 × 5 × 14-foot (1.5 × 1.5 × 4.3 m) container, but removed and assembled in less than thirty minutes with simple tools.

American Helicopter XH-26 Characteristics

rotor diameter	27 feet (8.2 m)	weight empty	298 lb (135 kg)
rotor blades	2	loaded	705 lb (320 kg)
span	27 feet (8.2 m)	service ceiling	7,500 feet (2,286 m)
length overall	12.3 feet (3.7 m)	speed, max.	84 mph (135 kph)
height overall	6 feet (1.8 m)	cruise	70 mph (113 kph)
rotor area	573 feet² (53 m²)	range, combat	104 miles (167 km)
fuel	50 gal (189 l)		

Both services evaluated the five helicopters American delivered in 1952 and found they met the specification, but the noise and hazardous autorotation were discouraging. There was no follow-up order.

The heavy-lift flying crane idea did generate a navy requirement for a Class HC vertical replenishment helicopter in 1951 to which several firms replied. The blade propulsion was still the only workable approach, and McDonnell won the competition with its offering. Their Model 86 planned to use two T58s turboprops only to supply compressed air to 12JP20 "pressure jets" (understood to mean combustors) at the tips of a 65-foot (19.8-m) rotor. The mission called for a 15,000-lb (6,804-kg) sling load

The diminutive American Helicopter Company XH-26 used ramjets to spin the rotor, though with a single-blade tail rotor added for directional control. The simple single-place machine was to be dropped in a container and assembled in just thirty minutes by aircrew who parachuted into an inaccessible area. The pulsejets were excruciatingly noisy, and autorotation would have likely ended badly. (*National Archives*)

with a dedicated aft-facing winch operator paired with a pilot. Empty weight was projected at 14,878 lb (6,749 kg) and maximum gross as 42,000 lb (19,051 kg), with a top speed of 115 mph (185 kph) and a 23-mile (37-km) operating radius. The USN ordered three XHCH-1s in April 1952 and inspected a mock-up in May 1953, but the program failed due to funding limitations following the end of the Korean Conflict.[18]

The XHCH-1 rotor continued to be tested on a whirl rig into 1956, perhaps marking the last official interest in tip propulsion. By then, the new turboshaft engines held the promise for practical flying crane helicopters, but with many more years before approaching military practicality.

The addition of very small turbine engines to replace the inefficient and noisy ramjets was a goal pursued by some. In 1951, small Williams Research turbojets were tested on Hiller whirl rigs at up to 140 g in hopes of powering their long-sought flying crane. However, the advent of turboshaft engines provided a more practical solution.

Turbine Aspirations

The helicopter manufacturers remained chained to recips through 1953 and beyond, with only tip propulsion as a demonstrably unsatisfactory alternative. The rotorcraft market was too small to motivate engine manufacturers to develop new products just for these aircraft. By the end of World War Two, piston engine designs were nearly as efficient as they were going to get (power generation per unit weight). The two R-2800s hung on the HR2S/H-37 weighed together on the order of 4,400 lb (1,996 kg) for the 3,800 hp (2,834 kW). A parallel problem was dealing with the noise plus heat and exhaust of the engine. The time between overhauls could be as little as 20 percent that for a fixed-wing installation given that the engines were run hot and at near full power all the time.[19]

The years following the war saw jet engines mature suitably for thrust production, but not shaft horsepower. The turboshaft engine was not among the initial projects the Americans started during the war to exploit the new gas turbine technology. Turboprops—a path to turboshafts—were pursued, but with slow progress and too many failures and heavy units. In their December 1950 proposal for the HR2S, Sikorsky had offered a version powered by a pair of T38 turboprops driving propellers as well as the rotor.[20] The navy had passed on this owing to the added technical risk. The piston engine, and mostly aero engines from the war, remained the only practical powerplant for helicopters. Their limitations were stunting the growth of these aircraft as practical military machines.

The growing Pentagon acquisition of helicopters, especially as this surged with the Korean Conflict, was the impetus for bringing to production more efficient powerplants suitable for rotorcraft. As with the recip, the rotation rate of the gas turbine had to be stepped down through a gearbox to be suitable for a rotor. Analysis suggested the power:weight ratio of a turboshaft was far superior to recips and, likely requiring less installation volume, and so could be mounted above the cabin for more loadable volume and better CG management.

Kaman was responsible for the first turbine application to a helicopter using the Boeing 502 (T50). The 212-lb (96-kg) turboshaft generated 190 hp (142 kW), fueled by propane or natural gas, replacing the 430-lb (195-kg) O-435 at 220 hp (164 kW).[21] The work was performed under a navy contract as the YH-22 (K-225). The first turbine-powered helicopter flight was then in 1951. This was followed by a modified HTK-1 in 1954 employing two of the engines with both navy and USAF funding. The two-engine powerplant weighed the same as the 240-hp (179-kW) engine they replaced, but it produced 37 percent more power.

The French beat the Americans with the first turboshaft aero engine—the Turboméca Artouste that first ran in 1947. This was built under license in the U.S. as the Continental T51, although it did not enter full production. The army funded a test of a 400-hp (298-kW) T51 on a YH-18A replacing the Franklin, but placed above the aft fuselage. This flew in July 1953 as the YH-18B (49-2890), which aptly demonstrated the weight savings expected to be realized with turbines. This was joined in 1954 by 49-2891 for static tests, and both were greatly modified as H-39s.[22]

With the helicopter market insufficient for engine firms to strike out on their own, the military provided the seed money. The USAF sought a 500–700 hp (373–522 kW) turboshaft and issued a request for proposals in 1952. Lycoming responded and development extended to 1959 on the T53, the initial model delivering 600 hp

While the military sponsored the development of turboshaft engines for helicopters, these were multi-year efforts. In the interim, a Boeing 502 (insert, later T50) gas turbine engine was adopted for experimental purposes. This had been employed as an auxiliary power source and to provide compressed air, but it delivered 190 hp as an engine. The T50 is seen installed on the Kaman K-225 testbed for the first flight of a turbine-powered helicopter in 1951 with Bill Murray at the controls. The volume consumed by the powerplant is considerably less than for the recip it replaced. (*National Archives*)

(447 kW) from a roughly 600-lb (272-kg) unit. The navy acted similarly with a 1953 requirement seeking 800 hp (600 kW) and under 400 lb (180 kg). General Electric was already conducting early work on a suitable engine and told the navy their requirements were too liberal. General Electric's T58, which flew in 1957, was lighter and more powerful. These new engines were put to immediate use in new rotorcraft designs.

10

Sea Missions

Classical naval missions continued to be executed by vintage aircraft as well as new, though the latter largely with World War Two technology. Countering submarines threatening naval task forces and convoys, day and night, remained a critical mission given their demonstrated lethality during the war by both Germany in the Atlantic and the U.S.A. in the Pacific. Aircraft had come to be a vital element in ASW operations. However, it had been a high workload/low yield endeavor. Crews could fly hundreds of hours without even a suspected contact, much less seeing or engaging a submarine. Yet the war had made clear that successful submarine combat ops could significantly affect the course of a conflict. Helping to protect the fleet with an airborne early warning (AEW) continued to grow from its introduction during the war. The scout and observation seaplanes catapulted from ships were on their way out while airborne means of addressing mines was just gestating.

Slingshots

Catapult floatplanes faded rapidly as surface combatants were decommissioned or mothballed, and their aircraft stored or broken up. The outstanding Curtiss-Wright SC-1 Seahawk carried on, all other types being withdrawn. Production continued until October 1946, though 166 were stored and never operated. The EDO OSE development was carried forward, with its first flight in December 1945. The XOSE-1 suffered directional control deficiencies, requiring an enlarged vertical tail and added ventral strakes for the XOSE-2. Only a pair of this model and two dual-seat XTE-1 trainers joined the ten OSE-1s completed before the program was closed out. The scout-observation mission was suitably filled by flying boats, land-based aircraft, or carrier types, if ship radar was itself inadequate to the task. Operating the "slingshot warriors" was manpower-intensive and complex, and it disrupted other ship operations. They were dropped entirely four years following the war.

The excellent Curtiss SC-1 carried on the catapult floatplane mission postwar and production continued until October 1946—though most were stored until being scrapped. Many of the ships employing the scout were decommissioned or mothballed, and the mission was assumed by less operationally cumbersome aircraft. An SC-1 (35299) is seen in flight and two others aboard the battleship USS *Iowa* (BB-61) in May 1949. (*Naval Aviation Archives*)

The renowned aircraft float manufacturer, EDO, took on a catapult floatplane development program towards the end of the war with the OSE. Powered by the 550-hp V-770 inverted Ranger inline, it had good low-speed handling with flaps, leading-edge slats, and drooped ailerons. It was a worthy design, optimized postwar, but the mission faded away. A production OSE-1 (75212) is shown in testing at Pax River on June 18, 1949. (*National Archives*)

Counter Mine

The landing at Wonson, Korea, in October 1950, emphasized the continuing threat from mines. Four vessels stuck mines. Initially, helicopters were used to spot the mines and allow them to be avoided, but this was shown to be a flawed tactic. Only the hard work of minesweeping would be effective. Yet the possibility of helicopters continuing to assist was explored. BuAer began an Airborne Mine Countermeasures R&D project in 1951. This came to focus on a helicopter dragging a sweeper through the water, as demonstrated in Key West during 1952 with a HRP-1. This was followed during the next two years by trials with H-21s at the US Navy Mine Defense Laboratory in Panama City, Florida. The helicopters towed thousands of pounds of equipment through the water at low speed, requiring a severe nose-down attitude at less than a fuselage length above the sea. Added floatation bags were mandated. This technology would continue to improve over the decades as a new naval air mission was born.

ASW Maturation

Much of the ASW equipment developed during World War Two continued afterward while slowly being upgraded with the pace of improving electronics and moved to more efficient aircraft. However, finding the sub was getting harder. The growing Soviet submarine fleet, based on the new diesel-electric boats (derived from the German Type XXI U-boat), was a worry that had to be addressed. A snorkel permitted operation of the diesel engines versus relying just on batteries (though they had a great number of batteries) and so could remain submerged for long periods while underway. The chance of catching the boat on the surface had decreased markedly. These boats were quieter, more streamlined (deck guns were eliminated), and designers worked to make the snorkels and periscopes more difficult to detect by radar. Their top speed under the water exceeded many surface pursuers and the homing torpedoes of the period. Radio transmissions from the sub were in bursts to make them more difficult to use in locating the boat.

The lesson from the Battle of the Atlantic was that one had to stay ahead of the threat with continuous development and fielding of improved technology. Hence, renewed ASW technology development was required to address the new threat; the U.S. Navy, who retained the mission, saw to this with vigor.

All the existing technology was improved, particularly making it more sensitive. The "hunter" improved radar and sound detection equipment while the "hunted" worked to sense the pursuit and take suitable measures. Detection of the snorkel or periscope via radar was challenging, particularly in any elevated sea state. It required considerable energy in a narrow beam with a large antenna. Radar detectors added to the snorkel could sense the presence of the search aircraft beyond the radar's detection range. A passive acoustic search was superior, but the sub needed to be localized first. This corner of the arms race continued for decades.

Airdropped sonobuoys, new at the end of the war, became standard equipment. Descending under a parachute, these would float with a hydrophone hanging beneath the surface and a radio antenna projecting above. They were normally passive and non-directional, listening for the sound of a submerged submarine that was then transmitted to the aircraft for analysis by an operator. A pattern of sonobuoys could be laid to determine a bearing to the boat and range via triangulation. More would be dropped as batteries expired or the target evaded. Active buoys sent an acoustic signal through the water that rebounded off a submerged hull to be detected by the hydrophone. Alternatively, small explosive echo-ranging devices could produce the sound wave.

Another ASW technology from the war was magnetic anomaly detection (MAD) that employed a sensitive magnetometer to detect the disturbance in the earth's magnetic field caused by the concentrated ferrous material of the submarine. The need to place the magnetometer as far as possible from the influence of the aircraft's metallic structure meant that MAD was commonly characterized by the tail-boom "stinger" projecting out the aft fuselage. The search for a contact by MAD alone was generally not practical. Initial detection by radar was typically necessary. Where the boom could not be retrofitted as a modification to an existing aircraft, a podded-sensor mounted at the extremity of the aircraft—wingtip or tip of the vertical tail—was used. MAD equipment continued to improve with additional research and development performed by NADC.[1] Seeking to further separate the sensitive detector from the aircraft, experiments were performed with towed MAD. The towed magnetic detectors were flown behind a PBY in 1951 and a R4D in 1952, the shape reeled out from an underwing mount. Work was also performed with blimps towing third-scaled models. Testing continued beyond 1953 with Neptunes. The technology was ultimately not adopted operationally.

Aircraft flying search patterns to locate the sub for engagement, guided by the sonobuoy operator, might drop floating sea markers to aid in navigation. At night, these were float lights or flares, while in daylight, smoke markers were employed. If the sub was determined to be within range for an attack, it could be engaged by acoustic homing torpedoes—another product of World War Two. Smaller and lighter models were under development to equip submarines. Depth charges were also used. If the boat was forced to the surface, it could be attacked with rockets to damage the hull and make diving inadvisable. A nuclear depth charge was in development by the end of the period under study. Such a weapon would eliminate the need to locate the submarine precisely enough for engagement by conventional weapons as the detonation would rupture the hull of a boat within miles.

Sensing the submarine in the area by radar, visual sighting, or sonobuoy location was generally the first step. In the war, when MAD was first deployed, retro-bombs were also used to permit immediate engagement of contact by allowing an abrupt downward trajectory to strike the boat before it dived. These, however, were not pursued postwar. Some of the floating smoke markers and flares were propelled aft from the aircraft as a "retro" store to fall almost vertically behind and reduce drift to more accurately mark the search box.

Another outstanding submarine detection technology was sonar (Sound, Navigation And Ranging). This sent out a series of sound waves in the water ("pings") that, when reflected back to the source by an object in the sea, enable range and bearing to be determined. This had been strictly ship-based, but the passage of the ship and blind spots reduced the sonar's effectiveness. The ship itself was subject to attack by the presumed prey. Deployment from an airplane was impractical as the sonar gear would have to be dragged through the water on an electrical line. Apart from the hazard to the aircraft, the tension on the line would be prohibitive, and the noise of the passage would further reduce effectiveness.

In early 1945, a team of navy and coast guard helicopter instructors and experimenters at Coast Guard Air Station Floyd Bennett Field in Brooklyn, New York, conceived of dipping (or dunking) sonar gear into the water from a hovering helicopter. The team had worked to explore naval missions for the helicopters that the army had in production and were rapidly maturing. In one effort, they worked with a prototype dipping sonar from the Naval Research Laboratory (NRL) as a more benign means of locating submerged submarines. Employing a Sikorsky XR-6A (XHOS-1), with excess power for the task, it was fitted with a dipping sonar and operating off a cutter. The tests involved lowering the sonar ball into the sea from the hovering helicopter to detect a participating submarine. It was important that the helicopter remain motionless above the surface, not dragging the device through any motion and generate self-induced noise. This was difficult to judge, and the use of float lights and dye markers was ineffective because the rotor downwash blew them away. The answer was a Sunday comics page thrown out into the sea where it clung to the water as a fixed and colorful reference point. The insightful development was not enough for navy brass to commit more fully to helicopters, and the Brooklyn operation was eventually shut down.

Work had continued after the war to optimize the self-guiding torpedoes developed during the conflict. These battery-powered projectiles were acoustically guided, either actively or passively, and generally weighed on the order of 2,000 lb (907 kg). They initially had standard diameters of around 20 inches (51 cm) to fit existing tubes aboard vessels. However, a few could be carried by aircraft. However, late in the period, lighter and narrower weapons were produced, approximately 13 inches (33 cm) and 300 lb (136 kg), though with shorter range and less explosive charge.

The technology developed for ASW was best adapted to purpose-built aircraft. The torpedo (VT) and bombing (VB) or scout (VS) missions had been combined as attack (VA). However, the first new naval anti-submarine aircraft was a rework of a planned torpedo bomber.

Ship-Based ASW

At the end of the war and immediately after, the ship-based ASW platform was the TBM-3Es variously equipped with APS-3 radar, sonobuoys, searchlights, depth charges, and rockets. Threat detection was improved by the TBM-3W2 ("W" for warning) with the APS-20 optimized for submarine detection, or more likely periscopes or snorkels protruding above the waves, with a range of about 62 miles (100 km). This S-band search radar was originally applied for AEW (see page 381), the 8-foot (2.4-m) antenna enclosed in an enormous radome under the belly of the Avenger. As the radar precluded carrying weapons in the bomb bay, this "hunter" was teamed with a TBM-3S ("S" for anti-submarine) "killer" equipped with homing torpedoes, 5-inch rockets, and depth charges, and sometimes a searchlight under a wing as night ops were common. A podded radar under the starboard wing might also be fitted, monitored by an operator under the aft end of the canopy that was extended over the space created by removing the turret. The TBM-3S2A was upgraded with improved electronics. This hunter/killer team began operating in 1950 with a peak strength of 156 machines in 1953.[2] However, the old aircraft were too limited for the full ASW equipment available and needed to be replaced.

The Grumman TB3F was under development at the end of the war to replace the TBF Avenger as the next heavy torpedo bomber. As originally envisioned, the large airplane was powered by an R-2800 supplemented with a Westinghouse 19 turbojet (J30) in the aft fuselage for heavy take-offs and sprints during combat. This speed allowed the gunner's turret to be eliminated. A voluminous weapons bay could accommodate two torpedoes or 4,000 lb (1,814 kg) of bombs. Two 20-mm cannon in the wings were also considered. A radar pod was to be placed under a wing, with the operator beside the pilot in the cockpit. Hydraulic wing fold was the usual Grumman design with the panels aligned along the fuselage.

The TBM-3S "killer" worked with its TBM-3W "hunter" partner to locate and engage the submarine discovered via the latter's radar. The -3W's radar operator was aft of the pilot under the enclosure that extended over the space previously occupied by the Avenger's gun turret. The changes necessitated the addition of the vertical fins on the horizontal stabilizers. The -3S's searchlight was commonly augmented with a radar pod under the starboard wing. The weapon pylons under the wings could be fitted with rockets while the bomb bay could carry homing torpedoes or depth charges. The photographs were shot in 1949 and 1950. (*National Archives*)

Development proceeded at a modest pace after the war, out-prioritized by the F9F. Delays in obtaining the J30 and then issues with intake ducting design meant Grumman never operated the turbojet in flight. The first prototype flew in December 1946, but almost immediately, the navy ordered Grumman to halt work. Two months later, direction was given to rebuild the next two prototypes for the ASW mission. With such aircraft as the Douglas AD that could carry torpedoes, a lumbering giant was not needed. The jet engine was not required nor were the wing cannon. Fighters would provide protection for ASW airplanes.

The resulting aircraft were large and complex given the technology of the day. One model, the XTB3F-1W flying in October 1948, had the APS-20 in the large belly radome. The aircraft also carried sonobuoys and float lights dispensed from chutes in the aft fuselage. An RCM receiver facilitated the identification of transmitter signals—perhaps a submarine radio transmission or radar sweep—via a pulse analyzer and homing equipment. All this gear meant a crew, apart from the pilot, of a radar operator and a sonobuoy/RCM operator in the aft fuselage. The TB3F-1W hunter worked with the TB3F-1S killer teammate that first flew in January 1949. The latter could be variously equipped with APS-31 radar under the starboard wing to pick up the contact, a searchlight under the port wing, sonobuoys, float lights, and sea markers in the bomb bay or in pods under the inboard wings. Weapons could be torpedoes and depth charges under the wings or in the bay, plus up to six under-wing rockets. A Douglas wing-mounted sonobuoy dispenser was also used, some versions with a searchlight in the nose. The bombsight and searchlight were slaved together, and azimuth-bearing information was transmitted to the pilot's direction indicator. The crew was, apart from the pilot, a radar or sonobuoy operator and a bombardier/ navigator/searchlight operator in the aft fuselage. The -2S also had an ECM set, and both aircraft were equipped with identification transponders.

The development and flight testing encountered routine design issues to be corrected and a few that took more effort. One prototype was lost in a crash that took the life of the engineering observer. Both aircraft had the tail reworked for suitable stability to include increasing the area of the vertical stabilizer and adding "finettes" to the horizontal. Control surfaces were still fabric-covered. Slots in the outer wing panel leading edges ensured suitable roll control at approach airspeeds. This was augmented by a hydraulically powered "flaperon" ahead of each flap, at the outboard end, to augment roll rate while reducing adverse yaw. These were essentially spoiler panels with the trailing edge hinged to rotate up separately as a "flaperette" with initial lateral stick motion. The rudder was also hydraulically boosted. Owing to their size and distance from the pilot, spring tabs aided the deflection of the ailerons and elevators.

These were "low-level" machines without even crew oxygen. Consequently, they were powered by a 2,300-hp (1,715-kW) R-2800 with a single-stage/single-speed supercharger. This turned a large Hamilton Standard four-blade propeller of 13.2-foot (4-m) diameter, giving just 9 inches (23 cm) of ground clearance in the two-point attitude. Torque was eased by canting the engine 3 degrees right. A 3-degrees down cant improved low-speed stability while affording the pilot a bit better view forward. Both models could be fitted with a pair of 150-gal (568-l) drop tanks.

These would be the largest single-engine (piston) aircraft to operate from a carrier in the U.S. Navy. They also flew from the short-deck escort (CVE) flat tops, though the vessel's slow speed could make flight ops marginal or hazardous. The "fast" CVL light carriers were more suitable in this regard, but with a narrower flight deck. Yet maneuvering the enormous airplanes on either deck was sometimes a nail-biting affair, especially if the brakes faded with heat owing to over-use. Beginning in 1953, the squadrons began to be moved to *Essex*-class (CV) vessels where they enjoyed an easier life.

Production of the hunter-killer Guardian ASW aircraft was ordered in May 1948, soon with a designation change to AF-2W and AF-2S. Flying from the end of 1949, deliveries were underway before carrier qualifications had been completed and it was in squadron service before spin testing. Some changes were required to permit suitable traps, and spins were dicey, claiming one test aircraft. A stick shaker was added. The USN ultimately bought 153 AF-2Ws and 193 -2Ss, entering fleet service in 1950. More killers allowed for on-station replacement or even two working the same contact simultaneously—though this was a tremendous burden on the "W."

Grumman AF-2S Characteristics (Best of Four Attack Configurations)

span, spread	60 feet (18.3 m)	weight empty	14,658 lb (6,649 kg)
folded	24 (7.3 m)	combat	18,123 lb (8,221 kg)
length	43.4 feet (13.2 m)	max. take-off	23,015 lb (10,439 kg)
height	16.6 feet (5.1 m)	speed, max. (4,000 feet)	275 mph (443 kph)
wing area	549 feet² (51 m²)	cruise (1,500 feet)	166 mph (267 kph)
fuel, int.+ext.	320+300 gal (1,211+1,136 l)	range, combat	915 miles (1,473 km)
service ceiling	22,900 feet (6,980 m)	maximum	1,140 miles (1,835 km)
climb rate, 1,500 feet	2,280 fpm (695 mpm)		

An AF-3S model was also developed with an ASQ-8 MAD gear. The retractable boom extended from a fairing grafted to the starboard side of the fuselage. First entering service in 1950, the navy bought forty through April 1953. These were also equipped with the APS-31 radar in a large pod. The "W" could still offer AEW for the fleet. Although ostensibly intended to replace the TBM-3 hunter/killer teams, they served largely concurrently until 1953. So more squadrons were established and others retired around the same time.

During this same period, there were versions of Skyraiders capable of sub-hunting using much the same equipment as Avengers and Guardians. This amounted to several hundred aircraft, though they were not devoted entirely to ASW and not available at the same time. In 1945–1950, Douglas delivered fifteen AD-3Ns (night) aircraft equipped with the usual sub-hunting gear, with two operators in the rear fuselage. Equipment included an APS-31 radar pod, searchlight, sonobuoy dispenser, and sea markers. They retained two 20-mm cannon. This was only the beginning.

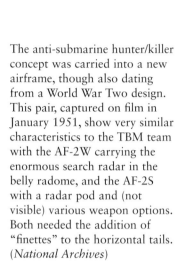

The anti-submarine hunter/killer concept was carried into a new airframe, though also dating from a World War Two design. This pair, captured on film in January 1951, show very similar characteristics to the TBM team with the AF-2W carrying the enormous search radar in the belly radome, and the AF-2S with a radar pod and (not visible) various weapon options. Both needed the addition of "finettes" to the horizontal tails. (*National Archives*)

Two of the aircraft were made specific ASW models with the AD-3S designation. They were paired with two AD-3E hunters created from AD-3Ws (see page 382), the APS-20 radar retuned for surface scanning. This also explored the viability of the AD-3S successfully operating on its own. This improvised hunter/killer team appeared the most successful, but the Skyraider was never devoted to the role. Other night attack models (307 AD-4N and 239 AD-5N) still had ASW as a secondary mission. They could be paired with the 164 AD-4Ws and 218 AD-5Ws, the underwing pylons allowing various tanks and weapons to be carried.

The proceeding history suggests hundreds of sub-hunting aircraft were in service on a relatively small fleet of carriers, although they flew from land bases as well. In actuality, accident rates were comparatively high owing to the nature of the aircraft and carriers of the period.[3] Various other factors either reduced the number of aircraft or ensured they were not in active service.

The hunter/killer concept worked well—when it worked. With two aircraft of World War Two vintage and equipment not much more modern, failures were discouragingly frequent. If one aircraft aborted, the other had to do the same or have a replacement join the formation for a reduced mission duration. With sonobuoys and MAD being the most effective ASW means, a purpose-built aircraft could accommodate the equipment more efficiently than the adapted machines.

The navy put together a requirement for an all-weather aircraft for detecting, tracking, and attacking subs. It would also be able to locate other surface targets, photograph them and attack. The tricycle landing gear would improve deck operations, especially with a view over the nose during taxi and approach. Dimensions

These January 1950 images capture another ASW hunter/killer team created from the versatile Douglas Skyraider. The AD-3E (top) carried the powerful search radar while the AD-3S (bottom) had a smaller radar to pinpoint the contact and then engage with a variety of weapons. Other models of the Skyraider also performed some elements of the ASW mission. Although a more forgiving airplane than the AF, this solution was still more of the same. (*National Archives*)

were to be smaller than the hefty Guardian. Although the navy requirement did not specify twin engines, more than half the proposals featured this layout. The safety of two engines was desirable for the long over-water mission. Experience with the F7F gave some confidence these features were compatible with carrier ops. All intended to use World War Two piston engines to meet the six-hour endurance.

Even as the TBM, AF, and AD aircraft were being deployed in the ASW role, the new aircraft was ordered into development. After inviting bids in January 1950, Grumman and Vought were selected in June 1950 to develop prototypes for the next ship-based ASW aircraft. The Vought XS2U-1W (later TWU-1) had a large radome for the APS-20 atop the fuselage. While initial construction started, Vought was still struggling with suitable wing fold when the project was canceled. The Far East war was draining development funds, and only one contractor could be sustained. Reflecting navy confidence in Grumman and the low technical risk in the type, the two prototypes were supplemented by fifteen preproduction aircraft. Then, before the first aircraft had flown, 284 production examples were ordered in spring 1952.

The S2F-1's APS-33 X-band radar was small enough to fit into a retractable radome, first tested on a modified AF-2W. For production, this became the APS-38. The MAD boom extended from the aft fuselage while sixteen sonobuoys were dispensed from the aft ends of the engine nacelles. A bomb bay, on the port side of the centerline, could accommodate one torpedo, bombs, and depth charges while stations on the wings allowed for six rockets or other light weapons. A searchlight was fitted snug under the starboard wing. Also, ECM gear was common. The pilot deployed all weapons via gunsight, with the bombardier being eliminated. The crew was two pilots on the flight deck and two ASW system operators in a cabin forward of the bomb bay with the radar farther aft. Pilot side windows were bulged for downward vision as well as comfortable shoulder room in as narrow a fuselage as practical.

Wing leading-edge slots ahead of the ailerons supported good low-speed lateral control. De-icing boots were featured on the wings and tails. Prop blades were de-iced via heating elements. There were the usual heated pitot tubes and alcohol spray over the windscreen. Grumman's design for a safe single-engine flight was a major factor in its win. A two-segment rudder improved efficiency for suitable control on a single-engine approach, with the forward hydraulically powered segment operating mostly during take-off and landing while the aft manually operated segment was the principal up-and-away surface without excessive yaw authority where the forward segment remained for trim.

Flaps extended to 85 percent of the span. The small "feel" ailerons, displaced by spring tabs, were supplemented by spoilers. The aircraft was limited to 3 g and a limiter was installed to ensure against over-g. A control column shaker was also installed to make up for the lack of natural stall warning. At a certain engine rpm, the horizontal stabilizer shook heavily and threatened structural failures in the empennage. This was corrected with an added mass at the tips ("dynamic damper").

The S2F-1 had a high wing with a fold that placed one outboard panel ahead of the other across the top of the airplane. The nose wheel was not steerable, but varying engine power side-to-side and generous use of rudder was sufficient. A tail wheel/bumper was required for over-rotation incidents, and it was pressed against the deck when all was tensioned in preparation for catapult. The 11-foot (3.4-m) three-blade Ham Standard props were turned by 1,525-hp (1,137-kW) R-1820s with single-stage/single-speed superchargers—a powerplant dating from the 1920s. The airplane featured overhead throttles and a yoke control.

Work was slowed by the Korean Conflict prioritizing F9F work over the ASW machine. The first XS2F-1 Tracker flew in December 1952. Despite the progress, the navy also ordered a single example of an ASW version of the Skyraider with MAD. A converted AD-5 (132479), the AD-5S had the MAD boom stowed within the fuselage, an APS radar pod under the starboard wing, and a sonobuoy dispenser under the port wing that was combined with a searchlight at the front. Flying in December 1952, it was not an all-weather machine and the radar was not omnidirectional. With the Grumman project making satisfactory strides, the Douglas effort was shelved.

The second XS2F-1 took to the air in October 1953. Yet the first preproduction example had flown in July and was delivered in September to begin fleet evaluation the next February and then to sea trials later in 1954. It entered production soon after the period under review and left the Guardian with just five years of fleet service.

Grumman S2F-1 Characteristics

span, spread	69.7 feet (21.2 m)	weight empty	17,357 lb (7,873 kg)
folded	27.3 feet (8.3 m)	design	23,042 lb (10,452 kg)
length	42 feet (12.8 m)	max. take-off	24,500 lb (11,113 kg)
height	16.3 feet (5 m)	speed, max. (3,100 feet)	272 mph (438 kph)
wing area	485 feet² (45.1 m²)	cruise	150 mph (241 kph)
fuel	544 gal (2,059 l)	range, combat	968 miles (1,558 km)
service ceiling	22,800 feet (6,949 m)		
climb rate	2,330 fpm (710 mpm)		

A S2F-2 was being planned with a larger bomb bay (bulged doors) to take the Mk 90 nuclear depth charge. The special weapon was about 10 feet (3.1 m) long and 31 inches (79 cm) in diameter; it weighed roughly 2,500 lb (1,134 kg).

With updates of new equipment, the Tracker served into the 1970s with over 800 produced.

Flying Boat ASW

Although by the end of World War Two the USN flying boats were being used largely as transports, they still held value for ASW. These aircraft had long endurance for the patrol mission and could operate where airfields were lacking for shore-based airplanes. Consolidated Catalinas and Martin PBMs initially continued to serve. The PBYs were principally employed as utility aircraft, and almost all were gone by 1948.

The PBM-5 continued in production through 1947. Of these, the PBM-5S was lightened—dorsal turret particularly eliminated, though waist guns were added—to enhance its endurance and was fitted with the latest ASW gear from the wartime Lockheed-Vega PV-1. The APS-15 "doghouse" fairing radome was prominent above the forward fuselage. A radio altimeter, RCM antennae and operator station, plus drift markers and dispenser, were all included. A searchlight was added under the starboard wing and the ASQ-1 MAD sensor atop a stinger projecting from the port wingtip. The number of PBM-5Ss generated is unclear, though certainly less than 200 and presumably replacing the remaining ninety-four underpowered PBM-3Ss.[4] A number of these aircraft were modified in 1951 as PBM-5S2 with an APS-31 bullet radome replacing the APS-15, plus sonobuoys with receiver station. Other gear from the P2V Neptune (see page 371) was also adapted to the Mariner. They had mounts for two JATO bottles on each of the two side waist hatches and storage for bottles inside. The bottles could be removed and restored in flight.

The Mariner design still had life in it, and twins seemed the most efficient large patrol flying boat given the wartime experience with the Consolidated PB2Y Coronado—an airplane retired soon after the war. The navy looked ahead to the next evolution with modern ASW gear. This, too, fell to the Glenn L. Martin Company.

Top, the second of two prototype XS2F-1 Trackers (129138) is shown at NAS Patuxent River on August 19, 1953, undergoing flight testing. Bottom is a March 1955 image of the S2F-1 in service. The general layout of the aircraft, intended for shipboard operation, is evident with the underwing weapon pylons and searchlight. The radar antenna dome retracted into the belly, and the MAD boom extended out the aft end of the fuselage, the sonobuoy tubes at the aft end of the engine nacelles. (*National Archives*)

What is likely a PBY-6A is equipped with an APS-3 search radar antenna above the flight deck in what became a common installation. The legendry amphibian served a few years beyond the war with navy units, in ASW, SAR, and utility functions. (*San Diego Air & Space Museum*)

The Martin Mariner continued in production after the war and had its ASW role enhanced with the adoption of the PBM-5S configuration. This example (February 1, 1949, image) shows the searchlight and the radar "doghouse" above the flight deck. The MAD sensor on the port wing is hidden and the ECM additions are not visible. The PBM-5S2 changes included sonobuoys and a bullet fairing for the radar. (*National Archives*)

The new airplane was derived from the wartime PBM-4 project that was to substitute R-3350s for the Wright R-2600s. This was not carried forward at the time, largely because of B-29 priority for the engines. The navy felt that a single vertical tail with low horizontals versus the familiar "pinwheel tail" was a necessary match with the more powerful engines. The service and Martin also chose to lengthen the hull for a 8.6:1 length:beam ratio with a single step versus the more standard 6.5:1 as based upon R&D (see page 88). An amphibious gear was not incorporated given the example of the PBM-5A (see page 310), which had been so much heavier than the non-amphibious Mariner that it was withdrawn from patrol and ASR duties.

The P5M-1 Marlin was an entirely new design, though following the features of the XP5M-1 demonstrator (see page 88) and overall larger. The 3,250-hp (2,423-kW) R-3350 turbo-compound was selected, promising excellent fuel economy for range and endurance benefits. It had a single-stage/two-speed supercharger and turned a 15-foot (4.6-m) four-blade Hamilton Standard prop. Along with the reversing props, Martin added "hydroflaps" that rotated to the side from the stern keel to either aid in turning or slowing on the water. The design incorporated mounts for four JATO bottles. Fuel could be carried in droppable tanks for the bomb bay that lay behind the engines in the nacelles. These supplemented a considerable internal capacity. The flight deck was raised to ensure vision over this nose. Roll was enhanced with spoilers. There was also an APU backup. The tip floats were of a new low drag profile on stronger mounts. The tall vertical tail was hinged to rotate down for the aircraft to fit in more hangars when on beaching gear. The ASQ-8 MAD fairing was mounted atop the tail. A large nose radome enclosed the 7.5-foot (2.3-m) diameter antenna of the new APS-44 C- and X-band radar. This radar was specifically developed to detect snorkels and periscopes with its narrow beam and had the highest energy of any airborne radar at that time. The radar demanded a high voltage alternating current electrical system from the airplane that required a constant speed drive for the alternators regardless of engine rpm changes. Aero surface leading edges were fitted with de-icing boots.

Turrets were reduced to two 20-mm cannon in the tail. The nacelles' voluminous bomb bays accommodated all current ASW weapons. Stores up to 1,090 lb (494 kg), including rockets, could also be carried on underwing mounts. There was a searchlight at the starboard wingtip and a camera could be carried to photograph contacts. Along with sea markers, sonobuoys were stored and dispensed from the cabin where the operator sat with his equipment. He was joined by the radar and ECM operators for a crew of nine.

Martin P5M-1 Characteristics

span	118.2 feet (36 m)	weight empty	47,861 lb (21,709 kg)
length	92.3 feet (28.1 m)	ASW mission	74,601 lb (33,838 kg)
height	35.2 feet (10.7 m)	max. overload	85,000 lb (38,555 kg)
wing area	1,406 feet² (131 m²)	speed, max. (1,500 feet)	269 mph (433 kph)
fuel, int.+bay	2,809+1,150 gal (10,633+4,353 l)	cruise	157 mph (253 kph)
service ceiling	21,000 feet (6,401 m)	range, normal	3,000 miles (4,828 km)
		ferry	3,600 miles (5,794 km)

Deliveries of 114 Marlins to the USN ran from 1951 through 1954, with fleet service beginning at the end of 1952. These were challenging aircraft to maintain, with versions supplied to the USCG and the French returned after a time. Extensive use of magnesium in the aircraft structure eventually led to accelerated corrosion issues that had to be dealt with later in the service life. By 1953, the navy and Martin were planning a P5M-2 model with a lighter T-tail to clear the horizontals from spray and a revised bow to reduce spray into the props. The tip of the tail was also to be the location of a trailing stinger with a MAD detector. A more sensitive radio direction-finder was also to be mounted above the forward fuselage, and the tail turret was replaced with another antenna radome. The revised tail was tested on a modified P5M-1 (130286), and production of the new model followed in 1954 with a water-injected R-3350. The P5M-2 was produced through 1960 and the Marlin was in active service until 1967. It proved to be the navy's last fleet flying boat.

In an attempt to introduce newer technology, the navy sought a fast patrol flying boat powered by turboprops. They also sought superior handling on the water with little or no porpoising and skipping potential. Responding to a December 1945 requirement, a contract was awarded in August 1946 to Convair for two XP5Y-1 prototypes with its first flight projected for December 1948.

The new boat was to have a hull with a length:beam ratio of 10:1—about half again that for prior flying boats. Research into designing the hull included use of tow tanks, both at the San Diego plant and at NACA, and a one-tenth scale flying model of the aircraft—this last a first in the industry—as well as resources at the Stevens Institute of Technology and the Massachusetts Institute of Technology.

This Martin Marlin was photographed on October 10, 1951, on the occasion of the first fleet delivery of the P5M-1 (124912) at Norfolk, Virginia. The aircraft continued the U.S. Navy's tradition of seaplane ASW patrol. The most evident features are the large radome nose, the MAD sensor above the vertical tail, and the searchlight under the starboard wing. (*National Archives*)

Plans for a P5M-2 included adopting a T-tail. This was tested during 1953 on P5M-1 130286 as seen here. The tail also has an extended MAD "stinger." (*National Archives*)

The development of the chosen powerplant, the Westinghouse T30, was running long, hounded by grave technical and labor issues. It ultimately proved another Westinghouse failure. The USN chose to change to the 5,100-hp (3,803-kW) T40 that also suffered a lengthy development. Convair nestled the four T40 units into the aft end of the wing with two long, three-segment power shafts extending forward to gear cases placed at the leading edge. These drove two three-blade, 15.1-foot (4.6-m) diameter Aeroproducts contra-rotating propellers. An electro-mechanical engine-prop control combined the operations into a single power lever, save for reversing and feathering. This arrangement had many engineering challenges, apart from Allison's troubles.

The wing did not permit a retractable float design and so these remained fixed. Instead of a watertight hull, Convair used a multi-cell design. The four twin-20-mm cannon barbettes were distributed around the fuselage and another station in the tail, all remotely controlled. Deployed ASW weapons, amounting to 4,000 lb (1,814 kg), were to be carried in four wing bays while there were also provisions for 8,000 lb (3,629 kg) accommodated on external stations. The flight deck and engines would be protected by 721 lb (327 kg) of armor. Instead of hydraulics, the aircraft employed pneumatics to actuate heavy equipment. An APS-30 radar antenna was placed in the nose. A crew of eleven would operate the boat.

The first aircraft was not completed until 1949 and then waited for engines. Years behind schedule, the first aircraft took flight in April 1950. Most flights collected data on the T40 and their installation that was still immature. Engine changes were frequent, seldom getting more than ten hours from any single unit—then the identified time between overhauls—and propeller control was balky. The propulsion system was also exceedingly noisy and burned more fuel than specified such that range fell short. The second aircraft, with full mission equipment, was used for some ground and tow tests, but otherwise was idle awaiting engines.

By 1950, the navy was changing course, deciding that other systems contributed sufficient combat potential such that the costly patrol flying boats were no longer needed. The mission of the P5Y had focused solely on ASW and then minelaying, the latter not requiring armament. These were too narrow for the investment. The project was canceled in August 1950 with another contract to turn the design into a transport, the R3Y (see page 311). The only XP5Y-1s to fly was claimed by a flutter incident and the second was scrapped.

Convair XP5Y-1 Characteristics

span	145.8 feet (44.4 m)	weight empty	71,824 lb (32,578 kg)
length	127.9 feet (39 m)	gross	123,500 lb (56,019 kg)
height	44.8 feet (13.7 m)	maximum	140,374 lb (63,673 kg)
wing area	2,102 feet² (195 m²)	speed, max. (20,000 feet)	383 mph (615 kph)
fuel	8,762 gal (33,168 l)	cruise	198 mph (319 kph)
service ceiling	37,500 feet (11,430 m)	range, 2,600-lb weapons	2,785 miles (4,482 km)
climb rate	3,000 fpm (914 mpm)	ferry	3,450 miles (5,552 km)

An attempt to create a fast patrol flying boat a few years after the war yielded the Convair XP5Y-1 with turboprop engines turning contra-rotating propellers. The aircraft was very stable and easy to handle on the water, but the engines remained developmental and proved the downfall of the airplane. Just one of the XP5Y-1s flew. The evolution of other weapons was spelling the eventual demise of the big flying boats. (*San Diego Air & Space Museum*)

Shore-Based ASW

The purpose-built naval land-based patrol bomber, developed during the war, was the Lockheed P2V.[5] This aircraft promised to fulfill many shore-based patrol and ASW missions more efficiently than the converted World War Two aircraft. However, it would be several years before production met the need. In the meantime, others would have to serve.

The Lockheed-Vega PV Harpoon was the most effective shore-based patrol airplane at the end of the war. However, it was derived non-optimally from a commercial aircraft adapted during the war emergency. An unclear number of PB4Y-2 aircraft were converted for ASW, the first (59857) by the NAF. At least five patrol squadrons were equipped with these PB4Y-2S machines—perhaps twelve each, though not simultaneously—suggesting perhaps forty were adapted. The designation became P4Y-2S in 1951. The variant had a searchlight under the starboard wing, sonobuoy receiver, and two radio altimeters. The two bomb bays were altered to take, depending upon configuration, up to two homing torpedoes, forty sonobuoys, four depth charges, and a large number of night sea drift markers. The aircraft did not have the ground clearance for the APS-20 radome and so were fitted with an APS-15 radar bombsight. This was unsuitable for ASW operations and so the P4Y-2S would have to work in cooperation with such an aircraft to locate the submarine.[6] The aircraft required a

A Consolidated PB4Y-2 (59862 photographed on June 16, 1948) is in the external configuration common to postwar ASW and weather patrol missions. Dated and unpopular, the type served until the Lockheed P2V could be fielded. They continued years longer in the reserves and contributed in Korea. (*National Archives*)

crew of twelve for the mission. It became available in 1949 and served while units began transitioning to P2V in 1953.

This P2V was powered by two R-3350s with a two-stage supercharger. These turned reversing Hamilton Standard propellers. For favorable handling in the pitch axis, while avoiding an overly large horizontal tail and elevator or the need for boost, Varicam (variable camber) was adopted. An aft portion of the horizontal stabilizer was electrically articulated, with the manually displaced elevator hinged off this. Fowler flaps were augmented with drooped ailerons. The tricycle gear featured a steerable nose wheel. The airplane carried up to 8,000 lb (3,629 kg) of weapons in the bomb bay, with two torpedoes, up to a dozen depth charges, or various bombs. Up to sixteen rockets could be carried under the wings. Hot air from four combustion heaters was directed into the wing and empennage leading edges for anti-ice/de-ice. Props were de-iced by electrical heating elements within the blades.

The Neptune was slow in maturing during the period immediately following the war. Only fourteen P2V-1s were delivered through March 1947, followed by eighty P2V-2s taken up through August 1948. Most of the -2s dispensed with the nose turret and its .50-cals to place six fixed 20-mm cannon in a "solid" nose, and the cannon replaced the MGs in the tail turret. The dorsal turret with the twin .50-cal MGs was retained. More importantly, sonobuoy dispensers were added. However, the APS-8 radar in these airplanes was a common surface-search system not suitable for efficient snorkel or periscope detection. The guns and cannon had little relevance to ASW, and the potential for interception by a fighter on deep-ocean patrols was remote. The underwing rockets were becoming anachronistic as well.

While appearing formidable in the mid-1940s, within a few years, it would be a matter of pure luck for a Neptune crew to locate one of the new diesel subs. Without a suitable radar and MAD, it could not be effective.

The P2V-3 was powered by R-3350s with water injection for 3,200 hp (2,386 kW) matched to jet-augmenter exhausts. Fifty-three were built. This was followed by fifty-two

P2V-4s delivered from January 1950 through March 1951. This got the APS-20 radar in a larger belly radome. With the sonobuoy operator, the crew rose to eight. Fuel was increased internally and with wingtip tanks, the port tank incorporating a searchlight in the front. As weight grew with all the modern ASW kit, an engine change helped to sustain favorable performance. The R-3350 Turbo-Compound found its first production application in the P2V-4, giving 3,350 hp (2,948 kW) and with lower fuel consumption.

The definitive Neptune was the P2V-5 that emerged in several sub-variants as equipment was added or retrofitted. The principal features were a MAD sensor within an extended fuselage tail cone, larger tip tanks, improved flight deck visibility, and ECM with an operator. The MAD installation eliminated the tail turret, so a nose turret with two 20-mm cannon was reintroduced. Eventually recognizing the low value of the weapons, the dorsal turret was soon deleted, and then the nose turret was replaced with an observation bubble.

Lockheed P2V-5 Characteristics (With MAD Boom, No Cannon)

span	104 feet (31.7 m)	weight empty	41,754 lb (18,939 kg)
length	81.7 feet (24.9 m)	design	67,500 lb (30,617 kg)
height	28.1 feet (8.6 m)	max. gross	76,152 lb (34,542 kg)
wing area	1,000 feet² (93 m²)	speed, max.	341 mph (549 kph)
fuel	4,200 gal (15,899 l)	cruise	207 mph (333 kph)
service ceiling	26,000 feet (7,925 m)	range, combat	3,195 miles (5,140 km)
climb rate, initial	1,640 fpm (500 mpm)	maximum	3,885 miles (6,252 km)

This P2V-5 has many of the common features of the model that had many variations during the long production run. The most significant is the MAD sensor at the end of the aft fuselage extension and the large wingtip tanks, the starboard tank incorporating a searchlight. First delivered in 1950 (this photo from September 8, 1953), this definitive version of the Neptune served for decades and was the primary land-based ASW platform for much of that period. (*National Archives*)

The P2Vs began to replace Harpoons and PBYs a few years after the war. The new aircraft also had utility in minelaying and shore attack, naval gunfire spotting, and weather reconnaissance. Owing to the Korean Conflict and the growing Soviet submarine fleet, hundreds of P2V-5s were delivered beginning in April 1950. Production averaged sixty-one machines *per annum* from 1948 through 1952, which then rose to 241 in 1953—though Lockheed had to subcontract 51 percent of the work to keep pace. Many were exported. The type was in production through 1962 and served the USN into the 1970s.

Martin had been tasked during 1944 with developing a four-engine ASW aircraft to replace the PB4Ys. Their solution was a hybrid with two R-4360s and two J33s. The jet was installed behind the "round" engine in the nacelle, the intake being a retractable bottom "sugar scoop." The jet thrust would assist heavy take-offs, add safety during landings, and aid in evasion with bursts of speed. The recips served for the long-endurance "droning" patrol lasting as long as twelve hours. All burned the same 100-octane fuel. Nose, tail, and dorsal turrets plus waist gunner stations carried a mix of .50-cal and 20-mm ammunition. There was 668 lb (303 kg) of armor. The bomb bay accommodated the usual mix of naval weapons. This P4M-1 program moved slowly in the last year of the war and even after due to the press of other work and lack of urgency.

The first Mercator prototype flew in September 1946 and the second about a year later. Problems to be resolved included changing from an inadequate 2,000-psi (13,790-kPa) to 3,000-psi (20,684-kPa) hydraulic system. Different airfoils were selected for the inboard wing segments (optimized for high lift) and outboard (optimized for high speed). Unfortunately, the outboard stalled first for poor stall characteristics.

The navy funded a production run of just nineteen P4M-1s from 1949 to 1950, enough for two squadrons. The aircraft was expensive and the P2Vs—already in service—were handling the ASW mission well. The production Mercators had a lengthened fuselage and vertical tail. They were powered by the 3,250-hp (2,424-kW) R-4360 with single-stage, variable-speed superchargers, and J33 at 4,600 lbf (2.5 kN) static trust. The 15-foot (4.5-m) diameter Aeroproducts four-blade propellers were reversible. The bomb bay could accommodate 12,000-lb (5,443-kg) of weapons or up to four extended-range fuel cells. The aircraft kept all the electrically operated turrets, but the waist guns were deleted. The airplane was served by a crew of nine that included an RCM operator. The aircraft was quite fast with all four engines operating at full power, though the instances where this was needed were few. Yet the advantages of the jet "boosters" were noted, and the navy began to think about adding a pair of podded J34 turbojets under the wings of the P2V. That modification occurred beyond the period under review.

While the Mercator had a respectable search radar in the APS-33, plus a bombing radar in the APA-5, and a single sonobuoy chute and receiver, it did not have MAD. On the east coast, they worked with blimps for ASW. This and minelaying seemed the better missions. However, they always seemed a "fifth wheel," being far outnumbered by the well-performing and lower-priced Neptunes. They appeared excess to need, and a costly one at that. A better role for the handful of fast and roomy aircraft appeared to be in the growing EW field. The fleet began to be heavily modified as electronic "snoopers" as the P4M-1Q (see page 417), and the Mercators passed out of patrol use by 1953.

Martin P4M-1 Characteristics

span	114 feet (34.7 m)	weight empty	48,536 lb (22,016 kg)
length	86.2 feet (26.3 m)	gross	81,463 lb (36,951 kg)
height	29.2 feet (8.9 m)	maximum	83,378 lb (37,820 kg)
wing area	1,311 feet² (122 m²)	speed, max. (20,100 feet)	410 mph (660 kph)
fuel, wings+bay	2,800+1,400 gal (15,899 l)	cruise	168 mph (270 kph)
service ceiling	34,600 feet (10,546 m)	range, 2 torpedoes	2,840 miles (4,571 km)
climb rate, initial	2,730 fpm (832 mpm)	maximum	3,800 miles (6,116 km)

Rotorcraft ASW

The urgency of ensuring effective ASW capability drove the navy to look more closely at the helicopter dipping sonar means. During the last year of the war, as previously described, the naval helicopter clique had demonstrated hovering hydrophone dipping and dropping small depth charges, although this was primarily a gambit to keep interest in naval rotorcraft alive. The USN brass still did not have the vision of bringing helicopters aboard their carriers. However, subsequent improvements in the new technology had continued at the NRL and further flight demonstrations were encouraging. Interest was kindled.

Things still changed slowly, but rotorcraft began to gain acceptance. By 1950, the service was seeking a helicopter with sufficient performance to hover, lower a dipping sonar, and possibly launch a homing torpedo. Helicopters would never have the range and endurance of airplanes, and likely rarely the payload capacity. Particularly if the helicopter was to be an effective sonar platform, it had to be able to carry heavier gear and a torpedo, as well as remain on station longer than the World War Two models.

Development of the dipping sonar had continued with flight tests using available helicopters. Sending out pings or listening passively, lowered to variable depth, it was superior in range and at bearing information. The operationally representative gear weighed 325 lb (147 kg) with reasonable power requirements and a dedicated operator.[7] The navy still believed that the tandem-rotor layout was the best choice of a cabin-class machine, with equipment and crew. They already had the HRP as an example. A production HRP-1 Rescuer (111818) tested the gear operating from a Landing Ship, Tank (LST) in 1948–1949. This machine was so underpowered that the team stripped off the fabric skin to lighten the ship.

A Sikorsky HO2S-1 (75690, one of two ex-Army YR-5As, 43-46618) was employed in the next trials in early 1946 given its greater lifting capacity and roomier cabin. The sonar ball was lowered from the nose and the operator was in the front seat. The tests included operating from an LST against participating submarines to include a German Type XXI boat. The results were favorable, much more so than airplane-based systems. Consequently, the sonar equipment was redesigned to be more compact and then manufactured as the AQS-1. However, follow-up was slow.

The navy decided in 1949 to seek a production application of the dipping sonar approach and put Bell on contract in 1950 for three XHSL-1 single-engine, tandem-rotor helicopters to operate from carriers. Bell was, like all others, compelled

Above: A wartime project that flew only after, the Martin P4M-1, was built in small numbers. Although intended for ASW, its lack of MAD diminished it in the shadow of the Neptune. The photo, dating from 1949-1950, shows the open "sugar scoop" intakes for the jet engines, two of the three turrets, the two radar radomes, and the bomb bay. The aircraft were soon turned to electronic snooping. (*Naval Aviation Archives*)

Below: Exploring the potential for the helicopter to perform the ASW mission, a "naked" Piasecki HRP-1 was fitted with the experimental dipping sonar gear for sea trials, flying from an LST. The sonar ball can be seen under the fuselage and the operator above in the exposed cabin. The fabric covering has been removed to lighten the underpowered aircraft, and inflated flotation bags were installed. (*National Archives*)

to use a radial airplane engine. To generate the requisite performance, they selected a 1,900-hp (1,417-kW) R-2800, the most powerful engine yet mounted in an American helicopter for what was to be the heaviest U.S. rotorcraft yet. This had a single-stage/single-speed supercharger and speed reduction gearbox. The aircraft employed Bell's two-blade, semi-rigid rotor. However, the blades needed to fold to allow the machine to fit on an elevator and then into the hangar deck. The crew was two pilots and a sonar operator, with the option of a relief operator. There was a mount on both sides of the fuselage to carry a homing torpedo.[8]

The rotor blades were wood covered in fiberglass with a steel leading edge for erosion protection. They had blade de-icing via an electrical element—a Bell innovation. Cooling the enormous engine within the aft fuselage was a challenge, and the engine bay was essentially open to the air. The sonar dome was lowered on a cable from a well in the belly of the craft. The pilots had a drift indicator from which they sought to hover with the ball directly below. The autopilot, among the first in a helicopter, was important for night ops, but could also hold the hover and zero-out the drift angle via inputs from two "feeling fingers" where the sonar cable exited the fuselage.[9] The helicopter also carried float lights. The radar altimeter was becoming standard equipment. The helicopter was also equipped with a rescue hoist. Survivors could be winched aboard through the door or the sonar well hatch if that equipment was absent.

With the need judged urgent, the USN had ordered fifteen pre-production articles for service trials and a second lot of production aircraft. Contracts for at least 160 machines were let. However, the large, tandem-rotor machine was a considerable challenge for Bell. Problems included drive and control system issues plus understrength forward gear struts. Blade stow was quite an effort. The excessive empty weight caused many desirable features to be eliminated, including blade de-icing. Range and speed were roughly 20 percent less than initial projections, and the hover ceiling was also lower. Rotor tip speeds and forward rotor tip vortex interaction with the aft rotor created excessive blade slap noise in cruise. This contributed to a very loud interior and high vibrations. The cabin noise complicated the sonar operator's job, leading to soundproofing. There were high avionics failure rates due to the vibration, the vacuum tube technology not being very robust, which had to be dealt with via redesigned mounts.

After delays deriving from the numerous development problems, the maiden flight of the first XHSL-1 was in March 1953, nearly a year late. Deliveries began in December 1954. It was well into 1955 before the capabilities of the machine were evident via navy evaluation and shipboard trials, and the HSL-1 was clearly deficient.[10] Apart from the noise, even the 1,900 hp was not enough for a full complement of crew, fuel, sonar, and weapons. It handled well and was otherwise a good performer. The HSL set unofficial payload lift and time-to-climb records for its weight class. Endurance of up to 3.4 hours was laudable. Outright termination was delayed because of the great value of the helicopter dipping sonar. The navy was contemplating fielding the HSL until a fatal accident added the last straw. Production was halted at fifty-three machines completed. While a few HSL-1s were used for follow-on tests, most were stored and then broken up.

Bell HSL Characteristics (ASW Mission Loading Where Applicable)

rotor diameter, each	51.5 feet (15.7 m)	weight empty	13,000 lb (5,897 kg)
rotor blades	4	gross	16,000 lb (7,258 kg)
span	51.5 feet (15.7 m)	overload	18,100 lb (8,210 kg)
length overall (folded)	39.9 feet (12.2 m)	climb rate (sea level)	1,640 fpm (500 mpm)
height overall	14.5 feet (4.4 m)	service ceiling	15,500 feet (4,724 m)
rotor area, total	3,840 feet² (457 m²)	speed, max. (sea level)	115 mph (185 kph)
fuel	425 gal (1,609 l)	cruise	96 mph (155 kph)
endurance	3.4 hours	range, combat	350 miles (563 km)

Given the HSL disappointment, when Sikorsky demonstrated the S-55 with its greater performance, the navy seized on this. Already in production for the air force and army as the H-19, placement of the engine in the nose and rotor above the cabin gave respectable CG options, eliminating one of the BuAer objections to a single rotor machine. The navy ordered ten H-19As as the HO4S-1 in April 1950 for assessment in the dipping sonar role. Evaluations in 1951 found it was underpowered for the role, with the engine struggled in the hot and humid conditions of the Florida Keys, where the sea trials were performed. Endurance was also disappointing.

The navy also procured a dozen HUP-2Ss with dipping sonar, added fuel, and floatation devices should it have to ditch. It had a mechanism indicating sonar cable angle so that the pilot could adjust hover to keep it directly below instead of dragging through the water. The autopilot aided in this with a side-stick controller for fine adjustments. The mission taxed the engine, however, and the failure rate was intolerable.

The navy felt vulnerable in Korean waters, but they were still looking for a suitable sonar-dipping helicopter. With temperatures more moderate there than in Florida, the utility version of the HO4S-1, the marine HRS-1 transport helicopter was deemed suitable. A squadron of the helicopters was rapidly fitted with sonar and fielded. A production version with a 700-hp (522-kW) R-1300 engine, the HO4S-3, was ordered in the meantime, though fielded beyond the conflict. It was not an all-weather machine and lacked many of the desirable features of the HSL favorable to efficient ASW operations. The useful load was low and range short. It was clearly a stopgap.

By June 1952, the USN had stood up four helicopter ASW squadrons that were largely bereft of aircraft apart from ASW evaluation machines and utility helicopters.[11] With the HSL appearing moribund and the HO4S-3 marginal, BuAer set out requirements for a suitable helicopter. Sikorsky had a design in work that improved on the S-55. Four prototypes of the S-58 were ordered in June 1952 as the XHSS-1 Seabat. The air force placed orders in 1953 as the H-34. It was larger, with a different undercarriage and engine, with a four-blade versus a three-blade rotor. Yet the similarity allowed the program to move comparatively rapidly. It would be March 1954 before this helicopter flew, though production contracts were placed even before this. The 1,525-hp (1,137-kW) R-1820 answered the power needs. It was always meant to be the hunter rather than the killer, as it would be unarmed. Progress was so fast that the program was nearly neck-and-neck to the HSL, yet still falling beyond the period of this book.

One of the few Bell's HSL helicopters, developed specifically for ASW with a dipping sonar, is shown aboard the USS *Talbot County* (LST-1153) for sea trails, still wearing the Naval Air Test Center logo on the tail. The bottom of the sonar ball can be seen beneath the helicopter, and the shrouded engine is also evident. (*National Archives*)

The Sikorsky H-19 appeared a good candidate as a makeshift sonar-dipping platform, and it was pressed into service as the HO4S-1. However, it labored to perform the task and a replacement was sought concurrently. Here the helicopter is lowering the sonar dome into the sea. (*National Archives*)

Lighter-Than-Air ASW

Like other forms of naval aviation, the non-rigid airships had expanded from a small nucleus to a relatively large force during World War Two, then shrank after. In December 1941, the USN had ten blimps. This grew to a peak of 148 by June 1944. Other than anchored and unmanned barrage balloons, only the US Navy employed airships militarily during the war. They ended the war with 139 on hand, which was halved by 1947 with the wartime operational structure disbanded.

For the Allies facing the U-boat menace, the American airships were valuable additions to the ASW arsenal. They could fly at the low speed of shipping convoys, remain on station at low altitude for dozens of hours unrefueled, and persist in the area of sub sightings with continuous observation—all unlike airplanes. When eventually equipped with MAD and radar, the airship could escort a convoy into the night. The blimps were armed with the usual ASW weapons of the period. However, the ability to detect and track the enemy was potentially more important than their attack capabilities. Ancillary duties include ASR and on-deck resupply.

Although there were a small number of other types for training and tests, the navy focused on the K-type airship (formally ZNP-K) of which 134 were built during the war by Goodyear Aircraft in Akron, Ohio. Reliable and easy to handle, this became the most mass-produced airship in history. The last was delivered in April 1944 and each cost on the order on $320,000. Commonly filled with helium, the envelope encompassed 425,000 feet³ (12,035 m³) and was 251.7 feet (76.7 m) long and with a 57.9-foot (17.6-m) maximum diameter. They were powered by two R-1340 engines generating 425 hp (320 kW) each. With a cruise speed of 58 mph (93 kph), the airship could cover 2,198 miles (3,537 km) and thirty-eight hours. The maximum speed was 77 mph (125 kph). It was crewed by four officers and six enlisted men. These "King" ships operated in both oceans plus the Caribbean. Several also crossed the Atlantic to patrol off North Africa. The airship force flew more than 57,700 flights for more than 545,500 hours and escorted 89,000 vessels. They claimed no ships sunk while under airship escort.

In contemplating the next war, the value of the airship was questioned. Yet in sustaining the capability in the meantime, the remaining K-ships got equipment upgrades from Goodyear. This yielded ZP2K and ZP3K versions (later ZSG-2 and ZSG-3). The initial ZP2K was delivered in August 1951 with a total of forty-four converted. Included were improved radios and navigation systems, radar, autopilot, sonobuoy receiver, electrical landing gear, inflight refueling system, and bomb racks. The envelopes increased in volume to 527,000 feet³ (14,923 m³) with the ZP3K to provide the necessary lift as GW grew. Thirty ZP2K were reworked to this configuration from November 1952. During this period, the crews worked for more mission flexibility with "hovering" above carrier flight decks to exchange personnel and to refuel or rearm. The ships would also release floating bladders of fuel for the airships to haul aboard. Experiments were performed with bow planes, but their disadvantages outweighed their advantages.

When money became available for new airships, the navy issued a contract in May 1948 for a new Goodyear design. This initially flew in April 1951 as the ZPN-1 N-type. The envelope was 875,000 feet³ (24,777 m³), length 324.4 feet (98.9 m), and maximum diameter

Sustaining the airship fleet in the lean budget years following the war meant upgrading the K-ships that constituted the majority of the wartime fleet. This ZP2K is shown at Key West, Florida, on July 10, 1950, with an indication of the ground personnel and resource footprint to launch and recover the lighter-than-air machine. Among the improvements for enhanced ASW was the addition of MAD gear with the sensor seen attached to the starboard bow of the envelope. (*National Archives*)

73.5 feet (22.4 m), with X-oriented fins. These attributes made it the largest non-rigid airship ever flown to that time. They featured a double-deck car with quarters for the crew of eight above and workspaces below. The mission equipment typical of the Ks was included plus ECM. The two supercharged R-1300 engines were within the car and shafts drove the reversible propellers mounted outboard via gearboxes in small nacelles. One engine could drive both propellers for an efficient cruise a bit short of the best speed. It cruised at 46 mph (74 kph) to 3,913 miles (6,297 km) with eighty-five hours of endurance. The 800-hp (597-kW) engines delivered power needed for the towed sonar sled then under development. Tests of the capability included towing a whaling boat in full reverse power and with sea anchors deployed. At its peak, this created a towing tension of 9,500 lb (4,309 kg).

The production N-type did not fly until March 1953. With changes from the prototype, these twelve aircraft became ZP2N-1s (later ZPG-2). They substituted a 975,000-foot³ (27,609-m³) envelope to match the anticipated weight growth of avionics. In a few years, large mine detection radar and AEW suites were integrated into the blimps. Hence, airship development continued into the mid-1950s with the final new aircraft delivered in 1960.

With war coming again in 1950 and a potential need for added operational resources, the navy sought more airships to replace the aging Ks. However, with a single manufacturer building airships in only small numbers, it was not possible to "surge" production with new types. The attention and resources turned to these activities were in no way comparable to World War Two experience. The navy chose more on that scale of the K-type rather than the enormous ZPN-1s.

Although designated ZP4K and 5K, and also using R-1340s, these were new designs. The ZP4K (soon ZSG-4) was ordered in 1951 and only fourteen were ultimately constructed for $40 million. First delivered was after the Korean Conflict in

The largest non-rigid airship until recent decades was the Goodyear ZP2N-1, the first shown here at Akron, Ohio, on April 16, 1953. Seeking a persistent AEW capability, this aircraft has at least a trial radome beneath the car in addition to a smaller radar forward under the envelope. In few years, a small radome would be added above the envelope and a very large scanner within the envelope. (*National Archives*)

1954. Performance was very similar to the K-ships from the war. The ZP5Ks (ZS2G) were ordered in 1952 and featured a 650,000-foot³ (18,406-m³) envelope with three rather than the standard four fins and a longer car. Eighteen were manufactured with R-1300 engines and first deliveries in 1955.

The navy maintained a fleet of about sixty airships into 1955 when it began to dwindle steadily to fourteen in 1961. These machines required considerable labor to maintain plus enormous shore installations. Given the increasing capabilities of airplanes and helicopters, plus the greater ability of subs to evade, especially with speed, it appeared to many that the airship was anachronistic. The avionics-heavy K-ships of the 1950s cost approximately $2.7 million each.[12] The navy appeared to retain the small force more as a way to possess a unique aviation type to stand apart from the air force rather than truly enhance ASW capabilities. The end appeared inevitable to most. The last left the DoD in 1962.

Airborne Early Warning

Aircraft radar warning was born during the war to give earlier alert to approaching enemy aircraft than ship-based radar. This enabled vital additional time to launch and/ or vector fighters to intercept and protect the vessels. It gained more importance with the advent of Japanese Kamikaze tactics. The ship-based AEW platform was initially the TBM-3Ws equipped with the APS-20, with the radar operator/navigator in the aft fuselage. This capability was ready for service just as the war wrapped up.

About forty of these aircraft were created from TBM-3 and -3Es. All armament and armor were deleted. The system allowed the detection of aircraft threats at up to a 100-mile (161-km) radius from 20,000 feet (6,096 m), or as much as four times the range of ship-based equipment. However, they normally flew at a few thousand feet and 30–70 miles (48–113 km) from the fleet. The radar data were relayed to ship Combat Information Centers (CIC) to assess and react as required. These aircraft served for a few years until the Ws were turned to ASW beginning in 1950 (see earlier), although they still provided some AEW capability.

The AEW Avengers were replaced by newer aircraft based on the AD-3s Skyraider of greater reliability and performance. These "Guppies" had a similar arrangement of the belly radome for the APS-20 and two radar operators in the aft fuselage. Thirty-one of these AD-3Ws were built. Fuselage fuel was displaced to the wings and "finlets" had to be added to the horizontal tails. These were augmented over the years by variants based on the AD-4W and -5W.

Eager to find a more suitable solution, the navy turned to their long-time contractors Grumman and Vought for ideas. Grumman got the nod with their proposed conversion of the S2F with a radome above the forward fuselage. Their summer 1951 proposal met with favor and two XWF-1s were ordered. However, the press of more urgent efforts during the Korean Conflict saw the program canceled after about six months. It was resurrected after the war.

Shore-based AEW initially came in the form of thirty-one new B-17Gs, including a single B-17F upgraded to the "G" standard, transferred to the navy in 1945. Some may have been used for spares such that fewer were actually converted at NAMU. The modification added the APS-20 radar and large radome beneath the sealed bomb bay that held long-range fuel tanks. An operational unit took up the first of these PB-1Ws in 1946. A few years later, a few had the radome moved to the top of the aircraft.

Four B-29s were acquired and modified for the role as two P2B-1Ss and a pair as P2B-2Ss with radar and fuel cells in the bomb bays. However, the department chose not to employ the machines.[13]

The APS-20 was incorporated into a modified P2V-2 (39320) as the sole P2V-2S that flew in April 1948. The radar consumed some bomb bay volume. This proving satisfactory and the navy had Lockheed build thirty Neptunes as P2V-3Ws with the APS-20. The two radar operators were added to the normal crew of seven. The airplanes were delivered in 1949 and 1950.

The finishing of two Lockheed Model 749 Constellations in 1949 as navy AEW platforms saw enormous antenna radomes added above and below the fuselage. The Constellation was selected—as opposed to the DC-6—because the three vertical tails were easily expanded in area to ensure suitable directional stability. Designated PO-1Ws (later WV-1s), the long-endurance, four-engined airplane was found eminently suitable for the role. The aircraft had an airborne CIC to direct air battles, along with EW capabilities, and were shown as valuable during NATO exercises in 1950 and 1951. The standard crew was ten with the ability to carry a full relief crew. The aircraft then served as the template for WV-2s based on the L-1049 Super Constellation, replacing the PB-1Ws, though deliveries followed the period under review. The air force would also take up the airplane as the RC-121 and later EC-121 that would serve for many years in vital AEW and reconnaissance roles.

A late-war project was to create an airborne radar post for the U.S. Navy fleet that could observe much farther than ship-based radar. This first airborne early warning platform employed the Avenger with an enormous antenna radome grafted to the belly. This TBM-3W is prepared to be shot off the USS *Franklin D. Roosevelt* (CVA-42). (*Grumman History Center*)

Photographed on November 10, 1949, this AD-3W (122879, a flight test asset) appears much like the TBM-3W it replaced for the shipboard AEW. The radar antenna was in the large belly radome and the operators were within the aft fuselage. Additional vertical surface area at the tail was necessary for suitable stability. (*National Archives*)

Above: Thirty-one new Boeing B-17Gs were passed to the navy and many modified for the shore-based AEW mission. Initially delivered in 1946, this aircraft (77258, formerly 44-85863) carries external tanks. It was photographed prior to being painted in the deep blue that characterized later service of the PB-1Ws, and so probably dates to the late 1940s. All armament is retained, though some turrets were deleted in later years. (*National Archives*)

Below: A radome was added beneath this Neptune to become the P2V-3W. It is seen at Patuxent River in March 1951. The aircraft, 124270, was among thirty built for the AEW mission. Note that the nose weapons were deleted from the P2V-3Ws. (*National Archives*)

Undergoing test at Pax River in August 1950 (an AJ in the background), this Lockheed Constellation shows the large radomes affixed mid-fuselage and a "forest" of other antennae. The large radar antennae supported the land-based AEW mission. The bottom radome was the same as those used on the AF-2W and PW-1. The two PO-1Ws had a Combat Information Center and respectable electronic warfare systems, all accounting for the many additional "aerials" on the aircraft. (*National Archives*)

11

Special Types

Often less glamorous missions required either distinct aircraft types or adaptations of those from more standard combat roles. Yet many of these demanded unique engineering solutions and pushed certain aspects of what was considered state of the art. Among these missions were photo and weather reconnaissance, electronic warfare, liaison, air-sea rescue, training, targets or other applications of unmanned drones, and more for special missions. The period was particularly noted for replacing World War Two equipment and adopting new technology such as jet engines and electronics to this military work.

Reconnaissance Ancillaries

Photoreconnaissance continued to be an important field for all services for which some veteran aircraft from the war carried on and several wartime projects were sustained. The norm had been to adapt existing bomber and fighter types to the role. For the army, the B-29 conversion for PR, the F-13, was the common strategic type with the F-6 version of the P-51 fighter adaptation for tactical PR. The navy carried on with its shipboard recce assets from the war, most commonly the few F4U-4Ps with camera windows in the bottom and port side of the fuselage.

One such project for the air force was the Northrop F-15 spin-off of the XP-61E long-range fighter, itself a two-seat variant of the P-61B night fighter. An order for 175 aircraft had been issued in June 1945, and the XF-15, created from one of the two XP-61Es, flew in July. The production-representative XF-15A followed in October after being created from a P-61C. Postwar, the F-15A Reporter order was cut to thirty-six machines, likely owing to budget and eagerness to introduce jets. The airplanes were delivered from September 1946 through April 1947, being redesignated RF-61C in 1948. They were retired in 1949 after less than two years in operation. With jet interceptors sure to be introduced by potential adversaries, the prop-driven recce types were seen as too vulnerable. Jets needed to take over the role.

Northrop F-15A Characteristics

span	66 feet (20.1 m)	weight empty	22,900 lb (10,387 kg)
length	49.6 feet (15.1 m)	gross	32,015 lb (14,522 kg)
height	13.3 feet (4.1 m)	ferry	40,365 lb (18,309 kg)
wing area	662 feet² (62 m²)	speed, max.	440 mph (708 kph)
fuel, int.+ext.	1,130+1,240 gal (4,278+4,694 l)	cruise	315 mph (517 kph)
service ceiling	41,000 feet (12,497 m)	range	4,000 miles (6,437 km)
climb rate, initial	2,000 fpm (610 mpm)		

The F-15s and other PR platforms were busy in the immediate postwar period photographing previously little documented areas, particularly in the Pacific region. The results were useful to civil authorities while also potentially supporting future military operations. The operator of the F-15As in Japan, the 8th Photoreconnaissance Squadron, undertook missions over the Korean peninsula. Their prints proved invaluable when war broke out.

Two purpose-built recce types were under development. The objectives were high speed and altitude, and better optimization for the mission. One was the Hughes F-11, which had had a sordid history owing to inexperience at Hughes Aircraft, difficulty with the company president, the mercurial Howard Hughes, and late delivery of the propulsion elements. The program ran so late that, by the end of the war, it had been reduced to the static test article and the two XF-11s. It used two R-3350 engines with twin turbosuperchargers and Hamilton Standard contra-rotating propellers. The

The Northrop F-15A 45-59302 of the 8th Photoreconnaissance Squadron, possibly shot in Japan, was a PR adaptation of the XP-61E spin-off of the Black Widow night-fighter, but with cameras replacing the nose guns. The aircraft was built in small numbers, but it was an important early postwar imaging platform. The camera compartment was easily accessible and readily altered for different camera arrangements. (*Gerald Balzer collection and National Museum of the United States Air Force*)

two-place airplane had only a single set of controls, and few if any of the cameras could be accessed in flight. It had a high-aspect-ratio wing for efficient high-altitude cruise. Flaps were nearly full span and with small ailerons above the outboard segments. Roll was augmented at low speed with spoilers.

The maiden flight was finally achieved in July 1946 only to end in a crash that nearly cost the life of Hughes, who chose to pilot the sortie. The problem had laid in the immature propellers, and so this was reduced to just single-rotation Curtiss Electric units for the second prototype. This aircraft flew in April 1947 with the much-battered Hughes again the self-appointed test pilot. The aircraft was sleek and fast, but it fell short of other performance goals as well as having a deficient roll rate. It appeared just another fighter imperfectly adapted to the PR mission, of which there were already many waiting to be replaced by jets. The F-11 had just too little to offer for the high cost. The effort had cost taxpayers some $14 million.

Hughes XF-11 Characteristics

span	101.3 feet (30.9 m)	weight empty	39,392 lb (17,868 kg)
length	65.4 feet (19.9 m)	gross	53,530 lb (24,281 kg)
height	23.2 feet (7.1 m)	ferry	58,315 lb (26,451 kg)
wing area	983 feet² (91 m²)	speed, max. (33,000 feet)	450 mph (724 kph)
fuel, int.+ext.	2,650+380 gal (10,031+1,439 l)	cruise	400 mph (644 kph)
service ceiling	48,000 feet (14,630 m)	range, normal	4,000 miles (6,437 km)
climb rate, initial	2,025 fpm (617 mpm)	ferry	5,000 miles (8,047 km)

The F-11 was a high-speed, long-range airplane championed by Howard Hughes, but in search of a mission. During the war, it was placed on contract for the PR role, though the narrow fuselage made fitting cameras in an accessible manner quite challenging. The dual-rotation propellers gave way to single-rotation after a maiden flight crash that nearly killed Hughes, but there was no money to pursue the design to production in any event. (*National Museum of the United States Air Force*)

By contrast, the Republic XF-12 was the PR team's dream machine. With four engines and room for dedicated photographers, unbroken pressurized volume from the cockpit to aft fuselage, readily accessible cameras, and even an onboard darkroom to process film before the aircraft returned to base, there was little more to wish for. The design was exceptionally clean. The R-4360s had tight cowling with a cooling fan and translating annular ring flap. Turbosupercharger exhausts were expelled through nozzles for thrust amounting to 10 percent of the total at cruise. The wing leading edges featured hot air de-icing and the props electric heating. Roll was assisted via spoilers, and control forces were reduced through the use of tabs versus hydraulic boost. There were double-slotted Fowler flaps and underwing speedbrakes. To avoid potential distortion, the elegant ogive nose was to have a transparent section that could rotate aside to expose the flat windscreen for take-off and landing. The rotating portion may not have made it into the test aircraft.

The first XF-12 flew from the Farmingdale plant in February 1946, late and well over budget. The second followed in August 1947, but it was lost in a crash in November 1948 to an engine fire. The Rainbow performed well and was acclaimed as the fastest multi-engine (or four-engine) prop-driven airplane ever. However, the program was shut down in fall 1948. Fast as it was, it would be vulnerable to enemy jet fighters. A proposal to fit the airplane with VDT engines to gain 30 mph (48 kph) was not taken up. By 1949, there was just no money for such efforts.

Republic XF-12 Characteristics

span	129.2 feet (39.4 m)	weight empty	70,500 lb (31,978 kg)
length	93.8 feet (28.6 m)	gross	100,845 lb (45,743 kg)
height	28.3 feet (8.6 m)	ferry	108,435 lb (49,185 kg)
wing area	1,640 feet² (152 m²)	speed, max.	460 mph (740 kph)
fuel	5,514 gal (20,873 l)	cruise	348 mph (560 kph)
service ceiling	45,000 feet (13,716 m)	range, normal	3,460 miles (5,568 km)
climb rate, initial	1,600 fpm (488 mpm)	ferry	4,270 miles (6,872 km)

From this postwar disappointment came a further adaptation of existing types as stopgap waiting jets. For air force strategic reconnaissance, extended range and altitude remained priorities—though these sometimes worked against each other. The "boneyard" offered numerous B-29 airframes for immediate conversion. Nearly 120 of the airplanes got some manner of recce modifications through the late 1940s as F-13s—RB-29s after June 1948. The cameras grew in sophistication beyond those of the war and so several configurations were applied. The Superfortress also got meteorology equipment for the important weather reconnaissance mission. Weather reconnaissance had been used in the war to scout ahead of bomber streams and advise on conditions, and this became a distinct mission. These WB-29s were the last of the old breed to leave the air force.

The B-50 was turned to the role beginning in the late 1940s to slowly replace the B-29s. All but one of the B-50Bs were immediately modified to RB-50Bs after

The Republic F-12 was a dedicated fast, high-altitude photoreconnaissance prototype. It had many unique features matched with remarkable performance and would have served well. However, the immediate postwar budget did not support production and so the very worthy design died. (*National Museum of the United States Air Force*)

Boeing B-50s were turned to reconnaissance soon after they began emerging from the production line. Models were specialized for photoreconnaissance, weather reconnaissance, and EW, and flew many hazardous missions along or over hostile borders. This RB-50F (47-144, a modified B-50B) was imaged on July 4, 1953, and shows, among many antennae, a signals direction-finder system "bump" ahead of the bottom rear turret. (*National Museum of the United States Air Force*)

manufacture. These had a pressurized capsule in the aft bomb bay with nine cameras plus associated personnel. They were also fitted with external tanks and equipment to perform looped-hose refueling. In 1950, fourteen of these became RB-50Es with upgraded gear, followed into 1951 by fourteen others as RB-50Fs with the addition of SHORAN and focused on photo mapping.

Reconnaissance versions of the B-36 were conceived from early in the life of the bomber. These emerged beginning in June 1950 as twenty-four new RB-36Ds (eleven from B-36Bs never delivered as such) and RB-36Es made up of twenty-one remanufactured B-36As and the YB-36, though not operational for a year. These were followed by twenty-four RB-36Fs and seventy-three RB-36Hs, the last of the recce 36s handed over in September 1953. Ultimately, one-third of the Peacemakers were devoted to the mission.

The forward bomb bay was converted to a pressurized compartment with fourteen vertical and oblique cameras, an operator station, and a darkroom. The second bay held up to eighty 100-lb (45-kg) photoflash rounds and the third the long-range fuel cell. Total crew complement went to twenty-two and mission duration up to fifty hours. Equipment was added for a basic weather reconnaissance role as well. However, after 1953, it would be observed that the RB-36's speed was quite a deficit as interceptors grew in capability. These were soon turned back to bombers with a single bay devoted to weapons while recce remained an ancillary mission.

The RB-49 (see page 237), attempting to squeeze something from the flying wing investment, was dropped to pay for additional B-36Ds. The long-awaited jet strategic reconnaissance airplane finally arrived in 1950 as adaptations of B-45s. In keeping with precedence, the Tornados were turned to photo work as they rapidly grew irrelevant

Among the reconnaissance assets created from bombers was the RB-36, the range and altitude performance of the giant bomber making it a good photography and EW platform. These ultimately made up a third of the Peacemaker fleet. An RB-36D (49-2688) is shown with bright aluminum aft of the belly radome, indicating the pressurized compartment occupying the forward bomb bay and the three EW antenna fairings beneath the unpressurized aft-most bomb bay. (*San Diego Air & Space Museum*)

as bombers. Most of the B-45C production—thirty-three airplanes of forty-three—was devoted to the mission. These RB-45Cs had a lengthened nose for the cameras, the bomb bay revised for parachute flares and flash bombs, the tail guns removed, and additional fuel capacity. There were a dozen cameras in four locations within the aircraft. The airplanes were delivered from June 1950 through October 1951.

Cameras in the aft fuselage were common equipment in the B-47. Intended principally for bomb damage assessment, they could support PR objectives. A reconnaissance version of the high-performance Stratojet was being assembled by the end of 1953 via conversion of twenty-four B-47Bs. The cameras were placed in a pod within the bomb bay. The aircraft ended up primarily as trainers for a more advanced model to follow, the RB-47E, which first flew in July 1953. A PR version of the B-66 (see pages 251–252) was planned from the beginning of the program in 1952. These jets were not delivered until 1955. Seeking means of performing penetrating overflights of the USSR and China with reduced risk of intercept, the USAF began a program seeking alternatives. Several unique solutions were eventually followed, like the U-2, though beyond the study period.

The navy had to avoid intruding in the USAF's strategic reconnaissance domain, limiting itself to naval objectives. So, cameras added to existing land-based patrol assets were their limit. Examples were the PBM-5S with a camera in a bottom hatch and the P4M-1 with two vertical and two oblique cameras peering out each side. For shipboard assets, the navy had NAA manufacture a photo spin-off of the Savage bomber with thirty AJ-2Ps carrying five cameras distributed in the revised nose and bomb bay and a fourth crewmember accommodated. These airplanes were built in Columbus so as not to disturb the high-priority bomber line in Inglewood. Deliveries occurred in 1952, and they performed missions over China and North Korea.

On the tactical scale were such aircraft as the RB-26. This possessed improved observation with the substituted glass nose and possibly flares or photo-flash bombs carried in the bomb bay for night work, all gun turrets removed. The standard camera installation had these in the bomb bay along with any photoflash cartridge dispensers.[1] However, speed was still vital for survival in tactical recce, and jets were required as soon as possible.

An RF-80 model was produced very early in the life of this type. Lockheed manufactured 114 FP-80As (initially F-14A, later RF-80As) with cameras replacing the nose guns and sixty-six more via modification. Given the night capabilities of the modern warplane, recon in periods of darkness was more practical. Photo versions of the XF-87, XF-88, and XF-89 were sought in the late 1940s, but always stillborn.

When Republic developed the swept-wing Thunderstreak, it also built a prototype RF-84F that initially took flight in 1952. This was in direct response to the Korean Conflict experience where enemy interceptors could best every recce platform. Yet this was a radical redesign in that the annular inlet was sacrificed to a camera nose and wing root inlets were added.[2] Four wing MGs were featured and fences were added. For the period, this was close to a dedicated PR type. Deliveries began in August 1953.

By 1950, the USAF was making or planning PR versions of most new fighters as they were developed. As the B-57 was defined, its suitability as a photoreconnaissance

The high-performance navy bomber, the North American AJ, was a fine platform for photography. Capable of shipboard operations and with a sprint permitted by the jet engine in the tail supplementing the two R-2800s, cameras could be fitted in the revised nose and voluminous bomb bay. Thirty AJ-2Ps were delivered, like the one shown on December 16, 1952. (*National Archives*)

Reconnaissance versions of the P-80 were built in parallel with the initial deliveries of the new jet fighter at the end of World War Two, and then many more were created later via modification. These served for years as the most common fast reconnaissance platform, including into the Korean Conflict where this RF-80A (44-85269) is seen. Save for cockpit controls, all camera gear was in the revised nose displacing the guns. (*National Museum of the United States Air Force*)

Short of creating a dedicated aircraft for PR work, the conversion of the F-84F for the role was going quite far. Revising the wing to add inlets at the roots and free up the nose for cameras was an extensive change that stretched the credulity of it being just another variant of the Republic fighter. Yet the work went well and the RF-84F (the second example, 51-1829, shown) was popular and effective. (*National Museum of the United States Air Force*)

asset was clear, solving some of the problems encountered in Korea. Minimal changes seemed necessary to meet the mission demands, and the aircraft could be reverted to bomber standards with modest effort. Cameras were installed aft of the weapons bay in the early production aircraft as RB-57As, and photoreconnaissance was then seen as the Canberra's greatest contribution. As it happened, most of the A-model jets, sixty-seven in total, were devoted to the mission. Greater capabilities came with as later models emerged. Likewise, the RF-101 was among the first, developed simultaneously with the initial fighter version.

For the Navy, the NAF devised an oblique camera tested in a reworked Bearcat, the singular F8F-1P (90441) during 1946. Thirty fully armed F4U-5P camera ships were built and introduced during 1947–1948. These had lens windows on both sides of the aft fuselage and in the bottom, each covered by a sliding panel. The rotating camera mount allowed photography out any of the three windows. Engine exhausts were also angled to prevent the hot air from distorting imagery. Adding to the mix, sixty F8F-2Ps, reworked -2s giving up a pair of 20-mm guns, were delivered from February 1948 through May 1949.

With the McDonnell F2H-2 appearing the first practical naval jet fighter, turning it to photorecce was a natural consideration. An entirely new nose for six cameras was devised that eliminated armament. Apart from the environmental operation, there were also controls to rotate cameras between vertical and horizontal angles. A pair of pods for twenty photoflash cartridges each were also carried under the wings. The changes cut 50 mph (81 kph) off the top speed of the Banshee, but the range and ceiling remained quite respectable. Fifty-nine F2H-2Ps were acquired from late 1950 through May 1952 for navy and USMC employment. These served until 1960.

An F2H-2P of VC-61 is shown with the *USS Princeton* (CVA-37) beyond in the sea off Japan on May 27, 1953, as well as the camera nose of the model. The F2H-2 was the first practical naval jet fighter, with reputable range and speed, and so conversion to the fast photo recce mission was a natural choice. It became a reconnaissance workhorse during the Korean Conflict. (*National Archives*)

   While the F2H-2Ps were still being finished, war broke out on the Korean peninsula. Consequently, camera-hauling Panthers became the navy's first jet-powered recce aircraft. Some F9F-2s were converted by USN shops with cameras replacing the cannon in a lengthened nose. Thirty-six similar F9F-5Ps were manufactured. They were lightened by the removal of wing weapon pylons, but also given an autopilot. Requiring more speed, the swept-wing Cougar was also adapted for recce with sixty F9F-6Ps assembled, though most beyond the end of the Korean Conflict and none seeing combat.

Trainers Climb Slowly

The services initially carried on with the menagerie of training aircraft emerging from the war, but tight budgets forced the consolidation and elimination of types. Those that remained had to be refurbished or reconditioned to serve years beyond what had been expected when they were hastily built. The rapid changes in aircraft technology made it imperative that training aircraft kept up. However, it was years before the money could be turned to the need. The new USAF had more funds than the navy, and the army was even poorer. The Korean Conflict opened coffers and permitted reequipping. The comparatively low cost and complexity of the machines facilitated rapid fleet shifts, replacing inadequate and aging types.

Apart from pilot instruction, there were many other aircrew training requirements to include bombardiers, navigators, radio operators, and EW specialists. Associated aircraft were usually created as modifications of existing service aircraft, given a T-prefix in the air force. For heavy aircraft such as transports and bombers with two pilot seats, this worked suitably well for instruction. Some purpose-built machines were procured.

The navy had neglected trainers until just after the war. It then formulated a new training plan that was to include acquiring new basic and primary/advanced trainers. Fortunately, the service had specified a new primary trainer in early 1945 and gave a contract to Fairchild in September. This airplane had classical trainer lines with low wing, retractable undercarriage, sliding canopy over tandem pits, and all-metal construction save for fabric over control surfaces. A 300-hp (224-kW) Lycoming R-680 spun a two-blade Hamilton Standard metal prop. Flaps and gear were electrically operated. This was among the first aircraft developed under the new military specifications that guided design to help ensure uniformity and suitability. The first XNQ-1 went aloft October 1946 and was quite sound, but no immediate procurement decisions were made given funding limitations. The navy's Boeing-Stearman N2Ss biplanes were let go and all instruction was conducted on North American SNJs.

The navy and USAF cooperated on trainer selection during 1949, evaluating several designs for primary instruction. They decided to retain propellers given that jets were then limited to fighters and a few bombers. The air force tested the Fairchild trainer as the T-31, competing against a Beech YT-34 (see page 399) and the Temco YT-35 Buckaroo. This last was a development of the Globe GC-1 Swift with a 145-hp (108-kW) Continental engine and sliding canopy for tandem seats. Although the T-31 was pronounced the winner in March 1949, and the air force planned to procure 100 at $8 million, the budget battles that year saw trainer funding cut. Furthermore, the services came to loggerheads over fundamental characteristics. Among the debate topics was tricycle versus conventional and whether pilots should start in such light machines or more powerful and complex airplanes. Ultimately, the heavy trics camp won out, and so the worthy Fairchild (a taildragger) was left to history.

Fairchild XNQ-1 and T-31 Characteristics

span	41.3 feet (12.6 m)	weight empty	2,817 lb (1,278 kg)
length	27.9 feet (8.5 m)	loaded	3,750 lb (1,701 kg)
height	9.8 feet (3 m)	speed, max.	166 mph (267 kph)
wing area	236 feet² (21.9 m²)	cruise	142 mph (229 kph)
fuel	80 gal (303 l)	range	880 miles (1,416 km)
service ceiling	19,300 feet (5,883 m)		
climb rate, max.	1,070 fpm (326 mpm)		

The navy had also funded the North American XSN2J-1 in September 1945 as a primary/advanced trainer. This also followed classical layout, to include the conventional gear, but was overall larger at 5,948 lb (2,698 kg) empty and powered by a 1,100-hp (820-kW) Wright R-1830 turning a three-blade Ham Standard airscrew.

The navy lent some attention to training after the war. They gave Fairchild a contract for the XNQ-1, a straightforward trainer that performed well. However, budgets did not permit a production contract and so the naval aviators pressed with their tired wartime mounts. (*National Archives*)

Competing for a light trainer role in 1949–1950, Temco reworked the Globe Swift with common military trainer features. For the USAF evaluation, the type was designated the YT-35. The conventional undercarriage was growing archaic and the aircraft was not selected for production. (*National Archives*)

It was designed for carrier ops training and so featured an arresting hook and had suitable structural strength. This airplane began flight testing in February 1947. With tricycle gear beginning to dominate naval aviation, the worthy NAA machine was found wanting. The budget did not support production in any event.

With the creation of the USAF, its Air Training Command chose to combine the primary and basic courses into a single basic curriculum employing AT-6s carried over from the war. However, AMC began looking for a replacement. In 1948, it had NAA and DAC prepare concepts of the XBT-28 and XBT-30, respectively—simplified, as were others, to XT-28 and XT-30 in mid-1947. The Douglas airplane was to have an 800-hp (597-kW) R-1300 engine buried within the fuselage and driving the forward propeller via a long shaft. This allowed the front cockpit for the student pilot to be far forward for good visibility. The NAA concept was selected in 1948 for prototyping.

Even as North American worked up a detailed design for the T-28, the decision was made to retain the Texans for a bit longer as an economical measure and to ensure sufficient resources given the growing tensions with the USSR. Between 1949 and 1954, using service airplanes and those bought back from civilian operators, NAA restored 1,802 Texans at four locations. Redesignated T-6G, these featured cockpit improvements, new radios, a steerable and locking tailwheel, and a pair of 15-gal (57-lit) wing tanks. During 1952, the USN upgraded perhaps 266 of its Texans to approximate T-6G standard as SNJ-7s.[3] An order for 240 further-improved SNJ-8s was dropped.

The T-28 was the SN2J reworked to introduce changes meeting air force specifications until there was little in common save for general layout. The new airplane had a tricycle undercarriage with nose wheel steering and was powered by the 800-hp (597-kW) R-1300 with Aeroproducts two-blade constant-speed prop. The service was impressed with the preliminary design and gave NAA go-ahead for two prototypes. Soon redesignated the T-28A, the first Trojan took to the air in September 1949. The flight testing was largely trouble-free. The belly speedbrake was judged unnecessary and so deleted. Production commenced and the type began serving in April 1950. With communication and navigation gear, as well as underwing accommodation for weapons, the type could be employed in many training scenarios. However, the T-28A entered production with a seriously flawed engine that limited service until rectified. It could certainly have used more power, but it met needs and nearly 1,200 were assembled through 1953. The Trojan worked in the training role until 1956, replaced by the Cessna T-37 jet (see page 404).

North American T-28A Characteristics

span	40.1 feet (12.2 m)	weight empty	5,111 lb (2,318 kg)
length	32 feet (9.8 m)	normal loaded	6,365 lb (2,887 kg)
height	12.7 feet (3.9 m)	max. take-off	6,759 lb (3,066 kg)
wing area	268 feet² (24.8 m²)	speed, max. (5,900 feet)	283 mph (455 kph)
fuel, wing+ext.	125+52 gal (473+197 l)	cruise	190 mph (306 kph)
service ceiling	24,000 feet (7,315 m)	range, max.	1,008 miles (1,622 km)
climb rate, max.	2,570 fpm (783 mpm)		

In seeking a replacement for the legendary but aging SNJ, BuAer awarded a contract to North American Aviation for the XSN2J-1. This image from December 14, 1949, shows the classical training lines but stubby with the single-row engine and tall canopy over the two tandem seats. Although a sound design, the conventional landing gear no longer met needs and so the USN moved on. (*Naval Aviation Archives*)

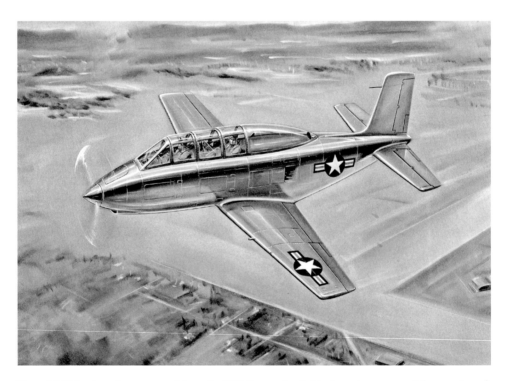

For a 1948 basic trainer competition, the USAF examined this Douglas proposal for an aircraft of common size for the mission. Unusual was the engine set amidships with a cooling inlet below the fuselage and exhausts on the side. The XT-30 was not selected for prototyping. (*National Archives*)

North American's T-28A Trojan (49-1507 shown) was a rework of a design for the navy to meet USAF trainer needs for the 1950s. First flying in September 1949, it was on flight lines by spring of the following year. Although a bit under-powered and plagued initially with engine troubles, nearly 1,200 were built over the next few years to train thousands of air force pilots. (*USAF via The Peter M. Bowers Collection/The Museum of Flight*)

When budgets next justified looking for a SNJ replacement in early 1952, BuAer judged that the T-28, with changes, could meet navy requirements. The alterations included substituting the R-1820 manufactured by Lycoming at 1,425 hp (1,063 kW) with a three-blade Ham Standard prop and the reintroduction of the speedbrake. Nose wheel steering was deleted because disconnecting the steering link to allow larger steering angles during repositioning aboard the ship was too cumbersome. With these features and general structural strengthening, the weight rose 1,300 lb (590 kg), yet speed went up 60 mph (97 kph). This became the T-28B, with its first flight in April 1953. Production aircraft were introduced to the fleet in 1954. The carrier-capable T-28C emerged in 1955. With nearly 800 built, the Trojan served for decades in many roles and in many countries.

The USAF reconsidered training a cadet from beginning to end in one airplane, concluding that a student pilot needed time in a more benign airplane for *ab initio* instruction before proceeding to the Trojan. Returning to the entrants for the 1949 competition, they performed another evaluation in August 1951 with the YT-34 and YT-35. The Beech YT-34 was a development of the commercial Model 35 Bonanza though with cruciform tail, sliding canopy, and structural strengthening for aerobatics. Developed on Beech's dime, the first Model 45 flew in December 1948 and a representative YT-34 in May 1950. It was powered by a 225-hp (168-kW) Continental O-470 six-cylinder engine. Nearly three years of evaluation transpired, awaiting the best time for a production contract. Well satisfied with the Beech, this was finally granted in March 1953 for 450 T-34A, with deliveries starting in 1954. These airplanes served into the early 1960s when an all-jet curriculum took hold. Late in the 1950s, the navy also bought the T-34.

The first North American T-28B is shown on climb-out from the Los Angeles International Airport on April 6, 1953, for its maiden flight. Derived from the air force's T-28A, the navy had a more powerful engine installed, among other changes. Production provided a respectable trainer that served for a long period. (*National Archives*)

Beech T-34A Characteristics

span	32.8 feet (10 m)	weight empty	2,156 lb (978 kg)
length	25.8 feet (7.9 m)	loaded	2,950 lb (1,338 kg)
height	9.6 feet (2.9 m)	speed, max. (sea level)	189 mph (304 kph)
wing area	178 feet² (10.9 m²)	cruise (10,000 feet)	173 mph (278 kph)
fuel	50 gal (189 l)	range, max.	737 miles (1,186 km)
service ceiling	20,000 feet (6,096 m)		
climb rate, sea level	1,230 fpm (375 mpm)		

For USAF twin instruction, replacing the venerable Beech C-45 and advanced TB-25 lash-up of the medium bomber, the USAF launched a competition in summer 1950. A year later, Beech won a contract for the T-36A. This tricycle-gear machine was to fly as fast as 300 mph (483 kph) with three students or a dozen passengers. The R-2800s and Ham Standard props were all conventional and the maximum GW was to be 25,000 lb (11,340 kg). Its first flight was but hours away when, in June 1953, the USAF abruptly pulled the plug and ordered all material scrapped. The service was concerned with the number of engineering changes and potential delays, plus worried that the aircraft would fall short of requirements.[4] It carried on with twins from other missions for such instruction.

To retire various World War Two airplanes employed in navigator training, the air force had Convair adapt their 240 Convair-Liners to the role. This commercial twin-engine, forty-passenger transport had been in production since 1947, powered by two R-2800s

Beech built a light military trainer from their Model 35 Bonanza, though the ancestry was barely evident. The type was put into production in 1953 as the T-34A to serve as an *ab initio* trainer for the USAF, which was later adopted by the navy after undergoing changes. Powered by a 225-hp, six-cylinder Continental, it got the job done with little fuss. (*National Archives*)

Beech was looking forward to manufacturing 195 of the T-36s for the USAF beginning in 1953 within a new building erected at its Wichita, Kansas, facility. The program was a major element of its projected income and so the abrupt cancelation of the effort in June 1953 was a big blow to the company. The first prototype was hours from its maiden flight when the government instructed Beech to promptly scrap everything. (*Air Force Test Center*)

turning Curtiss reversible pitch props. It had "aspirated cooling" whereby the exhaust helped entrain cooling air through the cowlings and also obtained a tiny bit of thrust via the exhaust ducts out the end of the fairings atop the wing. This arrangement, however, was also the source of heightened cabin noise. It used heat exchangers to warm leading edges for de-icing. The airliner was the first twin-engine with a pressurized cabin.

The USAF took its first T-29A in March 1950, though unpressurized. This had fourteen student navigator stations with access to radar (a belly radome for the antenna), Long Range Navigation (LORAN), five drift meters, and four astrodomes. Forty-six were delivered before moving to the pressurized T-29B that also featured greater fuel volume and radio operator training capability. The USAF took 105 of those from 1952. A version with a bombardier nose, the YT-32, of which ninety-two were planned, was not proceeded with.[5] The T-29C used a different model engine and a medivac version, the C-131 and R4Y Samaritan, were all produced beyond the period of review. Suffice to say, the plain-as-paper Convair served many military duties for decades.

For advanced training of attack/fighter pilots, only the USAAF initially had anything beyond the AT-6 with a small number of TP-51 two-seat Mustangs. It was very soon recognized that a jet equivalent was highly desired, before being judged mandatory. The P-59 and P-80 were suitable for introduction to jet fighters without an instructor. The Navy even took up fifty F-80Cs as TO-1 (later TV-1) to bridge the gap until its own jet combat aircraft appeared in suitable numbers. Yet nearly 600 were acquired in total. Although intended for training, a squadron of marine TV-1s had a combat role. The naval team replaced the Lockheed ejection seats with Martin-Baker units in many of the airplanes. Deck trials were also performed with three P-80As fitted with the requisite equipment, but the service saw no advantages over the FD-1. All of these aircraft lacked a second seat.

A proper trainer version of the likable Lockheed jet had been proposed by the company from about the origin of the Shooting Star. The USAAF initially had no funds for this, though a jet trainer was clearly needed given the many differences with high-performance prop aircraft and the high accident rate in the P-80s. The slow response of the early jet engines and the care with which they had to be handled, lack of propwash over tail control surfaces, and a sometimes-high stall speed of the newer thin wings, were some of the more important differences. By 1947, the training regimen included 180 hours with the T-6 and fifty with the P-51, but only ground runs of a P-80.

In May 1947, Lockheed began designing a trainer version of the P-80 on its own initiative. After a short time, the USAAF permitted the company to modify a P-80C (48-356). Additional fuselage length was added forward and aft of the wing for the second seat and new canopy, internal fuel reduced, and just two MGs retained. It was January 1948 before the service could finally contract with Lockheed for the first batch of two-seat TF-80Cs, soon known as T-33As. The first prototype took off just two months later and initial training operations began in June 1949. The T-33As also served as proficiency mounts in fighter/attack squadrons or just about any other aviation unit that could establish a need. The navy also adopted the Lockheed trainer as TO-2 (TV-2) starting in 1949. The type saw wide international use from its earliest service. Ultimately, Lockheed produced 5,691 T-Birds through 1960 and more abroad; they served well beyond that.

Replacing World War Two training aircraft with more modern equipment encompassed navigator and radio operator training with the T-29. The aircraft was a spin-off of the Convair 240 airliner and did little beyond wartime aircraft apart from tricycle undercarriage and leading-edge de-ice. This XT-29 (49-1910) shows the prominent belly radome, multiple astrodomes, redundant navigation antennae, and extended engine tailpipes. (*National Archives*)

The USAAF had ten two-seat TP-51Ds created towards the end of the war for advanced fighter pilot training, with full dual controls. Afterward, fifteen additional examples were ordered via conversion by Temco during 1951, these with a better canopy not confining the rear instructor's noggin as much. Shown is an example of these later TF-51Ds (44-84662). (*Jim Hawkins collection via Dennis Jenkins*)

Lockheed and the USAF sought to improve the T-33 and had 51-4263 built with a twin tail for better post-stall directional control. While this did not lead to a production change, Lockheed continued along different avenues with its own funding, including converting a T-33A (52-9255) in 1952. The aft seat was raised to give the instructor better visibility forward, and inlets redesign to maintain efficiency at higher AoA, the vertical tail enlarged and the horizontal raised, and single-point refueling added. Stall speed was lowered and low-speed handling improved with a larger wing possessing leading-edge slats. Engine compressor bleed air was also blown over the flaps as a measure of BLC. An uprated J33 gave marginally more thrust. When this aircraft flew in December 1953, it was found necessary to increase the dorsal fin area to compensate for disturbed flow from the heightened canopy, revise the inlets, and adjust the tailpipe area.

The USAF was not interested in the design, but the USN saw more naval training value squeezed from the worthy Lockheed mount, especially for carrier operations. They ordered a modified version as the T2V-1 Seastar with structural strengthening and catapult plus arrestment accouterments added. This prototype T2V was under construction by the end of the period under review. Changes were made during flight testing and a modest number were manufactured for brief naval service.

By the end of the Korean Conflict, it was clear that primary training aircraft had to be improved in order to produce pilots ready for the more advanced aircraft to which they would be streamed. Both the USAF and USN sought an all-jet training force. For the air force, they launched the TX program in April 1952 for a lightweight jet with ejection seats. The early 1953 evaluation of design submittals yielded a win for Cessna. Their offering had line-abreast seating and a pair of 920-lbf (4.1-kN) Continental J69s—the license-produced Turboméca Marboré II. This would bear fruit a few years later as the T-37A, a trainer that would serve for the next fifty years. The navy's efforts did not generate contracts until past the period of this book.

Liaison Frustrations

Army liaison aviation continued with just a few types from the war. After the formation of the USAF, the army retained Piper L-4s and Stinson L-5s. Aeronca supplied the L-16 (Model 7BCM Champion) as National Guard trainers. Likewise, the Piper L-18 and similar L-21 were other versions of the Cub purchased to replace the L-4. Many of these new types were pressed into service in Korea, though judged deficient.

The purpose-built, do-it-all L-13 was designed at the end of the war by the Stinson Division of Consolidated-Vultee. Two YL-13s were built in Wayne, Michigan, and first flown in March 1946. It was powered by a 245-hp (183-kW) Franklin O-225 with a constant-speed prop. A 52.5-gal (199-l) auxiliary fuel tank could be installed in the cabin. The externally strutted wing had double-slotted ailerons, outboard leading edge slots, and wide-span slotted flaps. The stall speed of 44 mph (71 kph) allowed operation within a 500-foot (152-m) field length, though typically much less. The airplane could be towed aloft at up to 150 mph (241 kph). The fixed undercarriage featured swiveling main wheels for ease of ground movement. Floats and skis could be

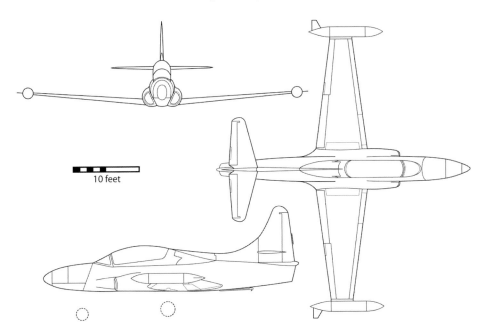

Lockheed worked to improve the T-33 trainer as a company initiative. It had the aft seat raised, the vertical tail enlarged, and lowered stall speed with a larger wing possessing slats and blown flaps, among other new features. Flying in December 1953, this eventually attracted a navy contract as the XT2V-1 shown in the drawing. (*Author*)

The Korean Conflict had highlighted the need for jet primary trainers, with line abreast seating and ejection seats preferred. Cessna won this TX competition with the conceptual T-37 shown in a drawing from late 1952. This aircraft would fly a couple of years later and go on to serve for half a century. (*National Archives*)

fitted. The wing and horizontal folded for crating or truck and air transport. Sloped windows provided an outstanding all-around vision for observation. The line-abreast seating in front and a third in the back was the standard layout. However, in an emergency, up to five could be carried in addition to the pilot. All seats but the pilot's seat could be removed to allow two litters to be loaded.

Although the army rejected the airplane, the USAF ordered 300 L-13As, built in San Diego. Slowed by funding shortfalls, deliveries began in 1947. Twenty-eight were converted to L-13B with combustion heaters for Arctic ops. The L-13 suffered engine problems that truncated its service.

Consolidated-Vultee L-13A Characteristics

span	40.5 feet (12.3 m)	weight empty	2,083 lb (945 kg)
length	31.8 feet (31.8 m)	gross	2,900 lb (1,315 kg)
height	13.8 feet (4.2 m)	speed, max.	115 mph (185 kph)
wing area	270 feet² (25 m²)	cruise	92 mph (148 kph)
fuel, wing + aux.	60 + 52.5 gal (227 + 199 l)	range, normal	368 miles (592 km)
service ceiling	15,000 feet (4,572 m)	with aux. tank	750 miles (1,207 km)
climb rate, initial	830 fpm (253 mpm)		

The similar Boeing Wichita L-15 Scout was the result of a competition and late 1946 contract. Boeing participated only because of the dearth of other work. The first article flew in July 1947. The two-place airplane was powered by a Lycoming O-290 at 125 hp (93 kW), turning a two-position Sensenich prop—later changed to a fixed-pitch

Consolidated-Vultee built 300 L-13s for the air force beginning in 1947, the army having rejected it. Devised during the war, it was a "do-it-all" dream of a liaison airplane that could operate on floats or skies and carry up to two litters as shown here. However, it suffered engine problems that marred its short career. (*San Diego Air & Space Museum*)

McCauley. The full-span slotted flaps and roll spoilers permitted operations from a 600-foot (183-m) field with a 35-mph (56-kph) stall speed. The fuselage was a pod with generous transparencies and the rear observer in a swiveling seat for an excellent view. The observer seat could be removed for light cargo, cameras, or other equipment, but there was no room for a stretcher. The airplane could be towed by another at up to 165 mph (266 kph), operated with skis or floats, performing airdrop, wire-laying, and airborne pickup (snatch, see page 104). There were provisions for a belly drop tank that could more than double endurance, and fittings for Brodie gear installation.[6] The wings and tail boom could be removed in thirty-nine minutes by six persons, and main landing gear wheels rotated to the inside of the strut, to fit a volume of 24 × 9 × 7 feet (7.3 × 2.7 × 2.1 m) for transport in a 2.5-ton truck and C-97. It could be reassembled in less than an hour.

After two XL-15s, ten YL-15s were delivered in 1948–1949 for thorough service evaluation. While liked, with an order for forty-seven in work, the budget did not permit a largescale purchase and the program was dropped in late 1949.

Boeing YL-15 Characteristics

span	40 feet (12.2 m)	weight empty	1,509 lb (685 kg)
length	25.3 feet (7.7 m)	loaded	2,050 lb (930 kg)
height	8.7 feet (2.7 m)	speed, max.	112 mph (180 kph)
wing area	269 feet² (25 m²)	cruise	101 mph (163 kph)
fuel, wing+ext.	21+24 gal (80+91 l)	range, normal	217 miles (349 km)
service ceiling	16,400 feet (4,999 m)		
climb rate, initial	628 fpm (1,011 mpm)		

The simpler Cessna L-19 was the real winner, derived from the commercial Model 170 and selected in a 1950 competition. Although provided additional transparent panels and with accommodations for a litter, the Bird Dog lacked nearly all the special features of the purpose-built airplanes indicated by the past war. The 213-hp (159-kW) Continental O-470 and slotted flaps gave good short field performance. Deliveries of the L-19A began in December 1950, and they were immediately shipped to Korea. The USMC also took up sixty as OE-1s for Korean ops.

Cessna L-19A Characteristics

span	36 feet (11 m)	weight empty	1,498 lb (680 kg)
length	25 feet (7.6 m)	max. loaded	2,430 lb (1,102 kg)
height	7.5 feet (2.3 m)	speed, max.	130 mph (209 kph)
wing area	174 feet² (16.2 m²)	cruise (5,000 feet)	104 mph (167 kph)
fuel	42 gal (159 l)	range, cruise	800 miles (1,288 km)
service ceiling	22,000 feet (6,706 m)		
climb rate, initial	1,485 fpm (453 mpm)		

The army tried again for a do-it-all liaison type, although discarding the litter-carrying requirement. The Boeing L-15 had many unique features to include easy disassembly/assembly, full-span flaperons for outstanding short-field performance, and an unparalleled observer view. However, the program was dropped in 1949 owing to a shallow budget. (*National Archives*)

Restricted largely to liaison airplanes, the army sought a replacement for World War Two vintage types. The selection of the Cessna Model 305A was made just as the war in Korea broke out, and the first was delivered within months. This L-19A (51-4829) was among the first of nearly 2,500 to follow. (*National Museum of the United States Air Force*)

A Cessna Bird Dog was fitted with an experimental Boeing 502 engine, reworked as a turboprop, to become the XL-19B. Designated the T50, the 210-hp powerplant carried the ship to a light-plane record 37,000 feet in 1953. It is shown on December 16, 1952. (*National Archives*)

A Bird Dog was fitted with an experimental Boeing 210-hp (157-kW) T50 turboprop in 1952 to become the XL-19B. The next year, it set an altitude record for light aircraft of 37,063 feet (11,297 m).

For a larger and rugged transport on the scale of the World War Two C-64 Norseman, the de Havilland of Canada DHC-2 Beaver was acquired as the L-20 with a 450-hp (335-kW) R-985. It could carry 1,200 lb (544 kg) with access through large double doors or accommodate seven passengers. It had outstanding STOL performance via wide-span flaps and drooped, slotted ailerons. The army had been interested in this type from its early development, but Congress had resisted allowing the procurement of foreign products, and the USAF had hesitated to relax the weight restrictions. Korean combat resulted in an attitude adjustment, and the air force also bought the L-20 (initially as the C-127). As with the L-19, the aircraft could be fitted with skis or floats. The similarly flexible Helio Courier was evaluated as the YL-24, but the budget did not permit the useful airplane to be acquired for many years.

de Havilland of Canada L-20A Characteristics

span	48 feet (14.6 m)	weight empty	2,775 lb (1,259 kg)
length	30.3 feet (9.2 m)	loaded	4,650 lb (2,109 kg)
height	10.6 feet (3.2 m)	speed, max. (5,000 feet)	179 mph (288 kph)
wing area	250 feet² (23 m²)	cruise (5,000 feet)	153 mph (246 kph)
fuel	72 gal (273 l)	range, economical cruise	480 miles (773 km)
service ceiling	26,000 feet (7,925 m)		
climb rate, initial	1,290 fpm (393 mpm)		

An L-20 of the 10th Liaison Squadron is seen operating from the barest of runway surfaces in Korea during October 1952. A de Havilland of Canadian DHC-2 Beaver, it was bought to meet the combat needs, overcoming resistance to purchasing a foreign airplane. Performance was outstanding and it proved a vital payload and STOL addition to army aviation. (*National Archives*)

Among the commercial purchases, with modest order numbers, were the single-engined North American L-17 Navion and Cessna LC-126 (Model 195). Korean experience suggested the need for aircraft with better performance and instruments for adverse weather operations. Acquired were the Beech Model 50 Twin Bonanza (L-23 Seminole) and the Aero Design and Engineering Aero Commander (L-26), as the first light twins.

Air-Sea Rescue

Air-sea rescue continued to be an important mission supported by the services, with operations executed regardless of whose aircraft had gone missing or ship was in distress. The Air-Sea Rescue Agency had been established in 1944 headed by the coast guard, becoming the Search and Rescue Agency after September 1946. Except in times of war, the USCG operated from U.S. soil in American or international waters. When the USAF was created, it assumed responsibility for worldwide ASR and focused on regions beyond coast guard purview. The role fell under MATS. Specially modified aircraft performed the mission, with seaplanes having a crucial role. Another vital element was the long-range landplanes with underslung boats to be dropped to survivors in the water. Helicopters began to take on some of the short-range rescues, but they needed much maturation before they could begin to replace airplanes.

The USAF's SC-47s and SB-17s (designations assumed in 1948) continued to support the ASR mission. Some two dozen or so SB-29s were created following the war and, like the SB-17s, carried airdropped boats and had radar for sea search. The coast guard also adopted seventeen SB-17s, though with the navy's PB-1G designation. All had an added radar.

Very similar to the USAF SB-17s, the USCG PB-1Gs were Flying Fortresses converted to the air-sea rescue mission. The radar helped locate vessels at sea which the boat could be dropped to personnel in the water. All the equipment dated from World War Two, serving into 1959. This example (82855, the former B-17G 44-85837) was photographed in San Francisco. (*Military Aircraft Photographs*)

The air force continued to operate SB-29s (44-84078 shown over Japan in April 1951) for deep-sea ASR, carrying the droppable boat for survivors in the water. The rescue gear was all developed during the war and the model served for many years as the Cold War developed. As this meant the potential for search and rescue operations where the flight might be challenged by hostile air defenses, the armament was retained. (*National Archives*)

The ubiquitous PBY Catalina had persisted as the flying boat end of these assets with the USAAF/USAF as the amphibious OA-10A (PBY-5As) and -10B (-6As). Although it had few peers, the air force did not consider these flying boats the ideal sea rescue craft and were eager to replace the older aircraft. Still, it operated five J2F-6 Duck biplanes as OA-12As beginning in 1948 for Alaskan service. The Republic Seabee was evaluated, and an order for twelve OA-15s promulgated but then canceled.

The Catalinas faded from navy and USCG service during 1946. The navy also let go of their "Dumbo" PBMs the same year after which the coast guard took these up. The "Coasties" focused on a version of the Mariner, the PBM-5G, that was specially lightened, had all armament removed, and fitted with reversible propellers for more positive control on the surface. The use of JATO assisted in take-offs, and mounts for the bottles were added to the aft fuselage hatches. Many open-ocean landings were made to affect rescues, but these remained dicey. The hazards occasionally claimed an airplane damaged beyond repair or sunk. The PBM-5A amphibians produced after the war (see page 310) were specifically intended for ASR, but the USCG judged them too heavy after a mishap. Instead, they operated their twenty-four PBM-5Gs until 1958.

By 1951, the PBMs were aging and the USCG sought an ASR version of the new Martin Marlin. For the first time, the seaplane was built to coast guard specifications, though it still amounted to removing all military gear and optimizing what remained for rescue. The P5M-1Gs did not begin to arrive until near the end of 1953 and served to 1958.

In 1947, the USAF took up a navy contract with Grumman for the new amphibian that the USN had originally called the JR2F-1 then the PF-1 when it had been considered (then rejected) for anti-submarine ops. The design dated from 1944, but it had moved very slowly to its first flight in 1947. The hydrodynamic design leveraged off all the lessons from the war and proved superior. The two 1,425-hp (1,063-kW) R-1820 engines had two-speed, single-stage superchargers and turned three-blade reversible propellers. The Albatross had fixed floats and slots ahead of the ailerons for improved low-speed control, could carry drop tanks, and lacked armament. The normal crew of four was commonly supplemented with two observers. The air force had the seaplane optimized for ASR with a radar pod under the port wing, a sea rescue platform to be deployed out the waist hatches, and JATO mounts on a panel that could be opened inward for bottle changes in flight. The AN/APS-31 radar would soon be moved to the nose.

The first of these SA-16s was delivered in 1949 and soon replaced the Catalinas and SC-47s. The navy piled on with an order for the nearly identical UF-1 utility airplane. The USCG adopted the navy craft as the UF-1G in 1952 that eventually displaced the Marlins. Subsequent models would further improve and optimize the design, including adding fuel tanks within the floats. The Albatross would assume the heroic mantel of the Catalina with many rescues of civilians and military personnel. They arrived in time to assist in Korea and would go on to serve for decades.

An air force OA-10A (44-33950) rests on an Alaskan lake during October 1948, JATO bottles attached to assist take-off. It is fitted with radar above the flight deck for sea search and rescue via water landings or dropping of survival gear to aircrew in the water. The Catalina amphibian performed yeoman duty in ASR with the USCG and air force until retirement. (*National Archives*)

A coast guard PBM-5G rests on beaching gear in San Francisco awaiting another emergency call, a PB-1G beyond. Note the radome atop the forward fuselage and the JATO bottle mounts on the aft access hatch, plus the complete lack of armament. (*San Diego Air & Space Museum*)

Grumman SA-16A Characteristics

span	80 feet (24.4 m)	weight empty	19,820 lb (8,990 kg)
length (nose radar)	62.1 feet (18.9 m)	loaded	28,670 lb (13,004 kg)
height	24.3 feet (7.4 m)	max. take-off	33,000 lb (14,969 kg)
wing area	833 feet² (77 m²)	speed, max. (sea level)	238 mph (383 kph)
fuel, wing+ext.	676 gal (2,559 l)	cruise	150 mph (241 kph)
service ceiling	24,800 feet (7,559 m)	range, normal	1,150 miles (1,851 km)
climb rate, max.	1,432 fpm (437 mpm)	maximum	2,680 miles (4,313 km)

For arctic rescues, where the airplane might be landing on water, ice, or snow, the air force explored a means of adapting the aircraft for all three. An amphibian so-equipped should also be able to operate on semi-prepared fields.[7] They turned to EDO for a solution to this "pantobase" goal. EDO modified a JRF-5 (37795 operated by the USAF as 48-128) with a principal ski under the hull and auxiliary skis on the tail and each wing float. Test operations on all surfaces were successful and demonstrated that only the principal ski was essential. Subsequently, a similar arrangement was developed and tested for the SA-16. This "triphibian" equipment was created in 1950 with two 1-foot (0.3-m) wide, shock-mounted, centerline keel skids and light skis attached to the floats. The keel skids fit into a recess created by altering the hull. The modifications to the triphibian kit were added to the production line and kits produced. Later, the aft keel skid was determined to be unnecessary under most circumstances. The USAF would go on to explore pantobase adoption of other aircraft. However, they ultimately adopted Piasecki H-21As for arctic rescue, and the USCG took the similar HRP-2 for ASR (see page 330).

The SA-16 began service with the USAF in 1949 as the principal air-sea rescue platform, but it was soon adopted by the navy and coast guard as well. This example (49-093) is seen in Korea during September 1951 in the company of an H-5 helicopter. It is equipped with underwing tanks and nose radar. (*National Archives*)

This JRF-5 Goose ("buzz" number OA-128), under USAF operation, has been modified by EDO with four added skis. This arrangement was to permit the aircraft to operate on sea, snow, and ice for arctic rescue as the "pantobase" concept. Testing showed promise. (*Jay Miller collection*)

Adoption of the pantobase to the air force's principal ASR aircraft, the Albatross, required only a keel skid and float skis. The production "triphibian" kit is seen on the prototype SA-16 (48-588). The colored field on the nose, black-bordered yellow, would be duplicated on other surfaces as an identification of a rescue aircraft. (*Jay Miller collection*)

Electrons Battle

The mounting tensions with the USSR and then the wider communist front countries, all remaining secretive behind closed borders, compelled an expansion of both strategic photoreconnaissance and electronic intelligence gathering or surveillance. The Americans, British, Taiwanese, and others—especially as NATO capabilities grew—worked together on these endeavors. Missions were commonly launched from bases retained in foreign lands. The electronic element initially mapped surveillance radar coverage to permit camera ships to come and go without detection. In time, monitoring communications and air defense reaction time also allowed those capabilities to be defined such that any future offensive penetration could be executed with greater success. In such eventualities, the electronic order of battle could be as important as imagery, and only the bombers themselves appeared suitable for these missions. As EW expanded on both sides, seeking to jam communications and radar (ECM), plus thwart those efforts (ECCM), additional detection and characterization of adversary emissions became important. Aircraft remained the most efficient means of collecting all these data.

Existing air force aircraft were modified for these missions and, typically, given an "R" prefix to their designation. Their forest of antennae was evidence of their capabilities. Yet they remained secretive, parked in remote areas of airfields, patrolled by armed guards, and with photography strictly forbidden. Even aircrew were sometimes prohibited from entering the aft areas of their aircraft. As few as one and no more than a few of any single configuration were created, and those changed frequently. As the Soviet, Chinese, and North Korean air defenses solidified, these lone covert "Ferret" flights over denied areas became increasingly hazardous. Flights were more often conducted only along the borders or flying toward the borders to prompt a reaction then turning away. Some of the aircraft and crew did not return.

Air force transports and bombers were best suited to this ancillary role owing to their range and endurance, the safety of multiple engines, interior volume, and excess electrical power generation capacity. This last could be enhanced with generators of greater output installed on the engines or APUs mounted. All or most defensive armament was removed to lighten the airplane. The interior was characterized by racks of electronics, operator stations, and recording devices. Photography and EW capabilities were frequently combined during these early years.

The B-29 was again the ready platform for early EW installations. Fifteen of the RB-50Bs were modified in 1951 as RB-50Gs with revised radar gear and equipment for the EW mission. The fourth bomb bay of the RB-36s were fitted with ECM gear and the EW operators were in the aft compartment. On a more tactical scale were such aircraft as the RB-26 with various "black boxes" and a monitoring station in the bomb bay. Even C-54s and C-97s were fitted for EW. The modifications were highly classified and performed by government shops and at a select few contractor sites. To manage these growing projects, the USAF set up an office within its headquarters in 1952 with codenamed "Big Safari."

The navy did identical work on a smaller scale and focused on detecting and defining potential adversary naval capabilities. Among its aircraft converted for the role, for which speed and weapons were largely irrelevant, included a small number of Avengers denoted as the TBM-3Q with the bulbous radome common to the TBM-3W (see page 357). Taking over aboard ship were eighteen AM-1Qs, with added crewmember and electronics, that served briefly. Then, each model of the AD through 1950 had 118 built as Q-birds with the RCM operator in the aft fuselage. Similarly, several Mariners were fitted with EW gear as PBM-5Es in 1946 that served until 1947. The P4M-1Qs became available for their new EW role in 1951 through 1953 after extensive internal modifications. With a crew of fourteen, the black boxes and support equipment were altered repeatedly as the mission demanded. These "Cold Warriors" served until 1960 throughout the world.

The Central Intelligence Agency also undertook such work to catalog the national technical capabilities of potential adversaries and other data sought to assess intentions and national economic means. One method for doing this was to send thousands of gas balloons carrying cameras and other recording devices across these borders in the hopes of collecting data thousands of miles away in accessible areas. This was conducted between 1952 and 1956 with minor results.

Beyond data collection were aircraft modified to perform EW combat missions in the event of hostilities. Penetrating bombers carried their own jammers and chaff with associate crewmen. Other aircraft would also drop chaff. Few aircraft dedicated to these tasks existed during this time, but that would change in the future during which many of the aircraft from this period, once rendered second-tier combat assets, were turned to these roles.

Drones Soldier On

Towing target sleeves remained a routine job for outdated aircraft. Targets for high-altitude and high-speed towing, up to 35,000 feet (10,668 m) and 450 mph (724 kph) saw the navy contract with Vought to develop the X-27 with a slender, V-tailed shape.[8] It was of all-metal construction for the flight conditions and to create radar reflection. The testing likely began with a subscale variant before moving to the full-size X-27A glider possessing a 24-foot (7.3-m) span. Forward V canards were probably meant only to create two cable attach points above the center of gravity for a three-point attachment, as the associated photo shows. Towing was on a 200-foot (61-m) line. To help slow the glider upon landing, there was also a drag chute deployed when the nose skid touched down and automatically released the towline. The production variant was the X-28A that probably had larger tail surfaces. Thirty-five were delivered. The USAF also acquired the Vought product in 1950 for towing via the B-45.

Both the army and navy continued operating target drones and developing more capable follow-ons. The fiscal environment meant that many of these did not leave the drawing board, and those that did seldom proceeded beyond testing. There were a great many of these from many sources, some serving more as inexpensive technological demonstrations than promising new weapon systems. All manner of propulsion and

The few Martin P4M-1s were quickly turned to EW and performed important missions in this capacity. This example (124369) was photographed in July 1951 and shows added fairings testifying to many additional antennae for ELINT collection. Many navy and air force machines grew such "warts," though they were seldom photographed and their exact capabilities or missions were classified. (*National Archives*)

This AD-1Q (09354) carries "window" (chaff) dispensers under the wings, and unseen radio countermeasures operator station inside, in this August 1949 image. This was to be employed coincident with an attack by jet fighter-bombers to confound enemy radar tracking of the attack force. Such offensive EW support capabilities were small during this period but growing. (*National Archives*)

Towed targets for high altitude and airspeed required advancement beyond the sleeves previously used. The navy had Vought develop such a shape in the X-27. This saw X-27A and X-28 versions of which the USAF also bought. The images show a JD-1 (77215) at Pax River on July 30, 1947, preparing to pull aloft what is likely a subscale X-27 version of the glider since the other image is of a much larger X-27A known to span 24 feet. (*National Archives*)

launch methodology was employed. For the navy especially, this became a bewildering assortment with frequently altered alphanumeric-soup designations. Most of the test flying was conducted at the remote Holloman AFB, New Mexico, for the air force, and Point Mugu plus China Lake for the navy. No effort is made here to document the numerous system that came and went during this period.

The USAF continued operating Culver Q-14 optionally piloted target drones while Radioplane produced more of its small radio-controlled targets. Radioplane had produced many thousands of inexpensive gunnery targets during the war, powered by small piston engines, and continued working on many more advanced designs of increasing performance and complexity. Globe built similar small airplanes, most recip-powered. Some of these were produced and operated for many years.

Radioplane development yielded the Army OQ-19 (KDR-2 for the navy) with a 60-hp (90-kW) engine. During 1950, this was improved through several models. The basic drone spanned 11.5 feet (3.5 m), weighed 323 lb (147 kg), and could reach 207 mph (333 kph). The wooden wing had slots and there was an antenna embedded in the vertical stabilizer. It was commonly catapult-launched but could get airborne from a wheeled trolley or be air-launched. Parachute recovery was common, and it could also be fitted with a floatation kit. This target remained in use into the 1980s with nearly 48,000 built for use by twenty-five nations.

A high-speed jet-powered target, for both air-to-air and surface-to-air gunnery, was needed given the introduction of jet aircraft and missiles. Outdated fighters converted as high-speed maneuvering targets (Full-Scale Aerial Targets) were especially useful for missile tests. For a more permanent solution in larger numbers, the air force let several contracts, while the navy had many such vehicles in work. For small drones, the use of simple pulsejet engines appeared a practical option.

The navy sponsored a small and inexpensive turbojet engines for missiles and drones. This meant they were expendable, and so the cost was to be low. From this program, Fairchild developed the J44 at 280 lb (127 kg), 1.8 feet (0.6 m) in diameter, and delivering 1,000 lbf (4.4 kN) of thrust. A service life of just ten hours was specified. In the same vein, Continental worked up various models of the J69, ultimately achieving 1,915 lbf (8.5 kN) in a 350-lb (159-kg) unit. This evolved into more advanced products that remained in production for decades, eventually pushing

The small radio-controlled target drones from World War Two were hastily and simply built to keep costs down, plus make repair quick and easy. These were continued postwar by the same company, Radioplane, but made more durable. This quickly converged on the OQ-19 (navy KDR-2) that typified the small target drone for the next couple of decades. (*National Museum of the United States Air Force*)

the J44 from the market. Westinghouse tried with the 0.8-foot (0.2-m) diameter J32 at 175 lbf (1.2 kN), but it proved too costly.

Curtiss developed the air-launched, jet-powered KD2C-1 Skeet target, built around Continental and McDonnell pulsejets. Tested in 1947 through 1949, it was produced in modest numbers. The McDonnell TD2D-1 Katydid was fitted with an 8-inch (20-cm) pulsejet of the manufacturer's design and extensively tested. Globe built the KD2G Firefly with McDonnell PJ42 and Solar PJ32 pulsejets, and this went into production for a few years of service from 1947. Radioplane manufactured twenty-eight XQ-1s for the army, powered by the Giannini XPJ33 pulsejet engine buried within the fuselage. This boosted the 14.4-foot (4.4-m) span drone to 330 mph (531 kph) after a catapult launch with a single vertical tail or an air launch with an H-configuration tail. The inlets for the engine were ducts beneath the straight wings. Recovery by parachute required an initial drogue to slow the vehicle before main chute deployment.

The XQ-1 testing in the first half of 1953 showed the pulsejet was a crude and fuel-inefficient motor, albeit inexpensive. The 880-lbf (3.9-kN) J69 turbojet was substituted. Eliminating the long pulsejet tailpipe allowed for a shorter airframe, and a single annular nose intake served. These XQ-1A and Bs were flight tested at Holloman beginning in late 1953. It was subsequently altered for an anti-radiation mission with a sensor in the nose. This forced a ventral intake for the J69 on what became the B-67 (later GAM-67) Crossbow.[9] Radioplane's drone work continued on to greater complexity with jet engines pushing the aircraft supersonic. The company eventually became part of Northrop who produced target drone to the date of writing.

The air force also gave Ryan a contract in 1948 for a high-speed target. This featured swept surfaces and a nose inlet for the small turbojet. The aircraft spanned 11.2 feet (3.4 m) and grossed around 1,200 lb (544 kg). The first glide flight of the XQ-2 was in March 1951 followed by powered flights that summer. This entered production as the Q-2A Firebee powered by a 1,060 lbf (4.7 kN) version of the J69. The navy also acquired the drone as the KDA-1, although with the 1,000-lbf (4.5-kN) J44 requiring a bullet fairing protruding from the inlet that was also swept back more sharply. The most common launch technique was to drop it from under a wing of a B-26 (JD-1 for the navy), but ground launch from a short rail with a JATO booster was also employed. Recovery was via parachute. The army also operated this variant and it was exported to Canada. The Firebee would continue to evolve over the coming decades for greater altitude and speed performance before being turned to reconnaissance. Many thousands were built.

The remotely controlled QB-17s from the war were employed to penetrate the radiated zones created by Pacific atomic bomb tests. Other airplanes were turned to this role using similar remote control technology. Such drones were given a "Q" prefix to their designations by the air force and the "K" suffix by the navy. Some flew in the region of the explosion to test the blast and radiation effects while other collected air samples.

This work brought thoughts of using robot planes for other dull, dirty, and dangerous missions. Towards the end of the period under review, the armed forces began to consider unmanned aircraft for reconnaissance roles.

The navy had Globe develop the KD2G target drone powered by a McDonnell PJ42 pulsejet engine. This could be ground- or air-launched. For the latter, one option was to drop from an F7F for which the navy had the sixty-five F7F-2Ns modified with a Bearcat canopy over the second cockpit for the drone controller, creating the F7F-2D. (*Naval Aviation Archive*)

The need for a high-speed target drone in the jet age meant an aircraft powered by a jet engine, an example being the 880-lbf Continental J69 turbojet (inset image). Radioplane began with an internally mounted pulsejet engine in the conservative XQ-1. This was both catapult-launched and dropped from an airplane such as the B-29 seen here. Launch preparation includes measuring the control surface deflections via scales seen installed. (*National Museum of the United States Air Force*)

Ryan also answered the call for the high-speed target drone, in their case with swept surfaces. The company developed the Q-2 Firebee for the USAF, but it was also adopted by the U.S. Navy as the KDA-1. This navy JD-1 carries a KDA-1 for launch, though it was also boosted aloft from the ground with a JATO rocket. (*Naval Aviation Archives*)

Drone conversions of manned aircraft, performed even before World War Two, continued into the postwar era. They served as targets for new technology missiles, but also to observe the effects of nuclear weapon blasts as well as collect radiation and fallout cloud samples. The wingtip pods of the QF-80 (P-80B 45-8599) are for the latter "sniffer" purpose during Nevada tests in 1952. (*National Archives*)

Ames Aeronautical Laboratory performed remote control testing with this navy SB2C-5 (83135) that had been modified with a raised drone control station. The NACA added a manually controlled periscope sight to visually track a target and the resulting signals used as control inputs to the remotely operated vehicle. This work became more important as some air-launched missiles required at least initial guidance by the launch aircraft crew. (*Jay Miller collection*)

The guidance and control of remotely operated aircraft for test purposes also bled over into missiles guided by the launching aircraft. These brought the detailed attention of NACA Ames given their experience with variable stability aircraft (see page 56). They performed much analytical, lab, and flight test work in this area of research that included uniquely modified aircraft. The use of remotely operated aircraft for testing to envelope extremes, such as diving pull-outs to maximum g, was nearing its end given the growing importance of onboard pilot compensation and the safety of ejection seats.

Special Missions

All services put standard aircraft to use on special missions with modifications. Airdrop of clandestine operatives saw some special methods to ensure against discovery. In one case, a B-26 was modified with wooden benches installed in the bomb bay for up to six jumpers.

Igor Bensen's work at GE included adopting the Rotachute autorotating kite idea (see page 343) to the soft delivery of airdropped articles. The blades would self-deploy and begin spinning on the descent after release.[10] Kaman took this further in adopting the rotachute idea for dropped bundles. Opening soon after release, the attached free-spinning rotor lowered the bundle via autorotation and with greater precision.[11]

12

Aerial Weapons

There were some benefits from insights into German wartime work, but American rocket and guidance plus radar technology were superior and propulsion systems matured rapidly. Guided missiles became a DoD priority with all the services championing a multitude of programs, some duplicative. Measures to create order and efficiency proved at best partially successful. Many projects died of funding starvation, testing failures, rapid obsolescence, or mission shifts. Much money was spent and much was learned, but the nation's defense was little enforced by systems that were generally inefficient if not ineffective. Most were developed without clear mission need stated by the warfighter.

Guns, Cannon, and the Like

By the end of the war, the .50-cal M-2 had become ubiquitous. However, this MG lacked penetrating momentum against more modern targets. Although an advanced model, the M-3, was introduced, with a rate of fire from 800 to 1,200 rpm plus pneumatically charged and electrically heated, this was but a brief reprieve. The 0.60-cal developed during the war was tested postwar on at least a P-38L and an XP-83 with hopes the higher muzzle velocity and round mass could match the lethality of the slower-firing 20-mm cannon. However, this weapon was not adopted.

An exploding cannon round served well against air and ground targets. Although greater ammunition capacity countered the arguments of too few rounds, complaints of a slow rate of fire had to be endured until Korean combat showed this to be acceptable as the new normal. The 20-mm cannon was also improved.

In Korea, an F-86 could put numerous 0.5-inch holes in a MiG that would still get away and be in the air again in a day or two. However, a few hits by the MiG's cannon would normally cripple the Sabre. In early 1953, eight F-86E and -F jets, fitted with four 20-mm each replacing the six machine guns, underwent sixteen weeks of combat evaluation. Three suffered flameouts at high altitude owing to gun gas ingestion, with two ending in the Yellow Sea. This was corrected, but the evaluation results were inconclusive. This effort was part of the USAF's Project Gun-Val that ran from early 1951 through late

1954 to assess the various guns, cannon, and rocket weapons then available, including foreign products, to inform future installations. This funded a number of experimental weapon installations on existing interceptors and fighter-bombers. Among these was four 30-mm cannon installed on F-89C 51-5766, with pluses and minuses documented. Quad 20-mm in a P-80A shifted the CG too far forward. One of the YF-94Ds (51-5500, see page 168) was fitted with a new GE 20-mm rotary-barrel cannon for testing.

In 1947, a P-80A (44-85044) was modified to permit four nose machine guns or two cannon to be rotated up to 90 degrees and fired. The recoil caused the fighter nose to drop, spoiling the shot, and the idea was dropped.[1] Four normally oriented cannon were substituted by Curtiss for the nose MGs for testing, but they moved the aircraft's CG too far forward.

The navy took the pivoting gun idea one step further in late 1949, experimenting with a gun turret making up the nose of a F9F-2 (re-engined F9F-3 122562) containing four .50-cal guns. This electro-hydraulic Emerson unit was fitted during summer 1950 and tested at Pax beginning in September. The guns pitched as a unit at up to 200 degrees per second and to 20 degrees beyond vertical, while the nose rotated up to 100 degrees per second, to allow firing in a large portion of the field around the aircraft. This would especially eliminate the need to dive on a strafing target. Unfortunately, the radar and fire control system to permit the aiming of the guns to actually hit anything was delayed for years until the project was dropped in early 1954.

Martin built a similar electrically operated turret with two paired 20-mm guns in elements that rotated up through 105 degrees (15 degrees beyond vertical) while the nose rotated 360 degrees. The turret was radar directed by a FCS. This was tested on F-89A 49-2434, but it also went nowhere.[2] The turret displaced most or all of the intercept radar gear that was essential to the F-89 mission.

The air force also fitted a P-80A (44-85116) with a nose "rocket gun" in which six 38-lb (17.2-kg), 4.5-inch (11.4-cm) folding fin rockets—a seemingly inadequate number and rate of fire—were launched individually out a tube projecting from the nose. The firing mechanism replaced the guns, and rocket exhaust gases were vented down through louvers. This was also left as experimental.

This P-80A (44-85044) shows off the experimental elevated nose gun and cannon installations at Wright-Patterson AFB. Presumably, these could allow the fighter to pass into a defensive armament blind spot of a bomber to shoot it down. Apart from causing the nose to drop during firing, the challenge was then to aim the weapons for which no practical sight was developed for this or a similar navy system. (*National Museum of the United States Air Force*)

Some better means of deploying rockets than underwing mounting was sought, freeing up the wings for other stores. A single launch tube and mechanism for revolving fire of stored rounds was explored. This image shows the tube in the nose of the P-80A 44-85116 test aircraft, the firing mechanism within for just six rounds, and a firing event with rocket exhaust expelled through two bottom vents. Clearly, six rounds were few and the rate of fire surely too low, and so the "rocket gun" was not adopted operationally. (*National Museum of the United States Air Force*)

A more "practical" rocket gun was evaluated during Gun-Val. This used fin-stabilized 2.75-inch projectiles and a gun system, both developed by the Army's Ordnance Corps. Two of the guns, with twenty-five rounds each, were fitted in the nose of F-89C 51-5795. The barrels projected from both sides of the nose leaving the radome unaltered. During flight testing in 1953, a number of problems arose and were resolved to include gun gas purge, adverse structural consequences of firing, and engine flameouts. This, too, was left as an experiment.[3]

A B-17 was modified with a proposed gunner station in a wingtip pod. While the bomber's wings seemed quite stiff, in flight, the wingtip oscillated up and down enough to complicate any targeting plus induce motion sickness—another idea set aside.

Around 1950, the services began testing and soon adopted low-drag tanks and bombs that were longer and narrower, with "pointy" ends. Multiple ejector racks were being thought of.

The Beginning of Aircraft Missiles

Among the earliest work on American AAM was undertaken by the USAAF. In 1946, it contracted with Ryan to study and then develop the AAM-A-1 Firebird. The initial goal was for use by an interceptor to knock down an enemy bomber. As developed, this became a subsonic missile guided during the first portion of the flight manually with microwave signals from the launch aircraft. Terminal guidance was via a small radar in the nose of the missile (semi-active radar homing, SARH) and warhead detonation via a proximity fuse. The technology of the period ensured it was a large weapon at a 7.5-foot (2.3-m) length, weighing 260 lb (118 kg). A solid fuel booster kicked the missile off the launch pylon and a liquid sustainer motor took over for the fly-out. Initial flight tests occurred in October 1947 from an A-26, and later a P-82, with hundreds of missiles fired. Engagement was necessarily limited to daylight and good visibility, with an expected range of 5–8 miles (8–13 km). Perhaps no more than four missiles could be carried by a fighter. Firebird was canceled in 1949 when its technology was being overtaken by more effective systems.

The navy carried on programs from the war and initiated others. The Massachusetts Institute of Technology and Bell worked on various aspects under AAM-N-5 Meteor. This evolved to a SARH system of about 500 lb (227 kg) in weight. Although some good test firings were performed from a JD-1 and F3D, it was ultimately set aside for more promising programs. Martin was also developing the AAM-N-4 Oriole with active radar homing (ARH), but no flight testing occurred before cancelation in 1953. Its weight of 1,500 lb (680 kg) may have been one impediment.

Beginning in 1947, the navy undertook the development of three versions of a missile called Sparrow, with testing at Point Mugu. This was initially to be an adaptation of the HVAR rocket, but it grew beyond those dimensions to 8-inch (20.3-cm) body diameter and 12.3 feet (3.7 m) in length. It had an Aerojet solid-propellant motor and weighed 315 lb (143 kg). The radar beam-riding version by Sperry was called AAM-N-2 Sparrow I. The radar was slaved to an optical sight and so required suitable visibility of the target, with a 6.2-mile (10-km) range. The ARH version was the AAM-N-3 Sparrow II by Douglas. The SARH AAM-N-6 Sparrow III was from Raytheon.

The earliest flight tests of Sparrow rocket and components were in 1948. The first guided Sparrow I shot, from the ground, was in April 1951. The initial inflight launch was in July 1952 from a F6F-5K drone. In December 1952 it hit a QB-17 drone—possibly the first air-to-air guided missile "kill." Sparrow II was first launched in July 1952. Sparrow III did likewise in February 1953 from an A3D, followed by a guided shot in October. By that time, the missile was already in production, though it would not be deployed to the fleet until 1956.

In 1950, NOTS began work on the infrared-guided Sidewinder, initially as a local effort and then, in 1952, as a sanctioned program. This missile was converging on a 175-lb (86-kg), 9 feet (2.7 m) in length, and 5-inch (12.7-cm) diameter round with a 10-mile (16-km) range. Apart from the sensitive seeker head, it also had the innovation of aft fin tip "rollerons." These were notched wheels in pivoting tabs. The wheels were spun by the airstream and, if the missile rolled, would precess like a gyroscope and cause the tab to deflect to correct the roll. From initial tests in 1951 on AD-4s (and an F3D-1 the next year), the first full-up round shot followed in September 1952. After a dozen missiles were fired, the initial intercept was in September 1953, passing within lethal range of a F6F-5K, then hitting a QB-17 in January 1954.[4]

Sparrow and Sidewinder did not enter service for years, then took many more to be reliable and effective. Both would also be adopted by the USAF and served for many decades.

The Ryan Firebird air-to-air missiles are shown under the wing of an A-26 in preparation for a test flight, apparently dated December 12, 1947. It was guided manually after firing by radio signals from the launch aircraft before radar took over for terminal guidance. The manual guidance required daylight and good visibility, rendering it of such marginal value that it was set aside awaiting more suitable products. (*National Archives*)

The navy began developing the Sparrow air-to-air missile in beam-rider, semi-active homing, and active homing versions during the first half of the 1950s. The gestation was long and difficult, and initial products had low reliability and effectiveness. This photo shows a Sparrow dummy round mounted on an F3D at NAS Seattle on April 16, 1953. (*National Archives*)

The IR-seeking Sidewinder was also developed by the navy at China Lake. This was a protracted effort as well but yielded a worthy product. This Sidewinder XAAM-N 7 is seen on F3D at Inyokern. (*National Archives*)

The advent of practical air-launched missiles brought thoughts of aircraft optimized for their employment. The navy was contemplating Skyknights, with cannon removed, fitted with APQ-36 radar and four underwing mounts for the Sparrows. These F3D-1Ms and F3D-2Ms became operational in 1954. Yet Sparrow performed poorly for more than a decade to come.

Hughes was contracted in 1946 to develop a SARH missile with solid propellant and impact fuse for launch from aircraft to destroy aerial targets with a 7.6-lb (3.5-kg) warhead. Development and test continued through the mid-1950s. Initially the AAM-A-2, it later became the XF-98 Dragonfly—suggesting an unmanned interceptor aircraft—then YGAR-1 (Guided Aircraft Rocket). The program came to include an infrared-guided version. It was a subsonic missile with an approximate range of 5 miles (8.1 km). Initially intended for bomber self-defense, the launch had to be from higher speeds although, it was soon learned, not supersonic. The intended target became slow-moving bombers when launched from an interceptor, and this became a program objective in March 1949.

The initial XF-98 was 6.5 feet (2 m) long and had an 8-lb (3.6-kg) warhead with only an impact fuse. It had a range of about 5,000 feet (1,524 m). Testing began in 1949 with the first launch in May 1951 from a B-25. An F-89 fired one for the first time in September 1952. However, development progressed slowly and the first production missile, then dubbed Falcon, was not delivered until 1954, becoming the first such operational missile with the USAF. By 1953, there was still concern with the ability of interceptors to clear the sky of enemy bombers preparing to deliver nuclear bombs. That year, the USAF began the development of a nuclear warhead for the Hughes missile to wipe out formations of aircraft.

Among the first air-to-air guided missiles deployed by the U.S. was the Hughes Falcon. The first application was from the tip pods of the F-89 (as seen here), though it did not become operational until 1956. The Falcon was built in semi-active radar homing and IR-guided versions, but neither were reliable. (*National Archives*)

Smart Bombs

The guided bomb program from the war was sustained postwar. The VB-3 Razon (Range and Azimuth Only guidance) was a 1,000-lb (454-kg) bomb fitted with control fins, tail flare, and radio guidance. The bombardier visually guided the tail flare to the target via a joystick.

The 12,000-lb (5,443-kg) VB-13 Tarzon, by Bell, was a similar guided bomb (ASM-A-1 after 1948). This was a variant of the Tallboy "earthquake" bomb with added stability and control surfaces, and range plus azimuth steering employing World War Two technology. Also added was a gyroscope to aid in stability and a pneumatic system to power the surfaces during the brief fall. An accuracy of 290 feet (88 m) was measured in tests. The VB-13 program was begun during the war, but it was shelved until 1950. In addition to B-29s, eighteen B-36Bs were equipped to deploy the VB-13. The reliability of such weapons remained low.

The navy carried on with several programs from the war and added others. In the former field was the Bat radar-guided glide weapon that was subjected to a practical demonstration in July 1948 when four were launched from PB4Ys at the USS *Nevada* battleship, scheduled for destruction. All failed or missed by a large margin. The similar McDonnell Gargoyle anti-ship glide bomb was tested, beginning during the war and continued after, eventually simply as a research effort through the end of 1950. The store weighed 1,517 lb (688 kg) and had an 8.5-foot (2.6-m) span. It was guided manually via radio signals from the launch airplane by reference to a flare in the tail. Once diving into the target, a 1,000-lbf (4.5-kN) JATO rocket in the aft end was ignited to drive the 1,000-lb (454-kg) armor-piercing bomb to more than 600 mph (966 kph) and through deck plating. The wings stretched range to nearly 5 miles (8 km)—possibly the limit for the operator to see the flare—when dropped from 27,000 feet (8,230 m). The full 200-missile production was not expended before being set aside.

The navy continued several wartime air-launched weapon programs, some just for research and experience purposes. One such was the McDonnell Gargoyle anti-ship glide bomb with a rocket engine to drive the warhead through armored deck plates. This example is mounted under a SB2C and shows the fittings in the aft end for the flare and rocket motor. (*Air Force Test Center*)

The navy also carried on the Kingfisher program from the war seeking a torpedo with aero surfaces to permit engagement of ships and surfaced submarines from beyond the range of anti-aircraft defenses. The work converged on the Petrel missile by 1952. This added a 1,000-lbf (4.5-kN) J44 to the rear of the torpedo in addition to wooden wings and an empennage. The weapon weighed some 3,900 lb (1,769 kg), was 23.5 feet (7.2 m) long, and spanned 13.3 feet (4.1 m). Range was perhaps 23 miles (37 km). Two could be carried externally by heavy naval patrol aircraft such as the Neptune and Marlin. The missile would be dropped on the radar return and continued to guide to the radar reflects off the target as illuminated by the mother aircraft (SARH). When within range of the torpedo run, the aero appendages were shed and the weapon dropped into the water for independent engagement.

Petrel was developed throughout the early 1950s and fielded in the mid-1950s. With the aircraft having to remain in the area, and even continue to close while "painting" the target, the mission profile was less than ideal. Additionally, with the Soviet Navy becoming largely a submerged force against which Petrel was unsuited, the program was canceled in 1959.

With concern about the growing defenses against strategic bombers, that may not have a fighter escort, the USAF began to look at the potential for what would come to be known as standoff ordnance. The effort had begun in July 1945, and Project Mastiff was formed in March 1946 to produce air-to-surface missiles more practical than the JB-2 (see page 436), and launched from the B-29. The goal was an autonomous weapon with a 300-mile (583-km) range propelled by a rocket motor to supersonic speeds. Bell won the contract in April 1946. Their preliminary work concluded that only a 100-mile (161-km) range was a reasonable objective, and the requirement was altered accordingly.

With the advent of nuclear weapons, there was a desire to increase the payload of the missile that required its size to grow markedly. In January 1948, the existing contract then became a risk-reduction project while a parallel effort was kicked off for a larger production missile. The RTV-A-4 (rocket test vehicle) Shrike sought to develop the propulsions and guidance technologies while also permitting experience to be gained with very large air-launched weapons. The vehicle was initially powered by a 4,500-lbf (20-kN) motor from Solar Aircraft and a 1,500-lbf (6.7-kN) unit from Aerojet Engineering, both using acid and monoethylaniline (aniline).

Later missiles had the Bell XLR65-BA-1 liquid propellant motor. Burning jet fuel with a white fuming acid oxidizer, this employed two thrust chambers producing a combined 3,000 lbf (13.3 kN). The missile was 22.8 feet (6.9 m) long with a 1.8-foot (0.6-m) body diameter, spanned 7.8 feet (2.4 m), grossed 3,495 lb (1,585 kg), and flew at Mach 1.5 to 2 to about 50 miles (81 km). It was released from a B-50 after being lowered from beneath the bomb bay on a dual-rail trapeze. Eventually designated X-9, twenty-eight units were dropped or launched in 1949 through 1953 of thirty-one built. The program achieved its objectives with fewer failures than other early missile efforts.

The weapon program became the Bell B-63 RASCAL (Radar Scanning Link, initially ASM-A-2). It closely followed the X-9 design, though scaled-up. This "Parasite Pilotless Bomber" was an 18,200-lb (8,255-kg), 32-foot (9.8-m) long missile spanning 16.6 feet (5.1 m) and with a diameter of 4 feet (1.2 m). It was powered by the XLR67-BA-1, then generating 10,440 lbf (46.4 kN) with three thrust chambers arranged in a vertical line. Circular error probable (CEP) accuracy was from 1,500 to 3,000 feet (457–914 m).

Just one missile was to be air-launched from the two aft bomb bays of a B-36 from which it was to be only partially retracted, leaving aero surfaces just below. Additional electronics were in the forward-most bay. The RASCAL could strike a target 110 miles (177 km) away, flying at up to Mach 2.95 and carrying a 3,000-lb (1,361-kg) nuclear warhead. The guidance system was developed by a team of Bell, Radio Corporation of America, and Texas Instruments. For the initial portion of the flight, the missile would be guided to a heading reference from the bomber using the onboard inertial system. Terminal guidance was from the B-36 bombardier using radio links, with the antenna in a radome retractable into the aft fuselage, and reference to video from the missile's radar. Each missile cost about $2.3 million.

The first air-launch of a RASCAL was from a B-50D in September 1952. Like the X-9, the missile was carried on a cradle extending from the bomb bay. The conversion of eleven B-36Hs as RASCAL carriers began in May 1953. The bombers were to be capable of conversion back to standard configuration within twelve hours. Captive carriage and separation trials occurred in summer 1953. Firings began in 1955 but suffered many failures. However, the B-47 was subsequently selected as the carrier, with the missile tucked up against the starboard side of the fuselage. Thirty of those bombers were to be converted for the role. The first launch from the Stratojet was in 1955. The project, by then the GAM-63, was eliminated entirely in 1958. Other emerging technologies appeared eminently more practical than the large and heavy RASCAL.

Various guided air-to-ground missiles were pursued, principally by the Navy. They worked on a series of Gorgon-guided missiles and drones, designed and built by

A large RASCAL missile is prepared for a test firing from B-50D 48-075. The supersonic missile was planned as a standoff nuclear strike weapon for the B-36, then the B-47, with an approximately 110-mile range propelled by a rocket motor. After years of testing, the project was abandoned. (*National Archives*)

NADC, for various missions. They used the first generation of turbojets, pulsejets, ramjets, and rockets. Launch methods included air and ground (rocket-boosted or catapult on rails). The guidance and control systems derived from World War Two, though with further development. These were marginal systems that performed poorly.

One such system, under development by the NAF, was the air-launched Gorgon, which had started during the war. It had a version powered by a Naval Engineering Experimental Station, Annapolis, Maryland, liquid-propellant rocket motor, a Navy 14-inch pulsejet, and the Westinghouse 9.5 turbojet. Some were simple shore bombardment weapons and others to be guided by remote control via television for anti-ship and anti-aircraft applications. Another version was to be the turbojet-powered TD2N high-speed target. The basic airframe was a canard design of molded plywood construction. The air-launched air-to-ground version (Gorgon III or KU3N) retained the fuselage but adopted a more conventional wing and empennage design with rocket propulsion. Several of each variant were constructed for testing that showed the general lack of reliability endemic to all such systems of the period. Some 100 Gorgon II-C (KUN) pulsejet-powered, remotely guided missiles were built at NAMU, though few were actually delivered. The effort was terminated in early 1951.

An unpowered version of the Gorgon IV, normally with underslung ramjet, had an aerosol dispenser and chemical tank installed in the ramjet nacelle to create the Gorgon V chemical attack glide weapon. Released from high altitude, the Plover could glide over 20 miles (35 km) descending steeply, leveling off at a few hundred feet via a radar altimeter to disperse the chemical over a 6-mile (9-km) swath. Tests in 1953 were favorable, but the weapon did not go operational.

Navy testing of its myriad postwar missile and drone programs, with all manner of launch, propulsion, and guidance methodology, was insightful and informed later endeavors that were more productive. Shown is the Naval Aircraft Factory Gorgon II-C (a.k.a. KUN-1) during a test of the navy's 14-inch pulsejet engine at the Naval Aircraft Modification Unit in Johnsville, Pennsylvania, on December 24, 1946, with an individual providing restraint. Also shown is a glide or captive carry version of the Gordon III (KU3N-1) to be powered by a rocket motor, being mounted to a launch airplane at Johnsville, also on December 24, 1946. (*National Archives*)

Robot Planes

Early work was being done on what would later be called cruise missiles—autonomous jet-powered winged missiles. With conventional weapons and the poor accuracy permitted by extant technology, these were intended for mass bombardment. With a nuclear warhead, once these were reduced in size to fit such weapons, fewer missiles would be required to hold targets at risk. Various ranges were sought, up to intercontinental. The USAAF/USAF and navy competed to quickly develop and field these systems and claim the associated missions. There were many programs in work at the end of the war, yet still failing to address every mission need. Postwar budget cuts winnowed these down. By the middle of 1946, the USAAF projects were cut from nearly fifty to roughly half.[5] Some of them were "insurance" programs aimed at characteristics short of requirements while waiting for technology to catch up, after which a more advanced model would be ordered.[6] The navy likely took a similar approach, and its myriad programs were likewise culled. The air force saw the extent of the navy's efforts as seeking to saturate the contractors and addressing all mission types to reduce the AAF's potential for claiming roles and missile types. There was never a comprehensive and stable national guided missile program with the concurrence of all services.

Certainly, there was a potential benefit in a low-cost unmanned system that required less ground support than bombers. A disposable missile carrying an atomic weapon could be a significant saving. However, missile programs suffered the same frustration as manned aircraft when it came to information about atomic warheads required for detailed design. They might satisfy strategic weapon delivery over an oceanic range while the ballistic missile was developed—a weapon with few antecedents and so a potentially long gestation. The cruise missile had the disadvantage of not being recallable once launched; it also lacked a pilot to deal with the unexpected or a navigator to update and adjust the routing. It would "cruise" to the target and so not evade intercept and might be at an altitude to allow ready radar tracking. None of the systems aimed at strategic missions with "intercontinental" range even approached the unrefueled range requirements to meet such a definition. Indeed, apart from the early but impractical B-36, no manned or even unmanned winged system would ever meet such goals without inflight refueling—unsuitable for a missile.

Key to the success of such weapons was accurate autonomous navigation via an independent source. Inertial navigation systems were maturing, but they struggled to reduce accumulated errors over hours of flight that could sum to miles. Updates via celestial references were being introduced at the end of the period under review. Additionally, such systems weighed literally a ton.

Towards the end of the war, the army sought to divide the emerging new weapons between its branches to avoid certain disputes over roles and responsibilities. Winged missies (pilotless airplanes) and air-launched weapons would lie with the USAAF while ground-launched rockets directly affecting ground combat belonged to the ground forces. Later this was more finely honed to focus on the mission type. Strategic objectives or those in support of air operations, especially guided missiles, belonged to the air force. Ground bombardment or anti-aircraft were the responsibility of ground forces. This division continued to evolve but, of course, ignored the navy. That service also launched weapons from aircraft and ships—winged and otherwise. Consequently, this brewed into another postwar dispute between the services, resulting in some duplication of effort. The evolution of the weapons also created systems falling between clean categorization.

Initially, testing continued with the wartime JB-2 launched from mobile ramps by the army and by the navy. The USAAF treated this as gaining experience, while the navy explored creating an operational system from the simple missile. Labeling it "Loon" (also KUW and LTV), and using units built during the war, these were modified for radio control and incorporated a radar beacon. This permitted the flight path to be adjusted by reference to radar track until issuing a dive command to impact the target. The effective range with this method was 200 miles (322 km).

Work was done, primarily at Point Mugu, to improve the system. Testing included launch from shorter ramps with powder charges, zero length using the rocket-propelled launch sled and ramp, and a catapult. The mounting of the rocket boosters was not always true and the off-axis thrust could sometimes overpower the flight controls, leading to a crash on launch. A gimbaled nozzle or "jetevator" was developed, controlled by the autopilot, to overcome this problem. Methods for reliable flight termination were also explored, finally settling on fuel cutoff and blowing off the wings. This contributed to the accuracy of impact to within a square mile of the target. Following over two and a half years of progressive improvements with 152 launches, system reliability was raised to just 62 percent.[7] Yet a submarine was modified to launch the missile, with a deck rail and large "hangar" canister for missile storage (wings removed), and another sub with the command ground station. The launching sub would be on the surface for fifteen–twenty minutes during the operation. Efforts were then made to improve guidance, to include using a pulsed radar signal in place of radio, and reduce vulnerability to jamming.

Republic Loon Characteristics

span	17.7 feet (5.4 m)	weight, launch	5,025 lb (2,279 kg)
length	27.1 feet (8.3 m)	warhead	2,100 lb (953 kg)
height	4.7 feet (1.4 m)	speed, launch	220 mph (354 kph)
wing area	60.5 feet² (1.7 m²)	cruise (optimal)	385mph (620 kph)
fuel	180 gal (681 l)	range, max.	150 miles (241 km)
service ceiling	6,000 feet (1,829 m)	endurance	25 minutes
climb rate	1,000 fpm (305 mpm)		

Loon testing stretched into 1951, with proficiency shots into 1953, with the conclusion that submarine-launched cruise missiles were practical and potentially effective, though Loon itself was not suitable. With the advent of diesel-electric subs, the quiet nature that made them difficult to detect also made them a suitable missile platform. They could approach a coast, surface to fire missiles, then submerge and evade engagement. This became the navy's goal for the next two decades.

The conversion of combat-weary bombers to cruise missiles during the war was extended after with B-29s, seeking a 1,000-mile range, under the USAAF Banshee program. The success of this effort was important in establishing AAF dominance in the guided missile field. However, Banshee suffered the same reliability issues as the wartime projects. Elements were tested during manned flights, and no unmanned sorties were conducted. One aircraft crashed in 1948 during this work, with the deaths of many crewmen. The program was dropped in April 1949.

A Loon is prepared for firing from a catapult erected at Point Mugu, California. The U.S. Navy tested dozens of the missiles to include incorporating them into a submarine and practiced guiding the missile via radio. Though unsuitable as a naval weapon, the experience gained fed directly into guided missile programs to follow. (*US Navy*)

The navy attempted something similar with the deck-launched AJ bomber converted to drone control. A one-way mission with an atomic weapon permitted a 1,400-mile (2,253-km) range, although it would have to be controlled remotely from another aircraft. This Taurus program was canceled in 1948 as the improbability of mission effectiveness and the coming Regulus missile overcame any exuberance.[8]

The USAAF sought a half measure between the JB-2 and Banshee with a ground-launched winged missile of respectable payload and range. This began with an August 1945 requirement for a 600-mph (966-kph) craft flying 175–500 miles (282–805 km) with a CEP of 500 feet (152 m). It was to be radio-guided from a ground or airborne controller. Martin was obligated in March 1946 to study both a supersonic and subsonic version of the B-61 Matador (later TM-61A, Tactical Missile). Budget cuts saw the supersonic variant dropped. Going was still slow, paced by funding and modest enthusiasm within higher ranks. The development contract was placed in May 1947, and the Korean Conflict would compel a priority rise.

The Matador had swept surfaces with spoilers for roll and a T-tail. The wing used honeycomb internal support rather than conventional semi-monocoque construction. The 4,600-lbf (20.4-kN) J33 engine was fed by a flush NACA inlet in the belly. A 57,000-lbf (254-kN) Picatinny Arsenal T-50 booster (also manufactured by Goodyear) kicked the missile airborne off a zero-length launcher. The missile took approximately 1.5 hours to prepare to fire once assembled, erected, and inspected. The optimal mission profile was a climb to 35,000 feet (10,668 m) and then cruise-climb to 44,000 feet (13,411 m) as fuel was burned, the missile accelerating throughout until the dump command was sent.

Matador's maiden flight was at Holloman in January 1949. As the German V-1 experience had shown, it took a great many test flights, with a great many missiles, to perfect the system. Martin struggled with suitable structural strength to keep the aircraft together during the terminal dive. Of the initial design, forty-six were flown through March 1954, followed by eighty-four pre-production and initial production models flown between December 1952 and spring 1954, then versions with strengthened wings and empennage between August 1953 and February 1954. Production B-61As began being tested in November 1952. Three ground stations provided remote microwave guidance by reference to radar tracking. This meant line-of-sign (LOS) transmission limiting range to, at best, about 250 miles (402 km) with high-altitude cruise, though it was vulnerable to jamming.

An autonomous guidance system was introduced with the TM-61C, though linked to ground stations emitting radar pulses. Hence, this still required LOS, limiting range, and was subject to jamming, in addition to limiting range. However, it got accuracy down to 1,800 feet (549 m) CEP—potentially acceptable with a nuclear warhead depending on the target. Overall system reliability was just 71 percent. This weapon, each missile costing $60,000, was produced and deployed operationally in 1955, by then with W-5 nuclear warheads replacing the conventional. Work also brought the transport and launch hardware from 40 tons down to 17.5 tons. Yet it required twenty-eight vehicles to transport, erect, and launch. The wings were moved separately and installed prior to flight.

Martin TM-61A Matador Characteristics

span	28.7 feet (8.8 m)	weight empty	5,410 lb (2,454 kg)
length	39.7 feet (12.1 m)	launch	12,660 lb (5,743 kg)
height	9.7 feet (3 m)	warhead	3,500 lb(1,588 kg)
wing area	180 feet² (16.7 m²)	speed, max. (44,000 feet)	596 mph (959 kph)
fuel	400 gal (1,514 l)	launch	200 mph (322 kph)
max. altitude	44,000 feet (13,411 m)	range, max.	794 miles (1,278 m)
		endurance	1.3 hours

A radar terrain map matching guidance system was introduced in 1954 on a missile that had been lengthened, wings shortened, a more powerful propulsion system substituted, and radar added. All this substantially increased weight. This TM-61B (later TM-76A) was named Mace and began flight testing in 1956. Its range was substantially extended, and the missile could be flown at low altitude for greater survivability. Later still, an inertial guidance system was installed, though the unit cost quadrupled to $250,000.[9] This system went operational in 1959.

The navy, building on the Loon experience, had explored many possibilities and conducted numerous experiments. However, the Matador prompted them to kick off a development program to ensure the air force did not solely claim offensive guided missiles, capable of carrying nuclear warheads. They initiated a new submarine-launched cruise missile program in December 1947 with Vought as the developer of Regulus. Within months, the DoD, seeking budget reductions, asked for an evaluation

The Matador was the air force's first production cruise missile. It was powered by a jet engine once launched by a JATO rocket, then guided by radio control, though later changes introduced more autonomous navigation. Hundreds were flown (to destruction) in the course of years perfecting the system, which still had low reliability and accuracy. (*Air Force Test Center*)

given that Matador and Regulus were nearly identical systems. Considering the changes needed in Matador to make it suitable for submarine deployment, the navy managed to keep Regulus alive. However, they also tried to accelerate their program.

Vought developed a 10,000–12,000-lb (4,536–5,443-kg) missile of 30 feet (9.1 m) in length boosted off a short, 11-ton rail launcher via two 33,000-lbf (147-kN) JATO rockets. The craft had swept wings and only a vertical tail for empennage. "Ailavators" and a rudder served as the only flight controls. Regulus employed a J33 fed by an annular inlet. It was to carry a 3,000-lb (1,361-kg) warhead to a range of 435 miles (926 km) at Mach 0.85 with a CEP of 0.5 percent of the range from the nearest controlling station. It was guided to its target via two stations aboard submarines or surface ships. Vought built their flight test and training vehicles with retractable landing gear and drag chute to permit recovery for cost savings. The vehicle initially had a ventral fin that was blown off prior to landing, but the fin was eventually deemed unnecessary. The four "slippers" that engaged the launch rails were also blown off after flight was achieved. The production articles would have folding wings and tail.

Regulus's maiden flight was in March 1951 at Edwards, with recovery on the lakebed. Initially, control was from a chase airplane. The first rail launch with rocket boost was in January 1952 from Point Mugu. The initial shipboard launch was in November 1952, and the first submarine launch in July 1953. The highest speed reached was Mach 1.08 in a dive from 35,000 feet (10,668 m). During 1952, the aircraft was also turned to use as an assault missile, to be guided to target impact by a chase control aircraft, for potential use in Korea—though this did not occur.

Chance Vought Regulus Characteristics (Flight Test)

span	21 feet (6.4 m)	weight empty	10,685 lb (4,847 kg)
length	34.3 feet (10.5 m)	launch (submarine)	14,522 lb (6,587 kg)
height	18.2 feet (2.5 m)	warhead	3,000 lb (1,361 kg)
wing area, approx.	115 feet² (10.7 m²)	speed, max. (diving)	Mach 1.1
ceiling	40,000 feet (12,192 m)	cruise	600 mph (966 kph)
		range, max.	575 miles (925 km)
		practical tactical	200 miles (322 km)

Several submarines were modified to carry and fire the missiles. This was a major alteration for hangars in large hull fairings for two to five missiles. Several cruisers were also fitted for Regulus, and carriers launched the missile for assault missions, guided by one of its aircraft. Improvements in Regulus included a revised guidance system reducing the shipboard or airborne stations to one. Carrier operations included shooting the missile aloft off a cart via the catapult. It was still unpopular on the carrier, seriously disrupting other ops.

Regulus went operational in 1955, with a reduction in the weight of nuclear weapons permitting the W-5 warhead to be fitted. The submarines made "deterrent patrols" in the Western Pacific, ready to launch nuclear-armed missiles into the USSR. Ultimately, 514 missiles were produced by the end of 1958. Testing and training, to include

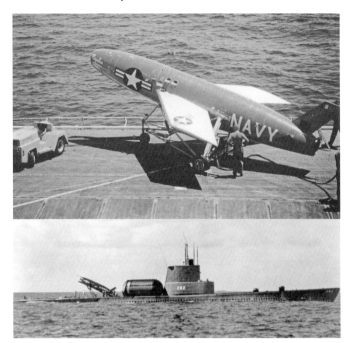

The navy developed its own shipboard, jet-powered cruise missile in the Vought Regulus. It was guided by ground stations and so had a modest range and initially a conventional warhead. This image shows the missile being prepared for flight from its rail launcher on the USS *Hancock* (CVA-16), and the other on the USS *Tunny* (SSG 282) with the on-deck hangar. (*National Archives and Air Force Test Center*)

using them as targets, saw 1,033 flights. System reliability reached approximately 80 percent. Its practical range was 200 miles (322 km) with vulnerability to jamming and intercept operational realities that increased year-to-year. The CEP was 3,300 feet (1,006 m).[10] Each missile cost approximately $307,000 including support equipment.

Taking the basic Regulus design to a supersonic platform with more range appeared a short path to a vehicle that was less likely to be intercepted. Vought began the design effort in April 1952 and was under contract in June 1953. Regulus II added small canards and a ventral intake to a slimmer body and a new afterburning J79, but the weight went up some 10,000 lb (4,536 kg). A single launch booster was to be used. The missile was to carry a 3,000-lb (1,361-kg) warhead for 650 miles (1,046 km) at Mach 2, or 1,300 miles (2,092 km) at slower airspeed. It first flew in 1956 and forty-four more flights with eighteen missiles followed. It proved marginally more successful during flight tests than its predecessor—that is, it had fewer failures. Production was ordered in 1958 with one submarine modified to fire the missile, which cost $1 million apiece. However, the program was dropped the same year in favor of ballistic missiles.

Navy long-range plans had been to get Regulus operational in 1953, the Grumman Rigel in 1955, and Triton in 1960. Rigel was to be a 19,000-lb (8,618-kg) launch weight cruise missile powered by a 48-inch (1.2-m) Marquardt ramjet with 20,000 lbf (89 kN) of thrust to fly at Mach 2 to 450-575 miles (724-925 km). While the very large ramjet was under development, challenged by the lack of a suitable test facility, subscale systems were flown with a 28-inch ramjet. This first flew in March 1950. However, the tests suffered many failures and the obstacles to success appeared insurmountable. Likewise, tests of a one-sixth scale model of the missile were not encouraging. The program was killed in August 1953.

The navy's Mach 2 Rigel cruise missile was in development for many years by Grumman before being abandoned. The large Marquardt ramjet powerplant is under test in this 28-inch scale version prepared for launch from Point Mugu in the early 1950s. Many ramjets and high-speed aircraft designs were tested in this fashion during the period. (*US Navy*)

Triton was worked by navy organizations as the "ultimate cruise missile." It was hoped the system could use the Regulus launchers, though Triton's launch weight crept up. Through many iterations, it became a 30,000-lb (13,608-kg) launch weight weapon reaching for 1,000–1,300 miles (2,222–2,408 km) at Mach 3.5 and 80,000 feet (24,384 m), with ramjet propulsion. Inertial navigation with radar mapping for terminal corrections was to permit the 1,550-lb (703-kg) warhead to be delivered within 1,800 feet (549 m) of the target. Started in 1946, it went into full-scale development in 1955 but was killed in 1957 with the focus shifting to submarine-launched ballistic missiles. Besides, Regulus II was targeting very similar goals.

In the final month of the war, the USAAF had sought a turbojet-powered missile with a 5,000-mile (8,047-km) range flying at 600 mph (966 kph) with a 2,000 lb (907 kg) payload. Of the respondents, Northrop offered only 3,000 miles (4,828 km), yet they won a study contract in March 1946 to look at 1,500-mile (2,414-km) subsonic and 5,000-mile range supersonic missiles with a warhead weighing up to 5,000 lb (2,268 kg). A development contract for the B-62 followed, but budget cuts saw the supersonic variant killed, and Northrop had to fight to keep the subsonic alive.

Northrop's N-25 Snark spanned 42 feet (12.8 m), was 52 feet (15.9 m) long, and weighed 28,000 lb (12,701 kg) at launch. It employed a J33, fed by a flush ventral inlet, inside a simple airframe. It had just a vertical tail and a swept wing, with only elevons as control surfaces. The launch was from a sled track using two 33,000-lbf JATO boosters while a drag chute and retractable skids allowed recovery. The company sought to achieve a 1,550-mile (2,495-km) range at Mach 0.85 cruise. Even as it was coming together, the USAF was altering requirements. In summer 1950, they specified a supersonic dash at the end of a 6,350-mile (10,219-km) flight with a 7,000-lb (3,175-kg) warhead and an accuracy of 1,500 feet (457 m) CEP. The N-25 was then well along, aiming at a December first flight, and had no hope of meeting such objectives. A revised design was started while Northrop pressed ahead with the N-25.

For flight testing, the N-25 was directed from a B-45 "mothership" and ground station. The initial two flight attempts at Holloman at the end of 1950 were failures, but a successful first flight was achieved in April 1951. Over the next year, twenty-five flights on sixteen vehicles were made through March 1952 with only five test articles surviving. Yet they achieved an endurance of 2.8 hours and a maximum Mach 0.9 when level and 0.97 when diving. Concurrent with this work were trials of the inertial navigation system, with celestial updating, performed on several manned platforms across hundreds of flight hours. The shocks across the star tracker window from supersonic flight introduced navigation errors. This system weighed nearly 2,000 lb (907 kg) and drifted such that a CEP of 1.6 miles (2.6 km) was anticipated at maximum range. Overall, Snark was costly and running well beyond schedule, losing some support.

The follow-on N-69 Snark design was nearly twice as heavy with a lengthened fuselage, enlarged wing area, and substituting the J71 with a ventral inlet. To collect design data, the remaining N-25s were modified for heavier GW and flight from a zero-length launcher with a more powerful booster. This work was done at Cape Canaveral where N-69 testing was to be conducted.

Its first flight attempt with the new missile was in August 1953 and failed, as did the next few. Successes were slow in coming, and few vehicles were recovered. Stability and other issues saw variations in the design. Even the terminal dive was found to be unworkable as the aircraft lacked adequate control authority at such speeds. A detachable nose with a warhead for ballistic delivery via fin stabilizers had to be designed. Weight and complexity crept up. The initial operational date in 1953 came

After the war, the USAAF sought a jet-powered, long-range, subsonic cruise missile and placed Northrop on contract. Their N-25 Snark was a simple vehicle with a complex and heavy navigation system, but it was destined to be passed over for a more capable successor even as testing was underway. Results with the sixteen N-25 test articles were respectable. (*Dennis Jenkins collection*)

and went. Testing dragged on into 1956, achieving some impressive long-range flights and Mach 0.9. Yet outside evaluators and even SAC were questioning the practicality of the system given the low expected accuracy and the vulnerability of the vehicle. Operational testing in 1957–1959 was dismal, with gross inaccuracy and very low reliability. Yet the system went operational in 1960. It was scrapped little more than a year later owing to defense cuts and the advent of ballistic missiles.

The USAAF was reaching for an intercontinental winged missile with another supersonic platform. Aware of the army's ambitious goals, NAA suggested in December 1945 a winged rocket based on the German V-2, though substituting a ramjet engine with a first-stage booster. The service began funding this work in April 1946, and it went through several evolutions in the coming years as the B-64. The requirements stabilized in September 1950 as a twin ramjet aircraft atop a rocket booster for a 6,300-mile (9,656-km) range at Mach 3.25.

North American began design work in May 1950 and initially tested the aircraft with turbojet engines to perfect aerodynamics, flight control, and the stellar-updated inertial auto-navigation system. The radio-controlled X-10 was powered by two afterburning 10,900-lbf (48.5-kN) J40s and was launched and recovered on a conventional retractable undercarriage. It had an aft-mounted delta wing, forward all-moving canards, and a V-tail. Pitch control via the canards were supplemented with wing elevons. The craft spanned 28.2 (8.6 m) with 66.2 feet (20.2 m) in length with a maximum take-off weight of 42,300 lb (19,187 kg). Titanium was used where the heating of Mach 2 flight was a concern. Noteworthy was the use of the fuel as a sink for vehicle system heat, collected by circulated hydraulic fluid. Also interesting was the departure from the standing shock supersonic inlet with a convergent/divergent design. This gradually reduced the speed for more ideal conditions at the engine compressor face. The X-10 also used then-common bleed splitter plates on the inlets.[11]

The supersonic, long-range Snark was markedly different with a larger engine, ventral intake, and overall greater size. Launch attempts began in late summer 1953 at Cape Canaveral from a zero-length launcher with twin booster rockets. This image shows the arrangement. (*Air Force Test Center*)

The vehicle's autopilot was tested on a modified T-33, F-80, and F-86. The company began conducting taxi tests of the X-10 at Edwards in September 1953. Control was from a ground station or following T-33. The craft first flew in October, and over twenty-seven flights with eleven vehicles were conducted at Edwards and Cape Canaveral. The maximum airspeed was Mach 2.05. The full B-64 Navaho project slipped years owing to multiple issues to include the RJ47 ramjets, expected to generate 40,000 lbf (177.9 kN). From the first flight attempts in late 1956, spectacular failures were emblematic until the effort was terminated in 1957 with $700 million invested.

Surface-to-air missiles were also being developed to intercept Soviet bombers. One such was a winged missile effort begun in 1945 as the Ground-to-Air Pilotless Aircraft along with two study efforts. A gap was perceived between bomber intercept by fighter aircraft and point-defenses (guns and missiles) that needed to be addressed. The army development program was initiated in 1947 as XSAM-A-1, and it matured over many years and budget swings to an objective to hit a target at 60,000–70,000 feet (18,288–21,336 m) and 200 miles (322 km) downrange at supersonic airspeeds with a 1,000-lb (4,536-kg) conventional or nuclear warhead. Boeing conducted considerable research into the subject from 1946, including rocket-boosted test shapes, and they won the 1949 development contract.

The program evolved by 1951 into the XF-99 BOMARC—Boeing and University of Michigan Aeronautical Research Center, the latter working the intercept control systems.[12] The missile was to be boosted to supersonic airspeed by a rocket after which ramjets would take over for wing-borne flight to intercept. For supersonic maneuvering, Boeing used pivoting tips on the wings and vertical tail, plus all-moving horizontal tails, for effective control in the presence of shocks. It was propelled initially by a 35,000-lbf (156-kN) Aerojet LR59 liquid rocket. This employed hazardous hypergolic propellants of hydrazine and nitric acid that were loaded in the two minutes before launch. The rocket accelerated the vehicle to speed for ignition of the two 11,500-lbf (51-kN) Marquardt RJ43-MA-3 ramjets—a rare production application for ramjets. Fly-out was to be around Mach 3 at altitudes beyond 60,000 feet (18,288 m) to engage bombers at up to 250 miles (402 km) range. The missile was to be guided from a ground station except for terminal homing via an onboard radar. The missile eventually spanned 18.2 feet (5.5 m) with its delta wing, was 46.8 feet (14.3 m) long, and grossed 15,619 lb (7,085 kg) at launch. The wing was just 5 percent thick and with a symmetrical biconvex section.

Testing of the XF-99 began in 1951 at Cape Canaveral, with its initial flight in September 1952 without the ramjets. This progressed slowly through multiple failures and design changes. Flights with the ramjets did not begin until 1955, then with the full-up system in 1957.

A production contract was issued in 1957 for what had become IM-99 (intercept missile), and the system became operational in 1959. It was upgraded, with the liquid rocket replaced by a Thiokol solid, improved Marquardt ramjets, and the vacuum tubes replaced with solid-state electronics. The missile remained in production for a decade with 715 delivered to U.S. and Canadian forces.

Above: The turbojet-powered North American X-10 was a precursor to a more ambitious Navaho missile with ramjets and boosted aloft on a rocket for true intercontinental range. While the X-10 performed many flights from its first in October 1953, eventually topping Mach 2, the ultimate system suffered spectacular failures and was canceled. The first X-10 (51-9307) is seen on the Edwards AFB lakebed in preparation for early testing. (*Air Force Test Center*)

Left: The initial testing of the rocket-boosted BOMARC anti-aircraft missile was without the side ramjets, as shown here. The missile struggled with both propulsion elements such that testing was protracted. Yet the system was fielded in 1959. (*45th Space Wing History Office via Dennis Jenkins*)

13

The Test: Korea

Starting just five years after World War Two and the massive demobilization, the reorganization that included the creation of the USAF, and the introduction of many new weapon systems, the Korean Conflict was a significant test of American airpower. It was not a war that was expected or for which American forces were best equipped. However, the U.S. adapted and fought well beside the allies, with many hard-learned lessons for aviation.

The outlines of Korean history and the war can be readily found in other sources. The People's Democratic Republic of Korea (PDRK) in the north was trained and equipped by the USSR. The U.S. had been the patron of the Republic of Korea in the south but withdrew nearly all of its military presence by June 1950. Seeking to bring the entire peninsula under communist rule, PDRK forces crossed the frontier that month. Only the Americans, deploying initially from Japan and flying combat missions from same, were prepared to resist the aggression as part of a U.N. force that eventually counted sixteen nations. The USSR would not see their proxy defeated, but hesitated to intervene themselves for fear of sparking a major conflict with the Americans. Instead, the Chinese were compelled to intervene. The struggle continued for three years, but the U.N. was constrained to combat within the peninsula to avoid provoking a stronger response by the Soviets that could grow to a wider conflict and use of atomic weapons.

Airpower Dimension

Airpower was a powerful force in the war for the U.N., though it was not decisive given the enemy's ability to absorb staggering losses and damage. The small North Korean air force was quickly destroyed, most on the ground by bombing. Though the U.N. was always superior, the introduction of the MiG-15 caused short-term consternation until the Americans brought in comparable jets. From that point, the enemy losses were tremendous, but they kept coming. Even as Soviet and Chinese aircraft were substituted, the force never reached a state to attack the aircraft carriers offshore or hit bases in Japan. Even attacking U.N. facilities in Korea was too ambitious.

As in World War Two, delivery of almost all Air Force fighters, light-planes, and helicopters to the war zone in Korea was via sea transport, usually U.S. Navy aircraft carriers. The USS *Boxer* (CV-21) is seen loading F-51s at Alameda, California, in July 1950. This transport bottleneck was only moderated in later decades as many airplanes became air refuelable to support self-deployment, but rotorcraft would continue to be shipped by sea or flown in via transports. (*National Archives*)

Too much was expected of airpower at the beginning by the Americans. It was an extremely destructive war owing mostly to the preponderance of airpower, with some 80 percent of the Korean infrastructure smashed. Tactical aviation and air defense fighters had been combined under Continental Air Command, and this undermined the training of vital ground attack skills. Coordination between the USAF, Navy, and marines was rocky initially, but it then worked out to an acceptable if not ideal level.

The USAF initially had difficulty operating jets on the peninsula because of short or unimproved runways. Flying from Japan shortened time in the combat zone. Bombers were almost exclusively B-29s and B-26s. For such World War Two vintage aircraft, spares quickly became scarce. "Boneyards" and stored aircraft became vital in filling some needs. Many of those machines were essentially scrapped as they were disassembled and parted out. Early in the war, combat was consuming aircraft and aircrew faster than they could be replaced by reserves being brought up to strength and required skill level, and stored aircraft made ready. Restoring and modifying aircraft quickly exceeded depot capacity, and additional resources had to be allocated with contracts let, all taking valuable time.

The war caught the U.S. Navy in a transitional phase to shipboard jet combat aircraft. Only seven of its carriers had the steam catapults almost always essential for launching the heavy aircraft. Only three of these carriers were in the Pacific.

The navy had 14,036 aircraft at the start of the war, with 9,422 combat types, increasing by a thousand or so during the conflict. Propeller-driven aircraft still outnumbering jets, on decks and especially ashore. The jets had shorter "legs" and carried a smaller war-load, but had a roughly 100-mph (161-kph) top speed advantage. They were somewhat safer on approach and landing, but wave-off was marginal owing to slow engine response time. They all had to be shot off the decks and so were confined to the large carriers. The Essex-class CV, modernized Essex Attack CVA, Light CVL, and large Midway class Battle CVB carriers were equipped with F9Fs, F4Us, and ADs. The Escort CVEs were all prop jobs with F4Us, F7Fs, F8Fs, and ADs. The F8F and Midway carriers did not serve in the warzone. All also carried special types like night-fighters and recce aircraft. By 1952, the USN usually had four carriers in Korean waters persistently.

Fighters

It was the first workout for the new jet fighters, and they did well even in ground attack, though ground fire was their bane. The new ejection seats got an extensive trial with nearly 2,000 egresses, though only 63 percent without difficulties.[1] The initial problem with jets was that their short range greatly limited their utility when sortieing from Japan. Not only did USAF prop planes like the F-51 have a range and endurance advantage, but they could also operate from short and unpaved runways. So, the veteran recip fighters proved invaluable initially. It was also found that the ordnance from the last war was no longer entirely suitable.

For close air support, the marines began the war with 223 Corsairs in ten squadrons and the navy 370 in twenty. Reduced to seven and three squadrons, respectively, by the end, they were still more numerous than any other fighter-bomber and augmented by the AU-1. The first ten months of combat saw the Corsairs fly more than 80 percent of all naval strike missions. The USMC birds also operated ashore, but many of the Korean airfields were initially poor and this took its toll on aircraft until improved. Yet the readiness of the recips frequently led the jets. Many of the new features introduced with the F4U-5 were not welcome and some had unintended consequences that undermined safety. Apart from the night fighter and photorecce version, the "dash-4" Corsairs soldiered on in Korea while the new model was sent back home.

Of the prop-jobs, the AD-1 was the champ owing to its toughness and payload. One of their most notable actions was eight delivering torpedoes into the Hwachon Dam on May 1, 1951, breeching it to flood a river and hinder enemy crossing. Douglas stripped 100 AD-4Ns of night-fighting gear to carry heavier ordnance, and added two more cannon, to become AD-4NAs after combatants noted how effective such an attacker could be.

Above: A December 26, 1950, shot shows numerous F4U-4Bs on the deck of the USS *Valley Forge* (CV-45) preparing to launch on a mission over Korea. These World War Two vintage fighters performed so well, and the need was so urgent, that new models of the Vought aircraft were placed into production. Behind all the Corsairs are F9Fs. (*National Archives*)

Below: This is the typical condition of a carrier hangar deck during combat. The USS *Boxer*, off Korea on May 28, 1953, has F9Fs in the bay and numerous bombs being prepared, plus crates of other stores. The Korean Conflict was a good workout for the new naval jet combat aircraft and their adoption to carrier decks, from which much was learned. (*National Archives*)

The P-51D exited World War Two with a sterling reputation and was retained into the Korean Conflict. It did well in ground attack, although the engine cooling elements on the bottom of the aircraft were vulnerable to ground fire. This example (44-64004) from the 18th Fighter Bomber Wing is armed with bombs and rockets for a mission from a flooded Korea air base during September 1951. (*National Archives*)

Close air support (CAS) meant different things to the different services. The marines expected aircraft to hit the enemy as close as 100 yards (91 m) away from friendlies. During the first ten months of the war, the Corsairs flew 82 percent of navy and marine CAS missions. North American T-6 trainers and AD-1 attackers were pressed into service as airborne forward air controllers. These "Mosquito" missions launched from forward strips and overflew enemy lines with trained observers delivering spotting calls via radio, improving CAS effectiveness.

The North Korean People's Army employed Soviet T-34 tanks that generally proved impervious to the 5-inch HVAR Holy Moses. In response, a substitute 6.5-inch shaped-charge warhead was developed to create the Anti-Tank Aircraft Rocket (ATAR or "Ram Rockets"). China Lake conceived, built, tested, and shipped the first 200 rounds in just nineteen days. The HVAR was having other problems, addressed with improvements to including making the fins folding. The FFAR, designed to engage bombers aloft, had a fuse change to permit it to be fired against ground targets and from six-round tube launchers built by Douglas. This was so successful that the weapon survived into the Vietnam War and beyond.

The F-80Cs performed respectably in Korea, although predominately devoted to ground attack. Larger tip tanks were devised to give the jets more time over the battlefields when sortieing from Japan.[2] Aircraft would fly to Korea in the morning, refuel at a suitable base, fly a combat mission, refuel again, and then fly back to Japan for a long day of operations. Air-to-air, they did well against prop-jobs, scoring the first American kill with a jet, but only superior airmanship allowed them to triumph against the MiG-15 flown by Soviet, Chinese, and Korean pilots. The first successful

Above: The air force had fifty Texans rebuilt for forward air control duties. These served in an important role during the Korean Conflict where these machines were photographed on March 9, 1953. Actually designated LT-6G (49-3558 shown in foreground), these could carry light armament. (*National Archives*)

Below: Ready stores of ATARs and napalm tanks are seen with F4Us at an airfield in Korea. China Lake developed and delivered the ATAR "Ram Rocket" in under a month after the need was identified. (*Naval Aviation Archives*)

all-jet combat was an F-80C versus a MiG-15 on November 8, 1950, in which the American emerged victorious. The Shooting Stars flew more than 95,000 sorties and suffered 287 aircraft lost, though only fourteen to enemy aircraft while 40 percent were to ground fire and 39 percent to operational accidents. They knocked down thirty-one aircraft and destroyed twenty-one more on the ground.

The F-84D, -E, and -G models fought in Korea, supplementing and then largely replacing the F-80s. The D-model jets were considered so marginal that half sent to theater were not operated. As with other straight-wing jets, the Thunderjets contributed air-to-air but turned predominantly to air-to-ground missions—destroying 60 percent of targets—after the introduction of the MiG-15. They knocked down nine opposition machines but traded eighteen in the bargain. In total, they flew 86,408 sorties and saw 122 airplanes dropped by anti-aircraft artillery (AAA), thirteen to unknown causes, and 182 lost to mishaps. The Thunderjets were among the most successful jet-powered USAF air-to-ground workhorses of the conflict.

Aerial refueling held promise to address the combat efficiency deficit for fighters flying from Japan. The recent work with probe-and-drogue refueling was a potential solution, and a crash program was launched. The idea was worked out at Wright-Patterson while detailed design and fabrication were left to the individual manufacturers. Performing the intrusive system changes for single-point refueling was too much in theater, but another solution was found. A probe was added to wingtip tanks of F-80s and F-84Es to permit refilling these tanks alone and individually.[3] Where weight or runway length suggested the use of JATO, the resulting dust and smoke were intolerable. Instead, the aircraft would take off at a light fuel load then immediately join a tanker to top off the tip tanks. The F-86E was more challenging given the low/swept wing with drop tanks placing the tips outside the pilot's field of view. The probe from the tanks was quite long and close to the fuselage. Although fabricated and tested, the F-86 system was not used operationally.[4]

An EB-29 (44-69704) was modified to serve as the tanker for fighter AR flight trials.[5] The YKB-29T and possibly the other hose tanker modified in England during 1950 were brought into the theater by June 1951 to service the modified jets. Six KB-29Ms from SAC were modified by FRL in England with the hose reel in the aft bomb bay.[6] As a full tip tank on one side alone could destabilize the fighter, the pilot had to fill one to half full, disconnect and move to fill the other side, then return to top-off the first. The cumbersome process nonetheless permitted combat persistence and range advantages previously denied by too few Korean bases.

The first-ever combat AR was performed in July 1951 with three RF-80As topped off to allow them to reach objectives deep inside North Korea and return. Later in the month, a RB-45C was boom-refueled by a KB-29P for a mission over the north. After suitable if hasty training, AR operations moved from an emergency expedient to a more routine if limited capability. Eventually, three squadrons of fighters were modified for tip tank AR. In September 1952, a F-80 flew a 14.24-hour strike mission with the aid of multiple tanker "hits." Modified F-84s were soon flying aerial-refueled strike missions. During July 1952, a wing of F-84Gs was deployed to Japan with the use of AR from KB-29Ps, saving considerable time and effort over shipping via sea.

The Thunderjet was the mainstay of the air force's fighter/attack teams when the Korean Conflict broke out. It fought well, even after the MiG-15 appeared with its superior performance. This pair of F-84Es are fitted with AR probes in their tip tanks to refuel from KB-29s equipped during the conflict with hose-reel systems to extend the range and endurance of TAC fighter-bombers. (*National Museum of the United States Air Force*)

The F2H-2 service in Korea was comparatively brief. It was considered among the most capable fleet defense fighters and priority was given to equipping Atlantic and Mediterranean carriers. Among the Banshee's war duties were escorting B-29s to targets in the far north that were beyond the range of USAF fighters out of Japan.

Grumman F9F-2s scored the first jet aerial victories for the navy in Korea, including a MiG-15. The Panther went on to claim three more MiGs for no loss to themselves. However, their primary role was providing fighter screens for piston-powered attackers until the F9F-2B appeared in theater to become the naval service's first jet attacker. The Grumman ultimately flew 78,000 sorties during the conflict. One unexpected discovery during the war was the nose blowing off the Panthers during gun firing owing to trapped gasses being ignited explosively. Grumman devised vents to ensure against gas accumulation.

Air superiority was secure, ensuring Allied forces had little to fear from enemy air. The MiG-15 was a rude surprise for aircraft but suitably dealt with. It was observed that the machine guns of the past were losing effectiveness air-to-air, and the cannon fired too slowly for the pilot's liking. Missiles would clearly soon be required.

When the Chinese intervened in Korea, they were supported by Soviet-piloted MiG-15s. This swept-wing fighter was lighter than its American counterparts, with the U.S. choosing to build heavy combat aircraft with more armor and safety systems than most contemporaries. The MiGs held superior speed and maneuverability, doing much harm against straight-wing jets and bombers, with a 2:1 exchange ratio in the communists' favor. Eventually, Chinese and North Korean pilots assumed the duty,

The Grumman Panther quickly became the most reliable and capable naval jet fighter of the war. This F9F-2B of VF-721 off USS *Boxer* (CV-21) is making a strafing pass over Korean terrain on July 15, 1951. The B-model was specifically created to enable attack missions for the jet. (*Naval Aviation Archives*)

but the Americans quickly brought in their F-86s. In the end, the U.N. pilots were enjoying a more than 10:1 exchange ratio.

The F-86 teams became the "glamour boys" of Korea with their high score against the vaunted MiG-15. Initially, F-86As flew over Korea beginning in December 1950, but they were replaced within a year with E-models. The F-86F (see page 174) was rushed to the combat units as soon as possible after they emerged from production lines, being introduced during June 1952. North American supplemented Inglewood output by opening another production line in Columbus, Ohio (the wartime Curtiss-Wright plant), to meet demand. The F-86Fs with the "6-3" wing began arriving in January 1953, and kits were shipped to modify aircraft in the field. This pushed the Sabre past the MiG-15 in capabilities (except ceiling) and even more of the opposition fell. In May 1953, the Sabres shot down seventy-seven MiGs with no losses in exchange. Another change was more of a field test with a handful of Sabres modified with four 20-mm cannon replacing the MGs. They quickly discovered that only two could be fired simultaneously without risking engine compressor stalls and flameouts.

The final tally was 87,177 Sabre sorties with seventy-six dropped by MiG-15s, nineteen to ground fire, thirteen to unknown causes, and 114 to operational accidents. In exchange, they destroyed an astonishing 792 MiGs. Of the 926 communist aircraft downed air-to-air during the war, 86 percent were lost to Sabres.

Improvisation could still win dividends, even with advanced jet fighters. The F-86 engine start required a large electric cart that could be absent at some fields. However, it was found that the engine could be brought to start rpm by a T-33 running up to 80 percent power about 16 feet (5 m) ahead of the fighter to allow its exhaust to windmill the J47.[7]

Left: A line of F-86As of the 336th Fighter Interceptor Squadron occupies a pierced steel planking flightline at Suwon (K-13), South Korea, during June 1951. This initial production model did well enough during the first year of the war, but the F-86E and then F-model dominated air-to-air combat in the theater with a remarkably imbalanced exchange ratio. (*National Archives*)

Below: The Allies got the opportunity to examine an intact MiG-15 up close when a Polish defector brought one over in March 1953, and a North Korean pilot in September 1953. The aircraft were evaluated, the Korean jet seen here on Okinawa in October 1953. It was lighter and less complex than American counterparts, but it represented the same state of the art in jet fighter design—with the engine a derivative of the Rolls-Royce Nene that also powered some U.S. types. (*National Archives*)

Bombing

Strategic bombing was meant to suppress North Korean fighting capabilities and cause such destruction and dismay as to prompt the PDRK to desist. The USAF employed B-29s almost exclusively in the role, with lighter B-26s and fighter-bombers executing interdiction and special missions. However, precision bombing remained a goal with, for example, hundreds of tons of explosives dropped on bridges ineffectually. Consequently, enormous resources were brought to bear. There was the realization that the costly A-bombs would likely have very limited application short of a war with the USSR or China.

Strategic Air Command deployed B-29s to the Far East, flying from Japan and Okinawa. They were employed in both strategic and tactical roles with good effectiveness, including the use of radar bombing and radio navigation. At first, they faced little air defenses, but the introduction of the MiG-15 emphasized the aging bomber's vulnerability. Operations switched to night and radar bombing for a time. Their EW suite was poor given little volume or electrical capacity for improvement. The R-3350 engines still gave fits, with overheat failures and some fires. Encountering icing on any flight would mean mission termination.

Available for general radio navigation was LORAN, though this required aircraft to be upgraded. Likewise, equipment had to be added to B-26s and B-29s to enable SHORAN use. The USAF employed SHORAN in Korea beginning in spring 1951, but only forty aircraft could utilize the system simultaneously. It required LOS between the aircraft and ground stations and so had a practical range of around 200 miles (322 km). This usually demanded an altitude above 14,000 feet (4,267 m), over the mountains that dot Korea. This was a struggle for the B-26 that removed its gun turrets, replacing the top unit with SHORAN antennae under a radome. In particular, the Invader had difficulty accommodating the SHORAN equipment and operator in the narrow space.

The new radio navigation gear and other equipment, plus training, eventually enhanced night bombing above that employed during the last war. Accuracy improved again with the introduction of the simpler AN/MPQ-2 beacon tracking and ground control guidance. The practical range was 60 miles (97 km), though 175 miles (282 km) was possible under ideal conditions.

Between July and September 1950, the Superforts destroyed all the large targets assigned. Throughout the war, this force dropped 167,100 tons of ordnance in 21,328 effective combat sorties, in addition to flying 1,995 reconnaissance and 797 psychological warfare sorties. Twenty bombers were lost to enemy action and two RB-29s downed north of Japan, but more than 100 were written off due to severe battle damage and operational mishaps.

The B-29s dropped 489 of the 1,000-lb (454-kg) radio-controlled Razon bombs, initially with only 67 percent system reliability. The bomb mass was too light to penetrate hardened targets, if they hit at all. They also dropped thirty 12,000-lb (5,443-kg) Tarzons. Eight are recorded as having struck their bridge targets, but use was discontinued when it was determined that jettisoning the bomb could result in detonation. The navy also employed their drone conversion technology for a precision strike. Six F6F-5Ks were launched from the USS *Boxer* (CV-21) in August 1952. Guided by controllers aboard two AD-2Qs, they targeted a heavily defended railyard. One aircraft struck home while four missed and the sixth malfunctioned. These unimpressive results saw no follow-up.

Interdiction of resupply convoys moved to night ops as the enemy sought to avoid Allied aircraft. Marine F4U-5Ns and F7F-3Ns performed their "Firefly" interdiction missions with PB4Y-2s dropping flares. The Ns also lead standard fighter-bombers to locate a target and dispense flares so the others might work, or led the attack themselves. While flares illuminated the target, they also undermined the night adaptation of the pilots' eyes, which then had to be regained while trying to avoid hitting rising terrain or their mates. The Tigercat, particularly, had good persistence but its lack of de-icing gear was lamentable.

At the beginning of the war, the USAF did not possess any unit proficient in night intruder missions, nor did it have any suitable aircraft. Night fighters and B-26s contributed the most. The F-82 was ill-suited for the role, and single-seat fighters were particularly challenged given the many tasks the pilot had to perform to be safe and effective. The B-26—with 1,054 aircraft in service, though many stored—assumed the mission as its principal role, day or night. Invader crews had to change tactics and relearn safe and effective procedures for the mission. Ordnance was bombs, rockets, and napalm. This still remained an improvised fit. The bombsight was not suitable and firing the guns in the nose risked temporarily blinding the pilot, as would underwing rockets.

Black-painted aircraft or RB-26s carried parachute-retarded flares (paraflares) to illuminate targets. Additionally, C-47 "Fireflies" could drop 150 flares from racks installed in the cargo compartment. Many of the World War Two-era flares proved defective, even when substituting navy ordnance. A few of the B-26s were fitted with war-surplus navy underwing searchlight pods, but with mixed operational success. They could be operated for only brief periods before cooling and they made the aircraft more vulnerable to ground fire. They were soon set aside. Some Invaders had their "solid" noses swapped for the transparent nose to permit the bombardier to get a better view of potential targets in the dark.[8] Other B-26s were fitted with radar to aid night flying as Pathfinders and target detection. One configuration had the radar under the forward fuselage, requiring the bomb bay to be shortened and bombs to be carried routinely underwing. Another had it in the nose, above the transparent sighting area.

States-side modification of bombers always seemed to lag combat need. The RB-26 and SHORAN installations produced a large number of configurations of the Intruder sent to theater. This was another frustration, the press of time and shortage of spares not allowing for standardization. The B-26 remained effective, although 154 were lost—with as many or more aircrew.

The introduction of variable-time fusing bombs and airburst using a radar altimeter were assessed as effective innovations. The air force also dropped "tacks" to puncture tires, the immobilized vehicles to be destroyed in daylight. Helping to locate locomotives at night, a Bell Laboratories infrared detector was added to the nose of some B-26Bs.

The 12,000-lb VB-13 Tarzon was guided to impact manually by the bombardier using radio signals and reference to a flare in the tail of the weapon. The enormous bomb was credited as providing "earthquake" like effects, apart from the blast. Thirty of the weapons were dropped by B-29s in Korea, with eight recorded as having struck the bridges targeted. (*National Archives*)

An F6F-5K drone and controller is seen on February 13, 1951, at Johnsville (NADC), and launching from USS *Boxer* (CV-21) bound for Korea in August 1952. The drone was developed during World War Two and put to use in Korea as an expedient. However, reliability and accuracy were low as testified by all but one of those employed in Korea failing or missing their targets. (*Naval Aviation Archives*)

Night Combat

Night fighters were successful in disrupting enemy intercept of U.N. nocturnal ops. However, it remained a difficult task that saw equipment evolution in the middle of the war.

Air force F-82G night-fighter squadrons in Japan when the war broke out were, as with much of the USAF, not fully fit to fight. There was also a critical shortage of spares. By that time, the Twin Mustang was anachronistic, but there were no other choices given the poor progress with jet all-weather fighter programs. Hence, they were pressed into combat and downed the first enemy aircraft. The units flew 1,868 sorties, destroying four aircraft in the air and sixteen on the ground, but the air force was eager to replace them. With enemy air little active at night, many of the missions were weather reconnaissance before the F-82 disappeared from the theater by February 1952, and the USAF entirely in November 1953.

The F-94A and -B jet all-weather interceptors were the preferred successor, arriving in-theater beginning December 1951. While they saw combat, they were initially forbidden to fly over enemy areas for fear of their advanced technology being revealed via downed airplanes. However, in a bid to reduce B-29 losses to enemy interceptors, they were pressed into flying "barrier patrols" about 30 miles (48 km) ahead of the bombers. They scored several kills, including the first credited as solely on instruments.

The navy and marines had a similar experience. Their pilots flew F4U-5N and F7F-3Ns from bases ashore. This did not approach the scale of the USAF efforts but experienced similar success—though the navy's only ace of the war flew an F4U-5N. However, it was discovered that the cannon recoil in the Corsair, harsher than the .50-cals, damaged radar components, and MTBF was low until rectified.

The marines took up the new F3D-2s in 1952, also operating from land bases. They began escorting B-29 formations and soon had contact with the enemy. They enjoyed more success than any other type in night combat by knocking down six adversaries. This included history's first jet-on-jet night combat kill. During 1953, the Skyknights also began night bombing missions. Two aircraft and crews were lost to unknown causes.

Maritime Dimension

In 1950, the U.S. Navy's active patrol force—mixing in ASW—had eight P2V and six PB4Y-2 landplanes squadrons, and six PBM-5 flying boat units with nine aircraft each—mostly PBM-5Ss and soon enforced to twelve boats. The reserves still had eleven units with PV-2 and nine with PBY-5As. Some of the reserve outfits would be activated during the emergency.

A naval blockade of North Korea was enforced by all available means. The U.S. was also sustaining a Formosa Straits patrol to forestall any mainland Chinese attempt to invade the nationalist enclave. There were no enemy submarines to counter, but floating mines were a threat. The guns in the aircraft proved valuable in detonating the mines. Minelaying and directing naval gunfire were other tasks.

Neptunes performed some ground attack and flare-dropping missions until one was hit by AAA and had to ditch. Thereafter, they were devoted to patrolling, flying mostly from Japan and Formosa. By this point, the Neptunes were flying more patrol sorties than seaplanes, marking a shift in navy operations.

Search and Rescue

The ASR role was vital in recovering personnel from aircraft going down in transit between Japan and the combat zone. The new Albatrosses were very busy and effective. The Dumbos would follow a bomber strike force to Korea then orbit off the coast until the force returned to be followed back to Japan. The PDRK's ability to occasionally intercept and destroy slow-movers in the Sea of Japan made it necessary to restore the armament previously eliminated from the repurposed bombers. The SB-29s also got a flare dispensing pod under the wings to support night rescue ops, although no such occurred.

Helicopters began to see wider use, though in limited roles. Medical evacuation was quite important given the poor road system and rugged terrain. Some 80 percent of all frontline casevacs—thousands of men—were evacuated by Bell H-13/HTL choppers. The first H-19s in the theater were USAF YH-19s undergoing evaluation in March 1951, and more followed for SAR.

An H-13B became the first army helicopter flown into combat, at the end of November 1950. Helicopter casevac could make the difference between life and death. Yet the mountainous terrain challenged the power of the extant rotorcraft. To ensure a ready start in the cold season, engines were enclosed in a specially fabricated housing that also permitted preheating from ground equipment. The original stokes litter accommodations were unsatisfactory, so army personnel devised a windscreen

Thirty-nine H-5Gs were optimized for air force rescue with a litter pod on either side. Procured in 1948, they served well in Korea as shown by this example. (*National Museum of the United States Air Force*)

over the soldier's head and some even piped exhaust-heated air to the litter area and added plasma bottle mounts on the outside of the cabin.

Recce and Special Missions

During Korea, the F4U-4Ps were fitted with a 90-degree lens prism to permit photography behind as the aircraft pulled up from an attack pass, capturing immediate post-strike imagery. The RB-26s pioneered the adoption of SHORAN to help locate their targets. Several B-26s got the gear to identify and locate enemy air defense radar.

The RF-80s flew the highest number of jet-powered recce missions. Field modifications produced F-80Cs with recce cameras until seventy or so RF-80Cs were created via conversion at Lockheed for the emergency. The recce F2H-2P were as prevalent. Found in composite squadrons and marine units afloat and ashore, their workload was high and persistent, though always escorted on missions.

The RB-45s were quite important for high-speed and high-altitude photorecce. Yet with so few in service, they suffered from a spares shortage. However, three RB-45s were deployed to Japan with missions extended over the Far East to include photo mapping all of Manchuria. This mission was considered so vital that, when the canopy was found to be deficient and risked cabin depressurization, reworked parts were rapidly fabricated and airlifted to the theater. The risk to recce jets posed by the MiG-15 was cause to adapt a small number of Sabres with cameras replacing some of the guns in the nose. These RF-86As were a field modification devised by the operators.

The presence of the RB-45C detachment offered an opportunity to supplement the RB-29s that were finding missions over some areas greatly restricted by enemy air defenses. The Tornados began flying sorties in early 1951 and evaded the opposition until April when a crew barely escaped a MiG encounter. They continued to fly into the northwest corner of North Korea with fighter escort after the RB-29s were banned entirely. The RB-45Cs were then restricted from the area beginning in November following another close call. One of the aircraft was shot down by a MiG-15 in December 1950 as the USAF's first loss of a jet bomber to an interceptor. An attempt was made at night recce only to find that buffeting with the bay doors open for the release of photoflash expendables spoiled the photography—an astonishing discovery for an aircraft supposedly thoroughly tested and deployed operationally.

The Americans continued their wide-ranging photo and ELINT reconnaissance missions with higher tempo to assess Soviet and Chinese capabilities and intentions. There was clearly an expanding role for airborne radar and electronic warfare assets. However, through summer 1953, these adversaries downed eleven air force and navy aircraft.

Liaison and Assault

Initial deployments to the peninsular were by L-4s and L-5s flying from Japan with Jeep fuel tanks installed in the back seat and plumbed into the aircraft's supply. Along with

A workhorse of the American photorecon effort in Korea was the navy's F2H-2P, like that shown here (123366). Both ship- and land-based units contributed. Unarmed and a straight-wing jet, it had to be escorted on its missions. (*Naval Aviation Archives*)

its motley collection of aircraft, the U.S. Army also found itself with a severe shortage of ground crew and pilots at the outbreak of war. Mobilization of reservists helped answer the immediate needs of the emergency. Thirty-day refresher training was provided before crews were deployed to theater. The flying was tough given the mountainous terrain with few options for an emergency landing. The H-13 light helicopters were the best answer to this. However, more than 100 small strips were eventually bulldozed to accommodate the operations. Units moved frequently until the front stabilized. The legacy of the last war was revisited with parcel drops from under the wings.

The vintage L-5s were not in the best of shape and parts were in short supply, while the other "grasshoppers" were barely suitable. The great need for liaison machines compelled the army to take up forty-three L-13As from the Air Force. Most were employed stateside to permit standard L-types to be deployed overseas. The civilian types, like the Ryan L-17, would normally have had no role in a warzone, but were pressed into service nonetheless. New equipment eventually made it to Korea. The L-19, when first arriving in February 1951, was very welcome, especially with its VHF radio and blind-flying instruments. The first L-20 arrived in December 1951.

Army helicopters began to undertake important replenishment missions. The first mass helicopter airlift missions were also flown. The promise was there and the need for more capable rotorcraft was evident. Although desiring five H-19C transport companies, USAF opposition and aircraft delivery rate permitted only two in the near-term. These were active in the last months of the war. Also, H-21s were on order.

The marines had a similar experience with their OE-1 versions of the L-19 and Sikorsky HRS-2s.

Transports

The transports would have had much more difficulty, if not for proximity to Japan. Much freight was flown directly from the U.S. mainland by C-124s, and C-97s contributed especially in bringing home wounded. However, true strategic airlifters were needed. Much good work was performed at minimal forward airstrips, but true assault airplanes were also needed.

Both USAF and USMC C-119s/R4Qs contributed in Korea. The USAF contingent especially supported airdrops to include the two large-scale paratroop assaults of around 3,300 troops each. These were supported by parachute delivery of heavy equipment that involved jeeps, trucks, and howitzers, plus 2,000,000 lb (907,180 kg) of fuel. This was the first combat test of such airdrop capabilities, and more followed. Notable was heavy equipment dropped to the marines at Chosen Reservoir. These included eight Bailey Bridge segments delivered from 900 feet (274 m) under heavy ground fire. They were quickly assembled and facilitated troop movement south. Transports also performed ersatz bombing with experimental night drops of 55-gallon drums of napalm.

The early model Flying Boxcars suffered from maintenance issues and parts shortages. The propeller blades developed fatigue cracks that could produce a sudden catastrophic failure and potential aircraft loss. Until resolved, the aircraft were prohibited from carrying passengers except for urgent airdrops.

A C-46 takes on a jeep in support of Korean combat in a laborious operation given the side cargo door and sloping deck of the airplane. Such complications and the need to operate from minimal airfields under combat conditions emphasized the need for true assault transports. Such were under development, but too late for Korea. (*National Archives*)

The navy was learning that operating very small fleets of unique aircraft like the JRM and R6O transports were costly and inefficient. These and its transport squadrons had been an expression of independence with the formation of MATS, and strong suspicion that the USAF could not suitably meet particular navy needs. However, Korea and other experiences showed such attitudes and pique to be unfounded and undercutting best use of funds for specific naval missions. Things began to change after the war.

In Sum

Many aircraft capabilities fell short in Korea, especially at the beginning. Yet much excelled as well, especially the ability to react with improvements, introducing new types, and adapting to a limited war. Innovative tactics, battlefield alterations, and rapid modifications back home helped respond to the unexpected. Fortunately, aircraft and weapons were then still built relatively quickly and simply enough for designs to be optimized for the war's conditions and new models to be introduced in the span of the war.

14

Precipitous

The eight years between the end of World War Two and the end of the Korean Conflict was a period of extraordinary advancement in American military aviation. Many new aircraft and systems were introduced in quick succession of ever-increasing capabilities. Trying to meet the new warfare dimensions of nuclear weapons, intercontinental reach, and supersonic speeds brought forth systems without precedence, while others faded. The Korean experience showed how some of the preparation has sound and others wanting. Efforts were redoubled as the communists showed they were willing to push the West into shooting wars, at least by proxy. In retrospect, it all appeared a precipitous rush to create military assets on an enormous and costly scale to confront the Soviet Union that responded in kind.

Another Step Forward

The American military aviation and aerospace industry grew in competencies throughout the period. While the number of aircraft procured was small by the measure of the recent total war, and initially paced by shrinking budgets, resources were built, many new weapon types established, and a steady growth in performance was produced with each new system and model. Development resources were adjusted in response to new programs and operating regimes sought.

The rapid advance in aircraft design, flight regime, and military aviation expectations drove continuous technical risk in designs. Analytical and ground test capabilities moved ahead to keep pace, but they were occasionally imbalanced or design teams were behind available means. Wind tunnels, engine test cells, inflight testbeds, research aircraft, and more supported the industry, academia, and government laboratories. The military/NACA partnership in research was sustained and published detailed design guidance and standards to help reduce risk. Yet even a team as capable as Grumman developed a shockingly deficient airplane in the XF10F-1.

Technologies moved just as rapidly during World War Two. However, although the U.S. conducted robust R&D and experimentation, it pushed comparatively fewer technologies into new designs. Wartime production focused on upgrading existing designs, with nearly 90 percent of the aircraft manufactured consisted of just nineteen types. Consequently, the U.S. companies and labs had some catching up to do postwar.[1] Manufacturing was at a more modest volume, but more varied, while R&D continued apace. More design innovations were attempted and some pushed to fleet assets in seeking operational advantages during a time in which anything seemed possible.

It was a period of extraordinary change and progress in propulsion systems as the jet engine dominated and matured rapidly, both as the turbojet and ramjet. The military services rapidly adapted to the operational implications of jets. There was initially enough uncertainty in the reliability of the powerplants that the services developed fighter types with both recips and jet engines, and non-combat types were still being developed using vintage piston motors at the end of this period. The initially modest performance of the turbojet compelled the development of augmentation and adjustable area nozzles, and these were just becoming commonplace. The immediate solution for practical take-off performance was the addition of JATO rockets in several forms, including semi-permanent installations. The added complexity and cost were taken as a necessary evil until engine thrust could compensate—which it did within a few years.

The engine tumult was very disruptive. Many a worthy airplane design fell by the wayside owing to engine development shortcomings. For example, after Westinghouse produced the J34, a good and reliable engine, all their products were problem-plagued and under-performing, including the J40 and J46. The navy, particularly, had invested heavily in these powerplants and most of its second-generation jets were initially

An RB-45C (48-033) and a B-29 (44-69862, in October 1948) are taking off at Muroc with the assistance of liquid propellant rocket boosters. These experimental Aerojet units suggest the efforts made to augment the take-off thrust of bombers and other heavy aircraft. By summer 1953, turbojets had grown in thrust to the extent that such measures were bound to fade in time. (*Air Force Test Center*)

directed to fit them. When the engines fell well short and efforts were made to replace them, programs were greatly delayed and resulting performance below expectations. This outcome saw Westinghouse exit the jet engine business entirely. Early turboprops gave much the same desultory outcomes.

The following table shows, for turbojet engines, the progress made.[2] For a quadrupling in thrust, a roughly 65 percent improvement in SFC was achieved, addressing one of the greatest grievances with the first generation of turbojets.

Aircraft Engine Characteristics

Engine	Developer	Year Introduced	Thrust (lbf)	SFC	Weight (lb)	Thrust:Weight	Notes
J30 (19XB)	Westinghouse	1944	1,350	1.27	732	1.85	
J31 (I-16)	GE	1944	1,650	1.20	805	2.05	
J33 (I-40)	GE	1944	4,000	1.19	1,850	2.15	Allison production
J35 (TG-180)	GE	1944	4,000	1.08	2,399	1.67	Allison production
J34 (24C)	Westinghouse	1945	2,650	1.05	1,257	2.11	
J40	Westinghouse	1948	6,000	2.20	3,499	1.72	canceled
J42	P&W	1948	5,000	1.09	1,715	2.92	licensed Nene
J47	GE	1948	5,200	1.03	2,524	2.06	dry thrust
J48	P&W	1949	6,255	1.00	2,002	3.13	equivalent Tay
J57	P&W	1950	9,000	0.82	4,839	1.86	twin spool
J71	Allison	1950	8,090	0.88	4,090	1.98	
J65	Wright	1951	7,400	0.93	2,796	2.65	licensed Sapphire
J73	GE	1952	7,825	0.81	3,649	2.15	

As in other periods of aviation history, engines could make or break a program. For example, the Allison preproduction T40 never reached acceptable reliability and brought down numerous programs employing it—though all had other deficiencies. However, every failure generates experience and lessons. These disappointments placed Allison on the path to their very successful T56, first run on the bench in September 1953, which would be the first standout success of American turboprops. As always, relying on a developmental engine to power a developmental aircraft greatly increased the technical risk of the program. Yet during this period, there appeared few options as requirements kept pressing the state of the art in both realms.

The significant achievements during the period reviewed are listed in the accompanying table. There were few comparable periods in aviation history, during peace or war.

Development of the turboprop engine was begun concurrent with the turbojet, but it took longer to mature into reliable products. Several aircraft projects attempted to employ the early models, usually to their grief. In particular, the Allison T40, shown here, was the bane of several, including the Convair P5Y seen beyond. (*San Diego Air & Space Museum*)

Summary of Significant Achievements

Developmental
Transonic wind tunnels achieved, displacing other data collection methods
Design guidance for transonic flight perfected and used widespread
Initial moves to investigate hypersonic flight
Computers began to be used in design
Variable stability testbeds developed
Formal X-plane research aircraft adopted
VSTOL and VTOL aircraft being developed experimentally, to include "tailsitters"
First vertical flight on jet engine efflux with reaction controls
Many new aircraft configurations flown and some adopted as fleet assets
Fighter carry-along demonstrated (towing and hookup) but soon dismissed
Tracked undercarriage developed, to include fully retractable
The tanker-transport aircraft class created
Airborne Early Warning become standard and flying command posts inaugurated
Second-generation jet fighters in production

Flight to Mach 2.6 and nearly 80,000 feet, Mach 2 combat aircraft in development
Turboprop transports and fighters maturing
Ultimate combat gliders developed, then entire category eliminated
Heavy lift helicopter demonstrated and fleet assets in development
Joint production by multiple manufacturers of vital systems and aircraft undertaken
Systems
Ejection seat perfected and adopted as common
Speedbrakes and drag parachutes become common
Runway arrestment barriers introduced and tailhooks for land-based airplanes under development
Tricycle undercarriage and nose wheel steering becomes common
Bomber and patrol aircraft turrets reduced to just tail units
High-pressure hydraulic systems developed and adopted
Fully boosted and irreversible flight controls adopted
Redundancy and safety emphasized
Cabin pressurization, anti-ice and deice, and other features made common
Avionics as integral and essential elements of combat aircraft established
Radar adopted as common combat aircraft equipment
Night and all-weather fighters disappear as unique types
EW operationally common and with dedicated aircraft
Airborne ASW assets matured to resources carried to present day
Airplane and helicopter towing perfected but set aside
Propulsion
End of the era of high-powered piston engine development, except for turbo-compound
Hybrid propulsion, with recip and jet, fielded and then dismissed
Podded jet units begin to be added to recip airplanes as a means to boost speed
In-flight investigation of supersonic propellers, and in supersonic flight, imminent
Turbojet augmentation perfected
Optimal jet fuels developed to accepted standard and widely fielded
Small turbojets developed for missiles and drones
Work on turboprop and turboshaft engines about to pay off
Ramjet and pulsejet engines perfected and deployed, first manned aircraft flown on ramjets
Tip jet propulsion for rotorcraft developed to operational level
Rockets as supplemental thrust source thoroughly explored
Weapons
The rocket adopted as an air-to-air weapon
Air-to-ground guided weapons accepted and maturing
Functional air-to-air guided missiles developed, but much refinement lay ahead
Rotary-barrel 20-mm cannon (later Vulcan) under test, to become primary armament in later fighters
Fission weapons made practical, produced in large numbers, and reduced to size for fighter-bomber employment
Flight
Supersonic achieved, allowed in service types, and achievable in level flight for combat aircraft
Highly swept surfaces in multiple planforms developed and adopted to fleet aircraft
Demonstrated variable geometry in manned aircraft

Fully booted aircraft controls and stability augmentation becoming common
Supersonic seaplane fighter demonstrated
Navy began flying the largest aircraft it would ever operate from a carrier, and the largest flying boat
The Air Force operated the largest aircraft in its history
Cruise missiles and other wing-borne missiles developed, including submarine launch
Operational
Operational adaptation of jets completed, to include introduction of barriers
Jet fighter-bombers shown to be operationally effective in ground support
Highly swept aero surface aircraft adopted as common
Aircraft carriers greatly altered in adaptation to jets with safety innovations
Jet bombers become common, with markedly smaller crews and self-defense weapons
Unrefueled intercontinental bomber range achieved, but then surrendered
Unrefueled long-range bomber escort pursued then abandoned
Three methods of aerial refueling perfected and made operational as essential combat support resource
The age of tip tanks and JATO, though end in sight
Jet trainers on the verge of adoption
Tactical airlifter perfected
Tactical airdrop developed to operational level
Final evolution of military flying boat, but demise in sight
Helicopter reliability and performance made acceptable, in all rotor configurations, permitting them to become commonplace in many roles to include large cabin-class types
Navy adopted helicopters a carrier-based asset
The form of ASW aircraft for decades to follow were established
Heliborne assault and replenishment adopted, including amphibious ops
The largest operational lighter-than-air airship adopted, but end in sight
Combat gliders and catapult seaplanes eliminated
All services aptly fought a war while in a equipment transitional phase

The push out in airspeed and altitude seemed to have no limit. By summer 1953, the experimental flights had reached just shy of Mach 2 and 80,000 feet (24,284 m) manned and Mach 2.6 unmanned. Supersonic airspeed in level flight had been reached with a combat aircraft, and production was imminent in summer 1953. Supersonic combat was shaping up as only a dash capability given the very high fuel consumption of AB. Transonic and supersonic flight drove marked changes in aircraft design to sustain the stress of the flight regime, reduce drag, and ensure suitable S&C.

Due to the rapidly changing powerplants, onboard systems, weapons, and flight regimes, the reliability of the new aircraft and missiles did not advance markedly. They were all labor-intensive, demanding levels of support much greater than present-day equivalents. Fortunately, personnel costs were relatively low. Performance was emphasized over such factors. Additionally, the fast pace of change meant the costly aircraft were often modified and upgraded rather than replaced. In some cases, this was to correct deficiencies built-in during a precipitously quick move to production.

The development of aerial refueling to large-scale operational employment was a monumental achievement. This went from concept to practical fleet application in just a few years as perhaps the innovation with the greatest long-term implications. Three AR schemes were adopted, productionized, and fielded, owing to the urgency. Large contracts for tankers and receiver modifications were promulgated, and operational means were growing rapidly. The Americans led in AR deployment and would field more tankers and receivers than all other nations combined from then to now.

Aerial refueling helped to ameliorate the combat implications of high turbojet fuel consumption rate, restoring range and endurance. It was especially important for the long-range bomber, permitting intercontinental range without carrying all the fuel required for the mission in an enormous aircraft. It could also have answered, in part, the bomber escort conundrum, although the mission had largely been dismissed by summer 1953 as impractical and possibly unnecessary. The potential as a force multiplier for tactical aviation was clear and the capability was set to grow. It was shown as operationally effective over Korea.

Helicopters became commonplace and moved into many roles. The army and Marine Corps' move towards transport helicopters for battlefield mobility had begun, though with marginal rotorcraft. The machines were on the verge of a marked performance and suitability increase with turboshaft engines within reach.

There was only a gradual change in nuclear weapons and delivery systems through the end of the period, but the stage was set for rapid advancement. Weapon weight and size were reduced while kiloton yield increased, and the associated fielded weapons plus warheads were just being released. They could be carried by fighter-bombers and more easily delivered by carrier-based aircraft. The weapons became more flexible and easier to use.

The KB-29 was important in refueling jet bombers that suffered range deficits owing to the high fuel consumption of the turbojet's engines. The first to be refueled by a boom from the XB-29P (44-86363 shown) was the B-45, although here represented by a RB-45C (48-012). The scene is likely testing over Edwards AFB in 1950. (*Air Force Test Center History Office*)

Above: A marine HRS-2 hauls a sling load from the USS *Sicily* (CVE-118) to a Korean location on September 2, 1952, with another helicopter on the deck preparing to do the same. The USMC and the army had come a long way in a few years in introducing rotorcraft as a common element in their battlefield transportation, propelled by the conflict. (*National Archives*)

Below: From 1945 when the U.S. Navy was openly suspicious of helicopters and swore that the "whirlybirds" would never appear on an aircraft carrier deck, within a few years, they were spending serious money on rotorcraft and betting the lives of fixed-wing aviators on the ability of plane-guard helicopters to rescue them from the sea. Naval helicopters and those supporting marine operations had become essential. Here, a HUP-1 works to recover the crew of an AF, from the USS *Block Island* (CVE-21), that went into the "drink" on August 12, 1953. (*National Archives*)

Guided munitions and autonomous weapon systems were growing in number under development, though few were produced in quantity. The vacuum tube technology of the period, with high power, cooling, and volume demands, brought integration and reliability difficulties. Indeed, nearly all of the long-range, wing-borne, and autonomously guided missiles of the era were costly and resource-consuming failures or persisted in unusually prolonged developments. While it may be said that the airmen of both services were at best ambivalent regarding the success of these systems, their leadership committed tremendous money and credibility to the programs that impacted airplane programs.

The push into new types of weapons with expanded capabilities engendered much waste, though barely evident at the time owing to the proliferation of programs, secrecy, and the immaturity of the systems. An example is the 268 Navy F3D night fighter that only went to sea on a carrier once and was only operated in its intended role by the marines. While the new defense establishment sought to contain redundant and ineffective acquisitions, this was only marginally successful. Many systems were placed into production early in development to ensure capabilities were field as soon as possible given the rapid advancements in the field. However, some were also to keep the contractor in the "black" and take advantage of available funds before budget cuts. One can argue that even troubled developments should be pushed to yield the necessary lessons making the next weapon more successful, especially in a period of new potential. Yet many of these weapons were fielded despite their glaring flaws and marginal capabilities in performing their missions. They were also pressed into service for the sake of influencing Soviet behavior, plus showing progress and results so that funding would continue for the next system.

The extensive and largely fruitless work on cruise missiles was emblematic of the waste, yet also an eagerness to press ahead with the technology to gain ultimately a truly effective system. For example, squadrons of Matadors, developed during this period, and its brother Mace, were deployed to Europe in the latter half of the 1950s with 200 missiles. With the low reliability and accuracy of these cumbersome weapons, the 200 were too few for a significant operational impact employing conventional warheads. All would likely have to have been fired at a single enemy air base to have any reasonable expectation of knocking it out. With atomic warheads, they would become more effective, though expanding the risk of employing such weapons.

One might conclude that the pursuit of the possible exceeded the practical. This led to some excessively risky developments that, not surprisingly, failed or found no operational applications. The tailsitting vertical take-off and landing fighters were but one example, added to flying by periscope. Some seriously deficient systems were fielded regardless, making them "hollow" weapons. There was simply too little experience with the new technologies for clear perception and too much faith in the technologies. The link between requirements and programs was unclear in some cases; the development agencies pursuing what appeared useful in pushing performance. The navy, particularly, was prone to reach for risky mission solutions to justify and sustain its aviation arm.

Both the navy and air force developed examples of the first generation of cruise missiles. The navy launched its Regulus from submarines (shown) and ship decks while the air force's Matador was shot from land. Both were very similar in technology and capabilities, meaning that they were unreliable and inaccurate. Fielded nonetheless, only the addition of nuclear warheads in the late 1950s made them of any meaningful value. (*Air Force Test Center*)

Future Indicative

The capabilities and advancement trends established during the eight-year period were a guide to what was coming. Fundamentally, the system types and capabilities that would persist to the present day were established, and some of the individual aircraft and weapons served for decades.

From Korea, the Americans came to appreciate the limitations in the application of military power. It had to accept war with limited goals, then a negotiated armistice. More tons of bombs were dropped on Korea than on Japan in the last war, and most of the North Korean industry was destroyed. China and the USSR sustained the enemy with impunity. The North Koreans always managed to move supplies to the front despite the repeated destruction of their transportation system. A third world war, with the exchange of atomic munitions, was avoided, and so the Cold War would be waged with limited objectives and political restraints. Given the confrontation around the world, and especially helping defend allies in Europe, there was always a "balancing act" meeting projected threats and operational exigencies. This would affect national choices in the future, with Vietnam a similar experience.

The Department of Defense's structure of leadership and development resources would remain fundamentally unchanged beyond 1953. The worse of the air force and navy acrimony over roles and missions passed, but all services continued to battle over the budget and which programs should be continued. Influenced by these and contractor lobbying, oversight by Congress of all the DoD programs continued to lack the "teeth" to require more rigorous accounting and cancelation of poorly performing efforts. Despite the ever-increasing costs of systems, the services and industry were only diffidently pushed to economize during the coming decade before another war opened coffers again.

The navy had won its relevance in the new realities of strategic reach and nuclear delivery. It was grim up until Korea demonstrated the continued necessity of conventional weapons and the hesitancy to employ nuclear ordnance. The aircraft carrier and its aviation assets were vital and so revitalized. Carrier upgrades proceeded and the first Forrestal class "super carrier" would be commissioned in 1955. However, it was only the reduced size of atomic weapons and the advent of submarine-launched ballistic models that would cement the navy's strategic role. Mobile Basing and the Sea Strike Force were shown to be impractical. Most of the department's efforts at carrier-based and seaplane bombers, VTOL fighters, cruise missiles, and the like either came to naught, were ineffective or too costly, or generated inefficient systems soon adapted to other roles.

The flying boat and airship were a very costly and labor-intensive way to perform sea patrol. By the mid-1950s, landplane alternatives were superior and carrier-based counterparts suitably effective. Efforts to develop the flying boat into a high-speed, jet-powered bomber to deliver nuclear weapons—though not the stated goal of the P6M—was also beached by the advent of newer super carriers with heavy strike aircraft capable of delivering the "nukes." The Polaris ballistic missile was being developed to be fired from nuclear-powered submarines to hit distant targets with nuclear warheads. The flying boat and airship were simply no longer needed. Yet the navy's struggle saw considerable funds expended over many years and interesting aircraft developed.[3]

The reduced size of atomic weapons permitting fighter-bombers to become delivery platforms, ensuring greater accuracy and survivability than the ineffectual cruise missiles. It would be decades before the latter became effective with autonomy, solid-state electronics, and superior navigation subsystems. The H-bomb was just around the corner to start the cycle again.

The push for greater speed for combat survivability and more assured intercept soon appeared to become an end unto itself. This undermined the mission flexibility of the aircraft. The USAF and USN also seemed determined to continue producing heavy and complex specialized airplanes despite the evidence of Korea that multirole machines were advisable. The army and marines, particularly, repeatedly emphasized the apparent neglect in supporting ground force operations. Although standoff weapons for air-to-air and air-to-ground were expected to compensate to some degree, these were still more than a decade from becoming effective.

The deployment of B-29s to begin quickly operating against the North Koreans demonstrated the effectiveness of SAC mobility plans and training. The air force as a whole was becoming more operationally mobile. The ability of these bombers to also assume tactical roles after strategic targets were destroyed, or as demanded

Among the improvements being introduced in U.S. Navy carriers was the "canted" deck. This permitted aircraft to land on this deck and execute a bolter if the trap was missed, while launches were executed on the starboard side. As shown in this January 14, 1953, image—an F9F-5 being positioned on the "cat" while an AD-4N flies off the canted deck—this greatly reduced risk of collisions on the deck that had grown with the introduction of jet aircraft. (*National Archives*)

The complex naval aviation missions, serviced by numerous aircraft categories carried over from the war, made for a very diverse fleet of aircraft during the decade following World War Two. Illustrating this, the image shows a portion of the NAS Patuxent River, Naval Air Test Center, *c.* August 1950. Visible is a Grumman F8F, a developmental Vought F7U-1, a Douglas AD-3W in the company of another AD, and a Grumman UF-1 Albatross. (*National Archives*)

Above left: Progress with ballistic missile development showed such promise by summer 1953 that the potential was beginning to affect aircraft acquisition decisions by the services. This Viking rocket, launching from White Sands in late 1952, is exemplary of the achievements. (*National Archives*)

Above right: In just eight years, the U.S. jet fighter had grown from underpowered airplanes reminiscent of the war's prop-driven types to supersonic, swept-wing warplanes with several times the thrust. This is exemplified by a subsonic Lockheed P-80B (45-8480) powered by a General Electric J33 delivering 5,200 lbf with water injection and the supersonic North American YF-100A (52-5754) with a Pratt & Whitney J57 giving 15,000 lbf in afterburner. The latter was the first of what would become the famous Century Series of the 1960s and serve in America's next Far East Asia war. (*National Museum of the United States Air Force*)

by battlefield circumstances, was a good lesson. However, it was an open question whether the newer jet bombers could perform similarly.

The AR resources born in the early 1950s served for decades and were the foundation for that which survives to the present day. Receiver capability would thereafter become part of specifications for each new combat type. Tactical Air Command had initially played second fiddle to SAC for AR resources. However, in the latter half of the 1950s, TAC would take up castoff B-50s as tankers with underwing turbojet engine pods added to partially address speed incompatibility. The KC-97s also received podded jets, extending their usefulness while awaiting the jet-powered KC-135. The navy's own move into AR for its shipboard aircraft—with tankers, suitably equipped receivers, and a "buddy" AR pod—only bore operational fruit in the late 1950s.

A Convair B-36D (49-2657), photographed in perhaps 1951, is contrasted with one of the Boeing YB-52s (49-231) photographed on November 21, 1952. The B-36 was a World War Two program that, postwar, was central to true American intercontinental bombing with atomic weapons, and subjected to extensive rework over a decade to include adding the jet engine pods to become a ten-engine bomber. The eight-engine B-52 was still developmental in summer 1953 and relied on aerial refueling for its intercontinental reach. (*National Archives*)

The early difficulties in moving forces into Korea, and then sustaining them, was a lesson taken to heart. More effort would be made for strategic transports in addition to the associated base resources. Most aircraft could not self-deploy because of a short range or the unacceptable wear-and-tear of such a long ferry—if such was possible or safe at all. A great many USAF aircraft had to be brought over on the decks of aircraft carriers—risking the common saltwater corrosion—or the holds of transports. Self-deployment of fighters via AR was demonstrated in Korea, but many other aircraft such as light-planes and helicopters would remain bound to sea transport. It would be many decades before they could be airlifted into theater.

The USAF continued working to meet the commitment to the Army in providing mobility via tactical transports. The tactical resupply and airdrop successes during Korea pointed to the future, but more investment would be essential. Continuing to employ reciprocating engines, these were little advanced beyond those from the world war until the advent of the Lockheed C-130. In the same vein, the stage was set for the rotorcraft that would support the next war. As combat aircraft, the prop-equipped aircraft were clearly on their way out. The last Corsairs were retired from naval service in the latter half of the 1950s, but the AD persisted in navy and air force service through the next war.

Jet engines continued improving at a fast pace and would power some of the finest American combat aircraft, on the drawing boards at the end of the period. It meant accepting the risk of applying a developmental engine to a developmental aircraft, despite warnings evident in recent experience. The greater thrust and augmentation would see the end of routine JATO use during the next decade. Likewise, integral rocket motors for combat enhancement were shelved with jet engine progress and the advent of AAM making such measures of too little benefit. The introduction of swept wings spelled the general demise of tip tanks as well.

Essentially, the form of turbine engines to follow, and the problems to address, were well established. The turboprop would mature in a few years to improve greatly transport performance and sustainability—likewise for the turboshaft, which was so important for helicopters. Tip propulsion for rotors was dismissed. Only the turbofan and thrust reversing were yet to be explored. Variable geometry inlets to improve efficiency across a range of operating conditions became necessary as airspeed moved significantly supersonic. Attempts to push ramjets to very large dimensions and power generation had failed, and they were soon limited to missile applications.

Given the Cold War, R&D funding continued to flow following the end of the Korean Conflict. Although there were some cuts, the decline experienced at the end of the world wars was not repeated. Indeed, many of the larger development efforts had not been intended for operation in Korea, but rather the wider confrontation with the USSR. This would continue to grow to mammoth proportions. Yet development began to slow as aircraft served effectively longer.

Flight safety continued to advance as a design priority. Ejection seat tests progressed to higher speeds and more severe conditions, including supersonic flight. Wheel brakes improved in energy capacity and use of anti-skid. Crash safety, subsystem redundancy and reliability, and more were introduced with each new type and many new models. Yet development and fielding of these increasingly complex machines were growing longer and more costly. The B-52 would be seven years from concept to combat capability, and the development up to initial production ran approximately $100 million.

Among the miscellany, the zero-launch capability, using rocket boost, for winged missiles would be extended to manned aircraft for evaluation, though not adopted. The hydro-ski work continued for a few more years, although full-scale experience had been disappointing, and then extended to the potential for hydrofoil application to aircraft. This faded away with the seaplane itself as helicopters assumed the associated roles.

Doing Better

World War Two had taught the Americans that the nation had to be prepared for farsighted threats and eventualities. It did not want to be caught unprepared again. Yet Korea found the country only beginning to equip suitably to meet the communists in a shooting war anywhere, and so still short of the required capabilities. This was especially true when it became clear national leadership and the U.N. would contain the conflict within Korean borders and nuclear armaments employment was *verboten*. The Cold War would see continuing progress and more lethal weapons fielded. This became a seemingly endless arms race for the next weapon to exceed projected adversary capabilities. It is questionable whether all the weapons contained communist adventurism—if also making them feel beleaguered by superior hostile forces.

In preparing for the next wars, it is always a question of which weapons, to what quantity, and at what cost to the nation. Responding to a perceived need, as skewed by the parochial interests of each military service, the number and variety of armaments continued to mount, and the Treasury to be further strained. Beyond summer 1953, acquisitions sought to meet another limited war as well as an international nuclear exchange, with acquisition meeting these ends often competing and filling only one mission. The weapons for the conventional war fell short again as demonstrated by the Vietnam experience a decade later. The nuclear combat capabilities were, fortunately, never tested in combat.

National capabilities would continue to grow to meet the weapons sought, creating an enormous and costly network feeding seemingly insatiable military demand. What President Dwight Eisenhower would warn about with the phrase "military industrial complex" had taken root and would grow for the next couple of decades. It wielded considerable influence in sustaining appropriations addressing the communist foe of the ever-expanding threat level.

As a matter of aviation technology advancement and history, it was all fascinating and stimulating. However, with the Soviets and Chinese responding in kind, and more proxy wars emerging, the world became a more dangerous place.

This is Convair's concept of the NX-2 nuclear-powered bomber with direct-cycle General Electric engines in the aft fuselage and conventional turbojet "boosters" under the wings. The layout, with canards, placed the nuclear engines and aircrew the greatest distance apart to facilitate radiation shielding. The exciting period of aircraft advancements, with numerous radical designs, facilitated such concepts. (*San Diego Air & Space Museum*)

Endnotes

Chapter One

1   It was learned later that it was 1951 before the USSR tested their first aircraft-delivered bomb, and years more before a significant number of weapons were in service.

2   Meyer, C. C., *Grumman F9F Panther, Part One: Development, Testing, Structures*, Naval Fighters Number Fifty-Nine (Simi Valley, California: Steve Ginter, 2002) p. 23, and Winchester, J., "Type Analysis—Vought F7U Cutlass, The Navy's 'Widowmaker,'" *International Air Power Review*, Volume 15, 2005, p. 111.

3   A C-54 flew from Dayton, Ohio, to Brize Norton, U.K., and returned in September 1947 under automatic control. The author assumes that the aircraft was landed manually since auto-coupled landing systems did not then exist.

4   Knaack, M. S., *Encyclopedia of US Air Force Aircraft and Missile Systems, Volume II: Post-World War II Bombers, 1945–1973* (Washington, D. C.: Office of Air Force History, 1988), p. 488, note 21.

5   Abel, A., *Fairchild's Golden Age*, The Golden Age of Aviation Series (Brawley, California: Wind Canyon Books, 2008), p. 120.

6   The armed services collaborated on the development of jet fuels. The first was JP-1 (Jet Propellant) from the war that was pure kerosene and had an unacceptably high flashpoint and low freezing value. JP-2 raised the freezing point but saw limited use while JP-3 was even less used. JP-4 was introduced in 1951 and was a 50-50 blend of kerosene and gasoline, reducing the flashpoint. The navy adopted JP-5 in 1952 with an even lower flashpoint. This was for use on aircraft carriers where the risk of fire is particularly grave. JP-4 and JP-5 became the standard jet fuels for decades.

7   Darling, K., *NAA B-45 Tornado*, Warpaint Series No. 118 (Bedfordshire, England: Warpaint Books, date not specified), p. 40. The occasional turbine failures were the reason the services began to mark on the cowling or fuselage the location of the turbine ring within as a caution zone for those working around the jet during ground operations. Likewise, warning markings were applied, indicating the jet exhaust and intakes. Even more insidious was the example of the Westinghouse J46 that used magnesium compressor cases that grew "whiskers" of material when contaminated by salt water in sea ops. The compressor blades were soon brushing the case walls. Cleaning away the contamination was done by spraying fresh water and ground walnut shells into the operating engine. Another interesting aspect of the adoption of jet engines to aircraft was that standard aircraft instruments had needles that tended to stick because they lacked the vibration common with propeller-driven aircraft. Until improved instruments were developed, some aircraft had vibrators attached to instrument panels to counter sticking needles.

8   Even in 1948, the new GE J47 needed an inspection at 7.5 hours and then, if passed, could
     operate another 7.5 hours before overhaul. Knaack, *Post-World War II Bombers*, p. 75.
     This was improving steadily, but it would still be years before turbojets had time-between-
     overhauls exceeding recips. Even the reliable J35 suffered excessive tailpipe temperatures with
     the early F-84 installations and had a mean life of just forty hours. Even in the seemingly
     mature F-84E, the mean time between overhauls was 100 hours. Willis, D., "Warplane
     Classic—Republic F-84 Thunderjet, Thunderstreak & Thunderflash," *International Air Power
     Review*, Volume 24, 2008, pp. 136–137.

9   The leap in performance represented by the J57 was so remarkable that the 1952 Collier
     Trophy went to Leonard S. Hobbs, chief engineer of United Aircraft Corporation (of which
     P&W was a division).

10 Loftin, L. F., Jr., *Quest for Performance, The Evolution of Modern Aircraft*, SP-468
     (Washington, D.C.: National Aeronautics and Space Administration, 1985), p. 138.

11 For the Douglas C-74, the fabric-covered control surfaces and tabs caused a problem in flight
     testing when, during a 340-mph (547-kph) dive of the second aircraft, ballooning of the
     fabric ahead of the elevator tabs disturbed the flow to an extent the tabs oscillated. This drove
     elevator motion that produced severe pitching and overloaded the outer wing panels. The
     panels broke away and the airplane had to be abandoned.

12 In June 1948, the Pursuit types were thereafter referred to as fighter, and aircraft designations
     changed from "P" to "F." Other classes of aircraft were also redesignated.

13 Munroe, C. L., Colonel, USAF, Chief, Maintenance Division, D/MS&S, Office, Deputy Chief
     of Staff, Materiel, "'Gem' Program Summary," Memorandum for Major General Whitten,
     August 26, 1948. See also Campbell, R. H., *The Silverplate Bomber, A History and Registry
     of the Enola Gay and Other B-29s Configured to Carry Atomic Bombs* (Jefferson, North
     Carolina: McFarland & Company, 2005), p. 23, and Pace, S., *Boeing B-29 Superfortress*
     (Wiltshire, United Kingdom: The Crowood Press, 2003), p. 108.

Chapter Two

1   Francillon, R. J., in *Grumman Aircraft Since 1929* (Annapolis, Maryland: Naval Institute
     Press, 1989), p. 214, Borchers, P. F., Franklin, J. A., and Fletcher, J. W., *Flight Research at
     Ames: Fifty-Seven of Development and Validation of Aeronautical Technology*, NASA/
     SP-1998-3300 (Moffett Field, California: National Aeronautics and Space Administration,
     1998), p. 29, and Hartman, E. P., *Adventures in Research, A History of Ames Research Center
     1940–1965*, NASA Center History Series, SP-4302 (Washington, D.C.: National Aeronautics
     and Space Administration, 1970), pp. 165–166.

2   Matthews, B., *Cobra!, Bell Aircraft Corporation 1934–1946* (Atglen, Pennsylvania: Schiffer,
     1996), pp. 226–230, provides a most thorough summary of this project and notes that the
     airplanes were given bureau numbers 90061 and 90062.

3   Corky Meyer, test pilot for the XF10F-1, admitted that a dual-redundant system was not then
     the norm, suggesting that the aircraft would have benefited from such for a critical function
     like wing sweep. Meyer, C. C., *Grumman Swing-Wing XF10F-1 Jaguar*, Naval Fighters
     Number Twenty-Six (Simi Valley, California: Steve Ginter, 1993), p. 7.

4   Meyer, *Grumman Swing-Wing XF10F-1 Jaguar*, p. 9.

5   *Ibid*, p. 21, points out that the aircraft required more than 2 miles to lift off at 130 mph (209
     kph).

6   These flights were conducted over sparsely populated and remote areas. When NACA Ames
     began supersonic dives with an F-86 in 1949 near the San Francisco Bay area, reports of
     explosions and buildings rattling began to come in. Soon, the mystery of the sonic boom was
     explained. However, Wright-Patterson AFB testers also claim to have determined the source of
     booms reported by the public.

7   Several rocket motor mishaps were caused by the deterioration of ulmer leather seals in the
     presence of LOX until this problem was identified and corrected.

8   Johnsen, F. A., *Testbeds, Motherships & Parasites, Astonishing Aircraft from the Golden Age of Flight Test* (North Branch, Minnesota: Specialty Press, 2018), p. 35, credits the XB-29G as being instigated by G.E. This contradicts other sources that have P&W as initially creating the testbed. Johnsen suggested on p. 54 that the P&W airplane was a different airframe, previously a Navy P2B, but fails to identify the serial or bureau number. The most often published photos of the aircraft with the tail number visible, and included with this text, are credited as showing it with the P&W J42. Andrade, J. M., *U.S. Military Aircraft Designations and Serials 1909–1979* (Leicester, United Kingdom: Midland Counties Publications, 1997), p. 206, does not reflect any of the four P2Bs as being used as an engine testbed. Pearcy, A., *Flying the Frontiers, NACA and NASA Experimental Aircraft* (Annapolis, Maryland: Naval Institute Press, 1993), p. 191, identifies the NACA B-29A engine testbed as 42-1808, which is a serial number not corresponding to any recorded production Superfortress.

9   The Germans made several flights of manned V-1 missiles dropped from a bomber and with the pulsejet operating. Also, as reported in Chapter 9, McDonnell claimed to be the first with their XH-20 rotorcraft with ramjet tip propulsion flying from mid-1947.

10   Chilstrom, K., and Leary, P., *Test Flying at Old Wright Field* (Omaha, Nebraska: Westchester House Publishers, 1995), p. 79. Despite this hazard, several civilian-owned Mustangs had ramjets added to the wingtips for racing or airshow displays.

11   The ram air turbine became common equipment for many jet aircraft that followed, though as emergency equipment.

12   Piet, S. and Raithal, A., *Martin P6M SeaMaster* (Bel Air, Maryland: Martineer Press, 2001), p. 25.

13   Boyne, W. J., "The Custer Channel Wing Story," *Airpower*, May 1977, Vol. 7 No. 3, p. 15.

14   Norton, B., "Tilt-Rotor Patriarch, Bell's XV-3 Convertiplane," *Air Enthusiast*, No. 115, January/February 2005, pp. 46–49, provides a more complete summary of Transcendental Aircraft's efforts.

15   Francillon, R. J., *McDonnell Douglas Aircraft Since 1920: Volume II* (Annapolis, Maryland: Naval Institute Press, 1990), pp. 412–414, provides the most complete HRH account.

Chapter Three

1   Neufeld, J., Watson, G. M., Jr., and Chenoweth, D. (ed.), *Technology and the Air Force, a Retrospective Assessment* (Washington, D.C.: Air Force History and Museums Program, United States Air Force, 1997), p. 98, note 37.

2   Hays, G., *Boeing B-50*, Air Force Legends Number 215 (Simi Valley, California: Steve Ginter, 2012), pp. 197–198.

3   Jenkins, D, R., *Magnesium Overcast, The Story of the Convair B-36*, (North Branch, Minnesota: Specialty Press, 2001–2002), p. 17, with reference. Wachsmuth, W., *B-36 Peacemaker*, In Detail & Scale Vol. 47 (Carrollton, Texas: Squadron/Signal Publications, 1997), p. 49, offers, without attribution, that the drag and weight of the tread gear imposed a 20 percent take-off distance penalty.

4   Chilstrom, K. and Leary, P., *Test Flying at Old Wright Field* (Omaha, Nebraska: Westchester House Publishers, 1995), pp. 22–23, Dorr, R. F., "Beyond the Frontiers: McDonnell XF-85," *Wings of Fame*, Vol. 7, 1997, p. 30, and Dorr, R. F., "Lockheed P-80 Shooting Star Variant Briefing," *Wings of Fame*, Vol. 11, 1998, pp. 132–133. This account highlights the bold flight testing being undertaken at the time, with risks accepted only slightly less than during the war. However, the poor test safety planning and lack of redundant mechanical systems evident for this and other projects would certainly not be allowed to stand for long.

5   Approaching the coupler from ahead of the wing would avoid the worse of the vortex effect, but also encounter the upwash or upward flow ahead of the wing.

6   The November 1947 range derives from Neufeld, *Technology and the Air Force*, p. 87.

7   Aerial refueling has also been known as air refueling, air-to-air refueling, flight refueling, and inflight refueling. This text will stick with AR.

8   Smith, R. K., *75 Years of Inflight Refueling Highlights, 1923–1998*, Air Force History and Museums Program (Washington, D. C.; U.S. Government Printing Office, 1998), p. 23. Tanner,

R. M., *History of Air-to-Air Refueling* (Barnsley, South Yorkshire, England; Pen & Sword Aviation, 2006), p. 39, states that the orders amounted to ninety-two kits to convert B-29s to KB-29Ms, seventy-four B-29 and fifty-seven B-50A receivers, plus B-36 receivers. This is a rare mention of B-36 AR that saw no material follow-up to the author's knowledge.

9   Single-point ground refueling meant that each tank or group of interconnected tanks of the aircraft had to be joined to a manifold valve that permitted fuel to be directed to all at once or individually, under pressure. Theretofore, the tanks usually had to be fueled individually from the top of the airplane via gravity in a time-consuming, cumbersome, and more hazardous process. So, despite the aerial refueling requirements that demanded such a manifold, the single-point refueling had operational benefits in permitting more rapid ground refueling.

10   Smith, *75 Years of Inflight Refueling Highlights*, p. 30.

11   *Ibid*, p. 31, and Air Mobility Command Office of History, *Aerial Refueling Highlights in the Air Force's First Decade 1947–1957* (Scott Air Force Base, Illinois: Air Mobility Command, US Air Force, May 1997), p. 12.

12   Lloyd, A. T., *Boeing's B-47 Stratojet*, (Atglen, Pennsylvania: Schiffer Publishing, 2005), p. 202, whereas Habermehl, C. M. and Hopkins III, R. S., *Boeing B-47 Stratojet, Strategic Air Command's Transitional Bomber*, (Manchester, England: Crécy Publishing, 2018), p. 225, states that the testing was in 1952 at Eglin AFB.

13   Byrd, V. B., *Passing Gas, The History of Inflight Refueling* (Chico, California: Byrd Publishing, 1994), p. 70.

14   McLaren, D. R., *Lockheed P-80/F-80 Shooting Star, A Photo Chronicle* (Atglen, Pennsylvania: Schiffer Publishing, 1996), p. 47.

15   Tuttle, J., *Eject!, The Complete History of U.S. Aircraft Escape Systems* (St. Paul, Minnesota: MBI Publishing, 2002), pp. 63 and 79.

16   Amtmann, H. H., *The Vanishing Paperclips; America's Aerospace Secret, A Personal Account* (Boylston, Massachusetts: Monogram Aviation Publications, 1988), pp. 90–95, Chilstrom, K., and Leary, P., *Test Flying at Old Wright Field* (Omaha, Nebraska: Westchester House Publishers, 1995), pp. 111–113, and McLaren, D. R., *Lockheed P-80/F-80 Shooting Star, A Photo Chronicle* (Atglen, Pennsylvania: Schiffer Publishing, 1996), pp. 51–52.

Chapter Four

1   Pilots would fly a curving approach to see the landing signals officer until leveling for a straight-in just prior to the trap.

2   The first American pilot to employ an ejection seat in an emergency was a navy pilot leaving his F2H-1 on August 9, 1949.

3   The fleet Combat Air Patrol mission at the time was a 2.5-hour flight with two hours on station 170 miles (280 km) from the carrier. This gave time for the vessel to launch two more squadrons. Returning early would disrupt this cycle time.

4.   Dorr, R. F., "Northrop F-89 Scorpion Variant Briefing," *Wings of Fame*, Vol. 6, 1997, p. 129. It is fair to say that operating military aircraft, particularly fighter-bombers, was a hazardous occupation in the 1950s. Dorr points out that in the first thirty months of the decade, the USAF suffered 1,833 major jet aircraft mishaps that claimed 429 lives.

5   Davis, L., "North American F-86 Sabre," *Wings of Fame*, Vol. 10, 1998, pp. 44 and 67.

6   Francillon, R. J., in *Grumman Aircraft Since 1929* (Annapolis, Maryland: Naval Institute Press, 1989), p. 550, credits the 3,000-lbf (13.3-kN) Westinghouse 24C (later J34) as the selected engine. Given that this was described as a jet-powered F7F Tigercat, and likely lighter than the exceptionally large F3D-1 powered by two J34s, it appears that the J30 was the engine selected.

Chapter Five

1   Several authors and speakers at technical symposia have asserted that the XP-86 inched past the speed of sound in November 1947 or April 1948, with the early engines. This

would have been only the second airplane to perform the feat since the air-launched XS-1. See Avery, N., *North American Aircraft 1934–1998, Volume 1* (Santa Ana, California: Narkiewicz/Thompson, 1998), pp. 170-171. However, this is examined in detail, and refuted, in Kempel, R. W., *The Conquest of the Sound Barrier*, X-Planes Book 7 (Beirut, Lebanon: HPM Publications, 2007), pp. 54–59. It is true that the production F-86s could get a few hundredths of a Mach number beyond 1 in a dive, but this was very unlikely with the prototypes.

2   Bradley, R. E., "The Birth of the Delta Wing," *AAHS Journal*, Vol. 48 No. 4, Winter 2003, p. 244.

3   McDonnell's chief engineer and the XF-88's project engineer observed that other teams selected a similar sweep angle, likely based upon the same conclusion from the same data. Pace, S., *McDonnell XF-88 Voodoo*, Air Force Legends Number 205 (Simi Valley, California: Steve Ginter, 1999), p. 11.

4   As evident throughout the text, the period was marked with a continuation of type designation being extended to models that bore little if any commonality with those that preceded it. This began as a means of using existing program monies for continuing aircraft evolution without having to seek funding approval for an entirely new program in an era of tight budgets. Even past the time when money was scarce, the appearance of upgrading an existing design helped avoid close Congressional scrutiny and uncomfortable questions.

5   A 2-inch version of the weapon was to be adopted but ultimately set aside in the interest of simplified logistical support.

6   Kinzey, B. and Roszak, R., *F-102 Delta Dagger*, In Detail & Scale Vol. 6 (Wroclaw, Poland: Detail & Scale, 2018), p. 12.

7   An F-84G (51-843) was modified to flight test the periscope with a fairing containing the device obstructing the usual view from the windscreen.

8   Ginter, S., *Douglas F3D Skyknight*, Naval Fighters Number Four (Simi Valley, California: Steve Ginter, 1982), p. 87, reports the order quantity as 102 while Swanborough, G., and Bowers, P. M., *United States Navy Aircraft Since 1911* (Annapolis, Maryland: Naval Institute Press, 1990), p. 199 and Francillon, R. J., *McDonnell Douglas Aircraft Since 1920: Volume I* (London, England: Putnam, 1988), p. 420, records the number as 287.

Chapter Six

1   McDowell. E. R., "Ryan's Fireball," *AAHS Journal*, Vol. 8 No. 4, Winter 1963, p. 240, and McDowell, E., *FR-1 Fireball*, Mini in Action Number 5 (Carrollton, Texas: Squadron/Signal Publications, 1995), p. 20, would appear to suggest that the XFR-2 was flown, but offers no corresponding BuNo.

2   Markgraf, G., *Douglas Skyshark A2D Turbo-Prop Attack*, Naval Fighters Number Forty-Three (Simi Valley, California: Steve Ginter, 1997), p. 45.

3   van Pelt, M., *Rocketing into the Future, The History and Technology of Rocket Planes* (New York, New York: Springer, 2012), p. 157.

4   The rocket installation is partially evident in a drawing in Bradley, R. E., *Convair Advanced Designs II: Secret Fighters, Attack Aircraft and Unique Concepts 1929–1973* (Manchester, England: Crécy Publishing, 2013), p. 115. Donald, D., "Pioneers & Prototypes—Convair F2Y Sea Dart," *International Air Power Review*, Volume 12, Spring 2004, p. 167, states there were to be forty-four rockets.

5   The change was initially to make eight of the F2Y-1s into pre-production YF2Y-1s, canceling the second prototype. The contract was altered further to make it four YF2Y-1s and twelve F2Y-1s plus a static article. Donald, *International Air Power Review*, Volume 12, pp. 166–167, and Andrade, J. M., *U.S. Military Aircraft Designations and Serials 1909–1979* (Leicester, United Kingdom: Midland Counties Publications, 1997), p. 193. All this may have been more of a political move to lend the appearance of success.

6   Long, B. J., *Convair XFY-1 and YF2Y-1 SeaDart*, Naval Fighters Number Twenty Three (Simi Valley, California: Steve Ginter, 1992), pp. 5 and 21.

7   Piet, S. and Raithal, A., *Martin P6M SeaMaster* (Bel Air, Maryland: Martineer Press, 2001), p. 163.

8   Treadwell, T. C., *Strike from Beneath the Sea, A History of Aircraft-Carrying Submarines* (Stroud, Gloucestershire, England: Tempus Publishing, 1999), pp. 166 and 181.

9   Lockheed, via its flying model tests, had identified a possible technique of cutting power for the last foot or two of descent to allow the aircraft to pass rapidly through this difficult region of control to a positive touchdown. Coleman, S. and Ginter, S., *Convair XFY-1 Pogo*, Naval Fighters Number Twenty-Seven (Simi Valley, California: Steve Ginter, 1994), p. 4. They did not have the opportunity to demonstrate the technique with the full-size aircraft.

Chapter Seven

1   The earlier Martin B-26 was retired with the termination of hostilities, save for Navy JM-1s.

2   The use of an "A" suffix to the initial production variant of the B-50 reflected a change from the prior policy of having no suffix for the first model of a new type.

3   Convair initially tested the spoiler roll control with "guide" aileron on a modified B-32. Boyne, W. J., "Convair's Needle-Nosed Orphan," *Airpower*, September 1976, Vol. 6 No. 4, p. 15.

4   Knaack, M. S., *Encyclopedia of US Air Force Aircraft and Missile Systems, Volume II: Post-World War II Bombers, 1945-1973* (Washington, D. C.: Office of Air Force History, 1988), p. 530, observes that the engines had adjustable tailpipes. This is repeated in Boyne, W. J., "XB-48 ... Martin's Pipe Dream—Pipe Organ Bomber!," *Airpower*, September 1975, Vol. 5 No. 5, p. 10. The nature of these is unclear and the feature is not mentioned in other text nor visible in photographs.

5   Jenkins, D, R., *Magnesium Overcast, The Story of the Convair B-36*, (North Branch, Minnesota: Specialty Press, 2001–2002), p. 146.

6   At least the elevator tab, as designed, produced excessive control power at maximum deflection. There was an in-flight breakup likely caused by an elevator tab that produced pitching moments that the pilot was unable to counter with boost deselected or failed. This demonstrates that there were still things to learn about failure modes of such power-assisted controls and that, as has been true too often in aviation design, such lessons are "written in blood."

7   SHORAN was a ground-based radio-navigation system to guide bombers over a target at night or when obscured by clouds.

8   Lloyd, A. T., *Boeing's B-47 Stratojet* (Atglen, Pennsylvania: Schiffer Publishing, 2005), p. 242.

9   Wright worked on turboprop versions of the J65 with a twin-spool T47, which led nowhere, and the single-spool T49 that ran in December 1952 at 8,000 hp (5,966 kW). It would find no production applications.

10 The use of store ejectors predated this period but became more prevalent given the high speeds being sought.

11 Libis. S, *The Martin XB-51*, Air Force Legends Number 201 (Simi Valley, California: Steve Ginter, 1998), p. 44. Additionally, Glenn Martin had supported the Navy during its struggles with the USAF, and this allegedly earned the ire of air force leadership (pp. 44 and 46, and Boyne, W. J., "Attack! The Story of the XB-51, Martin's Phantom Strike Ship," *Airpower*, July 1978, Vol. 8 No. 4, pp. 23–24).

12 Knaack, *Encyclopedia of US Air Force Aircraft and Missile Systems, Volume II*, p. 309.

13 Accelerating to rotate speed and then aborting, braking to a stop in the remaining runway, determines accelerating/stopping distance. Climb gradient is a function of climb rate; a low rate meaning a shallow gradient and the height of obstacles off the departure end of the runway becomes more critical. The use of JATO for the operation of the B-36 is not mentioned in available literature.

14 SAC boasted of an official ceiling (possibly absolute ceiling) of 47,000 feet (14,326 m) and some missions were flown as high as 50,000 feet (15,240 m). Such would leave the bomber with little maneuver margin. The combat ceiling numbers provided are from Knaack, *Encyclopedia of US Air Force Aircraft and Missile Systems, Volume II*, p. 55, though it is assumed that the service and combat numbers are switched since the altitude for 500 fps will be lower than or 100 fps.

15 Knaack, M. S., *Encyclopedia of US Air Force Aircraft and Missile Systems, Volume I: Post-World War II Fighters, 1945–1973* (Washington, D. C.: Office of Air Force History, 1978), p. 554, reports that the configuration also permitted a longer ground roll in a flat attitude before rotation, shortening the overall take-off distance.

16 The engines are mentioned in many accounts without specifics. The bulk of this account is drawn from Mutza, W., *Lockheed P2V Neptune, An Illustrated History* (Atglen, Pennsylvania: Schiffer Publishing, 1996), pp. 52–57, but which fails to mention these engines. The aircraft were flown to a much higher altitude for the nuclear bomb drop than for its typical maritime patrol mission.

17 Barlow, J. G., *Revolt of the Admirals: The Fight for Naval Aviation. 1945–1950* (Washington, D.C.: Naval Historical Center, Department of the Navy, undated e-book edition), e-book p. 2656.

18 Piet, S. and Raithal, A., *Martin P6M SeaMaster* (Bel Air, Maryland: Martineer Press, 2001), p. 37.

Chapter Eight

1 In the mid-1950s, the C-119s would be given a twin nose wheel installation.

2 Cox, G. and Kaston, C., *American Secret Projects 2, US Airlifters 1941 to 1961* (Manchester, England: Crécy Publishing, 2019), p. 158.

3 The first purpose-built Carrier Onboard Delivery (COD) was a transport version of the S2F (see page 363). Grumman initially conceived this at the end of 1951, but it was well into 1953 before the Navy moved on the proposal. Martin proposed a COD version of the AM-1 that got the designation JR2M-1 Mercury, but this did not proceed. Breihan, J. R., Piet, S., and Mason, R. S., *Martin Aircraft 1909-1960* (Santa Ana, California: Narkiewicz/Thompson, 1995), p. 145–146.

4 Ginter, S., *Convair XP5Y-1 & R3Y-1/-2 Tradewind*, Naval Fighters Number Thirty-Four (Simi Valley, California: Steve Ginter, 1996), p. 15.

5 *Ibid.*

6 *Ibid*, p. 112.

Chapter Nine

1 Placing the engine in front, where passing air in forward flight could assist engine cooling, compromises the superior forward visibility that makes the helicopter so attractive, but also complicates weight, balance, and routing of the power shaft to the rotor past the aircrew. Additionally, liquid-cooled was too heavy for the application.

2 Boyne, W. J. and Lopez, D. S. (ed.), *Vertical Flight, The Age of the Helicopter* (Washington, D. C.: Smithsonian Institution, 1984), p. 200.

3 It is unclear if this was an overt policy and coordinated effort. However, it remained an area of rare joint cooperation for decades to the present day.

4 Boyne and Lopez, *Vertical Flight,* p. 92.

5 Francillon, R. J., *McDonnell Douglas Aircraft Since 1920: Volume II* (Annapolis, Maryland: Naval Institute Press, 1990), p. 72.

6 Boyne and Lopez, *Vertical Flight,* p. 60.

7 Kowalski, R. J., *Grumman AF Guardian*, Naval Fighters Number Twenty (Simi Valley, California: Steve Ginter, 2016), p. 17.

8 Spenser, J. P., *Whirlybirds, A History of the U.S. Helicopter Pioneers* (Seattle, Washington: University of Washington Press, 1998), p. 145. This competes with Kaman's claim to have done the first loop with an HTK-1.

9 Spenser, *Whirlybirds*, p. 152.

10 This shared collective had been a feature of the wartime Sikorskys as well. It would not persist long as learning to use a different hand for collective and cyclic depending on the seat the pilot occupied was difficult and undermined flight safety.

11 Swanborough, G. and Bowers, P. M., *United States Military Aircraft Since 1909* (London, England: Putnam Aeronautical Books, 1989), p. 743.

12 Most of this account is from Story, R. W., "Igor Bensen, The GE Years," *AAHS Journal*, Vol. 46 No. 4, Winter 2001, p. 284.

13 Igor Bensen would go on to form his own company in 1953 in which he focused on autogyros, initially with ramjet tip propulsion.

14 Gunston, B. and Batchelor, J., *Helicopters, 1900–1960* (London: Phoebus Publishing, 1977), p. 43.

15 Porter, D. J., "Howard Hughes' Impromptu Beginning as a Helicopter Manufacturer," *AAHS Journal*, Vol. 58 No. 3, Fall 2013, p. 196.

16 Spenser, J. P., *Vertical Challenge, The Hiller Aircraft Story* (Bloomington, Indiana: 1st Books Library, 2003), p. 89.

17 Spenser, *Vertical Challenge*, p. 95.

18 Francillon, *McDonnell Douglas Aircraft Since 1920: Volume II*, pp. 414–416, provides the most complete HCH account.

19 Igor I. Historical Sikorsky Archives, S-56/HR2S-1/H-37 Helicopter product history, sikorskyarchives.com/S+56%20HR2S-1H-37.php, accessed July 24, 2018.

20 *Ibid.*, accessed July 27, 2018.

21 Boeing began developing gas turbines in 1943 and initiated production in 1947. Applications were usually as supplemental power generation and compressed air for main engine starting, power boost, and boat propulsion. The low-powered engine saw the experimental application to aircraft that benefited from the low weight and lower complexity. The 502's first flight application was as a turboprop installed in a Cessna L-19A to become the XL-19B (see page 409).

22 Most accounts mention the H-39 only, but the Igor I. Historical Sikorsky Archives, S-52 product history (sikorskyarchives.com/S-52.php, accessed July 22, 2018) has a photograph of a minimally modified YH-19 in flight with a single Artouste installed.

Chapter Ten

1 Mutza, W., *Lockheed P2V Neptune, An Illustrated History* (Atglen, Pennsylvania: Schiffer Publishing, 1996), pp. 100–101.

2 Francillon, R. J., *Grumman Aircraft Since 1929* (Annapolis, Maryland: Naval Institute Press, 1989), p. 175. Goodspeed, M. H., "Grumman TBF/TBM Avenger," *Wings of Fame*, Volume 13, 1998, p. 62, reports that the numbers reached 160.

3 Kowalski, R. J., *Grumman AF Guardian*, Naval Fighters Number Twenty (Simi Valley, California: Steve Ginter, 2016), reports on p. 14 an astounding accident rate of one per 292.6 flight hours (twenty-nine mishaps) during a one-year period for one squadron, though not all resulted in airframe write-off.

4 Ginter, S., *Martin PBM Mariner*, Naval Fighters Number Ninety-Seven (Simi Valley, California: Steve Ginter, 2013), p. 70.

5 The bomber aspect of the mission was de-emphasized, despite the presence of a bomb bay and a respectable weapons capacity, and so the designation lacked the previously common "B."

6 Veronico, N. A. and Ginter, S., *Convair PB4Y-2/P4Y-2 Privateer* (Simi Valley, California: Steve Ginter, 2012), p. 88, describes the equipment fit for the PB4Y-2s in detail, and no radar is listed. The Wikipedia entry for Patrol Squadron 23 (en.wikipedia.org/wiki/VP-23) lists the APS-15 but incorrectly identifies it as an ASW radar. Other non-detailed sources mention unspecified sea-search radar equipment while not reflecting the ASW-unique equipment. See Cary, A. C., *Consolidated-Vultee PB4Y-2 Privateer* (Atglen, Pennsylvania: Schiffer Publishing, 2005), p. 24, Andrade, J. M., *U.S. Military Aircraft Designations and Serials 1909–1979* (Leicester, United Kingdom: Midland Counties Publications, 1997), p. 213, Wegg, J., *General Dynamics Aircraft and their Predecessors* (London, England: Putnam Aeronautical Books, 1990), p. 100, and Swanborough, G., and Bowers, P. M., *United States Navy Aircraft Since 1911* (Annapolis, Maryland: Naval Institute Press, 1990), p. 106.

7 Thomason, T. H., *The Forgotten Bell HSL, U.S. Navy's First All-Weather Anti-Submarine Warfare Helicopter*, Naval Fighters Number Seventy (Simi Valley, California: Steve Ginter, 2005), p. 27.

8   The complete account of the HSL project is found in Thomason, *The Forgotten Bell HSL*.

9   Development of the autopilot was conducted on a Bell H-12B while the first HSL was still coming together. Lambermont, P. and Pirie, A., *Helicopters and Autogyros of the World* (South Brunswick, Great Britain: A.S. Barnes and Company, 1970), p. 227.

10   Thomason, *The Forgotten Bell HSL*, p. 31, provides the foundation for the Characteristics summary table, though this reference includes projected figures. Elsewhere in the book, there are hints of actual characteristics. Lambermont and Pirie, *Helicopters and Autogyros of the World*, pp. 227–228, and Pelletier, A. J., *Bell Aircraft Since 1935* (London, England: Putnam Aeronautical Books, 1991), p. 102, also provide some numbers of unknown veracity, but useful as a guide for adjustment of the projections.

11   Thomason, *The Forgotten Bell HSL*, pp. 15 and 51.

12   Shock, J. R., *U.S. Navy Pressure Airships 1915–1962* (Smyrna Beach, Florida; M & T Printers, 1994), p. II–38.

13   Willis, D., "Warplane Classic—Boeing B-29 and B-50 Superfortress," *International Air Power Review*, Volume 22, 2007, pp. 149–150.

Chapter Eleven

1   Thompson, S., *Douglas A-26 and B-26 Invader* (Ramsbury, Marlborough, Wiltshire, United Kingdom: The Crowood Press Limited, 2002), p. 100, indicates that the RB-26 designation emerged in 1948 and replaced the earlier FA-26. This suggests an interim scheme of using the F for 'photo' (as in F-15) as a designation prefix. The website US Warplanes (uswarplanes.net/a26.html) lists a single FA-26C with cameras and radar for night reconnaissance.

2   In late 1949, Republic modified one of the YP-84As (45-49482) with side NACA flush inlets and a streamlined, enclosed nose for testing. This experience likely informed the RF-84F design effort.

3   Swanborough, G. and Bowers, P. M., *United States Military Aircraft Since 1909* (London, England: Putnam Aeronautical Books, 1989), p. 455, gives a total number of 2,068 airplanes upgraded of which 1,802 were for the USAF. This leaves 266, which the navy typically credited as "some."

4   Pelletier, A. J., *Beech Aircraft and their Predecessors* (Annapolis, Maryland: Naval Institute Press, 1995), p. 111, and Johnson, E. R., *American Military Training Aircraft, Fixed and Rotary-Wing Trainers since 1916* (Jefferson, North Carolina: McFarland & Company, 2015), e-book p. 2,676.

5   Swanborough Bowers, *United States Military Aircraft Since 1909*, p. 192, and Johnson, E. R., *American Military Training Aircraft, Fixed and Rotary-Wing Trainers since 1916* (Jefferson, North Carolina: McFarland & Company, 2015), e-book p. 2,323.

6   Bridgman, L. (ed.), *Jane's All the World's Aircraft 1949–50* (New York, New York: McGraw Hill Book Company, 1949), p. 201c, and Murphy, D. "Boeing's Slow-Flying Scout," *Airpower*, July 1994, p. 40. The Brodie device was created during the war to permit light airplane operations in areas unsuitable for take-off or landing. The pilot flew the aircraft such that a hook on a truss arrangement affixed to the top of the aircraft engaged a sling sliding on a cable and was then slowed. Take-off was the reverse of this action. The cable was 500 feet (152 m) long. Norton, B., *American Aircraft Development of the Second World War, Research, Experimentation and Modification 1939–1945* (Stroud, England: Fonthill Media, 2019), pp. 204–215.

7   Semi-prepared fields were those that, at a minimum, had been checked that the surface was sufficiently firm to support the aircraft given its expected "footprint" loading that was a function of gross weight and tire pressure. Some obstructions might also be cleared.

8   Moran, G. P., *Aeroplanes Vought 1917–1977* (Temple City, California: Historical Aviation Album, 1977), pp. 105 and 127.

9   The USAF began giving bomber designations to long-range missiles at this time. Several more are highlighted in this text. Add to these are the two developmental ballistic missiles Atlas as the B-65 and Titan as B-68.

10   Story, R. W., "Igor Bensen, The GE Years," *AAHS Journal*, Vol. 46 No. 4, Winter 2001, p. 288.

11   Lambermont, P. and Pirie, A., *Helicopters and Autogyros of the World* (South Brunswick, Great Britain: A.S. Barnes and Company, 1970), p. 313.

Chapter Twelve

1   McLaren, D. R., *Lockheed P-80/F-80 Shooting Star, A Photo Chronicle* (Atglen, Pennsylvania: Schiffer Publishing, 1996), pp. 48–49 and 52. Francillon, R., *Lockheed Aircraft Since 1913* (Annapolis, Maryland: Naval Institute Press, 1988), p. 241, also credits the gun installation as including a rotating nose. The images provided here do not support this ascertain. The idea may have originated with a German wartime experiment called *Schräge Musik*, and the outcome would appear to have been readily foreseen.

2   Dorr, R. F., "Northrop F-89 Scorpion Variant Briefing," *Wings of Fame*, Vol. 6, 1997, p. 137, and Balzer, G., and Dario, M., *Northrop F-89 Scorpion*, Aerofax Datagraph 8 (Arlington, Texas: Aerofax, 1993), pp. 49–50.

3   Dorr, "Northrop F-89 Scorpion Variant Briefing," p. 139, and Balzer and Dario *Northrop F-89 Scorpion*, pp. 50–54.

4   Westrum, R., *Sidewinder: Creative Missile Development at China Lake* (Annapolis, Maryland: Naval Press, 1999), e-book pp. 114–115, and Babcock, E., *Magnificent Mavericks: History of the Navy at China Lake, California, Volume 3, Transition of the Naval Ordnance Test Station from Rocket Station to Research, Development, Test, and Evaluation Center, 1948–1958* (China Lake, California: Chine Lake Museum Foundation, 2008), pp. 303–305 and 309.

5   Werrell, K. P., *The Evolution of the Cruise Missile* (Maxwell Air Force Base, Alabama: Air University Press, September 1985), p. 81. Rosenberg, M., *The Air Force and the National Guided Missile Program 1944–1950* (Newtown, Connecticut: Defense Lion Publications, 2012), pp. 42–47 and 66–68, lists these programs.

6   Rosenberg, *The Air Force and the National Guided Missile Program*, p. 46.

7   Numerous contributors and editors, *Days of Challenge, Days of Change: A Technical History of the Pacific Missile Test Center*, The Pacific Missile Test Center (Washington, D. C.: U.S. Government Printing Office, 1989), p. 24.

8   Werrell, *The Evolution of the Cruise Missile*, p. 114, Armitage, M., *Unmanned Aircraft*, Brassey's Air Power: Aircraft, Weapons Systems and Technology Series, Volume 3 (Exeter, England: Brassey's Defence Publishers, 1988), p. 46, Bruins, B. D., *U.S. Naval Bombardment Missiles, 1940–1958: A Study of the Weapons Innovation Process*, Doctoral Dissertation (Ann Arbor, Michigan: Columbia University, 1981), p. 7, and Rosenberg, *The Air Force and the National Guided Missile Program*, p. 45, caption.

9   Werrell, *The Evolution of the Cruise Missile*, p. 111.

10   Stumpf, D. K., *Regulus, The Forgotten Weapon* (Paducah, Kentucky: Turner Publishing, 1996), p. 58, note 7.

11   Use of an X-series designation for a missile prototype was unusual in that the designations were typically reserved for true research vehicles.

12   The USAF felt strongly that air defense of any form, including ground-based missiles, lay within its purview. Yet, DoD ordained that the Army would bear this responsibility, and that service was developing the Nike missile for the purpose. To give the impression that BOMARC was more than a missile, being wing-borne for the terminal phase of flight, the F-99 designation was imposed in 1951. The gambit worked in that the two duplicative programs were sustained into production and fielding.

Chapter Thirteen

1   Tuttle, J., *Eject!, The Complete History of U.S. Aircraft Escape Systems* (St. Paul, Minnesota: MBI Publishing, 2002), p. 63.

2   These initially were 285-gal (1,003-l) unbaffled "Misawa" tanks devised by a team in Japan, replacing 165-gal (625-l) units. The lack of baffles contributed to several fatal accidents

during early operations from fuel slosh causing severe pitching motions of the jet that could lead to loss of control and structural failures. Chilstrom, K. and Leary, P., *Test Flying at Old Wright Field* (Omaha, Nebraska: Westchester House Publishers, 1995), pp. 102–103. Fletcher 230-gal (871-l) units were also carried.

3   Byrd, V. B., *Passing Gas, The History of Inflight Refueling* (Chico, California: Byrd Publishing, 1994), p. 84, describes how refueling with 265-gal (1,003-l) tip tanks was not practical while 165-gal (625-l) was successful. However, he describes on p. 89 a combat refueling in Korea with 265-gal tanks.

4   Smith, R. K., *75 Years of Inflight Refueling Highlights, 1923–1998*, Air Force History and Museums Program (Washington, D. C.; U.S. Government Printing Office, 1998), p. 34, and Tanner, R. M., *History of Air-to-Air Refueling* (Barnsley, South Yorkshire, England; Pen & Sword Aviation, 2006), p. 52.

5   Byrd, *Passing Gas*, p. 84.

6   The number of tankers in the theater was eight or nine, but the source of each is unclear. Smith, *75 Years of Inflight Refueling*, p. 34 says that ten tankers were lent to the effort by SAC while Tanner, *History of Air-to-Air Refueling*, p. 52, has FRL modifying six KB-29Ms to hose tankers. Others may have been modified in the U.S. Whether the EB-29 was sent to the theater is unclear.

7   Kay, A. L., *Turbojet, History and Development 1930–1960, Volume 2* (Wiltshire, England: The Crowood Press, 2007), p. 136.

8   Some confusion was introduced by the aircraft with the gun nose being referred to as B-26B and those with the glass nose B-26C, regardless of the original delivery designation.

Chapter Fourteen

1   This catching up included exploiting material collected in Germany and employing engineers from that country. However, while the German weapons were inspirational, they were neither copied nor of significant detailed design guidance.

2   Derived in part from Kay, A. L., *Turbojet, History and Development 1930–1960, Volume 2* (Wiltshire, England: The Crowood Press, 2007), pp. 257–258. The table is specific to factors relevant to aircraft performance and neglects such important propulsion system parameters as pressure ratios, mass flow, and other efficiencies plus electronic engine controls that were all similarly improved to facilitating the others.

3   As an example of this excess, Breihan, J. R., Piet, S., and Mason, R. S., *Martin Aircraft 1909–1960* (Santa Ana, California: Narkiewicz/Thompson, 1995), p. 197, gives a figure of $400 million spent on the P6M over the decade of work with sixteen aircraft built and none fielded.

Bibliography

Books

7th Bomb Wing B-36 Association, *"Peacemaker," The History of the B-36 at Carswell Air Force Base, Fort Worth, Texas, 1948-1958* (Fort Worth, Texas: Taylor Publishing, 1995)

Abel, A., *Fairchild's Golden Age*, The Golden Age of Aviation Series (Brawley, California: Wind Canyon Books, 2008)

The Airlift/Tanker Association, *Airlift Tanker, History of U.S. Airlift and Tanker Forces* (Paducah, Kentucky: Turner Publishing, 1995)

Amtmann, H. H., *The Vanishing Paperclips; America's Aerospace Secret, A Personal Account* (Boylston, Massachusetts: Monogram Aviation Publications, 1988)

Anderson, F., *Northrop, An Aeronautical History* (Century City, California: Northrop Corporation, 1976)

Andrade, J. M., *U.S. Military Aircraft Designations and Serials 1909–1979* (Leicester, United Kingdom: Midland Counties Publications, 1997)

Apostolo, G., *The Illustrated Encyclopedia of Helicopters* (New York, New York: Bonanza Books, 1984)

Armitage, M., *Unmanned Aircraft*, Brassey's Air Power: Aircraft, Weapons Systems and Technology Series, Volume 3 (Exeter, England: Brassey's Defence Publishers, 1988)

Avery, N., *North American Aircraft 1934–1998, Volume 1* (Santa Ana, California: Narkiewicz/Thompson, 1998)

Babcock, E., *Magnificent Mavericks: History of the Navy at China Lake, California, Volume 3, Transition of the Naval Ordnance Test Station from Rocket Station to Research, Development, Test, and Evaluation Center, 1948–1958* (China Lake, California: Chine Lake Museum Foundation, 2008)

Balzer, G., and Dario, M., *Northrop F-89 Scorpion*, Aerofax Datagraph 8 (Arlington, Texas: Aerofax, 1993)

Barlow, J. G., *Revolt of the Admirals: The Fight for Naval Aviation. 1945–1950* (Washington, D.C.: Naval Historical Center, Department of the Navy, undated e-book edition)

Beck, S. D., *Fairchild C-82 Packet, The Military and Civil History* (Jefferson, North Carolina: McFarland & Company, 2017)

Bilstein, R. E., *Orders of Magnitude, A History of the NACA and NASA, 1915–1990*, SP-4406, The NASA History Series (Washington, D.C.: National Aeronautics and Space Administration, 1989)

Borchers, P. F., Franklin, J. A., and Fletcher, J. W., *Flight Research at Ames: Fifty-Seven of Development and Validation of Aeronautical Technology*, NASA/SP-1998-3300 (Moffett Field, California: National Aeronautics and Space Administration, 1998)

Bowers, P. M., *Boeing Aircraft Since 1916* (Annapolis, Maryland: Naval Institute Press, 1989); *Curtiss Aircraft 1907–1947* (Annapolis, Maryland: Naval Institute Press, 1979); *Fortress in the Sky* (Granada Hills, California: Sentry Books, 1976)

Bowman, M. W., *Vought F4U Corsair* (Wiltshire, United Kingdom: The Crowood Press, 2002)

Boyne, W. J., and Lopez, D. S., ed., *Vertical Flight, The Age of the Helicopter* (Washington, D. C.: Smithsonian Institution, 1984)

Bradley, R. E., *Convair Advanced Designs II: Secret Fighters, Attack Aircraft and Unique Concepts 1929–1973* (Manchester, England: Crécy Publishing, 2013)

Breihan, J. R., Piet, S., and Mason, R. S., *Martin Aircraft 1909-1960* (Santa Ana, California: Narkiewicz/Thompson, 1995)

Bridgman, L. (ed.), *Jane's All the World's Aircraft 1949–50* (New York, New York: McGraw Hill Book Company, 1949); *Jane's All the World's Aircraft 1950–51* (New York, New York: McGraw Hill Book Company, 1950); *Jane's All the World's Aircraft 1952–53* (New York, New York: McGraw Hill Book Company, 1952)

Brown, E., *Testing for Combat* (Shrewsbury, England: Airlife, 1994)

Buttler, T., *American Secret Projects: Bombers, Attack and Anti-Submarine Aircraft 1945 to 1974* (Surrey, England: Ian Allan Publishing, 2010); *Early US Jet Fighters: Proposals, Projects and Prototypes* (Manchester, England: Hikoki Publications, 2013)

Butzum, R. A., *50 Years of Target Drone Aircraft* (Newbury Park, California: Northrop, 1985)

Byrd, V. B., *Passing Gas, The History of Inflight Refueling* (Chico, California: Byrd Publishing, 1994)

Campbell, R. H., *The Silverplate Bomber, A History and Registry of the Enola Gay and Other B-29s Configured to Carry Atomic Bombs* (Jefferson, North Carolina: McFarland & Company, 2005)

Cary, A. C., *Consolidated-Vultee PB4Y-2 Privateer* (Atglen, Pennsylvania: Schiffer Publishing, 2005)

Chilstrom, K., and Leary, P., *Test Flying at Old Wright Field* (Omaha, Nebraska: Westchester House Publishers, 1995)

Coates, S., with Carbonel, J. C., *Helicopters of the Third Reich* (Hersham, Surrey: Classic Publications, 2002)

Cox, G., and Kaston, C., *American Secret Projects 2, US Airlifters 1941 to 1961* (Manchester, England: Crécy Publishing, 2019)

Chorlton, M., *Convair* (Stroud, England: Amberley Publishing, 2018)

Crane, C. C., *American Airpower Strategy in Korea, 1950–1953* (Lawrence, Kansas: University Press of Kansas, 2000)

Dawson, V. P., *Engines and Innovation: Lewis Laboratory and American Propulsion Technology*, The NASA History Series, SP-4306 (Washington, D.C.: National Aeronautics and Space Administration, 1991)

Dean, F. H., and Hagedorn, D., *Curtiss Fighter Aircraft, A Photographic History* (Atglen, Pennsylvania: Schiffer Publishing, 2007)

Elward, B., *Grumman F9F Panther/Cougar, First Grumman Cat of the Jet Age* (North Branch, Minnesota: Specialty Press, 2010)

Francillon, R. J., *Grumman Aircraft Since 1929* (Annapolis, Maryland: Naval Institute Press, 1989); *Lockheed Aircraft Since 1913* (Annapolis, Maryland: Naval Institute Press, 1988); *McDonnell Douglas Aircraft Since 1920: Volume I* (London, England: Putnam, 1988); *McDonnell Douglas Aircraft Since 1920: Volume II* (Annapolis, Maryland: Naval Institute Press, 1990)

Frankel, M., *Killer Rays, Story of the Douglas F4D Skyray and F5D Skylancer* (North Branch, Minnesota: Specialty Press, 2010)

Friedman, N., *US Naval Weapons* (London, England: Conway Maritime Press, 1983)

Gibson, J. N., *The History of the US Nuclear Arsenal* (Greenwich, Connecticut: Brompton Books, 1989); *The Navaho Missile Project, The Story of the "Know-How" Missile of American Rocketry* (Atglen, Pennsylvania: Schiffer Publishing, 1996); *Nuclear Weapons of the United States, An Illustrated History* (Atglen, Pennsylvania: Schiffer Publishing, 1996)

Gray, G. W., *Frontiers of Flight, The Story of NACA Research* (New York, Alfred A. Knopf, 1948)

Grimes, B., *The History of Big Safari* (Bloomington, Indiana: Archway Publishing, 2014)

Gunston, B., *The Illustrated Encyclopedia of the World's Rockets & Missiles* (New York, New York: Crescent Books, 1979); *Night Fighters, A Development & Combat History* (New York, New York: Charles Scribner's Sons, 1976); *World Encyclopedia of Aero Engines* (Wellingborough, England: Patrick Stephens, 1986)

Habermehl, C. M., and Hopkins III, R. S., *Boeing B-47 Stratojet, Strategic Air Command's Transitional Bomber*, (Manchester, England: Crécy Publishing, 2018)

Hallion, R. P., *The Naval Air War in Korea* (Tuscaloosa, Alabama: The University of Alabama Press, 2011)

Hansen, C., *U.S. Nuclear Weapons, The Secret History* (Arlington, Texas: Aerofax, 1988)

Hansen, J. R., *Engineer in Charge, A History of the Langley Aeronautical Laboratory, 1917–1958*, SP-4305 (Washington, D.C.: National Aeronautics and Space Administration, 1987)

Harding, S., *U.S. Army Aircraft Since 1947, An Illustrated Reference* (Atglen, Pennsylvania: Schiffer Publishing, 1997)

Harkins, H., *F-84 Thunderjet, Republic Thunder* (Glasgow, United Kingdom: Centurion Publishing, 2013)

Hartman, E. P., *Adventures in Research, A History of Ames Research Center 1940–1965*, NASA Center History Series, SP-4302 (Washington, D.C.: National Aeronautics and Space Administration, 1970)

Harwood, W. B., *Raise Heaven and Earth, The Story of Martin Marietta People and Their Pioneering Achievements* (New York, New York: Simon & Schuster, 1993)

Heinemann, E., and Rausa, R., *Ed Heinemann, Combat Aircraft Designer* (Annapolis, Maryland: United States Naval Institute, 1980)

Hoffman, R. A., *The Fighting Flying Boat, A History of the Martin PBM Mariner* (Annapolis, Maryland: Naval Institute Press, 2004)

Isham, M. J., and McLaren, D. R., *Northrop F-89 Scorpion, A Photo Chronicle* (Atglen, Pennsylvania: Schiffer Publishing, 1996)

Jackson, R., *Air War at Night, The Battle for the Night Sky Since 1915* (Charlottesville, Virginia: Howell Press, 2000)

Jenkins, D, R., *Magnesium Overcast, The Story of the Convair B-36*, (North Branch, Minnesota: Specialty Press, 2001-2002)

Jenkins, D. R. and Landis, T. R., *Experimental & Prototype U.S. Air Force Jet Fighters* (North Branch, Minnesota: Specialty Press, 2008)

Johnson, E. R., *American Military Training Aircraft, Fixed and Rotary-Wing Trainers since 1916* (Jefferson, North Carolina: McFarland & Company, 2015)

Johnsen, F. A., *Testbeds, Motherships & Parasites, Astonishing Aircraft from the Golden Age of Flight Test* (North Branch, Minnesota: Specialty Press, 2018)

Jones, B. *English Electric Canberra and Martin B-57* (Wiltshire, England: The Crowood Press, 1999)

Jones, L. S., *U.S. Bombers* (Fallbrook, California: Aero Publishing, 1974)

Kay, A. L., *Turbojet, History and Development 1930-1960, Volume 2* (Wiltshire, England: The Crowood Press, 2007)

Knaack, M. S., *Encyclopedia of US Air Force Aircraft and Missile Systems, Volume I: Post-World War II Fighters, 1945–1973* (Washington, D. C.: Office of Air Force History, 1978); *Encyclopedia of US Air Force Aircraft and Missile Systems, Volume II: Post-World War II Bombers, 1945–1973* (Washington, D. C.: Office of Air Force History, 1988)

Kennedy, G. P., *The Rockets and Missiles of White Sands Proving Ground 1945–1958* (Atglen, Pennsylvania: Schiffer Publishing, 2009)

Lambermont, P. and Pirie, A., *Helicopters and Autogyros of the World* (South Brunswick, Great Britain: A.S. Barnes and Company, 1970)

Latimer-Needham, C. H., *Refueling in Flight* (London, England: Pitman & Sons, 1950)

Leary, W. M., *"We Freeze to Please," A History of NASA's Icing Research Tunnel and the Quest for Flight Safety*, The NASA History Series, NASA SP-2002-4226 (Washington, D. C.: National Aeronautics and Space Administration, 2002)

Libis, S., *Skystreak, Skyrocket, & Stiletto: Douglas High-Speed X-Planes*, (North Branch, Minnesota: Specialty Press, 2005)

Lloyd, A. T., *Boeing's B-47 Stratojet* (Atglen, Pennsylvania: Schiffer Publishing, 2005); *Fairchild C-82 Packet and C-119 Flying Boxcar* (Hinckley, England: Midland Publishing, 2005)

Loftin, L. F., Jr., *Quest for Performance, The Evolution of Modern Aircraft*, SP-468 (Washington, D.C.: National Aeronautics and Space Administration, 1985)

Lonnquest, J. C., and Winkler, D. F., *To Defend and Deter: The Legacy of the United States Cold War Missile Program* (Bodega Bay, California: Hole in the Head Press, 2014)

Lorell, M., *The U.S. Combat Aircraft Industry 1909–2000: Structure, Competition, Innovation* (Santa Monica, California: RAND, 2003)

Matthews, B., *Cobra!, Bell Aircraft Corporation 1934–1946* (Atglen, Pennsylvania: Schiffer, 1996)

McLaren, D. R., *Lockheed T-33, A Photo Chronicle* (Atglen, Pennsylvania: Schiffer Publishing, 1996); *Lockheed P-80/F-80 Shooting Star, A Photo Chronicle* (Atglen, Pennsylvania: Schiffer Publishing, 1996)

Mikesh, R. C., *Martin B-57 Canberra, The Complete Record* (Atglen, Pennsylvania: Schiffer Publishing, 1995)

Miller, J., *The X-Planes, X-1 to X-45*, third edition (Hinckley, England: Midland Publishing, 2001)

Mitchell, K. A., *Fairchild Aircraft 1926–1987* (Santa Ana, California: Narkiewicz/Thompson, 1997)

Moran, G. P., *Aeroplanes Vought 1917–1977* (Temple City, California: Historical Aviation Album, 1977)

Mutza, W., *Convair F-102 Delta Dagger, A Photo Chronicle* (Atglen, Pennsylvania: Schiffer Publishing, 1999); *Grumman Albatross, A History of the Legendary Seaplane* (Atglen, Pennsylvania: Schiffer Publishing, 1996); *Lockheed P2V Neptune, An Illustrated History* (Atglen, Pennsylvania: Schiffer Publishing, 1996)

Neufeld, J. (ed.), *Research and Development in the United States Air Force* (Washington, D.C.: Center for Air Force History, United States Air Force, 1993)

Neufeld, J., Watson, G. M., Jr., and Chenoweth, D. (ed.), *Technology and the Air Force, a Retrospective Assessment* (Washington, D.C.: Air Force History and Museums Program, United States Air Force, 1997)

Newdick, T., *Postwar Air Weapons 1945-Present* (London, England: Amber Books, 2011)

Norton, W., *American Aircraft Development of the Second World War, Research, Experimentation and Modification 1939–1945* (Stroud, England: Fonthill Media, 2019); *American Aircraft Development in World War 2; Special Types 1939–1945* (Manchester, England: Crécy Publishing, 2016); *American Bomber Development in World War 2* (Surrey, England: Midland Publishing, 2012); *American Military Gliders of World War II* (Atglen, Pennsylvania: Schiffer Military History, 2012); *U.S. Experimental & Prototype Aircraft Projects, Fighters 1939–1945* (Atglen, Pennsylvania: Specialty Press, 2008)

Numerous contributors and editors, *Days of Challenge, Days of Change: A Technical History of the Pacific Missile Test Center*, The Pacific Missile Test Center (Washington, D. C.: U.S. Government Printing Office, 1989)

Ordway, F. I., III, and Wakeford, R. C., *International Missile and Spacecraft Guide* (New York, New York: McGraw-Hill Books, 1960)

Pace, S., *Boeing B-29 Superfortress* (Wiltshire, United Kingdom: The Crowood Press, 2003)

Pape, G. R., Campbell, J. M., and Campbell, D., *Northrop P-61 Black Widow, A Complete History and Combat Record* (Atglen, Pennsylvania: Schiffer Publishing, 1995)

Pearcy, A., *A History of U.S. Coast Guard Aviation* (Shrewsbury, England: Airlife Publishing, 1989); *Flying the Frontiers, NACA and NASA Experimental Aircraft* (Annapolis, Maryland: Naval Institute Press, 1993)

Pelletier, A. J., *Beech Aircraft and their Predecessors* (Annapolis, Maryland: Naval Institute Press, 1995); *Bell Aircraft Since 1935* (London, England: Putnam Aeronautical Books, 1991)

Piet, S. and Raithal, A., *Martin P6M SeaMaster* (Bel Air, Maryland: Martineer Press, 2001)

Politella, D., *Operation Grasshopper, The Story of Army Aviation in Korea* (Wichita, Kansas: Robert R. Longo Company, 1958)

Polmar, N., *Historic Naval Aircraft* (Washington, D. C.: Potomac Books, 2004)

Porter, D. J., *Howard's Whirlybirds, Howard Hughes' Amazing Pioneering Helicopter Exploits* (Stroud, England: Fonthill Media, 2013)

Rawlins, E. W., *Marines and Helicopters 1946–1962* (Washington, D. C.: U.S. Government Printing Office, 1976)

Rosenberg, M., *The Air Force and the National Guided Missile Program 1944-1950* (Newtown, Connecticut: Defense Lion Publications, 2012)

Ross, F., Jr., *Guided Missiles: Rockets and Torpedoes* (New York, New York: Lothrop, Lee & Shepard, 1951)

Rubinstein, M., and Goldman, R. M., *To Join with the Eagles: A Complete History of Curtiss-Wright Aircraft from 1903 to 1965* (Garden City, New York: Doubleday & Company, 1974)

Ryan, C., *The Pre-Astronauts, Manned Ballooning on the Threshold of Space* (Annapolis, Maryland: Naval Institute Press, 1995)

Shock, J. R., *U.S. Navy Pressure Airships 1915–1962* (Smyrna Beach, Florida; M & T Printers, 1994)

Shortal, J. A., *A New Dimension, Wallops Island Flight Test Range: The First Fifteen Years*, NASA Reference Publication 1028 (Washington, D. C.: National Aeronautics and Space Administration, 1978)

Simpson, R. W., *Airlife's Helicopters & Rotorcraft* (Shrewsbury, England: Airlife, 1998)

Spenser, J. P., *Vertical Challenge, The Hiller Aircraft Story* (Bloomington, Indiana: 1st Books Library, 2003); *Whirlybirds, A History of the U.S. Helicopter Pioneers* (Seattle, Washington: University of Washington Press, 1998)

Stoff, J., *The Thunder Factory, An Illustrated History of The Republic Aviation Corporation* (Osceola, Wisconsin; Motorbooks International, 1990)

Stumpf, D. K., *Regulus, The Forgotten Weapon* (Paducah, Kentucky: Turner Publishing, 1996)

Swanborough, G., and Bowers, P. M., *United States Military Aircraft Since 1909* (London, England: Putnam Aeronautical Books, 1989); *United States Navy Aircraft Since 1911* (Annapolis, Maryland: Naval Institute Press, 1990)

Tanner, R. M., *History of Air-to-Air Refueling* (Barnsley, South Yorkshire, England; Pen & Sword Aviation, 2006)

Thompson, K., *North American Aircraft 1934–1999, Volume 2* (Santa Ana, California: Narkiewicz/Thompson, 1999)

Thompson, S., *Douglas A-26 and B-26 Invader* (Ramsbury, Marlborough, Wiltshire, United Kingdom: The Crowood Press Limited, 2002)

Tierney, R, and Montgomery, F., *The Army Aviation Story* (Northport, Alabama: Colonial Press, 1963)

Treadwell, T. C., *Strike from Beneath the Sea, A History of Aircraft-Carrying Submarines* (Stroud, Gloucestershire, England: Tempus Publishing, 1999)

Trimble, W. F., *Wings for the Navy: A History of the Naval Aircraft Factory, 1917–1956* (Annapolis Maryland: Naval Institute Press, 1990)

Tuttle, J., *Eject!, The Complete History of U.S. Aircraft Escape Systems* (St. Paul, Minnesota: MBI Publishing, 2002)

Vaeth, J. G., *They Sailed the Skies, U.S. Navy Balloons and Airship Program* (Annapolis, Maryland: Naval Institute Press, 2005)

van der Aart, D., *Aerial Espionage, Secret Intelligence Flights by East and West* (New York, New York: Arco/Prentice Hall Press, 1985)

van Pelt, M., *Rocketing into the Future, The History and Technology of Rocket Planes* (New York, New York: Springer, 2012)

Ventry, L. and Koleśnik, E. M., *Jane's Pocket Book of Airships* (New York, New York: Collier Books, 1976)

Wagner, R., *American Combat Planes of the 20th Century* (Reno, Nevada: Jack Bacon & Company, 2004)

Wegg, J., *General Dynamics Aircraft and their Predecessors* (London, England: Putnam Aeronautical Books, 1990)

Werrell, K. P., *The Evolution of the Cruise Missile* (Maxwell Air Force Base, Alabama: Air University Press, September 1985)

Westrum, R., *Sidewinder: Creative Missile Development at China Lake* (Annapolis, Maryland: Naval Press, 1999)

Wooldridge, E. T., Jr., *The P-80 Shooting Star, Evolution of a Jet Fighter*, Famous Aircraft if the National Air and Space Museum, Volume 3 (Washington, D. C.: Smithsonian Institution Press, 1979)

Yenne, B., *US Guided Missiles, The Definitive Reference Guide* (Manchester, England: Crécy Publishing, 2012)

Monographs

Anderson, H. G., *The Lockheed P2 Neptune*, Number 204, (Leatherhead, Surrey, England: Profile Publications, date not specified

Balch, A. M., *Sikorsky S-55/H-19 Chickasaw and Westland Whirlwind*, Warpaint Series No. 106 (Buckinghamshire, England, Guideline Publications, undated)

Cary, A. C., *Lockheed F-94 Starfire*, Air Force Legends Number 218 (Simi Valley, California: Steve Ginter, 2015)

Coleman, S., and Ginter, S., *Convair XFY-1 Pogo*, Naval Fighters Number Twenty-Seven (Simi Valley, California: Steve Ginter, 1994)

Cunningham, B., *Douglas A3D Skywarrior*, Naval Fighters Number Forty-Five (Simi Valley, California: Steve Ginter, 1998)

Curtis, D., *QF-86E/F/H/Sabre Full Scale Aerial Target*, Naval Fighters Number Fifty-Eight (Simi Valley, California: Steve Ginter, 2001)

Darling, K., *Lockheed Neptune*, Warpaint Series No. 51 (Bedfordshire, England: Warpaint Books, date not specified); *NAA B-45 Tornado*, Warpaint Series No. 118 (Bedfordshire, England: Warpaint Books, date not specified)

Davis, L., *F-80 T-33/F-94 Shooting Star in Action*, Aircraft No. 40 (Carrollton, Texas: Squadron/Signal Publications, 1980); *F-82 Twin Mustang, Mini in Action*, Mini Number 8 (Carrollton, Texas: Squadron/Signal Publications, 1996); *F-86 Sabre in Action* (Carrollton, Texas: Squadron/Signal Publications, 1978); *P-51 Mustang in Action* (Carrollton, Texas: Squadron/Signal Publications, 1981)

Davis, L. and Menard, D., *F-84 Thunderjet in Action*, Aircraft No. 61 (Carrollton, Texas: Squadron/Signal Publications, 1983); *F-89 Scorpion in Action* (Carrollton, Texas: Squadron/Signal Publications, 1990)

Doll, T. E., *Night Wings: USMC Night Fighters, 1942–1953* (Carrollton, Texas: Squadron/Signal Publications, 2000)

Doyle, D., *TBF/TBM Avenger in Action* (Carrollton, Texas: Squadron/Signal Publications, 2012)

Fahey, J. C., *U.S. Army Aircraft 1908-1946* (New York, New York: Ships and Aircraft, 1946)

Frankel, M., *Temco TT-1 Pinto*, Naval Fighters Number Seventy-Two (Simi Valley, California: Steve Ginter, 2006)

Ginter, S., *Consolidated Vultee XB-46*, Air Force Legends Number 221 (Simi Valley, California: Steve Ginter, 2016); *Convair XP5Y-1 & R3Y-1/-2 Tradewind*, Naval Fighters Number Thirty-Four (Simi Valley, California: Steve Ginter, 1996); *Douglas AD/A-1 Skyraider, Part One*, Naval Fighters Number Twenty-Eight (Simi Valley, California: Steve Ginter, 2014); *Douglas F3D Skyknight*, Naval Fighters Number Four (Simi Valley, California: Steve Ginter, 1982); *Douglas F5D-1 Skylancer*, Naval Fighters Number Thirty-Five (Simi Valley, California: Steve Ginter, 1996); *Early Banshees, The McDonnell F2H-1, F2H-2/-2B/-2N/-2P*, Naval Fighters Number Seventy-Three (Simi Valley, California: Steve Ginter, 2006); *Grumman H-16 Albatross*, Naval Fighters Number Eleven (Simi Valley, California: Steve Ginter, 1984); *Grumman Goose*, Naval Fighters Number Sixty-Three (Simi Valley, California: Steve Ginter, 2004); *Lockheed C-121 Constellation*, Naval Fighters Number Eight (Simi Valley, California: Steve Ginter, 1983); *Lockheed R6O/R6V Constitution*, Naval Fighters Number Eighty-Three (Simi Valley, California: Steve Ginter, 2009); *Lockheed T2V-1/T-1A Seastar*, Naval Fighters Number Forty-Two (Simi Valley, California: Steve Ginter, 1999); *Lockheed XFV-1 VTOL Fighter*, Naval Fighters Number Thirty-Two (Simi Valley, California: Steve Ginter, 1996); *Martin P4M-1/-1Q Mercator*, Naval Fighters Number Thirty-Seven (Simi Valley, California: Steve Ginter, 1996); *Martin PBM Mariner*, Naval Fighters Number Ninety-Seven (Simi Valley, California: Steve Ginter, 2013); *McDonnell Banshee F2H-1, -2, -B, -N, -P, -3, -4*, Naval Fighters Number Two (Simi Valley, California: Steve Ginter, 1980); *McDonnell FH-1 Phantom*, Naval Fighters Number Three (Simi Valley, California: Steve Ginter, 1981); *McDonnell F2H-3/4*, Naval Fighters Number Ninety-One (Simi Valley, California: Steve Ginter, 2011); *McDonnell F3H Demon*, Naval Fighters Number Twelve (Simi Valley, California: Steve Ginter, 1985); *North American AJ Savage*, Naval Fighters Number Twenty Two (Simi Valley, California: Steve Ginter, 1992); *North American FJ-2 Fury*,

Naval Fighters Number Ten (Simi Valley, California: Steve Ginter, 1984); *North American T-28 Trojan*, Naval Fighters Number Five (Simi Valley, California: Steve Ginter, 1981); *Republic XF-84H Thunderscreech*, Air Force Legends Number 219 (Simi Valley, California: Steve Ginter, 2015); *Ryan FR-1 Fireball and XF2R-1 Darkshark*, Naval Fighters Number Twenty-Eight (Simi Valley, California: Steve Ginter, 1995)

Ginter, S. and Picciana, R., *North American FJ-1 Fury*, Naval Fighters Number Seven (Simi Valley, California: Steve Ginter, 1983)

Ginter, S. with Taylor, N. and Romano, A., *Douglas R4D-8/C-117D Super Gooney, Part One*, Naval Fighters Number Ninety-Five (Simi Valley, California: Steve Ginter, 2013)

Ginter, S. and Williams, N., *Convair T-29 Flying Classroom, R4Y/C-131 Samaritan & CC-109 Cosmopolitan*, Naval Fighters Number Fourteen (Simi Valley, California: Steve Ginter, 1987)

Guenther, B., and Miller, J., *Bell X-1 Variants*, Aerofax Datagraph 3 (Arlington, Texas: Aerofax, 1988)

Gunston, B. and Batchelor, J., *Helicopters, 1900-1960* (London, England: Phoebus Publishing, 1977)

Hays, G., *Boeing B-50*, Air Force Legends Number 215 (Simi Valley, California: Steve Ginter, 2012)

Hoffman, R. A., *Martin P5M Marlin Patrol Seaplane*, Naval Fighters Number Seventy-Four (Simi Valley, California: Steve Ginter, 2007)

Hughes, K. and Dranem, W., *Douglas A-1 Skyraider*, WarbirdTech Series Volume 13 (North Branch, Minnesota: Specialty Press, 1997)

Jackson, P. A., *Republic F-84F Thunderstreak and RF-84F Thunderflash in European Air Forces*, Warpaint Series No. 1(Bucks, England: Alan H W. Hall Publications, 1976)

Jenkins, D, R., *Convair B-36 "Peacemaker,"* WarbirdTech Series Volume 24 (North Branch, Minnesota: Specialty Press, 2002)

Johnsen, F. A., *Douglas A-26 Invader*, WarbirdTech Series Volume 22 (North Branch, Minnesota: Specialty Press, 1999)

Kempel, R. W., *The Conquest of the Sound Barrier*, X-Planes Book 7 (Beirut, Lebanon: HPM Publications, 2007)

Kinzey, B., *AD Skyraider*, In Detail & Scale Vol. 67 (Carrollton, Texas: Squadron/Signal Publications, 2003); *F-84 Thunderjet*, In Detail & Scale Vol. 59 (Carrollton, Texas: Squadron/Signal Publications, 1999); *F-101 Voodoo*, In Detail & Scale Vol. 22 (Blue Ridge Summit, Pennsylvania: Tab Books, 1986); *F4U Corsair Part 2, F4U-4 Through F4U-7*, In Detail & Scale Vol. 56 (Carrollton, Texas: Squadron/Signal Publications, 1998); *F11F Tiger*, In Detail & Scale Vol. 17 (Fallbrook, California: Aero Publishers, 1984); *FJ Jury*, In Detail & Scale Vol. 68 (Carrollton, Texas: Squadron/Signal Publications, 2003); *P-51 Mustang Part 2 P-51D Through F-82H*, In Detail & Scale Vol. 51 (Carrollton, Texas: Squadron/Signal Publications, 1997); *TBF & TBM Avenger*, In Detail & Scale Vol. 53 (Carrollton, Texas: Squadron/Signal Publications, 1997)

Kinzey, B., and Roszak, R., *F-102 Delta Dagger*, In Detail & Scale Vol. 6 (Wroclaw, Poland: Detail & Scale, 2018)

Koehnen, R., *Chance Vought F6U Pirate*, Naval Fighters Number Nine (Simi Valley, California: Steve Ginter, 1983)

Kowalski, B., *Martin AM-1/1-Q Mauler*, Naval Fighters Number Twenty-Four (Simi Valley, California: Steve Ginter, 1994)

Kowalski, R. J., *Grumman AF Guardian*, Naval Fighters Number Twenty (Simi Valley, California: Steve Ginter, 2016)

Kowalski, R. J. and Thomason, T. H., *Grumman S2F/S-2 Tracker, Part One, Development, Testing, Variants, and Foreign Users*, Naval Fighters Number Twenty (Simi Valley, California: Steve Ginter, 1991)

Libis, S., *Douglas D-558-1 Skystreak*, Naval Fighters Number 56 (Simi Valley, California: Steve Ginter, 2001); *Douglas D-558-2 Skyrocket*, Naval Fighters Number 57 (Simi Valley, California: Steve Ginter, 2002); *The Martin XB-51*, Air Force Legends Number 201 (Simi Valley, California: Steve Ginter, 1998)

Lloyd, A. T., *B-17 Flying Fortress Part 2 Derivatives*, In Detail & Scale Vol. 11 (Blue Ridge Summit, Pennsylvania: Tab Books, 1983)

Long, B. J., *Convair XFY-1 and YF2Y-1 SeaDart*, Naval Fighters Number Twenty Three (Simi Valley, California: Steve Ginter, 1992)

Lundh, L., *H-34 in Action*, Aircraft Number 146 (Carrollton, Texas: Squadron/Signal Publications, 1994); *Sikorsky H-34, An Illustrated History* (Atglen, Pennsylvania: Schiffer Publishing, 1998)

Markgraf, G., *Douglas Skyshark A2D Turbo-Prop Attack*, Naval Fighters Number Forty-Three (Simi Valley, California: Steve Ginter, 1997)

McDowell, E., *FR-1 Fireball*, Mini in Action Number 5 (Carrollton, Texas: Squadron/Signal Publications, 1995)

Meyer, C. C., *Grumman F9F Panther, Part One: Development, Testing, Structures*, Naval Fighters Number Fifty-Nine (Simi Valley, California: Steve Ginter, 2002); *Grumman F9F-6/7/8 Cougar, Part One: Development, Testing, Structures and Blue Angles*, Naval Fighters Number Sixty-Six (Simi Valley, California: Steve Ginter, 2005); *Grumman F11F Tiger*, Naval Fighters Number Forty (Simi Valley, California: Steve Ginter, 1997); *Grumman Swing-Wing XF10F-1 Jaguar*, Naval Fighters Number Twenty-Six (Simi Valley, California: Steve Ginter, 1993)

Meyer, C. C. and Ginter, S., *Grumman F7F Tigercat*, Naval Fighters Number Seventy-Five (Simi Valley, California: Steve Ginter, 2007)

Mesko, J., *FH Phantom/F2H Banshee in Action*, Aircraft Number 182 (Carrollton, Texas: Squadron/Signal Publications, 2002)

Migliardi, R. D., *HU-16 Albatross in Action*, Aircraft Number 161 (Carrollton, Texas: Squadron/Signal Publications, 1996)

Myhra, D., *Messerschmitt P.1101* (Atglen, Pennsylvania: Schiffer Publishing, 1999)

Mutza, W., *H-13 Sioux Mini in Action*, Mini Number 6 (Carrollton, Texas: Squadron/Signal Publications, 1995)

Pace, S., *Bell Aircraft P-69 Airacomet*, Air Force Legends Number 208 (Simi Valley, California: Steve Ginter, 2000); *McDonnell XF-88 Voodoo*, Air Force Legends Number 205 (Simi Valley, California: Steve Ginter, 1999); *Republic XF-91 Thunderceptor Rocket Fighter*, Air Force Legends Number 210 (Simi Valley, California: Steve Ginter, 2000)

Panopalis, T., *Convair F-102 Delta Dagger*, Warpaint Series No. 64 (Buckinghamshire, England: Warpaint Books, date not specified)

Scarborough, W. E., *F7F Tigercat in Action*, Aircraft Number 79 (Carrollton, Texas: Squadron Signal Publications, 1986)

Simone, W., *Lockheed XF-90 Penetration Fighter*, Air Force Legends Number 222 (Simi Valley, California: Steve Ginter, 2020)

Smith, B., *PBM Mariner in Action*, Aircraft Number 74 (Carrollton, Texas: Squadron Signal Publications, 1986)

Smith, R. K., *75 Years of Inflight Refueling Highlights, 1923-1998*, Air Force History and Museums Program (Washington, D. C.; U.S. Government Printing Office, 1998)

Sullivan, J., *F4U Corsair in Action* (Carrollton, Texas: Squadron/Signal Publications, 2010); *S2F Tracker in Action*, Aircraft Number 100 (Carrollton, Texas: Squadron/Signal Publications, 1990); *Skyraider in Action*, Aircraft Number 60 (Carrollton, Texas: Squadron/Signal Publications, 1983); *P2V Neptune in Action*, Aircraft Number 68 (Carrollton, Texas: Squadron Signal Publications, 1985)

Taylor M. J. H. (ed.), *Jane's Pocket Book of Helicopters* (New York, New York; Collier Books, 1978)

Thomason, T. H., *The Forgotten Bell HSL, U.S. Navy's First All-Weather Anti-Submarine Warfare Helicopter*, Naval Fighters Number Seventy (Simi Valley, California: Steve Ginter, 2005)

Veronico, N. A. and Ginter, S. *Convair PB4Y-2/P4Y-2 Privateer* (Simi Valley, California: Steve Ginter, 2012)

Wachsmuth, W., *B-36 Peacemaker*, In Detail & Scale Vol. 47 (Carrollton, Texas: Squadron/Signal Publications, 1997)

Wagner, R., *North American F-86D/K/L Sabre Jet: Part One, Design / Structure / Testing*, Air Force Legends Number 202 (Simi Valley, California: Steve Ginter, 1999)

Periodicals

Allen, F., "Ambitious 'Eggbeater', Kellett's XR-8—Far Ahead of its Time," *Air Enthusiast*, No. 111, May/June 2004, pp. 26–30; "The McDonnell XV-1," *AAHS Journal*, Vol. 38 No. 1, Spring 1993, pp. 2–19; "Kellett's Whirling Eggbeater," *Wings*, August 1990, pp. 34–45

Bodie, W. M., "Breaching the Walls of Fortress Europe," *Airpower*, September 1973, Vol. 3 No. 5, pp. 36–55; "A Fighter for All Weather ..., Curtiss XF-87 Blackhawk," *Wings/Airpower*, date unknown, Vol. ? No. ?, pp. 30–38 and 5?; "Penetration Fighter, The Lockheed F-90," *Airpower*, March 1981, Vol. 11 No. 2, pp. 20–37 and 49–51; "Attack! The Story of the XB-51, Martin's Phantom Strike Ship," *Airpower*, July 1978, Vol. 8 No. 4, pp. 20–39; "Boeing B-52, The Once and Future Emperor of Airpower," *Airpower*, March 1982, Vol. 12 No. 2, pp. 12–49; "Bomber 47, How Boeing's B-47 Brought America into the Jet Age," *Wings*, August 1981, Vol. 11 No. 4, pp. 9–27 and 46–51; "Convair's Needle-Nosed Orphan," *Airpower*, September 1976, Vol. 6 No. 4, pp. 8–19 and 67; "The Custer Channel Wing Story," *Airpower*, May 1977, Vol. 7 No. 3, pp. 8–19 and 58; "The First, the Last, the Only: The Douglas XB-42/42A/43," *Airpower*, September 1973, Vol. 3 No. 5, pp. 6–15 and 67; "XB-48 ... Martin's Pipe Dream—Pipe Organ Bomber!," *Airpower*, September 1975, Vol. 5 No. 5, pp. 8–21

Bradley, R. E., "The Birth of the Delta Wing," *AAHS Journal*, Vol. 48 No. 4, Winter 2003, pp. 242–260

Buttler, T., "Flight Test—Bell XP-83, Bell's Last Fighter," *Aeroplane*, May 2021, Issue 577, Vol. 49 No. 5, pp. 80–83.

Daniels, C. M., "Skymaster, The Douglas DC-4/C-54, Aviation's First Intercontinental Airliner," *Airpower*, January 1974, Vol. 4 No. 1, pp. 46–60

Davis, L., "Air Combat—67th TRW in Korea," *International Air Power Review*, Volume 10, Autumn/Fall 2003, pp. 98–111; "Air Force Search & Rescue, Part 1," *Wings of Fame*, Vol. 13, 1998, pp. 142–157; "North American F-86 Sabre," *Wings of Fame*, Vol. 10, 1998, pp. 34–99

Donald, D., "Beyond the Frontiers: All the Fours, Republic XF-12 Rainbow," *Wings of Fame*, Vol. 3, 1996, pp. 26–33; "Pioneers & Prototypes—Convair F2Y Sea Dart," *International Air Power Review*, Volume 12, Spring 2004, pp. 162–173

Dorr, R. F., "Beyond the Frontiers: Convair R3Y Tradewind 'The Flying LST'," *Wings of Fame*, Vol. 18, 2000, pp. 4–15; "Beyond the Frontiers: McDonnell XF-85," *Wings of Fame*, Vol. 7, 1997, pp. 26–35; "Convair F-102 Delta Dagger," *Wings of Fame*, Vol. 17, 1999, pp. 30–97; "Lockheed P-80 Shooting Star Variant Briefing," *Wings of Fame*, Vol. 11, 1998, pp. 114–133; "Lockheed F-94 Variant Briefing," *Wings of Fame*, Vol. 13, 1998, pp. 126–141; "Martin Flying-Boats: Mariner, Mars and Marlin," *Wings of Fame*, Vol. 7, 1997, pp. 114–133; "McDonnell F-88/F-101 Voodoo Variant Briefing," *Wings of Fame*, Vol. 1, 1995, pp. 166–187; "Northrop F-89 Scorpion Variant Briefing," *Wings of Fame*, Vol. 6, 1997, pp. 128–147; "'T-birds' & Silver Stars, Lockheed T-33/T2V Variants," *Wings of Fame*, Vol. 16, 1999, pp. 102–125

Francillon, R. J., "'Connies' in Uniform, Lockheed Constellations/Super Constellation Military Variants," *Wings of Fame*, Volume 20, 2000, pp. 112–139

Goodspeed, M. H., "Grumman TBF/TBM Avenger," *Wings of Fame*, Volume 13, 1998, pp. 32–91; "Warplane Classic—Douglas AD/A-1 Skyraider: The 'Spad' in US Navy and Marine Corps Service," *International Air Power Review*, Volume 17, 2005, pp. 128–157

"Grumman's Guardian," *Air International*, August 1974, Volume 7 Number 2, p. 101

Gunston, B., "Beyond the Frontiers: Pogo! Convair XFY-1 and Lockheed XFV-1," *Wings of Fame*, Vol. 16, 1999, pp. 4–11

Hayes, K. E. and Power, E. C., "The Mars—Long Lasting Flying Boat," *Air-Britain Digest*, July-August 1981, pp. 75–80

Johnson, S. O., "Hunter/Killer," *Airpower*, March 1980, Volume 10 Number 2, pp. 30–36 and 51

Kuhn. G. G., "The Northrop YC-125 'Raider'," *AAHS Journal*, Vol. 6 No. 1, Spring 1961, pp. 38–41

Lake, J., "Martin P4M Mercator: Cold War Elint-gathering Operations," *Wings of Fame*, Volume 19, 2000, pp. 139–149; "Variant File—Boeing B-52 Stratofortress," *International Air Power Review*, Volume 8, Spring 2003, pp. 106–121; "Warbird Classic—North American F-100 Super Sabre," *International Air Power Review*, Volume 11, Winter 2003/1004, pp. 120–157

Machat, M., "The Trio that Tried," *Airpower*, May 2005, Vol. 35 No. 5, pp. 12–27 and 52–55

Machat, M. and Accurso, A., "Winged Missiles of the U.S. Air Force," *Airpower*, May 2004, Vol. 34 No. 5, pp. 14–27 and 54–59

Martin, G., "Pioneers & Prototypes—Jet Bomber Pioneer: North American B-45 Tornado," *International Air Power Review*, Volume 23, 2007, pp. 162–173

McDowell. E. R., "Ryan's Fireball," *AAHS Journal*, Vol. 8 No. 4, Winter 1963, pp. 231–247

Miska, K. H, "Development of the Grumman XTB3F and the AF 'Guardian,'" *AAHS Journal*, Vol. 18 No. 4, Winter 1973, pp. 218–225

Mitchell, K. A., "Endless Track Landing Gear," *AAHS Journal*, Vol. 38 No. 1, Spring 1993, pp. 55–57; "Mr. Custer and his Channel Wing Airplanes," *AAHS Journal*, Vol. 43 No. 1, Spring 1998, pp. 62–73

Moore, G., "Mustang Whirlybird, Hughes' XH-17," *Flight Journal*, April 2001, Volume 6 Number 2, pp. 76–83

Murphy, D. "Boeing's Slow-Flying Scout," *Airpower*, July 1994, pp. 36–43

Norton, B., "Tilt-Rotor Patriarch, Bell's XV-3 Convertiplane," *Air Enthusiast*, No. 115, January/February 2005, pp. 44–64; "Forgotten Airlifter, Douglas C-133 Cargomaster," *Air Enthusiast*, No. 110, March/April 2004, pp. 45–53

Porter, D. J., "Howard Hughes' Impromptu Beginning as a Helicopter Manufacturer," *AAHS Journal*, Vol. 58 No. 3, Fall 2013, pp. 194–199

Richards, C., "An Industry of Prototypes: Martin XB-51," *Wings of Fame*, Vol. 14, 1999, pp. 4–13

Scheppler. R. H., "Aviation Instruments Part 4," *AAHS Journal*, Vol. 7 No. 3, Fall 1962, pp. 197–204

Slayton, B., "The Lockheeds That Never Were, Part II," *AAHS Journal*, Summer 1999, Vol. 44 No. 2, pp. 102–113

Story, R. W., "Helicopter Projects at GE's Schenectady Flight Test Center," *AAHS Journal*, Vol. 48 No. 2, Summer 2003, pp. 138–140; "Igor Bensen, The GE Years," *AAHS Journal*, Vol. 46 No. 4, Winter 2001, pp. 284–289

Thompson, W. E., "B-26 Invader in Korea," *Wings of Fame*, Volume 13, 1998, pp. 112–125; "Fighter Combat Over Korea, Part 1: First Kills," *Wings of Fame*, Volume 1, 1995, pp. 4–33, "Fighter Combat Over Korea, Part 2: Jet Aces," *Wings of Fame*, Volume 2, 1996, pp. 4–23, "Fighter Combat Over Korea, Part 3: A Year of MiGs," *Wings of Fame*, Volume 3, 1996, pp. 96–113, "Fighter Combat Over Korea, Part 4: The Final Year," *Wings of Fame*, Volume 4, 1996, pp. 78–97; "Air Combat—Twin Mustangs in Korea," *International Air Power Review*, Volume 3, Winter 2001/2002, pp. 156–167

Thompson, W., "Air War Korea—Heavy Haulers," *Wings of Fame*, Volume 20, 2000, pp. 98–111; "Superfortress in Korea, Boeing's B-29 at War in the Far East," *Wings of Fame*, Volume 16, 1999, pp. 12–29; "Northrop P-61 Black Widow," *Wings of Fame*, Volume 15, 1999, pp. 36–101

Willis, D., "Variant File—Douglas A-26/B-26 Invader," *International Air Power Review*, Volume 18, 2005, pp. 104–127; "Variant File—Martin B-57, The American Canberra—Part 1," *International Air Power Review*, Volume 20, 2006, pp. 94–107; "Warplane Classic—Boeing B-29 and B-50 Superfortress," *International Air Power Review*, Volume 22, 2007, pp. 136–169; "Warplane Classic—Republic F-84 Thunderjet, Thunderstreak & Thunderflash," *International Air Power Review*, Volume 24, 2008, pp. 132–165

Winchester, J., "Type Analysis—Vought F7U Cutlass, The Navy's 'Widowmaker,'" *International Air Power Review*, Volume 15, 2005, pp. 98–115

Yenne, B., "Variant File—Boeing B-47 Stratojet," *International Air Power Review*, Volume 6, Autumn/Fall 2002, pp. 156–171; "Warplane Classic—Convair B-36 Peacemaker," *International Air Power Review*, Volume 13, Summer 2004, pp. 116–151

Yenne, B., additional material by Aloni, S., and Donald, D., "Warplane Classic—Boeing C/KC-97 Stratofreighter," *International Air Power Review*, Volume 13, Summer 2004, pp. 108–151

Reports and Studies

Air Mobility Command Office of History, *Aerial Refueling Highlights in the Air Force's First Decade 1947–1957* (Scott Air Force Base, Illinois: Air Mobility Command, US Air Force, May 1997)

Army Aircraft Characteristics, Production and Experimental, Report No. TSEST—A2, ATSC, United States Army, 1 April 1946

Case History of the XF-87 All-Weather Fighter, Historical Office, Air Technical Services Command, Wright Field, Ohio, reproduced in *AAHS Journal*, Vol. 38 No. 1 Spring 1993, pp. 20–31

Hanson, J. R., *A Digest of V/STOL Aircraft Flight Test Programs*, Report B754 (St. Louis, Missouri: McDonnell Flight Test Division, July 1, 1965)

Historical Office, *Case History of Air-to-Air Refueling*, Air Materiel Command, Wright-Patterson AFB, Ohio, March 1949

Rotary Wing Branch (TSEOA-5) Aircraft Projects Section, Engineering Division, *Summary of Rotary Wing Projects of Aircraft Projects Section (By Model)*, Air Materiel Command, February 1947

Self, M. R., *History of the Development and Production of USAF Heavy Bombardment Aircraft, 1917–1949*, Study No. 195 (Wright-Patterson AFB, Ohio: Historical Office, Executive Secretariat, Air Materiel Command, December 1950)

Manuals

Flight Handbook, USAF Series B-36H-III Aircraft, T.O. 1B-36H (III)-1, 26 November 1954

Flight Handbook, USAF Series H-13C H-13D, Navy Models HTL-4, Helicopters, T.O. 1H-13C-1, 15 September 1954

Flight Handbook, Navy Model HR2S-1 Helicopter, NAVWEPS 01-230HKA-1, revised 15 March 1961

Flight Handbook, Navy Models HUP-1, HUP-2 and HUP-3 Helicopters, NAVWEPS 01-250HCA-1, 1 July 1960

Flight Handbook, Navy Models R3Y-1 and R3Y-2 Airplanes, AN 01-5MRA-1, 15 March 1955

Pilot's Handbook, Navy Model HTK-1 Helicopters, AN 01-260HAA-1, 1 September 1952

Pilot's Notes, Hiller H.T. Mk.1, A.P. 4534A.-P.N., Ministry of Supply, reprinted March 1955

Pilot's Flight Operating Instructions for Helicopters Army Model R-5A Navy Model HO2S-1, AN 01-23OHB-1, 5 September 1945

Preliminary Flight Handbook, USAF Model YH-21 Helicopter, AN 01-250HDA-1, 23 March 1953

Preliminary Pilot's Handbook for Navy Model F6U-1 Aircraft, AN 01-45HEA-1, 15 April 1949

Correspondence

Munroe, C. L., Colonel, USAF, Chief, Maintenance Division, D/MS&S, Office, Deputy Chief of Staff, Materiel, ""Gem" Program Summary," Memorandum for Major General Whitten, August 26, 1948, found within Self, Mary R. *History of the Development and Production of USAF Heavy Bombardment Aircraft, 1917–1949*, Study No. 195 (Wright-Patterson AFB, Ohio: Historical Office, Executive Secretariat, Air Materiel Command, December 1950)

Other

Bruins, B. D., *U.S. Naval Bombardment Missiles, 1940–1958: A Study of the Weapons Innovation Process*, Doctoral Dissertation (Ann Arbor, Michigan: Columbia University, 1981)

Fahrney, D. S., *The History of Pilotless Aircraft and Guided Missiles*, unpublished manuscript (prepared for US Navy Bureau of Aeronautics, undated but likely 1958)

History of Kellett Aircraft Corporation, September 1952, Kellett Aircraft Corporation press release

The XH-10 Helicopter, undated, Kellett Aircraft Corporation press release

Signor, P. W., *Cruise Missiles for the U.S. Navy: An Exemplar of Innovation in a Military Organization*, (Newport, Rhode Island: Naval War College, June 1994)

USAF Historical Division, *Development of Night Air Operations, 1941–1952*, U.S. Air Force Historical Study No. 92 (Maxwell Air Force Base, Alabama: Air University, 1953)

Internet

Igor I. Sikorsky Historical Archives, Sikorsky Product History, sikorskyarchives.com, accessed July 2018

U.S. Warplanes, uswarplanes.net/a26.html, accessed August 2019

Marquardt Corporation, wikiwand.com/en/Marquardt_Corporation, accessed 4-10-20

Index

academia 51, 55, 466; Massachusetts Institute
of Technology 367, 428; Stevens Institute of
Technology 88, 367; University of Michigan
Aeronautical Research Center 445

aerial minelaying 35-36, 270-271, 369, 373, 460

aerial refueling (AR) 24, 42, 52, 100, 102, 108,
112-124, 142, 166, 168, 181, 240, 244,
252, 257, 259-262, 453, 471-472, 478-479,
484-485; D-704 "buddy refueling" pod 123,
478; Korea experience 118, 453-454

aerodynamic testbeds 56, 92, 95-96, 99-100, 178,
319, 337, 343

Air Rescue Service (ARS) 314, 330-331

air-sea rescue (ASR) 314, 410-415; Air-Sea Rescue
Agency 410

aircraft, airborne early warning (AEW) and as
variants 358, 360, 380-384, 469; PO/WV 382,
384; WF 382

aircraft, anti-submarine warfare and as variants
43, 263, 315, 355-381, 412, 460, 489; PV
Harpoon 364, 370, 460; S2F Tracker 43,
362-365, 382, 488; S2U/TWU 362; TBF/TBM
Avenger 357-358, 360-362; TB3F/AF Guardian
358-362, 384

aircraft, attack 205, 220; A-43 155, 245-246;
A-45 245; A2D Skyshark 190, 198-199,
205-207; A4D Skyhawk 123, 198-199; AD/
BT2D Skyraider 136-138, 268, 360-361-363,
382-383, 418, 428, 449, 451, 458, 477;
AM Mauler 135-137, 417, 488; AU Corsair
134-135, 449; BT2D/AD Skyraider 136-138,
268, 360-363, 382-383, 418, 428, 449, 451,
458, 477; BTC 135

aircraft, autogyro 96, 489; O-60 343; R-3 343

aircraft, bomber escort 31, 104-105, 107, 110,
112-113, 133, 142-144, 152, 175, 179,
181-182, 203, 205, 220, 432, 454, 460,
462, 472

aircraft, bombers (air force) 220; A-20 Havoc 99;
A-26/B-26/JD Invader 73, 75-76, 79-80, 99,
127-128, 220-222, 239, 245, 247-249, 391,
416, 418, 421, 423-424, 428-429, 448, 457-458,
462, 490, 492; A-44/B-53 232, 245-246; B-54
225-226; B-17/PB Flying Fortress 24, 73-74, 77,
84, 114, 128-129, 221, 284, 382, 384, 410-411,
413, 421, 427-428; B-24 Liberator 74, 77, 104,
114, 129, 221, 242; B-25 Mitchell 400, 430;
B-26/JM Marauder 233-234, 247, 487; B-29/
P2B Superfortress 24, 42, 52-53, 59, 66-68, 70,
75, 77-78, 82, 104-107, 110-123, 129, 142, 181,
203, 220-226, 236, 242-243, 277-278, 366, 382,
385, 388, 410-411, 416, 422, 431-432, 437,
448, 453-454, 457, 459-462, 467, 472, 476,
484-485, 492; B-32 221, 487; B-35 60, 105,
225, 227-230, 235-238, 260; B-36 Peacemaker
31-33, 42, 50, 52, 83-84, 100-101, 104-113,
119, 121, 154, 175, 181-182, 223, 225, 228,
237, 244, 253-262, 264, 281-284, 306-307,
390, 416, 431, 433-434, 436, 479, 485, 487;
B-42 75-76, 230-232; B-43 77, 231-232; B-45
Tornado 24, 41, 43, 77-78, 116, 230, 233, 237,
239-241, 249, 390-391, 417, 443, 453, 462,
467, 472, 482; B-46 230-234; B-47 Stratojet
49, 51, 79, 113, 118-121, 181, 225, 230,
233, 240-245, 257, 259-261, 391, 433-434;
B-48 230, 233-235, 242, 487; B-49 228, 230,
235-238, 390; B-50 Superfortress 44, 52-53,
71-72, 77-78, 82-83, 100, 102, 113, 115-117,
124-125, 222-226, 228, 237, 241, 255, 257,
278, 388-390, 416, 433-434, 478, 485, 487;
B-51 247-250, 487; B-52 Stratofortress 42,
113, 118, 243, 260-264, 479-480; B-55 260;

B-56 243; B-57 Canberra 249-252, 391, 393; B-58 Hustler 263-264, 287; B-59 263; B-60 258, 262-264; B-66 Destroyer 251-253, 391; B-68 252, 490; Generalized Bomber Study 263; intercontinental 24, 31, 42, 113, 228, 244, 253, 257, 260, 435-436, 444, 446, 466, 472, 479

aircraft, bombers (navy) 263, 265-272; A2J Super Savage 268-269; A3D Skywarrior 33, 251-253, 268-271, 488; AJ Savage 123, 249, 266-268, 391-392; High-Speed Minelayer 36, 270; P6M SeaMaster 88-89, 271-272, 472, 492

aircraft, convertible (convert-o-planes, convertiplanes) 93-98, 343; 1-G 95-96; compound helicopters 11, 93-97; Convertible Aircraft Congress 93; Convertible Aircraft Program 93; H-33/XV-3 95, 97; H-35/L-25/ XV-1 94, 96, 343; Project Hummingbird 93; S-57/XV-2 94

aircraft, drones/targets and as variants 417-424, 433, 435, 438; drone control aircraft 422, 424; for flight test 428; Full-Scale Aerial Targets 420; KD2C Skeet 421; KD2G Firefly 421-422; Korea experience 457, 459; OQ-19/ KDR 419-420; PQ-14 110-111; Q-1 421-422; Q-2/KDA Firebee 421, 423; Q-14 419; TD2D Katydid 421; TD2N/Gorgon III/KU3N 434-435; X-27 417, 419; X-28 417, 419

aircraft, electronic warfare, as variants 416-418, 457

aircraft, fighters (air force, intercept, pursuit) 30-32, 104, 133, 168-169, 201, 205, 207, 449; 1,000-mile per hour fighter 181; 1954 Interceptor 153, 183; F-84/P-84 Thunderjet 27, 75, 84-86, 107-112, 118, 121-122, 132, 140-142, 170-171, 181, 211-212, 248, 391, 393, 453-454, 483, 486, 490; F-85/P-85 Goblin 105-107, 144; F-86/P-86 Sabre 49, 119, 127, 132, 146, 153, 157, 159, 162-164, 170, 172-175, 179, 181-182, 184, 190-191, 211, 239, 425, 445, 453, 455-456, 462, 483, 485-486; F-88/P-88 Voodoo 86, 152, 175-177, 181-182, 193, 391; F-89/P-89 Scorpion 40, 153, 156-162, 170, 391, 426-427, 430-431; F-90/P-90 57, 152, 157, 175, 178-179; F-91/P-91 Thunderceptor 55-56, 152, 157-158, 207, 210-212; F-92/P-92 Thunderceptor 60, 62, 152, 185, 207-209; F-93/P-93 Sabre Cat 155, 180-181; F-94 Starfire 56, 153, 157, 159-162, 168, 170-172, 426, 460; F-95 163; F-96 170; F-100 Super Sabre 41, 183-184, 187, 189, 478; F-101 Voodoo 181-182, 393; F-102 Delta Dagger 60, 127, 153, 184-186; F-103 185, 187; F-104 Starfighter 187-188; F-105 Thunderchief 187-189; F-106 85, 185; F-107 189; hybrids 73, 76, 203-205, 245; P-38 Lightning 57-58, 104,

178, 425; P-47 Thunderbolt 133; P-51/F-51 Mustang 40-41, 79-80, 133-134, 143, 175, 385, 402-403, 448-449, 451; P-59 Airacomet 124, 137, 139, 144, 402; P-63 King Cobra 55, 58-59; P-79 60; P-80/F-80 Shooting Star 31, 48, 50, 77, 79, 81, 101-106, 125, 127-128, 130, 137, 139-141, 157, 160, 178, 248, 391-392, 402, 423, 426-427, 445, 451, 453, 462, 478; P-81 203, 205; P-82/F-82 Twin Mustang 79, 133, 142-143, 153-155, 160, 428, 458, 460; P-83 79, 81, 143-144, 425; parasite 105, 107, 109-110, 144; Penetration Fighter 152, 155, 157, 175, 178-181

aircraft, fighters (navy/marine) 133, 144, 189, 201, 211, 215; F2D/F2H Banshee 33, 46, 148-149, 166-168, 176, 393-394, 454, 462-463, 485; F2R Darkshark 202-204; F3H Demon 66, 193-195; F4D Skyray 193, 196-199; F4U Corsair 22, 134-135, 164-166, 385, 393, 449-452, 458, 460, 462, 479; F5D Skylancer 198; F5U "Flying Flapjack" 137-138; F6F Hellcat 22, 56, 64, 428, 458-459; F6U Pirate 77, 145; F7F Tigercat 79, 134, 164, 362, 422, 449, 458, 460, 485; F7U Cutlass 193-197, 477; F8B 135; F8F Bearcat 41, 134, 393, 449, 477; F8U Crusader 199-200; F9F Cougar 63, 65-66, 191-193, 198, 394; F9F Panther 34-35, 41, 46, 63, 123, 150-153, 166, 190-192, 359, 363, 394, 426, 449-450, 454-455, 477; F10F Jaguar 63-66, 193, 466, 483; F11F Tiger 198, 200; F15C 201-202; FD/FH Phantom 147-149, 402; FJ Fury (straight wing) 146-147, 172; FJ Fury (swept wing) 190-191; FR Fireball 201-203; FV 98, 216-219; FY 39, 98, 216, 218-219, 487; hybrids 49, 201-204, 373; Model 640 (Douglas) 214-215

aircraft, fighters (all-weather, night) and as variants 152-168, 460; All-Weather (Night) Interceptor 155, 179; all-weather interceptor 30-31, 158, 160-162, 164, 172, 189, 460; F3D Skyknight 156-158, 165-167, 191, 193, 428-430, 460, 474, 485; P-61/F2T Black Window 58, 79, 127, 129, 153, 164, 228-229, 385-386; P-87/F-87 Blackhawk 153, 155-157, 160, 245, 391

aircraft, foreign, BV 222 88; Canberra 249-251; CF-100 249; DH 108 58; DM-1 61; Fa 330 343-344; H8K Emily 88; H.8 Rotachute 343, 424; He 162 126; Lancaster 118; Me 163 58-59; Me 262 173; Meteor 118; MiG-15 63, 172, 181, 189, 211, 223, 447, 451, 453-457, 462; P.1101 62; Tu-4 24, 153; WN 342 341-343

aircraft, gliders 292-299; CG-4/G-4 124, 126, 293; CG-14 294-296; CG-15/G-15 124, 126, 293,

304-305; CG-18/G-18 294, 296-301; CG-19 294-295; CG-20/G-20 Avitruck 297-301, 306-307; deceleration devices 293; TG-32/LNE 129; towing 124-126

aircraft, helicopters 28-30, 37, 42, 56, 86, 93, 314-315, 374, 461, 463, 472; autopilots for 56, 332, 376-377; Class HC 349; flying crane/sky crane 341-343, 345-346, 349-350; H-18/HO5S/S-52 325-327, 351; H-19/HO4S/HRS/S-55 334-335, 377-378, 461, 463, 473, 489; H-20 Little Henry 341, 343, 484; H-21 Work Horse/HRP Rescuers 315, 329-332, 335, 355, 374-375, 414, 463; H-22/K-225 327, 351-352; H-23 Raven/HTE/UH-12/Model 360 321, 323-324, 332-333; H-24/S-4 Skyhawk 323-324; H-25 Mule/HJP/HUP Retriever 332-333, 377, 473; H-26 Jeep/A-8 340-350; H-27 339; H-28 346; H-29 341; H-30/HUM/MC-4/JOV 323, 325; H-31/LZ-4 333-334; H-32/HOE/HJ Hornet 96, 347-349; H-34/HSS Seabat/S-58 377; H-37 Mojave/HR2S/S-56 96, 316, 339-340, 351; H-39 351, 489; HCH 350; HJD/HJH Whirlaway 330, 336-337, 490; HJS/S-53 330-331; HOK/K-600 327-328; HRH 97; HSL 333, 374, 376-378; HTK/K-240 327-328, 351, 488; Model 30 (Bell) 317; Model 79 Big Henry 343; piston engine limitations for 315; R-1 336; R-4/HNS 315; R-5/HO2S/HO3S/S-51 56, 124, 315-318, 326, 374; R-6/HOS 37, 315, 333, 357; R-8 Synchrocopter 336; R-9/H-9 317-318, 320, 322; R-10/H-10 336-337; R-11/H-11 317, 319; R-12/H-12/Model 42 320-321, 325-326, 490; R-13/H-13 Sioux/HTL/Model 47 315, 319-322, 461, 463; R-14 320, 322; R-15/H-15 320, 322; R-16/H-16 Transporter 338-339; R-17/H-17 341, 344-346; S-3 (Seibel) 323; turbine engines sought for 350-352

aircraft, liaison (light-plane) 28-29, 404-410, 462-463; BC-12 92; Cub 91, 293; L-4 Cub 404, 462; L-5 404, 462-463; L-13 101, 404, 406, 463; L-15 Scout 101, 406-408; L-16/7BCM Champion 404; L-17 Navion 29, 410, 463; L-18 404; L-19 Bird Dog/OE/Model 170 29, 407-409, 463, 489; L-20/C-127/DHC-2 Beaver 409-410, 463; L-21 404; L-23 Seminole/Model 50 Twin Bonanza 410; L-24/Helio Courier 409; L-26/Aero Commander 410; LC-126/Model 195 101, 410

aircraft, lighter-than-air (blimp, non-rigid airship) 129, 356, 373, 379-381, 476; balloons 129, 131, 379, 417

aircraft, patrol 221, 263, 364, 367, 369-371, 460-461, 476; P2V Neptune 44, 101, 103,

121, 123, 265-266, 356, 364, 370-373, 375, 382, 384, 432, 460-461; P4M Mercator 88, 373-375, 391, 417-418; PB4Y/P4Y Privateer 121, 370-371, 373, 431, 458, 460, 489

aircraft, reconnaissance (photo, weather) and as variants 108, 373, 385-394, 460, 462; F-6 385; F-11 38, 386-387; F-12 Rainbow 388-389; F-13 385, 388; F-14 391; F-15 Reporter 57-58, 129, 385-386; U-2 391

aircraft, research 66-73; C-113 73-74, 469; CCW Channel Wing 37, 91-93; D-558 Skystreak 67, 69; D-558-2 Skyrocket 69-70, 72, 90; L-39 58-59, 71; M-270 88-89; variable stability research 56, 64, 66, 424, 469; X-1/XS-1 66-71, 486; X-2 47, 71-72; X-3 Stiletto 69-71, 186, 188; X-4/XS-4 Bantam 60-61; X-5 63; X-7 57, 81-83; X-13 98; X-15 73

aircraft, seaplanes/floatplanes/flying boat 36, 42, 48, 88-91, 123, 211-215, 263, 270-272, 308-313, 364-370, 410, 412, 460-461, 476, 480; catapult ("slingshot") 315, 353-355; F2Y SeaDart 91, 211, 213-215, 271, 486; hull design/testing 88-91; hydroflaps 88, 265, 271, 366; hydro-skis 88, 90-91, 211, 270, 480; J2F/OA-12 Duck 308, 412; J4F Widgeon 88-89, 308-309; JL 308-309; JRF Goose 91, 308, 414-415; OA-15/Seabee 412; OSE 353-354; P5M Marlin 88-89, 271, 312, 366-368, 412, 432; P5Y 88, 311-313, 367, 369-370, 469; P6M SeaMaster 88-89, 271-272, 476, 492; PB2M/JRM Mars 310-311, 465; PB2Y Coronado 364; PBM Mariner 88-89, 214, 310, 312-313, 364, 366, 391, 412-413, 417, 460; PBY/OA-10 Catalina 310, 356, 364-365, 373, 412-413, 460; R3Y Tradewind 88, 215, 271, 311-313, 369; SA-16/UF/PF/JR2F Albatross 308-309, 412, 414-415, 461, 477; SC Seahawk 353-354; Skate 211, Y2 211

aircraft, tankers and as variants 114-124, 272, 279, 286, 308, 312, 453-454, 472, 478, 485, 492; KC-135 Stratotanker 118, 478; tanker-transport 117, 119, 279, 283, 286, 469

aircraft, trainers and as variants 394-404; AT-10 55; N2S 395; NQ 395-396; T-6/AT-6 Texan/SNJ 90-91, 395, 397-399, 402, 451-452; T-28 Trojan/BT-28/SN2J 395, 397-400; T-29 402-403; T-30/BT-30 397-398; T-31 395; T-32 402; T-33/TF-33/TO/TV "T-bird" 31, 56, 124-125, 127-128, 160, 162, 402, 404-405, 445; T-34/Model 35 Bonanza 395, 399-401; T-35 Buckaroo/GC-1 Swift 395-396, 399; T-36 400-401; T-37 397, 404-405; T2V Seastar 91, 404-405; TE 353, TP-51 402-403

aircraft, transports, commercial 274, 287; CV-240 Convair-Liner 400; CV-240 Turboliner 73,